ORGANIZATIONAL BEHAVIOR

An Experiential Approach

Prentice-Hall International, Inc.

0-13-638636-9

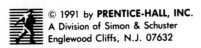
Organizational Behavior: An Experiential Approach
David A. Kolb, Irwin M. Rubin, and Joyce Osland

Printed in the United States of America

10 9 8 7 6 5 4 3 2 1

ISBN 0-13-638636-9

Prentice-Hall International (UK) Limited, *London*
Prentice-Hall of Australia Pty. Limited, *Sydney*
Prentice-Hall Canada Inc., *Toronto*
Prentice-Hall Hispanoamericana, S.A., *Mexico*
Prentice-Hall of India Private Limited, *New Delhi*
Prentice-Hall of Japan, Inc., *Tokyo*
Simon & Schuster Asia Pte. Ltd., *Singapore*
Editora Prentice-Hall do Brasil, Ltda., *Rio de Janeiro*
Prentice-Hall, Inc., *Englewood Cliffs, New Jersey*

To Jonathan
Beth, Steven, Cory
Asbjorn, Jessica, Michael, Katrina,
Bergit, and last but not least, Ellie

Contents

Foreword

This book—or better, the body of experiences it proposes—seeks to communicate some knowledge of general psychological principles, and some skill in applying that knowledge to social and organizational situations. Science tries to illuminate concrete reality by disclosing the general laws and principles that make the reality what it is. The generalization gives meaning to the concrete instance, but the instance carries the generalization into the real world—makes it usable. Experiencing social situations and then analyzing that experience brings generalization and concrete reality into effective union.

In teaching undergraduate and graduate management courses, I have frequently encountered students who hold a magical belief in a real world, somehow entirely different from any world they had hitherto experienced, and different, too, from the world of their textbooks. In teaching experienced executives, I have as frequently encountered men who balked at the proposal to apply general psychological principles to the concrete experiences of their everyday world. If there are skeptics of either variety in a group that undertakes one of these exercises, they can conduct their own tests of the relevance of theory to experience and vice versa. That is what the exercises are about.

But are the exercises themselves "real"? Can you really simulate social or organizational phenomena in a laboratory? The answer hangs on what we know of people—of their readiness to take roles, or, more accurately, their *inability not* to take roles when they find themselves in appropriate social situations, but this in itself is a psychological generalization: Man is a role taker. Like any generalization, it should be tested empirically; and the exercises do just that. Each participant can be his own witness to the reality—or lack of it—of what has gone on.

But the purpose of the exercises is not just to increase understanding of principles, or understanding of concrete situations in terms of principles. They can be useful also as a means of developing skills for group situations: skills of observing, skills of self-insight, skills of understanding the behaviors and motives of others, skills of adapting behavior to the requirements of a task and the needs of groups and persons.

There is no magic to it. Learning here, like all learning, derives from time and attention directed to relevant material. The exercises provide the material. The time, attention, and active participation must be supplied by those who take part in them.

Herbert A. Simon

Preface

This fifth edition of *Organizational Behavior: An Experiential Approach* is the latest improvement on an experiment that began over 20 years ago. The first edition of this book was developed at MIT in the late 1960s and was the first application of the principles of experience-based learning to teaching in the field of organizational psychology. Since then the field has changed, the practice of experience-based learning has grown in acceptance and sophistication, and we, the authors, have changed.

The field of organizational behavior has grown rapidly in this time period and is today a complex tapestry of historical trends, contemporary trends, and new emerging trends. In the Introduction that follows we will describe these trends in more detail. However, one of these developments—the expanding multi-disciplinary base of the field—should be mentioned here, since it has led us to change the title of the book from Organizational Psychology to Organizational Behavior in this fifth edition. This change reflects the increasing contribution from sociology, organization theory and management fields to the study of organizational behavior, giving the field and this new edition both a "macro" and "micro" perspective on human behavior in organizations.

Since the publication of our first edition, a number of other experience-based texts have been published in organizational behavior and other management specialties, and experiential-learning approaches have become widely accepted in higher education, particularly in programs for adult learners. The value of educational approaches that link the concepts and techniques of academia with learners' personal experiences in the real world is no longer questioned. In this latest edition we have attempted to reflect the state of the art in the practice of experiential learning and to bring these approaches to bear on the latest thinking and research in the field of organizational behavior.

The biggest personal change for us in the preparation of our fifth edition has been the addition of Joyce Osland to our co-author team. Joyce is professor of organizational behavior at INCAE in Costa Rica. She brings to our efforts the special perspectives of global issues, cross-cultural management, and the management of diversity. Her innovations can be seen throughout this new textbook. The chapter opening vignettes, the action tips for managers, the concept summaries, and the chapter-specific personal application assignments are just a few of the improvements she has introduced.

This book is intended for students and managers who wish to explore the personal relevance and conceptual bases of the phenomena of organizational behavior. It is designed with a focus on exercises, self-analysis techniques, and role plays to make the insights of behavioral science meaningful and relevant to practicing managers and students. Each chapter is designed as an educational intervention that facilitates each stage of the experience-based learning process. Exercises and simulations are designed to produce experiences that create the phenomena of organizational behavior. Observation schemes and methods are introduced to facilitate understanding of these experiences. Theories and models are added to aid in forming generalizations. And finally, the intervention is structured in a way that encourages learners to experiment with what they have learned in new experiences related to their personal life.

A companion readings book, *Organizational Behavior: Practical Readings for Managers,* Fifth Edition, is also published by Prentice Hall. Many footnotes in this volume make reference to articles which have been reprinted there. That these articles appear in our readings book may be abbreviated as *Readings* at the end of the footnote entry.

A preface is a place to publicly thank the many people who have helped us. Our feelings of pride in our product are tempered by the great indebtedness we feel to many others whose ideas and insights preceded ours. It is a tribute to the spirit of collaboration that pervades our field that the origin of many of the exercises recorded here is unknown. We have tried throughout the manuscript to trace the origins of those exercises we know about and in the process we may, in many areas, fall short of the original insight. For that we can only apologize. The major unnamed contributors are our students. In a very real sense, this book could never have been completed without their active participation in our explorations.

We wish to thank James McIntyre, our co-author in the first four editions of this book, for his generous and creative contributions. While much has changed and will continue to change through successive editions of the book, Jim's presence will always be there.

The many instructors who, as users of previous editions of our text, have shared their experiences, resources, insights and criticisms have been invaluable guides in the revision process. Our colleague, Donald McCormick, was particularly helpful in his detailed feedback and suggestions for improvement.

Clifford Bolster, Richard Boyatzis, William Pasmore, and Mary Ann Sharp gave generously of their time and effort to allow the videotaping of their class sessions to demonstrate their approaches to teaching via the experiential learning method. Mary Ann Sharp has also made a major contribution by authoring an Instructor's Manual containing tips for the conduct of specific class sessions and additional teaching resources. The chapter "Managing Diversity" was jointly developed by a Case Western Reserve University project team consisting of David Akinussi, Lynda Benroth, Rafael Estevez, Elizabeth Fisher, Mary Ann Hazen, David Kolb, Dennis O'Connor, and Michelle Spain.

Alison Reeves, our Prentice Hall Editor, has been patient, persistent, and supportive throughout the revision process. Several innovations in this edition, such as the video supplements, were her idea. She is a true editor in the classic tradition. We owe a special debt of gratitude to Retta Holdorf who managed the production of the final manuscripts and brought this project together.

David A. Kolb
Irwin M. Rubin
Joyce S. Osland

Introduction
to the Workbook

I hear and I forget
I see and I remember
I do and I understand

CONFUCIUS

As teachers responsible for helping people learn about the field of organizational behavior, we have grappled with a number of basic educational dilemmas. Some of these dilemmas revolve around the issue of *how* to teach about this most important and intensely personal subject. The key concepts in organizational behavior (indeed, in social science in general) are rather abstract. It is difficult through the traditional lecture method to bring these ideas meaningfully to life. Other problems concern issues of what to teach, since the field of organizational behavior is large and continues to grow. Relevant concepts and theories come from a variety of disciplines, and no single course could begin to scratch the surface. Another dilemma is one of control. Who should be in control of the learning process? Who should decide what material is important to learn? Who should decide the pace at which learning should occur? Indeed, who should decide what constitutes learning? Our resolution of these and related dilemmas is contained within this book. The learning materials in this book are an application of the theory of experiential learning to the teaching and learning of organizational behavior. In this method, primary emphasis is placed upon learning from your own experience. Each of the 20 chapters in the workbook begins with an introduction that raises key questions and provides a framework for your experiences in the unit. The core of each unit is an action-oriented behavioral simulation. The purpose of these exercises is to allow you to generate your own data about each of the key concepts to be studied. A format is provided to facilitate your ability to observe and share the personal reactions you have experienced, while the summaries at the end of each unit help to integrate the unit experiences and stimulate further questions and issues to be explored. If there is an overriding objective of the book, it is that you learn how to learn from all your experiences.

LEARNING ABOUT ORGANIZATIONAL BEHAVIOR

It has been over 20 years since we first began developing and testing the feasibility of experiential learning methods for teaching organizational behavior. Our initial attempts to substitute exercises, games, and role plays for more traditional educational approaches were met in many quarters by polite skepticism and resistance. Today experiential learning approaches are an integral part of management school curricula and management training programs everywhere. During these years, the subject matter of organizational behavior has undergone much change as well. Some of this change has been subtle and quiet, involving the consolidation and implementation of trends that began years ago. Other changes have been more dramatic. New vital perspectives have come alive, reorganizing and redirecting research, theory, and teaching in the field. Still other trends loom on the horizon, as yet underdeveloped, pointing the way toward the future shape of the field.

As we began to work on this fifth edition, we felt that it was time to take stock of these changes so that we might faithfully, in new selection of topics and experiential exercises, portray the field of organizational behavior as it is today—a complex of vital themes enduring from the past, alive in the present, and emerging in the future. Such a stocktaking is difficult to achieve objectively. Organizational behavior is a vast field with indefinite boundaries overlapping sister disciplines of social psychology, sociology, and anthropology, and management fields such as operations research, business policy, and industrial relations. One could convincingly argue that any patterns one sees in such diversity and complexity lie more in the eye of the beholder than in objective reality. At the very least, where one stands in defining organizational behavior is greatly influenced by where one sits, by one's particular experience and orientation to the field. Recognizing that any organization of the field is constructed from a combination of objective reality and subjective preference, we nonetheless felt that there is value in making explicit our view of the field, since it was on the basis of that view that choices of topics and exercises were made. By understanding our view, you, as learners, may be better able to articulate your own agreements and disagreements, thereby helping to sort the actual state of the field from our individual viewpoints.

In Table I-1 are summarized the changes we have seen in the field in the last 50 years in six general areas: the way organizational behavior is defined, the way management education is conducted, the field's perspective on the nature of persons, its view as to how human resources are to be managed, its perspective on organizations, and the nature of the change/improvement process. In each of these areas there are three kinds of trends: *historical foundations of trends,* previous historical development that is now widely influential in shaping the field; *contemporary trends,* current research and development that is capturing the excitement and imagination of scholars and practitioners; and *emerging trends,* new issues and concerns that seem destined to shape the future of organizational behavior in research and practice.

Definition of the Field

Paul Lawrence[1] traces the origin of the field of organizational behavior back to the early 1940s. He cites as the first key contribution to the field the group climate experiments of Kurt Lewin and his associates in 1943. Early scholars in the field came from industrial and social psychology and later from sociology. Organizational behavior departments were housed administratively in business schools, but in general they maintained their separate identity from the profession of management. Today we see major changes in the orientation as organizational behavior departments have become more integrated units within professional business schools. Most new faculty today have Ph.D.s in management as opposed to basic disciplines, and interdisciplinary research around the managerial task has burgeoned. Concepts are now more often defined in managerial terms (e.g., work team development) as opposed to behavioral science terms (group dynamics).

Active developments in organizational behavior today involve the expansion of the field from an industrial-business focus to a wider application of behavioral science knowledge in other professional fields—health care management, law, public administration, education, and international development. Perhaps because of this expansion into more complex social and political institutions, an emerging trend is toward a focus on sociological and political concepts that increase our understanding of management in complex organizational environments. In recent years the issue of environmental determinism has been raised, an even more "macro" approach to organizations. The population ecologists study the rise and fall of organizations within an entire industry and maintain that it is the environment, rather than actions by humans, that influences organizations. There is an active intellectual debate in the field between those who see strategic leadership and choice as the determinant of organizational success and those who subscribe to the environmental determinist position.

---

[1]Paul Lawrence, "Historical Development of Organizational Behavior," in Jay Lorsch (Ed.), *Handbook of Organizational Behavior* (Englewood Cliffs, N.J.: Prentice Hall, 1987).

TABLE I-1 Thematic Trends in Organizational Behavior, 1940–1990

	HISTORICAL TRENDS		CONTEMPORARY TRENDS		EMERGING TRENDS	
1. Definition of the field	Behavioral science discipline orientation	to Professional orientation	Industrial-business focus	to Management focus	Micro psychological emphasis	to Balance of macro and micro views systems focus environmental determinism
2. Perspective on organizations	Job satisfaction human fulfillment	to Organization productivity	Internal organizational functioning	to Organization, environment adaptation	Organizations as dominant, stable structures	to Organizations as symbolic entities networked with industries, institutions, careers in a global economy
3. Perspective on persons	Tender (communication, intimacy, growth)	to Tough (power and influence)	Socioemotional factors	to Cognitive problem-solving factors	Deficiency orientation (adjustment)	to Appreciation orientation (development)
4. Human resource management	Human relations	to Human resources	Management of people	to Management of work	Organization development	to Career development
5. Change processes	Expert, content consultation	to Process consultation	Change created by change agents	to Management of change by the system	Change via change intervention, action research	to Change via vision-based strategic transformation
			Simple, global technologies	to Highly differentiated problem-specific technologies		
6. Management education	Academic	to Experiential	Creating awareness	to Skill building	Performance orientation	to Learning to learn orientation

Perspective on Organizations

Early work in organizational behavior took a somewhat limited view of organizations, being primarily concerned with job satisfaction and human fulfillment in work. The recent past has included much research aimed at organizational productivity as well. But until recently the primary focus on the study of organizations has been on internal functioning. Some of the most vital research activity in the field stems from what is known as the open systems view of organizations. This view states that since organizations, to survive, must adapt to their environment, organizational functioning cannot be understood without examining organization-environment relationships. This led to the contingency theory of organizations, which states that there is no one best way to organize and manage; it depends on the environmental demands and corresponding tasks for the organization.

The open systems view of organizations leads to an important emerging trend in the study of organizations. In most research to date, the organization is the focal point of study, conceived as the dominant stable structure around which the environment revolves. Yet in many cases the organization is but a part of a more pervasive and dominant industry, institutional, or professional career structure. Utilities, for example, cannot be understood without understanding the impact of their relationship with governmental regulatory institutions, and medical organizations such as hospitals are dominated by the medical profession as a whole and particularly by the socialization and training of M.D.s. Improvements in the effectiveness of these organizations can be achieved only by consideration of the system of relationships among the organization and the institutions and professions that shape it.

Interorganizational networks are replacing the traditional view of the organization as the primary entity. Quasi-firms, such as construction jobs, which consist of subcontracted work teams, are becoming more common. The influence of the global economy is felt everywhere. Current research portrays organizations as symbolic systems in which members interpret their shared social reality. In this approach, reality is what is agreed upon, rather than an objective fact. The importance of organizational culture and shared values has also become an important trend.

Perspective on Persons

In their perspective on persons and human personality, organizational psychologists have added an emphasis on power and influence processes to an earlier concern with the more "tender" aspects of socioemotional behavior (e.g., communication, intimacy, and human growth). These concerns with the social-motivational aspects of human behavior are currently being expanded by many researchers to consider cognitive processes—learning, problem solving, decision making, and planning—thus contributing to a more holistic view of human behavior. A most promising future perspective on human functioning is emerging from the work of adult development psychologists in personality development, ego development, moral development, and cognitive development. Researchers in these fields are providing frameworks for human functioning in organizations that emphasize developmental-appreciative processes as opposed to the deficiency-adjustment perspective that has dominated much work on human behavior in organizations in the past.

Human Resource Management

The changes in perspectives on the person, which we have just discussed, have been mirrored in changes in philosophy about how human beings are to be managed. From our current historical vantage point, early approaches to management in organizational psychology seem defensive and vaguely paternalistic. People were involved in work decisions and attention was paid to "human relations" to keep workers happy and to avoid resistance to change initiated by management. Recently participative management has come to be viewed more as a positive tool for improving organizational functioning. People are involved in decision making not only to make them feel more satisfied, but also because the improved information and problem-solving capability resulting from a participative process is more productive and effective.

Current research takes a more systematic approach to human resource management, shifting the perspective from management of people and the social-motivational techniques of management style, organizational climate, management by objectives (MBO), and so on, to a management of work perspective. This perspective considers the whole person as he or she adapts to the work environment. Work is seen as a sociotechnical system, considering the content of jobs as well as the management process. Managing work involves designing technological systems, organizational arrangements, and jobs themselves to obtain effective organizational adaptation to the environment *and* maximum utilization of human resources and talents.

An important emerging trend in human resource management involves the addition of a career development perspective to the organization development perspective we have outlined. A host of trends are occurring in the labor market, including an older population, a more balanced male-female work force, a more culturally and racially diverse work force, and increasing career mobility and change among workers through their work lives.

There is an emergent trend that encourages greater responsibility on the part of workers to develop their own careers. As a result of downsizing leaner structures and the clog of baby boomers, some companies are making it clear to employees that they can no longer guarantee a lifelong career within the company. While many companies still manage the careers of those in the "fast track," career responsibility belongs primarily to workers themselves.

Change Processes

Concern with change and organization improvement has been central to organizational behavior from its inception. Kurt Lewin's action research methodology has been a dominant approach to integrating knowledge generation and practical application following his dictum: "If you want to understand something, try to change it." In the last decade the specialized field of organization development (OD) has emerged from the Lewinian tradition as a powerful practical approach for using behavioral science knowledge to improve organizational effectiveness and human fulfillment in work. A major contribution of OD has been an understanding of the process of introducing change. Process consultation, an approach that helps the organization to solve its own problems by improving the problem-solving, communication, and relationship processes in the organization, has emerged as an alternative to expert consultation, the approach where outside consultants generate problem solutions and present them for consideration by the organization. Currently the technologies for introducing and managing change are expanding and becoming more sophisticated and problem-specific as OD programs are being initiated in organizations of all types. As change becomes a way of life in most organizations, there is a shift of focus from change as something created and managed by external consultants to a concern with the manager as change agent, managing the change process as part of his or her job function. As a result there is less concern today with training OD professionals and greater concern with improving managers' OD skills.

With greater change and complexity in organizational systems, the dialectic in Lewin's action research model seems to be shifting from an emphasis on action to an emphasis on research. Policy development and strategy planning techniques are being developed to assist organizations in their adaptation to increasingly complex and turbulent environments. These approaches seem to be reversing Lewin's dictum—"If you want to change something, try to understand it."

Management Education

From the beginning, the field of organizational behavior has been concerned with educational innovations, particularly those aimed at communicating abstract academic knowledge in a way that is helpful and meaningful to pragmatically oriented professional managers and management students. The two dominant innovative traditions in this respect have been the development of the case method, particularly at the Harvard Business School, and the experiential learning approaches that have grown from Kurt Lewin's early work on group dynamics and the sensitivity training movement that followed. Both these traditions have developed educational technologies that are sophisticated in their application of theory to practice. Today, most management schools offer a mix of educational approaches—the traditional lecture, the case discussion, and experiential exercises, sometimes combining them in new and innovative ways, such as in computer-based business simulations. With these new educational technologies, management educators have begun to raise their aspirations from increasing student awareness and understanding to improving skills in interpersonal relations, decision making, managing change, and other key managerial functions. These new aspirations create new challenges for the design of management education and training programs, where the criteria for success are based on performance rather than cognitive comprehension. Yet the future poses an even greater challenge. The rapid growth of knowledge and increasing rate of social and technological change are making specific skill training more and more vulnerable to obsolescence. The answer seems to lie not in learning new skills, but in learning how to learn and adapt throughout one's career. An emerging concern in management education and research is, therefore, how individuals and organizations learn; developing the basic processes and adaptive competencies that facilitate effective individual and organizational adaptation to a changing world.

THE PLAN OF THIS BOOK

In choosing topics and exercises for this book, we have attempted to represent all the major current trends in organizational behavior: those that are mature and established, those that are the focus of current research excitement, and new ideas that suggest the future shape of the field. The book is organized into five parts progressing generally from a focus on the individual to a focus on larger units of organizational analysis: the group, the organization, and the organization-environment interface. Part I examines the individual in the organization. Chapters 1 and 5 consider the individual's relationship with the organization over time through the concepts of the psychological concept and organizational socialization and career development. Chapter 2 reviews the principal theories of management. Chapters 3 and 4 focus, respectively, on the learning/problem-solving and motivational determinants of human behavior in organizations—on how individual motivation and skill in problem-solving influence organizational performance. Part II examines the creation of effective work relationships. It begins with an examination of interpersonal communication in Chapter 6 and progresses to the study of perception in Chapter 7. Chapter 8 focuses on group dynamics, while Chapter 9 deals with problem management. Managing multigroup work and intergroup conflict are addressed in Chapter 10. Managing diversity, both in the United States and abroad, are examined in Chapter 11. The chapters in Part III examine critical leadership functions in the managerial role—creating and maintaining organizational culture (Chapter 12), decision making (Chapter 13), power and influence (Chapter 14), supervision and employee development (Chapter 15), and performance appraisal (Chapter 16). Part IV is concerned with managing effective organizations. It portrays the organization as a sociotechnical system that exists as an open system in a wider, changing environment. Chapter 17 examines the organization-environment relationship via the concept of open systems analysis; Chapter 18 examines issues of organization structure, communication, and design; Chapter 19 is concerned with the sociotechnical design of work and its impact on worker motivation, and Chapter 20 describes processes of planned change and organization development.

YOUR ROLE AS A LEARNER

You will find as you work with this book that a new role is being asked of you as a learner. Whereas in many of your prior learning experiences you were in the role of a passive recipient, you will now find the opportunity to become an active creator of your own learning. This is an opportunity for you to develop new and different relationships with faculty members responsible for this course. As you may already have sensed, the experiential learning approach provides numerous opportunities for shared leadership in the learning process.

ORGANIZATIONAL BEHAVIOR

1

THE PSYCHOLOGICAL CONTRACT AND ORGANIZATIONAL SOCIALIZATION

OBJECTIVES   After completing Chapter 1, you should be able to:

A. Define the terms "psychological contract" and the "self-fulfilling prophecy."

B. Describe examples of changing expectations in our society.

C. Explain the "pinch model."

D. Make a psychological contract with your professor.

I   Premeeting Preparation

II   Topic Introduction

III   Procedure for Group Meeting: Instructor/Participant Interviews

IV   Follow-up

V   Learning Points

VI   Tips for Managers

VII   Personal Application Assignment

A Cold Slap in the Face . . . Past Graduates, Corporate Managers Explain why you Probably Can't 'Have it All'

Douglas A. Campbell

Kreig Smith believed he knew what to expect in the business world after earning a master's degree from Brigham Young University last year. Successful internships, including four months with IBM Corp. in Rochester, Minn., had prepared him for the rigors of life after college, he thought.

Kreig's confidence was buoyed when he met the chief executive of the small computer concern that had recruited him. The man spoke of team effort, hard work and family. "He used to refer to himself as the father of the company, and he was proud to be a father," recalls Kreig, who says his ideals are as important to him as career success.

The job lasted one year. By the time Kreig left, he was calling management in American business a sham and was totally disillusioned with the man to whom he had looked for leadership.

Marie Robard, a recent University of Denver graduate, took a sales job with an electronics industry giant when she graduated two years ago. She worked hard enough in college to get decent grades, but no more. So the demands of her new job, where she spent from 7 A.M. until after the dinner hour, were unexpected. Still, Marie dived into her work, and soon she was outperforming her peers and exceeding her sales quotas by a remarkable margin.

Then Marie (not her real name) discovered the reward for her effort: Her quota was doubled, and the big bonuses that once fell into her pocketbook each month now had to be chased.

Like many new college graduates, Marie and Kreig were surprised newcomers to business. Although many graduates manage smooth transitions into their chosen careers, the road from the classroom to the conference room can be riddled with unexpected hazards.

"It's a complete change of cultures," says Victor R. Lindquist, director of placement at Northwestern University.

"Most people get a perception in their minds (of what work will be like)," adds Robert K. Armstrong, manager of professional staffing for DuPont Co. "All too frequently, it turns out not to be that way," resulting in a high degree of turnover at most companies in the first five years of employment, says Mr. Armstrong.

Professionals who work with recent graduates report that they're often surprised by the level of pay they receive, the hours they're required to work, the effect of those hours on their social lives and on their expectations for developing a family. They're also unprepared for office politics and for the need to seek— and accept—the help of those with more experience.

Source: Reprinted from *Managing Your Career,* Fall 1987, Dow Jones & Co., Inc., pp. 6, 9.

Hedwin Naimark, a social psychologist, conducted a study of college seniors in 1985 and 1986 to find out what they expected from the workplace. "They seemed to focus on what it's like to be a student," Ms. Naimark says. "You go to class, you do your work and you receive a good grade if you do what you're supposed to do. The concept that there are other things involved when you got to the workplace was missing," she says.

"Their concept of how they are going to live their lives is deeply affected by the whole aura of the country, which right now is (that) everybody is going to do everything and everybody is going to have everything," Ms. Naimark says.

If you have been lured by the beer commercial asking, "Who says you can't have it all?" consider the experience of Marie Robard.

"I found that to be good at what I was doing, (the job) had to be the number one priority in my life," says Marie, who describes her college experience as "a whole lot of fun."

"I would say my first year out of college, I didn't have a social life," she says.

That didn't bother Marie, because she was establishing herself as a star salesperson and because she was being rewarded with early promotions. What did bother her were the office politics ("It's really frustrating. It's constantly going on, and you have to learn to play it.") and what she saw as a lack of cooperation between corporate departments ("It's like you're fighting against somebody instead of everybody working together").

And then there was the matter of quotas. "I was penalized for being successful," says Marie, who still works for the same company.

For Kreig Smith, it was the human interplay that drove him from his corporate job. With a degree in organizational behavior, Kreig took a job as an internal management consultant. After interviewing workers to determine what motivated them, he was convinced they were seeking "respect and dignity" as much as anything. And so when the CEO talked "about quality, quality that extended beyond the product to how we dealt with everyone," that hit a responsive chord in Kreig.

Then the company's business took a nosedive.

"When things got tough, (the CEO's) tune changed. I talked with him personally. He would say, 'I'm tired of being the father. They're a bunch of crying babies.'

"I heard him say, 'As president, I have to compromise my integrity. If I didn't compromise, I couldn't interact with the board of directors.'"

The reality of the workplace eventually drove Kreig to start his own business, a consulting firm where he and a partner call the shots and set the standards.

TOO MUCH TIME

One of the most common and unexpected realities for recent graduates is the time a job demands, according to Elizabeth A. Meyer, director of Stanford University's Career Management Center. Employers attempt to make time demands clear, Ms. Meyer says, "but it's still sometimes a shock.

"It's often lifestyle issues that are troubling—things they (recent graduates) hadn't anticipated or thought wouldn't be important, the location or hours of the job," Ms. Meyer explains. "Many of our people are on the job 80 hours a week, and they think: I can handle it. And then they see their marriages or social lives falling apart."

In some industries—computer concerns and financial houses in particular— recent graduates often find room for rapid advancement. But industries with slower growth paths offer less chance for promotion—and more frustration.

"A number one ticket item (among recent graduates) is the expectation . . . that advancement's going to take place quickly with a very well-defined path," says DuPont's Mr. Armstrong. But for that to happen, he says, there has to be a combination of a well-qualified employee and a company with a need.

"In becoming more competitive, more productive, companies have had to come to grips with how they can do business . . . with fewer people," Mr. Armstrong says. As corporations pare management levels, new recruits have fewer positions into which they can rise. At DuPont, for example, an engineer who once could expect a management post after five years now may find himself on the engineering bench for 10 years or more before advancement, Mr. Armstrong says.

"I have five engineers who have been here for a while. Business is so-so, so we really don't have a need to promote them," says Mr. Armstrong. "Yet they have a feeling there should be advancement."

LEARNING THE ROPES
On any new job, recent graduates will find it necessary to learn the ropes—the peculiarities of the particular company and its expectations of new workers. To do that, Mr. Lindquist suggests that on visits to prospective employers, job seekers should spend time with potential new colleagues "to see whether this is a group of people with whom you would like to work."

A big mistake is failing to ask questions. "You can expedite the learning process by asking the right questions," Mr. Lindquist advises. New hires also should be wary of "the person who offers all kinds of counsel gratuitously as to what's in and what's not, who's good and who's bad. Very often, this is a discontented employee who hasn't figured out the system and isn't likely to be moving on," Mr. Lindquist says.

Ms. Naimark, the psychologist who studied undergraduates for Catalyst, a nonprofit New York City organization that specializes in women's career development issues, says among the 1,000 students she surveyed, "both men and women think they're going to have demanding and exciting careers. They think they're going to increase their salaries, be married and have children and be good parents."

After dealing with the realities of the workplace, she says the students' attitudes change. "What you see is a great growth . . . of the understanding that there are options and trade-offs."

In other words, the experts say, you can't have it all.

I
Premeeting Preparation

    A. Read "A Cold Slap in the Face."
    B. Read the Topic Introduction.

II
Topic Introduction

All the recent graduates in Campbell's article, "A Cold Slap in the Face" had one thing in common—in each case the psychological contract between the employee and the employer had broken down.

    A psychological contract is implicitly formed between individuals and the organizations to which they belong. This contract, as do others, deals with the organization's expectations of the individual and his or her contributions to meet these expectations. It also deals with the individual's expectations of the organization and its contribution to meet these expectations. The psychological contract is unlike a legal contract in that the former defines a dynamic, changing relationship that is continually being renegotiated. Often important aspects of the contract are not formally agreed upon—key organizational and individual expectations, as well as implicit premises about the relationship, are sometimes unstated. Organizational contributions, such as a sense of challenge in one's job and individual contributions such as loyalty to the company, are expected but often not consciously weighed. Yet this contract is a reality that has a great many implications for productivity and individual satisfaction. A company staffed by "cheated" individuals who expect far more than they get is headed for trouble. The rebel who refuses to meet key company expectations becomes a stumbling block to production. On the other hand, individual creativity is likely to be stifled in a company that demands total compliance to peripheral expectations or norms such as manner of dress.

    The dynamic quality of the psychological contract means that individual and company expectations and individual and company contributions mutually influence one another. High expectations on the part of the company can produce increased individual contributions, and great contributions will likewise raise expectations. From the company's point of view, the questions become, "How can we manage our human resources so that we can maximize individual contributions?" "How can we socialize our members to accept our expectations and norms as legitimate?" For the individual, the questions are, "How can I get the satisfaction and rewards that I want from this organization?" "How can I manage my own career so that my socialization takes place in organizational settings that encourage my personal growth and development?" and "How can I fulfill the expectations of the organization and still have time for my personal life?"

Campbell suggested that "the cold slap in the face" might be avoided by asking more questions during the job interview process. Certainly both prospective employees and employers would be better off if their expectations were made explicit from the beginning. But often we are not aware of our expectations until they have been disappointed/transgressed. That's why mechanisms or forums that allow for continued discussions and renegotiations of the contract are so important throughout the term of employment.

Research evidence demonstrates the importance of early organizational experiences to future performance. Berlew and Hall,[1] in a study of managerial performance in a large public utility, report a very strong and consistent relationship between the company's *initial* expectations of the manager (during the first year on the job) and his or her future performance. Company expectations focused upon the type and quality of contributions expected of the manager, and performance was measured by rate of salary growth. In other words, the individuals for whom the organization had high initial job expectations were among the highest performers five years later. It is possible that new employees who are perceived to have high potential are given more challenging first assignments that allow them to develop performance skills and become visible more quickly.

Today, many large corporations formally label those employees for whom they have high expectations. Their succession management programs involve paying special attention to this group of "fast trackers" to provide them with the experiences and opportunities that will prepare them to take a top leadership role in the future. Such programs can be very effective but one of their by-products may be resentment and complaints (both valid and invalid) by "nonfast trackers" who feel that they, too, could shine if they received the special treatment that goes along with higher expectations of one's performance.

Support for the importance of the psychological contract between an individual and an organization comes from a number of other sources. Rosenthal's findings on the effect researchers have on the outcome of their behavioral research are particularly impressive and can be viewed as empirical verification of the power of the self-fulfilling prophecy.[2] First, Rosenthal gave the same strain of rats to different groups of students at Harvard.[3] The students' task was to teach their rats to run a maze. However, one group of students was told their rats were bright; the other group was told their rats were dull. Although there were no inherent differences between the two groups of rats, the so-called "bright rats" learned to run mazes better than did the "dull" rats. Further inquiry revealed that the students found the "bright" rats more likable" and therefore had treated them differently. Intrigued, Rosenthal and Jacobson tried the same experiment with school children.[4] They randomly chose one child out of every five and told teachers that these children were "academic spurters." At the year's end the "academic spurters" had improved their IQ by an average of 22 points. The teachers' expectations about these students affected the way they treated the children. The children's response to that treatment was to become "academic spurters." The critical variable in these examples is the teacher's (or rat handler's) expectation: higher expectations were associated with higher learning. The children (and the rats) became what the teachers thought they were, which is a perfect example of self-fulfilling prophecy.

---

[1]David E. Berlew and Douglas T. Hall, "The Socialization of Managers: The Effects of Expectations on Performance," *Administrative Science Quarterly,* Vol. 11, no. 2 (September 1966), pp. 207–223.

[2]Robert Rosenthal, *Experimenter Effects in Behavioral Research* (New York: Appleton–Century–Crofts, 1966).

[3]Robert Rosenthal and K. L. Fode, "The Effect of Experimenter Bias on the Performance of the Albino Rat," *Behavioral Science,* Vol. 8, 1968, pp. 183–189.

[4]Robert Rosenthal and L. F. Jacobson, "Teacher Expectations for the Disadvantaged," *Scientific American,* Vol. 218, 1968, pp. 19–23.

Zimbardo's research on life in prisons provides further confirmation of the power of the self-fulfilling prophecy.[5] A mock prison was set up on the campus of Stanford University. A group of 10 "prisoners" and 11 "guards" was selected from a group of 75 volunteers because they were judged to be emotionally stable, physically healthy, mature law-abiding citizens. The experiment, which was scheduled to continue for two weeks, had to be called off after six days. Everyone involved began to act in accordance with the expectations of their respective roles. Prisoners expected guards to be inhuman, insensitive, brutal, and so on. Guards expected prisoners to be surly, obdurate, plan rebellions and escapes, and so on. In a matter of hours, these expectations began to become reality, and, once begun, the cycle fed upon itself and the experimental nature of the venture was lost. The emotional risks of continuing were too high.

Lest we try anxiously to wriggle away from the implications of his research too quickly, Zimbardo points out that

> For the most disturbing implication of our research comes from the parallels between what occurred in that basement mock prison and daily experiences in our own lives—and we presume yours. The physical institution of prison is but a concrete and steel metaphor for the existence of more pervasive, albeit less obvious, institutions of the mind that all of us daily create, populate, and perpetuate.
>
> To what extent do we allow ourselves to become imprisoned by docilely accepting the roles others assign to us or, indeed, choose to remain prisoners because being passive and dependent frees us from the need to act and be responsible for our actions?[6]

What is the practical significance in the workplace of understanding that, to some degree "we become what others think we are"?

- Employees who are expected to do well will likely perform better than those who are not when, in fact, there may be no differences between them.
- Supervisors who have high expectations of their employees will be more likely to have their expectations met.

As a culture we have been experiencing significant changes in the psychological contracts we make. At present one of the major areas where expectations are changing is the workplace. Massive terminations in previously stable companies and the increased percentage of people who remain unemployed for a longer period of time has caused people to question the American Dream itself.[7] Previously the terms of the psychological contract between many Americans and their corporate employers was relatively simple. Employees were willing to work their way slowly up the corporate ladder in return for the promise of a sufficiently high promotion in their middle age to allow them to live comfortably during their retirement years. Massive terminations and the employment uncertainty resulting from widespread mergers and acquisitions has caused many Americans to change these expectations.

One of the exercises commonly used with MBA classes at Case Western Reserve University involves drawing a map of one's life. Prior to 1982, the majority of the executive MBAs (referred to as EMBAs) placed their jobs squarely in the center of their drawings, with family and other interests positioned on the sidelines. However, after the Rust Belt layoffs in 1982, many of the EMBAs began to place their family, in particular, and nonwork interests in the center of their life maps and their jobs on the periphery. The psychological contract regarding work and its

[5]Phillip Zimbardo, "A Priondellian Prison," *The New York Times Magazine,* April 8, 1973.
[6]Ibid., p. 60.
[7]Oxford Analytica, *American in Perspective* (Boston: Houghton Mifflin, 1986).

rewards has been broken, and the EMBAs were apparently placing more emphasis on other areas which seemed to offer more permanence. The sacrifices and the toll their work had taken on the rest of their lives no longer seemed reasonable when the outcome of such loyalty and hard work was not guaranteed.

An interesting aftermath of the organizational downsizing and shrinkage we have seen in the early 1980s is that many people—whether they were personally affected or not—were motivated to rethink and renegotiate their psychological contracts with the organizations which employ them. As a result, managers and human resource professionals are grappling with questions such as the following: How do organizations promote commitment on the part of employees who no longer trust in job security? How do companies satisfy employees who expect rapid promotions in an economy which is not expanding enough to create as many jobs at the top?

An equally powerful set of expectational shifts can be deduced from the value trends Boyatzis and Skelly have identified for the current decade.[8] Based upon annual national surveys, organizational surveys, and historical documents, they discern the following value trends for the 1980s:

1. A strategic, competitive will to win on the part of individuals.
2. Revival of the importance of the nuclear family.
3. Increased regional parochialism and nationalism which manifests a desire to belong to something you can believe in.

New value trends and changing norms result in revised psychological contracts. This last decade is noteworthy for its upheaval in relationships with significant others, particularly among men and women. As Yankelovich commented in 1981, "Changing norms of what a woman is 'supposed to do' as wife and mother and what a man is 'supposed to do' as husband and father are transforming the institutions of the workplace and the family."[9]

It is not surprising, therefore, that many people experience a vague sense of restlessness inside themselves and in relation to significant others. As our expectations change, in the ways just suggested, the threads that keep us feeling whole within ourselves and connected to others begin to stretch. These threads are literally the "ties that bind" and reflect the implied contracts we make with ourselves and others.

A MODEL FOR MANAGING PSYCHOLOGICAL CONTRACTS

Working with people from other cultures forces the realization that psychological contracts have a cultural flavor to them. The Japanese concept of lifetime employment is one of many examples of cultural differences. Another is the Latin American expectation that bosses will attend the family celebrations—baptisms, first communions, marriages, and funerals—of their employees. In multicultural settings it becomes quickly apparent that different cultures utilize different psychological contracts and that devoting energy to understanding them is critical. But, given the changing expectations within our own society and the varying expectations of different generations in the workplace, we may do well to follow the cross-cultural model and proceed on the assumption that other people's expectations are not the same as our own. Let us examine a model that may help us to see ways both to anticipate and to manage the multiplicity of contractual changes confronting us in all aspects of life.

[8]Richard Boyatzis and Florence Skelly, "The Impact of Changing Values on Organizational Life," D. A. Kolb, I. M. Rubin, and J. S. Osland, *Organizational Behavior: Practical Readings for Managers,* 5th ed. (Englewood Cliffs, N.J.: Prentice Hall, 1990).

[9]See Daniel Yankelovich, "New Rules in American Life: Searching for Self-fulfillment in a World Turned Upside Down," *Psychology Today,* April 1981, pp. 35–91.

Sherwood and Glidewell have developed a simple but powerful model that (1) describes the dynamic quality of psychological contracts and (2) suggests ways of minimizing the potentially dysfunctional consequences of shifting expectations (Figure 1–1). It provides a framework for the continuous management of the psychological contract in the day-to-day work setting. The first stage of any relationship between two individuals and/or an individual and an organization is characterized by a *sharing of information and a negotiating of expectations*. Suppose that an organization informed potential new employees that everyone was expected to work from 9 A.M. to 12 noon on Saturdays. The potential new employee expects to work only Monday through Friday. If this difference in expectations cannot be resolved at this point, the two will part ways. They have found out immediately that they have an irresolvable mismatch.

Assuming that both parties hear enough of what they expect to hear from the other, they make a *joint commitment*. The employee and employer both expect to move into a period of *stability* and productivity. It is time to get down to work.

Even with the best of intentions and full sharing of initial expectations, changes are likely to occur over time. One or both of the parties begins to feel a "pinch" as Sherwood and Glidewell term it. For example, an employee may have been more than willing to put in heavy overtime and cover weekend shifts when he or she was single and new in town. But a marriage involving certain expectations about the time a couple should spend together might change the employee's attitude toward

FIGURE 1–1   Model for Managing Psychological Contracts   *Source: Adapted from J. J. Sherwood and J. C. Glidewell, "Planned Renegotiation: A Norm Setting OD Intervention," in* Contemporary Organization Development: Orientations and Interventions, *edited by W. W. Burke (Washington, DC: NTL Institute, 1972), pp. 35–46.*

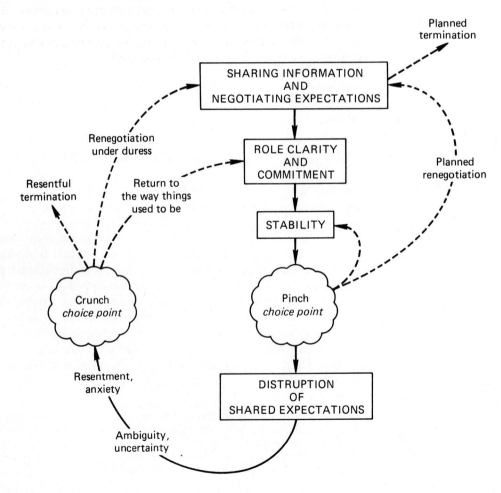

demanding hours and the automatic assumption that this particular employee will work them. Sherwood and Glidewell suggest that a pinch like this can be used as an early warning sign to manage the psychological contract process before situations become disruptive. Discussing and renegotiating expectations at this point will lead to either a return to stability or, if differences cannot be resolved, to a planned departure. Employees sometimes respond to pinches by saying, "I don't have time to test this issue with him" or "If I raise this issue with my boss, she'll think I'm just complaining so I'll ignore it." But pinches have a habit of growing into larger problems if they are not handled in a planned manner without the heat of emotion that accompanies a *disruption of shared expectations.*

Since the "rules" that were agreed to initially have been upset, one or both parties experience heightened *uncertainty,* which invariably results in heightened *anxiety.* Human nature being what it is, energy is thus invested in reducing this anxiety. Typically, what happens at this point is an effort to return to the way things used to be. The parties apologize for the misunderstanding, smooth over the conflict, and attempt to renew their commitment to one another under terms of the old contract. To the extent that two parties remain unsatisfied in this cycle, the result is invariably some form of termination—psychological (apathy: "I'll be darned if I'm going to do any more than I'm required to") or physical (absenteeism, lateness, quitting, etc.).

In the classroom, the psychological contract is also very important. Generally only one of the parties makes their expectations explicit. Teachers begin a course by stating their requirements of students. Students are rarely asked to reciprocate, but woe to the teacher who fails to meet students' unstated expectations! The purpose of this unit is to introduce you to the concept of the psychological contract as it exists in the learning organization you are about to enter. In this way you will be able to move as quickly as possible to a period of stability and productivity (learning) and set in motion the processes of communication needed to deal with any subsequent "pinches" that may develop. In this course we encourage participants to state their expectations in the following exercise because it is the first step in taking responsibility for one's own learning.

III

Procedure for Group Meeting: Instructor/Participant Interviews

Preparation

The goal in this part of the exercise is for the instructor to learn from the group members *their* expectations for the course: what they hope to learn, where they see these learnings as being useful. In addition, the instructor will try to learn what members feel they can contribute to the achievement of their expectations, how they can make these contributions, and what members feel they as learners can contribute to the learning process. In this part, the instructor will interview participants in the course via representatives.

STEP 1. The total group should divide into small discussion groups, four or five people per group.

STEP 2. Each group should elect a representative of the team that will be interviewed by the instructor.

STEP 3. Using the guide provided in the accompanying Instructor's Interview of Participants: A Question Guide, each group should discuss the general question areas in which the instructor will pose specific questions to the team representative during the interview.

Note: The instructor may add at this point any specific issues of concern not covered in the instructor's interview of participants: A question guide.

STEP 4. All representatives must understand their group's position on each of these questions so that they can accurately represent their views in response to the questions the instructor will pose during the interview. (You may want to jot these down on the guide provided.) (time allotted for steps 1–4: 30 minutes)

Instructor's Interview of Participants: A Question Guide

Few instructors ask group members to articulate their expectations for a class. During the ensuing interview, the instructor will try to gain an understanding of your views in the following general areas:

1. What are your goals for this course? To increase self-awareness? To learn theories? To get a grade? To apply learning in your job? Something else?

2. In what ways do you feel the instructor can best help you to achieve your goals? Lecture, give examinations, lead seminar discussions? Let you work on your own?

3. What, if anything, have you heard about this textbook and/or this course from others?

4. What reservations do you have about this course?

5. What is the "best" thing that could happen in this course? What is the "worst" thing?

6. What are your resources for this course (prior work experience, other courses in psychology, etc.)?

Notes

STEP 5. The representatives, one from each team, meet with the instructor. The instructor will interview them (using the Instructor's Interview of Participants: A Question Guide) to understand their expectations for the course.

STEP 6. The remainder of the class acts as observers, paying particular attention to the instructor's questions and the areas that seem most salient. You might find it helpful to jot down on the upcoming Participants' Interview of Instructor: A Suggested Question Guide the observations that you feel will help you prepare for the second round of interviewing. (time allotted for steps 5 and 6: 20 minutes)

PARTICIPANTS' INTERVIEW OF INSTRUCTOR

Preparation
The goal in this part of the exercise is for the course participants to find out what the instructor's expectations are for the course. What does the instructor hope they will learn from the course? What can the instructor contribute to the learning process? In this part, the participants will interview the instructor via representatives.

STEP 7. The class should form into the same small discussion groups used in Part A.

STEP 8. Each group should elect a member (other than the person they elected in step 2) as their representative to the team that will interview the instructor.

STEP 9. Using the guide provided as a starting point (Participants' Interview of Instructor: A Suggested Question Guide), each group should discuss any questions which they would like their representative to pose to the instructor.

STEP 10. Representatives should make certain that they understand the group's concerns so that they can accurately translate these concerns into questions to be posed to the instructor. (You may want to jot these down on the guide provided.) (time allotted for steps 7–10: 30 minutes)

Participants' Interview of Instructor: A Suggested Question Guide

You will have the opportunity to ask the instructor any questions you feel are relevant to effective learning during this course. (Note: It is important that you ask questions that are of real concern to you at this point. Only in this way can potentially important problems or conflicts be identified and be managed.) You probably have many ideas of your own and the questions asked by the instructor during the first interview should suggest others to you.

Some areas you may want to discuss are the following:

1. The instructor's objectives for the course—what does he or she hope to accomplish?

2. The instructor's theory of learning (i.e. how do people learn)

3. The instructor's feelings on the question of evaluation

4. The instructor's expectations of you

5. The instructor's role in the class

6. Anything else you think is important

Be sure to ask specific questions. Think about the assumptions that may underlie some of your questions; for example, why you feel this is an important question. Test these assumptions by asking the instructor's opinion if you feel it will be helpful.

Notes

STEP 11. Representatives interview instructor to understand the instructor's expectations for them and the course.

STEP 12. The remainder of the group acts as observers, paying particular attention to the following areas:

    a. In what ways do your (groups') expectations agree or disagree with the contributions the instructor feels he or she can make?

    b. In what way do the instructor's expectations agree or disagree with the contributions you feel you can make?

    c. In what way do you feel that you can contribute to the achievement of your own expectations?

    d. In looking back over your group discussions, how much diversity was there within the group concerning expectations?

(time allotted for steps 11 and 12: 30 minutes)

COMPARISON OF INTERVIEWS AND IDENTIFICATION OF POTENTIAL PINCHES

STEP 13. The total group should develop a list of (1) areas of difference that became apparent during the previous two interviews and (2) possible future conflicts—pinches—that will be important to watch for.

    a. To the extent possible, differences that will influence the learning process should be discussed further, with an eye toward a mutually acceptable negotiated resolution.

    b. With respect to potential future pinches, the group should discuss their expectations concerning

        (1) Whose responsibility it will be or should be to raise a pinch if and when it develops.

        (2) The mechanisms to be used for raising pinches (e.g., written comments, informal discussions at the end of meetings).

STEP 14. Instructor and participants should discuss their feelings and assessment of the value of this way of beginning a new course. (time allotted for steps 13 and 14: 30–40 minutes)

IV

Follow-up

Although we do not often view the processes in the same terms, entering a classroom environment the first time is very much like the first day on a new job. The typical orientation program in a company is usually very one-sided. Most company communication flows from the organization to the individual, "These are our policies, procedures, expectations."

One effect of this one-sided process is to cause "new employees" to feel that the organization is much more powerful than they are as individuals. This feeling of powerlessness often creates a situation in which new employees, when asked their expectations, try to second-guess the company's expectations. Instead of trying to formulate and articulate their own expectations, the new employees (participants) often repeat what they *think* the organization (instructor) wants to hear. Another effect is the organization's tendency to oversocialize new members. The new employee's feeling of powerlessness often results in more passivity than might ordinarily be felt appropriate in the situation.

Recall your last job interview. Remember how you tried to "look good" to the organization—to guess what it wanted, on what qualities it was evaluating you. How much time did you spend telling the interviewer what your expectations were and asking what the organization could contribute to your needs? Probably very little and then very cautiously. Our studies on individuals' entries into organizations and our work with orientation and training programs has led to the conclusion that in entering an organization, nearly everyone experiences a feeling of helplessness and dependency on the organization. From a functional point of view, this dependency seems necessary so that the organization can begin to socialize the incoming member to meet its norms and values, its way of doing things. Yet our observations have led us to conclude that most organizations overdo this—they tend to oversocialize their members. (For example, placing too much emphasis upon the organization's expectations of newcomers may result in conformity.) The phase of entry into an organization seems to be a critical period for the new members. Individuals who are overpowered and overcontrolled by organizational constraints become listless, passive members. Those who are challenged by the tasks they face and are encouraged toward responsibility can move toward success and mastery of their organizational life.

The organization often reads passivity as a sign that new employees want and need more direction and control—they want to be told exactly what to do. This situation can create a feedback cycle that, in the long run, operates to the detriment of both the individual and the organization. The organization needs people who are innovative, creative, and independent thinkers to survive and remain productive in a rapidly changing environment. Individual growth and satisfaction also demand these same kinds of behavior. Often, however, the new employee's (participant's) first contact with the organization sets in motion a cycle that acts directly counter to these long-range goals and needs.

There is another way in which we can view the process of organizational socialization and the notion of the psychological contract. In approaching any new organization, an individual makes two classes of decisions: a decision to join and a decision to participate.[10] In some cases, individuals have no control over their

[10]See J. G. March and H. A. Simon, *Organization* (New York: John Wiley, 1963), especially Chapter 4, for a fuller discussion of this conceptual scheme.

decisions to join, perhaps in the military or in a required course. When this condition exists, the organization often reacts by tightly controlling the socialization process, and the psychological contract becomes extremely structured (in the sense of policies, rules, and the like) and limiting (in the sense that legitimate behavior on the part of the organization members is clearly spelled out.)[11]

There are many cases, however, in which individuals do have control over their decision to join. One often finds, however, that the factors people use to help make the decision to join are unrelated to longer-run, higher-order goals they may have. For example, when interviewing a company for a job, most people ask questions about pay, fringe benefits, insurance plans, vacations, and the like. Fewer ask about the specific nature of their first job or the opportunities for personal growth and development. In the case of a class, most people, when given the chance, ask about the grading scheme, the amount of reading, the length of the required term paper, and the like. Few ask about the value of the course to them as individuals or about what they can expect to learn.

The process by which we join an organization has implications for the second class of decisions—the decision to participate. The focus here is on what happens after the individual has decided to join (voluntarily or otherwise) and has to do with the manner in which the person interacts with the organization on a day-to-day basis. In companies many people find that the job they are doing fails to meet many of their needs for challenge, responsibility, individual initiative, and so on. They become frustrated and dissatisfied and often leave after a few months.[12] Note, however, that these are expectations that they did not make explicit at the entry point— their decision to join.

In the classroom people often find a course dull, boring, and unexciting and feel that they are wasting their time. They sit passively in class every week (if they bother to keep attending), uninvolved in their own learning, and work to meet the organization's expectations to get a grade. Their own expectations for learning, involvement, and stimulation go unsatisfied, in large measure because they never made such expectations explicit.

You may have experienced some of these dilemmas during this unit. Learners often are unused to bearing much responsibility for their own learning. They are much more accustomed to the instructor's assuming full responsibility. Thus, when confronted with a genuine opportunity to participate in the learning process, they often became confused ("What kind of way is this to start a class?") and suspicious ("I wonder what the instructor is trying to do?").

When asked to articulate expectations, learners tend to be very vague and general, frustrating to all involved. Expectations are much more likely to be satisfied when a set of realistic, concrete goals can be developed. Instructors must realize that learners who are unused to controlling their own education will have to learn to accept that responsibility. The point is that *both* participants and instructor have a share of the responsibility for the learning process.

This point is an important one to reemphasize. A confusion often develops, as a result of this initial contracting session, of the form: "Why all this talk about our expectations and stuff? You [the instructor] already have the course laid out, the syllabus typed, and the schedule planned!" As is true in any organization, the general thrust or goals are given. This is not a course in art or home economics. It is a course in organizational behavior, but there are many areas of flexibility: what *specific* goals you as a participating learner set within the general objectives, how you relate to peers and staff, who takes what responsibility for *how* goals are achieved. Differences will exist around those issues, and they need to be explored during the initial socialization process.

[11]Edgar H. Schein, "How to Break in the College Graduate," *Harvard Business Review* (November–December 1964), pp. 68–76.

[12]A more complete description of the psychological contract may be found in Chapter 4 of Edgar H. Schein, *Organizational Psychology* (Englewood Cliffs, N.J.: Prentice Hall, 1965).

Clearly, within the context of a first class session of a few hours, all the possible conflicts that can arise will not be anticipated nor can all those anticipated be solved. More important than any concrete conclusions that may come out of this contract-setting exercise is a series of norms for dealing with conflicts. As a result of this contract exploration process, the legitimacy of conflict or difference can be established, the right to question each other and particularly the instructor can be demonstrated, and a decision-making process of shared responsibility to resolve conflicts can be introduced.

V

Learning Points

1. Psychological contracts are implicit or explicit (agreements on mutual expectations) that change over time.

2. People have psychological contracts with organizations and with individuals whether or not they are aware of them.

3. The pinch model is a way to avoid major disruptions by heeding early warning signs that expectations about the contract have changed and need to be reconsidered.

4. According to the concept of self-fulfilling prophecies, expectations about another person partly determine how he or she will act or perform.

VI

Tips for Managers

- Set aside time to establish and discuss expectations early.

- Remember that contracts are very likely to change over time. Therefore, make opportunities to check out whether the contract is still viable and renegotiate if necessary. Managers or leaders who take the initiative to do this checking are greatly appreciated because it is sometimes difficult for subordinates to bring "pinches" to their bosses' attention.

- "Pinches" are easier to handle than are full-blown breakdowns in expectations.

- Sample questions for checking out expectations:
    - What do you like/dislike about your job (or this relationship)?
    - Why do you continue with it?
    - Is there one thing that, if it were changed, would make you quit your job?
    - What are your expectations of me?
    - Do you think I am meeting them?
    - Is there any way I can help you do your job better?
    - What kind of supervision do you like best, or what type of supervision do you prefer to use with employees?
    - Does the organization or do I hinder you in completing your work?
    - Is there anything you would like to see changed?

- Some people use the following matrix to judge whether expectations are in line. The diagonal boxes should be fairly reciprocal. Using this matrix can be a good base for a discussion, but bear in mind that good human relationships are not based upon a uniformly tit-for-tat mentality, but upon a flexible give-and-take approach.

	Give	Take
Person A		
Organization/ Person B		

VII
Personal Application Assignment

The following is modeled after Kolb's adult learning cycle which appears in Chapter 3. Please respond to the questions and submit them at next week's class. Each section of the assignment is worth 4 points that will be assigned according to the criteria that follow.[13]

The topic of this assignment is to think back on a significant incident when you experienced a "pinch" in a psychological contract. Pick an experience about which you are motivated to learn more; that is, there is something about it that you do not totally understand, that intrigues you, that makes you realize you lack certain skills, that is problematical or very significant for you. It could have taken place in a work relationship or a social one (with a club or group) or within a personal relationship.

A. *Concrete Experience*

    1. *Objectively* describe the experience ("who," "what," "when," "where," "how" type information—up to 2 points).

    2. *Subjectively* describe your feelings, perceptions, and thoughts that occurred *during* (not after) the experience (up to 2 points). Does this section have too much detail? (If so, delete 1 point.)

B. *Reflective Observation*

    1. Look at the experience from different points of view. How many points of view did you include that are *relevant* (up to 2 points)?

    2. Use these perspectives to add more meaning to the incident (up to 2 points).

[13]This guideline was developed by Don McCormick, Ph.D., Antioch University, Los Angeles.

C. *Abstract Conceptualization*

1. Relate concepts from the assigned readings and the lecture to the experience (i.e., what theories that you heard in the lecture or read in the *Reader* relate to your understanding of this incident?).

2. Make reference to at least two sources. Use standard referencing format and include the page number to which you are referring. How many sources did you use and how clearly did you explain their theories (up to 4 points)?

3. You can also create an original model or theory, but it should not replace course concepts.

D. *Active Experimentation*

1. Write about what you will do in the future that will improve your effectiveness. Use rules of thumb or action resolutions.

2. Are they described specifically, thoroughly, and in detail (up to 4 points).

E. *Integration, Synthesis, and Writing*
1. Did you write about something personally important to you (up to 1 point)?
2. Was it well written (up to 2 points)?
3. Did you integrate and synthesize the different sections (up to 1 point)?

2

THEORIES OF MANAGING PEOPLE

OBJECTIVES   By the end of this chapter, you should be able to:

    A. Describe six theories of management and their "ideal" manager.

    B. Explain why it's important to identify your personal theories about management and organizational behavior.

    C. Describe your personal theory of management.

    D. Identify the managerial skills you need in today's environment.

    E. List the characteristics of organizational behavior.

The Education of a Modern International Manager

Jacques G. Maisonrouge

The novelist Gore Vidal once said that it is not enough to succeed; your friends must also fail. It is cleverly phrased—a true bon mot that speaks volumes about human psychology. But I do not agree, because success is not a zero-sum game in which there must be a loser for every winner.

This sentiment must sound odd coming from someone who has spent his adult life in the business world where the law of the jungle is supposed to prevail. But those of us who actually inhabit that world know that the modern business enterprise is too complex and too far-flung to be anything but a vast, cooperative effort with many interdependent parts. A multitude of skills and talents must mesh to make a large enterprise work. It is therefore in the common interest that as many people as possible succeed in what they do every single day. Toward that end, we learn from each other as much as we can.

Businesses have also learned to learn from each other—for example, through associations, through industry conferences, through consultants—and they have learned from universities. It is in this spirit that I am happy to share with you some thoughts on management education for an international career.

Throughout my career, I have met people with the same ambition, the same drive, even the same formal education—be they MBAs, graduate engineers, whatever—who did not achieve the same results at all. Those who are not successful—and I define success here as either rising on the hierarchical ladder or attaining professional distinction—share certain traits. First, they exhibit a lack of sensitivity in their relations with others. They become so mesmerized by the processes of management or the demands of their discipline that they lose sight of the human element. They forget that people are the sine qua non of working, planning, and decision making—in short, the ultimate resource of their operations.

Given these facts, it follows that the managers' quintessential responsibility is to help their people realize their own highest potential. They don't do this by intimidating them, or taking them for granted, or making them feel like "hired hands." They do it by inspiring them, recognizing their unique contributions to the general effort, and making them feel like valued members of a team. Certainly, a major reason for Japan's famous "economic miracle" has been its recognition that its chief resource—almost its only resource—is its people.

The second trait shared by the unsuccessful is a habit acquired first in

Source: Excerpt from a speech by Mr. Maisonrouge, senior vice president, IBM Corporation, and chairman of the board, IBM Word Trade Corporation, when he received the International Business Leader of the Year Award from the Academy of International Business in 1982. Reprinted in *Journal of International Business Studies,* Spring–Summer, 1983, pp. 141–146.

school. Having chosen to study only the subjects they liked, they continue that self-indulgence in business. What they like to do, they do well and neglect the rest. But to be successful in management, you must try to do well whatever needs doing.

Third, those who are unsuccessful never discard their youthful prejudices. To this day, they mistrust foreigners, members of the opposite sex, people who come from different regions of the country—anyone, in short, who differs from them. In the process, they miss the opportunity and benefits of learning from those who have another perspective.

So much for what the manager ought not to be or do.

Business has become subject to very rapid change. Alvin Toffler, the futurist, has dramatized this by translating the last 50,000 years into 800 lifetimes, then observing that of those 800 lifetimes, only the last 70 could communicate with their descendants through writing, only the last 8 ever saw a printed word, only the last 4 were able to measure time with any precision, only the last 2 used an electric motor, most of the material goods we use in our daily lives were developed within the 800th lifetime, and more technological progress will be made during the 801st lifetime than during the previous 800 combined.

Clearly, in a fast-changing environment the ability to plan for change becomes a managerial imperative. Consequently, tomorrow's managers will have to demonstrate more awareness of the world around them, more flexibility of mind, more "technological literacy" than ever before. In a world where new knowledge continues to accumulate rapidly, the most valuable managers of all will be those who have learned how to learn.

The two qualities I consider most essential to a manager's success in today's business world are a true global perspective and the ability to manage human resources. We in business look to the colleges and universities to impart the basic skills on which these qualities depend to the men and women who will someday take our places. In turn, we will do our best to translate what is being taught in the classroom into solid achievement.

I

Premeeting Preparation*

A. Think of four managers that you have had occasion to observe. Write their initials on the blanks. On the lines underneath, write adjectives that describe them.

_____ (MANAGER 1's INITIALS)   _____ (MANAGER 2)

_____   _____

_____   _____

_____   _____

_____   _____

_____   _____

_____ (MANAGER 3)   _____ (MANAGER 4)

_____   _____

_____   _____

_____   _____

_____   _____

_____   _____

B. Now write down the ways these managers behave differently from each other. Be specific. For example, if one manager strikes you as being a better communicator than another, don't stop with "M.G. communicates well; B.D. communicates poorly." Write down the specific behavior that is different, for example, "M.G. makes expectations clear; B.D. doesn't explain what she wants us to do."

*Note: This exercise was developed with Juliann Spoth, Case Western Reserve University, Cleveland, Ohio.

C. Return to the list you generated in B. Rank the items according to how important those behaviors are in terms of a manager's effectiveness. In other words, which are the most important behaviors for a manager to do if he or she wants to be successful?

D. Answer the following questions.

   1. How would you describe the ideal manager?

   2. How did you arrive at this ideal—previous experiences, values, role models, education, training, reading, and so on?

   3. What values underly your picture of the ideal manager?

   4. What were the significant learning points from the reading?

E. Read the Topic Introduction that follows.

II
Topic Introduction

As does Jacques Maisonrouge, whose speech was excerpted in the opening vignette, we all have our theories about what makes for successful managers and organizations. Peters and Waterman's list of attributes that characterize excellent companies is an example of a very popular current theory of management.[1] These attributes are:

1. bias for action,
2. close to the customer,
3. autonomy and entrepreneurship,
4. productivity through people,
5. hands-on,
6. value-driven,
7. stick to the knitting (the basic task),
8. simple,
9. lean staff, and
10. simultaneous, loose-tight properties.

Perhaps the most important piece they contributed to the management puzzle was the significance of shared values to the success of an organization.

Over the years, there have been numerous and varied contributions to our knowledge about organizations. Each reflected the theorists' model of what made for excellent organizations and managers within their sociohistorical context. Some of the major theories or schools of thought will be touched upon in the following paragraphs to set the stage for the study of organizational behavior.[2]

Frederick Taylor's *scientific management,*[3] the "one best way" of doing a job, which emerged in the late 1800s, emphasized the efficient division of labor into small, specialized, standardized jobs that were carefully matched with the capacities of workers. For the first time, Taylorism made it possible for engineers to research the most efficient way to do jobs. Taylor's goal was to develop workers to the best of their abilities and to convey the message that it was *cooperation* between capital and labor that resulted in success. By increasing profits, rather than arguing over their distribution, both labor and owners would prosper.

Taylor's name is often mistakenly associated with time-and-motion studies run amok and an inhumane emphasis upon output. In fact, Taylor was concerned about both the proper design of the job *and* the worker. In Taylor's eyes, the ideal manager (perhaps with the aid of an engineer) scientifically determined the goals that needed to be accomplished, divided the work up in the most efficient way, trained workers to do the job, and rewarded them by wage incentives such as piecework. However,

---

[1]Thomas J. Peters and Robert H. Waterman, Jr., *In Search of Excellence* (New York: Harper & Row, 1982).

[2]For fascinating histories of organizational theory, see Charles Perrow's *Complex Organizations: A Critical Essay* (New York: Random House, 1986) or Charles Perrow's "The Short and Glorious History of Organizational Theory," *Organizational Dynamics,* Summer 1973. For a comprehensive historical review that links management thought to economic, political, and social trends, see Daniel A. Wren's *The Evolution of Management Thought* (New York: John Wiley, 1979).

[3]Frederick A. Taylor, *The Principles of Scientific Management* (New York: W. W. Norton, 1911).

since foremen were cast as the "brains" who did planning rather than actual operations, workers came to be seen as little more than "a pair of hands." While that sounds pejorative, it was a perspective more easily understood when placed within the context of a country just beginning to industrialize. The labor force quite naturally consisted primarily of people from rural areas without prior factory experience. In that era, workers were viewed as one more resource, much like machines.

The next phase in management history was termed *administrative theory*. At that time, beginning about the late 1920s, managers were grappling with the problems of organizing larger and larger organizations and defining the emerging role of the professional manager. Administrative theory came up with answers to both issues. Fayol defined the functions of a manager as planning, controlling, organizing, and commanding and advocated the study of management as a discipline.[4] Weber contributed greatly to our understanding of the "ideal" bureaucracy and the different types of authority that were appropriate for it.[5] In those days, bureaucracy did not have the negative connotations it does today. Indeed, bureaucracy was then viewed as a solution to the nepotism, favoritism, and unprofessional behavior found in organizations of the day. During this era, people believed that if managers designed the organization correctly and followed the proven principles of management (e.g., having a limited number of people report to each supervisor, having only one boss for each worker, and engaging in merit-based selection of employees), the organization would succeed.

However, this formula for success was further complicated by the famous Hawthorne studies[6] that took place in the late 1920s and 1930s. It was a time when the credibility of business people was low due to the stock market crash and feelings of exploitation fueled the union movement. Decreased immigration had made labor scarce, and, as a result, the needs of workers began to receive attention. The Hawthorne studies contributed the idea that workers' output was also affected by the way they were treated; the way they felt about their work, their co-workers, and their boss; and what happened to them outside of work. The attention the workers received in the experiment, rather than the varied work conditions, caused them to work harder. This phenomenon has come to be known as the Hawthorne effect. The *human relations school* grew out of this research and acknowledged that workers had to be considered as more than "hands"; workers also had "hearts," feelings, and attitudes that affected productivity. And the norms or implicit rules of the work groups to which they belonged also affected productivity. Therefore, the effective manager was expected to pay attention to people's social needs and elicit their ideas about work issues.

March and Simon,[7] writing in the late 1950s, were proponents of the *decision-making school* and added yet another layer of complexity to our understanding of organizations with their description of organizations as social systems in which individual decisions were the basis of human behavior. For example, employees make the decision to join an organization, but once hired, they also have another decision to make—whether or not to participate and work as hard as they can. The outcome of this decision depends upon the employee's rational analysis of the situation and the rewards involved. Now managers also had to take into account workers' "minds." The effective manager set the premises for employee decisions and relied upon their rationality to make choices that would be best for both themselves and the organization. For example, if a CEO of a company in which marketing was seen as the springboard into top management decided that more emphasis needed

[4]Henri Fayol, *General and Industrial Management,* trans. C. Storrs (London: Sir Isaac Pitman, 1949).

[5]Max Weber, *The Theory of Social and Economic Organization,* trans. T. Parsons (New York: Free Press, 1947).

[6]F. J. Roethlisberger and W. J. Dickson, *Management and the Worker* (Cambridge, MA: Harvard University Press, 1939).

[7]James March and Herbert Simon, *Organizations* (New York: John Wiley, 1958).

to be placed upon operations, he or she would promote more rapidly from operations positions. Employees would then realize that operations was the area receiving top-level attention and ambitious workers would elect to work in that area. Manipulating the decision premises is an unobtrusive form of controlling the organization.

However, March and Simon also made the sobering observations that our decisions are limited by the number of variables our brains can handle, the time available, our reasoning powers, and so on; that is, the concept of bounded rationality. As a result, we learned that we "satisfied" rather than "maximized" when it came to decision making and that routine work drove out nonroutine work, which explained why it seems so much harder to launch important new projects than it is to maintain routine tasks. For theorists of this school, managerial effectiveness consisted of a thorough understanding of decision making for both themselves and others.

By the middle of the century, managers and scholars had identified many variables that were thought to be related to success: job specialization, managerial principles, worker attitudes and human relations, and rational decisions made by workers, among others. In the 1960s, many scholars converged on the idea that there was no "one best way" to manage. Instead, they tried to identify which variables would be successful for particular situations.

This is still the dominant perspective in the field of organizational behavior and is referred to as *contingency theory.*[8] The gist of this theory is that effectiveness varies according to the particular situation. We know now that individuals, groups, cultural groups, occupational subgroups, industries, types of technology, managerial styles, organizations, and external environments can all vary enormously. There are many examples of successful organizations that do things quite differently. For example, ITT under Harold Geneen and Matsushita under Konosuke Matsushita are examples of extremely well-managed, but exceedingly diverse, companies.[9] As long as the various aspects of the organization *fit* together, organizations seem to work. The building blocks of organizations are popularly referred to as the 7 Ss: strategy, structure, systems, staff, style, skills, and superordinate goals.[10]

AT&T, prior to the divestiture, had "good fit." The company's superordinate goals (universal service and serving the customer) and strategy were based upon a stable, regulated environment characterized by no external competition. It possessed staff who were primarily interested in stability and security, which fit with a promotion system based upon conformity. Its systems were highly routinized and suited to a stable environment. However, after the divestiture, AT&T found itself in a very competitive and turbulent environment. When the overall strategy changed to adapt to the new environment, the type of staff, the skills they had, the systems that were in place, and the managerial style were no longer appropriate. It has been a challenge for AT&T, as it is for any company, to learn the rules of a new game and transform itself to play a new game in a short period of time.

Being an effective manager now meant having an understanding of organizations as *open systems.* Systems theory maintains that organizations and all the subdivisions within them take in resources and transform them into a service or product that is purchased or utilized by a larger system. Acknowledging the inter-

---

[8]See D. A. Nadler and M. Tushman, "A Congruence Model for Diagnosing Organizational Behavior," *Readings.* For a famous example of research on contingency theory, see P. R. Lawrence and J. W. Lorsch," *Organization and Environment: Managing Differentiation and Integration* (Homewood, IL: Richard D. Irwin, 1969).

[9]Richard Tanner Pascale and Anthony G. Athos, *The Art of Japanese Management* (New York: Simon & Schuster, 1981).

[10]The 7S scheme, based upon the work of other organizational writers, was coined by Pascale and Athos and consultants of the McKenzie Company. It appears in *The Art of Japanese Management,* by Pascale and Athos (ibid.), and in D. A. Kolb, I. M. Rubin, and J. S. Osland, *Organization Behavior: Practical Readings for Managers* (Englewood Cliffs, N.J.: 1990).

dependence among different parts of the systems and seeing organizations as embedded in the larger environment added dealing with external entities as a crucial role for many managers. In this view, organization effectiveness is governed by three major factors: the individuals who make up the organization, the organization itself, and the environment in which the organization exists. Effective management of the interfaces between these factors—between the individual and the organization and between the organization and its environment—is central to organizational success. The relationship between the individual and the organization is often mediated or linked by a work group.

Figure 2–1 illustrates a systems model of organizations. It also includes most of the topics that are included in a study of organizational behavior. For each of these topics, scholars in the field have tried to answer the following questions:

1. What is the range of behavior to be found in organizations regarding the specific topic (what are the different ways in which people are motivated, appraise performance, etc.)

2. Which ways of behaving or organizing are most likely to be successful in a particular situation?

3. How can people, groups, and organizations learn to change and become more effective with regard to each topic?

Looking back upon these theories of organization, one is reminded of the parable of the blind men who each touched a different part of the elephant and assumed that they understood the entire animal. How is it that previous theorists only touched upon one part of organizing? One answer lies in the bounded rationality of their social context; most popular theories reflect ideas whose time has come, along with the personal predispositions and biases of the theorists themselves. Another answer is the increasing popularity of the concept of "paradox" regarding the process of organizing. Previous theories emphasized only one side of the equation (change ver-

FIGURE 2–1   The Open System View of Organizations

INDIVIDUALS	I/O INTERFACE	ORGANIZATION	O/E INTERFACE	ENVIRONMENT
Skills Goals Motives Expectations Perceptions	Psychological contract Socialization Culture Motivation Job design Appraisal/reward Leadership Supervision Employee development	Division of work among individuals and groups Coordination and integration of work done by individuals and groups	Problem-solving process Goals Strategic plans Feedback	Demands from relevant parts of environment such as: Government Customers Suppliers Special interest groups Labor market
	GROUP MEMBERSHIP	**G/O INTERFACE**		
	Group dynamics	Decision making Communication Power and influence Conflict management Management of diversity Problem solving		

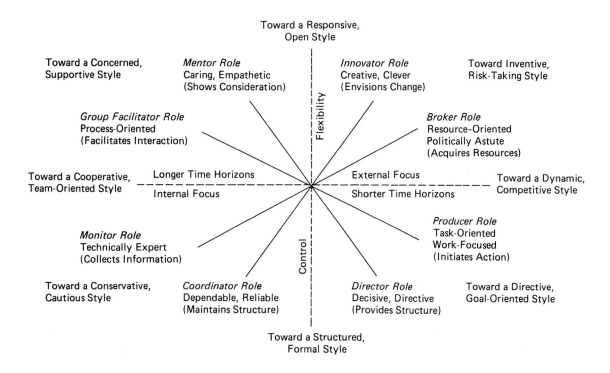

FIGURE 2–2   **Competing Values Framework of Leadership Roles**   *Source: Robert E. Quinn, Beyond Rational Management (San Francisco: Jossey-Bass, 1988), p. 86.*

sus stability, production versus social needs, Theory X versus Theory Y, etc.) rather than the balancing act that managers actually perform between them.

One of the most recent theories of organizing concerns the importance of mastering the paradoxes and competing demands of high performance. Quinn[11] maintains that parts of the different schools of management theory described in this chapter are still appropriate to modern organizations. (See Figure 2–2.) Organizational success comes from the ability to utilize the contradictory logic of all these theories. Each theory appears to be the opposite of the one it faces diagonally. Both the expectations and the value assumptions of opposite theories appear to be in competition. For example, maximizing output (rational goal model) is at odds with developing human resources (human relations model); growth and expansion (open systems model) appear to be the opposite of consolidation and continuity (internal process model).

According to Quinn, none of these models is the one best way to organize or manage; in fact, too much emphasis upon any one model will lead to failure. Figure 2–3 shows both positive and negative zones. When a model is used effectively, the organization will lie in the positive zone; however, too much of a good thing pushes the organization into the negative zone. Overemphasis upon productivity and lack of attention and sensitivity to human resources results in employee burnout and an oppressive sweat shop culture. In contrast, overemphasis upon human resources and lack of attention to productivity results in extreme permissiveness, irrelevance, and inappropriate participation, the irresponsible country club. The other two poles are

---

[11]Robert E. Quinn, *Beyond Rational Management* (San Francisco: Jossey-Bass, 1988).

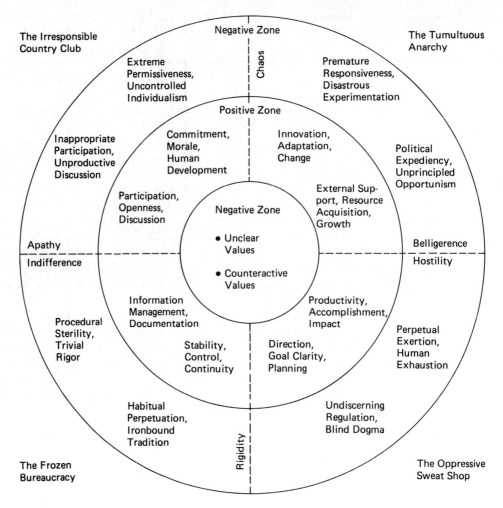

FIGURE 2–3   The Positive and Negative Zones   *Source: Robert E. Quinn,* Beyond Rational Management *(San Francisco: Jossey-Bass, 1988), p. 7.*

overemphasis upon the external environment and change—the tumultuous anarchy—and excessive control and stability, which results in the frozen bureaucracy.

As Quinn describes it, both organizations and people run the risk of becoming victims of their own success. Don Burr of People's Express was well known for his ability to create a vision for employees and be innovative. The vision was to create a high-volume, no-frills, cheap airline. In the beginning, the company thrived. Its growth was impressive. Employees were not constricted by formal roles and did whatever needed to be done, devoting long hours to the company. The company came up with many innovations. The shared values about how to work together were trust and providing opportunities to maximize people's abilities. However, at one point, Burr became dissatisfied with the organization; his response was to do what the company did well—grow. So it opened a route to London and acquired Frontier Airlines and was sold to the competition, Texas Air, four years later.

In retrospect, observers thought what the company needed was not more of the same but development of the bureaucratic underpinnings to sustain the company's growth and success—work that had little appeal or interest to Burr. His talents lay in Quinn's open systems quadrant rather than in the internal processes area. And, in the end, the organization's strengths became a weakness. When people or organizations are subjected to pressure, they usually resort to the mental maps or strategies that served them well in the past and do "more of the same." Unfortunately, it is often *new* strategies, theories, and ways of perceiving that are called for in times of crisis or upheaval.

How can managers learn to deal with paradox and be effective? How can they predict when following their strengths will result in success rather than failure? The summary of this chapter will go into this question in greater detail, but the first step is to become aware of one's own theories of management.

All of us have these theories, and it is these models that guide our behavior. For example, if manager A holds the belief that people are motivated primarily by money, he will see increased salary as a solution to low productivity. He may then see his role as little more than laying out the work that needs to be done and seeing that employees are well paid for doing it. In contrast, if manager B believes that people's attitudes affect their productivity, she will try to improve morale and see her managerial role as including mentoring and coaching. These examples indicate more than the ubiquitous presence of theories or models of behavior. They also show that our theories determine what we actually see in situations. Manager A may never consider the possibility that morale issues may be involved, while manager B may overlook the role of pay equity. Thus, our maps determine what we perceive when we look at situations and what role we are likely to take as a result of our theories.

Figure 2–2 also shows the different managerial roles that grow out of the different theories. These are placed in the inner ring. The outer ring shows eight different leadership styles that differ along three axes: flexibility–control, internal focus–external focus, and longer time horizons–shorter time horizons. One's theories about management determine the roles and leadership style one assumes.

The prework for today's lesson was assigned to help you clarify your personal theory about the role of effective managers.

III

Procedure for Group Meeting: Manager of the Year Acceptance Speech

STEP 1.   Divide into groups of five to seven participants.

STEP 2.   One of you (in each group) is about to receive the Manager of the Year Award. Your group can determine which member will receive this honor and the privilege of making a 5-minute acceptance speech, just as Jacques Maisonrouge did. The entire group should help to craft the speech, which should come close to representing all your views. You can draw ideas from your prework assignment. The speech should include two subjects:

   a. A brief description of today's business and social environment and the implications for management education.

   b. The qualities and skills essential to a manager's success in today's business world. (40 minutes)

STEP 3.   The award winner from each group presents a 5-minute speech to the entire class. (40 minutes)

STEP 4.   The class discussion includes the following questions:

   a. What were the common themes that ran through the speeches?

   b. Which of Quinn's quadrants appeared in the speeches? (15 minutes)

IV

Follow-up

The purpose of the group exercise was to identify some of your own theories about managing and organizing. This is the first step to being able to evaluate when your theories are adequate and when you need to learn or borrow other theories that may be more appropriate to specific situations. Quinn argued that master managers are capable of utilizing competing theories, either sequentially or simultaneously, to master the paradoxes found in organizations. Numerous management writers have written about the importance of managers' mental maps. Yankelovich and Immerwahr claim that the American work ethic has not disappeared, it is merely mismanaged by older managers who do not understand the values (and the mental maps related to them) of the younger generation.[12] Argyris states that one model of basic assumptions prevents organizational learning.[13] Streufert and Swezey claim that there is a correlation between reaching the executive suite and high "cognitive complexity."[14] Cognitive complexity refers to the extent to which people are multidimensional in their thinking and to the number of different relationships they can make between different dimensions or concepts. A manager with high cognitive complexity can see Quinn's four theory models and shuffle them around to choose the one that is most appropriate for a given situation. A manager with high cognitive complexity can be summed up as a person who possesses a variety of maps in his or her cognitive bank and who has the flexibility to play with them until an accurate combination is reached.

To be effective, today's managers must possess the capacity to analyze complex situations accurately and to choose appropriate responses. That may mean introducing a different theory or going against one's natural way of doing things. Perhaps when life was less complex, it was sufficient for managers to espouse a "one best way" for managing and have a knee-jerk response to all situations. Today's environment, however, is too turbulent for routine responses. How do you handle a joint venture with China or the issue of AIDS in the workplace? What managers need now is a behavioral repertoire that is appropriate for different situations and the analytical skill to know when to apply them. Effectiveness also requires the self-control and self-discipline to do something other than "what comes naturally" when one's natural style would not work. The key then is learning—learning as many models or theories as possible, learning what's involved in different or changing situations, learning about different people and what makes them tick, and learning what works and what doesn't.

COURSE OBJECTIVES

This course has three main objectives for students:

1. *To help you become more skilled at analyzing behavior in organizations.* We hope that you will learn to use the theories and models included in the work-

---

[12]Daniel Yankelovich and John Immerwahr, "Management and the Work Ethic," *Directors and Boards,* Fall 1983.

[13]Chris Argyris, "Double Loop Learning in Organizations," in D. A. Kolb, I. M. Rubin, and J. S. Osland, *Organizational Behavior: Practical Readings for Managers* (Englewood Cliffs, N.J.: Prentice Hall, 1990).

[14]Sigmund Streufert and R. W. Swezey, *Complexity, Managers, and Organizations* (Orlando, FL: Academic Press, 1986).

book and the reader to look at organizations through new lenses and to identify your own theories in the process. Organizations are like puzzles, and we would like to convey to you the challenge and fascination of figuring them out.

2. *To help you learn what actions are appropriate for different situations.* Understanding a situation is not enough; the next step is to know what action will produce the desired response.

3. *To help you acquire a repertoire of behaviors or skills.* The experiential nature of this course allows participants to see what effect their behavior has on others (and vice versa) and to experiment with new behaviors and receive feedback on them.

CHARACTERISTICS OF ORGANIZATIONAL BEHAVIOR

One of the criticisms sometimes leveled at organizational behavior is that it is just "common sense." In fact, many commonsense truisms are actually paradoxical; for example, "Nothing ventured, nothing gained" as opposed to "Better safe than sorry" or "Two heads are better than one" and "Too many cooks spoil the broth." The interesting question is, "If so much of organizational behavior is common sense, why is it not common practice?" One of the aims of this course is to find answers to the question, "What does it take to get common sense into common practice?"

Organizational behavior is characterized by the following traits.[15] It consists of *three levels of analysis: individual, group, and organizational.* One of the basic tenets of organizational behavior is that behavior is a function of the person and the environment, $B = f(P)(E)$.[16] For didactic purposes, the following equation is more helpful. Behavior is a function of the person (P), the group (G), the organization (O), and the external environment (E), or $B = f(P)(G)(O)(E)$.

While some scholars devote their time to *inquiry* or describing the phenomena one sees in organizations, there is also a strong emphasis upon *performance*—researchers are constantly asking what makes for success in organizations and what's the most effective way to do things? As such, organizational behavior is an *applied science*—its purpose is to develop knowledge that is useful to managers. Because of the emphasis upon both performance and application, it is a *change-oriented discipline.* Strategies for helping to improve performance or modify behavior have always been important to the field. Organizational behavior is a relatively young *interdisciplinary field* that pulls from the disciplines of psychology, sociology, anthropology, and political science. *Environmental forces* are perceived as having a major impact on behavior within organizations. An example of this can be found in Boyatzis and Skelly's[17] analysis of value trends and their implications for managers. And, finally, knowledge in the field is accumulated by using the *scientific method,* which means that theories and relationships are tested to see whether they can actually predict behavior.

Because of the variety and complexity of human behavior, there are few simple answers to questions about organizations. Organizational behavior scholars and consultants usually respond to questions with an "It depends," followed up by many questions about the particular situation, and maybe even a request to observe what's going on. For managers looking for quick answers, such a response may seem evasive, but an acknowledgment of the complexity involved is essential. Management

[15]Kurt Lewin, *A Dynamic Theory of Personality* (New York: McGraw-Hill, 1935).

[16]These characteristics are adapted from a comprehensive and up-to-date textbook by James L. Gibson, John M. Ivancevich, and James H. Donnelly, Jr., *Organizations: Behavior, Structure, Processes* (Plano, TX: Business Publications, 1985, p. 9).

[17]Richard E. Boyatzis and Florence R. Skelly, "The Impact of Changing Values on Organizational Life," D. A. Kolb, I. M. Rubin, and J. S. Osland, *Organizational Behavior: Practical Readings for Managers* (Englewood Cliffs, N.J.: Prentice Hall, 1990).

literature abounds with examples of companies who made policy and management decisions based upon a small fragment of the entire picture and lived to regret it. That's why this course is designed to broaden your appreciation of the complexity of organizational behavior. And since we can't teach you rules that will hold true for every situation, we have to focus upon teaching you to learn how to learn. In a rapidly changing environment, this is the most valuable skill of all.

V
Learning Points

1. Everyone has his or her personal theories about management and the role of managers.

2. Taylor's scientific management emphasized the efficient division of labor into small, standardized jobs that were matched to the capabilities of trained workers who received wage incentives.

3. Administrative theory focused upon understanding the basic tasks of management and developed guidelines or principles for managing effectively.

4. The human relations school acknowledged the effect of the informal social system with its norms and individual attitudes and feelings upon organizational functioning. This theory underlined the importance of employee morale and participation.

5. The decision-making school described organizations as social systems based upon individual decisions and contributed the idea of bounded rationality. Managers could control employee behavior by controlling the premises of decision making.

6. Contingency theory contends that there is no one best way to manage in every situation. Managers must find the appropriate method to match a given situation.

7. Successful organizations are characterized by "good fit" among strategy, structure, systems, staff, style, skills, and superordinate goals.

8. Open systems theory maintains that organizations and all the subdivisions within them take in resources and transform them into a service or product that is purchased or utilized by a larger system. All parts are interdependent, including the larger environment in which the organization is embedded.

9. Quinn's theory consists of a competing value approach and proposes that, to be successful, managers need to manage the paradoxes of the four different theories or quadrants: open systems model, rational goal model, internal process model, and the human relations model.

10. Too much emphasis upon any one model will lead to failure. Master managers are balanced in their ability to function in each of these quadrants and know when "more of the same" would not be warranted.

11. The first step in managing the paradoxes of organizational effectiveness is understanding one's own theories of management.

12. Our theories or mental maps determine what we see when we look at situations and determine the roles we perform.

13. Today's managers need to learn:

   a. How to analyze complex situations using a variety of models or theories.
   b. A repertoire of behaviors and the knowledge of when to use them.
   c. How to learn to adapt to a rapidly changing environment.

14. Organizational behavior has the following characteristics:

   a. Three levels of analysis: individual, group, organizational.
   b. Performance orientation.
   c. Application orientation.

    d. Change orientation.

    e. Multidisciplinary nature.

    f. Recognition of external environmental forces.

    g. Scientific method grounding.

VI

Tips for Today's Managers

- There are many good assessment instruments to help people determine how they usually behave at work. Completing them independently or attending seminars or taking courses may be useful. Having other people evaluate you is also valuable because it provides another perspective. If you are surprised by their evaluations, discuss the differences with an honest coworker or friend.

- Quinn made the following suggestions about developing oneself as a manager.[18]
  - Learn about yourself (similar to the previous point).
  - Develop a change strategy:
    - Keep a journal.
    - Identify specific areas in need of improvement.
    - Identify role models for your weak areas; read appropriate books on management skills.
  - Implement the change strategy:
    - Be honest about the costs of improvement (it may be high).
    - Develop a social support system (who will help you change or at least support your efforts?).
    - Constantly evaluate and modify your strategy.

- People with different theories often look down upon those whose theories are dissimilar. One way to develop yourself is to seek out and work with people who have different beliefs. Doing so may involve a cost to you, but the payoff should be greater complexity and understanding of different mental maps.

- Gathering as many perspectives as possible about situations is helpful. Just as there is no one best way of managing, there is no one best way to see a situation. Managers who can count on others to help them "see" what's going on and give their opinions on what could be done are fortunate. If, however, you give the impression that you don't like to hear bad news or receive advice, you won't—until it's too late to do much about it.

- Until it becomes second nature, use a framework like the one in Figure 2–1 to help you enumerate the different aspects you could consider when analyzing a situation. At the minimum, asking yourself, "Have I thought about what's taking place on the individual, group, organizational, and environmental level with regard to this particular situation?" is a good discipline.

- The interdependence aspect of open systems theory means that changes in one part of the system will have repercussions elsewhere. Try to determine these consequences *before* taking decisions and implementing changes.

[18]Quinn, *Beyond Rational Management,* p. 121.

VII

Personal Application Assignment

A. What is your own theory of management? You can describe it in words or draw it as a model. (Keep a copy for yourself so that you can modify it as the course proceeds.)

B. Based upon your theory of management and today's environment, answer the following questions.

1. What blind spots could your theory lead you to have?

2. What personal values seem to underlie your theory, that is, "people, managers, or organizations should/should not _____(what?)"

3. What implicit assumptions, if any, are you making about human nature or human motivation?

4. What skills do you think are necessary to be a "master" manager?

5. Which of these do you already possess?

6. What skills would you like to work on during this course?

7. Write up an action plan for learning these skills. How will you work on them? How will you know when they have improved?

3

INDIVIDUAL AND ORGANIZATIONAL LEARNING

OBJECTIVES By the end of this chapter, you should be able to:

A. Describe the model of adult learning.

B. Identify individual learning styles.

C. Improve the learning organization in this course by sharing learning objectives, available resources for learning, and learning environment preferences.

D. Understand the importance of continuous learning.

I Premeeting Preparation

II Topic Introduction

III Procedure for Group Meeting: The Learning Style Inventory

IV Follow-up

V Learning Points

VI Tips for Managers

VII Personal Application Assignment

Planning as Learning . . . At Shell, Planning Means Changing Minds, Not Making Plans

Arie P. DeGeus

Some years ago, the planning group at Shell surveyed 30 companies that had been in business for more than 75 years. What impressed us most was their ability to live in harmony with the business environment, to switch from a survival mode when times were turbulent to a self-development mode when the pace of change was slow.

Outcomes like these don't happen automatically. On the contrary, they depend on the ability of a company's senior managers to absorb what is going on in the business environment and to act on that information with appropriate business moves. In other words, they depend on learning. Or, more precisely, on institutional learning, which is the process whereby management teams change their shared mental models of their company, their markets, and their competitors. For this reason, we think of planning as learning and of corporate planning as institutional learning.

Because high-level, effective, and continuous institutional learning and ensuing corporate change are the prerequisites for corporate success, we at Shell[1] have asked ourselves two questions. How does a company learn and adapt? And, What is planning's role in corporate learning?

My answer to the first question, "how does a company learn and adapt," is that many do not or, at least, not very quickly. A full one-third of the *Fortune* "500" industrials listed in 1970 had vanished by 1983. And W. Stewart Howe has pointed out in his 1986 book *Corporate Strategy* that for every successful turnaround there are two ailing companies that fail to recover. Yet some companies obviously do learn and can adapt. In fact, our survey identified several that were still vigorous at 200, 300, and even 700 years of age. What made the difference? Why are some companies better able to adapt?

Sociologists and psychologists tell us it is pain that makes people and living systems change. But crisis management—pain management—is a dangerous way to manage for change.

The problem is that you usually have little time and few options. The deeper into the crisis you are, the fewer options remain. Crisis management, by necessity, becomes autocratic management.

The challenge, therefore, is to recognize and react to environmental change

Source: Excerpted from Arie P. DeGeus, "Planning as Learning," *Harvard Business Review,* March–April 1988, pp. 70–74.

[1]*Author's note:* I use the collective expression "Shell" for convenience when referring to the companies of the Royal Dutch/Shell Group in general, or when no purpose is served by identifying the particular Shell company or companies.

before the pain of a crisis. Not surprisingly, this is what the long-lived companies in our study were so well able to do.

All these companies had a striking capacity to institutionalize change. They never stood still. Moreover, they seemed to recognize that they had internal strengths that could be developed as environmental conditions changed.

Changes like these grow out of a company's knowledge of itself and its environment. All managers have such knowledge and they develop it further all the time, since every living person—and system—is continuously engaged in learning. In fact, the normal decision process in corporations is a learning process, because people change their own mental models and build up a joint model as they talk. The problem is that the speed of that process is slow—too slow for a world in which the ability to learn faster than competitors may be the only sustainable competitive advantage.

Some five years ago, we had a good example of the time it takes for a message to be heard. One way in which we in Shell trigger institutional learning is through scenarios.[2] A certain set of scenarios gave our planners a clear signal that the oil industry, which had always been highly integrated, was so no longer. That contradicted all our existing models. High integration means that you are more or less in control of all the facets of your industry, so you can start optimizing. Optimization was the driving managerial model in Shell. What these scenarios essentially were saying was that we had to look for other management methods.

The first reaction from the organization was at best polite. There were few questions and no discussion. Some managers reacted critically: the scenarios were "basic theory that everyone already knew"; they had "little relevance to the realities of today's business." The message had been listened to but it had not yet been heard.

After a hiatus of some three months, people began asking lots of questions; a discussion started. The intervening months had provided time for the message to settle and for management's mental models to develop a few new hooks. Absorption, phase one of the learning process, had taken place.

During the next nine months, we moved through the other phases of the learning process. Operating executives at Shell incorporated this new information into their mental models of the business. They drew conclusions from the revised models and tested them against experience. Then, finally, they acted on the basis of the altered model. Hearing, digestion, confirmation, action: each step took time, its own sweet time.

In my experience this time span is typical. It will likely take 12 to 18 months from the moment a signal is received until it is acted on. The issue is not whether a company will learn, therefore, but whether it will learn fast and early. The critical question becomes, "Can we accelerate institutional learning?"

I am more and more persuaded that the answer to this question is yes. But before explaining why, I want to emphasize an important point about learning and the planner's role. The only relevant learning in a company is the learning done by those people who have the power to act (at Shell, the operating company management teams). So the real purpose of effective planning is not to make plans but to change the microcosm, the mental models that these decision makers carry in their heads. And this is what we at Shell and others elsewhere try to do.

Fortified with this understanding of planning and its role, we looked for ways to accelerate institutional learning. Curiously enough, we learned in two cases that changing the rules, or suspending them, could be a spur to learning. Rules in a corporation are extremely important. Nobody likes them but everybody obeys them because they are recognized as the glue of the

[2]Pierre Wack wrote about our system in "Scenarios: Uncharted Waters Ahead," HBR September–October 1985, p. 72 and in "Scenarios: Shooting the Rapids," HBR November–December 1985, p. 139.

organization. And yet, we have all known extraordinary managers who got their organizations out of a rut by changing the rules. Intuitively they changed the organization and the way it looked at matters, and so, as a consequence, accelerated learning.

Several years ago one of our work groups introduced, out of the blue, a new rule into the corporate rain dance: "Thou shalt plan strategically in the first half of the calendar year." (We already had a so-called business planning cycle that dealt with capital budgets in the second half of the calendar year.)

In the first year the results of this new game were scanty, mostly a rehash of the previous year's business plans. But in the second year the plans were fresher and each year the quality of thinking that went into strategic planning improved.

A similar thing happened when we tried suspending the rules. In 1984 we had a scenario that talked about $15 a barrel oil. (Bear in mind that in 1984 the price of a barrel of oil was $28 and $15 was the end of the world to oil people.) We thought it important that, as early in 1985 as possible, senior managers throughout Shell start learning about a world of $15 oil. But the response to this scenario was essentially, "If you want us to think about this world, first tell us when the price is going to fall, how far it will fall, and how long the drop will last."

A deadlock ensued which we broke by writing a case study with a preface that was really a license to play. "We don't know the future," it said. "But neither do you. And though none of us knows whether the price is going to fall, we can agree that it would be pretty serious if it did. So we have written a case showing one of many possible ways by which the price of oil could fall." We then described a case in which the price plummeted at the end of 1985 and concluded by saying: "And now it is April 1986 and you are staring at a price of $16 a barrel. Will you please meet and give your views on these three questions: What do you think your government will do? What do you think your competition will do? And what, if anything, will you do?"

Since at that point the price was still $28 and rising, the case was only a game. But that game started off serious work throughout Shell, not on answering the question "What will happen?" but rather exploring the question, "What will we do if it happens?" The acceleration of the institutional learning process had been set in motion.

As it turned out, the price of oil was still $27 in early January of 1986. But on February 1 it was $17 and in April it was $10. The fact that Shell had already visited the world of $15 oil helped a great deal in that panicky spring of 1986.

By now, we knew we were on to something: games could significantly accelerate institutional learning. That's not so strange when you think of it. Some of the most difficult and complex tasks in our lives were learned by playing: cycling, tennis, playing an instrument. We did it, we experimented, we played. But how were we going to make it OK to play?

One characteristic of play, as the Tavistock Institute in London has shown, is the presence of a transitional object. For the person playing, the transitional object is a representation of the real world. A child who is playing with a doll learns a great deal about the real world at a very fast pace.

Successful consultants let themselves be treated as transitional objects. The process begins when the consultant says something like this to a management team: "We know from experience that many good strategies are largely implicit. If you let us interview people at various levels in your organization, we'll see whether we can get your strategy out on paper. Then we'll come back and check whether we've understood it."

Some weeks later the consultant goes back to the team and says: "Well, we've looked at your strategy and we've played it through a number of likely possibilities, and here is what we think will be the outcome. Do you like it?" The management team will almost certainly say no. So the consultant will say: "All right, let's see how we can change it. Let's go back to your original model and see what was built in there that produced this result." This process is likely to go through a number of iterations, during which the team's original model will change considerably. Those changes constitute the learning that is taking place among the team's members.

Like consultants, computer models can be used to play back and forth management's view of its market, the environment, or the competition. The starting point, however, must be the mental model that the audience has at the moment. If a planner walks into the room with a model on his computer that he has made up himself, the chances are slim that his audience will recognize this particular microworld.

But why go to all this trouble? Why not rely on the natural learning process that occurs whenever a management team meets? For us at Shell, there are three compelling reasons. First, although the models in the human mind are complex, most people can deal with only three or four variables at a time and do so through only one or two time iterations.

The second reason for putting mental models into computers is that in working with dynamic models, people discover that in complex systems (like markets or companies) cause and effect are separated in time and place. To many people such insight is also counter-intuitive. Most of us, particularly if we are engaged in the process of planning, focus on the effect we want to create and then look for the most immediate cause to create that effect. The use of dynamic models helps us discover other trigger points, separated in time and place from the desired effect.

Lastly, by using computer models we learn what constitutes relevant information. For only when we start playing with these microworlds do we find out what information we really need to know.

When people play with models this way, they are actually creating a new language among themselves that expresses the knowledge they have acquired. And here we come to the most important aspect of institutional learning, whether it be achieved through teaching or through play as we have defined it: the institutional learning process is a process of language development. As the implicit knowledge of each learner becomes explicit, his or her mental model becomes a building block of the institutional model. How much and how fast this model changes will depend on the culture and structure of the organization. Teams that have to cope with rigid procedures and information systems will learn more slowly than those with flexible, open communication channels. Autocratic institutions will learn faster or not at all—the ability of one or a few leaders being a risky institutional bet.

Human beings aren't the only ones whose learning ability is directly related to their ability to convey information. As a species, birds have great potential to learn, but there are important differences among them. Titmice, for example, move in flocks and mix freely, while robins live in well-defined parts of the garden and for the most part communicate antagonistically across the borders of their territories. Virtually all the titmice in the U.K. quickly learned how to pierce the seals of milk bottles left at doorsteps. But robins as a group will never learn to do this (though individual birds may) because their capacity for institutional learning is low; one bird's knowledge does not spread.[3] The same phenomenon occurs in management teams that work by mandate. The best learning takes place in teams that accept that the whole is larger than the sum of the parts, that there is a good that transcends the individual.

What about managers who find themselves in a robin culture? Clearly, their

---

[3]Jeff S. Wyles, Joseph G. Kunkel, and Allan C. Wilson, "Birds, Behavior and Anatomical Evolution," *Proceedings of the National Academy of Sciences, USA*, July 1983.

chances of accelerating institutional learning are reduced. Nevertheless, they can take a significant step toward opening up communication and thus the learning process by keeping one fact in mind: institutional learning begins with the calibration of existing mental models.

We are continuing to explore other ways to improve and speed up our institutional learning process. Our exploration into learning through play via a transitional object (a consultant or a computer) looks promising enough at this point to push on in that direction. And while we are navigating in poorly charted waters, we are not out there alone.[4]

Our exploration into this area is not a luxury. We understand that the only competitive advantage the company of the future will have is its managers' ability to learn faster than their competitors. So the companies that succeed will be those that continually nudge their managers towards revising their views of the world. The challenges for the planner are considerable. So are the rewards.

[4]Through MIT's Program in Systems Thinking and the New Management Style, a group of senior executives are looking at this and other issues.

I

Premeeting Preparation

(Time Allotted: $1\frac{1}{2}$ Hours)

A. Respond to this problem and answer the questions that follow: Identify a real learning situation that you have recently faced or are currently facing (e.g., learning to use a computer, play an instrument, understand the new income tax laws, master a new management technique, give a speech, play a new sport). Describe what you were (or are) trying to learn.

1. How did you go about learning to do it? What sequence of steps did you follow?

2. What was the outcome?

3. What was the best *group* learning experience you ever had? What was good about it?

4. What was your worst group learning experience? What made it that way?

5. In your opinion, what conditions promote adult learning?

6. What are the significant learning points from the readings?

B. Complete the Learning Style Inventory that follows.

C. Score the Learning Style Inventory and record your scores on the two normative profiles on the scale provided.

D. Read the entire unit *after* completing A, B, and C.

The Learning Style Inventory

This survey is designed to help you describe how you learn—the way you find out about and deal with ideas and situations in your life. Different people learn best in different ways. The different ways of learning described in the survey are equally good. The aim is to describe how you learn, not to evaluate your learning ability. You might find it hard to choose the descriptions that best characterize your learning style. Keep in mind that there are no right or wrong answers—all the choices are equally acceptable.

There are nine sets of four descriptions listed in this inventory. Mark the words in each set that are most like you, second most like you, third most like you, and least like you. Put a numeral "4" next to the description that is most like you, a "3" next to the description that is second most like you, a "2" next to the description that is third most like you, and a "1" next to the description that is least like you (4 = most like you; 1 = least like you). Be sure to assign a different rank number to each of the four words in each set; do not make ties.

EXAMPLE

0. __4__ happy   __3__ fast   __1__ angry   __2__ careful

(Some people find it easiest to decide first which word best describes them (4 happy) and then to decide the word that is least like them (1 angry). Then you can give a 3 to that word in the remaining pair that is most like you (3 fast) and a 2 to the word that is left over (2 careful).

1. __ discriminating   __ tentative   __ involved   __ practical
2. __ receptive   __ relevant   __ analytical   __ impartial
3. __ feeling   __ watching   __ thinking   __ doing
4. __ accepting   __ risk taker   __ evaluative   __ aware
5. __ intuitive   __ productive   __ logical   __ questioning
6. __ abstract   __ observing   __ concrete   __ active
7. __ present-oriented __ reflecting   __ future-oriented __ pragmatic
8. __ experience   __ observation   __ conceptualiza-   __ experimenta-
                                             tion   tion
9. __ intense   __ reserved   __ rational   __ responsible

SCORING INSTRUCTIONS

The four columns of words correspond to the four learning style scales: concrete experience (CE), reflective observation (RO), abstract conceptualization (AC), and active experimentation (AE). To compute your scale scores, write your rank numbers in the boxes below only for the designated items. For example, in the third column (AC), you would fill in the rank numbers you have assigned to items 2, 3, 4, 5, 8, and 9. Compute your scale scores by adding the rank numbers for each set of boxes.

Score items: Score items: Score items: Score items:

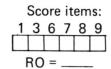
2 3 4 5 7 8

CE = ____

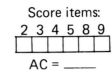
1 3 6 7 8 9

RO = ____

2 3 4 5 8 9

AC = ____

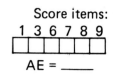
1 3 6 7 8 9

AE = ____

To compute the two combination scores, subtract CE from AC and subtract RO from AE. Preserve negative signs if they appear.

            AC   CE   AE   RO

AC–CE: □ – □ =   AE – RO: □ – □ =

To interpret the meaning of these scores read the introduction.

II

Topic Introduction

For most of us, the first associations we have with the word "learning" are teacher, classroom, and textbook. These associations belie some implicit assumptions that we tend to make about the nature of the learning process. Our years in school have trained us to think that the primary responsibility for learning lies with teachers. Their training and experience make them experts; we are more passive participants in the learning process. As students, our job is to observe, read, and memorize what the teacher assigns, and then to repeat "what we have learned" in examinations. Teachers have the responsibility of evaluating our performance and telling us what we should learn next. They set requirements and objectives for learning since it is often assumed that students do not yet have the experience to know what is best for themselves.

The textbook symbolizes the assumption that learning is primarily concerned with abstract ideas and concepts. Learning is the process of acquiring and remembering ideas and concepts. The more remembered, the more you have learned. The relevance and application of these concepts to your own job will come later. Concepts come before experience.

The classroom symbolizes the assumption that learning is a special activity cut off from the real world and unrelated to one's life. Learning and doing are separate and antithetical activities. Many students at graduation feel, "Now I am finished with learning, I can begin living." The belief that learning occurs only in the classroom is so strong that academic credentials are assigned great importance in hiring and promotions, in spite of the fact that psychological research has had little success in establishing correlations between performance in the classroom (grades) and success in later life.

As a result of these assumptions, the concept of learning seldom seems relevant to us in our daily lives and work. And yet a moment of deeper reflection says that this cannot be so. In a world where the rate of change is increasing rapidly every year, in a time when few will end their careers in the same jobs or even the same occupations that they started in, the ability to learn seems an important, if not *the* most important, skill.

This book is designed to create the learning environment that is most responsive to the unique needs of adult learners by addressing five characteristics of that environment. First, it is based on a *psychological contract of reciprocity,* a basic building block of human interaction. It is well documented that relationships that are based on a mutual and equal balance of giving and getting thrive and grow; those based on unequal exchange very quickly decay. This process of reciprocity is particularly important for creating an effective learning environment because many initial assumptions about learning run counter to it. Learning is most often considered a process of getting rather than giving. This is most evident in conceptions of traditional student/teacher roles: teachers give and students get. Yet in adult learning both giving and getting are critical. In getting, there is the opportunity to incorporate new ideas and perspectives. In giving, there is the opportunity to integrate and apply these new perspectives and to practice their use.

A second characteristic of an adult learning environment is that it is *experienced based.* Ideally the motivation for learning comes not from the instructor's dispensation of rewards and grades but from problems and opportunities arising from the learner's own life experience. Experience shows adults what they need to learn, but their experience also allows them to contribute to the learning of others.

Third, the adult learning environment emphasizes *personal application*. Since the adults' learning needs arise from their own experience, the main goal of learning is to apply new knowledge, skills, and attitudes to the solution of the individual's practical problems.

Fourth, the learning environment is *individualized and self-directed*. Just as every individual's experience is different, so are each person's learning goals and learning style. A major concern in the management of an adult learning environment is to organize program resources in such a way that they are maximally responsive to what each learner wants to learn and how he or she learns it. Essential to achievement of this kind of learning environment is the learners' willingness to take responsibility for the achievement of their learning objectives. Perhaps the most important of the learners' responsibilities is that of evaluating how well they are getting the learning resources needed to achieve their goals and alerting the community to problems when they arise since they are in the best position to make this judgment.

A final characteristic of an adult learning environment is that it *integrates learning and living*. There are two goals in the learning process. One is to learn the specifics of a particular subject matter. The other is to learn about one's own strengths and weaknesses as a learner (i.e., learning how to learn from experience). When the process works well, individuals finish their educational experience not only with new intellectual insights, but also with an understanding of their own learning style. This understanding of learning strengths and weaknesses helps in "back-home" application of what has been learned and provides a framework for continuing learning on the job. Learning is no longer a special activity reserved for the classroom; it becomes an integral and explicit part of life itself.

A MODEL OF THE LEARNING PROCESS

By examining the learning process we can come closer to understanding how it is that people generate from their experience the concepts, rules, and principles that guide their behavior in new situations, and how they modify these concepts to improve their effectiveness. This process is both active and passive, concrete, and abstract. It can be conceived of as a four-stage cycle: (1) concrete experience is followed by (2) observation and reflection, which lead to (3) the formation of abstract concepts and generalizations, which lead to (4) hypotheses to be tested in future action, which in turn lead to new experiences.

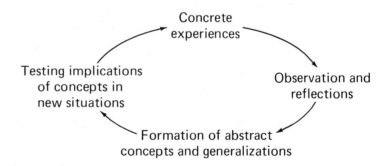

There are several observations to be made about this model of the learning process. First, this learning cycle is continuously recurring. We continuously test our concepts in experience and modify them as a result of our observation of the experience. In a very important sense, all learning is relearning and all education is reeducation.

Second, the direction that learning takes is governed by one's felt needs and goals. We seek experiences that are related to our goals, interpret them in the light of our goals, and form concepts and test implications of these concepts that are relevant to these felt needs and goals. The implication of this fact is that the process of learning is erratic and inefficient when personal objectives are not clear.

Third, since the learning process is directed by individual needs and goals, learning styles become highly individual in both direction and process. For example, a mathematician may come to place great emphasis on abstract concepts, whereas a poet may value concrete experience more highly. A manager may be primarily concerned with active application of concepts, whereas a naturalist may develop observational skills highly. Each of us in a more personal way develops a learning style that has some weak points and strong points. We may jump into experiences but fail to observe the lessons to be derived from these experiences; we may form concepts but fail to test their validity. In some areas our objectives and needs may be clear guides to learning; in others, we wander aimlessly.

INTERPRETATION OF YOUR SCORES ON THE LEARNING STYLE INVENTORY

The Learning Style Inventory (LSI)[5] is a simple self-description test, based on experiential learning theory, that is designed to measure your strengths and weaknesses as a learner in the four stages of the learning process. Effective learners rely on four different learning modes: *concrete experience* (CE), *reflective observation* (RO), *abstract conceptualization* (AC), and *active experimentation* (AE). That is, they must be able to involve themselves fully and openly, and without bias in new experiences (CE); they must be able to reflect on and observe these experiences from many perspectives (RO); they must be able to create concepts that integrate their observations into logically sound theories (AC); and they must be able to use these theories to make decisions and solve problems (AE).

The LSI measures your relative emphasis on the four learning modes by asking you to rank order a series of four words that describes these different abilities. For example, one set of four words is *feeling, watching, thinking, doing,* which reflects CE, RO, AC, and AE, respectively. Combination scores indicate the extent to which you emphasize abstractness over concreteness (AC-CE) and the extent to which you emphasize active experimentation over reflection (AE-RO).

One way to understand better the meaning of your scores on the LSI is to compare them with the scores of others. The "target" in Figure 3–1 gives norms on the four basic scales (CE, RO, AC, AE) for 1,933 adults ranging from 18 to 60 years of age. About two-thirds of the group are men and the group as a whole is highly educated (two-thirds have college degrees or higher). A wide range of occupations and educational backgrounds are represented, including teachers, counselors, engineers, salespersons, managers, doctors, and lawyers.

The raw scores for each of the four basic scales are listed on the crossed lines of the target. By circling your raw scores on the four scales and connecting them with straight lines you can create a graphic representation of your learning style profile. The concentric circles on the target represent percentile scores for the normative group. For example, if your raw score on *concrete experience* was 15, you scored higher on this scale than about 55 percent of the people in the normative group. If your CE score was 22 or higher, you scored higher than 99 percent of the normative group. Therefore, in comparison with the normative group, the shape of your profile indicates which of the four basic modes you tend to emphasize and which are less emphasized.

It should be emphasized that the LSI does not measure your learning style with

[5]The Learning Style Inventory is copyrighted by David A. Kolb (1976) and distributed by McBer and Co. 137 Newbury St., Boston, Mass. 02116. Further information on theory, construction, reliability, and validity of the inventory is reported in *The Learning Style Inventory: Technical Manual,* available from McBer and Co.

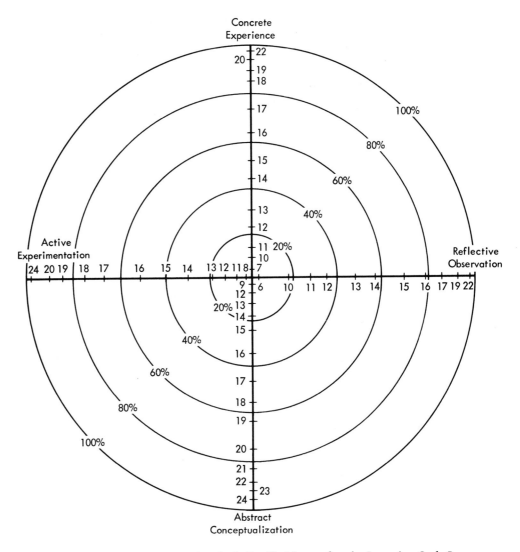

FIGURE 3–1   The Learning Style Profile Norms for the Learning Style Inventory
(Copyright 1976 by David A. Kolb)

100 percent accuracy. Rather, it is simply an indication of how you see yourself as a learner. You will need data from other sources if you wish to pinpoint your learning style more exactly (e.g., how you make decisions on the job, how others see you, and what kinds of problems you solve best). Beware of stereotyping yourself and others with your LSI scores. Your scores indicate which learning modes you emphasize in general. It may change from time to time and situation to situation.

The Learning Style Inventory was designed as an aid for helping you to identify your own learning style. The four learning modes—concrete experience, reflective observation, abstract conceptualization, and active experimentation—represent the four stages of the learning process. The inventory is designed to assess the relative importance of each of these stages to you so that you can get some indication of which learning modes you tend to emphasize. No individual mode is better or worse than any other. Even a totally balanced profile is not necessarily best. The key to effective learning is being competent in each mode when it is appropriate. A high score on one mode may mean a tendency to overemphasize that aspect of the learning process at the expense of others. A low score on a mode may indicate a tendency to avoid that aspect of the learning process.

An *orientation toward concrete experience* focuses on being involved in experiences and dealing with immediate human situations in a personal way. It emphasizes feeling as opposed to thinking, a concern with the uniqueness and complexity of present reality as opposed to theories and generalizations, an intuitive, "artistic" approach as opposed to the systematic, scientific approach to problems. People with a concrete experience orientation enjoy and are good at relating to others. They are often good intuitive decision makers and function well in unstructured situations. People with this orientation value relating to people, being involved in real situations, and an open-minded approach to life.

An *orientation toward reflective observation* focuses on understanding the meaning of ideas and situations by carefully observing and impartially describing them. It emphasizes understanding as opposed to practical application, a concern with what is true or how things happen as opposed to what is practical, an emphasis on reflection as opposed to action. People with a reflective orientation enjoy thinking about the meaning of situations and ideas and are good at seeing their implications. They are good at looking at things from different perspectives and at appreciating different points of view. They like to rely on their own thoughts and feelings to form opinions. People with this orientation value patience, impartiality, and considered, thoughtful judgment.

An *orientation toward abstract conceptualization* focuses on using logic, ideas, and concepts. It emphasizes thinking as opposed to feeling, a concern with building general theories as opposed to understanding intuitively unique, specific areas, a scientific as opposed to an artistic approach to problems. A person with an abstract conceptual orientation enjoys and is good at systematic planning, manipulation of abstract symbols, and quantitative analysis. People with this orientation value precision, the rigor and discipline of analyzing ideas, and the aesthetic quality of a neat, conceptual system.

An *orientation toward active experimentation* focuses on actively influencing people and changing situations. It emphasizes practical applications as opposed to reflective understanding, a pragmatic concern with what works as opposed to what is absolute truth, an emphasis on doing as opposed to observing. People with an active experimentation orientation enjoy and are good at getting things accomplished. They are willing to take some risk to achieve their objectives. They also value having an impact and influence on the environment around them and like to see results.

IDENTIFYING YOUR LEARNING STYLE TYPE

It is unlikely that your learning style will be described accurately by just one of the four preceding paragraphs. This is because each person's learning style is a combination of the four basic learning modes. It is therefore useful to describe your learning style by a single data point that combines your scores on the four basic modes. This is accomplished by using the two combination scores, AC-CE and AE-RO. These scales indicate the degree to which you emphasize abstractness over concreteness and action over reflection, respectively.

The grid in Figure 3–2 shows the raw scores for these two scales on the crossed lines (AC-CE on the vertical and AE-RO on the horizontal) and percentile scores based on the normative group on the sides. By marking your raw scores on the two lines and plotting their point of interception, you can find which of the four learning style quadrants you occupy. These four quadrants, labeled *accommodator, diverger, converger,* and *assimilator,* represent the four dominant learning styles. If your AC-CE score were −4 and your AE-RO score were +8, you would definitely occupy the accommodator quadrant. An AC-CE score of +4 and an AE-RO score of +3 would put you only slightly in the converger quadrant. The closer your data point is to the point where the lines cross, the more balanced is your learning style. If your data point is close to any of the four corners, this indicates that you rely heavily on one particular learning style.

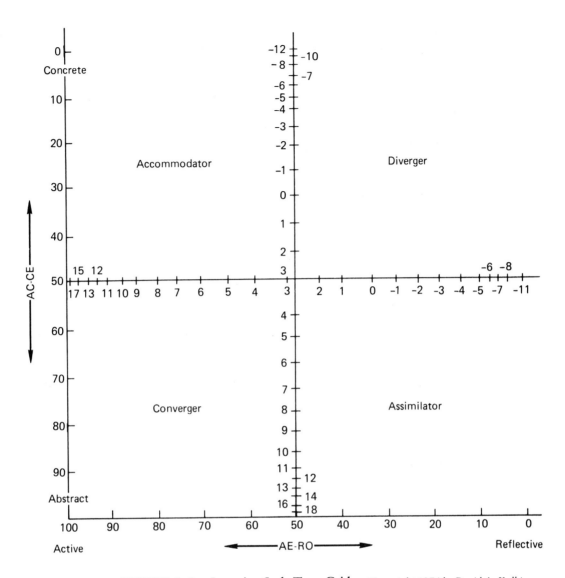

FIGURE 3–2 **Learning Style Type Grid** *(Copyright 1976 by David A. Kolb)*

The following is a description of the characteristics of the four basic learning styles based both on research and clinical observation of these patterns of LSI scores.

The *convergent* learning style relies primarily on the dominant learning abilities of abstract conceptualization and active experimentation. The greatest strength of this approach lies in problem solving, decision making, and the practical application of ideas. We have called this learning style the "converger" because a person with this style seems to do best in such situations as conventional intelligence tests where there is a single correct answer or solution to a question or problem. In this learning style, knowledge is organized in such a way that, through hypothetical-deductive reasoning, it can be focused on specific problems. Liam Hudson's research on individuals with this style of learning shows that convergent persons are controlled in their expression of emotion.[6] They prefer dealing with technical tasks and problems rather than with social and interpersonal issues. Convergers often have specialized in the physical sciences. This learning style is characteristic of many engineers and technical specialists.

The *divergent* learning style has the opposite strengths of the convergent style, emphasizing concrete experience and reflective observation. The greatest strength

[6]Hudson Liam, *Contrary Imaginations* (New York: Schocken Books, 1966).

of this orientation lies in imaginative ability and awareness of meaning and values. The primary adaptive ability in this style is to view concrete situations from many perspectives and to organize many relationships into a meaningful "Gestalt." The emphasis in this orientation is on adaptation by observation rather than by action. This style is called "diverger" because a person of this type performs better in situations that call for generation of alternative ideas and implications such as a "brainstorming" idea session. Persons oriented toward divergence are interested in people and tend to be imaginative and feeling oriented. Divergers have broad cultural interests and tend to specialize in the arts. This style is characteristic of individuals from humanities and liberal arts backgrounds. Counselors, organization development specialists, and personnel managers tend to be characterized by this learning style.

In *assimilation,* the dominant learning abilities are abstract conceptualization and reflective observation. The greatest strength of this orientation lies in inductive reasoning, in the ability to create theoretical models, and in assimilating disparate observations into an integrated explanation. As in convergence, this orientation is less focused on people and more concerned with ideas and abstract concepts. Ideas, however, are judged less in this orientation by their practical value. Here it is more important that the theory be logically sound and precise. This learning style is more characteristic of individuals in the basic sciences and mathematics rather than the applied sciences. In organizations, persons with this learning style are found most often in the research and planning departments.

The *accommodative* learning style has the opposite strengths of assimilation, emphasizing concrete experience and active experimentation. The greatest strength of this orientation lies in doing things, in carrying out plans and tasks, and in getting involved in new experiences. The adaptive emphasis of this orientation is on opportunity seeking, risk taking, and action. This style is called "accommodation" because it is best suited for those situations in which one must adapt oneself to changing immediate circumstances. In situations where the theory or plans do not fit the facts, those with an accommodative style will most likely discard the plan or theory. (With the opposite learning style, assimilation, one would be more likely to disregard or reexamine the facts.) People with an accommodative orientation tend to solve problems in an intuitive trial and error manner, relying on other people for information rather than on their own analytic ability. Individuals with accommodative learning styles are at ease with people but are sometimes seen as impatient and "pushy." This person's educational background is often in technical or practical fields such as business. In organizations, people with this learning style are found in "action-oriented" jobs, often in marketing or sales.

Reprinted courtesy of Mell Lazarus and Field Newspaper Syndicate

III

Procedure for Group Meeting: The Learning Style Inventory

SHARING INDIVIDUAL LEARNING STYLES, OBJECTIVES, AND RESOURCES
(Time Allotted: 1 hour)

STEP 1. Individual self-assessment. (5 minutes) Group members should individually review their Learning Style Inventory scores in the light of what they now know about learning styles and their own personal experiences in learning (e.g., their educational background, current job function, and positive and negative learning experiences).

    a. With this broader perspective, individuals should alter their position on the learning style type grid (Figure. 3–2) to reflect their current best judgment as to the learning style that best describes them.

    b. *Do this by placing an "X" on the grid spot that best defines your learning style.* You may agree with the position indicated by your LSI score. If so, place the "X" on top of the point you calculated earlier with the AC-CE and AE-RO scores. Or you may feel you are more extreme or centered on these dimensions. If so, move the "X" accordingly.

STEP 2. Portraying the learning style of class members. (10 minutes)

    a. A learning style type grid (see Figure 3–2) large enough for the entire class to stand on should be laid out on the floor of an open area.

    b. Individual group members should stand on this floor grid in the position corresponding to their X as positioned in step 1.

STEP 3. Individuals with similar learning styles join together in small groups of three to six. (20 minutes)

    a. Once the group members have positioned themselves on the spot that best indicates their learning style, they should form small groups (four to six persons) with their closest neighbors (i.e., those with similar learning styles).

    b. When this is completed, all members of these groups, in turn, should share with the group their thoughts on the following four topics. (The questions listed under these topics are suggestions only. Each person should speak about what he or she thinks is relevant.)

        1. Do your learning profile scores seem valid to you? How do you characterize the way in which you learn? Does your learning style profile relate to the way you went about the recent learning situation you described in the pre-work assignment earlier?

        2. What do you think is your greatest strength as a learner?

        3. What is your greatest weakness?

    Other members of the group may ask questions as each person speaks; however, the group should budget its time so that all participants get a chance to share their thoughts on these questions.

STEP 4. Reports to the total group. (25 minutes). Each small group should report its discussion briefly in the total group indicating

    a. Where they stood on the grid.

    b. The main points of their discussion—the *content* of the meeting.

    c. Observations about the process of their group meeting. How did it feel to be in a group of individuals who had learning styles similar to yours? Was the group's learning style reflected in the way the meeting ran? Do you prefer being in a group with similar or mixed learning styles?

    d. What connection can you make between this exercise and the readings for today's class?

CREATING A LEARNING COMMUNITY
(Time Allotted: 1 Hour)

Form learning groups of approximately six members. Diversity should be the criterion for group composition because this will maximize your learning. Try to have at least one person from each of the four learning styles and people of different ages, sexes, races, and occupations.

STEP 1. In your learning group discuss your answers to the premeeting questions. (20 minutes)

    a. What was the best group learning experience you ever experienced? What was good about it?

    b. What was your worst group learning experience? What made it that way?

    c. In your opinion, what conditions promote adult learning?

STEP 2. Prepare two lists on flipchart paper—a GIVE list and a GET list. (20 minutes)

    a. The GIVE list should record what individuals and/or the group as a whole are prepared to contribute to meet the learning needs of the class. These can be arranged in two categories:

        (1) Contributions to course content such as specific areas of expertise, relevant work experience, books, or other learning materials.

        (2) Contributions to the course learning process such as willingness to listen, willingness to share successes and failures candidly, and willingness to help manage time constraints.

    b. The GET list should record what individuals and/or the group as a whole want from the learning experiences. This list can also be arranged in two categories:

        (1) Content (specific knowledge, skills, or attitudes needed). (Your answers to the last chapter's questions about managerial skills you want to work on during the course fit in here.)

        (2) Process (the kind of learning environment characteristics individuals feel they need to learn most effectively).

STEP 3. The group should choose a spokesperson to report the results of the group's work and answer questions about the charts. The two lists for each group should be posted for viewing by the entire community. The spokesperson for each group should briefly describe their group's list. (20 minutes)

IV
Follow-up

Today's highly successful managers and administrators are distinguished not so much by any single set of knowledge or skills but by their ability to adapt to and master the changing demands of their job and career, that is, by their ability to *learn*. The same is true for successful organizations. Continuing success in a changing world requires an ability to explore new opportunities and learn from past successes and failures. So stated, these ideas are neither new nor particularly controversial. Yet it is surprising that this ability to learn, which is so widely regarded as important, receives little explicit attention by managers and their organizations. There is a kind of fatalism about learning; one either learns or one does not. The ability consciously to control and manage the learning process is usually limited to such childhood maxims as "Study hard" and "Do your homework."

Part of the reason for this fatalism lies in a lack of understanding about the learning process itself. If managers and administrators had a model about how individuals and organizations learn, they would better be able to enhance their own and their organization's ability to learn. This unit described such a model and attempted to show some of the ways in which the learning process and individual learning styles affect management education, managerial decision making and problem solving, and organizational learning.

LEARNING STYLES AND MANAGEMENT EDUCATION

Differences in learning styles need to be managed in management education. For example, managers who come to the university for midcareer education experience something of a "culture shock." Fresh from a world of time deadlines and concrete specific problems that they must solve, they are suddenly immersed in a strange slow-paced world of generalities, where the elegant solution to problems is sought even when workable solutions have been found. One gets rewarded here for reflection and analysis rather than concrete goal-directed action. Managers who "act before they think—if they ever think" meet the scientists who "think before they act—if they ever act." Research on learning styles has shown that managers on the whole are distinguished by very strong active experimentation skills and are very weak on reflective observation skills. Business school faculty members usually have the reverse profile. To bridge this gap in learning styles, the management educator must somehow respond to pragmatic demands for relevance and the application of knowledge, while encouraging the reflective examination of experience that is necessary to refine old theories and to build new ones. In encouraging reflective observation, the teacher often is seen as an interrupter of action—as a passive "ivory tower" thinker. Indeed, this is a critical role to be played in the learning process. Yet if the reflective observer role is not internalized by the learners themselves, the learning process can degenerate into a value conflict between teacher and student, each maintaining that theirs is the right perspective for learning.

Neither the faculty nor student perspective alone is valid. Managerial education will not be improved by eliminating theoretical analysis *or* relevant case problems. Improvement will come through the *integration* of the scholarly and practical learning styles. One approach to achieving this integration is to apply the experiential learning model directly in the classroom. This workbook provides games, role plays, and exercises (concrete experiences) that focus on central concepts in organizational behavior. These simulations provide a common experiential starting point for participants and faculty to explore the relevance of behavioral concepts for their work. In traditional management education methods, the conflict between scholar and practitioner learning styles is exaggerated because the material to be taught is filtered through the learning style of faculty members in their lectures or presentation and analysis of cases. Students are "one down" in their own analysis because the data are secondhand and already biased. In the experiential learning approach, this filtering process does not take place because both teacher and student are observers of immediate experiences which they both interpret according to their own learning style. In this approach to learning, the teachers' role is that of facilitator of a learning process that is basically self-directed. They help students to experience in a personal and immediate way the phenomena in their field of specialization. They provide observational schemes and perspectives from which to observe these experiences. They stand ready with alternative theories and concepts as students attempt to assimilate their observations into their own conception of reality. They assist in deducing the implications of the student's concepts and in designing new "experiments" to test these implications through practical "real-world" experience.

There are two goals in the experiential learning process. One is to learn the specifics of a particular subject matter. The other is to learn about one's own strengths and weaknesses as a learner (i.e., learning how to learn from experience). When the process works, participants finish their educational experience not only with new intellectual insights, but also with an understanding of their own learning style. This understanding of learning strengths and weaknesses helps in the back-home application of what has been learned and provides a framework for continuing learning on the job. Day-to-day experience becomes a focus for testing and exploring new ideas. Learning is no longer a special activity reserved for the classroom, but becomes an integral and explicit part of work itself.

THE ORGANIZATION AS A LEARNING SYSTEM

As do individuals, organizations learn and develop distinctive learning styles. They, as do individuals, do so through their transactions with the environment and through their choice of how to relate to that environment. This has come to be known as the open systems view of organizations. Since many organizations are large and complex, the environment they relate to becomes highly differentiated and diverse. The way the organization adapts to this external environment is to differentiate itself into units, each of which deals with just one part of the firm's external conditions. Marketing and sales face problems associated with the market, customers, and competitors; research deals with the academic and technological worlds; production deals with production equipment and raw materials sources; personnel and labor relations deal with the labor market; and so on.

Because of this need to relate to different aspects of the environment, the different units of the firm develop characteristic ways of thinking and working together—different styles of decision making and problem solving. These units select and shape managers to solve problems and make decisions in the way their environment demands. In fact, Lawrence and Lorsch define organizational differentiation as "the difference in cognitive and emotional orientation among managers in different functional departments."[7]

If the organization is thought of as a learning system, each of the differentiated units that is charged with adapting to the challenges of one segment of the environment can be thought of as having a characteristic learning style that is best suited to meet those environmental demands. The Learning Style Inventory should be a useful tool for measuring this organizational differentiation among the functional

---

[7]Paul Lawrence and Jay Lorsch, *Organization and Environment* (Boston: Division of Research, Graduate School of Business Administration, Harvard University, 1967).

units of a firm. To test this, we studied about 20 managers from each of five functional groups in a Midwestern division of a large American industrial corporation.[8] The five functional groups are described now, followed by our hypothesis about the learning style that should characterize each group given the environments to which they relate.

1. Marketing ($n = 20$). This group is made up primarily of former salespersons who have a nonquantitative "intuitive" approach to their work. Because of their practical sales orientation in meeting customer demands, they should have accommodative learning styles (i.e., concrete and active).

2. Research ($n = 22$). The work of this group is split about 50:50 between pioneer research and applied research projects. The emphasis is on basic research. Researchers should be the most assimilative group (i.e., abstract and reflective, a style fitted to the world of knowledge and ideas).

3. Personnel-labor relations ($n = 20$). In this company, workers from this department serve two primary functions: interpreting personnel policy and promoting interaction among groups to reduce conflict and disagreement. Because of their "people orientation," these people should be predominantly divergers, concrete and reflective.

4. Engineering ($n = 18$). This group is made up primarily of design engineers who are quite production oriented. They should be the most convergent subgroup (i.e., abstract and active), although they should be less abstract than the research group. They represent a bridge between thought and action.

5. Finance ($n = 20$). This group has a strong computer information systems bias. Financial personnel, given their orientation toward the mathematical task of information system design, should be highly abstract. Their crucial role in organizational survival should produce an active orientation. Thus, finance group members should have convergent learning styles.

Figure 3–3 shows the average scores on the active-reflective (AE-RO) and abstract-concrete (AC-CE) learning dimensions for the five functional groups. These results are consistent with the predictions with the exception of the finance group, whose scores are less active than predicted and thus fall between the assimilative and convergent quadrants. The LSI clearly differentiates the learning styles that characterize the functional units of at least this one company. Managers in each of these units apparently use very different styles in doing their jobs.

But differentiation is only part of the story of organizational adaptation and effectiveness. The result of the differentiation necessary to adapt to the external environment is the creation of a corresponding internal need to integrate and coordinate the different units. This necessitates resolving in some way the conflicts inherent in these different learning styles. In actual practice, this conflict gets resolved in many ways. Sometimes it is resolved through confrontation and integration of the different learning styles. More often, however, it is resolved through dominance by one unit over the other units, resulting in an unbalanced organizational learning style. We all know of organizations that are controlled by the marketing department, or are heavily engineering oriented, and so on. This imbalance can be effective if it matches environmental demands in a stable environment, but it can be costly if the organization is called upon to learn to respond to changing environmental demands and opportunities.

One important question concerns the extent to which the integrative conflict between units is a function of managers' learning styles rather than merely a matter of conflicting job and role demands. To get at this question, we asked the managers

---

[8]These data were collected by Frank Weisner as part of his Sloan School of Management M.S. thesis (1971). We have reanalyzed his data for presentation here.

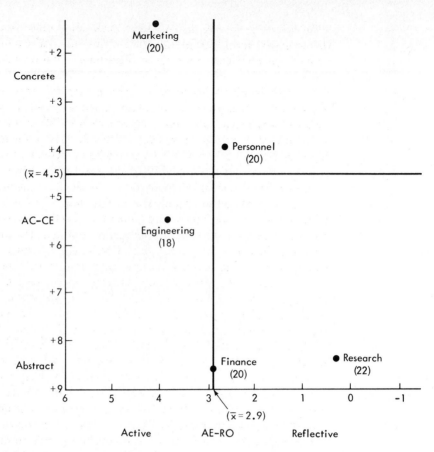

FIGURE 3–3 **Average LSI Scores on Active-Reflective (AE-RO) and Abstract-Concrete (AC-CE) by Organizational Function**

in each of the five functional units in the study to rate how difficult they found it to communicate with each of the other four units. If integrative communication is a function of learning style, there should be a correspondence between how similar two units are in their learning style and how easy they find it to communicate. When the average communication difficulty ratings among the five units are compared with differences in unit learning styles, we find that in most cases this hypothesis is confirmed (ie.., those units that are most different in learning style have most difficulty communicating with one another). To test this notion more rigorously, we did a more intensive study of communication between the two units who were most different in learning styles, marketing and research. To ascertain whether it was a manager's learning style that accounted for communication difficulty, we divided managers in the marketing unit into two groups. One group had learning styles that were similar to those managers in research (i.e., assimilators), while the other group had accommodative learning styles typical of the marketing function. The research group was divided similarly. The results of this analysis showed that when managers have learning styles similar to those of another group, they have little trouble communicating with that group. When style differences are great, communication difficulty rises. These results suggest that managers' learning styles are an important factor to consider in achieving integration among functional units.

MANAGING THE LEARNING PROCESS

To conclude, let us examine how managers and organizations can explicitly manage their learning process. We have seen that the experiential learning model is useful not only for examining the educational process but also for understanding managerial problem solving and organizational adaptation. But how can an awareness of the experiential learning model and our own individual learning style help improve individual and organizational learning? Two recommendations seem important.

First, learning should be an explicit objective that is pursued as consciously and deliberately as profit or productivity. Managers and organizations should budget time to learn specifically from their experiences. When important meetings are held or important decisions are made, time should be set aside to critique and learn from these events. All too few organizations have a climate that allows for free exploration of such questions as, "What have we learned from this venture?" Usually, active experimentation norms dictate: "We don't have time; let's move on."

This leads to the second recommendation. The nature of the learning process is such that opposing perspectives—action and reflection, concrete involvement, and analytical detachment—are all essential for optimal learning. When one perspective comes to dominate others, learning effectiveness is reduced. From this we can conclude that the most effective learning systems are those that can tolerate differences in perspective. This point can be illustrated by the case of an electronics firm that we have worked with over the years. The firm was started by a group of engineers with a unique product. For several years they had no competitors, and when some competition entered the market, they continued to dominate and do well because of their superior engineering quality. Today it is a different story. They are now faced with stiff competition in their original product area, and, in addition, their very success has caused new problems. They are no longer a small intimate company but a large organization with several plants in the United States and Europe. The company has had great difficulty in responding to these changes because it still responds to problems primarily from an engineering point of view. Most of the top executives in the company are former engineers with no formal management training. Many of the specialists in marketing, finance, and personnel who have been brought in to help the organization solve its new problems feel like "second-class citizens." Their ideas just don't seem to carry much weight. What was once the organization's strength, its engineering expertise, has become to some extent its weakness. Because engineering has flourished at the expense of the development of other organizational functions such as marketing and the management of human resources, the firm is today struggling with, rather than mastering, its environment.

V
Learning Points

1. The rapid degree of change present in today's business environment makes a necessity of continuous learning for both individuals and organizations.

2. Adult learning

   a. Is based on reciprocity.

   b. Is based on experience.

   c. Has a problem-solving orientation.

   d. Is individualized and self-directed.

   e. Integrates learning and living.

   f. Needs to be applied.

3. The adult learning process is a cycle composed of the following components: concrete experience, reflective observation, abstract conceptualization, and active experimentation.

4. Individuals usually see themselves as having a predisposition or a learned facility for one of the four stages in the learning model: divergence, assimilation, convergence, and accommodation.

5. The four learning styles differ along two dimensions. The first dimension represents the concrete experiencing of events at one end and the abstract conceptualization at the other (feeling versus thinking). The second dimension has active experimentation at one extreme and reflective observation at the other (doing versus watching).

6. Learning communities and organizations profit from having members with different learning styles because each style has its particular strengths and weaknesses.

VI
Tips for Managers

- Be aware of your personal learning style so that you understand how you approach work issues and how you react to others who have different styles.

- When you are training others (even if it's only breaking in a replacement), remember that people have a tendency to assume that everyone learns the same way they do. Since this is not true, find out how the trainee learns best and adapt your instruction accordingly.

- Ensure that people with different learning styles are valued for their strengths. If you find yourself in a situation where this is not the case, you may want to give the work team or the management group the Learning Style Inventory so that the differences can be understood in a positive manner. The LSI is often used as an opening exercise in team-building efforts.

- Make time to reflect upon work events and assume the stance, "What can we learn from this?" for both yourself and your employees.

VII

Personal Application Assignment

Please respond to the following questions in the upcoming week. Each section of the assignment is worth 4 points which will be assigned according to the criteria shown.

The topic of this assignment is to think back on a previous learning experience that was significant to you. Choose an experience about which you are motivated to learn more; that is, there was something about it that you do not totally understand, that intrigues you, that made you realize that you lack certain skills, that was problematical or significant for you. It may have been an academic one or a nonformal educational experience (e.g., tennis camp, a seminar, on-the-job training program).

A. *Concrete Experience*

    1. *Objectively* describe the experience ("who," "what," "when," "where," "how," information—up to 2 points).

    2. *Subjectively* describe your feelings, perceptions, and thoughts that occurred *during* (not after) the experience (up to 2 points). Does this section have too much detail? (If so, delete 1 point.)

B. *Reflective Observation*

    1. Look at the experience from different points of view. How many points of view did you include that are *relevant* (up to 2 points)?

    2. Use these perspectives to add more meaning to the incident (up to 2 points).

C. *Abstract Conceptualization*

  1. Relate concepts from the assigned readings and the lecture to the experience (i.e., what theories that you heard in the lecture or read in the *Reader* relate to your understanding of this incident?).

  2. Make reference to at least two sources. Use standard referencing format and include the page number to which you are referring. How many sources did you use and how clearly did you explain their theories (up to 4 points)?

  3. You can also create an original model or theory, but it should not replace course concepts.

D. *Active Experimentation*

  1. Write about what you will do in the future that will improve your effectiveness. Use rules of thumb or action resolutions.

  2. Are they described specifically, thoroughly, and in detail (up to 4 points)?

E. *Integration, Synthesis, and Writing*

  1. Did you write about something personally important to you (up to 1 point)?

  2. Was it well written (up to 2 points)?

  3. Did you integrate and synthesize the different sections (up to 1 point)?

4

INDIVIDUAL MOTIVATION AND ORGANIZATIONAL BEHAVIOR

OBJECTIVES By the end of this chapter, you should be able to:

A. Explain several theories of motivation.

B. Understand McClelland's three basic social motives and how they are defined.

C. Gain insight into your own motive patterns.

D. Explain how managers can direct individual motivation and behavior in organizations.

No Contest

Joyce Osland

Once upon a time a new sales manager who was highly motivated to earn a year-end bonus for bringing in new business decided to initiate a contest for his sales agents. He announced that he would pay $100 to the agent who had brought in the most new clients by the end of the month. Then he sat back in his chair to await the results and decide how he would spend his bonus money.

While visions of Porsches danced through his head, his sales agents were busily belly-aching for the following reasons:

1. They were used to working as a team and resented being encouraged to compete against close friends.
2. In the manager's last contest, a new sales agent had reportedly cheated and "stole" new clients from the old-timers.
3. The winner of the last contest was paid the prize money several months late, only after she had "shaken" it out of the sales manager.
4. One sales agent position had not been filled so the others felt they were already operating beyond full capacity and working extra hours because the new sales manager made them attend evening functions for clients, which they had never done in the past.
5. The sales manager had neglected to endear himself to the agents, and they felt he was just using them to get his bonus.
6. The sales agents felt as if they were being manipulated and perceived the $100 as an insult.

As a result, the sales agents decided to ignore the contest. The sales manager was angry when he saw the level of new business at the end of the month and concluded that the agents were lazy. He told them they were unprofessional and complained about them at staff meetings so that soon everyone in the organization had heard about their "laziness." Old-timers-in-the-know scratched their heads because they remembered how hard the sales agents used to work before the new sales manager was hired. And everyone lived unhappily ever after (except for a few agents who quit and went to work for a competitor) until the sales manager went back to school and learned about theories of motivation.

I

Premeeting Preparation

A. Read the Instructions for the Test of Imagination.[1]

B. Write stories on *four* pictures of your choice on the pages following those pictures. Do not take more than 5 minutes per story. Do this before reading further in this unit.

C. Read the Topic Introduction and the Procedure for Group Meeting: TAT Motive Analysis.

D. What were the significant learning points from the readings?

Please read the following instructions carefully before turning the page.

An important asset in the world is imagination. This test gives you an opportunity to use your imagination, to show how you can create ideas and situations by yourself. In other words, instead of presenting you with ready-made answers from which you choose one, it gives you the chance to show how you can think things up on your own.

On the following pages, write out four brief stories that you make up on your own. To help you get started, there is a series of pictures that you can interpret and around which you can build your stories. When you have finished reading these instructions, turn the page, look at the first picture briefly, then turn the page again and write a story suggested by the picture. To help you cover all the elements of a story plot in the time allowed, you will find four questions spaced out over the page:

1. What is happening? Who are the people?
2. What has led up to this situation? That is, what has happened in the past?
3. What is being thought? What is wanted? By whom?
4. What will happen? What will be done?

Please remember that the questions are only guides for your thinking and need not be answered specifically in so many words. That is, *your story should be continuous and not just a set of answers to these questions.* Do not take more than 5 minutes per story. You should complete the whole test 20 minutes after you begin, although you may finish in less time if you like (i.e., 4 stories at about 5 minutes each).

There are no right or wrong stories. In fact, any kind of story is all right. You have a chance to show how quickly you can imagine and write a story on your own. Do not simply describe the pictures; write a story about them. They are vague and suggestive of many things on purpose, and are just to help give you an idea to write about.

Try to make your stories interesting and dramatic. Show that you have an understanding of people and can make up stories about human relationships.

If you have read these instructions carefully and understand them, turn the page, look at the picture, and then write your story. Do not take more than 5 minutes. Then choose another picture, write out the story it suggests, and so on through the booklet.

[1]This test is a variation of the standard six-picture Thematic Apperception Test cited in John Atkinson, ed., *Motives in Fantasy, Action, and Society* (Princeton, NJ: D. Van Nostrand, 1958).

Just look at the picture briefly (10 to 15 seconds), turn the page, and write the story it suggests.

1. What is happening? Who are the people?

2. What has led up to this situation? That is, what has happened in the past?

3. What is being thought? What is wanted? By whom?

4. What will happen? What will be done?

When you have finished your story or your time is up, turn to the next picture. If you have not finished, go on anyway. You may return at the end to complete this story.

Just look at the picture briefly (10 to 15 seconds), turn the page, and write the story it suggests.

1. What is happening? Who are the people?

2. What has led up to this situation? That is, what has happened in the past?

3. What is being thought? What is wanted? By whom?

4. What will happen? What will be done?

When you have finished your story or your time is up, turn to the next picture. If you have not finished, go on anyway. You may return at the end to complete this story.

Just look at the picture briefly (10 to 15 seconds), turn the page, and write the story it suggests.

1. What is happening? Who are the people?

2. What has led up to this situation? That is, what has happened in the past?

3. What is being thought? What is wanted? By whom?

4. What will happen? What will be done?

When you have finished your story or your time is up, turn to the next picture. If you have not finished, go on anyway. You may return at the end to complete this story.

Just look at the picture briefly (10 to 15 seconds), turn the page, and write the story it suggests.

1. What is happening? Who are the people?

2. What has led up to this situation? That is, what has happened in the past?

3. What is being thought? What is wanted? By whom?

4. What will happen? What will be done?

When you have finished your story or your time is up, turn to the next picture. If you have not finished, go on anyway. You may return at the end to complete this story.

Just look at the picture briefly (10 to 15 seconds), turn the page, and write the story it suggests.

1. What is happening? Who are the people?

2. What has led up to this situation? That is, what has happened in the past?

3. What is being thought? What is wanted? By whom?

4. What will happen? What will be done?

When you have finished your story or your time is up, turn to the next picture. If you have not finished, go on anyway. You may return at the end to complete this story.

Just look at the picture briefly (10 to 15 seconds), turn the page, and write the story it suggests.

Work rapidly. Do not spend more than 5 minutes on this story.

1. What is happening? Who are the people?

2. What has led up to this situation? That is, what has happened in the past?

3. What is being thought? What is wanted? By whom?

4. What will happen? What will be done?

II

Topic Introduction

Concern over productivity levels in the United States raises the question of how well companies can compete in both the domestic or global marketplace. One of the many factors that affect productivity is motivation. Motivation has always been an issue of concern for managers; it has long been recognized as one of the classic managerial functions—planning, *motivating,* coordinating, controlling, and organizing. There persist, however, some common sense notions about motivation that are misleading and just plain wrong. First among these notions is the idea that there are persons who are not motivated. This is incorrect. Every living human being is motivated. What managers really mean when they say that a worker is not motivated is that the worker is not motivated to do what the manager wants the worker to do. The same "lazy" employee who just goes through the motions at work may stay up all night working with great intensity on a sports car or devote many hours outside of work to the Girl Scouts. While it is true that some people are more energetic than others, the most important factor to consider is how this energy is directed—toward what goals and objectives. The prime task for managing motivation, therefore, is channeling and directing human energy toward the activities, tasks, and objectives that further the organization's mission.

This leads to a second erroneous idea about motivation, namely, that managers "motivate" workers, that motivation is something you do *to* someone else. Motivation is an *internal* state that directs individuals toward certain goals and objectives. Managers cannot directly influence this internal state; they can only create expectations on the part of employees that their motives will be satisfied by doing the organization's work and provide the rewards that satisfy the employee's needs. Managers cannot motivate a worker to achieve, for example, but they can create expectations in the workplace that achievement will be rewarded.

This distinction may appear subtle, but it is important because failure to understand it often leads managers to attempt to use motivation to manipulate employees. (The opening vignette, "No Contest," is an example of such manipulation. In this example, the sales manager did not understand either his employees or theories of motivation well enough to realize that a contest of this sort contained more demotivators than motivators for this particular group of sales agents.) Manipulation is a very inefficient way of managing motivation because it requires that you as a manager maintain control of the carrot and stick. As a result you must spend time scheming about just how you will motivate those you supervise on a day-to-day basis. And you must do it alone. A more effective way of managing motivation is through understanding. If you understand the needs and objectives of those you supervise, you can work with them to develop an equitable psychological contract that recognizes their particular desires and creates conditions where these motives can be satisfied in the work setting. The same is true of your own motivation. By becoming more aware of your own motives and desires, you can better organize your own work and life activities to achieve satisfaction and productivity.

Motive is a word often used in mystery stories and among actors. All of us have some intuitive understanding of the meaning of the term in those contexts. The detective, for instance, in looking for the culprit, will always seek someone with a "motive," a *reason* for committing the murder. An actor or actress, in like manner, wants to understand the motivation of some character. In both instances the search for motive is the search for a process of thinking and feeling that causes a person to act in specific ways.

Our understanding of human motivation has increased substantially over the past few decades. Simplistic theories that argued that people worked primarily for money or primarily for social gratification have been replaced with more complex theories of human nature. Some of these theories are called content theories because they attempt to identify the factors within the individual that energize, direct, sustain, and stop behavior. They focus upon the specific internal needs that motivate people.[2] Maslow's work, for example, provided two important postulates concerning human motivation.[3] One is that human needs can be viewed in an hierarchical fashion. Lower-order needs—physical needs and security—must be satisfied to some extent before higher-order needs—needs for social belonging, self-esteem, and self-actualization—become activated. Second is the notion that a satisfied need is no longer a motivator of behavior.

Insights such as these can help us to understand why it is that beyond a certain point, a salary increase may be of marginal motivational value. Individuals can be at different levels in the motivational hierarchy at different times, causing different needs to be aroused. Herzberg suggests a two-factor theory of motivation that is based on Maslow's hierarchy.[4] *Hygiene factors*—extrinsic factors such as the attractiveness of the physical facilities, salary, company policy and administration, working conditions, and interpersonal relations—create dissatisfaction if they do not exist. Their presence, however, does not create positive motivation. A second set of intrinsic factors—*motivators* such as the work itself, challenge, responsibility, advancement, and recognition—are necessary to stimulate positive motivation. Once we have met a person's hygiene needs, "more of the same" yields marginal benefits.

Alderfer's ERG theory is also based upon Maslow's work. He identifies three categories of needs that are similar to Maslow's hierarchy: *existence needs* (food, air, water, pay, fringe benefits, and working conditions), *relatedness needs* (meaningful social and interpersonal relationship), and *growth needs* (creative or productive contributions). Alderfer subscribes to Maslow's idea that once a need is fulfilled, the individual will progress to a higher-order need, which is referred to as a fulfillment-progression process. However, Alderfer also maintains that when relatedness or growth needs are frustrated, the individual may regress to being motivated by a previously satisfied lower-order need. For example, if growth needs are continuously frustrated, individuals may redirect their efforts to satisfying relatedness needs. If relatedness needs are continuously frustrated, existence needs might become a motivating force even though they were satisfied in the past. This is referred to as a frustration-regression process.

Psychologists, most notably David McClelland of Harvard, have made a great deal of progress over the past 20 years in scientifically measuring and defining human motives.[5] McClelland began by looking not at external action but at the way a person thinks and feels. He used the Thematic Apperception Test (TAT), which you have taken in preparation for today, to record thought samples that could then be studied and grouped according to the dominant concerns, or themes, expressed in the stories. He and his coworkers were able to group the responses into three broad categories, each representing an identifiable human motive: need for affiliation (n-Aff), need for power (n-Pow), and need for achievement (n-Ach).

[2]The second category of motivation theories is process theories that attempt to describe how personal factors and environmental factors interact and influence each other to produce certain kinds of behavior. Examples of these theories are expectancy theory, equity theory, reinforcement theory, and goal setting. See the article by Nadler and Lawler, "Motivation: A Diagnostic Approach" in the *Reader* for a description of expectancy theory. Also, for a more complete discussion of various theories of motivation, see Edgar H. Schein, *Organizational Psychology,* 3rd ed. (Englewood Cliffs, NJ: Prentice Hall, 1981).

[3]Abraham Maslow, *Motivation and Personality* (New York: Harper & Row, 1970).

[4]Frederic Herzberg, B. Mausner, and B. Snyderman, *The Motivation to Work* (New York: John Wiley, 1959).

[5]See John Atkinson, *Motives in Fantasy, Action, and Society* (Princeton, NJ: D. Van Nostrand, 1958), David C. McClelland, *The Achieving Society* (Princeton, NJ: D. Van Nostrand, 1961), and David C. McClelland, *Human Motivation* (Glenview, IL: Scott, Foresman, 1985).

Most people, McClelland found, have a degree of each of these motives in their thoughts, but seldom in the same strength. A person may be high in the need for affiliation (n-Aff), low in the need for achievement (n-Ach), and moderate in the need for power (n-Pow). Such people would tend to think more about friendship than about doing a good job or controlling others. Their motivation to work will be of a different order than that of the employee who is high in achievement motivation and low in affiliation and power motivations. The needs identified in McClelland's framework are similar to Maslow's higher-order needs and Herzberg's motivation factors. McClelland states that these motives are learned from our parents and our culture. He discovered different motive patterns for different cultures, which is an important fact to bear in mind when engaged in international business.

We can sharpen our understanding of these motives in management settings by examining the motive patterns of some "typical" managers.

n-POWER

Many middle- and upper-level managers have a high need for power. Their effectiveness as creators of company climate depends not only on their need for power, but also on the other values they bring to their job. John Andrews's study of two Mexican companies is striking in this regard.[6] Both companies had presidents who scored high in n-Power, but one firm was stagnating whereas the other was growing rapidly. The manager of the growing company, although high in n-Power, was also high in n-Achievement and was dedicated to letting others in the organization satisfy their own needs for achievement by introducing improvements and making decisions on their own. The stagnant company, although well capitalized and enjoying a favorable market, was constantly in turmoil and experienced a high rate of turnover, particularly among its executives. In this company, the president's high n-Power, coupled with highly authoritarian values, led him to make all the decisions himself, leaving no room for individual responsibility on the part of his personnel. A comparison of motivation scores of upper-level managers of the two companies showed that the dynamic company's managers were significantly higher in n-Achievement than were those of the stagnant company, who tended to be more concerned with power and compliance than with individual responsibility and decision making.

The results of research have shown that a manager needs a reasonably high n-Power to function as a leader.[7] Whether he or she uses it well depends in large part on the other values and motives the individual holds. Being high in n-Power does not automatically make one autocratic or authoritarian. Good leadership may indeed be a function of the manager's ability to understand his or her need for power and to use it in creative, satisfying ways.[8]

n-AFFILIATION

Those persons high in n-Affiliation alone, since their concerns are more with warm, friendly relationships, are more likely to be in supervisory jobs (if they are in industry at all), jobs where maintaining relationships is more important than decision making. Kolb and Boyatzis[9] have shown that people high in n-Affiliation alone are

[6]John D. W. Andrews, "The Achievement Motive in Two Types of Organizations," *Journal of Personality and Social Psychology,* Vol. 6 (1967), pp. 163–168.

[7]Herbert A. Wainer and Irwin M. Rubin, "Motivation of Research and Development Entrepreneurs: Determinants of Company Success," *Journal of Applied Psychology,* Vol. 53, no. 3 (1969), pp. 178–184.

[8]This issue will be addressed in more depth in Chapter 14, Leadership: The Effective Exercise of Power and Influence.

[9]David A. Kolb and Richard Boyatzis, "On the Dynamics of the Helping Relationship," *Journal of Ap-*

seen as ineffective helpers, probably because they fear disrupting relationships by forthrightness and confrontation. They have also shown, however, that the people who are seen by others as effective helpers tend to have relatively even motive strengths across the three motives, not being extremely high or low on any of the three. Although strong n-Affiliation does not seem to be central to leadership and management performance, some concern with the feelings of others is necessary. Some concern with affiliation is important in understanding the needs of others and in generating a climate that takes those needs into consideration. Noujaim[10] has shown that high n-Affiliation managers spend more time communicating than do high n-Achievement or high n-Power managers. Communicating with others in warm, friendly ways is of real importance to the achievement of organizational goals particularly in achieving cooperation and effective coordination. When people can collaborate and communicate on task accomplishment, the climate of the organization is improved.

n-ACHIEVEMENT

Whereas a high need for achievement seems absolutely necessary for the entrepreneur, it is not always functional for managers, as creators of an organization's climate, to be extremely high in this motive. Noujaim[11] has shown that executives high in n-Achievement tend to have fewer meetings than do other executives and tend to want to work alone, despite the fact that many organizational problems would be better solved by collaborative effort. (For example, high n-Achievement managers spend significantly more time doing personal work alone.) As with executives high in n-Power, their effectiveness as managers depends more on their other values than on their motivation alone.

Persons high in n-Achievement want to take personal responsibility for their success or failure, like to take calculated (moderate) risks, and like situations in which they get immediate, concrete feedback on how well they are doing. Their need for feedback keeps them from getting too involved in open-ended exploratory situations with no concrete goal and no benchmarks along the way. Their sense of personal responsibility will keep them from delegating authority unless they hold values that let them see developing a responsive organization as a legitimate achievement goal. They will be task oriented, but the kind of climate they create in an organization will be healthier if their strong n-Achievement is balanced by moderate needs for power and affiliation and if they are committed to building an achievement-oriented organization that stimulates personal responsibility and calculated risks, getting feedback on how it is doing at each step along the way.

It is a truism in contemporary social psychology that behavior is a function of both the person and the environment. Atkinson and Feather have argued that the tendency (T) to act in these three ways (to fulfill needs for power, affiliation, or achievement) can be predicted by the strength of the individual's motivation (M) for power, affiliation, and achievement; times the individual's perceived expectation (E) that action in terms of one or more of these motives will be rewarded; times the reward value (R) of the power, affiliation, and achievement rewards that he or she expects to get. Thus, the individual acts to maximize satisfaction following the formula $T = M \times E \times R$ for three motives: power, affiliation, and achievement. While M refers to the individual's motivation, E and R refer to the individual's perception of the environment.[12]

plied Behavior Science (1970); D. A. Kolb, I. M. Rubin, and J. S. Osland, Organizational Behavior: Practical Readings for Managers (Englewood Cliffs, NJ: Prentice Hall, 1990).

[10]Khalil Noujaim, "Some Motivational Determinants of Effort Allocation and Performance" (Ph.D. thesis, Sloan School of Management, Massachusetts Institute of Technology, 1968).

[11]Ibid.

[12]J. Atkinson, An Introduction to Motivation (Princeton, NJ: D. Van Nostrand, 1964), and J. Atkinson and N. T. Feather, A Theory of Achievement Motivation (New York: John Wiley, 1966).

The equation in the preceding paragraph is based upon the assumption that employees make conscious choices about their behavior at work. They calculate whether a certain level of effort will result in a particular goal; they determine whether the reward is worth the effort, and they also compare whether their efforts and rewards are comparable to those of other people.[13] These decisions, which are based upon employees' perception of the environment and previous experiences, affect their behavior and level of productivity.

While individuals come to organizations with previously learned motive patterns and unique needs, managers can affect how employees perceive their environment. They shape and direct motivation by establishing expectations and rewards that tap into employee motives and further the organization's goals. The manager's task is to make sure there is a fit and a direct link—between employee needs and rewards, between performance and rewards, and between employees and jobs. The better the fit, the higher employee motivation.

One study asked workers and supervisors to rank ten job factors in order of their importance to the workers. Those factors that the workers ranked first, second, and third—appreciation for their work, being in on things, and sympathy for personal problems—were ranked eighth, ninth, and tenth by their supervisors! The supervisors mistakenly assumed that good wages, job security, and promotion were most important to the workers.[14] People often make the mistake of assuming that others have the same needs they do. If we return to the sales manager and his contest in the opening vignette, we see that he was not only mistaken about his employees' needs but also about what constituted incentives for them.

If he had had a better understanding of motivation theories, what might he have done differently? First, the sales manager could have explained the need for increased business and sought the agents' commitment and participation concerning this goal. This might have prevented the agents' feelings of being manipulated. Second, he could have investigated and attempted to remedy, if possible, any factors that were presenting the agents from bringing in new business. The understaffing issue, employee feelings about the previous contest, and maybe even work design concerns might have been raised. Perhaps as a team they could have looked for alternatives—ways to work smarter rather than harder.

Third, had the sales manager spent more time talking with the agents, he would have discovered that, since the agents already perceived themselves to be understaffed and overworked, $100 was not an equitable reward for the extra work required to generate new business. By knowing his employees better and discussing such matters with them, the sales manager could have discovered both what their individual needs were and what they saw as an equitable reward for increased effort.

And, finally, knowing that the agents were a tightly knit group who had worked as a team for several years should have told the manager that an individual prize in a contest that encouraged competition among peers would be a negative incentive. Had the manager set both a team goal and team incentive (*after* consulting the agents to discover what they would consider to be a positive incentive), he would have been more likely to connect with their needs for both affiliation and achievement. Competing against their own previous record or competing against other sales groups in the corporation would have been more motivating and appropriate for this particular group of sales agents.

[13]These are examples of the questions answered by process theories of motivation that were mentioned in footnote 1 of this chapter.

[14]Paul Hersey and Kenneth J. Blanchard, *Management of Organizational Behavior: Utilizing Human Resources* (Englewood Cliffs, NJ: Prentice Hall, 1977), p. 47.

III

Procedure for Group Meeting: TAT Motive Analysis and Money Auction

MOTIVE ANALYSIS AND SCORING
(Time Allotted: 1 Hour)

The purpose of this exercise is to help you identify (but not score in detail) the motivational themes you expressed in your TAT stories.

Divide the group into trios for the scoring and have one trio member read their first story to the other two. Using the criteria that follow, score the story and enter it on the individual scoring form provided. Repeat until all stories of each trio member have been scored and entered.

The following criteria, taken from the empirical scoring systems, will help you to decide which of the three motives, *if any,* is present in your stories. Record on the form provided those motives present in each story plus any other motivational concerns that you and your group may notice. It is possible for a story to contain none or all three of these motives as well as other motivational concerns, such as sex, aggression, hunger, or security.

In approaching the task, you should keep several things in mind. The TAT pictures and your responses are meant to be stimuli for reflection and discussion, not necessarily an absolute measure of your motives. In addition, you are not expected to become expert scorers, but to become familiar with general patterns. Finally, be wary of the pressure to reach consensus in your trio meetings. Each listener will, in fact, hear another's story through his or her own (the listener's) motivational filter. For example, a person high in the need for affiliation may well "see" considerable affiliation imagery in someone else's story.

The point of this exercise is that people *do* have different needs and that they *do* consequently see the world in different ways. The managerial task is to become aware of and effectively integrate these real differences.

Achievement motivation is present in a story when any one of the following occurs:

1. Someone in the story is concerned about a *standard of excellence.* The individual wants to win or to do well in a competition. The person has self-imposed standards for a good performance or is emotionally involved in attaining an achievement goal. Standards of excellence can be inferred by the use of words such as *good* or *better* or similar words when used to evaluate performance.

2. Someone in the story is involved in a unique accomplishment, such as an invention or an artistic creation. Here the standard of excellence can be inferred and need not be explicitly stated.

3. Someone in the story is involved in a *long-term goal,* such as an invention or

an artistic creation. Here the standard of excellence can be inferred and need not be explicitly stated.

Power motivation is present in a story when any of the following occurs:[15]

1. People describe actions in which they express their power. For example, strong, forceful actions which affect others, such as assaults, attacks, chasing or catching, verbal insults, threats, accusations, reprimands, crimes, sexual exploitation, and gaining the upper hand all indicate the presence of the power motive.

2. There are statements about someone giving help, assistance, advice, or support that has not been solicited by the other person.

3. There are statements which indicate that someone is trying to control another person through regulating his or her behavior, or through searching for information which would affect another person's life or actions. Examples of the last category are searching, investigating, and checking up on someone.

4. Someone is trying to persuade, influence, convince, bribe, make a point, or argue with another person, but not with the motive of reaching agreement or understanding. Mention of a disagreement is not sufficient to score the power motive here; there must be action or a desire for action that has the objective of changing another's opinion.

5. Someone is trying to impress another person or the world at large. Or someone in the story is described as being concerned about his or her reputation or position. Creative writing, publicity, trying to win an election or identifying closely with another person running for office, seeking fame and notoriety are all scorable for power.

6. Someone does something that arouses strong positive or negative emotions in others, such as pleasure, delight, awe, gratitude, fear, respect, jealousy and so forth.

Affiliation motivation is present when any of the following occurs:

1. Someone in the story is concerned about establishing, maintaining, or restoring a *positive emotional relationship* with another person. Friendship is the most basic kind of positive emotional relationship, and to mention that two characters in the story are friends would be a minimum basis for scoring imagery. Other relationships, such as father-son or lover-lover, should be scored *only* if they have the warm, compassionate quality implied in the definition given.

2. There is a statement that *one person likes* or *wants to be liked* by someone else or that someone has some similar feeling about another. Moreover, if a close interpersonal relationship has been disrupted or broken, imagery can be scored if someone feels sorrow or grief or takes action to restore the relationship.

3. Also, score if the story mentions such *affiliative activities* as parties, reunions, visits, or relaxed small talk as in a bull session. However, if the affiliative nature of the situation is explicitly denied in the story, such as by describing it as a business meeting or an angry debate, imagery is not scored. Friendly actions such as consoling or being concerned about the well-being or happiness of another person are scored, except where these actions are culturally prescribed by the relationship (e.g., father-son). In other words, there must be

---

[15]These categories were developed by David G. Winter, *The Power Motive* (New York: Free Press, 1973), pp. 251–255.

evidence that the nurturant activity is not motivated solely by a sense of obligation.

Discussion of Motive Scores

When a trio has finished scoring their stories, they should join with another trio and discuss the following questions:

1. How much similarity or difference was there in your group concerning the dominant motivational concerns expressed in the stories? Of what significance is this similarity or difference?

2. In what ways did the motivational concerns you expressed in the stories agree or disagree with the image you held of yourself *before* you took the test? Of what significance are any differences?

3. What kinds of things cause one person to express affiliation concerns, another person to express power concerns, and a third to express achievement concerns in response to the *same* picture? Consider immediate (e.g., "He hadn't had anything to eat all day") as well as historical (e.g., "She flunked math in high school") factors.

4. Were there any particular reasons that you chose the four pictures you did? In other words, you chose not to respond to two pictures in particular—why? Did others choose the same pictures as you?

5. What motives do you think are relevant or important within the context of a job?

6. Of what value, if any, do you feel are projective techniques such as the TAT in assessing human motivation? What other alternatives might be feasible or better?

7. What connections can you make between this exercise and the readings?

INDIVIDUAL MOTIVES AND BEHAVIOR
(Time Allotted: 1 Hour)

The focus in this part of the class is on the relationship between individual motives and behavior. The exercise has been designed to focus primarily upon the behavioral manifestations of n-Power, n-Affiliation, and n-Achievement.

The Money Auction
(Time Allotted: 1 Hour)

STEP 1. The first step in this exercise[16] is for the total group to divide into groups of three. If there are one or two individuals remaining after the trios are formed, they should join a trio as observers.

Each trio is made of *one auctioneer* and *two bidders*. This exercise will continue for three rounds, giving each member of the trio a chance to be the auctioneer. *During the exercise no talking is allowed except for stating bids.*

STEP 2. In the exercise itself the auctioneer should be considered the dispenser of funds. *It is not the auctioneer's money.* Auctioneers will offer for auction to the two bidders seven imaginary nickels, one at a time. Each nickel will be sold to the highest bidder. There is nothing special about these nickels (e.g., they are not rare coins). The opportunity for the first bid will alternate between the two bidders during the seven

[16]This game is a modification of an exercise introduced to us by Edgar H. Schein.

trials. Bidder 1 will bid first on the first trial, bidder 2 bids first on the second, and so on. Bids must be made alternatively between bidders in at least 1 cent units. Players should record the process of the auction on the accompanying Money Auction Record Form. *It is helpful to limit talking to the statement of bids until all three rounds are completed.*

STEP 3. Individual reflection. When all three rounds have been completed, each individual should take 5 minutes of time alone to record personal reactions to the questions that follow:

1. a. What was your goal in the nickel auction when you were a bidder?

   b. What strategy did you follow to reach your goal?

   c. Did you maintain the same goal and strategy throughout the exercise? If you changed, what caused you to do so?

2. What thoughts did you have before or during the exercise you just completed that you would say were reflective of the three motives under examination?

   a. n-Ach thoughts

   b. n-Pow thoughts

   c. n-Aff thoughts

3. In what ways was your behavior, in your view, reflective of each of the three motives under examination? Jot down some specific examples:

   a. n-Ach behavior I exhibited

   b. n-Pow behavior I exhibited

   c. n-Aff behavior I exhibited

4. In what ways did other members of your trio behave that you would say were reflective of each of the three motives under examination? Jot down some specific examples:

   a. n-Ach behavior others exhibited

   b. n-Pow behavior others exhibited

   c. n-Aff behavior others exhibited

STEP 4. *Trio discussion.* Each member of the trio should share his or her individual responses to the questions just raised. The following will help to guide and focus this discussion:

   a. How did n-Achievement, n-Power, and n-Affiliation behavior exhibited by individuals influence each other and interact; for example, what happened when one person was exhibiting n-Affiliation while another was exhibiting n-Power?

   b. What differences, if any, did you notice between the first, second, and third rounds of the auction? To what do you attribute these differences?

STEP 5. After you have finished discussing these points, read the next section, join another trio, and continue your discussion.

Individual Scoring Form
for Test of Imagination

Circle the motives present in each story and indicate other motivational concerns in the space provided.

	PRIMARY SOCIAL MOTIVES	OTHER MOTIVES PRESENT IN STORY
Story 1	Achievement Power Affiliation	
Story 2	Achievement Power Affiliation	
Story 3	Achievement Power Affiliation	
Story 4	Achievement Power Affiliation	
Story 5	Achievement Power Affiliation	
Story 6	Achievement Power Affiliation	
Summary	Number of stories with Achievement _____ Power _____ Affiliation _____	Other major concerns:

The average person ends up breaking even in the Money Auction Game (i.e., no profit, no loss). A few people make a little money—2 to 5 cents after seven trials. Many people *lose* money (as much as $2!) by bidding considerably more than 5 cents for a nickel! It is possible for each bidder to make as much as 28 cents in each of his or her two rounds. This can happen only under the following conditions:

1. Bidder 2 passes after an opening bid of 1 cent by bidder 1. (How many people even open the bidding at 1 cent?)
2. Bidder 1 then passes after bidder 2's opening bid of 1 cent, and so on.

To achieve this solution, one member must take the first step (risk) and *trust* the other to see that he or she is trying to *collaborate* and not to compete. Sometimes one person tries this strategy (trusting the other) and is betrayed. The other (B) thinks, "Have I got a sucker here!" But, "once burned, twice shy," A says, "I'm no fool," and the result is that neither makes any more money. B often comes away feeling as if he won. Did he? It depends on one's definition of the situation and the goals each is pursuing—achievement goals, such as winning money; power goals, such as getting the nickels from the other person at any cost; or affiliation goals, such as cooperation and sharing with the other person.

People often ask, "Are you saying affiliation and cooperation are the answer and that power and competition are no good?" The answer is yes; under certain conditions, competition has destructive effects. For example, competition between two departments in the same organization can hurt overall company achievement, whereas competition between two companies can be healthy.

It is important to note that n-Achievement has behavioral manifestations that are different from either n-Power or n-Affiliation in terms of the individual's relationships with people. n-Power and n-Affiliation are interpersonally oriented needs. Implicit in their definitions is the existence of other human beings who the n-Power- and n-Affiliation-motivated individual can influence and control or be friends with. n-Achievement, on the other hand, is a more individualized need. n-Achievement-motivated individuals may need other people to help them reach achievement goals, but the nature of their relationship with others and their strategies for dealing with other people will be determined by needs other than achievement.

The key point is this: we often define a situation as being a "zero-sum" power game (you win; ergo, I must lose). Our definition causes us to behave in a certain way (e.g., to compete instead of to collaborate to achieve our goals). This behavior on our part elicits comparable behavior from others, for example, the person who starts out collaborating (trusting) but is taken advantage of immediately begins to compete. A circle of events, a self-fulfilling prophecy, has begun that is extremely difficult to break!

The critical element in the point above is the crucial role played by our own definition of the situation—our goals and objectives. Two trio groups should now address the following questions:

1. The goals and objectives that people had for the money auction game (or might have had) can be categorized as primarily related to one of the three primary motives.
   a. What were (would have been) examples of n-Achievement-oriented goals and objectives (e.g., to maximize profit)?
   b. What were (would have been) examples of n-Power-oriented objectives (e.g., to beat the other person)?
   c. What were (would have been) examples of n-Affiliation-oriented objectives (e.g., not to make the other person look bad)?
2. After each person defined a goal or objective for the game, he or she presumably then began to behave in a certain way to reach that goal or objective.

    a. What were (would have been) examples of n-Achievement-oriented behaviors or strategies?

    b. What were (would have been) examples of n-Power-oriented behaviors or strategies?

    c. What were (would have been) examples of n-Affiliation-oriented behaviors or strategies?

3. In what ways can you see new or clearer connections between your own TAT results and your behavior in this game? In what ways did the structure of the game and/or your partner's behavior induce you to behave in a way different from that which your personal motive pattern might suggest? Did your motives remain constant throughout the exercise or did events arouse different motives at different times?

Reprinted by permission of the Chicago Tribune-New York News Syndicate

The Money Auction Record Form

Indicate how much the winner of each trial paid for each nickel and subtract from 5 to get profit or loss for the round.

ROUND ONE

AUCTIONEER _____	BIDDER 1 _____	BIDDER 2 _____
Nickel 1	5¢ − _____ = _____	5¢ − _____ = _____
Nickel 2	5¢ − _____ = _____	5¢ − _____ = _____
Nickel 3	5¢ − _____ = _____	5¢ − _____ = _____
Nickel 4	5¢ − _____ = _____	5¢ − _____ = _____
Nickel 5	5¢ − _____ = _____	5¢ − _____ = _____
Nickel 6	5¢ − _____ = _____	5¢ − _____ = _____
Nickel 7	5¢ − _____ = _____	5¢ − _____ = _____
	Total Earnings _____	Total Earnings _____

ROUND TWO

AUCTIONEER _____	BIDDER 1 _____	BIDDER 2 _____
Nickel 1	5¢ − _____ = _____	5¢ − _____ = _____
Nickel 2	5¢ − _____ = _____	5¢ − _____ = _____
Nickel 3	5¢ − _____ = _____	5¢ − _____ = _____
Nickel 4	5¢ − _____ = _____	5¢ − _____ = _____
Nickel 5	5¢ − _____ = _____	5¢ − _____ = _____
Nickel 6	5¢ − _____ = _____	5¢ − _____ = _____
Nickel 7	5¢ − _____ = _____	5¢ − _____ = _____
	Total Earnings _____	Total Earnings _____

ROUND THREE

AUCTIONEER _____	BIDDER 1 _____	BIDDER 2 _____
Nickel 1	5¢ − _____ = _____	5¢ − _____ = _____
Nickel 2	5¢ − _____ = _____	5¢ − _____ = _____
Nickel 3	5¢ − _____ = _____	5¢ − _____ = _____
Nickel 4	5¢ − _____ = _____	5¢ − _____ = _____
Nickel 5	5¢ − _____ = _____	5¢ − _____ = _____
Nickel 6	5¢ − _____ = _____	5¢ − _____ = _____
Nickel 7	5¢ − _____ = _____	5¢ − _____ = _____
	Total Earnings _____	Total Earnings _____

IV

Follow-up

It is easy to conclude from the Money Auction Game that competitive behavior, resulting from high n-Power, is bad and that collaborative behavior, resulting from high n-Affiliation, is good. The simplicity of such a conclusion should make clear its invalidity. The salient issues are

1. Under what conditions are the two forms of behavior—competitive versus collaborative—appropriate?
2. What kinds of factors cause us to misread a given situation and what are the consequences?

The reward structure existing in any social situation provides the key to whether it is logically a competitive or a collaborative situation. If there is only a limited amount of reward available, so that if one person wins, another must lose, the situation can be defined as competitive. If, on the other hand, it is possible for all participants to achieve their goals, and goal achievement by one person involves or leads to goal achievement by another, the situation is collaborative.

It is not difficult to think of examples of pure competitive and collaborative situations. A serious poker game or the interaction between a buyer and a used car dealer are purely competitive situations. An army squad in combat or several people working on a joint research project are examples of collaborative situations.

The behaviors most appropriate and effective in a competitive situation are quite different from, and often directly opposite to, behaviors that are most adaptive in a collaborative situation. The following is a partial list of behaviors or strategies appropriate and effective in each type of situation.[17]

EFFECTIVE COMPETITIVE BEHAVIOR	EFFECTIVE COLLABORATIVE BEHAVIOR
1. Behavior is directed toward achieving personal goals.	1. Behavior is directed toward goals held in common.
2. Secrecy.	2. Openness.
3. Accurate personal understanding of own needs, but they are either hidden or misrepresented. If others do not know just what you want and how much you want it, they do not know how much you are willing to give up to get it.	3. Accurate personal understanding of own needs and accurate representation of them.
4. Unpredictable, mixed strategies utilizing the element of surprise.	4. Predictable. Although flexible behavior is appropriate, it is not designed to take the other party by surprise.
5. Threats and bluffs.	5. Threats and bluffs are not used.

---

[17]This list and parts of the following discussion are reproduced from Richard Walton's paper, "How to Choose Between Strategies of Conflict and Collaboration," in R. Golembrewski and R. Blumberg, eds., *Sensitivity Training and the Laboratory Approach* (Itasca, IL: F. E. Peacock, 1970).

6. Logical, nonrational, and irrational arguments are used to defend a position to which you are strategically committed.

7. Where teams, committees, or organizations are involved, communicating bad stereotypes of the other, ignoring his or her logic, impugning his or her motives, and arousing in-group hostility. This tends to strengthen in-group loyalty, increase motivation, and convince others you mean business.

6. Logical and innovative processes are used to defend your views, if you are convinced of their validity, or to find solutions to problems.

7. Success demands that stereotypes be dropped, that ideas by given consideration on their merit regardless of source, and that good working relationships be maintained. Positive feelings about others are both a cause and an effect of collaboration.

SOME EFFECTS OF COMPETITIVE AND COLLABORATIVE BEHAVIORS

The use of competitive strategies, particularly, has some effects that often go unrecognized. These effects are probably functional if the persons or groups interact only under purely competitive conditions. However, they will make any subsequent attempt at joint problem solving much more difficult. Four such consequences of the use of competitive strategies are

1. *The development of a competitive, win-lose climate that emphasizes the separateness of "we" and "they."* We are superior—they are inferior. Individual factions or groups under competitive pressure invariably rate themselves above average in both cohesion and ability.

2. *Distortions in judgment.* Individuals or groups under competitive pressure invariably evaluate their own contributions as best and fall into downgrading the efforts of others.

3. *Distortions in perception.* Experiments demonstrate that under competitive pressure persons perceive that they understand the other's proposal when, in fact, they do not. Consequently, shared areas are likely to go unrecognized.

4. *Disruption of communication.* Individuals or groups in competition avoid interaction with each other. When forced to interact, communication is usually characterized by aggression and hostility, which further confirms each party's negative opinion of the other.

Unfortunately, most of the social situations in which we find ourselves are neither purely competitive nor purely collaborative. One complication is that we frequently have to play the competitive and the collaborative games simultaneously, such as when we are trying to problem solve with the same persons with whom we are competing for promotion, or when two work groups or departments that are trying to be "best" have to work together to complete a job.

A second complication arises from the fact that we frequently cannot accurately diagnose a situation as competitive or collaborative until we know how the other participants are viewing the situation and we have some expectations concerning how they will behave. In real-life situations, when asked why they do not collaborate in what logically appears to be a collaborative situation, people will respond that they do not behave collaboratively because they cannot trust the other participants to do the same. This is a common dilemma, and a very real one. But there is a possible alternative simply to relying on competitive strategies: it lies in the possibility of influencing the behavior of the other parties in the situation through communication and trust building.

Some people approach every situation as if it were a competitive game; that is, they will transform every discussion into a debate and automatically compete with peers. Others approach each situation as if it were a collaborative game. Still others tend to see the objective reality of the situation and choose approaches that are appropriate. The first type can be called cynical, the second naive, and the third realistic.

The common problem in industry today is cynicism—we characteristically approach situations as if they are competitive even when they are not. And this often results in a self-fulfilling prophecy. Similarly, the early decades of union-management relations were conducted in a strictly win-lose manner, as if the entire process were competitive bargaining—what labor gains, management must lose, and vice versa. However, attitudes changed over a period of time, and parties began to wonder if the game might have some collaborative aspects. Note the key role of attitude change in permitting collaborative behavior to substitute for competitive. The important thing is that the parties begin to know each other and have some trust in each other (if not positive feeling). They can begin to reexamine the situation to find the collaborative aspects that will facilitate the goal achievement of both parties.

A tendency toward either collaboration or competition may arise from individual motives, the organizational setting, and cultural background. However, analyzing the situation and adapting one's behavior to it are the requisite skills to be effective. This brings to mind the old management adage:

Know yourself

Know the employee (or other person)

Know the work

"Knowing yourself" means understanding oneself. In this case it means knowing what motivates you and realizing when you need to curb yourself to be effective. "Knowing the employee" or the person with whom you're dealing means understanding what motivates them and why they act as they do. "Knowing the work" in this instance refers to discerning whether the work calls for competition or collaboration.

V

Learning Points

1. Motivation is not something that is "done" to other people. It is an internal state that directs individuals toward certain goals.

2. Individuals are motivated by different needs. Managers sometimes have false assumptions about what motivates their employees.

3. The manager's job is to understand and channel the motivation employees already possess and direct it toward tasks that further the organization's objectives.

4. Maslow developed a hierarchy of needs—*physical safety, security, affiliation, self-esteem,* and *self-actualization.* Lower-order needs must be satisfied before higher-order needs become motivators. Once a need is satisfied, it no longer motivates behavior.

5. Herzberg identified extrinsic factors as *hygiene factors* and stated that they create dissatisfaction if they are not present. Once hygiene factors are present, intrinsic factors motivate people.

6. Alderfer's ERG theory maintains that people have three sets of basic needs: *existence needs, relatedness needs,* and *growth needs.* While incorporating Maslow's idea of satisfaction progression up the hierarchy, Alderfer also describes a process of frustration regression wherein a previously satisfied need may reemerge as a motivating force if a higher-order need is repeatedly frustrated.

7. McClelland's theory of motivation focuses upon three needs that are learned from the culture and the family: affiliation, achievement, and power. Almost everyone has these needs but in varying degrees.

8. McClelland measures need strength and motive pattern (scores for affiliation, power, and achievement) with the Thematic Apperception Test (TAT). Job performance is affected by people's motive pattern as well as by the values that individuals hold.

9. According to McClelland, high achievers
   a. Like to set their own goals.
   b. Tend to avoid either extremely difficult or extremely easy goals.
   c. Prefer tasks that provide immediate feedback on their performance.

10. People's needs for affiliation, power, and achievement often determine how they define a situation. The competitive behavior that results from high n-Power and the collaborative behavior that results from high n-Affiliation both have advantages and disadvantages. It's important to know which behavior is called for in a given situation rather than relying only upon one's need motivation.

11. In addition to internal need states, motivation is also affected by environment, the $T = M \times E \times R$ equation, where T = tendency to act, M = strength of motive, E = expectation that motive will be rewarded, and R = reward value.

12. Managers can create an environment in which goal-oriented behavior is encouraged and rewarded by making sure there are fits between employee needs and rewards, between performance and rewards, and between employees and jobs.

VI
Tips for Managers

- Managers often misdiagnose employee's motives for the following reasons:
  - They assume that everyone is motivated by the same factors that motivate them.
  - They hold stereotyped views of types of employees or make attributions about individual employees that prevent them from actually investigating motive patterns.
  - They overlook the individual differences in employee motive patterns.
  - They fail to comprehend that employee motives change over time.

- Figuring out what motivates each employee is not always a simple matter of asking them. Finding out about employees' nonwork activities, observing what they do with discretionary time at work, and determining what type of work or projects they enjoy are indirect methods of gauging an employee's motive pattern. The yearly performance appraisal provides a good opportunity to check whether the manager's assumptions about what motivates an employee are accurate. There is a close relationship between understanding what motivates your workers and negotiating and renegotiating an effective psychological contract with them.

- Establishing clear work objectives and standards of good performance and then providing periodic feedback will help to motivate people to achieve, to assist employees in setting challenging but attainable goals.

- Reward employees for behaviors that promote the organization's goals. Be sure the form of that reward is one that the individual employee finds valuable or motivating.

- Whenever you are contemplating changes in the organization, make sure you have taken motivation patterns into consideration. For example, a secretary with a very boring job that is redeemed only by a central location that allows her to satisfy a high need for affiliation will not be as excited as you are about a new work station placed in a remote location. The easiest way to avoid making errors of this sort is to understand what makes the job challenging or at least palatable for each employee and discuss possible changes with them before they are made.

- Put people in jobs they will find rewarding and recognize their contributions. Managers who always have their eyes on the next step of the career ladder often disparage workers who are content to remain in "dead-end" jobs. Doing a "boring" job well is just as great a contribution to an organization as doing any other job well.

- Organizations need to find ways to harness, channel, and stimulate higher levels of achievement motivation. One way of approaching this challenge is the concept of intrapreneuring. Internal entrepreneurs, according to Pinchot,[18] are individuals whose high need to achieve does *not* result in their leaving their organizations to start their own businesses. Rather, the organization strives to create the climate, conditions, structures, and procedures that allow and reward these budding entrepreneurs for staying, for becoming intrapreneurs. They are given the freedom and incentive to create and market their own ideas

[18]G. Pinchot III, *Intrapreneuring* (New York: Harper & Row, 1965).

for their own profit *and* for the company's. Intrapreneurs, Pinchot is quick to point out, are much more than inventors: "Intrapreneurs need team-building skills and a firm grasp of business and marketplace reality."[19] Like their entrepreneurial colleagues, they also have little understanding of the word "no." They are driven by their vision and are more than willing to take personal responsibility for their own success or failure. The challenge to the organization is to capture this innovative spirit.

VII

Personal Application Assignment

The topic of this assignment is to think back on a motivation experience that was significant for you. Choose an experience about which you are motivated to learn more; that is, there was something about it that you do not totally understand, that intrigues you, that makes you realize that you lack certain skills, that is problematical or significant for you, and so on. It may have been an academic one or a nonformal educational experience (tennis camp, a seminar, on-the-job training program, etc.).

A. *Concrete Experience*
1. *Objectively* describe the experience ("who," "what," "when," "where," "how," type information—up to 2 points).
2. *Subjectively* describe your feelings, perceptions, and thoughts that occurred *during* (not after) the experience (up to 2 points). Does this section have too much detail? (If so, delete 1 point.)

B. *Reflective Observation*
1. Look at the experience from different points of view. How many points of view did you include that are *relevant* (up to 2 points)?
2. Use these perspectives to add more meaning to the incident (up to 2 points).

[19]Ibid., p. 33.

C. *Abstract Conceptualization*

   1. Relate concepts from the assigned readings and the lecture to the experience (i.e., what theories that you heard in the lecture or read in the *Reader* relate to your understanding of this incident?). Make reference to at least two sources. Use standard referencing format and include the page number to which you are referring. How many sources did you use and how clearly did you explain their theories (up to 4 points)?

   2. You can also create an original model or theory, but it should not replace course concepts.

D. *Active Experimentation*

   1. Write about what you will do in the future that will improve your effectiveness. Use rules of thumb or action resolutions.

   2. Are they described specifically, thoroughly, and in detail (up to 4 points).

E. *Integration, Synthesis, and Writing*

   1. Did you write about something personally important to you (up to 1 point)?

   2. Was it well written (up to 2 points)?

   3. Did you integrate and synthesize the different sections (up to 1 point)?

5

PERSONAL GROWTH AND CAREER DEVELOPMENT

OBJECTIVES   When this chapter is completed, you should be able to:

A. Describe Levinson's theory of adult development.

B. Identify current trends in career management and planning.

C. Assess your current life-career situation.

D. Identify personal life goals.

E. Choose an immediate short-term goal that is personally important to you and develop a plan to achieve it.

I   Premeeting Preparation

II   Topic Introduction

III   Procedure for Group Meeting: The Life Line, Who Am I? and the Past Experience Inventory

IV   Follow-up

V   Learning Points

VI   Tips for Managers

VII   Personal Application Assignment

Your New Employment Contract

Walter Kiechel III

Fellow voyagers into the brave new world, let us face facts: Restructuring has put the final kibosh on traditional notions of corporate loyalty, whether of employee to employer ("As long as I do the work, my job will be secure, right?") or employer to employee ("As long as we take good, paternalistic care of you, you won't leave, right?"). The question now before our much thinned ranks is just what will replace the old understanding. What can a manager rightfully expect of his company these days, or it of him?

As some historians of scientific revolutions might put it, have I got an emerging paradigm for you. Corporations, particularly those that have been, as they say, leaned down, stoutly maintain that the New Employment Contract already exists. Its terms, in the short form: Hereinafter, the employee will assume full responsibility for his own career—for keeping his qualifications up to date, for getting himself moved to the next position at the right time, for salting away funds for retirement, and, most daunting of all, for achieving job satisfaction. The company, while making no promises, will endeavor to provide a conducive environment, economic exigencies permitting.

Everybody got that? Not quite. Preliminary reports from corporations, attempting to install the new regime—AT&T, for example—indicate that there are complexities involved that both sides are only beginning to grasp. Some surprises: To make the arrangement work, the company may actually end up having to pay more attention to individual employees. Worse, the boss himself may have to learn new skills.

Herewith, an Office Hours guide to the new rules, first for perplexed employee, then for equally befuddled employer:

Mr. or Ms. Employee, congratulations on your new responsibility. To discharge same, you're going to have to engage in career planning. At a minimum, this entails figuring out what and where you are now, what and where you want to be, and how you're going to get there. For starters, what will it take to provide you career satisfaction? Possible answers include money, promotion, security, and inherently interesting work. "All of the above" is not necessarily an available option; you should at least assign priorities.

Now wait a minute, comes the angry reply, isn't this all just a little too . . . selfish? Ah, my friend, to paraphrase the Wizard of Oz, movie version, you are the victim of disorganized, or at least outmoded, thinking. Wilbert Sykes, a psychiatrist and chief executive of the TriSource Group, a New York City firm that counsels so-called high-performance individuals, explains: According to the old model, loyalty was a zero-sum game. Whatever attention you devoted to

Source: *Fortune*, July 6, 1987.

yourself was subtracted from that available to your employer. The new model, by comparison, is win-win. Said employer will benefit more when an employee operates out of a decent and open-eyed self-regard.

Employees must be particularly open-eyed in assessing what they have to offer an employer. The experts at Career Development Team, a Manhattan firm brought in by the likes of AT&T and GE, observe that too often a person thinks of himself simply as his job title. No, no, you are an inventory of skills, experiences, and interests. The trick is finding a job that allows you to use that inventory, and maybe even add to it.

All right, you know what you want from a job and what you bring to it. With these in mind, consider your current position. Does it fill the bill? Could it, with a bit of tinkering, be made to? If, say, you were to take a broader view of what you're trying to accomplish for the company, and if this led you to take more initiative and apply a wider range of your talents to the job, might you not be more content with where you are right now? Career Development Team consultants report that most people in their program decide not that they want another job, but that they can take steps to be happier in the one they have. A middle-aged manager may find, for example, that he can use his hitherto smothered interest in teaching to help subordinates. In the trendy phrase of the new deal's proponents, it empowers employees.

The career planning exercise doesn't end here, though. Even if you're content with your job now, will you still be satisfied with it in five years? Will it even exist then? Are you doing it well enough to keep it? For answers, look first to your employer. As the experts genteelly put it, attempt to open a dialogue with your boss. Indeed, press him a bit; such info is critical to any serious responsibility-taking. If your efforts fail, try someone in human resources.

Also start chatting up your peers throughout the organization and the industry. Suggested topics of conversation: Where is the company headed? What are its fastest growing areas? If you do have to move on, but want to stay in the organization, that's where you should go, even if it entails retraining or stepping down a rung or two. The best spots, or at least the ones most likely to endure, are those where you can make an identifiable contribution to the bottom line.

You may in all responsibility conclude that to attain your career objectives, you will have to seek another employer. This is perfectly acceptable under the new rules. Indeed, if you're stalled, it's admirable. The experts offer lots of advice. In negotiating with a prospective employer, try to get points of agreement made explicit that would have been left implicit under the old rules, advises Paul Hirsch, a University of Chicago Business School professor whose forthcoming book is entitled *Pack Your Own Parachute*. Push to have your new job responsibilities, perks, and benefits spelled out, for example. It's still a rare manager who can command a full-fledged employment contract—an agreement, say, for x years at y salary. Headhunter William Gould observes, however, that an exec in the $100,000-a-year-or-more range can reasonably ask that the letter offering the job guarantee one year's pay if he's fired within the first three years.

Since your responsibilities now include making sure that you have enough squirreled away for retirement, look carefully at the state of your benefits. Have you been with your present employer long enough to be vested in the pension plan? If you stand to lose benefits by changing employers, will your prospective new organization make you whole, as the phrase goes?

Finally, in leaving one job and going on to another, be prepared to grieve a little. As psychologist Harry Levinson notes, "All change is loss, and all loss must be mourned." If you don't mourn, TriSource President Douglass Lind adds, you won't be prepared to commit yourself to the new job.

Now, as to Mr. or Ms. Employer: Believe it or not, you have some new responsibilities, too. You smirk. Don't. The much proclaimed reason for introducing the new rules was all the change out there—global competition, takeovers, deregulation, new technologies—and the promise of more change to come. But as Robert Gilbreath, an Atlanta management consultant for Theodore Barry & Associates, notes, good people are your single most adaptive resource with which to meet that change. Ignore the new rules and you won't be able to keep the good people you have, or hire replacements.

First off, you're going to have to tell your employees more. No bleating about the highly confidential nature of the corporate strategy, please; you want them to plan their careers at the company, so you have to give them the dope to do it with. William Morin, chairman of Drake Beam Morin, a big outplacement firm, takes the principle a step further: "If you don't know what's going to happen, you've got to tell them that too."

You also have to ensure that each employee knows how he or she is doing. This often represents the most critical piece of information for someone mulling his career; under the new rules, to withhold it is unethical, and lousy. Quick question for the top brass: How many of your managers can sit down with an employee and give him an honest performance appraisal? Troubling follow-up question: How many can act as career counselors, or as coaches? Remedial training may be required, as well as incentives—including, in some refractory cases, a swift kick in the executive downside—to take the new managerial responsibilities seriously.

To hold on to your better performers, under the new regime you may well have to do a better job of keeping pay up to market rates. As good career custodians, your folks increasingly will be out there in the world finding out what people with their inventory of qualifications can make. Nor can you buy them off with promises of future glories; you aren't making any promises, remember.

When a valued subordinate comes in to tell you he's going somewhere else, hold the hysterics about how deeply hurt you are, the cheap talk about how much the company has invested in him, or the animadversions on his character. If you want him to stay, match the offer or raise the ante. Otherwise, smile, shake El Responsible's hand, and wish him good luck. If you do it right, he just may come back someday.

Perhaps most revolutionary, if you're serious about the new rules, you will have to give your newly empowered employees the opportunity to do their jobs differently, more the way they think the work can best be done. But don't expect this to go down easily with your old-line, I-am-the-boss-and-I'll-tell-you-how-to-do-it managers. Outplacement consultant Morin, who is writing a book on the new regime, observes, perhaps a bit tongue in cheek, "It's the same stuff we were talking about back in the early Sixties. Back then, though, we called it participatory management."

I

Premeeting Preparation

A. Read the entire chapter.

B. Complete the Life Goal Inventory.

C. What are the significant learning points from the readings?

Life Goal Inventory

1. The purpose of The Life Goal Inventory is to give you an outline for looking at your life goals in a more systematic way. Your concern here should be to describe as fully as possible your aims and goals in all areas of your life. Consider goals that are important to you, whether they are relatively easy or difficult to attain. Be honest with yourself. Having fun and taking life easy are just as legitimate life goals as being president. You will have a chance to rate the relative importance of your goals later. Now you should try to just discover *all* the things that are important to you. To help make your inventory complete, we have listed general goal areas on the following pages. They are

   ■ Career satisfaction
   ■ Status and respect
   ■ Personal relationships
   ■ Leisure satisfactions
   ■ Learning and education
   ■ Spiritual growth and religion
   ■ Material rewards and possessions

   These categories are only a general guide; feel free to change or redefine them in the way that best suits your own life. The unlabeled area is for whatever goals you think of that do not seem to fit into the other categories.

   First fill in your own goals in the various sections of this inventory, making any redefinitions of the goal areas you feel necessary. Ignore for the time being the three columns on the right-hand side of each page. Directions for filling out these columns are on page 127.

CAREER SATISFACTION

General Description: Your goals for your future job or career, including specific positions you want to hold.

Individual Redefinition:

SPECIFIC GOALS	IMPORTANCE (H,M,L)	EASE OF ATTAINMENT (H,M,L)	CONFLICT WITH OTHER GOALS (YES OR NO)
1.			
2.			
3.			

STATUS AND RESPECT

General Description: To what groups do you want to belong? What are your goals in these groups? To what extent do you want to be respected by others? From whom do you want respect?

Individual Redefinition:

SPECIFIC GOALS	IMPORTANCE (H,M,L)	EASE OF ATTAINMENT (H,M,L)	CONFLICT WITH OTHER GOALS (YES OR NO)
1.			
2.			
3.			

PERSONAL RELATIONSHIPS

General Description: Goals in your relationships with your colleagues, parents, friends, people in general.

Individual Redefinition:

SPECIFIC GOALS	IMPORTANCE (H,M,L)	EASE OF ATTAINMENT (H,M,L)	CONFLICT WITH OTHER GOALS (YES OR NO)
1.			
2.			
3.			

LEISURE SATISFACTIONS

General Description: Goals for your leisure time and pleasure activities—hobbies, sports, vacations; interests you want to develop.

Individual Redefinition:

SPECIFIC GOALS	IMPORTANCE (H,M,L)	EASE OF ATTAINMENT (H,M,L)	CONFLICT WITH OTHER GOALS (YES OR NO)
1.			
2.			
3.			

LEARNING AND EDUCATION

General Description: What would you like to know more about? What skills do you want to develop? To what formal education do you aspire?

Individual Redefinition:

SPECIFIC GOALS	IMPORTANCE (H,M,L)	EASE OF ATTAINMENT (H,M,L)	CONFLICT WITH OTHER GOALS (YES OR NO)
1.			
2.			
3.			

General Description: Goals for peace of mind, your search for meaning, your relation to the larger universe, religious service, devotional life.

Individual Redefinition:

SPECIFIC GOALS	IMPORTANCE (H,M,L)	EASE OF ATTAINMENT (H,M,L)	CONFLICT WITH OTHER GOALS (YES OR NO)
1.			
2.			
3.			

MATERIAL REWARDS AND POSSESSIONS

General Description: What level of wealth is important to you? What possessions would you want?

Individual Redefinition:

SPECIFIC GOALS	IMPORTANCE (H,M,L)	EASE OF ATTAINMENT (H,M,L)	CONFLICT WITH OTHER GOALS (YES OR NO)
1.			
2.			
3.			

Definition:

SPECIFIC GOALS	IMPORTANCE (H,M,L)	EASE OF ATTAINMENT (H,M,L)	CONFLICT WITH OTHER GOALS (YES OR NO)
1.			
2.			
3.			

2. *Goal importance:* Now that you have completed the inventory, go back and rate the importance of each goal according to the following scheme:

H — Compared with my other goals, this goal is very important.

M — This goal is moderately important.

L — A lot of other goals are more important than this one.

Ease of goal attainment: According to the following scheme, rate each goal on the probability that you will reach and/or maintain the satisfaction derived from it.

H — Compared with my other goals, I easily reach and maintain this goal.

M — I reach and maintain this goal with moderate difficulty.

L — It would be very difficult to reach this goal.

Goal priorities: Select the goals from the inventory that seem most important to you at this time. Do not choose more than eight. Rank order them in terms of their importance.

(1)

(2)

(3)

(4)

(5)

(6)

(7)

(8)

3. *Anticipating conflicts:* One of the major deterrents to goal accomplishment is the existence of conflict between goals. The person who ignores the potential conflicts between job and family, for instance, will probably end up abandoning goals because of the "either/or" nature of many decisions.

The cross-impact matrix is one method of anticipating possible conflicts. List your goals on both axes of the matrix in order of priority (goal 1 is first on both horizontal and vertical axes). The next step is to estimate the potential impact of the vertical goal statements on the horizontal, using the following symbols:

(+) for a helpful impact ("working on goal 1 will help me with goal 3")

(−) for a hindering impact ("working on goal 2 will make it more difficult to accomplish goal 5")

(○) for no impact of any kind

The Cross-Impact Matrix

	Goal 1	Goal 2	Goal 3	Goal 4	Goal 5	Goal 6	Goal 7	Goal 8
Goal 1								
Goal 2								
Goal 3								
Goal 4								
Goal 5								
Goal 6								
Goal 7								
Goal 8								

List conflicts in order of importance:

1.
2.
3.
4.
5.

II

Topic Introduction

One of managers' most important tasks concerns the personal growth and career development of their employees and themselves. To this end an understanding of the process of adult development helps us to realize that others are making the same journey through life and are experiencing similar challenges or hardships at certain points. In addition to providing insight into our personal experience, theories of adult development also help us to understand the developmental phases and challenges facing our colleagues at work.

Figure 5–1 portrays the stages three different researchers have identified. Gould[1] concentrates upon the inner subjective experiences of individuals forming each period; his view asserts that we grow up with a mythical idea of adulthood and that, as we age, we need to let go of the myth and accept ourselves and the reality of our lives. Levinson, on the other hand, describes the developmental tasks

FIGURE 5–1*   Models of Adult Development

AGE	ROGER GOULD	GAIL SHEEHY	DANIEL LEVINSON
16	Escape from parental dominance	Pulling up roots	Leaving the family
18			
20	Substitute friends for family		
22		Provisional adulthood	
24			
26	Aspiring builders of future		
28			Getting into the adult world
30	What am I doing and why?	Age 30 transition	
32			
34			
36	A sense of urgency to make it	Major stabilization	Transition period
38			
40			Settling down and becoming one's own person
42		Midlife transition	
44	On terms with self as a stable personality		
46			
48			
50		Restabilization and flowering	
52	Mellowing of friendships—valuing of emotions		Midlife transition
54			
56			
58			Restabilization and entering into middle age
60			
			Another transition

Prepared by Dr. Eric Neilsen, Case Western Reserve University, Cleveland, Ohio.

[1] R. L. Gould, *Transformations* (New York: Simon and Schuster, 1979).

that must be mastered before one can successfully move on to the next stage of development.[2] Sheehy's stages are a synthesis of the preceding two.[3]

In *Passages,* Sheehy describes the Catch-30 syndrome—the bind that couples experience when their personal development is not coordinated. An example is the guilt some husbands in traditional marriages feel around age 30 when they are experiencing success in their work while their wife stays home with the children. The husband might suggest the wife work or take courses to relieve this guilt (and perhaps also make her more interesting to him). However, if the wife does enter the work force, the husband may well be jealous or resentful if he wants more children. The Catch-30 syndrome captures this paradox: the husband feels guilty if the wife stays home and jealous if she does not. The wife feels as if the husband is kicking her out of the home, but not really giving her the same freedom he had to establish himself while she maintained the home during their twenties.

Levinson developed his theory of adult development from biographical interviews with 40 men; he later expanded his research to include women. One of the gender differences Levinson found was that young men more easily formed a dream about what they would become than did young women. Another difference was that men were more likely to have a family and a career simultaneously if they so desired. In contrast, the women in the study made an either/or choice about family and career and had fewer cultural role models to guide them.

Statistically we find that more women are combining career with family. In 1985, half of the mothers with children under one year of age were working. Experts predicted that by the late 1980s, 70 percent of all women would be working. However at present, working wives still carry the major burden of household tasks in addition to their work roles.[4] Larger participation and more opportunities in the work force have not resolved the career/family dilemma for women, although it has changed the nature of their concerns.

The following explanation of Levinson's theory pertains to both sexes.[5] Levinson and his colleagues coined the term "life structure," which refers to the pattern or design of a person's life. A recurring developmental task is to establish an acceptable life structure which is appropriate for a particular era of life. The life cycle evolves through a series of four eras, each lasting about 25 years. Within each era are shorter developmental stages that consist of alternately stable periods (lasting 6 to 8 years) and transitional periods (4 to 5 years). This pattern of stability and transition occurs because people create life structures for themselves that are only viable for a certain time. The stable periods are followed by reexamination and replacement by yet another life structure during the transitional periods. Life structures become obsolete because no single life structure can contain all aspects of the self.

For example, the developmental challenge and dilemma facing people in their twenties (22 to 28) is to remain open enough to explore the world and stable and committed enough to make something of themselves. Some people keep all their options open and make few commitments, while others marry young and/or invest in a serious career effort. Whatever options people build into their early adult life structure, they are likely to question these early decisions when they reach the age of 30 and have enough years of adult experience to reassess their dreams. Similar transitions occur around ages 40 and 50. It is during these transitions that people make changes in their lives and try to build a life structure that is more attuned to the person they have become and that allows them to place more priority on areas

[2]D. J. Levinson, "A Conception of Adult Development," *American Psychologist,* Vol. 41, No. 1, January, 1986, pp. 3–13.

[3]Gail Sheehy, *Passages* (New York: Bantam Press, 1977).

[4]Oxford Analytica, *America in Perspective* (Boston: Houghton Mifflin, 1986).

[5]Daniel J. Levinson, in collaboration with C. N. Darrow, E. B. Klein, M. H. Levinson, and M. Braxton, *Seasons of a Man's Life* (New York: Ballantine, 1978), Ibid., 1986.

that are central to them and that they may have had to short-change in their earlier life structure. There is some evidence that people who do not resolve issues during one transition will eventually be forced to confront them in a later transition.

Whether or not these life transitions turn into full-blown crises depends upon the individuals and their circumstances. For some people it's more a matter of reform than revolution. A crisis occurs when individuals find their current life structure intolerable but are not yet able to create a new one. How can managers help people through this process?

1. First, by expecting the phenomenon and seeing it as a normal stage of healthy adult development rather than a sign of mental instability.
2. Second, by practicing active listening[6] or perhaps referring the individual to a professional counselor.
3. Third, by being as flexible as possible regarding the changes the employee feels he or she needs to make.

In addition to having an awareness of the stages of adult development, it is useful for managers to understand the current context of career management and career planning. Hall has identified current trends in these areas.[7] In career management, the necessity of tying strategic planning to human resource management is gaining greater acceptance, along with the expectation that managers should be trained to provide career counseling to employees. Leaner management hierarchies and the baby boom cohort have made assessment of management potential and succession management more appealing. Flatter organizations have also focused attention on the need for nontraditional career paths that provide alternatives to promotion such as lateral or rotational moves, dual-career ladders, downward moves, and early retirement.

In terms of career management, Hall reports more emphasis upon self-directed careers as a response to the economic recession. Midcareer choice points (the reevaluation that relates to Levinson's transition phases) seem to be occurring earlier due to the bulge of baby boomers in managerial jobs and the need for balance in dual-career families. Today's employees are more likely to question and reject transfers and even promotions. Opting for self-initiated career plateauing (a cap to upward mobility) due to family considerations or lack of desire to assume the burdens of greater management responsibility is becoming more common although it is still seen as un-American in some companies. Career planning is currently seen as a mutual responsibility of the individual and the company, which has resulted in greater employee need for information on company career opportunities.

At the same time that some writers speak of a trend toward lowered career expectations and voluntary career plateauing, business magazines are full of articles about young MBAs who are single-mindedly pursuing careers at the cost of company loyalty and their private lives. Perhaps these seemingly contradictory trends represent life structures of different age groups as well as the diversity found in our society.

Labor statistics reports indicate that Americans will, on the average, change jobs seven times and careers three times during their actual working life. This increasing pattern of career change has great implications for how organizations and educational systems manage career development. Although the career paths of many men and women may pass through two, three, or four distinct phases—each of which requires major new learning of knowledge, skills, and attitudes—education and training programs remain primarily oriented to the early stages of life. While

[6]For more details on active listening, see Chapter 6, Interpersonal Communication, and Rogers and Farson's article entitled "Active Listening" in the *Reader*.
[7]Douglas T. Hall, *Career Development in Organizations* (San Francisco: Jossey-Bass, 1986).

some education and training programs are beginning to adapt more to service the market of older people who wish to make career changes or reenter the job market, other educational institutions still treat adult and continuing education as low-status, low-priority activities done half-heartedly in the name of community service. The provision of midcareer educational programs has been left primarily to private industry. This is, in some cases, as it should be, but all too often the implicit price for admission is a further commitment to the organization and to one's previous career path. Changing careers is made more difficult by selection criteria that demand previous experience in that career and tax laws that allow deductions for job-related training but not for changing jobs.

The failure to provide avenues for career change produces great losses in social productivity and in human satisfaction. Organizations do not benefit by locking their employees into careers that long ago ceased to be rewarding and challenging. Society loses the creativity and productivity of those who are barred from entry into new careers in midlife. This is particularly true for traditional females who devoted the first part of their adult lives to marriage and family. Although social norms are changing, entry into careers in midlife when family demands are less pressing still remains difficult for many women.

While organization and educational system changes are essential to ensure access to education and learning throughout our life span, it is equally important that men and women in our society gain a greater awareness and insight into the problems and possibilities of adult development.

We are becoming more and more responsible for managing our own lives and careers. In earlier times, personal identity and continuity were sustained in relatively stable environments of expectation and demand. Career and life-style were ascribed, not chosen. Once on a life path, personal choice was primarily a process of affirming expectations. In today's "future shock" world, environmental complexity and change have denied us this easy route to personal identity. Now, more than ever, identity and continuity are forged through personal choices. These choices go beyond the computational selection of one alternative over another according to some predetermined values. They require the selection of the basic values themselves. In addition to asking, "What is the right thing to do?" we now ask, "What do I believe is right?" In addition to, "Who am I?" we ask, "Who do I want to be?" Our society grants many individuals great latitude, but the price of this freedom is often uncertainty about the "rightness" of the choices we make.

To cope with these increasing challenges for career self-management, we all need to develop our skills for planning and guiding the direction of our lives. The following exercises provide an opportunity to practice these skills and gain greater self-awareness.

My Life Line

III

Procedure for Group Meeting: The Life Line, Who Am I? and the Past Experience Inventory

SELF-ASSESSMENT AND LIFE PLANNING
(Time Allotted: 1 Hour, 15 Minutes)

Note: These are minimum times; you may want to take more time.

STEP 1.   Form trios for life planning. (5 minutes) The total groups should divide into groups of three for the purpose of sharing the Life Goal Inventory prework and working together on the life planning activities that follow.

STEP 2.   Life line exercise. (10 minutes) Each member of the trio should draw a line in the box on the preceding page to describe his or her view of his or her whole life from beginning to end.

Draw a line that corresponds to your own concept of your life line. Your life line can be any shape and can go in any direction. It could be a road, a river, a thread, a path, a graph line, or anything else you can imagine. Another way to think of it is as a route across a map. Place a mark on this line to show where you are right now. Discuss the feelings and thoughts you had in drawing the line and in placing your mark with others in your trio.

Notice that each life line has three distinct portions: your past, the place you are now (the "X"), and the portion of the line that represents your view of your future career path. These three portions represent the three basic perspectives for self-assessment and career planning.

The Past

Your unique experiences, acquired skills, and personal history.

■ The past has happened; we cannot change it.

■ Our past has a place in our current lives; we need to accept it and use it creatively but not be inhibited by it.

■ The past, creatively used, yields insight about our unfulfilled potential.

■ The past creates expectations for ourselves and can influence or limit the goals we set for the future.

The Present

The here-and-now of your life with all its joys and frustrations; your current priorities as they are embodied in your daily life situation and the way you spend your time.

■ Individuals can consciously plan their lives by assessing themselves, their environments, and their resources in the present.

■ You can choose where you would like to go on the basis of what satisfies you now.

■ We need symmetry and wholeness in our lives. Often we make choices in the present that lead to a lop-sided future (e.g., being too career oriented at the expense of a private life of fun, friends, and family).

■ Each person has a reservoir of undeveloped potential in the present that suggests directions for future development.

The Future

Your fantasies, dreams, goals, hopes, and fears, as well as specific commitments and responsibilities you have undertaken.

■ In large part, we can create our own future. (It's worth noting that the belief that we are masters of our own destiny represents an American value; many other cultures have a more fatalistic, and sometimes more realistic, attitude toward life. While this belief motivates us to take charge of our lives, it also makes us feel more responsible when life does not go as we had planned.)

■ To create a future, it must be linked to the present because we can only choose and act in the present.

■ Our future becomes self-determined to a large degree through the choices we make in the present.

■ We can try to create the future by the process of

By using the combination of these three perspectives on your life, it is possible to develop a more fulfilling life plan. By taking all three perspectives into account, a kind of triangulation occurs that identifies common themes from your past, your present, and your future.

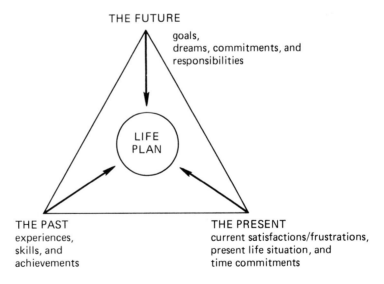

The next three exercises for your trio ask you to work together to assess yourselves from these three perspectives:

STEP 3. Who am I *now?* (20 minutes)

■ Write 10 separate short statements that answer the question, "Who am I?"

- ■ Then rank these statements according to their importance to you.
- ■ Discuss your answers and rankings with others in your trio.

RANK ORDER	WHO AM I?
_____	1. I am _____
_____	2. I am _____
_____	3. I am _____
_____	4. I am _____
_____	5. I am _____
_____	6. I am _____
_____	7. I am _____
_____	8. I am _____
_____	9. I am _____
_____	10. I am _____

STEP 4. Past experience inventory. (20 minutes) Complete the following questions and discuss them in your trio. (You may want to compose this trio of people of the same sex so you can discuss the role gender expectations have had on your life more readily.)

APPROXIMATE DATES

1. Who have been the most influential people in your life, and in what way have they been influential?

2. What were the critical incidents (events) that made you who you are?

3. What have been the major interests in your past life?

4. What were your significant work experiences?

5. What were the most significant decisions in your life?

_____ _____

_____ _____

_____ _____

6. What role have family, societal, and gender expectations played in your life?

_____ _____

_____ _____

_____ _____

7. Where do I feel fully alive, excited, turned on? Under what conditions does this occur? *

_____ _____

_____ _____

_____ _____

8. Where do I feel dull, routine, turned off? What conditions produce that?

_____ _____

_____ _____

_____ _____

9. What am I really good at? What strengths do I have to build on?

_____ _____

_____ _____

_____ _____

10. What do I do poorly? What do I need to develop or correct?

_____ _____

_____ _____

_____ _____

11. What do I want to stop doing or do much less of?

_____ _____

_____ _____

_____ _____

*Questions 7–12 were adapted by Donald M. Wolfe from the work of Herbert Shepard.

12. What do I want to start doing or do much more of?

_____ _____

_____ _____

_____ _____

13. What do I want to learn or develop in myself?

_____ _____

_____ _____

_____ _____

_____ _____

STEP 5. My future goals. (20 minutes) Share your Life Goal Inventory prework with each other. Your work on the previous exercise may suggest changes to you. If so, make them.

IV

Follow-up

Goal setting is a critical aspect of personal growth and career development. The ability to conceptualize life goals and to imagine future alternatives for living can free us from the inertia of the past by providing future targets that serve as guides for planning and decision making. Research results from several areas—management, psychotherapy, and attitude change—all confirm the importance of goal setting for personal growth and achievement of one's goals.[8] The increased likelihood of change resulting from the setting and articulating of goals is illustrated, for example, by Kay, French, and Myer, who found that improvement needs among managers were accomplished only about one-fourth of the time when they were not translated into goals in performance appraisal interviews. When these needs were transformed into clearly stated goals, the likelihood of accomplishment increased to about two-thirds.[9] It is not enough just to think about how you would like to change.

It is necessary to translate those visions into concrete goals. Commitment to clearly stated goals leads to achievement of those goals. Yet achieving commitment is not as easy as it sounds. There are several factors that make it difficult:

1. Reluctance to give up the alternative goals not chosen: to choose one goal is to reject others implicitly. Unless one clearly believes in the importance of the goal and its superior value, other goals will, as time passes, dominate and overshadow the initial decision.

2. Fear of failure: without goals and ideals, one never risks failure. Making a commitment to a future state involves a risk to one's self-esteem if the goal is not achieved. This fear of failure makes it difficult to commit oneself totally to a goal.

3. Lack of self-knowledge: it is difficult to choose goals and make future plans when one is not certain who one is and what one values. Confusion about oneself leads to confusion about what one's future self should be.

4. Lack of knowledge about the environment: lack of awareness of the opportunities available in the environment can also produce confusion and an inability to define goals that one can become committed to. An important part of the goal-setting process is researching the resources and opportunities afforded by the environment and using the information gained to discover new goals and redefine old ones.

5. Insecurity and low self-confidence: if circumstances or life-style lead one to feel like a hopeless victim of circumstances, one will have difficulty in planning one's future and becoming committed to future goals. To achieve goals implies a sense of self-control and control over one's environment. To become committed to a goal, the individual must feel as though he or she has ability to achieve it.

There are, however, some things that can be done to increase commitment to goals:

[8]David A. Kolb and Richard E. Boyatzis, "Goal-Setting and Self-directed Behavior Change," *Readings,* 1984 ed.

[9]E. Kay, J. R. P. French, Jr., and H. H. Myer, "A Study of the Performance Appraisal Interview" (Management Development and Employee Relations Services, General Electric Co., New York, 1962).

1. Explicit examination of the value of the chosen goal and comparison with rejected alternatives: by explicitly considering alternative opportunities that may arise, one can avoid being swayed in a weak moment by an unconsidered alternative. One especially useful technique here is linking short-term goals with long-term objectives. Awareness that a particularly difficult short-term goal is linked to a long-term objective can avoid its rejection for a more immediately gratifying but useless short-term pleasure.

2. Committing oneself to a continuous process of self-evaluation and goal setting: a person cannot in one sitting plan his or her future life. The world is changing far too rapidly for any of us to anticipate the future clearly, and our goals change as our experience increases. The risk of missing unforeseen alternatives by working blindly toward obsolete goals can be minimized by continued reassessment of goals. By seeking feedback from others about oneself and by using these data for continuing self-evaluation, one can achieve a more accurate self-image and a clearer conception of one's values.

3. Support from others: commitment to goals is best achieved in a supportive atmosphere. Those who play a significant role in one's life are invaluable for building self-confidence, helping to clarify thinking about the future, and getting helpful feedback about behavior. Personal growth cannot occur alone. It is through interactions with others that we discover ourselves and first experience our ideals.

4. Future visions and here-and-now awareness: planning for the future implies a continuing awareness of ways we can proactively shape our own futures. The goal-setting process means that I acknowledge that what I do at this moment in time will affect what I am able to do or be at some time in the future.

Reprinted courtesy of Mell Lazarus and Field Newspaper Syndicate

V

Learning Points

1. The manager's role is to develop both employees and themselves. Nowadays individuals are expected to assume greater responsibility for planning their own career and life.

2. Levinson's theory of adult development refers to life structures—the design or pattern of a person's life.

3. The life cycle consists of four evolving eras: childhood and adolescence, early adulthood, middle adulthood, and late adulthood.

4. People go through both stable and transitional periods. During the latter, individuals reevaluate and re-create their life structures. Transitions occur about the ages of 30, 40, and 50. If they are very turbulent, they are called crises.

5. Levinson found two gender differences: (a) it was easier for men to form a dream to guide their early adulthood, and (b) women made either/or choices regarding career and family.

6. Current trends in career management and planning can be traced to the economic recessions and lean management hierarchies, dual-career families, and demographic trends (beware the baby boom cohort), and changing social values.

7. Current trends in career management include tying strategic planning to human resource management, training managers in career counseling, assessment of management potential, succession planning, and nontraditional career paths.

8. Current trends in career planning consist of self-directed careers, earlier mid-career status, more questioning/rejection of job moves and promotions, increased self-initiated career plateauing, and career planning as a mutual responsibility of employee and organization resulting in greater employee need for information about company career opportunities.

9. Americans make an average of three career changes during their adult life, but educational institutions and organizations have not yet fully adapted to facilitate career changes.

10. People who set clearly stated goals are more likely to achieve them.

VI

Tips for Managers

- Encourage employees to plan for career goals and actively help them reach their goals. Employees with set goals are often more motivated and more likely to achieve their goals.

- Managers who sincerely try to help employees reach their career goals are usually rewarded with loyalty and commitment.

- Delegating not only provides the employee with an opportunity to grow, it also allows managers time to turn their attention to other facets of their role. It can be a growth opportunity for both parties.

- Managers who like to look indispensable to their superiors and who relegate to employees only those jobs they do not enjoy may be passed over for promotion because they have failed to develop anyone to replace them.

- Managers are more likely to provide effective career counseling to employees if they themselves also receive it from their superiors. It has to be modeled for them.

- Organizations that evaluate their managers on their ability to develop employees will generally see more positive results in this area. It's not enough to state that career development is important; measuring and rewarding it provides a clearer message that career development is valued.

- Career counseling requires that a manager try to support employees to assess their own strengths and weaknesses and to articulate their own goals. An authoritarian bulldozer approach is not effective.

- Personal growth or change is not a steady progression but rather a series of fits and starts.

- Once again, managers need to recognize that employees will have unique career goals and life situations. Too often managers who are single-mindedly pursuing a suite at the top find it difficult to value employees who are content to remain where they are. As long as employees perform their jobs well, lack of driving ambition should not be held against them.

- Managers need to bear in mind the different career stages of their employees. For example, a young "fast tracker" who may have many of the other skills needed for a managerial job may still be too involved in establishing his or her own career to mentor subordinates adequately. The best mentors are most likely to be found in the 40 to 60 age group because this coincides with a stage of adult development in which guiding the younger generation assumes greater importance.

- Managers who drive their employees so hard that it is impossible for them to have a personal life will usually have a higher degree of turnover.

- Take a careful look at workaholics. Sometimes working long hours is not a habit to admire but an indication of inefficient work habits and lack of a social life outside of work. If this is the case, their need to socialize on the job may actually prevent other employees from getting their work done.

- Work schedules that change constantly do not allow employees to create a life outside of work. This is generally not healthy for an extended period. Most people need a balanced life to keep a perspective on problems and find a measure of contentment.

VII

Personal Application Assignment

Eisenhower once said, "A plan is nothing; planning is everything." In career planning, too, the plan itself is not as valuable as the act of planning. Plans must give way to outside contingencies. But the process of planning—taking stock, devising objectives and possible means of reaching a goal, and then checking to see how one is faring and coming up with a new plan if necessary—is extremely valuable.

This assignment is "The Goal Achievement Plan and Achievement Progress Record." It is designed to help you create a plan for attaining a goal you select to work on in the immediate future. The steps in the plan are based on the factors that research has shown to be characteristic of successful goal achievers. Following these steps should help you improve your ability to achieve your goals.

A. From the goal inventory, pick the goal you most want to work on in the *next six months*. In choosing this goal you should consider the following issues. (See the ratings you made of goals.)

   1. Importance of the goal

   2. Ease of attainment

   3. Whether the goal is in conflict with other goals (and would therefore require working on those other goals)

B. The goal you choose to work on may include two or three of the goals you listed in the inventory. The main thing is to get clearly in mind what future state you are striving for. To do this, complete the accompanying Goal Definition form.

C. Now that you have defined your goal, the next step is to plan how to achieve it. There are four issues to be examined.

   1. Personal shortcoming to overcome

   2. Obstacles in the world to overcome

   3. Actions that you can take to achieve your goal

   4. Help you can get from others

   The first two categories refer to things that can prevent you from reaching your goal. The last two categories refer to things that you and others can do to achieve your goal.

D. The Goal Achievement Plan diagram that follows illustrates how these fit into the goal achievement plan. At the top of the page is your goal. The circle in the middle of the page represents your current self. Your personal shortcomings and obstacles in the world are forces that are keeping you from moving toward your goal. Your plan should try to accomplish two things:

   1. Reduce the personal shortcomings and world obstacle forces that keep you from your goals.

   2. Increase the force of your actions and help from others.

   The questions on the accompanying Removing Obstacles and Planning Action form are designed to help you accomplish this.

Goal Definition

State as exactly as possible what goal you want to achieve *in the next six months.*

_____

_____

_____

_____

Now think about your goal in terms of the following questions.

How important is it that you achieve your goal?

_____

_____

_____

_____

What conflicts are there with other goals? How will you manage the conflicts?

_____

_____

_____

_____

How will you feel when you attain this goal? (Try to imagine yourself with the goal achieved. What are your feelings?)

_____

_____

_____

_____

How will you feel if you do not attain this goal? (Try to imagine again. What are your feelings?)

_____

_____

_____

_____

What do you think about your chances of succeeding? What will happen if you do succeed?

_____

_____

_____

_____

What will happen if you fail?

_____

_____

_____

_____

Goal Achievement Plan

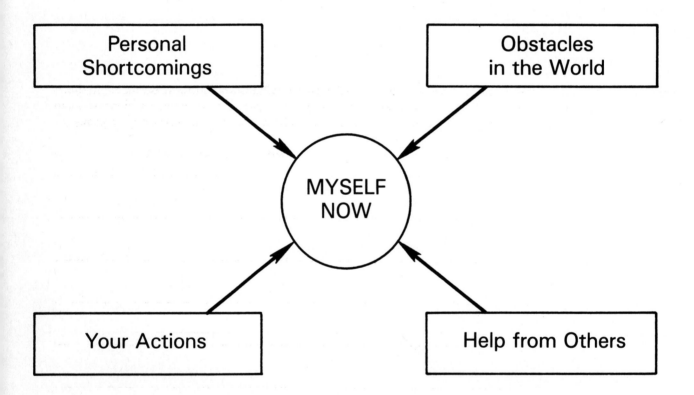

Removing Obstacles and Planning Action

What personal shortcomings will keep me from achieving my goal?

1.

2.

3.

4.

What obstacles in the world will keep me from achieving my goal?

1.

2.

3.

4.

What can I do to eliminate or lessen the effect of any of these obstacles or short-comings? (Note that you need not eliminate the block entirely. Anything you can do to lessen the force of the obstacle will start you moving toward your goal.)

OBSTACLE	WHAT CAN I DO ABOUT IT
_____	_____
_____	_____
_____	_____
_____	_____
_____	_____
_____	_____
_____	_____
_____	_____
_____	_____

What specific things can I do that will move me toward my goal?

1.

2.

3.

4.

5.

Circle the one that you are going to emphasize the most.

WHO CAN HELP ME ACHIEVE MY GOALS?	WHAT WILL I ASK OF THEM?
1. _____	_____
	_____
	_____
	_____
2. _____	_____
	_____
	_____
	_____
3. _____	_____
	_____
	_____
	_____
4. _____	_____
	_____
	_____
	_____

Achievement Progress Record

Now that you have made your plan, the next thing to do is to put it into effect. The achievement progress record is designed to help you keep a weekly record of your progress toward your goal. This record has two purposes.

1. It will give you an indication of where you stand, whether you are ahead or behind schedule in achieving your goal.
2. It will serve as a constant reminder of your goal and your desire to achieve it.

MEASURING YOUR PROGRESS

To accomplish the first purpose, it is necessary that you define for yourself just how you can measure progress toward your goal. The graph on page 151 lists the next 25 weeks along the bottom line. The left-hand side of the graph is anchored at the base by your position now. The top of the line represents your goal. You need to decide what units will indicate your progress up this line toward your goal. For some goals this is easy—for example, if your goal is to get better grades, you might want to indicate hours of study per week on the graph. Other goals are more difficult to measure. For these you may want to indicate each week what percentage of the total plan you have completed. You may want to keep more than one graph to record each of the actions you plan to use in achieving your goal. *Record in the space following how you plan to measure progress toward your goal.*

ACHIEVEMENT PROGRESS RECORD FORM

Goal _____

Units of Measurement _____

Name_____

Achievement_____

Plan Partner_____

Partner's Address_____

Phone_____

My Achievement Goal
Is Fully Accomplished

1 2 3 4 5 6 7 8 9 10 11 12 13 14 15 16 17 18 19 20 21 22 23 24 25

Week Number

Distance
from My Goal
When I Started to
Work Toward It

6

INTERPERSONAL COMMUNICATION

OBJECTIVES By the end of this chapter, you should be able to:

A. Understand the model of communication.

B. Discuss the arc of distortion and how to minimize distortion.

C. Describe and identify the five response styles.

D. Explain how to create a climate that encourages nondefensive communication.

E. Justify and improve your active listening skills.

Do you Have What It Takes?

Kurt Sandholtz

Thumb through almost any high school yearbook, and among the homecoming queens and football stars you'll probably find a picture of some clean-cut kid with the caption "Most Likely to Succeed."

It's a curious designation.

On one level, no one takes it seriously. How can a bunch of high school seniors possibly select from their classmates the one destined to succeed? Succeed at what?

On another level, everyone takes it seriously. However we define it, success is something we all pursue. And while the high school yearbook committee's pick is little more than a shot in the dark, researchers have spent years trying to pinpoint what makes a person "most likely to succeed."

Their efforts have produced reams of scientific and pseudo-scientific data. Perhaps the most comprehensive research to date comes from Stanford University and American Telephone & Telegraph Co. In separate long-term studies, research teams at these institutions have tracked managers from the college classroom to the executive suite. The basic question driving both inquiries was: Which characteristics of a student's background and personality are the best predictors of future business success, as measured by salary level and managerial rank 20 years after graduation?

The answers have been surprisingly consistent—and consistently surprising. "Some of the findings were totally unexpected," says Thomas Harrell, an emeritus professor of business and director of the Stanford study. "In retrospect, we shouldn't have been all that surprised. The results make a lot of sense."

Here, then, are summaries of key results from both studies. Like Prof. Harrell, you'll probably find much that stands to reason. But you may learn more from the surprises—those tidbits that prompt an "Aha!" or even a "No way!" Such reactions point to potential chinks in your armor.

COMMUNICATION SKILLS

"In our study, the single best question to predict high earnings was, "Do you like to make speeches?" says Prof. Harrell. "The correct answer, of course, is 'Yes.'"

This is no startling revelation. Even our nation's chief executive is often referred to as "The Great Communicator." But like many executive traits, verbal ability is more important at the top than at the bottom. So in tailoring your college curriculum, look beyond the entry level; blowing off that "waste-of-time" writing course could come back to haunt you.

Source: Reprinted from *Managing Your Career*, Fall 1987, p. 10. With permission of Dow Jones & Co., Inc.

"The most sought-after skill, from the CEO on down, is the ability to communicate with people," says John Callen, partner with executive recruiters Ward Howell International in New York. "The person who's comfortable with the press and public relations, who can make a speech on short notice—that person's always in demand."

INTERPERSONAL ABILITY

"The variable we found consistently related to management success was the personality trait of social extroversion or sociability," concludes one of Prof. Harrell's research papers.

That's academese for "Successful executives like people." And because they like people, they're good at managing them. "Dale Carnegie had most of it right," says Prof. Harrell.

If this sounds patently obvious, then why do most business administration programs emphasize the analytical at the expense of the interpersonal? Good question, says Ann Howard, an industrial psychologist who directed the studies at AT&T.

"Research shows that administrative skills—planning, cost/benefit analysis, decision making—do get cultivated in business programs. Those are certainly functional skills," she says. "But when you're promoted into your first management job, it's unlikely you'll be doing much strategic planning." Instead, you'll be stuck with a bunch of people who you're supposed to supervise—a task few business schools teach you how to do, she says.

Meryl Lewis, a Boston University business professor, has noticed the same weakness in business school training. As part of a study entitled "The First Years Out," she asked more than 200 graduates of top M.B.A. programs, "What were your most and least valuable courses?" Response from graduating students was nearly unanimous. "They said they hated their O.B. (organizational behavior) classes," she says.

When polled a year later, however, they'd done an about-face. "They said O.B. was among their most useful courses," says Prof. Lewis. "They were aware of a need for more of it than they got." In fact, organizational behavior was one of the few subjects the M.B.A.s were likely to brush up on, digging out old college notes and textbooks. "The bad rap that O.B. gets is washed away by the first year on the job," she says.

If you distrust the research, take it from a seasoned executive recruiter. "There are lots of brilliant people who can't relate with others," says Robert LoPresto, a senior partner with Korn/Ferry International in Palo Alto, Calif. "We replace that kind of person every day."

I

Premeeting Preparation

A. Fill out the Communication Climate Inventory that follows.

B. Then answer these questions:
1. What communication skills would you like to learn or improve?

2. How do you plan on going about it? How can your learning group help you in this?

3. What are the significant learning points from the readings?

C. Read the Topic Introduction.

Communication Climate Inventory

James I. Costigan and Martha A. Schmeidler

The following statements relate to how your supervisor and you communicate on the job. There are no right or wrong answers. Respond honestly to the statements, using the following scale:

1. Strongly Agree
2. Agree
3. Uncertain
4. Disagree
5. Strongly Disagree

	STRONGLY AGREE	AGREE	UNCERTAIN	DISAGREE	STRONGLY DISAGREE
1. My supervisor criticizes my work without allowing me to explain.	1	2	3	4	5
2. My supervisor allows me as much creativity as possible in my job.	1	2	3	4	5
3. My supervisor always judges the actions of his or her subordinates.	1	2	3	4	5
4. My supervisor allows flexibility on the job.	1	2	3	4	5
5. My supervisor criticizes my work in the presence of others.	1	2	3	4	5
6. My supervisor is willing to try new ideas and to accept other points of view.	1	2	3	4	5
7. My supervisor believes that he or she must control how I do my work.	1	2	3	4	5
8. My supervisor understands the problems that I encounter in my job.	1	2	3	4	5
9. My supervisor is always trying to change other people's attitudes and behaviors to suit his or her own.	1	2	3	4	5
10. My supervisor respects my feelings and values.	1	2	3	4	5
11. My supervisor always needs to be in charge of the situation.	1	2	3	4	5
12. My supervisor listens to my problems with interest.	1	2	3	4	5
13. My supervisor tries to manipulate subordinates to get what he or she wants or to make himself or herself look good.	1	2	3	4	5
14. My supervisor does not try to make me feel inferior.	1	2	3	4	5
15. I have to be careful when talking to my supervisor so that I will not be misinterpreted.	1	2	3	4	5
16. My supervisor participates in meetings with employees without projecting his or her higher status or power.	1	2	3	4	5
17. I seldom say what really is on my mind, because it might be twisted and distorted by my supervisor.	1	2	3	4	5
18. My supervisor treats me with respect.	1	2	3	4	5
19. My supervisor seldom becomes involved in employee conflicts.	1	2	3	4	5

	STRONGLY AGREE	AGREE	UNCERTAIN	DISAGREE	STRONGLY DISAGREE
20. My supervisor does not have hidden motives in dealing with me.	1	2	3	4	5
21. My supervisor is not interested in employee problems.	1	2	3	4	5
22. I feel that I can be honest and straightforward with my supervisor.	1	2	3	4	5
23. My supervisor rarely offers moral support during a personal crisis.	1	2	3	4	5
24. I feel that I can express my opinions and ideas honestly to my supervisor.	1	2	3	4	5
25. My supervisor tries to make me feel inadequate.	1	2	3	4	5
26. My supervisor defines problems so that they can be understood but does not insist that his or her subordinates agree.	1	2	3	4	5
27. My supervisor makes it clear that he or she is in charge.	1	2	3	4	5
28. I feel free to talk to my supervisor.	1	2	3	4	5
29. My supervisor believes that if a job is to be done right, he or she must oversee it or do it.	1	2	3	4	5
30. My supervisor defines problems and makes his or her subordinates aware of them.	1	2	3	4	5
31. My supervisor cannot admit that he or she makes mistakes.	1	2	3	4	5
32. My supervisor tries to describe situations fairly without labeling them as good or bad.	1	2	3	4	5
33. My supervisor is dogmatic; it is useless for me to voice an opposing point of view.	1	2	3	4	5
34. My supervisor presents his or her feelings and perceptions without implying that a similar response is expected from me.	1	2	3	4	5
35. My supervisor thinks that he or she is always right.	1	2	3	4	5
36. My supervisor attempts to explain situations clearly and without personal bias.	1	2	3	4	5

Reprinted from J. William Pfeiffer and Leonard D. Goldstein (Eds.), *The 1984 Annual: Developing Human Resources*. San Diego, California: University Associates, Inc., 1984. Used with permission.

Communication Climate Inventory
Scoring and Interpretation Sheet

Place the numbers that you assigned to each statement in the appropriate blanks. Now add them together to determine a subtotal for each climate descriptor. Place the subtotals in the proper blanks and add your scores. Place an X on the graph to indicate what your perception is of your organization or department's communication climate. Some descriptions of the terms follow. You may wish to discuss with others their own perceptions and interpretations.

PART I: DEFENSIVE SCORES

Evaluation	Neutrality
Question 1 _____	Question 19 _____
Question 3 _____	Question 21 _____
Question 5 _____	Question 23 _____
Subtotal _____	**Subtotal** _____
Control	**Superiority**
Question 7 _____	Question 25 _____
Question 9 _____	Question 27 _____
Question 11 _____	Question 29 _____
Subtotal _____	**Subtotal** _____
Strategy	**Certainty**
Question 13 _____	Question 31 _____
Question 15 _____	Question 33 _____
Question 17 _____	Question 35 _____
Subtotal _____	**Subtotal** _____

Subtotals for Defensive Scores

Evaluation _____   Neutrality _____

Control _____   Superiority _____

Strategy _____   Certainty _____

Total _____

18	25	30	35	40	45	50	55	60	65	70	75	80	85	90

Defensive   Defensive to Neutral   Neutral to Supportive   Supportive

Provisionalism

Question 2 _____

Question 4 _____

Question 6 _____

Subtotal _____

Empathy

Question 8 _____

Question 10 _____

Question 12 _____

Subtotal _____

Equality

Question 14 _____

Question 16 _____

Question 18 _____

Subtotal _____

Spontaneity

Question 20 _____

Question 22 _____

Question 24 _____

Subtotal _____

Problem Orientation

Question 26 _____

Question 28 _____

Question 30 _____

Subtotal _____

Description

Question 32 _____

Question 34 _____

Question 36 _____

Subtotal _____

Subtotals for Supportive Scores

Provisionalism _____

Empathy _____

Equality _____

Spontaneity _____

Problem Orientation _____

Description _____

Total _____

| 18 | 25 | 30 | 35 | 40 | 45 | 50 | 55 | 60 | 65 | 70 | 75 | 80 | 85 | 90 |

Supportive   Supportive to Neutral   Neutral to Defensive   Defensive

II

Topic Introduction

In a recent management development program after "listening" politely for 15 to 20 minutes to an exposition on the importance of interpersonal communications, one manager began waving his hand actively, had a grimace on his face, and even before being formally acknowledged, blurted out, "I can't spend all of my time with this interpersonal communications stuff—there's work to be done!" True! There is work to be done, and for that very reason, effective interpersonal communications become crucial.

Let us examine a few examples.

Much of a manager's job centers on effective problem solving and decision making. The "goodness" of any decision can be assessed along two criteria.[1] (1) Is the decision logically sound (i.e., were all the appropriate and available facts brought to bear in a rational way)? (2) Do those who are affected by the decision and/or are responsible for implementing it accept the decision (i.e., are they committed to the decision)? The "right" decision from a logical viewpoint to which people feel uncommitted (i.e., drag their heels, "forget" to implement, or actively resist) is, indeed, not a particularly good decision at all.

Effective interpersonal communication is important in this regard in several ways. Thoughts, facts, and opinions that go unheard and/or are misunderstood may seriously reduce the logical soundness of the decision. Picture yourself in a meeting where your ideas and inputs seem to be ignored or not seriously considered by others. The *feelings* this would create in you could make it very hard for you to act committed to the decision—you feel left out ("they decided" versus "we decided").

Effective interpersonal communication is also very important in ensuring the acceptance of certain decisions in another way. Consider the situation in which it has been decided, for example, to install a new computerized record system. The decision is very sound from a logical viewpoint (i.e., the new system will be more efficient and productive). However, some people are concerned that they will have to develop new skills or that many jobs will be eliminated by the new system. If these feelings (irrational as they may or may not be) are not expressed, heard, and dealt with, the introduction of the new system may encounter several snags.

A similar set of dynamics has been uncovered with respect to the selling process. The buyer, very often, appears to get cold feet just before the deal is to be completed. The seller had every rational reason to expect that things were going smoothly, but at the last minute, the sale is lost. The overt reason offered very often is that the price was too high (in spite of the fact that the price seemed acceptable all along). Follow-up research in these situations has documented that the overt reason offered had little to do with losing the sale. Most often, the buyer had concerns or anxieties related to the personal consequences of the purchase (i.e., "If this machine will make my department as productive as you say, my boss will think I'm trying to build my empire and get his job!") Effective interpersonal communication skills are essential to building the trust necessary to bring out these concerns and deal with them effectively.

Spouses who claim that they have a communication problem, children who feel their parents "just don't understand them," bosses who cannot understand why

---

[1]See Chapter 13, Leadership and Decision Making, for more detail on this point.

their performance evaluations of subordinates seem to have no impact—the situations where effective interpersonal communication is important are infinite.

Mintzberg's ground-breaking study on the nature of managerial work identified communication as the most frequent and important of managerial activities.[2]

> The manager's work is essentially that of communication and his (or her) tools are the five basic media—mail, telephone, unscheduled meetings, scheduled meetings, and tours. Managers clearly favor the three verbal media, many spending on the order of 80 percent of their time in verbal contact. Some managers, such as those of staff groups, spend relatively more time alone. But the greatest share of the time of almost all managers is spent in verbal communication.[3]

And even when managers are not trying to communicate, their actions (or lack thereof) are taken as messages. It's impossible to not communicate; rather the question for managers is, "Am I communicating effectively?"

To understand better this complex process of interpersonal communication, let's examine the basic model of communication.

THE COMMUNICATION MODEL

The Greeks believed that the God Mercury plucked ideas from the brain of the speaker, impaled the ideas on the end of a spear, and plunged them into the listener's brain. Today most people think of communication as the following process:

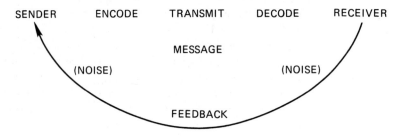

Very simply, senders think of what they want to convey to another person. The next step is to encode that message—to put it into verbal or nonverbal form and transmit it to the receiver. Receivers must then decode the message, that is, put it into a form which has meaning for them.

The potential for distortion in this process is very large. First, the way the sender encodes the message may not accurately reflect the message he or she wanted to transmit. "No, that's not what I meant," frequently accompanies communication attempts. Second, the form of transmitting the message may not succeed. For example, the new supervisor who tentatively touches upon an employee's habitual lateness may have failed to convey her displeasure with the employee's behavior and the consequences that lay in store.

Third, the way the receiver decodes the message is strongly related to the individual's background and personality. A feminist decodes a male boss's reference to "you girls" differently from a more traditional older woman. The recently hired low-level employee interprets a memo from the company president differently from the vice presidents. The most effective communicators are "receiver oriented" be-

---

[2]Henry Mintzberg, *The Nature of Managerial Work* (New York: Harper & Row, 1973).
[3]Ibid., p. 171.

cause they gear their messages to the receiver. They ask themselves, "If I were the receiver, how would this message strike me? How would I interpret it?"

Both encoding and decoding are heavily influenced by personal factors such as education, personality, socioeconomic level, family and child rearing, work history, culture, personal experience, and role in the organization. It is a fact of communication that people perceive messages differently; thus, meaning lies in people, not in words. Chapter 7, Interpersonal Perception, focuses more on the individualistic interpretations made in communication. The better one knows another person and understands their personal context, the easier it is to read their communications accurately.

Another likely source of distortion in the communication process is "noise," which is defined as interference with the intended message. In addition to physical conditions that make communication more difficult, emotional states can also create noise. The employee who arrives late for an 8:30 meeting because of a domestic skirmish is unlikely to capture all the messages coming his or her way.

Because the communication process is fraught with potential for distortion, the feedback part of the model is crucial. In this case, feedback refers to the receiver's attempts to ensure that the message he or she decoded is what the sender really meant to convey. Asking for clarification and paraphrasing the sender's words ("Let me see if I have understood you correctly. Do you mean . . . ?") are feedback methods. Senders can also check to see if their message got across. Managers often ask employees to paraphrase instructions to see if they were clear. The purpose of communication is *mutual understanding*. Unless we check with people, we are likely to make the mistake of assuming that communication occurred when it did not.

The normal result of an attempt to communicate is a partial misunderstanding because of the uniqueness of the sender and receiver. Asking for clarification in the communication process is similar to the renegotiation of expectations in the pinch model (Chapter 1). Feedback is a way to avoid communication failures. When communication does break down, a common response is to waste time and energy figuring out who is at fault. The result of this is generally a defensive reaction that further inhibits mutual understanding. However, if we accept misunderstandings as a basic reality of communication, we can stop looking for blame and start seeking better ways to communicate. A more effective response to breakdowns is, "How can we arrive at a level of mutual understanding that will allow us to accomplish our objectives?" and "How can we prevent a breakdown like this from happening again?"

Defensiveness is one of the most common barriers to good communication. People cannot hear the sender's message because they are busy defending themselves. Defensive communication in the work setting also means that some people are sitting on useful information to protect themselves, while others are reluctant to provide the feedback that could improve the performance of the organization. The following section shows the relationship between different responding styles and defensiveness.

RESPONDING STYLES

A study attributed to Carl Rogers, a famous psychologist, found that 80 percent of all responses fell into five categories, as follows:

1. *Evaluative.* "What a great report!" "That idea will never work." An evaluative response indicates that the listener has made a judgment of the relative goodness, appropriateness, effectiveness, or rightness of the speaker's statement or problem. With this type of response, the listener implies what the sender should do.

2. *Interpretive.* "You've just saying that because you lost the account." The interpretive response indicates that the listener's intent is to teach, to tell the sender what his or her statement or problem really means and how the sender really feels about the situation. With this type of response, the listener implies what the sender should think.

3. *Supportive.* "Don't worry, it'll work out." A supportive response indicates that the listener's intent is to reassure, to pacify, and to reduce the sender's intensity of feeling. The listener has in some way implied that the sender need not feel as he or she does.

4. *Probing.* "Why do you think you're going to be fired?" A response that indicates the listener's intent is to seek further information, provoke further discussion along a certain line, and question the sender. With this response, a listener implies that the sender needs to develop or discuss a point further.

5. *Understanding.* "So, you think your job's on the line and you're pretty upset about it?" An understanding response indicates that the listener's intent is only to ask the sender whether the listener correctly understands what the sender is saying, how the sender feels about the problem, and how the sender sees the problem. With this response, the listener implies nothing but concern that the sender's message is accurately received.

Our natural tendency as listeners is to evaluate and judge what others say to us. Rogers found that the most common responses are evaluative, but they are not always the most effective type of response to employ. Groups seeking creative solutions or resolution to a conflict are two examples of situations in which evaluative responses are clearly counterproductive.

Responses to messages communicate not only words but also a message about the relationship between the two people. By evaluating others, we place ourselves in a one-up position. The same is true when we interpret what others have said or try to pacify them and, even to some degree, when we use probing responses because they imply that the sender has not thought everything through. If our responses convey that we see ourselves in a one-up position with the sender, defensiveness results. The only type of response that communicates that the listener has positioned himself or herself on the same level as the speaker is the understanding response. This is the type of response that is used in active listening, which is explained in the next section. It is not appropriate for all situations; none of the responses described are. No response style can be said to be innately good or bad, but there are times when a certain type of response would be more appropriate or effective than another. A good communicator is aware of the type of response that is called for in each situation.

Rogers's work led him to believe that defensive communication could be avoided by being descriptive rather than evaluative and by assuming an equal rather than a superior stance. Gibb contributed four more ways to avoid provoking defensive communication: (1) assuming a problem-solving orientation rather than trying to control the situation, (2) being spontaneous rather than strategic, (3) showing empathy rather than neutrality, and (4) being provisional rather than certain.[4] An example of being certain rather than provisional is the manager who tears into employees when an error has been made before he or she has ascertained the facts of the situation. It's hard to repair the supervisor-employee relationship when this occurs because it signifies a lack of trust and respect for the employee and an unwillingness to give the employee the benefit of the doubt.

Our focus on defensiveness highlights how feelings affect communication. The

[4]Jack Gibb, "Defensive Communication," D. A. Kolb, I. M. Rubin, and J. S. Osland, *Organizational Behavior: Practical Readings for Managers* (Englewood Cliffs, N.J.: Prentice Hall, 1990).

distinction between the "content" and "process" aspects of interpersonal communication is very important.

THE WHAT (CONTENT) AND HOW (PROCESS) OF COMMUNICATION

The content of what we communicate can be thought of as relating primarily to thoughts and or feelings. *Thoughts* are the products of our minds. We imagine, muse about, remember, or reflect upon our thoughts. We experience thoughts as perceptions, ideas, reasons, rationales. We have thoughts about what we see, hear, touch, smell, and feel. *Feelings,* on the other hand, are the emotional reactions we have inside ourselves to our own or others thoughts, actions, and feelings. They are the "charge" or affect part of interpersonal communications.

Generally speaking, our facility to express, hear, and work with thoughts is much greater than our facilities with feelings. What is rational, concrete, objective, and quantifiable seems easier and safer than anything emotional. Feelings are considered "touchy," "too personal," and something "we don't talk about, especially in business." Yet feelings are another component of ourselves. Feelings are the way we personalize our thoughts, ideas, and reactions. We can "make believe" we have no feelings about a given situation (disassociate our feelings from our thoughts) for a while. In the long run, such a strategy (1) makes it difficult to communicate our thoughts clearly (it takes a lot of energy to communicate a thought dispassionately when you feel passionate!) and (2) is not terribly good for personal health (ulcers, stress, etc.).

Thoughts and feelings are clearly intertwined and the ability to differentiate between the two is an important communications skill. When we refer to the process of communication, the focus shifts from *what* (thoughts and feelings) to *how*— verbal and/or nonverbal. Many of our thoughts and our feelings are expressed via the words or phrases we speak. The words we express may be very concrete and direct, or they may be inferential and vague. This includes the tone, inflections, emphasis, and so on that we put on the words. The *channel* is *verbal.*

Much important communication is expressed via nonverbal means. A recent article on this topic concluded, "in spite of human garrulousness, perhaps as little as 20% of the communication among people is verbal,. . . . While people meander the earth through thickets of verbiage (theirs and others), many, perhaps most, do pay more attention to wordless signals and are more likely to be influenced and governed by nonverbal messages."[5] *Generally* speaking, our nonverbal signals relate to the feeling level of what (the content) is being communicated. And even when words are used, more meaning is taken from nonverbal signals. Mehrabian and Weiner found that words account for only 7 percent of the meaning we make out of communications; 55 percent of the meaning comes from facial expressions and posture, while 38 percent comes from vocal intonation and inflection.[6] Obviously, managers who continue doing paperwork while their employees are trying to talk to them are severely handicapping the communication process.

A second critical skill in enhancing the effectiveness of our interpersonal communications involves the concept of *congruence.* The verbal and nonverbal signals we send out need to be congruent with the thoughts and/or feelings we are experiencing inside ourselves and consistent with one another, so our verbal signals do not communicate a different message from our nonverbal signals (like the classic example of people who "say" verbally they are not angry while their face has turned beet red and they are pounding on the table).

[5]"Why So Much Is Beyond Words," *Time,* July 13, 1981, p. 74.

[6]A. Mehrabian and M. Weiner, "Decoding of Inconsistent Communications," *Journal of Personality and Social Psychology,* Vol. 6 (1967), pp. 109–114.

ACTIVE LISTENING: THE DYNAMIC SKILL
IN INTERPERSONAL COMMUNICATIONS

Before we talk about specifics, you may find yourself wondering, "How can *active listening* improve interpersonal communications?" The key lies in the word "active." We are *not* referring to sitting quietly like a bump on a log just waiting patiently for the other person to finish (although frequent interruptions do hurt the communication process). Rather, we are talking about taking *personal responsibility* to find out and be sure that (1) what we consciously communicated (thoughts and feelings) was received, (2) what you received (thoughts and feelings) was what was intended to be sent, and (3) any distortions uncovered by (1) and (2) are clarified before proceeding with the conversation.

We have a physiological excuse for not being excellent listeners. The rate of speech is 100–150 words per minute, whereas our brains are capable of thinking at a rate of 400–500 words per minute. People often use this slack time to daydream, to judge what the sender is saying, or to prepare what they want to say next. In contrast, active listeners use this slack time to concentrate fully on the sender's message. Active listening involves a different level of attending to the speaker.

The skills of active listening are demanding, but learnable. Guidelines for learning them are suggested in the paragraphs that follow. Some of the behaviors suggested may seem awkward and forced at first, but with practice, they will feel more natural. It is difficult to respond with patience, understanding, and empathy when the other person is expressing ideas that strike one as illogical, self-deceiving, or even morally wrong. However, the behaviors suggested will, if practiced faithfully, generate attitudes of tolerance and understanding that will make empathy and nonevaluative acceptance of the other come more easily.

Being Non-evaluative

Active listening includes a variety of verbal and nonverbal behaviors that communicate to the other that he or she is heard and understood, that the feelings that underlie the words are appreciated and accepted, that regardless of what the individual says or thinks or feels, he or she is accepted as a person by the listener. The object is to communicate that whatever the qualities of the ideas, events, attitudes, and values of the person who is talking, the listener does not evaluate the person or his or her ideas or feelings. The listener accepts the person for what he or she is without making judgments of right or wrong, good or bad, logical or illogical.

Paraphrasing the Manifest or Presented Content (Thoughts and/or Feelings)

This is simply to paraphrase what the talker has said in one's own words and repeat it back to the talker to test whether one has heard accurately. One uses such phrases as

"As I understand it, what you're saying is . . . "

"Do you mean that . . . "

"So your feeling is that . . . "

The key to this behavior, as to any active listening, is that one has to listen intently to what the other is saying. If we spend the time when the other is talking, thinking of what we are going to say next, or making mental evaluations and critical comments, we are likely not to hear enough of it to paraphrase it accurately.

The emphasis at this level is the *manifest* or *presented* content, that which is explicitly communicated verbally and/or nonverbally. The more indirect the content—*and people are generally less direct about feelings than they are about thoughts*—the more important are the next two active listening skills.

Reflecting the Implications

This requires going a bit beyond the manifest content of what the other is saying, and indicating to the speaker your appreciation of where the content is leading. It may take the form of building on or extending the ideas of the speaker, using such phrases as

"I guess if you did that, you'd then be in a position to . . . "

"So that might lead to a situation in which . . . "

"Would that mean that . . . ?"

"Are you suggesting that we might . . . ?"

"Would that help with the problem of . . . ?"

It is important in reflecting the implications to leave the speaker in control of the discussion. When this technique is used to change the direction of the speaker's thinking or to show how much more clever the listener is by suggesting ideas the speaker has not thought of, it ceases to build trust and becomes a kind of skillful one-upmanship. When, however, this technique is genuinely used to help the speaker, it communicates very strongly that the listener has really heard and understood the drift of his or her thinking.

Reflecting the Underlying Feelings

This technique goes still farther beyond the overt feelings content of what is said and brings into the open some of the underlying feelings, attitudes, beliefs, or values that may be influencing the speaker to talk in just this way. One tries to emphasize, to put oneself in the place of the speaker, to experience how it must feel to be in his or her situation. Then the listener *tentatively* expresses the feelings, using such phrases as

"I suppose that must make you rather anxious."

"If that happened to me, I'd be rather upset."

"Times when I've been in that sort of situation, I've really felt I could use some help."

"If I achieved that, I think I'd feel rather proud of myself."

"That must have been rather satisfying."

In reflecting the underlying feelings, delicacy is required so as not to overexpose the speaker or press him or her to admit to more than he or she would like to reveal. It is also important to avoid suggesting to the speaker that the feeling you reflect back is what he or she ought to feel in such a situation. This would tend to make the speaker feel evaluated, when what you are trying to do is to communicate acceptance of the underlying feelings. Often acceptance or evaluation is communicated more by the manner and tone of the listener than by the words used.

To the points just raised, we now can add the two final active listening skills.

Inviting Further Contributions

When one hasn't heard or understood enough yet to follow up with indications of understanding, empathy, and acceptance, one can at least communicate interest in hearing more. Phrases such as the following are useful:

"Tell me a bit more about that."

"How did you feel when . . . ?"

"Help me understand . . . "

"What happened then?"

Probing questions may lead to more and more exposure of the speaker, without letting him or her know the listener is receiving and evaluating the communication. Specific requests for information may constitute a unilateral demand for openness on the part of the speaker. To maintain balance, questions should not be used exclusively, but should be followed after a bit by rephrasing or reflecting. And, generally, open-ended questions create a more supportive trusting climate than do pointed questions fired in machine-gunlike fashion.

Nonverbal Listening Responses[7]

Active listening is often communicated as much by one's posture and nonverbal movements as it is by what one says. Such responses as the following examples communicate interest and understanding: eye contact; body posture leaning toward the speaker, head nodding, and receptive signals such as "um-hum."

Active listening skills, implemented in a climate of genuine concern and acceptance, help both parties in an interpersonal exchange understand, as fully as possible, the relevant content—facts and feelings—floating around on top and underneath the table.

[7]The range of nonverbal behavior is clearly extensive and often culturally determined. Most important, this is not intended to help people learn "trick" or "technique" to be applied mechanistically. Incongruent *listening* behavior contributes to ineffective interpersonal communications, as well.

III

Procedure for Group Meeting: Active Listening Exercise

STEP 1.   Individual work. (10 minutes) On the following pages you will find ten suggested stimuli for role-play situations. Each scenario has three basic roles:

1. An *Expresser* who gets a chance to enhance his or her ability to express thought and feelings in a congruent clear manner.

2. An *Active Listener* who practices listening and paraphrases what the expresser states. It is particularly critical that the active listener resists the temptation to give advice or try to solve the problem for the expresser.

3. Two *Observers* who watch the interaction silently, use the observer sheet on page 173 and provide feedback afterward.   Each participant should have the opportunity to play each of the three roles.

For each scenario there will be (1) a stage setting statement, (2) a scripted set of *words* to start the interaction, and (3) a suggested set of feeling states. The scenarios are listed roughly from easy to hard where easy or hard is determined by the range and intensity of feelings associated with the scenario. So, for example, scenario 1 is as follows:

Setting the stage: You are speaking with an outside consultant, brought in by your boss. The consultant has just delivered a copy of his or her final report.

Script: I want to know why I wasn't consulted on that report! You were researching my territory and the decision will impact my people.

Suggested feeling states: bothered, insulted, left out, angry.

The roles needed in this scenario would be

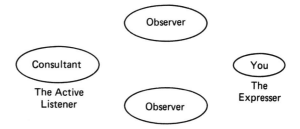

- ■ "You" would communicate the first line as scripted, for example, "I want to know why. . . . " In so doing, you would try to express some or all of the suggested feeling states (insulted, left out, etc.). "Consultant" would specifically practice the *active listening* skills described in the introduction. "Observers" would watch the interaction carefully.

- ■ As the "Consultant" (in the scenario) actively listens, "you" would carry on and add to the conversation in a manner consistent with the thoughts and feelings reflected in the original scripted opening. Carry on the communication at least five minutes.

Your first task is to read over the suggested scenarios and pick a scenario that, as the expresser (not the active listener),

> a. Seems *real* to you (i.e., you have been or could imagine yourself actually being in that situation).
> b. Involves some suggested feeling states that you would like to practice expressing that will stretch you but not immobilize you.

While this is meant to be a play-acting situation, it is also intended to be a serious opportunity to develop your interpersonal communication skills as *both* expressers and active listeners.

STEP 2.   Role plays. (10–15 minutes each round) Form groups of four. Each role play should take 10 to 15 minutes and consist of:

a. 5 to 8 minutes conducting the role-play scenario.

b. 8 to 10 minutes of feedback discussion initiated by the observers and then expanded by the expresser and the active listener.

During the feedback discussion, people should try to link insights gained from playing the different roles. For example, as an expresser, I *may* find out that I am more likely to give off mixed or confusing messages around high-intensity negative feelings than anything else. As the active listener, I *may* find that I am less likely to hear and pick up on high-intensity positive feelings.

Repeat this cycle until everyone has had an opportunity to play each role. If time permits, steps 1 and 2 can be repeated.

Suggested Scenarios

1. *Setting the stage:* You are speaking with an outside consultant, brought in by your boss. The consultant has just delivered a copy of his or her final report.

    Script: I want to know why I wasn't consulted on that report! You were researching my territory and the decision will impact on my people.

    Suggested feeling states: bothered, insulted, left out, angry.

2. *Setting the stage:* Linda and a colleague are talking in Linda's office. Linda is about to tell her colleague about an interaction she had with Ted, corporate vice president.

    Script: After the meeting, I was walking down the hall and Ted stopped me and said, "Linda, you did a really great job on that account!" (smiling) I thought so too!

    Suggested feeling states: proud, happy, contented, a sense of accomplishment.

3. *Setting the stage:* A subordinate is reporting to the boss on the status of his or her (the subordinate's) group. She or he knows, that in the boss's opinion, the group just has not been pulling its fair weight of late.

    Script: We finally had a breakthrough in that contract. After all the hours I spent researching the market, I finally got an idea that he liked (longish sigh). For a while I thought that the group would lose another one.

    Suggested feeling states: relieved, good, accomplished, productive, uncertain, scared.

4. *Setting the stage:* You are a secretary whose boss feels that you have more promise and can utilize your talents better and move ahead. You are about to speak to your boss.

    Script: Last week you mentioned that I could read those articles and compose an annotated bibliography. I know that you want to make my job more interesting. Maybe you even think that I'm bored. But, really, I just don't want to be challenged any more. I guess that I like things as they are.

Suggested feeling states: embarrassed, scared, resentful, frustrated.

5. *Setting the stage:* Charlie has just been offered a middle management position of considerable prestige. He is talking to his boss about it.

   Script: Frankly, I'm just not sure whether or not to accept the promotion. I should be overjoyed with the opportunity. It's a chance to influence some policy. Most people around here don't understand why I haven't left already. But parts of this job are very exciting. Marketing is always a challenge. So I just don't know.

   Suggested feeling states: ambivalent, uncertain, frustrated, unfulfilled, afraid of success and/or failure.

6. *Setting the stage:* You are the first and only female member of your audit team. You had hoped the market increase in travel would not be a problem because you love the work and do it very well. You are talking to your boss.

   Script: I know I said I would have no problem with the travel aspects of the job. I thought I would enjoy it. But, I find that two to three weeks is too long. I'm not really happy when I'm traveling, and my husband is complaining.

   Suggested feeling states: dissatisfied, concerned, uncomfortable, worried, nervous about relationship.

7. *Setting the stage:* You have just had an interaction with the division head, Mr. Samuels, who is your boss's boss. You are now telling your boss about it.

   Script: What was I going to say to him anyway. Mr. Samuels—the division head!—pats me on the back and tells me how concerned he is for my image. I knew this place was pretty straight, but that's the most ridiculous thing that I ever heard—that I can't have a typewriter in my office. I have every mind to put that typewriter right on top of the desk!!!!!

   Suggested feeling states: adamant, determined, angry, resistant, feeling pressured to fit into a mold.

8. *Setting the stage:* You and your boss have a lot of trouble agreeing on how things should be done and on priorities. Here we go again!

   Script: No! This is not a smokescreen for something else! Look, I really don't understand why I have to analyze the reports that way. I want to do an excellent job and I will. However, I'd like a little latitude in bringing some of *my* ideas into action.

   Suggested feeling states: annoyed, confused, frustrated, unchallenged.

9. *Setting the stage:* Given the problems you and your spouse have been having, it has been amazing to you that you've been able to function at all. Your boss has just called you in and read you the riot act.

   Script: Don't you think that I know that my work has been poor. Holy smokes, nobody is cooperating around here. I just . . . look . . . so I haven't been too pleasant. But I'm doing the best I can . . . under the circumstances.

   Suggested feeling states: exasperated, strung out, as if the "bottom has dropped out," tense, as if you have to keep up a front.

10. *Setting the stage:* Your long-time friend and colleague, Todd, has come to chat about his future career plans and long-term growth with the company. Your own career has been very much on your mind for months. So you almost interrupt Todd in midstream.

    Script: Todd, you sound like I did about 15 years ago. I'm 40 years old, Todd. I'm one of, maybe, a hundred middle managers. I've been working my ass off to become a CEO. Nothing was more important to me than my career. Yeah, I'm good, but my wife and kids—they're strangers to me—and I'm not going to become a CEO. Look at the years I wasted working for a goal I'll never reach.

Suggested feeling states: None—include whatever feelings you think you might have if you were this manager.

STEP 3.   Class Discussion (15 minutes)
Answer the following questions:
  a. What was it like to practice active listening?
  b. What did you learn about yourself and others by doing this exercise?
  c. When would it be a mistake to use active listening?
  d. What connections can you make between this exercise and the Readings?

Observer Sheet

Your role is an important one. You should silently observe the interaction and note specific examples of effective and ineffective communication as you see them. These data will be important in the feedback discussion.

ACTIVE LISTENING BEHAVIORS	EXAMPLES WHERE IT WAS EFFECTIVELY USED BY THE ACTIVE LISTENER	PLACES WHERE IT COULD HAVE BEEN USED AND/OR WAS USED INEFFECTIVELY*
1. Being non-evaluative		
2. Paraphrasing the content		
3. Reflecting possible implications		
4. Reflecting the underlying feelings		
5. Inviting further contributions		
6. Nonverbal listening responses		

*The observations you note in this column will give you the chance to provide feedback to the person who was the *expresser:* (1) thoughts and feelings *you* heard them expressing that the listener did not hear or pick up on and (2) mixed messages you observed being expressed (incongruities between words and nonverbals).

IV
Follow-up

A rational mechanical view of the process of communication could be depicted in the following manner:

Person A ⟷ Person B

In other words, A says something to B and B hears what A said. Were it so simple, we would never experience what Bennis has labeled "arc of distortion," which appears below.[8] A communicates something to B that was *not intended*. B reacts to this *unintended* communication, and this response confuses A, as well it would, since A is unaware of part of the message sent. *All behavior* conveys some message— it is a form of communication. In the broadest sense, therefore, when we study the concept of interpersonal communication, we are dealing with interpersonal relationships. The communication is the process vehicle through which relationships form, are managed, and, when necessary, dissolve.

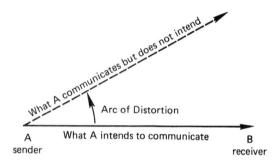

What A communicates but does not intend

Arc of Distortion

A sender — What A intends to communicate — B receiver

The first part of the exercise was intended to highlight the point that, while people's *experiences* and feelings are undoubtedly similar, the medium and mode of expression are generally very different. We all experience a wide range of feelings; it is our form of expression that varies tremendously. It is this reality of difference that makes active listening and communications skill important. I must learn to hear what you are saying, explicitly and implicitly, if I am to understand fully what you are experiencing from your point of view.

Active listening is an important skill in getting work done. Furthermore, *if* one of your subordinates, for example, is experiencing pressure from personal, nonwork-related areas, your ability to listen actively is critical (i.e., you can encourage and support their efforts to find someone who can help them to deal with this pressure). Ignoring this pressure or trying to persuade the person logically to forget personal problems while at work (or "let's keep personalities out of this" or "let's all be grown-ups") are unlikely to be effective in terms of helping to get jobs done effectively. Indeed, those types of responses may only serve to increase the pressure, making it even harder for the person to perform effectively.

[8]H. Baumgartel, Warren N. Bennis, and N. R. De, eds., *Reading in Group Development for Managers and Trainers* (New York: Asia Publishing House, 1967), pp. 151–156.

V

Learning Points

1. Communication is a major portion of a manager's job.

2. There is much potential for distortion in the communication process. Therefore, it's best to assume that any communication also involves a partial misunderstanding. Requesting and giving feedback on the message is one way to ensure that the message received is the intended message. Active listening is another way to minimize the arc of distortion.

3. The arc of distortion is the difference between what the sender intended to convey and what the receiver understood the message to be.

4. Meaning lies in people, not in words.

5. Defensiveness is a common barrier to communication because the energy devoted to defending oneself prevents attention to the message. Therefore, it's to a manager's advantage to learn to communicate in a manner that does not arouse defensiveness.

6. Rogers found five responding styles:
   a. Evaluative
   b. Interpretive
   c. Supportive
   d. Probing
   e. Understanding

   Evaluative responses are most common. These styles also contain a message about the relationship between the two parties. Only the understanding response reflects an egalitarian stance rather than a one-up position.

7. A nondefensive climate is created when people are descriptive, egalitarian, focused on problem solving, spontaneous, empathic, and provisional.

8. People have both thoughts and feelings. Both the sender and the receiver's feelings influence *what* thoughts get sent and received and *how* they get sent.

9. Both parties in an interpersonal exchange have the personal responsibility to use their active listening skills to enhance the quality of the messages sent and received and the dynamic interaction between the two.

10. More meaning is taken from nonverbal signals and vocal intonation and inflection than from words themselves.

VI
Tips for Managers

- It's very difficult to separate relationships from communication. Generally speaking, the better the relationship, the better the communication.

- Communication is a learned behavior that means that people usually send messages that maximize rewards and minimize punishment. Managers who are guilty of the "kill the messenger" syndrome will be told only the "good news," even though the bad news may be crucial to the organization's survival.

- Active listening is the appropriate response to use with people in a conflict situation. It's difficult to maintain anger when the listener is making a concerted effort to understand both your point and your feelings.

- Take for granted that communication is a flawed process and try to eliminate as many pitfalls as possible. It's a good idea to ask employees to paraphrase your instructions (i.e., "Would you please put the instructions in your own words so that I can see if I communicated them clearly?") and to paraphrase for them the problems or requests that they bring to you (i.e., "Let me see if I've understood the problem correctly . . . ").

- Some managers give written instructions along with verbal instructions to avoid both misunderstandings and later consultations.

- Self-concept serves as a filter through which we see all communication. People with low self-concepts present the greatest communication challenge because they can become defensive with no provocation. The specific content of your message is less important than what you are conveying to them about your relationship with them; if it's anything less than fully supportive, they become defensive.

- Before you communicate at work, ask yourself the following questions:
  What do I want to accomplish as a result of the following questions?
  How do I want the receiver to respond?
  Based on my knowledge of the receiver(s), how should I word this message and how should I transmit it?
  Am I the best person to send this message or would someone else have greater credibility or a better relationship with them?
  Will there be any likely resistance to the message that I need to take into consideration?

- Some managers deplore the power of the grapevine, the informal communication network. However, all organizations have grapevines, and some managers use the grapevine for their own purposes, as for example, floating trial balloons. The power of the grapevine can be decreased by more open sharing of information through formal channels. In a bureaucracy, information is often synonymous with power; providing greater access to information means that employees will devote less energy to ferreting it out.

- Most organizations are characterized by top-down information flows. Unless managers make a concerted effort to seek information from employees, they will remain in the dark on many issues. For senior managers it is not always enough to talk only with the layer of people immediately beneath them because this group may have a vested interest in presenting only positive information or self-serving interpretations of situations. This is why the concept of "managing by walking around" is so important.

■ The nonverbal cues that signify that you are attending to what another person is saying are: facing them squarely with an open posture (no limbs crossed), leaning forward, and maintaining eye contact and a relaxed posture. Studies have shown that more information is shared when people come out from behind their desks and sit closer to their visitors.

VII
Personal Application Assignment

At the beginning of this chapter you filled out an inventory in which you evaluated the type of communication climate your supervisor has established. That questionnaire was based upon Gibb's characteristics of defensive communication. This assignment is to gain insight into the type of communication climate you create. Choose one of the following ways to begin this assignment.

1. If you supervise employees, ask three of them to fill out a copy of the same questionnaire *anonymously*. If you're surprised at the results, discuss them and ask for clarification or examples from someone in your organization who you know will give you good, honest feedback. Take into consideration that your employees may be uncertain (or even terrified) about how you will accept feedback on your communication habits. Make sure they don't have to pay a price for their honesty.

2. Have a controversial discussion with someone (preferably someone difficult so you can test out the skills you practiced in this chapter). Try to create a supportive climate according to Gibb's framework. Afterward, evaluate the conversation. If it's possible, get the other person's evaluation of the conversation.

After you've completed (1) or (2), write up the experience in the usual format.

A. *Concrete Experience*
   1. *Objectively* describe the experience ("who," "what," "when," "where," "how" type information—up to 2 points).
   2. *Subjectively* describe your feelings, perceptions, and thoughts that occurred *during* (not after) the experience (up to 2 points). Does this section have too much detail? (If so, delete 1 point.)

B. *Reflective Observation*

1. Look at the experience from different points of view. How many points of view did you include that are *relevant* (up to 2 points)?

2. Use these perspectives to add more meaning to the incident (up to 2 points).

C. *Abstract Conceptualization*

1. Relate concepts from the assigned readings and the lecture to the experience (i.e., What theories that you heard in the lecture or read in the *Reader* relate to your understanding of this incident?). Make reference to at least two sources. Use standard referencing format and include the page number to which you are referring. How many sources did you use and how clearly did you explain their theories (up to 4 points)?

2. You can also create an original model or theory, but it should not replace course concepts.

D. *Active Experimentation*
1. Write about what you will do in the future that will improve your effectiveness. Use rules of thumb or action resolutions.
2. Are they described specifically, thoroughly, and in detail (up to 4 points)?

E. *Integration, Synthesis, and Writing*
1. Did you write about something personally important to you (up to 1 point)?
2. Was it well written (up to 2 points)?
3. Did you integrate and synthesize the different sections (up to 1 point)?

7

INTERPERSONAL PERCEPTION

OBJECTIVES   By the end of this chapter you should be able to:

A. Understand the factors that influence our perception of other people.

B. Explain the manner in which perceptions of other people influence interpersonal relationships.

C. Describe the Johari window and the implications for communication and interpersonal relationships.

D. Recognize and utilize good feedback.

E. Understand both the benefits and drawbacks of the perceptual process.

The Blind Men and the Elephant

John Godfrey Saxe

It was six men of Indostan
    To learning much inclined,
Who went to see the Elephant
    (Though all of them were blind),
That each by observation
    Might satisfy his mind.

The first approached the Elephant,
    And happening to fall
Against his broad and sturdy side,
    At once began to bawl:
"God bless me! but the Elephant
    Is very like a WALL!"

The second, feeling of the tusk,
    Cried, "Ho! what have we here
So very round and smooth and sharp?
    To me 'tis mighty clear
This wonder of an Elephant
    Is very like a SPEAR."

The third approached the animal,
    And happening to take
The squirming trunk within his hands,
    Thus boldly up and spake:
"I see," quoth he, "the Elephant
    Is very like a SNAKE!"

The fourth reached out an eager hand,
    And felt about the knee
"What most this wonderous beast is like
    Is mighty plain," quoth he:
"'Tis clear enough the Elephant
    Is very like a TREE!"

The fifth, who chanced to touch the ear,
    Said: "E'en the blindest man
Can tell what this resembles most;
    Deny the fact who can,
This marvel of an Elephant
    Is very like a FAN!"

The sixth no sooner had begun
    About the beast to grope,
Than seizing on the swinging tail
    That fell within his scope,
"I see," quoth he, "the Elephant
    Is very like a ROPE!"

And so these men of Indostan
    Disputed loud and long,
Each in his own opinion
    Exceeding stiff and strong,
Though each was partly in the right,
    And all were in the wrong!

I

Premeeting Preparation

A. Read the Topic Introduction.

B. What are the significant learning points from the readings?

II

Topic Introduction

People are not cameras or tape recorders. We do not take in, with our eyes, exactly what is "out there." We constantly respond to cues that have meaning for us. We see what we want or need to see to define ourselves or to advance our aims. We do not see people as they are; we see them for what they mean to us. The process of organizing and reading meaning into the stimuli that bombard us is called *perception.*

As stated in Chapter 6, perception is one of the barriers to good communication because our perceptual patterns filter the communication directed to us. There are four ways in which this occurs:

1. *Selective Exposure.* People expose themselves only to that which they want to hear or see. Students who daydream in class, atheists who avoid church, or managers who read only those reports that support their position engage in selective exposure.

2. *Selective Attention.* Even when people are listening or reading they tend to pick up only those items that interest them or support what they are looking for. Information that conflicts with what we believe is either ignored or distorted to conform to our preconceptions. Studies of both low-level supervisors and middle management executives revealed that these individuals perceived only those aspects of a situation that related to the goals and activities of their own departments.[1] This explains why two people can attend the same meeting or event and have contradictory stories about what occurred. The interesting part becomes, in Gestalt psychology terms, the "figure" for them—the dominant part. The rest is "ground." What do you see in the picture on page 187? This illustration is often used to reveal perceptual differences. Some people see an old woman, others see a young woman—proving that what is figural to some people is merely background to others.

    Our minds also organize and complete fragmented and partial perceptions. For example, some people will look at this figure, 13, and see a "B"; others will interpret it as a "13." In fact, the figure has no special meaning, but our minds adjust the lines for us to make it familiar. Part of the difficulty in introducing new ideas in organizations is this tendency to fit the idea into existing concepts. Stereotyping is a form of "adjusting the picture" whether or not the lines are really there.

3. *Distrusted Source.* Our expectations about people or sources of communication prevent us from an objective consideration of their message. Rabid liberals and conservatives block out reasonable arguments from each other because they distrust the source.

4. *Erroneous Translation.* Since each person's language is a reflection of his or her own experience, we often mistakenly assume that a word has the same meaning for everyone. Words themselves are ambiguous and mean what people think they mean.

[1]Dewitt Dearborn and Herbert Simon, "Selective Perception: A Note on the Departmental Identification of Executives," *Sociometry,* Vol. 21 (1958), p. 142, and Abraham Korman, "Selective Perception Among First Line Supervisors," *Personnel Administrator,* Vol. 26 (September 1963).

These are the ways in which perception can cause distortion in communication, but perception is also an extremely useful process. It helps us to make sense of a world full of stimuli in three ways: first, by *limiting* the amount of information that enters our mind to prevent overload; second, by *selecting* what input we will attend to; and, third, by *organizing* and classifying the input we receive.

Consider how we understand the world we live in, particularly those parts of it concerning ourselves and our relations with other people.[2] We organize the world according to *concepts,* or categories. We say that things are warm or cold, good or bad, simple or complex. Each of these concepts may be considered a dimension along which we can place events in the world, some closer to one end of the dimension, some closer to the other.

Any time we consider the qualities of ourselves, other persons, or events in the inanimate world, we have to use these concepts to do it. We are dependent for our understanding of the world on the concepts and categories we have for organizing our experiences. If we lack a concept for something that occurs in the world, we have to invent one or we cannot respond to the event in an organized fashion. How, for example, would a person explain his or her own and others' behavior without the concepts of love and hate? Consider how much behavior would simply puzzle or confuse a person or, perhaps, just go on by without really being perceived at all, for lack of this one dimension.

Most of us have developed our own set of concepts that we use to interpret others' behavior. These concept preferences are often related to our motivation. People with high affiliation motivation, for example, may tend to see the world in terms of love and hate, acceptance and rejection. They may be relatively insensitive to issues of leadership or excellence. Thus, an administrator who is overly sensitive to whether or not subordinates are friendly may, as a result, be in a poor position to judge other important aspects of subordinates' performance. The ability to develop differentiated perceptions of others is related to leadership effectiveness. Fiedler[3] has reported some research where he found that effective leaders, in contrast to ineffective leaders, were able to differentiate among their followers on a variety of dimensions. For example, whereas the captain of a losing basketball team tends to distinguish among his players only in terms of their overall ability, the captain of a winning team tends to be aware of who dribbles well, who passes well, who shoots well, who plays well under pressure, and so on. In other words, effective managers seem to have a large number of concepts in their conceptual schemes and tend to perceive differences among their subordinates along these dimensions.

Concepts do not exist in isolation; they are connected to one another by a network of relationships. Taken together, the concepts we use to understand a situation, plus the relationships among the concepts, are called a *conceptual system.* For example, we may say, "People who are warm and friendly are usually trusting, and hence they are often deceived by others." Here we have a conceptual system linking the concepts of *friendliness, warmth, trust in others,* and *proneness to deception.* Because concepts are linked to one another, the location of an event in one concept usually indicates where that event is located in each of a whole network of concepts. Thus, it is almost impossible to take in a small bit of information about a characteristic of a person or event without a host of implications about other characteristics.

Images and stereotypes operate this way. When we discover that a person is black, or a union leader, a social scientist, or a wife, the information on these concepts immediately calls up an entire network of expectations about other charac-

[2]See O. J. Harvey, D. E. Hunt, and H. M. Schroder, *Conceptual Systems and Personality Organization* (New York: W. W. Norton, 1955).

[3]F. E. Fiedler, *Leader Attitudes and Group Effectiveness* (Urbana: University of Illinois Press, 1958), also Irwin M. Rubin and M. Goldman, "An Open System Model of Leadership Performance," *Organizational Behavior and Human Performance,* Vol. 3, no. 2 (May 1968), pp. 143–156.

teristics of the person. In the case of stereotypes, these expectations may even be so strong that we do not check to find out whether our conceptual system worked accurately this time, but go to the other extreme of ignoring or distorting information that does not fit the conceptual system, so that the system may remain quite unaffected by contradictory experiences.

In other words, these concepts (or sets of dimensions) enable us to organize the multitude of experiences we have each day. Without them we would be in a continuous state of chaos, so, to this extent, they are functional and necessary parts of the human personality. The fact that we are so dependent on our conceptual system means that we are sometimes hesitant to accept any information that does not fit into it.

To protect ourselves from disconfirming experiences, we have at our disposal a host of perceptual defenses. These defenses[4] act as a screen or filter, blocking out that which we do not want to see and letting through that which we wish to see. The closer we get to conceptual systems concerned with our *self-perceptions* (self-image) and our relationships with important others, the more likely we are to call upon these defensive screens.[5]

These defensive screens help to create self-fulfilling or circular perceptual processes. Let us examine how these circular processes can (and often do) function with a few examples.

Example 1: The Stereotypical Female

1. As a woman, I believe that men prefer women who are passive and unassertive.
2. Since I would like to develop meaningful relationships with men, I behave in a passive and unassertive manner.

3. I tend to develop relationships with men who themselves expect women to be passive and unassertive.	or	3. I do not approach and/or am not approached by men who expect a woman to be active and assertive.
4. I am confirmed in my belief that men prefer women who are passive and unassertive.	or	4. I do not have the opportunity to develop my own assertiveness.

Example 2: A Managerial Dilemma

1. As a manager, I believe that subordinates are basically lazy and dislike work.
2. I assume, therefore, that to get the most out of subordinates, I must watch over their every move.
3. I behave in a strict manner, delegating little responsibility, and demanding that everything be cleared through me first.
4. My subordinates react to this parentlike stance by acting like rebellious teenagers. I have to lean on them all the time or they'll never do what I tell them.
5. Consequently, my original belief is confirmed; subordinates are basically lazy and dislike work.

The underlying pattern in these processes is one of (1) assumption or belief, (2) leading to behavior that is congruent with the assumption, followed by (3) ob-

[4]There is a large number of relevant sources here, some of which are Mason Haire and W. F. Grunes, "Perceptual Defenses: Processes Protecting an Organized Perception of Another Personality," *Human Relations*, Vol. 3 (1950), pp. 403–412, and M. Rokeach, *The Open and Closed Mind* (New York: Basic Books, 1960).

[5]For two excellent collections of material relevant to this point, see Warren G. Bennis et al., *Interpersonal Dynamics*, rev. ed. (Homewood, IL: Dorsey Press, 1968), and R. Wylie, *The Self Concept* (Lincoln: University of Nebraska Press, 1965).

servation of consequences, which, to the extent that selective perception is occurring, leads to (4) confirmation of the original assumption or belief. Testing the validity or desirability of this conceptual pattern is difficult, for several reasons.

One important reason is that normal social interaction is basically conservative—social norms operate to preserve existing interaction patterns and perceptions. Sociologist Erving Goffman[6] has described the tendency of people to preserve the "face" that others present to them. When someone acts "out of character," social pressures are mobilized to force them back into their role. In social situations we tend to act in such a way that we maintain our own self-image and the self-image we see others presenting. We resist telling someone that they have egg on their chin because we assume that this is not part of the image they want to present and we do not want them to "lose face" and be embarrassed. This conservative interaction norm tends to decrease the accuracy of interpersonal perception by relinquishing opportunities to test the accuracy of our perceptions of ourselves and others. The norm dictates that we cannot frankly tell others our impressions of them if these impressions differ from the face they are presenting. It also acts as an obstacle to our testing with others whether or not we are projecting the kind of self-image we think we are. "Do you see me the way I see myself?" If someone presents himself or herself as a leader, it is hard to tell him or her that you do not feel like following. Thus, we are denied information about others' true thoughts and feelings by the face we present.

A theoretical conceptualization of this process can be depicted in the following manner, called the Johari window, named after Joe Luft and Harry Ingram, its creators.[7]

	KNOWN TO SELF	NOT KNOWN TO SELF
Known to Others	Arena	Blindspot
Not Known to Others	Facade	Unknown

Arena. This cell includes all the factors upon which I and others have mutually shared perceptions; that is, people see me the way I see myself (e.g., I feel confident and people see me as confident).

Unknown. In this cell are factors that I do not see in myself nor do others see in me.

Facade. In this cell are factors that I see in myself but that I hide from others (e.g., I feel insecure, but I strive to project the image of a very secure person); that is, people see a "false me," and I must always be on guard not to let them see the "real me."

Blindspot. In this cell are factors that other people perceive in me but that I do not see in myself (e.g., others see my anxiety reducing my effectiveness but I do not see—or will not admit to myself—that I am anxious); that is, people know certain things about me, but they don't tell me ("Even your best friends won't tell you").

To move from the facade to the arena requires a sufficient level of trust and psychological safety to enable me to share my self-perceptions with another. To move from the blindspot to the arena

---

[6]E. Goffman, "On Face Work: An Analysis of Ritual Elements in Social Interaction," *Psychiatry,* Vol. 18 (1955), pp. 213–231.

[7]Joseph Luft, "The Johari Window," *Human Relations and Training News* (January 1961), pp. 6–7.

requires that people give me feedback as to how they see me. The conditions of trust and psychological safety are again critical—so that people will risk telling me and so I will not react defensively to what they say. It is only as we move from the facade and blindspot into the arena that true sharing of perceptions and understanding between people can develop.

III

Procedure for Group Meeting: How I See Myself and Others

SELF-PERCEPTIONS: INDIVIDUAL WORK
(Time Allotted: 30 to 40 Minutes)

The first part of this unit is designed to help you sharpen your understanding of the image and perceptions you believe you communicate to others. During the second part, you will have the opportunity to explore how others believe they see you.

STEP 1.   As you think about the *image you have of yourself,* list, in the appropriate spaces provided,

    a. The first five or six words that come to your mind

    b. An animal

    c. A musical instrument

    d. A food

       It is important that you work quickly. Let your first thought be the one you record.

STEP 2.   The words you have just listed are, at best, simplified cues or indicators of important elements of how you see yourself—your self-image. It is your own interpretation of what these words mean to you that contributes to your self-image. In this step you are asked to (a) interpret the meaning of those words and (b) decide whether or not each element of your self-image (known to self) is a part of your arena or your facade. Use the space provided to record these points.

    a. Elements of my self-image that I believe are in my arena (i.e., known to me and known to others):

    b. Elements of my self-image that I believe are in my facade (i.e., known to me but not known to others):

STEP 3.   Each of us *behaves* in ways designed to allow various aspects of our self-image (known to self) to be known to others—an arena. Similarly, we behave in ways to keep various aspects of our self-image in our facade (not known to others).

a. In the space provided, jot down examples of how you communicate to others important elements of your arena. (For example, if you feel confident and believe people see you as confident, how do you behave to communicate confidence?)

b. In the space provided, jot down examples of how you behave to keep elements of your self-image (known to self) in the facade. (For example, if you feel insecure, but try to project an image of confidence, how do you behave to "cover" your feelings of insecurity?)

How I See Myself

5–6 Words	
Animal	
Musical instrument	
Food	

TESTING SELF-PERCEPTIONS: SMALL-GROUP SHARING
(Time Allotted: 60 to 90 minutes)

In this part of the unit, you will have the opportunity to get a glimpse of how others see you. This will be a real test of your interpersonal skills. Giving and receiving feedback in a productive manner is difficult but important.

STEP 1.   In your learning group, fill out the Perception Matrix form on page 197 for others in your group. It is important in filling out the Perception Matrix that you work quickly. Let your first thought be the one you record. It is helpful if there is no communication during this step.

STEP 2.   (Read this paragraph to yourself.) The sharing process you are about to begin may not be an easy task. As was pointed out in the Topic Introduction, normal social interaction is basically conservative—social norms operate to preserve existing interaction patterns and perceptions. During this sharing process, you are, in effect, being asked to operate with an atypical set of social norms to share and discuss your impressions of one another.

In the discussions you have, it is important to remember that there is no one reality or truth. You have perceptions of yourself. Others have perceptions of you. Some of these perceptions will be shared—held in common. Others will be different. The issue is *not* whose perception is right or whose is wrong.

If I have a perception of someone and they do not share that perception of themselves, this discrepancy can serve as an important learning opportunity for *both of us*.

a. If I am the one being perceived, I may learn something about my blindspot. I may learn about behavior that serves to move elements from my facade to my arena.

b. If I am the perceiver, I may learn something about the perceptual filters I use (e.g., I assume all big people are confident). I may learn that I tend to see in others elements of how I see myself.

All of us can learn something more about our own inevitably circular self-fulfilling perceptual processes. This awareness is only a first step. Whether or not a person chooses to alter these perceptual patterns is clearly a matter of individual choice.

STEP 3.   People should share the perceptions they have of each other as recorded on their Perception Matrix.

STEP 4.   Groups should now discuss their perceptions using the following suggestions to guide their discussions.

a. What can you infer about the concepts in your cognitive map (the concepts or categories you most often use in perceiving other people) from the words you listed for each person in your group?

(1) Did you list mostly adjectives (which tend to be evaluative or difference oriented, e.g., good versus bad, big versus small) or nouns (which tend to be neutral or nondifference oriented, e.g., man, student) or verbs (which are behavior oriented as opposed to trait or characteristic oriented)?

(2) Did your lists of words differ for each person or did your lists reflect similar concepts for each person? What does this tell you about the breadth versus narrowness of your conceptual system; the degree to which the major concepts in your system are separate or highly interconnected?

b. Was your perception of some people generally closer to the ways they saw themselves than was true of your perception of other people? To what do you attribute any differences? Do some people project clearer self-images? Length of time or context within which you knew the person? Similarity to yourself?

c. Where two or more people saw the same person in substantially different ways, they should try to understand how these differences arise.

d. Based on the individual work you did in the beginning of this unit, some of you may have found

    (1) Elements that you thought were in your open arena were not known to others (i.e., they were in your facade).

    (2) Elements that you thought were in your facade were known to others (i.e., they are in your arena).

    (3) New perceptions in your blindspot.

In exploring these "surprises," it is most important that you listen to and understand others' descriptions of how you behave, which leads them to form the impressions they have.

e. It is very likely that you will uncover some typical circular perceptual processes such as those discussed in the Topic Introduction. The group may want to outline a few of their own such processes.

    (1) What does a person gain or achieve through the pattern?

    (2) What costs are incurred or opportunities forgone by maintaining the pattern?

    (3) What steps could be taken to change the nature of these circular patterns?

f. Finally, each of you chose, on some basis, to join this particular small group. What, if anything, have you learned during this exercise that might help to explain that choice process and its consequences?

g. What connections can you make between this exercise and the readings?

Perception Matrix
Own Perceptions

CATEGORY / MEMBER	HOW YOU SEE YOUR-SELF*	HOW YOU SEE A	HOW YOU SEE B	HOW YOU SEE C	HOW YOU SEE D
5–6 Words					
Animal					
Musical Instrument					
Food					

*These are the self-perceptions you recorded in step 1 of your individual work.

Perception Matrix
Others' Perceptions [*]

CATEGORY \ MEMBER	HOW I AM SEEN BY			
	A	B	C	D
5–6 Words				
Animal				
Musical Instrument				
Food				

[*]You may wish to use this space to record others' perceptions of yourself or themselves as people begin to share their matrices in the second part of this unit.

IV

Follow-up

It is as difficult for humans to understand the impact of their own conceptual system as it is for a fish to understand the concept of water. Yet our conceptual maps and the fish's water are equally important for survival. Without a conceptual system to simplify and order our experiences, we would become overwhelmed, helpless victims of our environment. Yet failure to recognize that our perceptions are to some extent our own creation can leave one closed, defensive, and unable to profit from new experiences. In the following analysis by an engineer of his reactions to the perception unit, we see one individual's struggle to understand his own way of perceiving others.

Again it seems I am going to write a paper about myself rather than the suggested topic. Whenever I reflect on the subject matter we study, I can directly relate it to myself. I have always considered myself "free of hang-ups"; however, there are many things I do that I do not completely understand. Previously I have never taken the time to question myself, but now, being forced to think about a concept, I can see how I have been influenced by that concept and can attempt to explain, but not always justify, the way I feel toward many things. Well, here goes!

I am the perfect example of a person blinded by his own perception of the world. Not all of the time, mind you, but mainly in one case—the case being when I become "snowed" by a girl. I'll begin by relating my current project in this area—at least I think the project is current, although I'm not sure as of this moment because of a possible misperception on my part. Being alone in a new city, I engaged in the well-known game of mixer this autumn in the hope of meeting someone interesting. I accomplished my goal without any difficulties, and here is where my problem began—I committed my unpardonable sin of becoming snowed.

I do not have many difficulties with first perceptions. I think I am pretty objective and usually make good judgments. First impressions are almost solely objective! As long as I do not become emotionally involved, that is, as long as there is no filter between what I see and how I perceive what I have seen, I am quite able to understand what is communicated. However, once I am personally involved with the reason behind the attempted communication, my vision of what is actually happening is, I believe, distorted.

This weekend, for example, I did not take Mary [a fictitious name] out because of our last date and a phone call I made after the date. Even though I wanted to take her out, I didn't; consequently, I have been asking myself all weekend what motivated me not to ask her out; and I do not have a specific answer—but I know it stems from how I perceived how she feels. However, this is what I think she feels, which just might not be what she does feel, and I do not let myself comprehend that there may be a difference between these two versions of the same feelings. I guess I feel that my logical reasoning of what a particular look or remark means necessarily is the correct idea. I completely leave out the possibility that everyone does not (thankfully) think about everything the same way I do.

Zalkind and Costello, in their article on perception, give five reasons of how a person misperceives.[8] These are

1. You are influenced by cues below your own threshold (i.e., the cues you don't know you perceived).
2. You respond to irrelevant cues to arrive at a judgment.
3. You are influenced by emotional factors (i.e., what is liked is perceived as correct).
4. You weigh perceptual evidence heavily if it comes from a respectable source.
5. You are not able to identify all factors (i.e., not realizing how much weight is given to a single item).

I feel I am guilty, if one can be "guilty," of most of the mentioned means of misperception. However, I feel that rather than imposing a perceptual defense upon myself, I project a perceptual offense, and this greatly compounds my misperception. Rather than looking for favorable acts of communication and not allowing unfavorable perceptions, I am forever (when I become emotionally involved with a girl) on the lookout for any signs of displeasure. And at the slightest hint, my mind begins to work on such questions as "What if that means . . . ?"

For example, to the question, "Did you have a good time?" I got the reply, "Yeah, I guess so." This was not perceived favorably. My perceptual offense was quickly in play and I have since been analyzing that statement. I don't know Mary well enough to say what anything she says really means, but because I was afraid the reply meant "I had a bad time," that is what I have convinced myself that she meant (although nothing else that was said even hinted at that idea; and to the friend who doubled with me, the opposite was obviously true). I didn't ask her out this weekend for reasons mainly based on this one perception of how she feels about dating me. Looking back on my action, I see I have committed three of the Zalkind-Costello means of misperception.

■ no. 2—I may have responded to an irrelevant cue—her remark probably just came out and didn't really have any deep meaning behind it.
■ no. 3—I was influenced by a (negative) emotional factor—I am so worried that she was not enjoying herself, with the repercussions that would have to my emotional happiness, that my perception might have been distorted.
■ no. 5—I did not realize how heavily I weighted this single cue.

Being apprehensive of how she felt, I ended up analyzing every little remark made. I did not take time to think that my ways of comprehending a perception may be inaccurate—the thought never seems to enter my mind. The handout on perception states, "These defenses act like a screen or filter . . . blocking out that which we don't want to see and letting through that which we wish to see." I, however, feel that I block out that which I want to see and let in that which I don't want to see. This is a definite problem, but one that I never thought of before. And to compound matters, the perceptions I let in are my

<hr/>

[8]Sheldon Zalkind and Timothy Costello, "Perception: Implications for Administration," *Readings*, pp. 211–222.

own personal version of what is perceived and may be the opposite of what is being communicated.

I do not have this problem until I begin to like a girl. Trained as an engineer, I think I am able to cope with objective matters; but when I try to understand another person, I seem to fail—especially when there are present emotional filters through which my perceptions are received. To take a statement *out* of context, Zalkind and Costello say, "A little learning encourages the perceiver to respond with increased sensitivity to individual differences without making it possible for him to gauge the real meaning of what he has seen." Well, I have had only a little learning about perception, and their statement applies to me perfectly. I try to play psychologist without knowing the first thing about what I am looking for. This is a habit I have gotten myself addicted to, and one I will have to break down in order to have a better understanding of the people around me. Right now the unknown (i.e., the human unknown—what people are thinking) confronts me and I am frustrated by it. In response to this frustration, I set up a perceptual defense (I guess my perceptual offense is nothing but a type of perceptual defense—there is an old football theory that the best offense is a good defense, which only adds to my frustration). Thus, to move from the unknown to perceptual understanding, I must first realize that I am reacting defensively to what is being communicated to me.

It seems I am now coming back to what seems to be a familiar theme in all the topics we have covered so far. Zalkind and Costello say, "The person who accepts himself is more likely to be able to see favorable aspects of other people." I feel this is especially true of myself. If I stop and realize that my date is probably thinking of the same things that I am (at the initial stages of human relations, most of the time is spent in the unconscious, hidden, and blind areas of perception), then I may prevent my perceptual defense from operating at the level it is now operating. If I continually look at weak points, and never strong points, and do not realize that I am doing such, I am not really aware of myself and therefore not aware of how others perceive me.

I feel I can improve myself in a number of ways. First, I must accept my own feelings and not worry or analyze them. As is stated in the pamphlet, "Each of us has both his tender and tough emotions." Second, I should stop analyzing everything logically—it's hard for me to accept the fact that all of my world is not logical. Third, I should experiment more in the giving and receiving of perceptual feedback. I spend too much time analyzing a date's behavior and not enough giving her feedback, thus blocking the understanding between us. Finally, the fourth area of improvement, and the factor that this paper has led me to explore, is increasing my own awareness and understanding of the causes of emotion. These steps of improvement exactly parallel those given in the pamphlet on how to use our emotional resources effectively. I hope I can put them to use and, once they are in use, build on them.

V
Learning Points

1. Perception is the process by which we read meaning into the stimuli that bombard us.

2. Perception is a common barrier to effective communication because each individual interprets communications differently.

3. Selective exposure, selective attention, distrusted source, and erroneous translation are aspects of perceptual processes that are barriers to communication.

4. The drawbacks to perception are that it prevents us from taking in everything we should, makes our interpretations open to question, and promotes stereotypes.

5. On the positive side, the process of perception organizes stimuli that would otherwise overwhelm us.

6. We organize the world according to constructs or categories, which are then grouped into conceptual systems.

VI
Tips for Managers

■ The most important lesson to be learned from perception is that no one's perceptions are ever totally accurate. Arguing about what different people really saw or heard is often futile. For this reason, it's best to take a provisional approach that allows for different perceptions:

Not: "I know I'm right; I heard him with my own ears!"

But: "I thought he said that, but perhaps I'm mistaken."

Not: "I'm positive the staff decided to approve my budget just as it is."

But: "Well, if we have different perceptions about the outcome of the decision, we'd better check it out with the rest of the staff. We both may have heard only what we wanted to hear."

■ Rephrase what is said to you so you're sure you really understand the message.

■ When people give you feedback, remember that their view of you may be distorted by their perceptions. It's a good idea to check feedback out with more than one person to make sure it is accurate.

■ Once again, knowing yourself is useful in managing perceptions. If you suspect you have a bias in regards to certain people or issues, you can make a special effort to use active listening and keep your mind from leaping to conclusions and/or check out your perceptions with an objective person.

■ Trying to put yourself in the other person's shoes—empathizing with them—prevents distortion and improves communication.

■ The more managers disclose their own feelings, opinions, and difficulties to others, the more likely that employees will reciprocate and share the same type of information. This is another instance where managers have to model the behavior they want from employees.

■ Self-disclosure is like a bell curve. Too much disclosure scares people off and makes them nervous. Too little disclosure doesn't give others enough information about the person to form a relationship with him or her.

VII

Personal Application Assignment

The topic of this assignment is to write about an experience that involved perceptions or misperceptions. Choose an experience that was significant to you and one about which you are motivated to learn more.

A. *Concrete Experience*

    1. *Objectively* describe the experience ("who," "what," "when," "where," "how" type information—up to 2 points).

    2. *Subjectively* describe your feelings, perceptions, and thoughts that occurred *during* (not after) the experience (up to 2 points). Does this section have too much detail? (If so, delete 1 point.)

B. *Reflective Observation*

    1. Look at the experience from different points of view. How many points of view did you include that are *relevant* (up to 2 points)?

    2. Use these perspectives to add more meaning to the incident (up to 2 points).

C. *Abstract Conceptualization*
   1. Relate concepts from the assigned readings and the lecture to the experience (i.e., what theories that you heard in the lecture or read in the *Reader* relate to your understanding of this incident?). Make reference to at least two sources. Use standard referencing format and include the page number to which you are referring. How many sources did you use and how clearly did you explain their theories (up to 4 points)?
   2. You can also create an original model or theory, but it should not replace course concepts.

D. *Active Experimentation*
   1. Write about what you will do in the future that will improve your effectiveness. Use rules of thumb or action resolutions.
   2. Are they described specifically, thoroughly, and in detail (up to 4 points)?

E. *Integration, Synthesis, and Writing*
   1. Did you write about something personally important to you (up to 1 point)?
   2. Was it well written (up to 2 points)?
   3. Did you integrate and synthesize the different sections (up to 1 point)?

8

GROUP DYNAMICS

A Fair Day's Work

R. H. Richard and G. Ray Funkhouser

For 18 years Ginny had been doing about the same thing: packing expandrium fittings for shipment. She was so well practiced that she could do the job perfectly without paying the slightest attention. This, of course, left her free to socialize and observe the life of the company around her. Today Ginny was breaking in a new packer:

"No, not that way. Look, Jim, if you hold it that way, well, then you have to twist your arm when you pack this corner, see. This way it's easier."

"But that's the way Mr. Wolfe [the methods engineer] said we had to do it."

"Sure he did, Jim. But he's never had to do it eight hours a day like me. You just pay attention to what I say."

"But what if he comes around and says I should pack the other way?"

"Oh, that's easy. When he's here you do it his way. Anyway, after a couple weeks you won't see him again. Slow down. You'll wear yourself out. No one's going to expect you to do eighty pieces for a week anyway."

"But Mr. Wolfe said ninety."

"Sure, he did. Let him do it. Look, here's how to pace yourself. It's the way I was taught, and it works. You know the 'Battle Hymn of the Republic'?" Ginny hummed a few bars. "Well, you just work to that, hum it to yourself, use the way I showed you, and you'll be doing eighty next week."

"But what if they make me do ninety?"

"They can't. Y'know, you start making mistakes when you go that fast. No, eighty is right. I always say, 'A fair day's work for a fair day's pay.'"

Reprinted and adapted with permission from *The Ropes to Skip and the Ropes to Know* by R. H. Richard and G. Ray Funkhouser (New York: John Wiley, 1982), p. 189.

I
Premeeting Preparation

A. Read "Eighty Pieces Is Fair."

B. Then read the Topic Introduction.

C. Third, do the following:

    1. Focus on an effective group to which you belong (or belonged).

        a. List the norms (unwritten rules of conduct) of this group.

        b. How do you think that group developed those norms?

    2. Now think about a poorly functioning group to which you belong(ed).

        a. List its norms.

        b. How do you think they developed?

    3. How would you go about changing the norms in a poorly functioning group?

    4. What are the norms in your learning group or class? How do they hinder or promote learning?

    5. What are the significant learning points from the readings?

II

Topic Introduction

"A camel is a horse put together by a committee." "Groupthink." These two cliches are often applied to group decision making. Most people believe that working in groups is inevitably less efficient, more time consuming, and very frustrating and that it creates conformity in thinking. Many of these deeply held beliefs are simply unsubstantiated or found to be less generally true than was originally believed. Stoner's work,[1] for example, on the riskiness of group versus individual decisions is a case in point. It is clear that, contrary to popular belief, under certain conditions groups make more *risky* decisions than do individuals.[2]

All of us have participated in groups of various sorts, family, gang, team, work group, and the like, but rarely have we taken the time to observe what was going on in the group or why the members were behaving in the way they were.[3] In thinking about groups, few people realize that in any group there are at least two classes of issues operating at any given point. One is the reason for the group's existence in the first place (e.g., to solve a particular problem). These are called *content* or *task issues*. A second, and equally important, set of issues concerns elements of how the group is going about achieving its formal task. These are called *process issues*.[4]

CONTENT VERSUS PROCESS

When we observe *what* a group is talking about, we are focusing on the *content*. When we try to observe *how* the group is handling its communication (i.e., who talks how much or who talks to whom), we are focusing on group *process*. The content of the conversation is often a good clue as to what process issue may be on people's minds when they find it difficult to confront the issue directly. It often seems that groups spend considerable time talking about things that, on the surface, have nothing to do with the task at hand. Discussing the worthlessness of their previous PTA meetings may mean that members are not satisfied with the performance of their present group. The assumption is that it is less threatening to talk about how we feel about PTA meetings (there-and-then) than it is to talk about our feelings about these (here-and-now) meetings.

COMMUNICATION

One of the easiest aspects of group process to observe is the pattern of communication:

---

[1]James A. F. Stoner, "Risky and Cautious Shifts in Group Decisions: The Influence of Widely Held Values," *Journal of Experimental Social Psychology,* no. 4 (1968), pp. 442–459.

[2]Roger Brown, "Group Polarization," in *Social Psychology,* 2nd ed. (New York: Free Press, 1986).

[3]The literature on group dynamics has grown to enormous proportions. See D. Cartwright and A. Zander, eds., *Group Dynamics: Research and Theory,* 3rd ed. (New York: Harper & Row, 1968); B. E. Collins and H. Guetzkow, *A Social Psychology of Group Processes for Decision Making* (New York: John Wiley, 1964); Linda N. Jewell and H. Joseph Reitz, *Group Effectiveness in Organizations* (Glenview, IL: Scott, Foresman, 1981); and Alvin Zander, *Groups at Work* (San Francisco; Jossey-Bass, 1977).

[4]For a discussion of the differences between content and process issues, see Edgar H. Schein, *Process Consultation: Its Role in Organizational Development* (Reading, MA: Addison-Wesley, 1969).

1. Who talks? for how long? how often?
2. Whom do people look at when they talk?
   a. Individuals, possibly potential supporters
   b. The group
   c. Nobody
3. Who talks after whom, or who interrupts whom?
4. What style of communication is used (assertions, questions, tone of voice, gesture, etc.)?

The kind of observations we make gives us clues to other important things that may be going on in the group, such as who leads whom and who influences whom.

DECISION-MAKING PROCEDURES[5]

Whether we are aware of it or not, groups are making decisions all the time, some of them consciously and in reference to the major tasks at hand, some of them without much awareness and in reference to group procedures or standards of operation. It is important to observe how decisions are made in a group, to assess the appropriateness of the decision to the matter being decided on, and to assess whether the consequences of given methods are really what the group members bargained for.

Group decisions are notoriously hard to undo.[6] When someone says, "Well, we decided to do it, didn't we?" any budding opposition is quickly immobilized. We can undo the decision only if we reconstruct and understand how we made it and test whether this method was appropriate or not.

Some methods by which groups make decisions are the following:[7]

1. The *plop:* "I think we should appoint a chairperson." . . . Silence.
2. The *self-authorized agenda:* "I think we should introduce ourselves. My name is Jane Allen . . . ".
3. The *handclasp:* Person A: "I wonder if it would be helpful to introduce ourselves?" Person B: "I think it would; my name is Pete Jones."
4. The *minority decision:* "Does anyone object?" or "We all agree, don't we?" Agreement or consensus may not be present but it's difficult for others to object sometimes.
5. *Majority-minority voting:* "Let's vote and whoever has the most votes wins."
6. *Polling:* "Let's see where everyone stands. What do you think?"
7. *Consensus seeking:* Genuine exploration to test for opposition and to determine whether opposition feels strongly enough to refuse to implement decision; not necessarily unanimity but essential agreement by all. Consensus does *not* involve pseudo-"listening" ("Let's hear Joe out") and then doing what you were going to do in the first place ("OK, now that everyone has had a chance to talk, let's go ahead with the original decision").

[5]Much of the following material has appeared in a variety of places and is a standard input into many training programs such as those conducted by the National Training Laboratory. This particular material was abridged with permission of the author from "What to Observe in Groups," from *Reading Book for Relations Training,* C. R. Mill and L. C. Porter, eds. (Arlington, VA: NTL Institute, 1982), pp. 28–30. The Collins and Guetzkow book, *A Social Psychology of Group Processes for Decision Making,* is also very relevant here.

[6]Literature on group conformity is relevant to this point. For a summary, see E. L. Walker and R. W. Heyns, *An Anatomy for Conformity* (Englewood Cliffs, NJ: Prentice Hall, 1962).

[7]This typology was developed by Robert R. Blake.

TASK, MAINTENANCE, AND SELF-ORIENTED BEHAVIOR[8]

Behavior in the group can be viewed in terms of what its purpose or function seems to be. When a member says something, is the intent primarily to get the group task accomplished (task) or to improve or patch up some relationship among members (maintenance), or is the behavior primarily meeting a personal need or goal without regard to the group's problems (self-oriented)?

As the group grows and members' needs become integrated with group goals, there will be less self-oriented behavior and more task or maintenance behavior. Types of behavior relevant to the group's fulfillment of its *task* are the following:

1. *Initiating.* For any group to function, some person(s) must be willing to take some initiative. These can be seemingly trivial statements such as "Let's build an agenda" or "It's time we moved on to the next item," but without them, little task-related activity would occur in a group. People would either sit in silence and/or side conversations would develop.

2, 3. *Seeking or giving information or opinions.* The clear and efficient flow of information, facts, and opinions is essential to any task accomplishment. Giving-type statements—"I have some information that may be relevant" or "My own opinion in this matter is . . . "—are important to ensure decisions based on full information. Information-seeking statements not only help the seeker but the entire group.

4. *Clarifying and elaborating.* Many useful inputs into group work get lost if this task-related behavior is missing. "Let me give an example that will clarify the point just made" and "Let me elaborate and build upon that idea" are examples of positive behaviors in this regard. They communicate a listening and collaborative stance.

5. *Summarizing.* At various points during a group's work, it is very helpful if someone takes a moment to summarize the group's discussion. This gives the entire group an opportunity to pause for a moment, step back, see how far they have come, where they are, and how much farther they must go to complete their work.

[8]K. D. Benne and P. Sheats, "Functional Roles of Group Members," *Journal of Social Issues,* Vol. 2 (1948), pp. 42–47, and Edgar H. Schein, *Process Consultation.*

6. *Consensus testing.* Many times a group's work must result in a consensus decision.[9] At various points in the meeting, the statement "Have we made a decision on that point?" can be very helpful. Even if the group is not yet ready to commit itself to a decision, it serves to remind everyone that a decision needs to be made and, as such, it adds positive work tension into the group.

7. *Reality testing.* Groups can take off on a tangent that is very useful when creativity is desired. However there are times when it is important to analyze ideas critically and see whether they will hold up when compared to facts or reality. This helps the group get back on track.

8. *Orienting.* Another way of getting a group back on track is through orienting behavior that helps the group to define its position with respect to goals and points of departure from agreed-upon directions. When questions are raised about the direction the group is pursuing, everyone is reminded of the group goal and has an opportunity to reevaluate and/or recommit to meeting it.

Following are types of behavior relevant to the group's remaining in good working order, with a good climate for task work and good relationships that permit maximum use of member resources, namely, *group maintenance:*

1. *Gatekeeping.* Gatekeeping, directing the flow of conversation like a traffic cop, is an essential maintenance function in a group. Without it, information gets lost, multiple conversations develop, and less assertive people get cut off and drop out of the meeting. "Let's give Joe a chance to finish his thought" and "If people would talk one at a time, I'd find it easier to listen and add to our discussion" are examples in this regard.

2. *Encouraging.* Encouraging also ensures that all the potentially relevant information the group needs is shared, listened to, and considered. "I know you haven't had a chance to work it through in your mind, but keep thinking out loud and we'll try to help." "Before we close this off, Mary, do you have anything to add?"

3. *Harmonizing and compromising.* These two functions are very important but tricky because their overuse or inappropriate use can serve to reduce a group's effectiveness. If smoothing over issues (harmonizing) and each party's giving in a bit (compromise) serve to mask important underlying issues, creative solutions to problems will be fewer in number and commitment to decisions taken will be reduced.

4. *Standard setting and testing.* This category of behavior acts as a kind of overall maintenance function. Its focus is how well the group's needs for task-oriented behavior and maintenance-oriented behaviors are being met. All groups will reach a point where "something is going wrong" or "something doesn't feel right." At such points, effective groups stop the music, test their own process, and set new standards where they are required. "I'm losing track of the conversation. If other people are willing, maybe it would help if someone could summarize the last 10 minutes."

5. *Using humor.* The use of humor to put people at ease and reduce tension is an important maintenance function. However, the inappropriate use of humor can prevent groups from reaching their goals quickly and stop them from tackling uncomfortable issues that need to be resolved.

[9]Not all decisions can/should be made by group consensus. For more details on this issue, see Chapter 13, Leadership and Decision Making, and Victor H. Vroom and P. Yetton, *Leadership and Decision Making* (Pittsburgh, PA: University of Pittsburgh Press, 1973).

For a group to be effective, both task-oriented behavior and maintenance-oriented behavior are needed.

EMOTIONAL ISSUES: CAUSES OF SELF-ORIENTED EMOTIONAL BEHAVIOR[10]

The process described so far deals with the group's attempt to work and the work-facilitating functions of task and maintenance. But there are many forces active in groups that disturb work, that represent a kind of emotional underground or undercurrent in the stream of group life. These underlying emotional issues produce a variety of self-oriented behaviors that interfere with or are destructive to effective group functioning. They cannot be ignored or wished away, however. Rather, they must be recognized, their causes must be understood, and as the group develops, conditions must be created that permit these same emotional energies to be channeled in the direction of group effort. What are these issues or basic causes?

1. The problem of identity: Who am I here? How am I to present myself to others? What role should I play in the group?
2. The problem of control and power: Who has the power in the situation? How much power, control, and influence do I have in the situation? How much do I need?
3. The problem of goals: Which of my needs and goals can this group fulfill? Can any of my needs be met here? To which of the group's goals can I attach myself?
4. The problem of acceptance and intimacy: Am I accepted by the others? Do I accept them? Do they like me? Do I like them? How close to others do I want to become?

Self-oriented behaviors tend to be more prevalent in a group at certain points in the group's life. Early in the life of a new group one can expect to see many examples of self-oriented behaviors. Members are new to one another and a certain amount of "feeling out" is to be expected. Sometimes this takes place in after-hours social situations—"Why don't we get together after work for a drink?" On a less intense scale, the same phenomenon can be observed at the start of a group meeting with an old, established group. Side conversations and social chatter characterize the first few minutes while people catch up on where they have been since the last meeting.

A third point in a group's life when self-oriented behaviors can be observed is when a newcomer joins an already established group. It is not unlike the dynamics that develop when a new sibling arrives in a family. Everyone else may be sincerely happy with the newcomer ("We really need her resources"); nonetheless, this is now a "new" group. The old equilibrium has been changed and a new one must take its place.

None of the foregoing sounds particularly like an undercurrent, an emotional underground, that could be potentially destructive to effective group functioning. While all these issues can be observed in a group, their potential destructiveness is highest at that time when the group most needs to be maximally effective—under stress. In that sense, they are akin to regressive individual behaviors: in times of stress, individuals will regress to an earlier stage of development. Different individuals handle their anxiety in different ways, thus generating many different kinds of reactions in groups.

---

[10]This section is based on Schein's *Process Consultation.*

Following are types of emotional behavior that result from tension and from the attempt to resolve underlying problems:[11]

1. Tough emotions: anger, hostility, self-assertiveness
   a. Fighting with others
   b. Punishing others
   c. Controlling others
   d. Counterdependency
2. Tender emotions: love, sympathy, desire to help, need for affiliation with others
   a. Supporting and helping others
   b. Depending on others
   c. Pairing up or affiliating with others
3. Denial of all emotion
   a. Withdrawing from others
   b. Falling back on logic or reason

Individuals have different styles of reducing tension and expressing emotion. Three "pure types" have been identified:

1. The "friendly helper" orientation: acceptance of tender emotions, denial of tough emotions—"Let's not fight, let's help each other"; can give and receive affection but cannot tolerate hostility and fight.
2. The "tough battler" orientation: acceptance of tough emotions and denial of tender emotions—"Let's fight it out"; can deal with hostility but not with love, support, and affiliation.
3. The "logical thinker" orientation: denial of all emotion—"Let's reason this thing out"; cannot deal with tender or tough emotions; hence shuts eyes and ears to much going on around him.

But: Friendly helpers will achieve their world of warmth and intimacy *only* by allowing conflicts and differences to be raised and resolved. They find that they can become close with people *only* if they can accept what is dissimilar as well as what is similar in their behavior.

Tough battlers will achieve their world of toughness and conflict *only* if they can create a climate of warmth and trust in which these will be allowed to develop.

Logical thinkers will achieve their world of understanding and logic *only* if they can accept that their feelings and the feelings of others (both tough and tender) are also facts and contribute importantly toward our ability to understand interpersonal situations (see Table 8–1).

These three, as described, are clearly pure types; the average person has some elements of each. What varies is emphasis or the most characteristic style. The three styles can be depicted as corners of an equilateral triangle:

11 For another view of emotional behavior in groups, see William C. Schutz, "Interpersonal Underworld," *Harvard Business Review,* Vol. 36, no. 4 (July–August 1958), pp. 123–125, and W. W. Liddell and J. W. Slocum, Jr., "The Effects of Individual Role Compatibility upon Group Performance: An Extension of Schutz's FIRO Theory," *Academy of Management Journal,* Vol. 19 (1976), pp. 413–426.

TABLE 8–1   Three Bests of All Possible Worlds

1. FRIENDLY HELPER	2. TOUGH BATTLER	3. LOGICAL THINKER
A world of mutual love, affection, tenderness, sympathy	A world of conflict, fight, power, assertiveness	A world of understanding, logic, systems, knowledge
Task-Maintenance Behavior		
Harmonizing Compromising Gatekeeping by concern Encouraging Expressing warmth	Initiating Coordinating Pressing for results Pressing for consensus Exploring differences Gatekeeping by command	Gathering information Clarifying ideas and words Systematizing Procedures Evaluating the logic of proposals
Constructs Used in Evaluating Others		
Who is warm and who is hostile? Who helps and who hurts others?	Who is strong and who is weak? Who is winning and who is losing?	Who is bright and who is stupid? Who is accurate and who is inaccurate? Who thinks clearly and who is fuzzy?
Methods of Influence		
Appeasing Appealing to pity	Giving orders Offering challenges Threatening	Appealing to rules and regulations Appealing to logic Referring to "facts" and overwhelming knowledge
Personal Threats		
That he or she will not be loved That he or she will be overwhelmed by feelings of hostility	That he or she will lose his or her ability to fight (power) That he or she will become "soft" and "sentimental"	That his or her world is not ordered That he or she will be overwhelmed by love or hate

We can learn to use emotional resources more appropriately by

a. Acceptance of our own feelings and awareness that each of us has both tender and tough emotions.

b. Understanding group behavior at the feeling level as well as at the logical level, since feelings are also part of the group's reality.

c. Increasing our awareness through experimentation and feedback of the consequences of expressing emotions and when it is appropriate to do so.

d. Increasing our awareness through observation and analysis of the causes of emotions. By learning to recognize which events in the here-and-now trigger emotions, we can gain better control of ourselves in a given situation and behave more appropriately.

GROUP NORMS

Another issue that must be addressed with respect to group functioning is group norms. A norm in a group is like an individual habit. It is an unwritten, often implicit, rule that defines what attitudes and behaviors characterize a "good" group member versus a "bad" group member. For example, in the opening vignette, "A Fair Day's Work," Ginny made sure Jim the newcomer learned the rules—that doing 80 pieces was good. Doing 90 would be bad because then the boss might pressure everyone to maintain that rate. Ginny was socializing Jim, teaching him the ropes. By doing so, she pointed out the difference between formal rules—those set by bosses and that may or may not be obeyed—and informal rules—norms that employees enforce among themselves. If a member does not comply with important group norms, the other members will pressure him or her to do so. If he or she still does not comply, the rest of the group may well ostracize the offending group member. If Jim, the newcomer, were to insist on making 90 pieces, he would soon be labeled a rate-buster and effectively ignored in the factory cafeteria.

All groups create norms as they develop and mature. In and of themselves, norms are neither good nor bad. The important point is whether or not the norms that do exist support the group's work or act to reduce effectiveness.

Let's take a real-world example. The president of a multimillion-dollar multinational corporation wanted to make a major change in the way he and his three vice presidents functioned. The general pattern of behavior was such that each vice president would argue for decisions that would benefit their particular department. Turf battles and tunnel vision were standard fare during group meetings.

It was the president's desire to create what he called "the Office of the Presidency." When he and his VPs met, he wanted everyone to look at the issues before them from an executive perspective. In other words, he wanted everyone to focus on the corporation as a whole, looking at decisions through the "eyes" of a president.

Clearly a host of group norms would have to change dramatically. Historically, no meeting ever began until the president arrived. After all, it was "his meeting." If the new philosophy was to be taken seriously, the "Office of the Presidency" had to function *irrespective* of who—as an individual—was present or absent.

One Monday morning the three VPs arrived for their normally scheduled meeting. But one "small" problem had arisen: a devastating weekend snowstorm caused the president to be stranded 1,000 miles away. Still, several critical topics were on the agenda.

After considerable anxious grasping for solutions (conference calls, private jets, and even prayer) and much nervous laughter, they bit the bullet. The "Office of the Presidency" was called to order. An old norm had been changed.

The pinch point occurred Tuesday morning at 8:00 A.M., only now it was the president who felt the anxiety. To his credit, he asked to be *informed* as to the decisions taken by the Office of the Presidency in his absence. Any other behavior on his part, such as reopening decisions he personally did not like, would have violated, and made a game of, the new normative expectations.

Many groups operate under the norm: "In this group, no one ever dares to question or suggest that we examine our norms." With respect to the maintenance behaviors discussed earlier, there is an absence of standard setting and testing and an implied punishment for anyone who engages in such behavior. Such a "Catch 22" norm is unlikely to facilitate the development of an effectively functioning group.

III

Procedure for Group Meeting: Lost at Sea

LOST AT SEA EXERCISE[12]
(Time Allotted: 1 Hour)

The purpose of the following exercise is to sharpen skills both in observing how a group goes about solving a task (diagnosing process) and in participating in the task. An effective group member is one who can function well at both of these levels—this person is a *participant-observer*.

STEP 1.   Turn to the Lost at Sea Individual Worksheet on page 221 and read the instructions. Without consultation or discussion, please rank the 15 items. (10 minutes)

STEP 2.   Now turn to the Lost at Sea Group Worksheet on page 223 and read the instructions. As a group, rank the 15 items, but do not change your individual rankings.

STEP 3.   Your instructor will give you the experts' rankings and the rationale behind them.

STEP 4.   Transfer your individual and group rankings to the Lost at Sea Scoresheet, page 235, and follow the scoring instructions found there.

DISCUSSION OF LOST AT SEA SIMULATION
(Time Allotted: 40–60 Minutes)

1. What behaviors helped or hindered the consensus-seeking process?
2. What patterns of decision making occurred?
3. Who were the influential members and how were they influential?
4. How did the group discover and use its information resources? Were these resources fully utilized?
5. What are the implications of consensus-seeking and synergistic outcomes for intact task groups such as committees and staffs of organizations?
6. What connections can you make between this exercise and the readings?

PARTICIPANT OBSERVATION IN GROUPS

STEP 1.   Each individual should fill out the Group Behavior Rating Form on page 225 based on the behavior they observed during the simulation.

[12]This exercise was developed by Paul M. Nemiroff and William A. Pasmore.
Source: P. M. Nemiroff and W. A. Pasmore, "LOST AT SEA: A Consensus Seeking Task" in J. W. Pfeiffer and J. E. Jones (Eds.), *The 1975 Annual Handbook for Group Facilitators*, San Diego, CA: University Associates, Inc., 1975. Used with permission.

STEP 2. The groups should then discuss the following questions:

    a. What task-oriented, maintenance-oriented behaviors seemed most frequently used? Least frequently used?

    b. In what ways, if any, did the group's work suffer because certain task/maintenance functions were underutilized?

    c. How did "friendly helpers," "tough battlers," and "logical thinkers" interact with and influence each other? What impact did these styles have on group functioning?

Lost at Sea Individual Worksheet

Name _____

Group _____

You are adrift on a private yacht in the South Pacific. As a consequence of a fire of unknown origin, much of the yacht and its contents have been destroyed. The yacht is now sinking slowly. Your location is unclear because of the destruction of critical navigational equipment and because you and the crew were distracted trying to bring the fire under control. Your best estimate is that you are approximately 1,000 miles south-southwest of the nearest land.

The following is a list of 15 items that are intact and undamaged after the fire. In addition to these articles, you have a serviceable, rubber life raft with oars large enough to carry yourself, the crew, and all the items listed below. The total contents of all survivors' pockets are a package of cigarettes, several books of matches, and five one-dollar bills.

Your task is to rank the 15 items that follow in terms of their importance to your survival. Place the number 1 by the most important item, the number 2 by the second most important, and so on through number 15, the least important.

_____ Sextant

_____ Shaving mirror

_____ Five-gallon can of water

_____ Mosquito netting

_____ One case of U.S. Army C rations

_____ Maps of the Pacific Ocean

_____ Seat cushion (flotation device approved by the Coast Guard)

_____ Two-gallon can of oil-gas mixture

_____ Small transistor radio

_____ Shark repellent

_____ Twenty square feet of opaque plastic

_____ One quart of 160-proof Puerto Rican rum

_____ Fifteen feet of nylon rope

_____ Two boxes of chocolate bars

_____ Fishing kit

Lost at Sea Group Worksheet

Group _____

This is an exercise in group decision making. Your group is to employ the group consensus method in reaching its decision. This means that the prediction for each of the 15 survival items must *be agreed upon by each group member before it becomes a part of the group decision. Consensus is difficult to reach. Therefore, not every ranking will meet with everyone's complete approval. As a group, try to make each ranking one with which all group members can at least partially agree. Here are some guides to use in reaching consensus.*

1. Avoid arguing for your own individual judgments. Approach the task on the basis of logic.
2. Avoid changing your mind if it is only to reach agreement and avoid conflict. Support only solutions with which you are able to agree at least somewhat.
3. Avoid "conflict-reducing" techniques such as majority vote, averaging, or trading in reaching your decision.
4. View differences of opinion as a help rather than a hindrance in decision making.

_____ Sextant

_____ Shaving mirror

_____ Five-gallon can of water

_____ Mosquito netting

_____ One case of U.S. Army C rations

_____ Maps of the Pacific Ocean

_____ Seat cushion (flotation device approved by the Coast Guard)

_____ Two-gallon can of oil-gas mixture

_____ Small transistor radio

_____ Shark repellent

_____ Twenty square feet of opaque plastic

_____ One quart of 160-proof Puerto Rican rum

_____ Fifteen feet of nylon rope

_____ Two boxes of chocolate bars

_____ Fishing kit

Group Behavior Rating Form

EXAMPLES OF: PROCESS DIMENSION/CATEGORY	IMPACT ON GROUP FUNCTIONING
1. Communication patterns	
2. Decision-making patterns	
3. Task-oriented behaviors	
4. Maintenance-oriented behaviors	
5. Self-oriented behaviors	
6. Group norms observed	

IV

Follow-up

As society becomes more complex and we continue to make major advances in our technological capability, more and more of organizational life will revolve around a team or group structure. The "information explosion" will guarantee that no one person can expect to have all the facts necessary to make many decisions. "Temporary systems," in which a group of people join for a short-term task and then disperse to form new and different task groups to tackle other problems will become more prevalent.[13] Groups play an important part in organizational life today, and every indication points toward increased importance in the future.

The distinction made in this exercise among task issues, maintenance issues, and self-oriented issues can be important in understanding how groups function. Most of us assume that if a group of people is called together to perform a task, nothing but the task is important or relevant. This assumption rests upon the belief that it is not only feasible but essential that we separate our emotional self (needs, wants, motives) from our intellectual, rational, problem-solving self. This is impossible. When people enter a group situation, they bring their total selves, the emotional as well as the intellectual. In fact, certain aspects of our emotional selves will become more salient because we are in a group situation. Attempts to bury, wish away, or ignore the interpersonal aspects of group interaction is much like sweeping dirt under the rug—sooner or later the pile gets big enough that someone will trip over it.

In some ways, the appointment of a chairperson or moderator reflects recognition of the fact that groups do not always "stay on the track." While this is often useful, there are two potential problems with this approach. First, seldom do the group members spend any time discussing why they are "off the track." More often the chairperson will say something like "We're getting off the main track, let's get back to it!" and that's all that happens. It is extremely important to realize that if people are having difficulty staying on the track, there are reasons for the behavior and simply saying "Let's get back to it" does nothing to eliminate the basic causes. Worse than that, this kind of behavior ("Let's quit wasting time and get to the task") may further accelerate the underlying reasons for lack of involvement and may make the situation worse.

Second, there is no inherent reason that only one person in a group should have the responsibility for worrying about how the group is progressing. Everyone can and should share this responsibility. To delegate this function or role to one individual is in some situations a highly inefficient utilization of resources. People can learn to be effective participant-observers at one and the same time. In such a group, *anyone* who feels that something is not right can and should raise the issue for the total group to examine. Anyone who observes a need for a particular kind of task or maintenance behavior can help the group. In a well-functioning group (working on something other than a routine programmable task), an observer looking in from the outside might not be able to pick out the formal leadership. The "leadership function" could pass around according to the group's need at a particular point.

[13]M. B. Miles, "On Temporary Systems," in M. B. Miles, ed., *Innovation in Education* (New York: Teachers College, Columbia University Press, 1964), pp. 84–112. See also Warren G. Bennis and Philip E. Slater, *The Temporary Society* (New York: Harper & Row, 1968).

It is important, in other words, to distinguish between leaders as persons and leadership as a function. To provide a summary or gatekeeping when these are needed by the group is to engage in an important act of leadership. To see the need and fail to respond can be viewed as a failure to fulfill one's membership responsibilities as well. A group is in some ways just like a machine. For a machine to continue to produce a high-quality product, it must continually be maintained. The maintenance function in a group is equally important, for, again, people bring their whole selves to a group, not just that part of themselves having to do with the task.

It is often argued that "We don't have the time to worry about people's feelings or to discuss how the group is working." Sometimes this is perfectly true, and under severe task pressure a different kind of process is necessary and legitimate. People can accept this, however, if they know from past experience that this situation is temporary. More often, however, lack of time is used as a defense mechanism to avoid the discussion completely. Furthermore, if a group really is under severe time pressure continually, some time ought to be spent examining the effectiveness of the group's planning procedures.

A group that ignores individual members' needs and its own process may well find that it meets several times to make the same set of decisions. The reason for this is that the effectiveness of many decisions is based on two factors[14]—logical soundness and the level of psychological commitment among the members to the decision made. These two dimensions are not independent; in fact, some people who are uncommitted (often because of process issues) may withhold, on a logical basis, information necessary to make the soundest decision. In any event, the best decision (on a task or logical level) forged at the expense of individual commitment is indeed not a very good decision at all.

Finally, what can be done to learn to use self-oriented emotional resources more appropriately? As a first step, it is important to accept our own feelings and to realize that everyone has both tender and tough emotions. Within American culture at least, managers (and particularly males) are expected to be tough, hard, aggressive, and the like. Any sign of "tender emotions" (warmth, affection) is taken to be a sign of weakness. But if we can accept the fact that feelings are a part of an individual's and therefore a group's reality, we can begin to explore ways of dealing with these realities rather than trying to clear them away. Given the opportunity to experiment with and get feedback on our emotional behavior (and a climate that supports such behavior), we can become more aware of when it is appropriate to be tough, tender, or neither.

The point here is that it is foolhardy to assume that simply because a group of people assembles to perform a task, it will somehow automatically know how to work together effectively.[15] A comparison between the behavior of a football team and the behavior of a management team highlights the essence of this paradox. The football team spends untold hours practicing teamwork in preparation for the 60 minutes each week that its members' performance as a team really counts. In contrast, most management teams do not spend even 60 minutes per week practicing teamwork in spite of the fact that for 40 or more hours every week their behavior as a team really counts. For this reason, in recent years many management groups

[14]This dichotomy of a decision's quality is analogous to issues raised during the discussion of the concept of psychological contract in the introduction of Chapter 1, Organizational Socialization. In that case, the dichotomy was the decision to join versus the decision to participate. See also Chapter 13, Leadership and Decision Making, for more detail on effective decision-making styles.

[15]One such process for learning how to work more effectively in groups is called broadly "laboratory training." For a full discussion of this and related educational techniques, see Edgar H. Schein and Warren G. Bennis, *Personal and Organizational Change Through Group Methods: The Laboratory Approach* (New York: John Wiley, 1965).

have undergone team-building training where they learn to identify their group norms and the roles that they play within the group. Much like we have done in this class, team-building participants learn to diagnose what is occurring with their group and focus upon discovering more effective ways to work together.[16]

V
Learning Points

1. In any group there are two types of issues operating at any given time: content and process. Content issues refer to the task, "what" the group is working on. Process issues refer to "how" the group is going about achieving its task.

2. By observing communication patterns and decision-making procedures, we can understand better how a group functions.

3. Task behaviors contribute to accomplishing the group task or goal. They consist of initiating, seeking, or giving information or opinions, clarifying and elaborating, summarizing, consensus testing, reality testing, and orienting.

4. Maintenance behaviors are geared toward creating a good climate for work and good relationships that permit maximum use of member resources. They are gatekeeping, encouraging, harmonizing and compromising, standard setting and testing, and using humor.

5. Groups need both maintenance and task behaviors to be effective. Groups that emphasize content and ignore their process are just as likely to fail as are groups that emphasize process at the cost of task.

6. Self-oriented emotional behavior interferes with effective group functioning. Issues of identity, inclusion, power, acceptance, intimacy, and goal agreement occur and reoccur at various points in a group's development.

7. There are three types of emotional behavior that result from tension and the attempt to resolve underlying problems:
   a. Tough emotions
   b. Tender emotions
   c. Denial of all emotion

8. The "pure types" that represent the three different styles of reducing tension and expressing emotion are:
   a. The "friendly helper"
   b. The "tough battler"
   c. The "logical thinker." However, each of these types can create only the

---

[16]For good descriptions of team building, see William G. Dyer, *Team Building: Issues and Alternatives* (Reading, MA: Addison-Wesley, 1977), and R. Fry, I. Rubin, and M. Plovnik, "Dynamics of Groups that Execute or Manage Policy," in *Groups at Work,* ed. by R. Payne and C. Cooper (New York: John Wiley, 1981), pp. 41–57.

type of climate in which they feel most comfortable by incorporating some of the perspectives of the other two types and accepting their dissimilarities.

9. We can learn to use our emotional resources better by
   a. Accepting our personal feelings.
   b. Trying to understand the feelings that occur in a group.
   c. Trying to identify what causes our emotions to be triggered in a group.
   d. Experimenting with expressing emotion differently and asking for feedback.

10. Group norms are unwritten, often implicit, rules that define the attitudes and behaviors that characterize good and bad group members. All groups have norms. By making them explicit, a group can determine whether their norms help or hinder their group's effectiveness.

11. Ideally, all members of a group should be participant-observers so everyone can contribute to keeping the group on track and bringing up the need to discuss process issues that may be hindering the group. Group leadership should be performed by more than just the designated leader.

12. Groups that ignore their process often take longer to resolve content issues because process problems prevent commitment and full sharing of information.

13. It takes practice and effort to transform a group into an effective team.

Tips for Managers

- Groups of employees can have either positive or negative impact on productivity and the work environment, depending upon the norms and stances they have taken. The more cohesive the group, the more likely they are to take a unified position.

- Informal leaders of employee work groups are important communication links for getting input, sending out trial balloons, and disseminating information about upcoming plans or events.

- Understanding group behavior is especially important at meetings. Heightening people's awareness of the roles they play is often helpful as is rotating the chairpersonship of the meeting so everyone has an opportunity to develop leadership skills and also see how difficult it is to run a good meeting.[17]

- Asking a work group to help establish norms can be very effective. It can be done by asking them
  What would be effective behaviors at work?
  How should we treat each other at work?
  How should we make decisions?
  How should we communicate?
  Do we have any norms that are keeping us from being effective?

[17]One of the best articles about running good meetings is Antony Jay's "How to Run a Meeting," in the *Harvard Business Review,* March–April 1976, pp. 43–57.

VII
Personal Application Assignment

The face-to-face group working on a problem is the meeting ground of individual personality and society. It is in the group that personality is modified and socialized; and it is through the workings of groups that society is changed and adapted to its times—Herbert Thelen

This assignment is to write about a group experience or incident about which you want to learn more. (You may wish to write about one of the exercises you did with your learning group in this course.)

A. *Concrete Experience*
   1. *Objectively* describe the experience ("who," "what," "when," "where," "how" type information—up to 2 points).
   2. *Subjectively* describe your feelings, perceptions, and thoughts that occurred *during* (not after) the experience (up to 2 points). Does this section have too much detail? (If so, delete 1 point.)

B. *Reflective Observation*
   1. Look at the experience from different points of view. How many points of view did you include that are *relevant* (up to 2 points)?
   2. Use these perspectives to add more meaning to the incident (up to 2 points).

C. *Abstract Conceptualization*

   1. Relate concepts from the assigned readings and the lecture to the experience (i.e., what theories that you heard in the lecture or read in the *Reader* relate to your understanding of this incident?). Make reference to at least two sources. Use standard referencing format and include the page number to which you are referring. How many sources did you use and how clearly did you explain their theories (up to 4 points)?

   2. You can also create an original model or theory, but it should not replace course concepts.

D. *Active Experimentation*

   1. Write about what you will do in the future that will improve your effectiveness. Use rules of thumb or action resolutions.

   2. Are they described specifically, thoroughly, and in detail (up to 4 points)?

E. *Integration, Synthesis, and Writing*

   1. Did you write about something personally important to you (up to 2 points)?

   2. Was it well written (up to 2 points)?

   3. Did you integrate and synthesize the different sections (up to 1 point)?

Lost at Sea Answer and Rationale Sheet[18]

According to the "experts," the basic supplies needed when a person is stranded in mid ocean are articles to attract attention and articles to aid survival until rescuers arrive. Articles for navigation are of little importance: Even if a small life raft were capable of reaching land, it would be impossible to store enough food and water to subsist during that period of time. Therefore, of primary importance are the shaving mirror and the two-gallon can of oil-gas mixture. These items could be used for signaling air-sea rescue. Of secondary importance are items such as water and food, for example, the case of army C rations.

A brief rationale is provided for the ranking of each item. These brief explanations obviously do not represent all the potential uses for the specified items but, rather, the primary importance of each.

1—Shaving mirror
Critical for signaling air-sea rescue.

2—Two-gallon can of oil-gas mixture
Critical for signaling—the oil-gas mixture will float on the water and can be ignited with a dollar bill and a match (obviously, outside the raft).

3—Five-gallon can of water
Necessary to replenish loss by perspiring, and so on.

4—One case of U.S. Army C rations
Provides basic food intake.

5—Twenty square feet of opaque plastic
Can be utilized to collect rain water, provide shelter from the elements.

6—Two boxes of chocolate bars
A reserve food supply.

7—Fishing kit
Ranked lower than the candy bars because "one bird in the hand is worth two in the bush." There is no assurance that you will catch any fish.

8—Fifteen feet of nylon rope
May be used to lash equipment together to prevent it from falling overboard.

9—Floating seat cushion
If someone fell overboard, it could function as a life preserver.

10—Shark repellent
Obvious.

11—One quart of 160-proof Puerto Rican rum
Contains 80 percent alcohol—enough to use as a potential antiseptic for any injuries incurred; of little value otherwise; will cause dehydration if ingested.

12—Small transistor radio
Of little value since there is no transmitter (unfortunately, you are out of range of your favorite AM radio stations).

13—Maps of the Pacific Ocean
Worthless without additional navigational equipment—it does not really matter where you are but where the rescuers are.

---

[18]Officers of the United States Merchant Marines ranked the 15 items and provided the "correct" solution to the task.

14—Mosquito netting
    There are no mosquitoes in the mid-Pacific.

15—Sextant
    Without tables and a chronometer, relatively useless.

The basic rationale for ranking signaling devices above life-sustaining items (food and water) is that without signaling devices there is almost no chance of being spotted and rescued. Furthermore, most rescues occur during the first 36 hours, and one can survive without food and water during this period.

Lost at Sea Scoresheet

	INDIVIDUAL RANKING (1)	GROUP RANKING (2)	EXPERT RANKING (3)	INDIVIDUAL SCORE (4)	GROUP SCORE (5)
Sextant			15		
Mirror			1		
Water can			3		
Mosquito netting			14		
C rations			4		
Maps			13		
Seat cushion			9		
Oil-gas mixture			2		
Radio			12		
Shark repellent			10		
Plastic			5		
Rum			11		
Nylon rope			8		
Chocolate			6		
Fishing kit			7		

Total   Group Score

SCORING INSTRUCTIONS

1. *Individual Ranking.* Copy your individual rankings from the Lost at Sea Individual Worksheet.

2. *Group Ranking.* Copy your group's rankings from the Lost at Sea Group Worksheet.

3. *Expert Ranking.* Column 3 already contains the experts' rankings.

4. *Individual Score.* Find the absolute difference (ignore plus or minus signs) between each item in columns 1 and 3. Total these numbers at the bottom of column 4.

5. *Group Score.* Find the absolute difference between each item in columns 2 and 3. Write the total of these differences at the bottom of column 5 to create your group score.

6. *Average Individual Score.* Total the individual scores (column 4) for each group member and divide by the number of people in your group. _____

7. *Gain/Loss Group Score.* Calculate the difference between the group score (column 5) and the average individual score (6). _____

8. *Lowest Individual Score.* What was the lowest individual score found in your group? _____

9. *Gain/Loss Individual Score.* Calculate the difference between the group score (column 5) and the lowest individual score (8). _____

9

PROBLEM MANAGEMENT

OBJECTIVES   By the end of this chapter, you should be able to:

A. Explain the four stages of managerial problem solving: situation analysis, problem analysis, solution analysis, and implementation analysis.

B. Describe the red/green modes of problem solving.

C. Explain the different roles a manager plays during problem solving.

D. Discuss the link between learning styles and problem-solving styles.

E. Identify what problem-solving stage a group is in and have some ideas about how to facilitate a group's progress.

The Pendulum Swings

Christopher M. Barlow

A group of construction specialists, attempting to reduce the cost of a new office building, proposed replacing a 10-story spiral staircase for the atrium with a 10-story brass pendulum. The architect was delighted. The owner was enthusiastic. Half a million dollars was saved!

This may give you visions of executives sliding down the brass pole, but it really made perfect sense. The function of the staircase was not to serve as a way to get from floor to floor. The building had elevators to do that. The spiral staircase was merely an architectural feature to convey an upsweeping dynamic vision to visitors.

The group realized that projecting an image was the key to the problem. They brainstormed a variety of different ways to project such an image. In the end they settled on the brass pendulum, partly because of the money it would save.

A group less skilled at problem solving would have proposed ways to build the spiral staircase more cheaply. This group got to the nub of the matter and focused on the *function* of the staircase. Groups need to manage their problem-solving and communication process to find the pendulums, not cheapen the staircase.

Used with permission from the author, Creativity and Value Consultant, Appleseed Associates, Cleveland, Ohio.

I

Premeeting Preparation

    A. Read the Cardiotronics Case.

    B. Read the Topic Introduction.

    C. What were the significant learning points from the readings?

    D. Make a plan to conduct tomorrow's meeting of Assembly Unit D as if you were Marion Andrews. Prepare a list of questions or statements on the following page that Marion could use during each stage of the problem-solving process described in the Topic Introduction. For example, what kinds of questions would facilitate good problem solving during the valuing stage, the priority-setting stage, and so on?

Role Play Preparation:
Questions/statements leaders can use during each stage of the problem solving process:

    A. Valuing/Exploration

    B. Priority Setting

    C. Information Gathering

D. Problem Definition

E. Idea Getting

F. Decision Making

G. Participation

H. Planning

Cardiotronics, Inc.

Cardiotronics, Inc., was started 17 years ago in a small New Hampshire town by two biomedical engineers whose goal was to produce a quality cardiac monitor (a device that continuously displays the wave pattern of the heart's function). The company originally produced customized monitors on a small scale. After 5 years the owners had perfected a quality monitor that was significantly less expensive than custom monitors and they decided to mass produce it.

The company currently has just over 200 employees. It remains nonunionized, but the labor union in this old New England milltown has from time to time made efforts to win a union election.

For the past 11 years, the company has enjoyed a strong competitive edge and has gained a reputation for a quality product and prompt service. Recently, however, the company's top management team has been informed that a similar monitor, reputed to be of equal or better quality than Cardiotronic's, will soon be introduced into the U.S. market by a large Japanese electronics firm.

Monitor Assembly Process. The cardiac monitors (excluding cables) are produced in four stages. In the first stage, circuit boards are produced largely by machine process. During the second stage, the circuit boards are placed by hand on a "mother" board and are connected to one another. The final step in stage 2 is the attachment of the mother board to the base panel. In the third stage, the casing is mounted by hand onto the base panel and external hardware and cables are placed. In the final stage, the monitors are tested for a week before shipping.

The Second-Stage Assembly Task. Four assembly teams are responsible for the second stage of monitor assembly, the manual assembly and the wiring of the "mother" board. Each team consists of five workers operating in a U-shaped area. The mother board is started at station 1. Each worker adds their circuit, connects it to the others, and passes it to the next worker. The assembly process requires some manual dexterity but is relatively easy to do. Each job on the line is of equal difficulty as determined by a recent industrial engineering study. The assembly arrangement for one of these teams, Team D, is as follows.

Assembly Team D

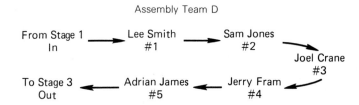

The following are the recently announced assembly team average daily production figures for the last month:

Team A = 40 boards
Team B = 32 boards
Team C = 43 boards
Team D = 35 boards

Your Problem as Marion Andrews, Supervisor of Team D. You are the new supervisor of Team D, Marion Andrews. You have been in the position for a month having recently been promoted from the quality control section where you worked for 5 years. During your second week you received a memo stating that to meet increased production requirements resulting from increased sales, all second-stage teams were to meet their minimum daily production rates. You informed the team in a brief meeting but had to leave for a week of supervisory training shortly thereafter. After returning from the training program you note that the daily production has increased to 36 but that your team is still 4 units below the daily minimum rate of 40 units. In looking into the problem you note the following:

- Work accumulates at the station of Joel Crane (station 3), and there are typically several "mother" boards waiting. Joel is 58 years old and has been with the company for 13 years. The supervisors of the other production teams do not consider Joel acceptable for transfer.
- Only one monitor from your team has been rejected in the past month by quality control.
- Assembly and test equipment is relatively new and in good working order.

Team D's assembly line will be closed for 30 minutes tomorrow, and you have decided to call a meeting for team D.

How do you plan to conduct this meeting?

II

Topic Introduction

For many scholars who study organizations and management, the central characteristic of organizations is that they are problem-solving systems whose success is measured by how efficiently they solve the routine problems associated with accomplishing their primary mission, be it manufacturing automobiles or selling insurance, and how effectively they respond to the emergent problems and opportunities associated with survival and growth in a changing world.[1] Kilmann's view is representative of this perspective:

> One might even define the essence of management as problem defining and problem solving, whether the problems are well structured, ill structured, technical, human, or even environmental. Managers of organizations would then be viewed as *problem managers,* regardless of the types of products and services they help their organizations provide. It should be noted that managers have often been considered as generic decision makers rather than as problem solvers or problem managers. Perhaps decision making is more akin to solving well-structured problems where the nature of the problem is so obvious that one can already begin the process of deciding among clear-cut alternatives. However, decisions cannot be made effectively if the problem is not yet defined and if it is not at all clear what the alternatives are, can, or should be.[2]

In this view, the core task of management is problem solving. While experience, personality, and specific technical expertise are important, the primary skill of the successful manager is the ability to manage the problem-solving process in such a way that important problems are identified and solutions of high quality are found and carried out with the full commitment of organization members.

THE NATURE OF PROBLEM SOLVING

This chapter describes a model of the problem-solving process that defines the stages and tasks involved in such a way that managers can better manage their own and their organization's problem-solving activities. This model of problem solving is based on three premises: first, that problem solving is basically a process of learning from experience; second, that problem solving involves the manipulation and control of the external world through one's mental processes (mind over matter); and third, that problem solving is by its nature a social process.

A Process of Learning from Experience

The experiential learning process presented in Chapter 3 identifies four phases: concrete experience, reflective observation, abstract conceptualization, and active experimentation. Common sense notions of problem solving tend to focus on the phases of concrete experience and active experimentation—on the specific difficul-

---

[1]The problem-solving model described here was developed in collaboration with Richard Baker and Juliann Spoth.

[2]Ralph Kilmann, "Problem Management: A Behavioral Science Approach," *Management Principles for Non-Profit Agencies and Organizations,* ed. by G. Zaltman, American Management Association, 1979, pp. 214–215.

ties experienced in immediate situations and the actions taken to overcome them. Traditional educational ideas about learning, on the other hand, tend to focus on the phases of reflective observation and abstract conceptualization—emphasizing the gathering of information and development of general concepts. Just as it has been proposed that the process of traditional education is improved when the concrete and active emphasis of problem solving is added,[3] it can correspondingly be suggested that the effectiveness of problem solving is enhanced by the addition of the academic learning perspectives of reflection and conceptualization. In both cases, what results is a more holistic and integrated adaptive process. More specifically, by viewing problem solving as a process of experiential learning, more attention is given to finding the right problem to work on, problems are more adequately defined, better quality solutions are found, and the implementation process is more effective.

Mind over Matter

The ability to solve complex problems is uniquely human resulting from the structure of the human mind, first, in its dialectic ability to perceive experiences in the world and to comprehend these experiences through words and other symbols. Second, human self-consciousness provides a perspective on and control over this process. We can choose which aspects of our experience to attend to and discipline ourselves to pursue a line of thought or action. As Kaplan described it, "The manager gives form to a problem in the way a potter sees and then shapes the possibilities in a lump of clay. The difference is that managers practice their craft using an intangible medium: information."[4] Thus, problem solving is the process of using our minds to control the world around us. It is literally the way we achieve the power of mind over matter. For centuries humans watched birds fly and dreamed that they, too, might fly. That vision of flight became a motivator of countless problem-solving efforts that have culminated today in flight achievements far beyond the dreams of our ancestors.

A Social Process

Problem solving is not just an activity of the mind; it is fundamentally a social process. Solutions to problems are inevitably combinations, new applications, or modifications of old solutions. From other people we get new dreams, new ideas, information, and help in getting things done. Language, communication, and conflict are central in problem solving. Particularly in organizations, it is difficult to conceive of a problem that does not in some way involve other people—in choosing the problem, supplying information about it, helping to solve it, or implementing the solutions. Given the social nature of problem solving, the effective management of problem solving involves four tasks:

1. The management of one's own and other's thinking processes to ensure an orderly and systematic process of analysis that determines the right problem or opportunity to work on, the most likely causes of the problem, the best solution given available alternatives and constraints, and a process for implementing the solution that ensures quality and commitment.

2. The proper organizational arrangements to promote cooperation among interdependent groups and assignment of problems to appropriate organizational units.

3. The management of relationships among people to ensure the appropriate involvement and participation of others.

4. The constructive use of conflict in an organization climate that removes in-

---

[3]M. Keeton and P. Tate, *Learning by Experience: What, Why, How* (San Francisco: Jossey-Bass, 1978), and A. Chickering, *Experience and Learning: An Introduction to Experiential Learning* (New York: Change Magazine Press, 1977).

[4]R. Kaplan, "Creativity in the Everyday Business of Managing," *Issues and Observations,* Center for Creative Leadership, Greensboro, NC, 1983, and *Reader.*

terpersonal and group barriers to information sharing and collaborative problem solving.

A MODEL OF PROBLEM SOLVING BASED
ON THE THEORY OF EXPERIENTIAL LEARNING

The model of problem solving derived from the theory of experiential learning describes an idealized problem-solving process that is characteristic of the fully functioning person in optimal circumstances. Ineffective problem solving is seen as the result of deviations from that normative process because of personal habits and skill limitations or because of situational constraints such as time pressure or the limited access to information that can result from one's position in the organization or from mistrusting relationships with subordinates. The model consists of four analytic stages that correspond to the four stages of the experiential learning cycle. Stage 1, situation analysis, corresponds to concrete experience; stage 2, problem analysis, to reflective observation; stage 3, solution analysis, to abstract conceptualization; and stage 4, implementation analysis, to active experimentation. These four stages form a nested sequence of analytical activities so that each stage requires the solution of a particular analytic task to frame the succeeding stage properly.

The four stages of problem solving and the basic questions each answers are presented in the paragraphs that follow.

Situation Analysis: What's the Most Important Problem?

The task of *situation analysis* is to examine the immediate situational context to determine the right problem to work on. While problem-solving activity is often initiated by urgent symptomatic pressures, urgency alone is not a sufficient criterion for choosing which problems to work on. As every manager knows, the press of urgent problems can easily divert attention from more important but less pressing long-term problems and opportunities. Every concrete situation contains a range of problems and opportunities that vary in urgency and importance. Some of these are obvious, whereas others are hidden or disguised. Situation analysis requires exploration to identify the problem that takes precedence by criteria of both urgency and importance. This is what is meant by the popular saying, "Managers do things right; leaders do the right thing." Problem finding is equally as important as problem solving.

Problem Analysis: What Are the Causes of the Problem?

Given the appropriate choice of a problem, the task of *problem analysis* is to define the problem properly in terms of the essential variables or factors that influence it. Here the task is to gather information about the nature of the problem and evaluate it by constructing a model of the factors that are influencing the problem. This model serves to sort relevant from irrelevant information and guides the search for further information to test its validity. The result of problem analysis is to define the problem so that the criteria to be met in solving it are identified.

Solution Analysis: What's the Best Solution?

Once the problem is analyzed correctly, the third stage, *solution analysis,* seeks to generate possible solutions and to test their feasibility for solving the problem against the criteria defined in stage 2. This is the most intensively studied stage of problem solving, best known through Osborn's early work on brainstorming.[5]

Implementation Analysis: How Do We Implement the Solution?

The solution chosen in solution analysis is next implemented in the fourth stage of problem solving: *implementation analysis.* Tasks essential for implementing the solution must be identified and organized into a coherent plan with appropriate time deadlines and follow-up evaluations. Responsibility for implementing the plan is developed through participation of those individuals and groups not already in-

[5]A. F. Osborn, *Applied Imagination* (New York: Scribners, 1953).

volved in the problem-solving activity who will be directly affected by the solution. Implementation activities from stage 4 are carried out in the situation identified in stage 1 and thus modify that situation, creating new opportunities, problems, and priorities. Effective problem solving is thus a continuing iterative cycle paralleling the experiential learning cycle. For example, when the participation of affected individuals is elicited in implementation analysis, new problems and opportunities may come to light as priorities for continuing problem-solving efforts. There is some evidence that the solution to one problem causes another.

THE DIALECTICS OF PROBLEM SOLVING

The process of problem solving does not proceed in a logical, linear fashion from beginning to end but rather is characterized by wavelike expansions and contractions alternatively moving outward to gather and consider alternatives, information, and ideas and inwardly to focus, evaluate, and decide. These expansions and contractions have been variously labeled green light/red light in brainstorming, ideation/evaluation, and divergence/convergence. The existence of such a pulsation process strongly suggests that problem solving is not the result of a single mental function such as logical thinking but rather that effective problem solving involves the integration of dialectically opposed mental orientations—red and green mode mind sets.

The red mode mind set facilitates analysis, criticism, logical thinking, and active coping with the external environment. The green mode mind set facilitates creative imagination, sensitivity to the immediate situation, and empathy with other people. The red mode mind set is therefore most appropriate for the contraction phases of problem solving—priority setting in situation analysis, problem definition in problem analysis, decision making in solution analysis, and planning in implementation analysis. The green mode mind set, on the other hand, facilitates the expansion phases of problem solving—valuing, information gathering, idea getting, and participation. Effectiveness in problem solving is enhanced by approaching the expansion/contraction phases of each problem-solving stage in the appropriate mind set. For problem solvers to accomplish this matching of mind set and problem-solving task, they must first become aware of when they are in the red or green mode of consciousness and then learn to shift from one mode to another. With some practice, this can be accomplished quite easily, and usually, practice in identifying and separating the two mind sets has the effect of increasing the intensity of both. This purity of conscious mind set increases problem-solving effectiveness by enhancing the dialectics of each analytical stage. Similarly, managing the problem-solving process with groups of people requires the creation of a climate that stimulates and reinforces the appropriate mind set in participants.

The problem-solving process is further guided by four role sets that focus the dialectic interplay of red and green mind sets on the relevant stage of the problem-solving process. In situation analysis, the problem solver adopts the role of a *leader* focused on identifying goals and values in the situation in the green mode and setting priorities in the red mode. In problem analysis, the role set is that of a *detective* focused on gathering information in the green mode and building and evaluating models in the red mode. In solution analysis, the role set is that of an *inventor:* generating ideas in the green mode and testing their feasibility in the red mode. In implementation analysis, the problem solver adopts the *coordinator* role: developing participation in the green mode and planning in the red mode. Conscious attention to these role sets serves to focus attention on the priorities of each analytic stage and shifting role set signals the transition from one stage to another. A diagram of this refined model is shown in Figure 9–1 and is described in the paragraphs that follow.

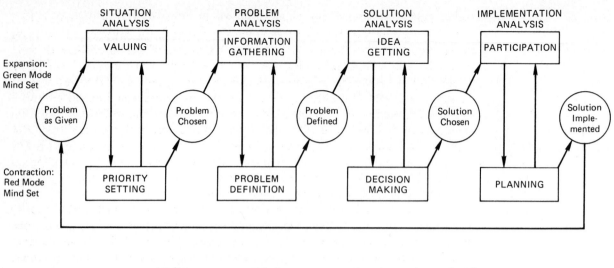

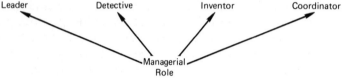

FIGURE 9–1   Problem Solving as a Dialectic Process

SITUATION ANALYSIS—VALUING AND PRIORITY SETTING

Most problem-solving activity begins with a problem as given—a specific circumstance, task, or assignment that demands attention. The task of situation analysis is to transform this problem as given into a problem that is consciously chosen to meet the dual criteria of urgency and importance. Urgent structured problems in organizations are often the result of failure to address unstructured problems that lie behind them (e.g., the continued urgent need to replace bank tellers may result from the failure to address more unstructured problems of worker morale or career opportunities). Structured problems are repetitive and routine, and definite procedures are developed for dealing with them. Unstructured problems are novel and not covered by ready-made procedures because they occur infrequently or are very complex. In addition, for many organizations in rapidly changing environments, aggressive opportunity seeking is essential to maintain stability and growth. Careful situation analysis is therefore most critical in those cases where long-term adaptation to a changing environment takes precedent over expedient action.

When people discuss problems, they devote time to talking about how they would like the situation to be. For example, the technique of visioning involves asking people to close their eyes and imagine about their ideal organization. This reflects the green mode, while the exploration of current realities represents the red mode. The result is a menu of problems and opportunities in the situation from which one can be chosen that satisfies the criteria of urgency and importance. The process of articulating desired goal states is the process of *valuing*. To be successful, the valuing process must overcome barriers that exist in most organizational settings to open sharing of values. Foremost among these barriers is the organizational press to be realistic. Wishing, wanting, and valuing must be explored independently of reality for them to develop fully. Two other barriers to the valuing process are the fear of conflict and the threat of isolation.

Charles Lindblom[6] noted some time ago that it is easier to find agreement on a course of action than it is to get agreement on the goals for the action. Discussion of values accentuates human individuality and emotional commitment with a resulting increase in conflict among viewpoints. In the dialectic view, such conflict is essential for the discovery of truth, although most managers shy away from conflict because it is unpleasant and they do not know how to use disagreement constructively. A related barrier to valuing is the threat of isolation that comes from holding values different from those of the majority. It is this barrier that gives rise to conformity and groupthink in problem finding.[7] A worker, for example, may suppress his or her genuine values for achievement and excellence so as not to violate group norms of mediocrity. For this reason an effective valuing process requires an environment that gives security and support for individuality.

The contrasting pole to valuing in the situation analysis dialectic is *priority setting*. As with any dialectic, valuing and priority setting mutually enhance one another—valuing gives direction and energy to priority setting and priority setting gives substance and reality to valuing. Every managerial decision reflects values; choosing one problem as a priority reveals the values of the decision makers. Priority setting has three specific tasks: (1) to explore the current situation for those features that facilitate or hinder goal achievement, (2) to test the feasibility of changing those features, and (3) to articulate reality-based goal statements that give substance to values and allow them to be realized. Priority setting is not a rational, analytic process of reflective planning. It is an active, intuitive process of trial and error exploration of what is going on in the situation. It involves "knocking on doors," listening to people, trying things out, and taking risks.

Taken as a whole, the central issue in situation analysis is leadership, and the basic social role of the problem solver is that of a leader whose responsibility is to guide the problem-solving attention of the organization to those problems and opportunities whose solution will be of maximum benefit to the long-run effectiveness of the organization. Someone once said that the key to successful leadership is to find out which way people are going and then run out in front of them. There is an element of truth in this, for the successful leader in situation analysis identifies the values and goals of those in the situation and then holds up those that are most important as priorities for action.

PROBLEM ANALYSIS— INFORMATION GATHERING AND PROBLEM DEFINITION

Problem analysis begins with the problem chosen in situation analysis and seeks to understand and define the problem in such a way that solutions to it can be developed. In the expansion mode, information about the concrete problem situation is gathered. The *information-gathering phase* of problem analysis is a receptive, open-minded phase in which all information associated with the problem is sought and accepted. This receptive stance has both a cognitive and interpersonal component. Cognitively, it is important in the information-gathering phase to avoid biases and preconceptions about the nature of the problem and its causes in favor of letting the data about the problem speak for themselves. Interpersonally, information gathering requires skills in the development of trusting relationships so that others do not hold back or modify information to say "what the boss wants to hear" or to avoid reprisals. In many organizations, these two components negatively interact with one another to produce a climate where the gathering of accurate information is very difficult. Mistrust and threat cause workers to withhold information, and

---

[6]Charles Lindblom, "The Science of Muddling Through," *Public Administration Review,* Vol. 2 (1959), pp. 78–88.
[7]Irving L. Janis, "Group Think," *Psychology Today,* November 1971; *Readings.*

this forces management to rely on its own prejudgments as to the nature of the problems. By acting on these prejudgments, they reinforce worker mistrust and perpetuate a cycle that restricts accurate information exchange.

In the contraction mode, *problem definition,* the task is to define the problem based on the information gathered. Problem definition is basically a process of building a model portraying how the problem works—factors that cause the problem, factors that influence its manifestation, and factors mediating the application of solutions. Two skills are critical in building a model that defines a problem: causal analysis and imagery. Causal analysis uses the inductive logic of experimental inquiry to evaluate data and identify those invariant causal relationships that define the problem. It is a means of sorting relevant from irrelevant information. Imaging is a way of refining the problem definition by imagining its dynamics and subjecting them to "thought experiments." Stated simply, imaging is the process of creating in one's mind a model or scenario of how the problem occurs and then subjecting that model to various transformations to understand how the model operates and how the problem might be solved. Prince describes this process nicely:

> Imaging is our most important thinking skill because it accompanies and facilitates all other thinking operations. I find it useful to think of my imaging as my display system or readout of my thinking processes.[8]

With practice, imaging can create richly detailed problem scenarios and can portray large amounts of information in complex interrelationships. When concrete information is juxtaposed against a conceptual model, it serves to evaluate that model. Furthermore, the model serves to guide the search for new relevant information. In a sense, the problem solver in the problem analysis is in the role of detective—gathering clues and information about how the "crime" was committed, organizing these clues into a scenario of "who done it," and using that scenario to gather more information to prove or disprove the original hunch. The dialectic between information gathering and the problem definition has a synergistic power over information or model alone. By combining them, one can learn from what does not occur or has not happened as well as from what has. As in Sherlock Holmes's famous case, "The Dog Who Didn't Bark," a model suggests events that should occur if the model is true and thus their nonoccurrence in reality can invalidate the model.

The output of the problem analysis phase is a model of the problem validated through the interplay of information gathering and problem definition—a problem as defined. The problem as defined describes the problem in terms of those essential variables that need to be managed to solve it.

SOLUTION ANALYSIS—
IDEA GETTING AND DECISION MAKING

Solution analysis achieved through the interplay between getting ideas about how the problem can be solved and decision making about the feasibility of ideas generated. This two-stage process has been highly developed in brainstorming. The first step of solution analysis focuses on creative imagination, the green light stage of brainstorming, where the aim is to generate as wide a range of potential solutions as possible in an atmosphere that is free from evaluation and supportive of all ideas. Research on both communication and meeting behavior reveals that most responses are evaluative. Obviously this does not promote either creativity or participation. The second substage, the red light stage of brainstorming, focuses on evaluation,

---

[8]George Prince, "The Mind Spring Theory: A New Development from Synetics Research," *The Journal of Creative Behavior,* Vol. 9, no. 3 (1975), pp. 159–181.

sorting through the ideas generated in the first substage and evaluating them systematically against the criteria that need to be met for a potential solution to solve the problem most effectively. In the solution phase, the problem solver is in the role of inventor creatively searching for ideas and then carefully evaluating them against feasibility criteria.

IMPLEMENTATION ANALYSIS—PARTICIPATION AND PLANNING

Implementation analysis is accomplished through the interplay of planning and the process of carrying out plans. Since implementation of solutions in organizational settings is most often done by or with other people, the critical expansion task is *participation*, enlisting the appropriate involvement of those actors in the situation who are essential to carrying out the problem solution. Three subtasks are involved here:

1. The anticipation of the consequences that will result from implementing the solution and the involvement of those who will experience these consequences in the development of ways to deal with them.
2. The identification of those key individuals who by virtue of expertise and/or motivation are best qualified to carry out the various tasks in implementation.
3. Sometimes in the process of accomplishing (1) and (2), it becomes necessary to ask these key individuals to recycle through the problem solving process to reevaluate whether the most important problem has been chosen, whether the problem is properly defined, and whether the best solution has been identified.

In the participation phase of implementation, the essential attitude to adopt is inclusion of others, receptivity, and openness to their concerns and ideas.

The *planning phase* of implementation analysis is an analytic process involving the definition of tasks to be accomplished in implementing the solution, the assignment of responsibility to qualified individuals, the setting of deadlines and planning for follow-up monitoring, and the evaluation of the implementation process. If the problem and its solution are very complex, planning may be quite complicated using network planning methods such as PERT (Program Evaluation Review Technique) or CPM (Critical Path Method) of analysis. Often, however, a simple chart listing key tasks, responsible individuals, and time deadlines is sufficient for planning and monitoring implementation.

As with the other three stages of our problem-solving model, there are two dialectically related processes involved in implementation analysis. The first involves developing plans for implementation and the concrete apprehension of the potential consequences of implementing these plans. An iterative process is often useful here—scout potential issues that may arise in implementation, develop a rough plan, share it with those involved in the situation to get reactions, and then modify the plan. The other dialectic can be termed the "who's" and the "what's." Managers appear to have distinct stylistic preferences about how they deal with this issue. Some prefer to define the "what's" first—the plan and tasks to be accomplished—and then assign these tasks to individuals to carry them out. Others begin with the "who's," seeking to identify qualified and interested individuals and then developing plans with them. While the best approach probably varies with the situation and task, beginning with the "who's" has the advantages of giving priority to often-scarce human resources and maximizing participation and delegation. In synthesizing these dialectics, the problem solver in implementation analysis adopts the role of coordinator, working to accomplish tasks with other people.

Reprinted by permission of Tribune Company Syndicate, Inc.

Procedure for Group Meeting: Cardiotronics Role Play

PART I. ASSEMBLY UNIT D MEETING
(Time Allotted: 45 Minutes)

During the meeting, groups will have the opportunity to practice problem solving on a real work problem by means of a role play.

STEP 1. In this role play each group of six class members will be Assembly Team D with individuals in your group assuming the role of Marion Andrews, Lee Smith, and so on. (In groups of five, combine the Lee Smith role with that of Sam, i.e., "Sam can speak for his friend Lee who is sick today." Groups larger than six should have observers. Observers should take notes on the group's problem-solving process during the role play using the form described in Part II, Analysis, step 2.)

STEP 2. Group members should choose roles. One person should play Marion Andrews and prepare to conduct the meeting. Role descriptions for the other team members are on the pages cited.

Lee Smith	page 265	Tear out the page describing your role and make a "name tent"
Sam Jones	267	
Joel Crane	269	
Jerry Fram	271	
Adrian James	273	

LEE SMITH

role instructions on back

STEP 3. Action.

Instructions for Team D workers

Place your name tent in front of you after you have read the role descriptions and prepare to be the person described.

Instructions for Marion Andrews

The assembly line just closed and the five workers from Assembly Team D have gathered in your office. You have 30 minutes to conduct the meeting before everyone goes back to work.

FOUR TIPS ON ROLE PLAYING:

■ Be *yourself* as much as you can.
■ Imagine yourself in that person's life.
■ Don't "ham it up."
■ Talk loudly enough for the observers to hear.

PART II. ANALYSIS
(Time Allotted: 1 Hour, 15 Minutes)

STEP 1.   After finishing the role play, write down the decision that was reached. (5 minutes)

> **IN OUR GROUP IT WAS DECIDED TO:**

STEP 2.   The group should prepare a group review of its problem-solving process by completing the following Cardiotronics Case Review (30 minutes):

STEP 3.   Results from each group should be summarized for discussion on a chalkboard or flip chart so the whole group can compare subgroup results. The "Summary of Role-Play Results" on page 263 gives one format for preparing this summary. The last row in this chart gives results for 10 groups of business executives for comparison purposes. (5 minutes)

STEP 4.   Everyone should read the summary. (5 minutes)

STEP 5.   Total group discussion. (30 minutes) Each group should share the solution it decided on and describe the highlights of the problem-solving process. Consider the following questions:

   a. What differences were there in the problem-solving process followed in each group?

   b. Were these differences related to the adequacy of the solutions arrived at (e.g., firing or removing Joel is not a particularly good solution since work would only pile up at Jerry's position—realizing this requires green mode-information getting so that Jerry feels free to share his role information)?

   c. What common obstacles to effective group problem solving came up? How were these dealt with by Marion Andrews? by other Team D members?

   d. What connections can you make between this exercise and the readings?

Cardiotronics Case Review

DESCRIBE HOW THE FOLLOWING PROBLEM-SOLVING ACTIVITIES TOOK PLACE	APPROXIMATE % OF TOTAL PROBLEM-SOLVING TIME SPENT IN THIS ACTIVITY	SEQUENCE IN WHICH ACTIVITY TOOK PLACE IN MEETING (1 = FIRST, 2 = SECOND, ETC.)
Valuing Examining the situation for opportunities and problems		
Priority Setting Agreeing on the most important problem		
Information Gathering Getting information on possible causes		
Problem Definition Choosing most likely cause		
Idea Getting Generating possible solutions		
Decision-Making Selecting ideas		
Participation Deciding how/when to involve others		
Planning Constructing a plan		

IV

Follow-up

Most experienced managers tend naturally to follow a problem-solving sequence that is close to that described in the four-phase model of situation analysis, problem analysis, solution analysis, and implementation analysis. There are, however, significant differences in the amounts of energy devoted to each of these phases that tend to inhibit effective problem solving. Perhaps the most significant of these is the tendency to spend too little time defining the problem at hand before generating possible solutions.[9] This tendency to be solution oriented often results in the treatment of symptoms as opposed to causes of the problem and time wasted working on solutions before relevant information is known. If this process is widely typical of an organization's problem solving, a crisis fire-fighting atmosphere develops where symptom-oriented solutions fail to resolve basic problems that recur over and over. This further reduces time available for thoughtful situation and problem analysis.

Effective problem solving requires balanced attention to each phase of the problem solving process and equal emphasis on the expansion/green mode and contraction/red mode mind sets. We learned in Chapter 3, Individual and Organizational Learning, that individual learning styles emphasize different aspects of the experiential learning cycle. There is a strong correlation between people's learning styles and the way they approach problem solving.

USING THE EXPERIENTIAL LEARNING MODEL TO ANALYZE PERSONAL APPROACHES TO PROBLEM SOLVING

Figure 9–2 overlays a model of the problem-finding and problem-solving process on the experiential learning cycle and identifies problem-solving activities that characterize different stages of the cycle. In this figure we can see that the stages in a problem-solving sequence generally correspond with the learning style strengths of the four major learning styles described earlier. The accommodator's problem-solving strengths lie in executing solutions and in initiating problem finding based on some goal or model about how things should be. The diverger's problem-solving strengths lie in identifying the multitude of possible problems and opportunities that exist in reality ("compare model with reality" and "identify differences"). The assimilator excels in the abstract model building that is necessary to choose a priority problem and create alternative solutions. The converger's strengths lie in the evaluation of solution consequences and solution selection.

Let us briefly examine two organizational studies to illustrate the practical implications of this theoretical model. The first study[10] was conducted in the Trust Department of a large U.S. bank. One aim of this study was to discover how the learning styles of investment portfolio managers affected their problem solving and decision making in the management of the assets in their portfolios. While the study involved only 31 managers, there was a strong correspondence between the type of decisions these managers faced and their learning styles. More specifically, nearly all the managers in the Investment Advisory section of the department, a high-risk,

[9]See Norman Maier, "Leadership Principles for Problem-Solving Conferences," *Readings.*

[10]Charles Stabell, "The Impact of a Conventional Computer System on Human Problem-Solving Behavior," unpublished working paper, Sloan School of Management, Massachusetts Institute of Technology, 1973.

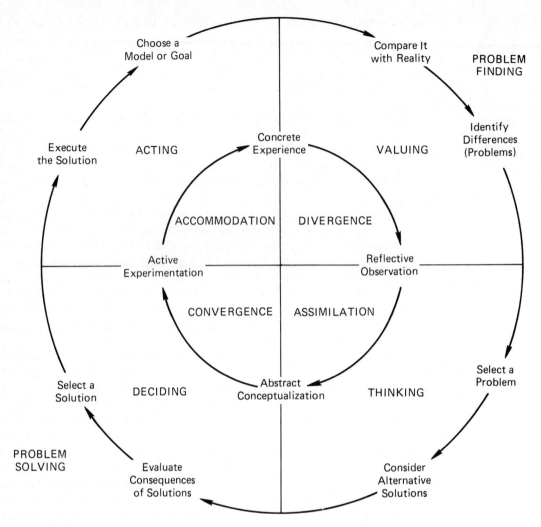

FIGURE 9–2 Comparison of the Experiental Learning Model and the Problem-Solving Process

high-pressure job (as indicated by a large percentage of holdings in common stock, a large percentage of discretionary accounts, and a high performance and risk orientation on the part of clients), had accommodative learning styles (scoring very high on the AE and CE LSI scales). On the other hand, the people in the Personal Trust section, where risk and performance orientation were low and where there were few discretionary accounts and fewer holdings in common stock, scored highest on reflective observation. This finding supports the view that high-pressure management jobs select and develop active experimentation learning skills and inhibit reflective observation learning skills.

The study also attempted to study differences on the basis of their LSI scores, in the way managers went about making investment decisions. The research focused on differences between managers with concrete experience (CE) learning skills and abstract conceptualization (AC) learning skills. Managers were asked to evaluate the importance of the information sources that they used in making decisions. CE managers cited more people as important sources (e.g., colleagues, brokers, and traders), while the AC managers listed more analytically oriented printed material as important sources (e.g., economic analyses, industry and company reviews). In addition, it seemed that CE managers sought services that would give them a specific recommendation that they could accept or reject (e.g., a potential list), while the AC managers sought information that they could analyze themselves to choose an investment. This analytic orientation of the AC managers is further illustrated by the fact that they tended to use more information sources in their decisions than the CE managers. These data fit well with the learning/problem-solving model. The concrete managers prefer go/no-go implementation decisions based on personal recommendations, while the abstract managers prefer to consider and evaluate alternative solutions themselves.

The second study of the relationship between learning styles and managerial problem solving was a laboratory computer simulation of a production "troubleshooting" problem where the problem solver had to determine which specific type of "widget" was failure-prone.[11] This experiment was conducted with 22 middle-level managers at the Massachusetts Institute of Technology's Sloan Fellows program. The study focused on the different types of problem-solving strategies that assimilators and accommodators would use to solve this problem. It was predicted that the accommodators would use a strategy that called for little complexity in use and interpretation, little inference from the data, and little cognitive strain in assimilating information, while assimilators would prefer a strategy that had the opposite characteristics—more complex use and interpretation and more assimilation strain and required inference. The former strategy, called successive scanning, was simply a process whereby the problem solver scans the data base of widgets for a direct test of his or her current hypothesis. It requires little conceptual analysis, since the current hypothesis is either validated or not in each trial. The latter strategy, called simultaneous scanning, is in a sense an "optimal" strategy in that each data point is used to eliminate the maximum number of data points still possible. This strategy requires considerable conceptual analysis since the problem solver must retain several hypotheses mentally at the same time and deduce the optimal widget to examine to test these hypotheses. The results of the experiment confirmed the hypothesis that accommodators would use successive scanning, while assimilators would use the more analytical simultaneous scanning strategy. It was further found that managers with accommodative learning styles tended to show more inconsistency in their use of strategies, while the assimilative managers were quite consistent in their use of the simultaneous scanning strategy. The accommodative managers seemed to be taking a more intuitive approach, switching strategies as they gathered more data during the experiment. Interestingly, the study found no differences between accommodative and assimilative managers in the amount of time it took them to solve the problem. Although the two groups used very different styles in this problem, they performed equally well.

The Guide for Analysis of Your Personal Problem-Solving Process that follows identifies more specifically the types of problem-solving activities that characterize the different phases of the learning/problem-solving process. Its purpose is to assist you in the analysis of problem situations and how you approach them in a manner similar to that used in the experiments just described. Activities that characterize the four learning style types are grouped together around the learning cycle so you can assess your stylistic emphasis in the problem-solving processes you reported.

[11] Jerrold Grochow, "Cognitive Style as a Factor in the Design of Interactive Decision-Support Systems," Ph.D. thesis, Sloan School of Management, Massachusetts Institute of Technology, 1973.

Guide for Analysis of Your Personal Problem-Solving Process

Describe the problem briefly. _____

Rate on a scale of 1 to 7 how much each of the following activities were a part of your approach to the problem you were trying to solve. Record the consensus score of your group.

		Very Little		Moderate			Very Much		
(spl)	Being sensitive to people's feelings	1	2	3	4	5	6	7	DIVERGER
(sv)	Being sensitive to values	1	2	3	4	5	6	7	
(lom)	Listening with an open mind	1	2	3	4	5	6	7	
(gi)	Gathering information	1	2	3	4	5	6	7	
(ii)	Imagining implications of ambiguous situations	1	2	3	4	5	6	7	
(oi)	Organizing information	1	2	3	4	5	6	7	ASSIMILATOR
(bcm)	Building conceptual models	1	2	3	4	5	6	7	
(tt)	Testing theories and ideas	1	2	3	4	5	6	7	
(de)	Designing experiments	1	2	3	4	5	6	7	
(aqd)	Analyzing quantitative data	1	2	3	4	5	6	7	
(cnw)	Creating new ways of thinking and doing	1	2	3	4	5	6	7	
(eni)	Experimenting with new ideas	1	2	3	4	5	6	7	CONVERGER
(cbs)	Choosing the best solution	1	2	3	4	5	6	7	
(sg)	Setting goals	1	2	3	4	5	6	7	
(md)	Making decisions	1	2	3	4	5	6	7	
(co)	Committing yourself to objectives	1	2	3	4	5	6	7	
(seo)	Seeking and exploiting opportunities	1	2	3	4	5	6	7	ACCOMMODATOR
(ilo)	Influencing and leading others	1	2	3	4	5	6	7	
(bpi)	Being personally involved	1	2	3	4	5	6	7	
(dp)	Dealing with people	1	2	3	4	5	6	7	

(transfer ratings to draw profile)

V
Learning Points

1. Some scholars characterize organizations as problem-solving systems whose success depends upon how well they perform that process.

2. The problem-solving model presented is based upon three premises:
   a. Learning from experience.
   b. Mind over matter.
   c. Problem solving as a social process.

3. The problem-solving model consists of four stages:
   a. Situation analysis.
   b. Problem analysis.
   c. Solution analysis.
   d. Implementation analysis.

4. The role of the manager is different for each stage and can be characterized as
   a. Leader.
   b. Detective.
   c. Inventor.
   d. Coordinator.

5. Problem solving is not a logical, linear process. Instead, it is characterized by wavelike expansions and contractions alternatively moving outward to gather and consider alternatives, information, and ideas and inwardly to focus, evaluate, and decide.

6. Each of the stages in the problem-solving model possesses two substages that reflect the two dialectics of problem solving, the expansion/green mode and the contraction/red mode.

7. Effective problem solving requires balanced attention to each phase of the problem-solving process and equal emphasis on the expansion/green and contraction/red mode mind sets.

8. There is a correlation between individual learning styles and the way people solve problems.

VI

Tips for Managers

- The management of group problem solving can be enhanced by avoidance of the following common obstacles to effective group problem solving:
    - *Preparation for the Meeting*
    Little or no preplanning.
    Low expectations.
    Failure to include the right people, inclusion of irrelevant people.
    Group's goal and function are ambiguous (e.g., is it advisory, information sharing, decision making?).
    - *Managing the Meeting*
    Lack of clarity about procedures and ground rules:
        Goals and agenda.
        How decisions get made (by voting or by consensus, etc.).
        Time.
        Structure (chairperson, recorder, etc.).
    Group members do not follow an orderly problem-solving sequence together.
    Failure to balance the discussion—dominance by high-status or aggressive members.
    Conflict is either avoided or allowed to become personalized as opposed to problem focused.
    Members do not understand what is being said and think they do.
    - *Situation Analysis*
    Urgent and structured problems take priority over important problems.
    Symptoms are treated as the problem (e.g., often people as opposed to situations are seen as the problem).
    Problems are accepted as given—reluctance to express hopes and dreams and to search for opportunities.
    - *Problem Analysis*
    Premature discussion of solutions.
    Critical facts are not made known to all.
    No distinction is made between facts and opinions.
    Problem situations are defined as choice situations.
    - *Solution Analysis*
    Generation and evaluation of ideas not kept separate.
    Premature focusing.
    Unproductive conflict and competition in evaluation.
    Undue weight given to secondary decision criteria—the primary criterion is—Does the solution solve the problem? Secondary criteria such as cost should not be allowed to overshadow the prime criterion.
    - *Implementation Analysis*
    Failure to gain commitment of those who will implement solutions.
    Failure to assign clear responsibility to individuals for tasks.
    Failure to follow up and monitor.
- Try to include people with different learning styles in problem-solving groups and see that their disparate skills are both valued and utilized.
- Feelings and perceptual biases influence the problem-solving process as do the

mental ruts that prevent us from generating creative solutions. Discussing the situation with neutral outsiders or objective insiders is often helpful.

■ The success of some quality circles and participative management projects has shown that employees are capable of solving problems that management either did not recognize or had not been able to resolve.

VII
Personal Application Assignment

In this assignment you will write about an experience involving problem management. Choose an experience about which you want to learn more.

A. *Concrete Experience*

1. *Objectively* describe the experience ("who," "what," "when," "where," "how" type information—up to 2 points).

2. *Subjectively* describe your feelings, perceptions, and thoughts that occurred *during* (not after) the experience (up to 2 points). Does this section have too much detail? (If so, delete 1 point.)

B. *Reflective Observation*

1. Look at the experience from different points of view. How many points of view did you include that are *relevant* (up to 2 points)?

2. Use these perspectives to add more meaning to the incident (up to 2 points).

C. *Abstract Conceptualization*

    1. Relate concepts from the assigned readings and the lecture to the experience (i.e., what theories that you heard in the lecture or read in the *Reader* relate to your understanding of this incident?). Make reference to at least two sources. Use standard referencing format and include the page number to which you are referring. How many sources did you use and how clearly did you explain their theories (up to 4 points)?

    2. You can also create an original model or theory, but it should not replace course concepts.

D. *Active Experimentation*

    1. Write about what you will do in the future that will improve your effectiveness. Use rules of thumb or action resolutions.

    2. Are they described specifically, thoroughly, and in detail (up to 4 points).

E. *Integration, Synthesis, and Writing*

    1. Did you write about something personally important to you (up to 1 point)?

    2. Was it well written (up to 2 points)?

    3. Did you integrate and synthesize the different sections (up to 1 point)?

Summary of Role-Play Results

GROUP NO.		SITUATION ANALYSIS		PROBLEM ANALYSIS		SOLUTION ANALYSIS		IMPLEMENTATION ANALYSIS		Solution Decided on by Assembly team D
		Valuing "Examine Situation"	Priority Setting "Agree on Problem"	Information Getting "Information on Causes"	Problem Definition "Choosing Cause"	Get Ideas "Generate Ideas"	Decision Making "Select Idea"	Participation "Involve Others"	Planning "Construct Plan"	
1	Sequence									
	% Time									
2	Sequence									
	% Time									
3	Sequence									
	% Time									
4	Sequence									
	% Time									
Averages for 60 managers (½ male, ½ female; 10 groups)	Sequence (av. rank)	1	3	2	4	5	7	6	8	
	% Time	5.2%	6.2%	7.7%	5.2%	43.0%	12.9%	6.2%	14.0%	

STATION 1
LEE SMITH

You find you can easily do more work, but you have to slow down because Joel gets behind. So as not to make Joel feel bad, you hold back. You don't want to get Joel into trouble. Right now, the job lacks challenge and is boring.

STATION 2
SAM JONES

You and Lee work closely together, and you are usually waiting for the board from Lee. Waiting for the board is more prevalent in the later part of the day than in the beginning. To keep busy, you often help out Joel who can't keep up. However, you are careful not to let the supervisor catch you helping Joel because Joel might be let go. Joel is a bit old for the pace set and feels the strain. For you, the job is easy, and you feel the whole job is slowed down too much because of Joel. "Why couldn't Joel be given less to do?" you ask yourself.

STATION 3
JOEL CRANE

You work hard, but you just aren't as fast as the others. You know you are holding things up, but no matter how you try, you get behind. The faster you try to go, the more difficult it is to make correct connections. You feel quality is important, and you don't want to make mistakes. The rest of the workers are fine people and have more energy than you do at your age.

STATION 4
JERRY FRAM

You are able to keep up with the pace, but on your last assembly job, you were pressed. Fortunately Joel is slower than you are, and this keeps the pressure off you. You are determined that Joel will not be moved off the job. Somebody has to protect people from speed-up tactics.

STATION 5
ADRIAN JAMES

You get bored doing the same circuit operations over and over. On some jobs you get variety by working fast for awhile and then slowly. On this job you can't work fast because the boards aren't fed to you fast enough. Why can't the supervisor see that Joel is a problem and needs to be moved out of the group? It gets you down to keep doing exactly the same thing over and over in slow motion. You are considering getting a job some place where they can keep a worker busy.

10

MANAGING MULTIGROUP WORK

OBJECTIVES   By the end of this chapter you should be able to:

   A. Describe how group conflict affects human behavior.
   B. Identify common sources of conflict.
   C. Understand the functional and dysfunctional nature of conflict.
   D. Explain the five styles of conflict management.
   E. Describe strategies for reducing group conflict.

Joe D'Amico's Better Idea

Larry R. London

Joseph B. D'Amico registered another first last year. Nobody had ever won four consecutive terms as union president at Ford's Walton Hills Stamping Plant. But Joe did. They weren't squeakers either. In all four elections he defeated his opponents by embarrassing margins. How did he inspire such loyalty from a local that was one of the most politicized in the United Auto Workers? His constituents offer a simple explanation:

"He's the reason I still have a job," said a production worker.

"If it hadn't been for Joe, Ford would have closed us down," added a machine repairman.

"If you have to give one person credit for keeping this plant open, it would have to go to Joe, hands down," said Terry Gray, UAW Local 420's benefits representative.

Ford had plenty of good reasons to shut down the Walton Hills Plant back in 1980. From the company's viewpoint, it was simply smart business.

Walton Hills had been an embarrassment to management since it opened in 1954. Tough managers were known to sit down and cry when told they were being transferred there. The 4,500-person work force was heavily populated with former miners from the coal fields of West Virginia and Pennsylvania. They brought with them a strong, militant brand of unionism. To control them, the company brought in its toughest managers; it was war from the start.

As soon as Local 420 received its UAW charter in December 1955, the strikes began. When one legal strike was settled, the union began compiling data for the next. Between legal strikes, there were wildcat strikes. In the 1960s they wrenched from management some of the most expensive contractual commitments Ford ever granted workers. They included an agreement that workers could stop working when they met production goals and that they did not have to make up for machine downtime. And the workers kept track of the downtime.

So when the automobile recession hit in the spring of 1980 and the company was faced with excess stamping capacity, Ford decided to pull the thorn known as Walton Hills from its side.

"They had threatened us with plant closings before," D'Amico said, "But then, it wasn't hard to tell they were bluffing. Hell, every stamping plant they owned had more work than it could handle. We knew there was no way they were going to shut us down."

But D'Amico knew that this time it was no bluff.

Excerpted from "Joe D'Amico's Better Idea," *Sunday Magazine, Cleveland Plain Dealer*, April 17, 1988 with permission of author, Larry R. London.

"This time it was different. We could see them hauling dies out every day, moving our jobs to other plants. All the stamping plants were down to about half our normal work force. The handwriting on the wall was plain to anyone who wanted to read it. Things weren't the same any more. We were in a different world.

"Do you know what really convinced me? They sent us a letter, signed by a company official, that told us if we didn't buy their package, we'd be phased out of existence by the end of 1980."

The company's take-it-or-leave-it offer was presented to the membership in a general meeting. It was greeted with cat calls, boos, and shouted obscenities at Ford's management.

But D'Amico swayed the vote with his speech. He told them things had changed and Ford wasn't bluffing.

"I see two choices. If we want jobs, we have to vote for it. If you don't, then vote against it. If it doesn't pass, make no mistake, they'll close us down by the end of the year. I'm voting to accept it. I don't like it, but that's the way it is."

After listening to D'Amico, the membership accepted the company's demands by a margin of 87 percent.

"These were scary times for Local 420," D'Amico remembers. "Even after we accepted it, they didn't stop laying off. We went down to 1,500 people. Lots of Ford's big shots felt we weren't going to make it, and they wouldn't give us any new work. Union and management realized we were all in the same leaky boat. When Ford closes a plant, about the only person they save is the plant manager. (Ford has since changed its policy on plant closings. In an effort to become a more people-oriented corporation, their current official position is to place or retrain as many incumbents as possible.) So we met regularly to resolve our differences. We tried for win-win solutions. With both sides cooperating, it worked.

To demonstrate to hourly and salaried employees that a new attitude was afoot at Walton Hills, D'Amico and plant manager, Ron Wallace, devised a simple yet very direct method of management-labor relations: the weekly plant tour. Each week they toured the plant together, an innovative and gutsy move, particularly for D'Amico. In the past, representatives of management and the union were seen together publicly only when there was trouble and then only to scream and shout at each other.

They stopped and chatted with workers and supervisors. They asked about their problems and concerns. When an immediate fix was possible, they took care of it. When it wasn't, they delegated responsibility to look into the matter and find a solution.

It worked. Supervisors and workers were being heard. It had a tremendous effect on plant morale.

Still it was an uphill struggle. Many had vested interests in the old ways. Some union and company people had earned their positions by being tough and uncompromising. "They didn't trust us, and we didn't trust them," D'Amico explains. "I mean, how do you tell a man who started on hourly and worked his way up to manager by kicking a-- and taking names that he was wrong? How do you make a union officer believe that he won't lose his next election if he behaves fairly toward management, particularly when that union guy feels he was elected for being hard-nosed? It was rough. Some on both sides haven't got the message."

The Employee Involvement process also helped. Employee Involvement (EI) was a provision of the UAW-FORD Master Agreement that encouraged the establishment of forums and procedures to allow workers greater involvement in the decision-making process.

In theory, EI would help a worker develop a sense of ownership toward his job. He would enjoy his work more and be more valuable to the company. Since nobody knows a job as well as the person performing it, his or her involvement would make for more efficient operations.

These are simple concepts, but they became lost in the highly mechanized, militaristic setup of modern industry. EI was designed to establish a win-win philosophy between management and labor. It was simply treating adults as adults and expecting them to respond in the same way. To Wallace and D'Amico, it was what the doctor ordered.

In an attempt to save the plant, Wallace had challenged Ford executives to send them any job, no matter how nasty, and give the plant a chance to prove its worth.

The work force, decimated by layoffs, took up the challenge. Aided by the new EI process, workers were able to channel the same energy that had made Walton Hills the most militant of Ford's plants into making it one of its most productive and profitable.

In the summer of 1987, the number of orders had reached the point that Walton Hills finally was able to recall all the employees with recall rights, many of whom had been laid off since 1979. "Things have changed so much since they were last here that we have orientation sessions for them before they go to work," D'Amico said. "The company explains the new rules and the new way we relate to each other. I talk to them, too. I tell them the same thing: 'We are working together now. Both sides work hard to develop and maintain an atmosphere of mutual respect and trust. That's the only way we can survive in today's world.

"'But never forget that there's still a difference. They're management and we're union. They want as much from us as they can get for as little as they can give. That's just the way it is. But at the same time don't forget that one of the principles of the UAW is that we owe them a fair day's work for a fair day's pay.'"

He was silent for a moment, thoughtful. "It was easier in the past. When they were wrong we'd just bust them. Shut them down. No boring meetings and all that. Today it's harder, working out ways so that everyone wins. The outcomes are better. And it's obvious to a blind man that our members are better off."

I

Premeeting Preparation

A. Answer the following questions before reading the Topic Introduction.

    1. What was the worst experience you ever had with intergroup conflict? What was so bad about it?

    2. What are some of the things that caused the conflict?

    3. What would you like to learn about intergroup conflict?

    4. What are the significant learning points from the readings?

B. Read the Topic Introduction.

II

Topic Introduction

Although the assumption is often made that our behavior is strictly an individual matter—that personality factors alone are responsible for specific actions—there is a growing body of research that points to membership in groups and the relationships between groups as major determinants of behavior, particularly when groups are in competition or conflict. The work of Sherif, the most successful field experiment ever conducted on intergroup conflict, has shown how easily behavior may be changed by putting individuals in a competitive, limited contact situation with another group.[1]

Sherif's research is called the Robbers Cave experiment, named after a summer camp at Robbers Cave, Oklahoma. A homogeneous group of 22 boys was divided into two groups of 11. During the first stage of the experiment the boys were unaware of the existence of the other group. Each group did a variety of cooperative tasks and developed their own group norms and leadership. During the second stage, the groups were informed they would be competing against each other in a week-long grand tournament. The counselors manipulated the scores so that the two groups were neck and neck until the last event. The groups became very antagonistic; there were several commando raids and the losing team robbed the winning team of their medals. When members of one group passed the other, they held their noses. In addition to this sound qualitative evidence of intergroup conflict, the researchers employed quantitative measures that proved that (1) the members of each group had an ethnocentric view of the other group, and strongly preferred "their own kind," (2) that each group overvalued the performance of its own members and devalued the performance of the other group, and (3) that each group stereotyped the other. One's ingroup was "brave, tough, and friendly," while the outgroup was comprised of "sneaks, stinkers, and smart-alecks." These adjectives and this story seem humorous but one sees the same dynamics with union-management conflicts and in companies undergoing less than friendly mergers.

What caused the intergroup conflict at Robbers Cave? We-they feelings are very common but they don't always blaze into open conflict. The key variable in this instance was the competition with its scarce resources. The winning team would receive wonderful prizes, while the losing team would win nothing. Since both groups already thought more highly of themselves than of the other group, whichever team lost would think the tournament was unfair.

During the third stage of the experiment, Sherif tested two of the most effective modes for reducing intergroup tensions: (1) noncompetitive contact in which the two antagonistic groups have equal status and (2) a superordinate goal that was important for all and attainable only by joint cooperation.[2] As Sherif suspected, the first solution, equal status contact, did not work with groups who had reached the antagonistic level that these had. However, the superordinate goal technique was effective; the boys had to cooperate in finding a leak in their water supply, to pool their money to rent a movie, and to pull a broken-down bus. By the end of the third week, the boys had ceased hostilities, eaten meals together, and opted to share a single bus on the trip home. Furthermore, they had begun to treat each other as

---

[1]M. Sherif, *Intergroup Relations and Leadership* (New York: John Wiley, 1962).

[2]M. Deutsch, "An Experimental Study of the Effects of Cooperation and Competition upon Group Process," *Human Relations,* Vol. 2 (1949), pp. 199–231, and G. W. Allport, *The Nature of Prejudice* (Reading, MA: Addison-Wesley, 1954).

individuals and chose friends for reasons other than common group membership. (Incidentally, the boys had a wonderful time at camp.)

A test of stereotyping at the end of the research revealed that the boys thought the members of the other group had *changed* and become more like themselves. In fact, the only difference was due to an environmental change from competition to cooperation.

From this study and others, we know that there are certain behaviors that are typical of conflict situations: stereotyping, overvaluation of one's own group, devaluation of the other group, polarization on the issues, distortion of perceptions, and escalation. Conflict is characterized by an unwillingness to give the other party the benefit of the doubt regarding their motives or actions.

In the opening vignette, "Joe D'Amico's Better Idea," union and management certainly exhibited these conflict behaviors. While the cause of this particular conflict was not solely related to competition over scarce resources, it was resolved in the same manner as in the Robbers Cave study. An overarching goal was established—keeping the plant open and retaining their jobs. Doing that required changing conflict behaviors that had become ingrained over the years and were not easy to modify.

The distinctive nature of group conflict is related to the effects of group membership on individual behavior. Many other studies[3] have since confirmed and added to the body of knowledge about the effects of group membership on individual behavior. Researchers have noted strong tendencies to believe whatever others in a strong reference group believe, even when it contradicts one's visual perceptions. Groups to which we belong, particularly the ones we value most, tend to affirm us in ways we cannot always do for ourselves. By accepting us, they let us know that we are "okay" and erase a lot of the doubts we may have had about our identity. But with that acceptance often comes a series of pressures, subtle and/or overt, to conform to a set of values or behaviors that the group deems acceptable.

In organizations there are different functional groups, professional specialties, geographical groupings, power levels, race, sex, and social class distinctions. Any or all of these can serve as focal points for the creation of strong reference groups that provide their members with a sense of acceptance and identity in exchange for group loyalty and commitment. To the individual, these reference groups are often the most immediate and tangible sources of a sense of belonging to the organization. As a result, these groups are a vehicle for gaining commitment to organizational goals and motivation to work.

Yet group loyalty and commitment lead group members to value their own priorities, goals, and points of view more highly than do other "out" groups. This difference in views often leads to a we-they competitive atmosphere between groups, which further strengthens internal group loyalty and outgroup hostility in a cycle of increasing intensity. Organizations often find this to be a major stumbling block in optimizing productivity and reaching the organization's goals. The people in production may see the marketing department as making inordinate demands on them for changes in products with insufficient lead time. Marketing, on the other hand, may see production as intractable, a group that does not understand the necessity of meeting the competition from other companies. As a result of the conflict, the energy of both groups is being expended in defense of their own position as well as attacking the position of the other group, all at the expense of organizational goals. Furthermore, in many cases, conflict is a major source of stress for the individuals involved.

Is this competition between groups always bad or dysfunctional? Not neces-

[3]For example, D. Cartwright and A. Zander, *Group Dynamics Research and Theory* (New York: Harper & Row, 1968); M. Deutsch, *The Resolution of Conflict* (New Haven, CT: Yale University Press, 1973); Clayton Alderfer and Ken K. Smith, "Studying Intergroup Relations Embedded in Organizations," *Administrative Science Quarterly* (March 1982), pp. 35–64; and Stephen P. Robbins, *Managing Organizational Conflict* (Englewood Cliffs, NJ: Prentice Hall, 1974).

sarily. There are numerous examples in our society of the advantages of intergroup competition. In the sports world one team is always competing against another. This phenomenon produces much excitement for audiences since they have an emotional identification with one or the other team and feel actively involved in the battle. The competitive nature of the encounter produces excitement for the players and motivates or induces them to exert maximum effort to reap the rewards of winning. In the business world, companies compete with one another for a larger share of the consumer dollar. Competition between organizations often increases the excellence of the product.

These situations where competition between groups is productive have several distinguishing characteristics. First, they involve entities (groups) that are not part of the same formal organizational structure. The Giants and the Colts are a part of the NFL, but they represent independent and autonomous operating organizations. Deliberate intergroup competition has been used by many government contracting agencies within the framework of parallel projects. The same task (usually a feasibility study) is given in two or more different companies with the understanding that the best proposal will win the follow-up contract. The assumption underlying this strategy is that the higher quality of the final product resulting from such a competitive structure will justify the duplication of effort and expenditure of funds. A second distinguishing characteristic is that seldom do any of these competing organizations (groups) find it necessary to work together to solve a common problem or to reach a common goal. Indeed, when they must come together, as in the case of two nations to resolve an international dispute or a group of baseball owners to elect a new commissioner, the competitive element that proved so beneficial in their other activities often gets in the way when they must collaborate. Finally, the prize for which these groups are competing is a scarce resource of relatively fixed amount—there will be only one recipient of the government proposal or there can be only one winner of the Super Bowl. The reward system is such, in other words, as to create a zero-sum, win-lose situation: for me to win, you must lose.

There are, then, two distinct kinds of competitiveness as far as organizations are concerned, each with its own sets of consequences. Competitiveness internal to an organization often results in energy being expended at the expense of the overall mission of the organization. Competition among organizations is the essence of the marketplace.

Conflict within organizations is inevitable. In addition to we-they situations resulting from group membership, conflict is likely to occur anywhere in the organization where there are "joints" or interfaces between different functions. Common causes of conflict are differences in values, personalities, education, culture, perceptions, and goals. Ambiguity often results in conflict when people battle over power or turf that has not been clearly assigned. Competition over scarce resources in whatever form—recognition, money, or even offices with windows—is also a source of conflict. Whenever the work is structured in such a way that groups are interdependent and their output depends upon that of another department, there is a potential for conflict.

To some degree the human factor determines whether conflict will actually occur at some of these interfaces. Individuals are comfortable with varying levels of conflict. In our culture we receive two somewhat contradictory messages: (1) fight and stand up for yourself, but (2) only when it is acceptable. Part of being politically savvy is understanding when conflict is appropriate. Some people thrive upon conflict and create it wherever they go; others go to great lengths to avoid it. Managers at either end of this continuum are likely to be less than effective in their jobs and in their ability to create a positive work environment for their employees. Research on individual conflict styles is summarized in Figure 10–1.[4]

---

[4]K. W. Thomas, "Conflict and Conflict Management," in *Handbook of Industrial and Organizational Psychology,* edited by M. D. Dunnette (Chicago: Rand McNally, 1976), pp. 889–935.

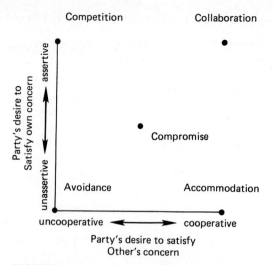

FIGURE 10–1   Five Conflict-Handling
Styles, Plotted According to Party's Desire to
Satisfy Own and Other's Concerns

The model of conflict styles has two axes: (1) the degree to which the individual wants to satisfy his or her own concerns and (2) the degree to which he or she wants to satisfy the concerns of the other party. The *competitive* orientation implies winning at the other's expense. This is an example of a win-lose power struggle. In contrast, the *accommodation* style represents appeasement or satisfying the other's concern without taking one's own needs or desires into consideration. *Compromising* reflects the midway point between these two styles and involves give-and-take by both parties. Both parties gain and give up something they want. The *collaborative* orientation differs from compromising in that it represents a desire to satisfy fully the concerns of both parties. People search for solutions that are mutually beneficial. The *avoiding* orientation implies lack of concern about the desires of either party. As with any taxonomy of styles, each conflict style has its advantages and disadvantages, which are shown in Table 10-1. As we stated at the beginning of the book, effective managers are capable of employing more than one style and know which one to use in a given situation.

The purpose of this exercise is to simulate a set of organizational relationships among groups. As you go through the exercise, try to be aware of your feelings about your group and other groups; there will be time after the exercise to reflect on your feelings individually and to discuss them with your group and the entire class.

TABLE 10–1 Gains and Losses Associated with Conflict Styles

	COMPETITION	AVOIDANCE	ACCOMMODA-TION	COMPROMISE	COLLABORA-TION
GAINS	Chance to win everything Exciting, games-manship Exercise own sense of power	No energy or time expenditure Conserve for fights that are "more important"	Little muss or fuss no feathers ruffled Others may view you as supportive. Energy free for other pursuits	No one returns home empty-handed "Keeps the peace" May or may not encourage creativity	Both sides win Better chance for long-term solutions Creativity in problem solving Energizing on both sides New level of understanding of situation Commitment, quality
LOSSES	Chance to lose everything Alienate others Discourage others from working with you Potentially larger scale conflicts in the future (*or* more avoidance of conflict)	Less stimulation Less creative problem solving Little understanding of the needs of others Incomplete comprehension of work environment	Lowered self-assertion and possibly self-esteem Loss of power Absence of your unique contribution to the situation Others dependent on you may not feel you "go to bat" for them	Since neither side is totally satisfied, conflicts are likely to recur later. Neither side realizes self-determination fully	Time, in the short run Loss of sense of autonomy

Developed by Ronald Fry, Jared Florian, and Jacquie McLemore, Department of Organizational Behavior, Weatherhead School of Management, Case Western Reserve University, Cleveland, Ohio.

III

Procedure for Group Meeting:
The Nadir Corporation Negotiation[5]

THE TASK

Throughout its 40-year history, the Nadir Corporation has been run by George Nadir, founder, president, and majority stockholder. Nadir rules with a heavy hand and takes part in all company decisions. He adjudicates disputes between the two major divisions of the company, marketing and manufacturing, insisting at all times that the divisions communicate through him on major issues. Nadir Corporation has been a very successful consumer-oriented manufacturing organization over the last 12 years, growing at an average annual rate of 8 percent in sales. It is an above-average performer in terms of profits in its industry. Further details about Nadir products and financial performance are not essential for this exercise.

Nadir's surprise sale of his stock to Apogee, Inc., has made Nadir Corp. a wholly owned subsidiary that must now operate without "the old man." Not being willing to impose a new president on Nadir without first finding out what the company's needs and executive resources are, Apogee has sent its executive vice president for acquisitions, Pat Cleary, to meet with Nadir personnel to get a clearer picture of what should be done—whether, for instance, a new president should come from the outside or from within and just what kind of manager he or she should be. Pat Cleary has sent a memo (below) to members of the manufacturing and marketing departments.

Half of you will represent manufacturing (group A). The manufacturing division is divided about evenly between managers who began their careers as engineers and managers who operated the facilities starting as hourly workers. Marketing (group B) is managed totally by college graduates, with about half having started as engineers, the other half coming to the company from liberal arts backgrounds.

APOGEE CORPORATION
INTEROFFICE MEMO

TO: Manufacturing Department
       Marketing Department
FROM: Pat Cleary, Executive Vice President
RE: Criteria for Choosing New President, Nadir Corporation

You are requested to hold a department meeting for the purpose of establishing criteria for choosing a new president for Nadir Corporation. Please prepare a brief report listing five criteria, in short phrases, that you think should be used in the choice. Please rank order them in terms of their importance to the Nadir Corporation.

When you have prepared your reports, we will have a joint meeting of the two departments to evaluate them.

---

[5]The intergroup exercise used in this unit is similar to many that have been developed previously. The original concept should probably be credited to Sherif, *Intergroup Relations and Leadership,* but has been further developed by many others, notably, Robert Blake.

STEP 1. The total group will be the Nadir Corporation, with half the learning groups representing marketing and the other half representing manufacturing. Assign or divide into the groups on whatever basis seems most appropriate, keeping the same number of members in each group. The group leader or instructor will act as Pat Cleary and will coordinate the simulation and discussion. (*Note:* If your total group size exceeds 18 people, you may want to run two separate, but simultaneous, sessions.) (10 minutes)

STEP 2. Marketing and manufacturing meet separately to prepare their response to Cleary's memo, listing their criteria for choosing a new president of the Nadir Corporation. In preparing these reports, you should take your role as members of marketing and manufacturing into account but rely primarily on your own personal judgments about what kind of person would make the best president of Nadir. Short phrases should be used, and there should be no more than five criteria listed by each group. They should be rank ordered in terms of importance to the company. *Each group member* should make a clear, legible copy of the group report for use in the next step. (30 minutes)

STEP 3. To evaluate the two reports, Cleary has asked individuals in marketing to pair off with someone in manufacturing. During this period you will be paired with a member of the other team. The pairings may be done as you wish. You will be expected to provide a copy of your group's criteria report for your discussion partner to review. (20 minutes)

Your task as a two-person team will be to decide which set of criteria is better in its entirety and by how much. You must allot 100 points between the two, but cannot allot 50 to each under the assumption that no two reports are ever exactly alike. Even if the wording is identical the thoughts behind them will not be. There must be a preference indicated, whether by 52:48 or by 90:10. Concentrate on the content of the list rather than on peripheral things such as style or elegance of wording.

At the end of 20 minutes (the instructor or leader should let you know when the time is up), return to your original group and total the number of points each member brought back to get the total group score. Give your numerical results to the instructor who will tabulate them and announce which is the better report.

STEP 4. Back in your original groups, discuss the preceding hour's events (20 minutes), focusing on
   a. What occurred between you and the representatives of the other group?
   b. How this group operated during the time in which you were generating the criteria report?
      (1) What was the predominant leadership style? What were its effects?
      (2) What were the effects of time and task pressures on group interaction?
      (3) How were conflicts handled? Decisions made?
   c. What is the state of this group now?
      (1) What is the climate in this group right now? Is it different from when you were doing the task?
      (2) How willing would you be to give or receive help from someone in the other group right now? How easy would it be for you to work with the other group now (e.g., to implement the winning criteria list)?
      (3) What effect did winning or losing have on your group?

STEP 5. Reconvene as a class. (30 minutes) Read the Follow-up in this chapter, and, using it as a guide, discuss
   a. What happened within the groups during the task? Were the summary predictions correct? How did they vary from the reality?

b. What happened between the two groups?

   c. In the group discussion (step 4), what was the winning group's discussion like? Were the summary predictions valid?

   d. What was the climate in the losing group? Were the summary predictions valid for them?

   e. What conclusions can you draw about the effect of intergroup competition on group behavior? On your behavior as an individual group member?

   f. How might Pat Cleary's memo be rewritten to reduce conflict?

   g. What connections can you make between this exercise and the readings?

OPTIONAL
   STEP 6.   Meet once again with your partner from the other group for purposes of giving each other feedback on your influence styles. (20 minutes, if time permits) Discuss

   a. Your perception of your partner's influence style during the interaction and your reasons for it.

   b. Your partner's perception of your influence style and the reasons for it.

   c. How these perceptions agree or conflict with your own perception of your influence style.

   (If you have completed the chapter, Leadership: Power and Influence, compare your style then and now. Do you perceive changes in your style of influencing others?)

IV

Follow-up

Schein, in *Organizational Psychology,*[6] provides a brief but lucid description of intergroup problems in organizations. This summary draws heavily upon his ideas. The simulation you have just experienced has been replicated many times with a variety of groups.[7] Because the results have been surprisingly constant, it is now possible to predict what will generally happen as a consequence of intergroup competition. These predictions are summarized here.

What Happens *Within* Groups?

The members of each of two competing groups begin to close ranks and quickly experience increased feelings of group loyalty and pride. Each group sees itself as the best and the other group as the enemy. Under the pressure of time and task deadlines, the group willingly accepts more structure and autocratic leadership. The group climate is characterized by work, as opposed to play or fight; task, as opposed to maintenance. Conformity is stressed and there is little tolerance for individual deviation.

What Happens *Between* Groups?

Whatever interaction there was between the members of the two groups before the competition decreases and becomes more hostile. Whatever communication there is becomes very selective, each group hearing only comments that confirm its stereotype of the other and support its own position.

What Happens to the *Winners*?

The winning group climate can be called "fat and happy." Tension is released; there is little desire to get on to work. People would prefer to play and rest on their laurels. There is little desire to explore earlier conflicts and possibly learn from them.

Generally, the winners not only retain their prior cohesion, but become more cohesive. The exception is when the group really does not feel as if it won or when the decision is close and they did not win decisively. Under these conditions, winners often act like losers.

What Happens to the *Losers*?

The members deal initially with having lost in one of two ways. Some groups deny reality—"We didn't really lose. It was a moral victory." Other groups seek a scapegoat, someone other than themselves to blame for the defeat. Rules, for instance, are often seen as at fault.

A losing group is, however, also a "lean and hungry" group. Tension increases, old conflicts are reexamined, and the group really digs in and learns a lot about itself in preparation for the next task.

What Happens to *Negotiators* Between Groups?

The negotiator often experiences significant role conflict between being a good judge and a good group member. Judges often find it difficult to ignore loyalties to their own groups and be completely neutral. If theirs happens to be a loser, they experience much difficulty reentering, and often bear the brunt of much of the scapegoating behavior (often in a jocular fashion).

People seldom realize how much responsibility a person feels when asked to represent a group and the tension that results from being put in such a position. In addition, it is often unclear just how free a representative really is to be himself or

---

[6]Edgar H. Schein, *Organizational Psychology* (Englewood Cliffs, NJ: Prentice Hall, 1965), pp. 80–86.
[7]The most systematic research in organizational settings is reported in Robert R. Blake, H. A. Shepard, and Jane S. Mouton, *Managing Intergroup Conflict in Industry* (Houston: Gulf, 1964).

herself as opposed to being what the group expects him or her to be. How flexible is the person to deviate from the group's mandate in response to changes in the situation? Finally, if the group loses, the representative often feels guilty and responsible.

We have, in this chapter, explored some of the dysfunctional consequences of intergroup competition and conflict, and it would be a simple step to assume that all conflict between groups in an organization is bad. More recent studies[8] have pointed to a different view of conflict—that too little expressed conflict between groups can be as dysfunctional as too much.

Brown maintains that conflict will exist between groups by their very nature and that the task of the manager is not necessarily to eliminate conflict but to maintain it at a level appropriate to the task. Too much conflict can lead to defensiveness and an inability to work collaboratively toward organization goals. Too little conflict can stifle ideas and innovation. Relative differences in power between groups, for instance, often lead to too little conflict being expressed as the "low-power" group finds the expression of such views to the "high-power" group much too risky.

The manager who wishes to manage conflict productively needs to develop skills in diagnosing dysfunctional situations at both extremes in terms of attitudes, behaviors, and structures that are needed to increase or decrease the level of conflict. Many conflicts in society (race, sex, age) require the effective manager to be aware of those larger conflicts, assessing as clearly as possible the extent to which his or her organization reinforces them, and working to change those attitudes, behaviors, and structures that institutionalize them.

As we have seen in the exercise, intergroup conflict is easy to induce. Getting the conflicts in the open and managing them effectively is another matter. Generally, it has been found that intergroup conflict, once it begins, is extremely hard to reduce.[9] The strategy of locating a common enemy or a superordinate goal is useful, but much work must be done to overcome the negative consequences that have already developed before such strategies become feasible. Educational techniques[10] exist and are being used with considerable success to help organizations deal with intergroup conflict that has dysfunctional consequences.

Given the difficulties of reducing intergroup competition, strategies for eliminating it in the first place may be desirable. Schein suggests four steps that have proved to be effective in helping organizations avoid the dysfunctional consequences of intergroup conflict.

1. Relatively *greater emphasis is given to total organizational effectiveness* and the role of departments in contributing to it; departments are measured and rewarded on the basis of their *contribution to the total effort* rather than on their individual effectiveness.

2. *High interaction* and *frequent communication* are stimulated between groups to work on problems of intergroup coordination and help; organizational *rewards are given partly on the basis of help* that groups give each other.

3. There is frequent *rotation of members* among groups or departments to stimulate high degrees of mutual understanding and empathy for one another's problems.

4. *Win-lose situations are avoided;* groups should never be put into the position of competing for the same organizational reward; emphasis is always placed on pooling resources to maximize organizational effectiveness; rewards are shared equally with all the groups or departments.

[8]L. Dave Brown, "Managing Conflict Among Groups," *Readings*.

[9]The reality of this is nowhere clearer than in our efforts to combat years of racial prejudice and discrimination.

[10]See Blake et al., *Managing Intergroup Conflict in Industry,* for discussion on this point and various publications of the National Training Laboratories, Washington, DC.

V

Learning Points

1. Individual behavior is influenced by membership in groups undergoing conflict.

2. Groups in conflict tend to stereotype the other party, see their own group as ideal, and overvalue the contributions of their own members, while devaluing those of the other group. Their perceptions of one another become distorted and hostilities tend to escalate.

3. Sherif's Robbers Cave experiment revealed that conflict behavior was induced by having two groups of boys compete for a scarce resource—limited prizes. The hostility that resulted decreased greatly when the researchers introduced superordinate goals that were important to all the boys and could only be obtained by collaboration.

4. Organizations are full of reference groups that provide individuals with a sense of belonging and identity in exchange for loyalty and commitment. However, a we-they attitude often develops when these groups come into contact with each other.

5. We-they attitudes between internal groups can foster competition and a lack of collaboration that hinders productivity and achievement of the overall goals of the organization. In contrast, competition with external groups can be very productive.

6. Common causes of group conflict in organizations are we-they attitudes of reference groups, competition for scarce resources, ambiguous authority, interdependence and differences in values, personality, perceptions, education, culture, and goals.

7. The five conflict management styles are based upon two axes:
   a. Desire to satisfy one's own concerns.
   b. Desire to satisfy the concerns of the other party.

8. The five conflict styles are
   a. Competition.
   b. Accommodation.
   c. Compromise.
   d. Collaboration.
   e. Avoidance.
   Effective managers use the style appropriate to the situation.

9. Too much or too little conflict are both dysfunctional states.

VI

Tips for Managers

- Try to reframe the situation from a "we-they" position to a "we versus the problem" approach.

- Look for mutual goals and values, or even a common enemy. Make sure common enemies are outside the company and not a person or group with whom it is important to have a collaborative relationship.

- Try to establish overarching goals that free employees from conflict positions. For example, the manager of an auditing department realized her efforts to incorporate the auditing department of a recently merged smaller bank were not succeeding. In fact, hostility between the two groups was increasing. Rather than remain at the level of fighting over whose procedures were best, the manager wisely reframed the situation and asked the entire group to start from scratch and use the merger as an opportunity to devise the best possible procedures. Their final product was "ours," and in the process, the two departments became a cohesive unit.

- Managing conflict may appear to be too time consuming in the short run, but conflicts that are allowed to fester can cause great harm and take up more time in the long run.

- Groups that cannot come to an agreement can sometimes be moved along by identifying what criteria should be used to solve the problem.

- Another way to avoid conflict is by clearly determining both authority and responsibility.

- Managers can sometimes decrease conflict by the use of a liaison or a buffer. Liaisons or boundary spanners absorb heat from both sides and try to interpret the actions of both groups to each other. Buffers can also be inanimate objects that prevent two groups from having to interact, for example, the order wheel in restaurants and automatic reordering systems in warehouses.

- Managers can set the stage for collaboration between departments or divisions by their actions: by having a clear understanding of the contribution each group makes and passing that on to others and by showing an interest in all groups and how they work together. The manager's attention is often one of the scarce resources in an organization. Therefore, managers who share their attention as equally as possible (or at least explain to the others why they are focusing upon a certain area) are more likely to have a collaborative climate.

VII

Personal Application Assignment

This assignment is to write about a situation involving intergroup conflict. Choose an experience about which you want to learn more. When you address the "Reflective Observation" section, answer these questions: How does the other group see you? How do you think you see them?

A. *Concrete Experience*

1. *Objectively* describe the experience ("who," "what," "when," "where," "how" type information—up to 2 points).

2. *Subjectively* describe your feelings, perceptions, and thoughts that occurred *during* (not after) the experience (up to 2 points). Does this section have too much detail? (If so, delete 1 point.)

B. *Reflective Observation*

1. Look at the experience from different points of view. How many points of view did you include that are *relevant* (up to 2 points)?

2. Use these perspectives to add more meaning to the incident (up to 2 points).

C. *Abstract Conceptualization*

1. Relate concepts from the assigned readings and the lecture to the experience (i.e., what theories that you heard in the lecture or read in the *Reader* relate to your understanding of this incident?). Make reference to at least two sources. Use standard referencing format and include the page number to which you are referring. How many sources did you use and how clearly did you explain their theories (up to 4 points)?

2. You can also create an original model or theory, but it should not replace course concepts.

D. *Active Experimentation*

1. Write about what you will do in the future that will improve your effectiveness. Use rules of thumb or action resolutions.

2. Are they described specifically, thoroughly, and in detail (up to 4 points).

E. *Integration, Synthesis, and Writing*
   1. Did you write about something personally important to you (up to 1 point)?
   2. Was it well written (up to 2 points)?
   3. Did you integrate and synthesize the different sections (up to 1 point)?

11

MANAGING DIVERSITY *

OBJECTIVES   By the end of this chapter you should be able to:

A. Define culture and ethnocentrism.

B. Understand the impact that one's cultural assumptions have on one's own behavior and the behavior of others.

C. Appreciate the positive aspects of diversity.

D. Explain what happens to tokens in organizations.

E. Understand how to manage diversity in organizations.

*This chapter was partially developed and written by David Akinnusi, Lynda Detterman, Rafael Estevez, Elizabeth Fisher, Mary Ann Hazen, David Kolb, Dennis O'Connor, and Michelle Spain.

What's Your Eccentricity Quotient?

Joyce Osland

How weird can you be in a major corporation and still keep your job? Kathleen McDonald, organization development team leader who was responsible for a project on managing diversity at Exxon, devised an eccentricity model to help employees answer that very question.

According to McDonald, the employee's goal is to balance their *perceived competence* with their *perceived eccentricity* (PC = PE). She defines perceived competence as how you and your job performance are seen by others in your organization. But note that this perception can be different from reality; perceived competence is how good others in the organization "think" you are.

Perceived eccentricity refers to those parts of you or your actions which do not fit neatly into the "ideal organization person" as defined by your organization. As McDonald describes it, perceived eccentricity is the corners of the square peg as you work in an environment that rewards round pegs. Obviously, some of those corners can be worn down, while others are difficult if not impossible, to remove. In most *Fortune 500* companies, anyone who is female, foreign born, or a person of color is likely to have a higher perceived eccentricity score than a WASP male. Likewise, people with different lifestyles, vocal religious beliefs, or a unique style of dress, mannerisms, or speech may also be perceived as eccentric in some organizations. In technical environments, perceived eccentricity can also relate to the degree of risk and innovation you display.

How you manage the perceived eccentricity side of your equation has to do with how much acceptance you seek and what that acceptance represents. How much of an insider can you be? How much of an insider do you want to be? How much of yourself are you willing to leave at home or to censor at work? These can be tough issues, especially for minorities who feel the strain of struggling to fit an "ideal type" which bears little resemblance to them.

McDonald described the experience of a white woman who moved from a plant to a technical service position. At the plant she and just about everyone else wore pants. For her new job she upgraded her wardrobe to slack suits. Eventually word drifted back to her that the sales people did not want to take her with them on customer calls because of her "eccentric" dress. She had a choice to make: she could work at raising her perceived competence so that her new colleagues would see her as an invaluable resource even in a burlap sack, or she could invest in a new wardrobe and decrease her perceived eccentricity. She went out and bought skirts—a quicker if more expensive route to correcting an imbalance in the eccentricity model.

Adapted with permission from an unpublished document by Kathleen McDonald.

However, it's easier to change clothes than skin color. The black man who entered a predominantly white company and was assigned to a supervisor who was also brand new, had more difficulty in overcoming the perceived eccentricity of his race. Because the new supervisor couldn't inform him about the company's norms early on or interpret his competence to others in the organization, it took longer for the black man to establish his perceived competence.

McDonald says that you can be as eccentric as you are competent. And it's usually a good idea to establish your competence before you test the company's tolerance of eccentricity. How do you scope out your perceived competence and eccentricity? From performance appraisals, the rewards that come your way and from feedback. And you may have to take an active role in seeking out feedback so you can decide how to manage yourself in the workplace. McDonald's eccentricity model is a good barometer for figuring out the consequences of your choices.

Examples of employees whose perceived eccentricity far outweighed their perceived competence come readily to mind. These are the folks who are no longer around to tell their tale or who are continuously passed over for promotion. The danger of that kind of imbalance is clear. However, McDonald sees no advantage in the opposite kind of imbalance, even though there are typically many people in organizations who are perceived to be more competent than they are eccentric. The danger here is that employees will lose valuable opportunities to grow, both personally and professionally, by playing it safe. And organizations won't learn how to live with and profit from the diversity of their employees. So if your organization perceives you as more competent than eccentric, even up the equation and break out a little. Let those at work know how wonderfully weird or innovative you can be. You'll be doing everyone a favor.

I
Premeeting Preparation

A. Read the entire chapter to become familiar with the topic and prepare for the group meeting. Do this first. Then

B. Complete the

1. Analysis of a Personal Experience of Being Different.

2. Intensity of Differentness Rating.

C. What are the significant learning points from the readings?

Analysis of a Personal Experience of Being Different

The experience of being different from others can be frustrating, isolating, and even painful. In our desire to avoid these feelings of difference, we are often tempted to deny our individual uniqueness and to "fit in"—to adopt the superficial characteristics of the majority. But doing so is not good for us as individuals for we are denying part of ourselves with resulting feelings of alienation (playing a role). It is ineffective as well, for our skills lie with who we are, not who we pretend to be. Nor is this denial of differences good for the organization, for without a variety of perspectives and alternatives for action, organizations become rigid and ultimately die.

Think of a recent experience you have had where you felt you were being treated as though you were "different," where others were not recognizing you as a unique person. It could be an experience in this course, at work, or anywhere. (Use another page if you need more space.)

1. Describe what happened in the situation.

2. How did you feel, think, and act?

3. How did others feel, think, and act?

4. What was the outcome of the situation?

When you have finished, score your experience for its intensity of differentness.

Premeeting Preparation Intensity of Differentness Rating

We are all unique individuals with unique cultural and subcultural backgrounds and identities. As a result, we all have experiences of being different, of being stereotyped and discriminated against. These feelings are most pronounced and intense:

- When the situation is very important (e.g., where a job is at stake, in personal relationships, or where physical safety is a concern).
- When our own cultural experiences are markedly different from the dominant culture around us.
- When these differences are visible to others (e.g., skin color, sex, age, language, manner of dress).
- When there are power differences between ourselves and the dominant culture (i.e., when we are "one-down" in influence or rank).
- When we are alone or isolated from others who share our culture or subculture.
- When others are stereotyping us in a way that we and others notice.
- When we have strong emotional reactions of frustration, anger, or humiliation.

Look back over your description of the situation where you felt "different." Score it on the following issues:

	CIRCLE THE NUMBER THAT APPLIES		
1. How important was the situation to you?	0 Relatively un-important	1 Important	2 Very critical
2. How different were you?	0 Very little difference	1 Some difference	2 Great difference
3. Were these differences visible to others?	0 No	1 A little	2 Obvious
4. Were there power differences?	0 I was one-up, in charge	1 Equal	2 I was one-down
5. Were you isolated from others similar to you?	0 I had several others like me for support	1 One other supportive	2 I was alone
6. Were you stereotyped?	0 I was treated as a unique individual	1 I felt stereotyped	2 There was direct evidence of stereotyping
7. Did the situation cause you to react emotionally?	0 No emotional reaction	1 I felt slightly upset	2 I had strong emotional reactions

Add the numbers circled to get your total intensity of differentness score: _____.

II

Topic Introduction

> But while he gains so much from culture, man is also brainwashed, to some extent by the culture to which he is exposed from birth. Equipped with a collection of stereotypes with which to face the world, man is apt to lose sight of possible alternative modes of behavior and understanding.[1]

Culture causes humans to see the world differently through their cultural lenses and is also a major determinant of behavior, even when it is not perceived. We accept Lewin's[2] theory that behavior is a function of personality and environment, but too often the cultural context of the person's environment is overlooked. People are usually introduced to their own culture in the act of confronting another. One learns what it means to be an American by rubbing up against other nationalities. And even then, one discerns mainly those aspects of one's own culture that come into conflict with those of the other culture. "What the observer notices about the culture he visits will depend not only on the society he chooses to study, but also his (or her) own cultural background."[3] We don't notice similarities as quickly because our eyes are drawn first to differences. Another way to explain this phenomenon is to cast it into the Gestalt scheme of figure and ground. What is ground in one's own culture and country becomes figural when thrown up against the relief provided by another culture. Figure 11–1 presents a list of American cultural values.

Hofstede[4] states that culture is to a human collectivity what personality is to the individual. The way humans react to the basic issues that confront all humankind is determined by culture. For example, old age and dying represent an inescapable problem for all societies, but the manner of approaching and resolving this problem derives primarily from particular cultural values and beliefs: the prestige and respect given to the elderly, beliefs about the afterlife, and economic values determine how a culture will handle the problem of old age and death.

Culture provides us with both ready-made solutions to basic human issues and a sense of identity. However, we must also acknowledge the price we pay for these provisions. The concept of trade-offs is a useful one when studying different cultures. Traditional cultures with clear norms may be more confining and slower to change, but their members usually possess a strong sense of identity. Creativity and adaptability are often identified as by-products of American culture; however, the price we pay for allowing people the freedom to go their own way in our polyglot and highly mobile society is insecurity and rootlessness. All cultures have advantages and disadvantages when considered objectively. However, human nature sometimes prevents us from appreciating the advantages or the good points of other cultures. This quality is referred to as ethnocentrism.

Ethnocentrism is defined as the "exaggerated tendency to think the charac-

---

[1]V. Barnouw in Ross Webber, *Culture and Management* (Homewood, IL: Richard D. Irwin, 1969), p. 69.

[2]Kurt Lewin, *A Dynamic Theory of Personality* (New York: McGraw-Hill, 1935).

[3]J. S. Wiggins, K. E. Renner, G. L. Clore, and R. J. Rose, *The Psychology of Personality* (Reading, MA: Addison-Wesley, 1971), p. 109).
Source: Reprinted from C. R. Mill, *Activities for Trainers: 50 Useful Designs.* San Diego, CA: University Associates, Inc., 1980. Used with permission.

[4]Geert Hofstede, *Culture's Consequences: International Differences in Work-Related Values* (Beverly Hills, CA: Sage, 1977, 1980, 1984).

1. **Action is good.**
   Change can be induced through individual or group action. "Getting things done" is commendable. Problems, once identified, can be solved.

2. **Man's environment can be controlled.**
   Nature is to be conquered and made over to suit man's needs.

3. **Progress is straight-lined and upward, not spiral.**
   Change is inevitable and Utopia is the result of achievement and progress.

4. **The material is more real than the spiritual.**
   The concrete and observable are relevant. Material comfort and convenience are emphasized.

5. **A person's success is self-made.**
   Social status accrues to one who succeeds in the face of competition.

6. **The individual is the keystone of society.**
   Individual responsibility is important, and "the greatest good for the greatest number" leads to a successful society. Minority rights must be protected.

7. **Man is a moral creature.**
   Personal conduct can be evaluated in universal moral terms. Clear-cut ethical distinctions can be made that affect all people equally.

8. **Time is money.**
   Time is a material thing. It should be actively mastered or manipulated to one's advantage.

9. **The world is rational.**
   Scientific reasoning is the unquestioned way of understanding the physical world.

10. **The American is open and friendly and so are other people when dealt with in an open and friendly way.**
    People of traditional, formal cultures often view as ill-mannered the openness, use of first names, personal questions, display of enthusiasm in public, and open displays of affection that are characteristics of Americans. Americans tend to overlook this disapproval.

FIGURE 11–1   Concepts Shaping the American Way of Life   *Source: Reprinted from C. R. Mill,* Activities for Trainers: 50 Useful Designs. *San Diego, Ca.: University Associates, Inc., 1980. Used with permission.*

teristics of one's own group or race superior to those of other groups or races."[5] Humans are preoccupied with the differences between their "own" kind and outsiders. Anthropologists have encountered many tribes whose name is literally translated as "the human beings"; this implies that those outside their tribe are not human and, therefore, are not treated with the same consideration.

Ethnocentrism is very obvious in the epithets used by countries at war, but it is not triggered only by military conflict. Within the United States our ethnocentrism is reflected in race issues, the deterioration of our neighborhoods, and promotions at work—all of which represent threats to the economic and social dominance of the white majority.[6] Because ethnocentrism in this country seldom results in all-out warfare, we should not be lulled into overlooking its existence. Everyone possesses some degree of ethnocentrism. For anyone who deals with people who are different, the first step is to acknowledge one's ethnocentrism and try to curb the natural thought that one's own group/culture/sex is, by definition, better than others.

[5]Ibid., 1977, p. 25.
[6]Ross Webber, *Culture and Management.* (Homewood, IL: R. D. Irwin, 1969).

As corporations grow larger and the world grows smaller, we find ourselves increasingly involved with coworkers who differ from us in their cultural and subcultural identities. Organizations exist in a multicultural environment and cannot avoid this reality. People in organizations bring with them aspects of their cultural experience, and thus, organizations come to mirror issues facing society and the world.

Brown,[7] for example, reminds us that the minorities of a society that allows discrimination tend to be particularly sensitive to discriminatory behaviors within the organizations that employ them. They perceive discriminatory intent in behaviors that may seem appropriate and nondiscriminatory to members of the dominant culture. As a result, members of the majority may feel insulted if accused of discrimination. They do not recognize that they are "beneficiaries" of institutional discrimination and do not understand why minorities are so sensitive about discrimination. People from different cultures or groups are likely to put outsiders through a testing period. Minorities who have had negative experiences with majority members or institutions are especially likely to watch for possible signs of discrimination or untrustworthiness in new relationships or settings and take longer to form relationships with majority members. This is sometimes mistakenly interpreted as standoffishness; in fact, it's merely a different timetable for forming relationships.

Because multicultural organizations are becoming a major feature of modern society, new issues are being raised about what constitutes effective management of human beings in these organizations. For example, Geert Hofstede, a Dutch psychologist, studied personnel in a very large multinational corporation with operations in nearly every country in the world.[8] He administered questionnaires to 166,000 employees of this firm in 40 different countries. The results showed that cultures varied on four dimensions:

1. Power distance: the extent to which a society accepts the fact that power in institutions and organizations is distributed unequally.

2. Uncertainty/avoidance: the extent to which a society accepts or avoids uncertain and ambiguous situations.

3. Individualism: the extent to which people are responsible for taking care of themselves and give priority to their own interests. Its opposite is collectivism in which individuals give their loyalty to a group and in return the group takes responsibility for the individual.

4. Masculinity: the extent to which the dominant cultural values are assertiveness, the acquisition of money and things as opposed to its opposite, femininity, which refers to dominant values of caring for others, quality of life, and people.

His findings cast doubt on the universal applicability of American management techniques. Americans, he found, value equality (low power distance), are individualists who willingly tolerate uncertainty, and have generally masculine values (achievement and striving versus nurturance and support). American management techniques, he argues, are largely based on these values. As a result, they do not work as well in a culture, for example, that values the collective over the individual, emphasizes feminine values, or desires great power distance. The practical implication of this research is that management practices need to be adjusted to the values and attitudes of the culture or subculture in which they are applied. This implication applies not only in cross-cultural management in other nations but in our day-to-day relationships with those who identify with different subcultures, whether these

[7]L. D. Brown, *Managing Conflict at Organizational Interfaces* (Reading, MA: Addison-Wesley, 1983).
[8]Geert Hofstede, "Motivation, Leadership and Organizations: Do American Theories Apply Abroad?" *Readings.*

are based on race, sex, education, religion, or geographic region. The focus of this chapter is on managing diversity in multicultural organizations. It underscores the importance of individual differences and seeks to develop skills in managing these differences.

STEREOTYPING

People entering organizations bring with them their own assumptions and preconceptions, and they use these ideas to form new impressions about other groups in the organization. These groups can be based on sex, race, ethnic background, professional associations, and so on. When we act toward individual members of a group based on our assumptions about the group to which they belong, we are engaging in a stereotypic behavior. Aronson[9] describes this as follows: "to stereotype is to assign identical characteristics to any people in a group regardless of the actual variation among members of the group."

A stereotypic perception of individual differences is called a prejudice. Stereotypes abound in organizations. The common ones are based on sex, race, and professional groups. For example, even during the last decade, researchers[10] discovered that women were not perceived by men and by other women to be as competent as men. Where a woman was successful, there was a tendency to attribute it to unusually high motivation or to luck. In either case there is an implied sense of female inferiority that, as Daryl and Sandra Bem[11] suggest, is a stereotype that the society has conditioned us to accept. This prejudice also prevails in matters of race.

One of the effects of stereotyping is to deny individual uniqueness. A person is often responded to only as a member of a group instead of as an individual with his or her own unique characteristics. This often creates difficulties in interpersonal communication and cooperation at work. Such differences are even more pronounced in decision-making and problem-solving situations where participants approach problems with different values, dispositions, and perspectives.

Another effect of stereotyping is that it blocks learning in organizations. If we view individuals and organizations as learning systems, then individual differences need to be fostered rather than suppressed if learning is to occur. Friedlander[12] asserts that "for an organism to learn, it must be sufficiently heterogeneous to contain differences. These are differences in perception, value, preferences, time orientations, plans, expectations, etc." Therefore, the multicultural organization provides an excellent opportunity for individual and organization learning because it accommodates people with unique differences and perspectives. For example, one occasionally sees references to the "feminine" values that are found in the management practices of certain successful companies. Presumably these companies tolerated the "deviance" of individual female managers and, in the process, discovered, that is, learned, that such practices had value. We know that culture constrains our ability to conceive of alternative behavior; therefore, seeking out different cultural and individual perspectives is a way of ensuring that we are not blindly pursuing solutions that would be better served by diverse views. Treating individuals as just

[9]Elliott Aronson, *The Social Animal* (San Francisco: W. H. Freeman, 1976, p. 175).

[10]D. C. Feldman, S. Summers, and S. B. Kiesler, "Those Who Are Number Two Try Harder: The Effect of Sex on Attributions of Causality," *Journal of Personality and Social Psychology,* Vol. 30, no. 6 (1974), pp. 836–845, and I. Deaux and T. Emswiller, "Explanations for Successful Performance or Sexlinked Tasks: What Is Skill for the Male Is Luck for the Female," *Journal of Personality and Social Psychology,* Vol. 29, no. 1 (1974), pp. 80–85.

[11]S. L. Bem and D. J. Bem, "Case Study on a Nonconscious Ideology: Training the Woman to Know Her Place," in D. J. Bem, ed., *Beliefs, Attitudes and Human Affairs* (Belmont, CA: Brooks/Cole, 1970, pp. 22–40).

[12]F. Friedlander, "Patterns of Individual and Organizational Learning," in S. Srivastva & Associates, *The Executive Mind* (San Francisco: Jossey-Bass, 1983), pp. 192–220.

one of a group and treating minorities as groups that have little to contribute greatly diminishes the opportunity for learning from them.

NETWORKS

To some extent every cultural group, including any minority group in an organization, tends to develop shared meanings, values, frameworks, and languages among the members of the subculture. Such groups are likely to have common interests and to share needs that the formal organization seldom meets. As a consequence these groups form their own networks in which they exchange the things they need and desire, such as support, advice, and collaboration.

Within an organization there exists a multiplicity of social networks that arise out of the many possible types of social relationships that tie people to one another. Researchers, however, show that kinship, ethnic, and minority ties are among the strongest links that hold together a network.[13] Each emergent network has its own social and functional logic, and it does not necessarily become part of one major structure that might be labeled "the informal organization." Such networks, however, can provide an alternative power base within an organization for its members.

As minority groups are empowered by this and other processes, and power becomes more equally balanced, there is more possibility for contact among the heterogeneous groups. For example, the chairperson of a university department would consult with a group of black students before hiring a black faculty member. In the ensuing discussion about the need for role models, both the administrator and the black students could learn more about the organization from a different perspective. Thus this empowerment allows organizational members to see cultural differences. The myth of cultural homogeneity, in which cultural differences are ignored and suppressed, can no longer be maintained. Similarly, a balance of power reduces cultural isolation in which members of different subcultures withdraw from interaction at the expense of their organizationally defined interdependence. Thus, balance of power "can produce multicultural problem solving in which exploration of cultural differences contribute to mutually beneficial outcomes, or multicultural bargaining, in which negotiations over cultural differences produce mutually acceptable compromises in spite of conflicting interests among the parties."[14]

However, this can also lead to a situation of too much conflict and "culture shock."[15] Individuals in culture shock cannot cope with the cultural context that surrounds them, and they may develop cultural biases. Too much conflict produces cultural polarization, distorted communications, and fighting among members of different cultures. Effective management of cultural diversity, therefore, allows conflict to permit awareness and problem solving but, at the same time, manages this conflict to prevent escalating cycles of misunderstanding and actions that polarize differences unproductively.

MULTICULTURAL ORGANIZATIONS

Merevitch and Reigle describe some characteristics of a multicultural organization that are important for managing individual differences. The five most relevant ones are

[13]J. P. Lafargue, "A Survival Strategy—Kinship Networks," *American Journal of Nursing,* Vol. 80, no. 9 (1980), pp. 480–495; M. F. Neitlin, L. Ann, and R. E. Ratcliff, "New Princes for Old? The Large Corporation and Capitalist Class in Chile," *American Journal of Sociology,* Vol. 80 (1974), pp. 87–123; R. D. Alba, "Ethnic Networks and Tolerant Attitudes," *Public Opinion Quarterly,* Vol. 42, no. 1 (1980), pp. 1–16.

[14]Brown, *Managing Conflict at Organizational Interfaces,* p. 68.

[15]Ibid.

1. It actively seeks to capitalize on the advantages of its diversity—rather than attempting to stifle or ignore the diversity—and to minimize the barriers that can develop as a result of people having different backgrounds, attitudes, values, behavior styles, and concerns.

2. Organizational resources (key jobs, income, perquisites, access to information, etc.) are distributed equitably and are not determined or affected by cultural characteristics such as race and sex.

3. The ability to influence decisions and the way they are carried out is shared widely, not differentially by cultural characteristics.

4. The organizational culture (assumptions about people and groups, take-it-for-granted norms, the way work gets done) is pluralistic in that it recognizes and appreciates diversity; it acknowledges both the need for "being the same" in some ways to work together effectively and the need for "being different" in some ways to recognize individual and group interests, concerns, and backgrounds.

5. Institutional policies, practices, and procedures are flexible and responsive to the needs of all employees.[16]

Developing these characteristics poses great challenges for employees and managers; among these are learning from their experiences and viewing differences as a challenge and an opportunity rather than as a set of problems. It also means being continuously sensitive to issues that arise in diverse work forces and legitimizing the discussion of such issues. Indeed, as Merevitch and Reigle assert, employees and managers must have "a high capacity for examination of thoughts, feelings, attitudes, and beliefs about race, sex, or people who are different on any cultural dimension: actively examining personally held assumptions, taking care not to view differences among people as indications that some of those people are inferior or strange." All these require, above all, an honest and dedicated leadership that is committed to the goals and values of a multicultural organization. As Tannenbaum and Davis[17] put it, "those who have the greatest, direct impact on and responsibility for creating, maintaining and changing the culture of an organization must assume direct ownership of the change effort."

[16]Jarrow Merevitch and Don Reigle, *Toward a Multicultural Organization* (Cincinnati, OH: Proctor & Gamble, January 1979).

[17]R. Tannenbaum and S. A. Davis, "Values, Man, and Organizations," *Industrial Management Review,* Vol. 10, no. 2 (Winter 1969), p. 67–83.
Adapted from C. R. Mill, *Activities for Trainers: 50 Useful Designs.* San Diego, California: University Associates, Inc., 1980. Used with permission.

III

Procedures for Group Meeting: The Embassy Reception

(Time Allotted: $1\frac{1}{2}$–2 Hours)

By considering an international culture, you will learn about American cultural characteristics.

STEP 1. Divide the class into two groups. One group is called the Embassy Crowd; the other group is the Host Country Nationals. Your instructions follow.

STEP 2. The groups should meet in two different locations so they can discuss their strategy openly. You and your co-patriots have been invited to an embassy reception that will start in half an hour. Your task is to create a culture from scratch, using Hofstede's dimensions of national culture. (30–45 minutes)

STEP 3. The embassy reception will take place; each group observes its cultural customs. (20–30 minutes)

STEP 4. The entire class discusses the following questions:

  a. What words would you use to describe the other group's culture?

  b. What was it like to interact with them? How did you feel when you were talking to them?

  c. What norms did you observe for the *other* culture?

  d. Which cultural value patterns do you think the other culture chose? Why?

  e. What were the norms of your own culture?

  f. Which cultural values did you choose?

  g. You filled out the Intensity of Differentness Rating as the prework assignment for this chapter. Did you feel different at any time during today's exercise? In what ways?

  h. If you didn't feel different, why not? How did the class exercise differ from the situation you thought of for the prework assignment?

  i. How did your group manage differences today?

THE EMBASSY RECEPTION INSTRUCTIONS

Your group task is to form your own culture. At the end of this planning period, you are invited to an embassy reception where the two cultures can meet and get acquainted.

A culture is the totality of the norms, standards, and behaviors that operate in a society. These attributes distinguish a society's members, individually and collectively, from other societies and cultures. Hofstede's four dimensions of national culture are examples of cultural differences.

  A. Read the characteristics of these dimensions on the following pages.

  B. Choose a cultural pattern by deciding whether you want your culture to be high or low on each of the four dimensions. Don't choose the American pattern because this is an opportunity to create a different culture.

YOUR CULTURAL VALUE PATTERN:	HIGH	LOW
Power Distance	_____	_____
Uncertainty Avoidance	_____	_____
Individualism Collectivism	_____	_____
Masculinity	_____	_____

C. Decide what norms and customs your group can develop to operationalize your cultural value pattern. For example, how would a person from a high uncertainty avoidance and low masculinity culture behave at an embassy reception? What would their conversation be like? Gestures, food rituals and habits, language, gender relationships, status differentials, and leadership are some of the many areas for which your group can develop norms. Your group's task for this period is to discuss this matter fully so that these norms become a part of you. You may wish to practice them with the use of role playing, or you may suggest additional supporting behaviors such as signs and symbols for use among yourselves.

You will heighten your uniqueness as a culture if you maintain the following ground rules.

1. When you are interacting with a member of your own group, be as open, spontaneous, and helpful as you can. Both give and seek support from your group members, whether you are alone with them or in the presence of outsiders.

2. When interacting with members of the other group, do everything you can to improve your understanding of them by being friendly and receptive. Openness in oneself invites openness in others, so strive for a free and outgoing society in this class exercise.

3. Don't tell the other group what cultural value pattern you chose.

Adapted from C. R. Mill, Activities for Trainers: 50 Useful Designs. *San Diego, California: University Associates, Inc., 1980. Used with permission.*

Cultural Value Dimensions

THE POWER DISTANCE DIMENSION	
Small Power Distance	**Large Power Distance**
Inequality in society should be minimized.	There should be an order of inequality in this world in which everybody has a rightful place: high and low are protected by this order.
All people should be interdependent.	A few people should be independent: most should be dependent.
Hierarchy means an inequality of roles, established for convenience.	Hierarchy means existential inequality.
Superiors consider subordinates to be "people like me."	Superiors consider subordinates to be a different kind of people.
Subordinates consider superiors to be "people like me."	Subordinates consider superiors as a different kind of people.
Superiors are accessible.	Superiors are inaccessible.
The use of power should be legitimate and is subject to the judgment as to whether it is good or evil.	Power is a basic fact of society that antedates good or evil. Its legitimacy is irrelevant.

Cultural Value Dimensions (cont.)

All should have equal rights.	Power-holders are entitled to privileges.
Those in power should try to look less powerful than they are.	Those in power should try to look as powerful as possible.
The system is to blame.	The underdog is to blame.
The way to change a social system is to redistribute power.	The way to change a social system is to dethrone those in power.
People at various power levels feel less threatened and more prepared to trust people.	Other people are a potential threat to one's power and can rarely be trusted.
Latent harmony exists between the powerful and the powerless.	Latent conflict exists between the powerful and the powerless.
Cooperation among the powerless can be based on solidarity.	Cooperation among the powerless is difficult to attain because of their low-faith-in-people norm.
exp.: U.S.A., Israel, Austria, Denmark, Ireland, Norway, Germany, New Zealand	exp.: Spain, France, Japan, Singapore, Mexico, Brazil, Indonesia.

THE UNCERTAINTY AVOIDANCE DIMENSION

Weak Uncertainty Avoidance	Strong Uncertainty Avoidance
The uncertainty inherent in life is more easily accepted and each day is taken as it comes.	The uncertainty inherent in life is felt as a continuous threat that must be fought.
Ease and lower stress are experienced.	Higher anxiety and stress are experienced.
Time is free.	Time is money.
Hard work, as such, is not a virtue.	There is an inner urge to work hard.
Aggressive behavior is frowned upon.	Aggressive behavior of self and others is accepted.
Less showing of emotions is preferred.	More showing of emotions is preferred.
Conflict and competition can be contained on the level of fair play and used constructively.	Conflict and competition can unleash aggression and should therefore be avoided.
More acceptance of dissent is entailed.	A strong need for consensus is involved.
Deviation is not considered threatening; greater tolerance is shown.	Deviant persons and ideas are dangerous; intolerance holds sway.
The ambiance is one of less nationalism.	Nationalism is pervasive.
More positive feelings toward younger people are seen.	Younger people are suspect.
There is more willingness to take risks in life.	There is great concern with security in life.
The accent is on relativism, empiricism.	The search is for ultimate, absolute truths and values.
There should be as few rules as possible.	There is a need for written rules and regulations.
If rules cannot be kept, we should change them.	If rules cannot be kept, we are sinners and should repent.
Belief is placed in generalists and common sense.	Belief is placed in experts and their knowledge.
The authorities are there to serve the citizens.	Ordinary citizens are incompetent compared with the authorities.
exp.: Denmark, U.S.A., Canada, Norway, Singapore, Hong Kong, Australia	exp.: Israel, Austria, Japan, Italy, Argentina, Peru, France, Belgium

Cultural Value Dimensions (cont.)

THE INDIVIDUALISM DIMENSION	
Collectivist	**Individualist**
In society, people are born into extended families or clans who protect them in exchange for loyalty.	In society, everybody is supposed to take care of himself/herself and his/her immediate family.
"We" consciousness holds sway.	"I" consciousness holds sway.
Identity is based in the social system.	Identity is based in the individual.
There is emotional dependence of individual on organizations and institutions.	There is emotional independence of individual from organizations or institutions.
The involvement with organizations is moral.	The involvement with organizations is calculative.
The emphasis is on belonging to organizations; membership is the ideal.	The emphasis is on individual initiative and achievement; leadership is the ideal.
Private life is invaded by organizations and clans to which one belongs; opinions are predetermined.	Everybody has a right to a private life and opinion.
Expertise, order, duty, and security are provided by organization or clan.	Autonomy, variety, pleasure, and individual financial security are sought in the system.
Friendships are predetermined by stable social relationships, but there is need for prestige within these relationships.	The need is for specific friendships.
Belief is placed in group decisions.	Belief is placed in individual decisions.
Value standards differ for in-groups and out-groups (particularism).	Value standards should apply to all (universalism).
exp.: Colombia, Pakistan, Taiwan, Peru, Singapore, Japan, Mexico, Greece, Hong Kong	exp.: U.S.A., Australia, Great Britain, The Netherlands, Canada, New Zealand

THE MASCULINITY DIMENSION	
Feminine	**Masculine**
Men needn't be assertive, but can also assume nurturing roles.	Men should be assertive. Women should be nurturing.
Sex roles in society are more fluid.	Sex roles in society are clearly differentiated.
There should be equality between the sexes.	Men should dominate in society.
Quality of life is important.	Performance is what counts.
You work in order to live.	You live in order to work.
People and environment are important.	Money and things are important.
Interdependence is the ideal.	Independence is the ideal.
Service provides the motivation.	Ambition provides the drive.
One sympathizes with the unfortunate.	One admires the successful achiever.
Small and slow are beautiful.	Big and fast are beautiful.
Unisex and androgyny are ideal.	Ostentatious manliness ("machismo") is appreciated.
exp.: Norway, Sweden, Denmark, Finland	exp.: Japan, Austria, U.S.A.

IV

Follow-up

Minorities in both cultures and organizations often pay a high price for their "differentness." Feeling the need to represent one's entire race, sex, or culture is quite a burden. As one black man who was tired of fielding questions in an all-white group stated, "I'm not putting on a charm school course on blacks for white folk." Kanter's study of "tokens" in a large corporation maintains that a small *number* of minorities (regardless of their group membership) to majorities calls forth three perceptual tendencies.[18]

1. Tokens receive *more attention* because they are more highly visible. In Gestalt psychology terms, the tokens become "figure" rather than "ground." (This concept was discussed in Chapter 7, Interpersonal Perception.) As a result, the tokens are constantly "in the public eye," and their behavior is scrutinized for symbolic content because they represent their entire group, not just themselves. Performance pressures are thereby magnified.

2. *Contrast* between the token and the majority group results in exaggeration and polarization of the differences between the two groups. Exposure to a minority makes the majority self-conscious and, therefore, uncomfortable and uncertain. As a result, the boundaries of the dominant group became even stronger and isolation of the tokens occurs.

3. *Assimilation* of the tokens is based upon the use of stereotypes. A larger number of "token-type" people would allow the majority to perceive that there are, in fact, many individual differences among this group. This perceptual tendency forces the tokens into limited and caricatured roles which Kanter refers to as "role encapsulation."

Sensitivity to the stress that accompanies tokenism can be partially alleviated by managers who understand the phenomenon. But the systemic answer to the problem is to hire and promote enough people from the minority group to make tokenism a moot point.

The ability to deal with people from other cultures is becoming more and more necessary in business. Technical competence is a necessary but insufficient condition for success. Effectiveness depends upon an ability to develop good interpersonal relationships that are built upon an acceptance and appreciation of differences, respect for the cultural beliefs of others, and a willingness to learn from people who are different.

[18]Rosabeth Moss Kanter, *Men and Women of the Corporation* (New York: Basic Books, 1977), pp. 206–242.

V

Learning Points

1. Culture provides us with ready-made solutions for basic human problems and a sense of identity, but it also limits our ability to see and sometimes appreciate alternative behaviors.

2. All cultures have both positive and negative aspects and are best understood as a series of trade-offs.

3. Ethnocentrism is the tendency to think one's own group or race is superior to other groups or races.

4. Everyone possesses a degree of ethnocentrism, but it must be curbed to work effectively with people from other groups or races.

5. Minorities in societies characterized by discrimination are especially sensitive to discriminatory behavior in the organizations that employ them.

6. Hofstede claims that American management techniques reflect American cultural values—low power distance (equality), individualism, tolerance of uncertainty, and masculinity (achievement versus nurturance). As such, they are probably not applicable in other countries or with people from different subcultures within our own country.

7. Stereotyping is assigning identical characteristics to any member of a group regardless of their individual differences. The prejudice that accompanies stereotypes prevents us from judging individuals fairly upon their own merit.

8. Power imbalances between groups decrease contact and an appreciation of heterogeneity. As a result the system's ability to learn from different perspectives is diminished.

9. Minority groups often form networks within larger organizations to share common interests and meet needs that the formal organization may not fill.

10. Managing diversity well allows minorities and eccentric people to feel comfortable and contribute as fully as possible at the work site, but it also allows organizations to profit from divergent viewpoints, which may be essential to its performance.

11. Multicultural organizations manage individual differences by
    a. Trying to capitalize upon diversity.
    b. Distributing organizational resources equitably.
    c. Allowing widespread participation in decision making that is not based upon membership in a particular group.
    d. Recognizing and appreciating diversity as a value of the organizational culture.
    e. Instituting policies, practices, and procedures that are flexible and responsive to the needs of all employees.

12. Three perceptual tendencies and their results affect tokens:
    a. High visibility leads to performance pressures on tokens.
    b. Contrast that exaggerates differences between the two groups leads the dominant group to heighten its cultural boundaries.
    c. Assimilation by stereotyping results in role encapsulation for the tokens.

13. These consequences, which cause stress for tokens, could be avoided by increasing the number of the minority group within the organization so minorities would be perceived as individuals rather than tokens.

VI

Tips for Managers

- Guidelines for dealing with people from different cultures:

  Know and understand your own culture (Why do we value certain things and behave in certain ways?).

  Know the other culture.

  Make an effort to understand why the other culture holds the values they do and behaves as they do.

  Look for strengths in the other culture rather than focus upon its weaknesses or differences.

  Respect the other culture and bear in mind that it's the ability to create relationships and work through others that leads to effectiveness.

  Recognize the degree to which you are ethnocentric and keep it in check.

  Listen actively so that people from the other culture can guide you and so the organization will benefit from its diversity.

  Use management techniques or intervention strategies that will be appropriate for the given culture or subculture.

- Multicultural groups can be the source of learning and creativity, but only when groups can be open about their differences and use them to enhance understanding.

- Conflict and tension do not disappear in a multicultural group when the differences are acknowledged, but they can become a source of learning.

VII

Personal Application Assignment

Quelle verité que ces montagnes burnent, qui est mensonge au monde qui si tient au dela?

What kind of a truth is this that is bounded by a chain of mountains and is falsehood to the people living on the other side?

(MONTAIGNE, ESSA is II, XII, p. 34)

This assignment is to write about a situation that involved cultural diversity. Choose an experience about which you are motivated to learn more.

A. *Concrete Experience*

1. *Objectively* describe the experience ("who," "what," "when," "where," "how" type information—up to 2 points).

2. *Subjectively* describe your feelings, perceptions, and thoughts that occurred *during* (not after) the experience (up to 2 points). Does this section have too much detail? (If so, delete 1 point.)

B. *Reflective Observation*

1. Look at the experience from different points of view. How many points of view did you include that are *relevant* (up to 2 points)?

2. Use these perspectives to add more meaning to the incident (up to 2 points).

C. *Abstract Conceptualization*

1. Relate concepts from the assigned readings and the lecture to the experience (i.e., what theories that you heard in the lecture or read in the *Reader* relate to your understanding of this incident?). Make reference to at least two sources. Use standard referencing format and include the page number to which you are referring. How many sources did you use and how clearly did you explain their theories (up to 4 points)?

2. You can also create an original model or theory, but it should not replace course concepts.

D. *Active Experimentation*
1. Write about what you will do in the future that will improve your effectiveness. Use rules of thumb or action resolutions.
2. Are they described specifically, thoroughly, and in detail (up to 4 points)?

E. *Integration, Synthesis, and Writing*
1. Did you write about something personally important to you (up to 1 point)?
2. Was it well written (up to 2 points)?
3. Did you integrate and synthesize the different sections (up to 1 point)?

12

LEADERSHIP AND ORGANIZATIONAL CULTURE

OBJECTIVES   By the end of this chapter you should be able to:

A. Define organizational culture.

B. Explain how it evolves and is maintained.

C. Describe the relationship between leadership and the organizational culture.

D. Identify the impact of organizational culture on the motivation and behavior of individuals in the organization.

E. Explain the role of socialization in maintaining organizational culture.

Best Corporate Culture Is a Melting Pot

Jack Falvey

Promoting from within has been a policy of misguided company loyalty that has damaged the foundations of organizations it seeks to build.

Because of promote from within policies, many companies are headed today by organization men of the 1940s. Many of these inmates-turned-wardens have never worked outside of the corporations they head. Is it any wonder they are having difficulty adjusting to a world marketplace? Take this example.

A major company introduced a new consumer product. The market for that product accelerated, and soon a foreign competitor entered the arena. As the company's share began to erode, top management met to determine strategy. The competitor's clever advertising was to be countered with trade deals and deep price cuts. The decision was unanimous. Why? Because everyone in the meeting was with the company 15 years before when a similar foreign product threatened another segment of the business. Everyone's experience was exactly the same. "We were successful before, so we will do the same thing again."

Unfortunately, the foreign challenge was slightly different this time and so were the results. There were layoffs, then several plant closings, and, finally, sale of the product, or what was left of it, to another company.

When I speak to management groups of established companies, the view from the podium is sometimes frightening. They look alike; they dress alike; unfortunately, they think alike. They are the products of a success profile. They are plain vanilla. But strength comes from diversity. When you face a problem, isn't it better to have five or six options, rather than just one?

When, on the other hand, there is "cross-pollution," some wondrous things begin to happen. A consumer goods president took over as chief executive officer of a computer company. He insisted that stock be available before a new product was launched, knowing that advertising backed by empty shelves was a waste. Consumer electronics companies usually had announced first, promoted and sold second, and delivered third. He reversed the order and filled the distribution pipeline first. He single-handedly caused a major shakeout of his competition by his product's success.

To compound the promote from within syndrome, companies have established traditional areas of the business from which all top managers will come. Organizations are headed by finance businessmen 20 years after they are no longer in the finance business. Engineers have headed computer companies that have consistently driven down prices and increased performance of their products with technical breakthroughs but that have failed to make the products usable in the marketplace. Family ownership imposes similar limitations when it gives each son a small division or sees to it that every cousin has an office somewhere.

Is it any wonder our industrial giants become targets of opportunity for anyone who chooses to pose a serious challenge to their products, services, or marketplace? (In some cases the challenge is directly to those companies' management teams in the form of takeover bids or green mail.)

One of the major moves in our business environment is the formation of ventures by talented, aggressive, well-trained managers who have left their companies. Most could not survive or contribute within an in-bred organization. The proliferation of prospering companies that have been spun off should tell us something about the company men who were unable to make a success of those subsidiaries.

Between 20 and 30 percent of all openings should be filled from outside. The broader the mix, the better. Every position should have outside talent included in the selection process. If inside people are not competitive, how can your organization be competitive in the marketplace?

Consultants who work across industry lines will confirm that the fundamentals in every industry are almost identical. There are no real barriers to mobility. Junior managers especially should be valued if they have three or four different work experiences because they have found that managing their own careers produces far better returns than delegating that responsibility to a single organization.

The mobile manager of the 1960s who did duty in six cities and then returned to the home office should now be replaced by the mobile manager of the 1980s who has worked across six different industries and deals comfortably in business on three different continents. The time of the generalized top manager is coming, and none too soon. Narrow specialists have always had difficulty with the big picture.

The rules of business have been shifting dramatically and rapidly for the past decade. Stable, secure management teams are remnants of the past. Dynamic, diverse management is needed for the present and the future. The rigid rules of organization construction must be broken.

The process of regenerating cannot be done overnight. Broaden your view and bring in more talent from nontraditional sources. Its addition will add new strength. It may already be long overdue.

I
Premeeting Preparation

    A. Fill out the accompanying Organizational Culture Questionnaire for an organization to which you belong(ed).

    B. Read the Topic Introduction.

    C. Complete The G.B.A. Construction Company, Part I, and prepare your individual analysis.

    Note: For your individual and collective learning, *do not* read Part II of the case in advance.

Organization Culture Questionnaire

For each of the seven organization culture dimensions described, place an (a) above the number that indicates your assessment of the organization's actual position on that dimension and an (i) above the number that indicates your choice of where the organization should ideally be on this dimension.

1. *Conformity.* The feeling that there are many externally imposed constraints in the organization; the degree to which members feel that there are many rules, procedures, policies, and practices to which they have to conform rather than being able to do their work as they see fit.

Conformity is not characteristic of this organization.   1 2 3 4 5 6 7 8 9 10   Conformity is very characteristic of this organization.

2. *Responsibility.* Members of the organization are given personal responsibility to achieve their part of the organization's goals; the degree to which members feel that they can make decisions and solve problems without checking with superiors each step of the way.

No responsibility is given in the organization.   1 2 3 4 5 6 7 8 9 10   There is a great emphasis on personal responsibility in the organization.

3. *Standards.* The emphasis the organization places on quality performance and outstanding production, including the degree to which the member feels the organization is setting challenging goals for itself and communicating these goal commitments to members.

Standards are very low or nonexistent in the organization.   1 2 3 4 5 6 7 8 9 10   High challenging standards are set in the organization.

4. *Rewards.* The degree to which members feel that they are being recognized and rewarded for good work rather than being ignored, criticized, or punished when something goes wrong.

Members are ignored, punished, or criticized.   1 2 3 4 5 6 7 8 9 10   Members are recognized and rewarded positively.

5. *Organizational clarity.* The feeling among members that things are well organized and that goals are clearly defined rather than being disorderly, confused, or chaotic.

The organization is disorderly, confused, and chaotic.   1 2 3 4 5 6 7 8 9 10   The organization is well organized with clearly defined goals.

6. *Warmth and support.* The feeling that friendliness is a valued norm in the organization, that members trust one another and offer support to one another. The feeling that good relationships prevail in the work environment.

There is no warmth and support in the organization.   1 2 3 4 5 6 7 8 9 10   Warmth and support are very characteristic of the organization.

7. *Leadership.* The willingness of organization members to accept leadership and direction from qualified others. As needs for leadership arise, members feel free to take leadership roles and are rewarded for successful leadership. Leadership is based on expertise. The organization is not dominated by, or dependent on, one or two individuals.

| Leadership is not rewarded; members are dominated or dependent and resist leadership attempts. | 1 2 3 4 5 6 7 8 9 10 \| \| \| \| \| \| \| \| \| \| \| | Members accept and reward leadership based on expertise. |

8. What are the dominant values of this organization?

9. What are some of the behavioral norms of the organization that an outsider or a newcomer would quickly notice?

10. How do the leaders of the organization reinforce these values and norms?

11. How are newcomers socialized in this organization?

12. Does this culture help or hinder the organization in terms of performance?

13. What do you want to learn about organizational culture and socialization?

14. What are the significant learning points from the readings?

The G.B.A. Construction Company, Part I[1]

INTRODUCTION

The G.B.A. Construction Company was started in the early 1930s by G.B.A., Sr. His son, G.B.A., Jr., took over as president in 1946. G.B.A., Sr., passed away a few years later. There are two major stockholders at present: G.B.A., Jr., who owns 65 percent of the stock, and A. H., who owns 35 percent. A.H. started the business with G.B.A., Sr., but in recent years has been relatively inactive in the business.

The following sketches provide a brief view of G.B.A., Jr., and the business history of the G.B.A. Co.

G.B.A., JR.—A SNAPSHOT

G.B.A., Jr., took over as president of the company in 1946. He is a tireless worker and through his many years of experience has become a consummate businessman.

Under his leadership the company has developed a reputation for excellence—highest-quality work, on-time delivery, and within-budget estimates. G.B.A., Jr.'s personal reputation has done much to build the company. While very knowledgeable in all aspects of the construction business, he is particularly skilled in financial matters.

His managerial style can best be described as that of a benevolent autocrat. He is used to making most, if not all, of the major decisions by himself. As he put it, "It's my company, so why shouldn't I make the decisions?"

The benevolent part of his style manifests itself in a somewhat paternal attitude toward employees. For example, he recently instituted a program wherein key employees received company pins with diamonds to signify their length of service to the organization. G.B.A., Jr., felt that rewarding people in this manner would motivate employees. According to the grapevine, however, many recipients felt these pins (and other similar awards) were "Mickey Mouse."

His relationships with his key officers are rather aloof: "He's not the kind of guy you can get very close to." The climate of the organization is very much influenced by his personal style. Secrecy is high (lots of closed files), and people maintain J/C files (*just in case* the boss asks). As is characteristic of benevolent autocrats, people fear and respect him at the same time.

He is presently in his mid-fifties and in good health. While not concerned overtly with his own personal health, he is somewhat concerned that his partner and other colleagues in the industry are increasingly suffering heart attacks.

He and his wife do some traveling and he looks forward to the time when he can relax more and travel, play tennis, and so on. His son has just entered an Ivy League school but shows few signs of interest in coming into the business. G.B.A., Jr.'s daughter is a budding commercial artist and is presently unmarried.

BUSINESS HISTORY

The history of the company has been solid and profitable. When the entire construction industry had lean years, the G.B.A. Co. continued to do as well as or better than comparable companies in the field. Its main business is in the area of shopping centers, office buildings, hotels, motels, and the like. Several recent trends are important.

Volume in 1973 was $200 million and is predicted to be $300 million in 1974

---

[1]Part I of this case was prepared early in 1974. Part II, which follows later, covers the period 1974 to 1981.

and $400 million to $500 million in 1975. Although no one expects this rapid rate of growth to continue at its present or projected pace, the long-range goal is to grow at about 15 to 20 percent per year in both volume and profit.

Job or project size has increased to the point at which the "average" job is now about $5 million per job. The company expects this trend to continue. The company expects, in other words, to be in a position to take on and successfully manage larger projects of longer duration rather than many small projects. Changes in the structure and functioning of the organization will be necessary to cope with this change in the nature of their business.

Increasingly, the company was finding itself in the position, and indeed was seeking such situations, in which it was brought in at the early planning stages of a project. In this way, the company worked directly with architects and planners, under a negotiated overall cost and fee, and was in a position to significantly influence design and specifications.

Although the company is always looking for ways to improve and grow, there is no expectation that the nature of its basic business will change substantially in the future (e.g., to go into the construction of nuclear power plants). G.B.A. Co. knows its business, knows that it can do it well, and plans to continue in this vein. Geographically, most of the business is in the South, Southeast, Midwest, and West of the United States. Division II is located in the same city as the corporate central offices. There are increasing opportunities coming across Mr. G.B.A.'s desk for expansion into new areas overseas, particularly in developing nations such as Saudi Arabia.

ORGANIZATION STRUCTURE

The company is organized into four divisions and a central office as follows:

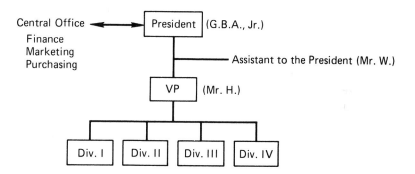

THE PROBLEM

Early in 1973, G.B.A., Jr., contacted a Boston-based consulting firm. He had seen a seminar flyer that described this consulting company's capability as being in the general area of the "human side of enterprise." He believed this group might be able to help him with some of his concerns. Discussions with G.B.A., Jr., and his top management group led to the specification of two major problem areas—succession and continuity of management.

G.B.A., Jr., recognized that the time would soon come when he could not or would not want to be as involved in the day-to-day problems of the company. The G.B.A. Co. would need a new president sometime soon, and he ought to be planning for it now.

From his viewpoint and that of his top management group as well, it was very undesirable to go outside for a new president. Most felt that this would be taken as a sign in the industry that the G.B.A. Co. did not have the backup strength or the internal capability to "grow its own new chief executive." An outsider, in addition, would find it hard to break into the organization and develop the necessary relationships with other key executives.

The candidates from within the organization were essentially four: the assistant to the president, division manager I, division manager II, and division manager III. (Division manager IV was very new and young and, therefore, not a candidate.) A sketch of each of these men follows.

ASSISTANT TO THE PRESIDENT—J. W.

J. W. is a man in his mid-forties who has worked for the company about ten years. He holds a B.S. in engineering. Prior to coming to work for G.B.A. Co., he worked as the equivalent of a division manager with a comparable company.

His main responsibilities have been to work with G.B.A., Jr., in the design and implementation of corporate policies and procedures. In this capacity he has become exposed to some of the modern thinking in the areas of recruitment, executive compensation, and so on. His technical skills in construction and his prior experiences have enabled him to be a "backup division manager." In other words, when the need arose, he has been more than able to step in and manage business as do the existing division managers.

He is very soft spoken, less overtly aggressive than his officer colleagues, and believes very strongly in loyalty as a motivation of people. He is very loyal to G.B.A., Jr., and the company—"They have treated me very well and I'll do anything I'm asked to do." His willingness to stay in the very difficult position of assistant to the president, with all its attendant home office and field office conflicts, is an example of his loyalty. His compensation is lower than that of the division managers because he is not as directly tied in to profits as they are.

In spite of the conflicts of his job, he gets along reasonably well with the key officers. They and he recognize that the problems encountered are a function of the role and not a function of J.W.'s personality.

MANAGER I

Manager I is the youngest of the division managers—late thirties. He graduated from a prestigious southern engineering school and came into the company about six years ago. He was hired to start a new division in the Southeast and worked closely with A. H., the vice president, to build this new division.

The first four to five years of this effort were very disappointing. His division was consistently the big loser. At officer's meetings when financial figures were reviewed, Manager I was always the target of digs and barbs from the others. That situation has changed dramatically and his division is now the biggest winner. In 1973, his division will account for a substantial portion of the total volume and profits.

Manager I is, in some ways, like Mr. G.B.A., Jr. He is hard-driving and level-headed and has a quiet charm and confidence that appeals to clients. He has a reputation of letting some details fall through the cracks; for example, he never answers phone messages, misses planes, and is often the last to arrive (often late) at an officers' meeting. His rationale is that selling new business and taking care of clients are his primary jobs—anything else comes second. This, of course, is consistent with the climate Mr. G.B.A., Jr., has set for the company.

MANAGER II

Manager II is in his early forties and a college graduate. He was hired eight years ago by G.B.A., Jr., to take over as manager of the Central Division. Prior to coming to the G.B.A. Co., he held a high-level position with a competitor.

His division has been a solid producer under his leadership—not outstanding but clearly adequate. The fact that he is physically located in the same building as the corporate offices is, in the minds of some people, the reason for his success. In other words, some people believe that G.B.A., Jr., is responsible for a large percentage of the business that Manager II gets for the company. From his point of view, his physical proximity to G.B.A., Jr., does not interfere with his ability to "be his own man."

Of all the division managers, Manager II's style is the most participative. He is a good group builder and has the reputation for developing his younger people very well. He is more willing and able to delegate responsibility. He demonstrates, in much that he does, a concern for the human side of issues. During officers' meetings, for example, he would be most likely to support someone who was under attack.

MANAGER III

Manager III is the senior man in the manager group (25 years), just a few years younger than G.B.A., Jr., himself. He is the only one of the division managers without a formal college education, having learned the business from the University of Hardknocks. His knowledge of the business is unquestioned, and he is respected by all.

His division, the Western Division, has always been a high-variance division in terms of profit performance. From a volume perspective, it has always been high—"He'll take any job" was the comment often made. Profits, however, have never been as high as expected, and others attribute this in large measure to Manager III's style.

"He does everything his own way by himself" is the comment most often made. He calls *every* site several times a day, issues orders, and makes all the decisions by himself. Not one of his subordinates does anything without checking with him first. As could be expected, this style creates many home and field office problems and conflicts. He resists most corporate policies and procedures and yields grudgingly only after direct intervention by G.B.A., Jr.; even then, there are some "special rules" for him (i.e., he is often allowed to ignore company policy).

These profiles of the candidates were constructed by the behavioral science consultants on the basis of interviews in the company. In addition, the consultants assessed the motivational patterns of the candidates using the McClelland framework (see Chapter 3 for a description of these motive patterns). Achievement, power, and affiliation motivation have considerable relevance for issues of leadership style, organizational climate, and organizational growth. The consultants prepared the following table indicating how each of the key people rank in terms of McClelland's three motives. (For example, G.B.A., Jr., himself, would be equally high in his power and achievement needs and lowest in his affiliation needs.)

	PRESIDENT	MANAGER I	MANAGER II	MANAGER III	ASSISTANT TO THE PRESIDENT
n-Achievement	High	High	High	High	Moderate
n-Power	High	Moderate	Low	High	Low
n-Affiliation	Low	Low	Moderate	Low	High

As a group the candidates were "a bunch of supreme primadonnas," by their own admission. Each believed that he could handle the job of president. While they all "said" they could work under the others, it was very clear that the choice of one would have to be handled delicately. Whoever among them was chosen might have a period of some tension, jealousy, and covert (if not overt) conflict until he "proved his mettle."

In spite of this dilemma, it was not considered desirable, unless no other alternative existed, to bring in someone from the outside. However, G.B.A., Jr., was smart enough to realize that some other changes might also be necessary to deal with the second of his concerns—continuity of management. Simply selecting a new president might not be enough. A new management strategy and climate would also probably be needed.

The concern over continuity of management comes from several sources. G.B.A., Jr., recognized that each of his key executives was in high demand. None of them would find it hard to switch jobs quickly and beneficially. Their individual compensations (with the exception of J.W., his assistant) were tied directly and heavily into their individual profit performance. In terms of both salary and bonus, they all did very well, but they wanted "something" more.

The key executives had several concerns regarding continuity. What would happen to the company if or when G.B.A., Jr., died? How could they get security? What would happen to them? As they put it, "We, too, have put our sweat and blood into this company. Do we fall to the whims of some trustees? Your wife?"

G.B.A., Jr., recognized that he had been the central, dominant figure in the life of the company during the past 25 years. It was not clear whether, even if he remained president, the company could continue to be managed in the same way and cope with all the normal problems of rapid and continued growth. So, in addition to succession, he was concerned with making any changes required to ensure continuity of management.

YOUR TASK

The concerns of succession and continuity are complex problems, and many factors are involved in successfully dealing with such problems.

In preparation for the upcoming group meeting you should answer these questions:

1. What do you see as the major strengths and weaknesses of the four main candidates?

2. Which candidate would you recommend as the new president of the G.B.A. Company?

3. What is your rationale for the choice? What kind of leadership style does the company need now?

4. How would you rank the other candidates?

5. In addition to a new president, what other changes should the G.B.A. Company consider to provide for the continuity of management and organizational culture it will need in the future? New structures? New procedures? New reward systems? Why?

II

Topic Introduction

Organizational culture has become an exceedingly popular topic in recent years. The publicity given to successful companies with strong cultures[2] has had several results. More attention is being paid to maintaining a culture that has proved to be effective in terms of the organization's performance. Some companies that lack a strong culture have decided that culture might be an answer to their problems and have hired consultants to help them develop one. And more attention is being paid to specific aspects of organizational culture and to the relationship between leaders and culture in particular. This relationship is not a new idea. Studies on leadership and culture's predecessor, "organizational climate," were done decades ago, but the concept has been better developed of late and has certainly captured the public's attention. Schein defines organizational culture as

> Organizational culture is the pattern of basic assumptions that a given group has invented, discovered, or developed in learning to cope with its problems of external adaptation and internal integration, and that have worked well enough to be considered valid, and, therefore, to be taught to new members as the correct way to perceive, think, and feel in relation to those problems.[3]

In simple terms, organization culture is the pattern of shared values and beliefs that lead to certain norms of behavior.[4] Culture reflects the values of the founders or strong leaders of the organization and the solutions to problems which other members have learned over time. The broader societal context also influences the culture of an organization. Many of our attempts to understand the success of Japanese industry center on characteristics of the Japanese culture that are reinforced in corporations.

A discussion of organizational culture raises once again the issue of "fit," both internally and externally. In choosing a management system and organization structure, the interaction between the following variables must be considered:

1. The *people* in the organization, their abilities, and motives.
2. The *organization's tasks* and the kinds of behavior needed to accomplish those tasks most effectively.
3. The *organization's external environment* and the demands it makes on the organization for creativity, flexibility, quality, and so on.
4. The *organization's culture* as determined by the leadership styles of management and the organization's structure.

---

[2]R. T. Pascale and A. G. Athos, *The Art of Japanese Management: Applications for American Executives* (New York: Simon & Schuster, 1981); Tom Peters and R. H. Waterman, *In Search of Excellence* (New York: Harper & Row, 1982); Tom Peters and N. A. Austin, *A Passion for Excellence* (New York: Random House, 1985); and T. E. Deal and A. A. Kennedy, *Corporate Cultures: The Rites and Rituals of Corporate Life* (Reading, MA: Addison-Wesley, 1982).

[3]Edgar H. Schein, "Coming to a New Awareness of Organizational Culture," *Sloan Management Review* (Winter 1984), pp. 3–16.

[4]Linda Smircich, "Concepts of Culture and Organizational Analysis," *Administrative Science Quarterly* (September 1983), p. 342.

Stated simply, the goal of organization design is to match people with tasks that require and inspire their motives and abilities and to design tasks that cope with environmental demands and opportunities. The most manageable variable of the four is organization culture. It can serve as an effective management tool for integrating individual motivation with the goals and tasks of the organization. Organizational culture, therefore, is an important concept for the manager to understand because it can be used to "manage the motivation of employees." Organization effectiveness can be increased by creating an organizational culture that satisfies members' needs while channeling their motivated behavior toward organizational goals. The shared values of an organizational culture generate commitment and cooperation. Furthermore, strong organizational cultures serve the same control function as the cultural rules we learn in childhood. When groups of people share the same behavioral norms, there is less need for external controls and close supervision.

An organizational culture must be reinforced internally—many things within the organization must fit together. A close look at organizations with strong cultures reveals the following characteristics.[5] People in the organization can easily identify the dominant values. The selection processes target people who are likely to fit into the culture and find it satisfying. Socialization and training convey to newcomers the "ropes" they need to learn. Employees who do not fit the culture or produce in accordance with its values are sometimes fired. People within the company are rewarded for acting in accordance with the dominant values of the organizations. Leaders and managers send clear, consistent signals about desired values and norms by their own behavior. Managers measure and control what is important to the culture.

It's not enough that organizational cultures simply be strong. They also have to fit with their environment. Both AT&T and the banking industry had strong cultures. But when their external environments changed, these cultures, bred upon stability and lack of competition, actually threatened their survival. Possible dangers of strong cultures are resistance to change and pressure for conformity.[6] If the culture is self-sealing and refuses to consider new assumptions, its very strength can become a weakness. This is one of the major dilemmas in organizations, finding the right degree of stability and flexibility. For this reason, it comes as no surprise that one study found that companies with well-organized workplaces and strong *participative* cultures performed better than did other firms.[7] Presumably, the value placed upon participation would allow for the expression of different opinions and different assumptions about the external environment.

Changing their culture is the strategic route some companies are taking to improve their performance. It is not a quick process because of all the "fits" within the organization. However, it is possible if an organization is willing to figure out the mission and values that are important to them and then bring their selection, socialization, training, reward, and management styles into alignment. Sometimes the organizational structure also has to be revised so that it fits the mission and cultural values. (See Chapters 17 and 18 for a discussion of organizational design issues.)

Often the first step in changing a culture involves a change in management style. Leadership can have a very strong impact on organizational culture, be it positive or negative. Managerial leadership style is a major force in determining the climate or culture of an organization. John Andrews's study of two Mexican companies is striking in this regard.[8] One firm was stagnating whereas the other was

[5]Edgar Schein, *Organizational Culture and Leadership* (San Francisco: Jossey-Bass, 1985).

[6]Richard Pascale, "The Paradox of 'Corporate Culture': Reconciling Ourselves to Socialization," *California Management Review* (Winter 1985).

[7]R. D. Denison, "Bringing Corporate Culture to the Bottom Line," *Organizational Dynamics* (Autumn 1984), pp. 5–22.

[8]John D. W. Andrews, "The Achievement Motive in Two Types of Organizations," *Journal of Personality and Social Psychology,* Vol. 6 (1967), pp. 163–168.

growing rapidly. The manager of the growing company, although high in n-Power, was also high in n-Achievement and was dedicated to letting others in the organization satisfy their own needs for achievement by introducing improvements and making decisions on their own. The stagnant company, although well capitalized and enjoying a favorable market, was constantly in turmoil and experienced a high rate of turnover, particularly among its executives. In this company, the president's high n-Power, coupled with highly authoritarian values, led him to make all the decisions himself, leaving no room for individual responsibility on the part of his personnel. A comparison of motivation scores of upper-level managers of the two companies showed that the dynamic company's managers were significantly higher in n-Achievement than were those of the stagnant company, who tended to be more concerned with power and compliance than with individual responsibility and decision making. Similarly, Wainer and Rubin[9] found correlations between the achievement motive scores of R&D entrepreneurs and the profitability of their companies. The leadership style of top managers tends to influence the culture of the whole organization through a kind of "waterfall" effect, whereby managerial styles are passed from boss to subordinate down through the organizational hierarchy.

Litwin and Stringer[10] defined six key variables in organizational culture and tested them in a laboratory situation in which they set up three companies that would be engaged in similar production and development work over a two-week period. The top managers of the companies, chosen for their personal styles of management, were given instructions on how their companies should be run. One company was set up on highly authoritarian lines designed to arouse the power motive. Communication was in writing, jobs were well defined, all decisions were made by the president, and little room was left for individuals to show initiative. A second company was organized along friendly democratic lines, emphasizing warm, friendly working relationships more than task accomplishment or formal organization. People were encouraged to talk and play, and interpersonal issues were confronted in daily group meetings. The president was always available to all employees and encouraged them to bring their problems to him. The third company was designed for an achieving culture. The president formulated objectives in collaboration with other executives, allowed groups to establish their own procedures, established a reward system for productivity, and constantly communicated his expectation of high performance by showing approval of good work. He was interested in everything, but he trusted his employees to make decisions affecting their own work. He posted progress reports for all to see every time he received any data on sales or new product acceptance.

Summarizing the data of Litwin and Stringer somewhat oversimplifies their study; nevertheless, job satisfaction was high in the achieving and friendly democratic cultures, low in the authoritarian group. In terms of profits made, the achieving group far outstripped the other two, who were relatively even in profits. The achieving culture also completed the experiment with a greater number of new products developed and accepted than the other two companies. In terms of overall performance, the achieving culture seemed far ahead, probably because it encouraged people to satisfy their achievement needs in the work situation, structuring the situation to stimulate that motive.

STAGES OF ORGANIZATION GROWTH

Organizational growth poses a further complexity concerning the relationship among leadership, motivation, and organizational culture. Organizations (like people) go

[9]Herbert A. Wainer and Irwin M. Rubin, "Motivation of Research and Development Entrepreneurs: Determinants of Company Success," *Journal of Applied Psychology,* Vol. 53, no. 3 (1969), pp. 178–184; *Readings.*

[10]George H. Litwin and Robert Stringer, "The Influence of Organizational Climate on Human Motivation" (Graduate School of Business Administration, Harvard University, May 1966); *Readings,* 1984.

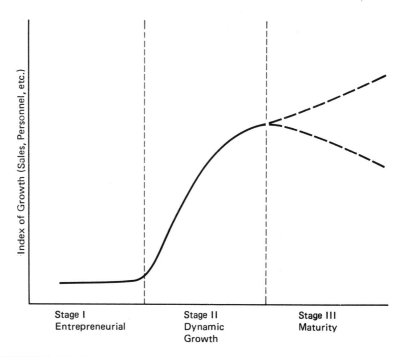

FIGURE 12-1

through stages of growth and development.[11] The "best" or most appropriate combination of personal motivational concerns and characteristics of organizational culture can only be answered by addressing the questions, "In what stage of growth are we now?" "Where are we trying to go?" "What kind of leadership style and organizational culture will be needed to ensure that we can cope with our next stage of development?" A simplified picture of the stages of organizational growth and development is shown in Figure 12–1. Stage I is the typical start-up base for the classical entrepreneur. It is often a very small show with a simple organization. The individual entrepreneur, high in n-Achievement, carries most of the weight with his or her energy, vision, and strong drive to succeed. Others get caught up in the excitement because they are in on the ground floor of a new venture.

If the organization survives this stage (and many do not), it then moves into a period of rapid growth (stage II). The morale and excitement, so high in stage I, begin to show the signs of stress. That old feeling of personal contact, easy access to the boss, and so on begins to wane as the organization grows in size. During this period of rapid growth the following problems often will be experienced:

1. Lower morale due to loss of close family feeling.
2. Lack of coordination among functional departments (now the organization structure has become more complex).
3. Missed deadlines, overrun budgets, poor or uneven quality control (things are falling through the cracks).
4. Chief executive officer overload—"I'd like to let go but I don't dare."
5. Frequent reorganization (about every six months).

If these normal stresses and strains are not managed effectively, the organization may find itself on a sharp downward spiral. While the forces are undoubtedly

[11]Larry Greiner, "Evolution and Revolution as Organizations Grow," *Harvard Business Review* (July–August 1972).

many and complex, a critical variable appears to be the organization's ability to reorganize and accept the fact that at different points in its life it needs different kinds of top management motivation and leadership and a different organizational culture. These transitional issues are particularly disconcerting to the entrepreneur-owner. The organization is his or her "baby" and letting go in certain areas and recognizing the need for more teamwork and group problem solving and conflict resolution, for example, is by no means simple.

III

Procedure for Group Meeting: The G.B.A. Construction Company Case

The class should divide up into their learning groups.

STEP 1.   The class should form groups of approximately five to six persons per group.

STEP 2.   Each group should prepare a 5-minute summary analysis of the G.B.A. case to share with the total class. (20 minutes) Use the accompanying G.B.A. Co. Case Summary form to write down your conclusions. This summary should touch on the following points:

a. What do you see as the major strengths and weaknesses of the four candidates?

b. Which candidate would you recommend as the new president of the G.B.A. Co.?

c. What is your rationale for this choice?

d. What other changes would you recommend to help the new president create the kind of organizational culture needed by the G.B.A. Co. over the next five to eight years?

STEP 3.   When the subgroups have completed their work in step 2, the entire class should reconvene for a summary discussion and analysis. (40 minutes)

a. Each of the subgroups should share its analysis with the total class. Others should ask questions of clarification during the process to ensure understanding. (20 minutes)

b. *After* sharing these analyses, the class should take a few moments to read over the G.B.A. Construction Company—Part II, and discuss the additional questions raised at the end of the case. (20 minutes)

G.B.A. Co. Case Summary

	ASSISTANT TO THE PRESIDENT (J. W.)	MANAGER I	MANAGER II	MANAGER III
MAJOR STRENGTHS				
MAJOR WEAK-NESSES				

a. GROUP CHOICE FOR THE NEW G.B.A. PRESIDENT	b. RATIONALE FOR CHOICE

c. CHANGES RECOMMENDED TO HELP THE NEW PRESIDENT CREATE THE ORGANIZATIONAL CULTURE NEEDED.

The G.B.A. Construction Company, Part II

THE IMMEDIATE RESULTS

Late in 1973, manager II was selected to be the new president of the G.B.A. Co. The major points in his favor, at the time, were as follows:

1. A high n-Achievement, combined with a moderate n-Affiliation, was felt to be critical in developing the teamwork needed among the top management group.

2. His ability and commitment to developing younger people would set a tone for the company that would help it develop the human resources needed to continue its rapid growth.

3. He seemed strong enough and had enough of a history with G.B.A., Jr., to "help" him keep his fingers out of the daily operations.

Manager I was also a strong candidate. His age and lack of experience were his major drawbacks. There was an underlying feeling that with more experience and "polish," he could be a strong candidate the next time around. For now, his strengths were best utilized as a division manager.

Manager III was not a serious contender. In a nutshell, he was too much like G.B.A., Jr.

The assistant to the president, J.W., was a hard candidate to exclude for a variety of reasons. Chief among these was a concern that if his loyalty were not rewarded, he might subsequently leave the company. These fears proved valid and he left a year later.

THE LONGER TERM*

So, it is late 1973, and manager II has taken over as president. Very shortly thereafter, as pointed out, the assistant to the president left the company. Manager III retired when manager II took over, and the Western Division was managed out of the home office for a while. A. H. also retired as had been expected.

Businesswise, the next 18 months were very favorable. Then, as the general economy took a downturn, so, too, did the construction business. Falling sales volume and reduced profits impacted all the senior managers, including the new president, for their compensation was still closely tied to bottom-line results.

This downturn was mitigated somewhat by the increasing business opportunities in Saudi Arabia. The new president had personally spearheaded this move overseas, and while this drained energy from other matters, it did keep sales volume and profits from dropping even further.

Stylistically, the new president appeared *not* to be working out as expected. His participative style was most reflective in his dealing one-on-one with people informally, as peers. This was his forte. For whatever reasons, he had considerable discomfort with the more formal group settings. G.B.A., Jr., commented, "He seemed to behave in an inferior way" (as if he felt very insecure). Consequently, he could not get the top team together much as it had appeared he might.

So, one day late in 1975, upon returning from one of his frequent trips to Saudi Arabia, he said almost in desperation to G.B.A., Jr., "I'm not sure I want to be the head of a big company!" He and G.B.A., Jr., subsequently negotiated an agreement wherein he would run the Saudi Arabian business on a contract basis for one year. G.B.A., Jr., thus took over again as president.

At the end of this one-year contract, they agreed to part company completely.

*G.B.A., Jr., was interviewed during April 1981 and graciously provided this current update.

So manager II left the G.B.A. Construction Company to start his own construction business in the same city as the G.B.A. Company's home office. According to G.B.A., Jr., he has taken on a lot of big jobs (although *not* as big as those taken by the G.B.A. Co., he is quick to point out) and has had dramatic turnover in staff. The causes of his dramatic turnover are unknown. What is clearer is the implication that "He deserves whatever he gets for being disloyal."

THE NEW AND CURRENT PRESIDENT

So, in the fall of 1976, G.B.A., Jr., turned over the reins of his company to manager I. Four and one-half years later, G.B.A., JR., talks glowingly and proudly of "his new president's" accomplishments. He has proven to be a very solid long-range planner and organizer . . . in spite of the fact that he is "much more intellectual" than anyone else in top management.

In comparison with the previous president (manager II, not G.B.A., Jr.), he finds it harder to communicate informally with peers on a one-to-one basis. On the other hand, he has proven to be very good in formal group settings. While the maturity of a few more years to develop undoubtedly helped manager I develop into presidential timber, it is important to examine briefly several other changes.

With respect to G.B.A., Jr., himself, by his own reports, he is still working hard. He is, however, much less involved now than he was during manager II's reign.

Several critical structural changes have also taken place that have had a very positive impact on the culture and behavior.

Flowing in part from his relative discomfort in informal one-on-one situations and relative comfort in formal group settings, the new president has instituted two important group structures. One, an operations committee of key managers from each of the divisions, was formed to focus on companywide (versus division specific) issues such as contracting, cost cutting, and policy. A similar Human Resource Committee was formed to focus on issues of personnel (benefits, recruitment, etc.) and training. The new president serves as formal chairperson for both committees.

Finally, a way was found in the last three years, to, in effect, create two companies. The new one is structured on a partnership format that is owned by G.B.A., Jr., and his senior top management team of officers and provides a trust for G.B.A., Jr.'s family. Ultimately, this new corporation will develop a solid equity base. When this happens, the family trust portion (and ultimately G.B.A., Jr.'s portion) will be bought out. While he was appropriately reticent to share the details, G.B.A., Jr., was clear that this new structure had virtually eliminated the previous concern among his officers about continuity and their long-run futures.

A POSTSCRIPT: THE 20:20 VISION OF HINDSIGHT

Several points about the concepts of motivation and organizational culture are highlighted—with the clarity afforded by 20:20 hindsight.

Let us begin by reexamining the original choice of manager II. The underlying question is "Was he the right or the wrong candidate?" and there is no absolute answer to this question. Several explanatory clues can be traced, however.

It is important to realize that a prime reason for the company's success under G.B.A., Jr.'s leadership was the fit or match between the elements that make up organization culture. G.B.A., Jr.'s personal skills and his personal style were matched to the types of people he gathered around himself as part of his executive team. These human factors were furthermore aligned and matched with key elements of the management operation systems, organizational structure, and strategy.[12] The

[12]For more detail on this concept of fit or alignment, see Pascale and Athos, *The Art of Japanese Management.*

combination and alignment or matching among all these elements created a coherent environment or climate that shaped and channeled individual behavior.

Manager II's personal style may well have been the one needed to carry the company through its next stage of development. We'll never know for sure. It is reasonably clear, however, that manager II did not have the time, skill, or support from G.B.A., Jr., to design and implement other environmental changes. These changes potentially could have created the alignment and matching that gives the concept of organizational culture such power in influencing behavior. A new president with a new style cannot function in an environment (e.g., executive team, organizational systems, structures, strategies, reward systems, and the like) *designed* to fit a very different presidential style (G.B.A., Jr.'s). The totality of culture variables, taken together, seem to far outweigh the power of a given personality in influencing the behavior of people in organizations.

This line of argument gains further support when we review the characteristics of manager I. While not identical to G.B.A., Jr., manager I was nonetheless like him in many ways. It is not surprising, therefore, that after a few years of seasoning, he should emerge as the replacement for manager II. The resulting stress on the organization—including very importantly the top executive team—was much less severe. The fit between manager I's style and the existing environmental variables was guaranteed to be closer since G.B.A., Jr., and manager I were more similar. Add to this the fact that important structural changes concerning equity (referred to earlier) did not get implemented until after manager II was relieved and manager I took over.

Pascale and Athos sum up these issues well:[13] "There is no quick fix in sight. Rather, each company's CEO and other top executives need to recognize that it takes time, discomfort, stamina, and commitment to strengthen what is weak in their organizational development. Moreover, there is no sure blueprint for success. Every firm has to be good at (the elements of climate or environment) and their fit to one another. . . . And each company, like each individual, has to develop in its own way."

The entire group should now discuss the following points in light of what actually happened:

1. Knowing how clear things can appear, in hindsight, what additional clues were there—*if any*—that manager II *may* have been an inappropriate choice?

2. Could manager I have handled the job in late 1973? Why or why not?

3. How might manager II have fared if comparable structural changes (i.e., operations committee, human resources committee, the creation of two companies) had been instituted during his rein? How might manager I have fared in the absence of these structural changes?

4. If you were the consultant in this case, would you feel successful? Why or why not?

5. What connections can you make between this exercise and the readings?

ASSESSING THE ORGANIZATIONAL CULTURE OF THE CLASSROOM
(Time Allotted: $1\frac{1}{2}$ Hours)

This exercise utilizes a technique known as the *nominal group technique*. It is designed to gather ideas or data quickly in a democratic fashion. The round-robin nature of this technique prevents influential people from controlling the air time or the vote. Once ideas are mentioned, they become the property of the group, not ideas advocated by specific individuals.

[13]Ibid., p. 206.

STEP 1. Write down three to five statements that describe

     a. The current state of the organizational culture of your learning organization—this course.

     b. The ideal state of this learning organization.

     c. The current state of your learning group.

     d. The ideal state of your learning group.

Note: (1) It's not necessary to write complete sentences as long as your words or phrases will be understood by others. (2) For the "current state" questions, try to think of both positives and negatives to "cover the waterfront." (3) For the "ideal state" questions, don't limit yourself by merely reversing negative characteristics you may have identified for the current state. Give yourself free rein here to be creative and think beyond the constraints of the current situation. (15 minutes)

STEP 2. The instructor will go around the room asking each participant to read out loud one statement from their list and write it on a flipchart or blackboard. Participants can "pass" when all the statements on their list have been recorded. (15 minutes)

STEP 3. The class will examine the statements to see if all are comprehensible and that there are no duplicates. Some statements may need to be combined. (10 minutes)

STEP 4. Each participant marks the three statements that are most significant to them as individuals with a marker or chalk mark. Put a "1" beside or beneath the three statements. This is a way of quickly ranking the statements. (10 minutes)

STEP 5. The marks will be counted, identifying the major issues regarding the organizational culture in the course.

STEP 6. The class as a whole can discuss the results, using the discussion questions that follow. (30 minutes)

DISCUSSION QUESTIONS ABOUT ORGANIZATION CULTURE

1. How did your motive pattern influence your choice of an ideal culture?

2. In your opinion, which dimensions of our culture stimulate or inhibit n-Achievement? n-Power? n-Affiliation?

3. Is there a fit between the task of our learning organization and the other aspects of our organizational culture?

4. During the unit on psychological contracts, a contract was formulated. To what extent is the culture supporting or inhibiting this contract.

5. What steps can be taken to change the culture in this classroom to enhance the realization of the psychological contract or to bring the reality closer to the ideal state?

IV

Follow-up

To summarize let us examine a couple of examples of the relationships among organizational structure, culture, and individual motivation. All complex organizations need standard operating procedures and policies to some degree. Policies and procedures that appear to an employee to require arbitrary, nonwork-related conformity have the effect of reducing n-Achievement behavior and increasing n-Power behavior (i.e., behaviors aimed at beating the system and its rules). High-n-Achievement persons must be able to take moderate risks, get frequent clear feedback on their actions, and see a direct link between their actions and desired rewards. Many organizational reward and performance appraisal systems have the unanticipated effect of reducing achievement-oriented behavior. In these systems, feedback is only a once-per-year event, rewards are tied to seniority versus performance, and failure (an inevitable consequence of risk taking) is punished rather than treated as a learning opportunity.

Many times the task of building an achieving culture in an organization is one of changing the concerns of management from power compliance ("Here is what needs doing, and here is how to do it") to one that offers warmth and support to each individual, communicating organizational goals and standards but not attempting to control the means of reaching those goals.

In a classroom "organization," Alschuler[14] gives an example of the effects this kind of climate change has on performance. An experienced typing teacher in a suburban Boston high school decided to stop prescribing goals for her pupils, to stop scheduling tests for all at the same time, and to stop enforcing behavior rules unrelated to typing skill (talking, gum chewing). She gave one speed test a week, at a time of the pupils' choosing, asked them to estimate their goals for the test in terms of speed and errors, and gave them as many tests as needed to reach their goals. When not taking the tests, pupils were free to practice as they wished, working on problems they felt most important. When they brought a record player and records to class, she merely asked them not to play it so loud that it would disturb other classes. In this climate, which emphasized affiliation and achievement and deemphasized compliance with authority, the pupils improved their speed and accuracy to an extraordinary degree. Compared with a previous class almost perfectly matched in IQ and manual ability, every one in the experimental group tied or outscored the highest scorer in the more conventional classroom climate. Clearly, the difference in culture increased performance and satisfaction.

Another example of how organization structure changes can produce improvements in organization culture and effectiveness occurred in the assembly division of an electronics company. The morale, productivity, and return rates on equipment were very bad in one group until management changed the physical structure of the group of assemblers from a linear assembly line to a circle. When they sat in a face-to-face group, worker morale improved as their affiliation needs were met. This resulted in improved production, sharing of work loads, and better quality control resulting from a sense of team spirit. It is important to note in connection with this case that culture must be changed by giving consideration to both the individuals' motives and the job demand.

[14]Alfred Alschuler, "How to Increase Motivation Through Structure and Climate," Achievement Motivation Development Project, Working Paper 10, Graduate School of Education, Harvard University, Cambridge, MA, 1968.

The preceding paragraphs have illustrated how organizational culture can be adapted to fit the needs of the individuals and groups better within the organization. However, in many organizations it is more common to try to fit the individual to the culture. Socialization is the way in which organizations introduce their members to the organizational culture. Let's examine two approaches to the task of socializing new members and the potential consequences.

For many Americans, a visit to the doctor follows this scenario: Your call to the physician is answered by a machine or harried-sounding person who puts you on hold. Eventually, you are assigned an appointment time several weeks hence. On the specified day you wait at least an hour in a crowded reception room trying to read magazines that were clearly intended for a minuscule segment of the population, and you wonder why only the doctor's time is worth money. By now your frame of mind is as aggravated as whatever occasioned your visit to the doctor in the first place.

The program at Disney World provides a strong contrast. There, customers are treated like guests in a private home. There are no information booths, only guest relations rooms. A summer employee whose work life with Disney will span 50 days spends the first 5 days in an orientation program, the purpose being to inculcate the organizational culture of guest relations. Ten percent of the expected summer employment is spent becoming socialized into the organization's normative expectations. Could it be done faster? Perhaps. Isn't it worth it to cut a few corners? Not to an organization serious about its search for excellence.

V

Learning Points

1. Organizational culture is defined as a pattern of shared values and beliefs that produce certain norms of behavior.

2. Organizational culture can be used to manage the motivation of employees, generate commitment and cooperation, and also serve as a control function.

3. Organizational culture is formed by

   a. The values of the founder or strong leaders.

   b. Learned solutions to problems over time.

   c. The larger societal context.

4. Fit is an important consideration with organizational culture. The people, the organization's task, and the environment and the culture should be complementary.

5. Strong cultures have the following characteristics:

   a. People in the organization can easily identify the dominant values.

   b. The selection processes target people who are likely to fit into the culture and find it satisfying.

   c. Socialization and training convey to newcomers the "ropes" they need to learn.

   d. Employees who do not fit the culture or produce in accordance with its values are sometimes fired.

   e. People within the company are rewarded for acting in accordance with the dominant values of the organizations.

   f. Leaders and managers send clear, consistent signals about desired values and norms by their own behavior.

   g. Managers measure and control what is important to the culture.

6. Strength of the culture does not result in high performance unless the culture fits the environment.

7. A strategy decision to change the organizational culture requires identifying the mission and dominant values of the organization and bringing all other aspects into alignment.

8. Managerial style plays a major role in determining the culture because the leader's motivation patterns affect performance and trickle down through the entire company.

9. Democratic, participative cultures designed to stimulate people's need for achievement were more effective than were autocratic cultures that emphasized compliance and stimulated the need for power or cultures that stimulated the need for affiliation.

10. Organizations go through stages of growth that have varying characteristics and require different types of leaders.

11. Socialization is the process of introducing new members into the organization.

12. Companies with strong cultures generally devote more time and effort to socialization.

VI

Tips for Managers

- Before you join an organization, try to read its culture and determine whether or not your values are compatible with those of the organization.

- Figure out your organization's cultural characteristics and use that understanding when making analyses and decisions. Awareness of the history of the organization can keep new managers from making errors.

- Establishing an effective organizational culture requires consistency. What managers do to reinforce culture is stronger than what they say.

- Encourage a certain degree of nonconformity. While it is more difficult to handle people who don't fit the culture very well, they are valuable in pointing out the assumptions that are guiding the dominant culture.

- Helping a work group or organization to make their norms explicit identifies what values need to be reinforced or changed.

- Creating traditions and events that emphasize the cultural values you deem important help form a culture (e.g., the Glorious Booboo Award in the R&D lab, roasts for people who get promoted or retire, and Friday afternoon TGIF parties).

- The organization's culture must be taken into consideration whenever changes are planned because culture can be a major impediment to change. Changes that utilize the culture, rather than fight against it are more likely to succeed.

VII

Personal Application Assignment

Rumor has it that one Friday, a CEO attended a speech on organizational culture. When the speaker had explained the advantages of a strong culture, the CEO leaned over to his assistant and said, "Get me one of those cultures by Monday!" Your assignment is to write about an experience involving organizational culture. Choose an experience about which you want to learn more.

A. *Concrete Experience*
   1. *Objectively* describe the experience ("who," "what," "when," "where," "how" type information—up to 2 points).
   2. *Subjectively* describe your feelings, perceptions, and thoughts that occurred *during* (not after) the experience (up to 2 points). Does this section have too much detail? (If so, delete 1 point).

B. *Reflective Observation*
   1. Look at the experience from different points of view. How many points of view did you include that are *relevant* (up to 2 points)?
   2. Use these perspectives to add more meaning to the incident (up to 2 points).

C. *Abstract Conceptualization*
   1. Relate concepts from the assigned readings and the lecture to the experience (i.e., what theories that you heard in the lecture or read in the *Reader* relate to your understanding of this incident?). Make reference to at least two sources. Use standard referencing format and include the page number to which you are referring. How many sources did you use and how clearly did you explain their theories (up to 4 points)?
   2. You can also create an original model or theory, but it should not replace course concepts.

D. *Active Experimentation*
   1. Write about what you will do in the future that will improve your effectiveness. Use rules of thumb or action resolutions.
   2. Are they described specifically, thoroughly, and in detail (up to 4 points)?

E. *Integration, Synthesis, and Writing*
   1. Did you write about something personally important to you (up to 2 points)?
   2. Was it well written (up to 2 points)?
   3. Did you integrate and synthesize the different sections (up to 1 point)?

13

LEADERSHIP AND DECISION MAKING

This unit is based on the research of Victor Vroom and his colleagues. Cases are used with permission of the University of Pittsburgh Press and the American Institute for Decision Sciences. Further information about training programs based on the model can be obtained from Kepner-Trego Associates, Inc.

Pajama Talk

Lester Coch and John R. French, Jr.

The Sleepytime Pajama factory was going great guns. Sales were up. The work force was expanding. There was only one hitch. To remain competitive, factory managers were constantly adapting both work techniques and products. Workers were often transferred to different jobs or had parts of their job modified, either in the name of progress or as a result of high turnover and absenteeism. The biggest problem facing Sleepytime was worker resistance to these changes. As soon as they became proficient at one job they'd be switched to another. They worked on a piece-rate incentive system, and it wasn't easy to work their way up to producing 60 units per hour, the standard efficiency rate. Some suspicious souls thought management just switched workers to new jobs when they had finally mastered their tasks and could begin to earn bonuses for producing more than 60 units. Even though workers received a transfer bonus that made up for the money lost learning new jobs, it didn't make up for the loss in status of being a "greenhorn" on a new task. Workers still hated to be transferred to a new job, and some quit rather than change. Others complained bitterly about management and fought with their supervisors and the time-study engineers. Statistics showed that old workers took longer to relearn new jobs and get up to speed than did new employees with no work experience! This convinced the company that the problem was really a question of motivation and resistance to change.

Mr. Sleepytime himself, Joe Berg, had the production people organize the output figures in relation to the changes that had been introduced during the last year. He was surprised to find that the work groups supervised by Kathy Johnson seemed to have fewer problems with changes. Her groups got back to speed quicker after the changes and had a higher level of output than the others. She also had fewer terminations, even after the job transfers. So Berg sent his industrial relations expert out on the floor to figure out what was going on.

After observation, the expert discovered that the difference lay in how the supervisors handled the changes. Supervisors of the low-productivity groups simply announced to their employees that a job had to be changed (so they could compete better in the marketplace), explained the new piece rate, and answered questions.

In contrast, Johnson used physical demonstrations with her workers in which she showed them samples of pajamas made using new and old techniques, explained the cost differential, and asked them if they could tell the difference between them. Or she'd bring in pajamas made by a competitor who was underselling them and show them why changes had to be made to respond to this challenge. Next, she'd ask the group how the new jobs should be designed.

Based on "Overcoming Resistance to Change," *Human Relations,* Vol. 1 (1947), pp. 512–531.

They'd come up with a blitz of ideas for improving the job, and then they worked *with* the time-study engineer to test out the innovations. Johnson let the workers do most of the talking and planning. She didn't have in her head a "one best way" to make the changes; she let them figure it out for themselves. As a result, they bought into the changes and became committed to making them work. Johnson made the factory workers participants in the change process rather than victims of it. And in the process Berg learned that the sooner people are brought into a change effort and allowed to participate in the decision making, the better.

I
Premeeting Preparation

(Time Allotted: 30 Minutes)

A. Read the descriptions of decision-making alternatives for individual and group problems in Table 13–1 and describe how you would handle each of the five decision-making cases that follows. Indicate whether the case describes an individual or group problem and which decision-making approach you would use. Choose your approach based on what you would do in the situation described. This will allow a comparison between your experience and the recommendations of the decision-making model described in this chapter.

B. After completing A, read the Topic Introduction and the Procedure for Group Meeting.

C. What are the significant learning points from the readings?

TABLE 13–1 Decision Styles for Leadership: Individuals and Groups

INDIVIDUAL PROBLEMS*	GROUP PROBLEMS†
AI. You solve the problem or make the decision yourself, using information available to you at that time.	AI. You solve the problem or make the decision yourself, using information available to you at that time.
AII. You obtain any necessary information from the subordinate and then decide on the solution to the problem yourself. You may or may not tell the subordinate what the problem is in getting the information from him. The role played by your subordinate in making the decision is clearly one of providing specific information that you request, rather than generating or evaluating alternative solutions.	AII. You obtain any necessary information from subordinates and then decide on the solution to the problem yourself. You may or may not tell the subordinates what the problem is in getting the information from them. The role played by your subordinates in making the decision is clearly one of providing specific information that you request rather than generating or evaluating solutions.
CI. You share the problem with the relevant subordinate, getting ideas and suggestions. Then *you* make the decision. This decision may or may not reflect your subordinate's influence.	CI. You share the problem with the relevant subordinates individually, getting their ideas and suggestions without bringing them together as a group. Then *you* make the decision. This decision may or may not reflect your subordinates' influence.
GI. You share the problem with one of your subordinates, and together you analyze the problem and arrive at a mutually satisfactory solution in an atmosphere of free and open exchange of information and ideas. You both contribute to the resolution of the problem, with the relative contribution of each being dependent on knowledge rather than formal authority.	CII. You share the problem with your subordinates in a group meeting. In this meeting you obtain their ideas and suggestions. Then *you* make the decision, which may or may not reflect your subordinates' influence.
DI. You delegate the problem to one of your subordinates, providing him or her with any relevant information that you possess, but giving him or her responsibility for solving the problem alone. Any solution that the person reaches will receive your support.	GII. You share the problem with your subordinates as a group. Together you generate and evaluate alternatives and attempt to reach agreement (consensus) on a solution. Your role is much like that of chairman, coordinating the discussion, keeping it focused on the problem, and making sure that the critical issues are discussed. You do not try to influence the group to adopt "your" solution and you are willing to accept and implement any solution that has the support of the entire group.

*The decision adopted will have potential effects on only one immediate subordinate. The problem is confined to that manager's area of responsibility.
†The decision adopted will have potential effects on all or some subgroup of immediate subordinates. The problem overlaps areas of at least some subordinates' responsibilities and/or expertise.
A = Autocratic.
C = Consultative.
G = Group decision.
D = Delegation.

Case 1: The Finance Case

You are the head of a staff unit reporting to the vice president of finance. The vice president has asked you to provide a report on the firm's current portfolio to include recommendations for changes in the selection criteria currently employed. Doubts have been raised about the efficiency of the existing system in the current market conditions, and there is considerable dissatisfaction with prevailing rates of return.

You plan to write the report, but at the moment you are quite perplexed about the approach to take. Your own speciality is the bond market, and it is clear to you that detailed knowledge of the equity market, which you lack, would greatly enhance the value of the report. Fortunately, four members of your staff are specialists in different segments of the equity market. Together, they possess a vast amount of knowledge about the intricacies of investment. However, they seldom agree on the best way to achieve anything when it comes to investment philosophy and strategy.

You have six weeks before the report is due. You have already begun to familiarize yourself with the firm's current portfolio and have been provided by management with a specific set of constraints that any portfolio must satisfy. Your immediate problem is to come up with some alternatives to the firm's present practices and select the most promising for detailed analysis in your report.

How would you go about doing this?

Is it an individual or a group problem?

What decision-making method would you use?

Circle the box that indicates the approach you would use in this case.

Individual	A1	A11	C1	G1	D1
Group	A1	A11	C1	C11	G11

Case 2: International Consulting Company

You are regional manager of an international management consulting company. You have a staff of six consultants reporting to you, each of whom enjoys a considerable amount of autonomy with clients in the field.

Yesterday you received a complaint from one of your major clients to the effect that the consultant whom you assigned to work on the contract with them was not doing his job effectively. They were not very explicit as to the nature of the problem, but it was clear that they were dissatisfied and that something would have to be done if you were to restore the client's faith in your company.

The consultant assigned to work on that contract has been with the company for six years. He is a systems analyst and is one of the best in that profession. For the first four or five years his performance was superb, and he was a model for the more junior consultants. However, recently he has seemed to have a "chip on his shoulder," and his previous identification with the company and its objectives has been replaced with indifference. His negative attitude has been noticed by other consultants, as well as by clients. This is not the first such complaint that you have had from a client this year about his performance. A previous client even reported to you that the consultant reported to work several times obviously suffering from a hangover.

It is important to get to the root of this problem quickly if that client is to be retained. The consultant obviously has the skill necessary to work with the clients effectively. If only he were willing to use it!

Is it an individual or a group problem?

How would you as regional manager deal with this problem?

Circle the box that indicates the approach you would use in this case.

Individual	A1	A11	C1	G1	D1
Group	A1	A11	C1	C11	G11

Case 3: The Engineering Work Assignment

You are supervising the work of 12 civil engineers. Their formal training and work experience are very similar, permitting you to use them interchangeably on projects. Yesterday your manager informed you that a request had been received from an overseas affiliate for 4 engineers to go abroad on extended loan for a period of six to eight months. For a number of reasons, he argued and you agreed, this request should be met from your group.

All your engineers are experienced in and are capable of handling assignments such as this. From the standpoint of present and future work projects, there is no particular reason why any one should be chosen over any other. The problem is somewhat complicated by the fact that the overseas assignment is in what is generally regarded in the company as an undesirable location.

Is it an individual or a group problem?

How would you deal with this problem?

Circle the box that indicates the approach you would use in this case.

Individual	A1	A11	C1	G1	D1
Group	A1	A11	C1	C11	G11

Case 4: The Pharmaceutical Company

You are executive vice president for a small pharmaceutical manufacturer. You have the opportunity to bid on a contract for the Defense Department pertaining to biological warfare. The contract is outside the mainstream of your business; however, it could make economic sense, since you do have unused capacity in one of your plants, and the manufacturing processes are not dissimilar.

You have written the document to accompany the bid and now have the problem of determining the dollar value of the quotation that you think will win the job for your company. If the bid is too high, you will undoubtedly lose to one of your competitors; if it is too low, you would stand to lose money on the program.

There are many factors to be considered in making this decision, including the cost of the new raw materials and the additional administrative burden of relationships with a new client, not to speak of factors that are likely to influence the bids of your competitors, such as how much they *need* this particular contract. You have been busy assembling the necessary data to make this decision, but there remain several "unknowns," one of which involves the manager of the plant in which the new products will be manufactured. Of all your subordinates, only she is in the position to estimate the costs of adapting the present equipment to its new purpose, and her cooperation and support will be necessary in ensuring that the specifications of the contract will be met. However, in an initial discussion with her when you first learned of the possibility of the contract, she seemed adamantly opposed to the idea. Although she has been an effective and dedicated plant manager over the past several years, her previous experience has not particularly equipped her to evaluate the overall merits of projects like this one. From the nature of her arguments, you inferred that her opposition was ideological rather than economic. You recall in this context that she is involved in the local nuclear freeze movement.

Is it an individual or a group problem?

How will you go about determining the amount of the bid?

Circle the box that indicates the approach you would use in this case.

Individual	A1	A11	C1	G1	D1
Group	A1	A11	C1	C11	G11

Case 5: The Oil Pipeline

You are general supervisor in charge of a large gang laying an oil pipeline. It is now necessary to estimate your expected rate of progress to schedule material deliveries to the next field site.

You know the nature of the terrain you will be traveling and have in your records the historical data needed to compute the mean and variance in the rate of speed over that type of terrain. Given these two variables it is a simple matter to calculate the earliest and latest times at which materials and support facilities will be needed at the next site. It is important that your estimate be reasonably accurate. Underestimates result in idle supervisors and workers, and an overestimate results in tying up materials for a period of time before they are to be used.

Progress has been good, and your five supervisors and other members of the gang stand to receive substantial bonuses if the project is completed ahead of schedule.

Is it an individual or a group problem?

How would you go about scheduling material deliveries?

Circle the box that indicates the approach you would use in this case.

Individual	A1	A11	C1	G1	D1
Group	A1	A11	C1	C11	G11

II

Topic Introduction

To a manager, executive, or administrator, no other job function encapsulates the frustrations and joys of leadership more dramatically than decision making.[1] It is in making decisions that managers most acutely feel the responsibilities, the power, and the vulnerability of their jobs. This central focus of decision making in the experience of leadership is illustrated in the autobiographies of political leaders, who characteristically organize their life stories around major decision points they faced, the dilemmas and pressures they experienced, and how in the end the "buck" stopped on their desks, confronting them with lonely moments of decision. Harry Truman described his decision to fire General MacArthur and his decision to drop the atomic bomb in this way. Richard Nixon's "six crises" were phrased as major decision points that called for lonely soul searching and personal commitment to the right course of action. Most of us in our life and work face decisions of less than presidential magnitude; nonetheless, from time to time we share the existential loneliness of making an important decision.

Yet there are two things wrong with using this admittedly powerful subjective experience of decision making as the focus for analyzing and improving the decision-making process in organizations. First, this experience would suggest that decisions can be thought of as independent solitary events relatively unconnected to other decisions and the process that brought the decision point to a head. If there is anything to be learned from the Bay of Pigs fiasco or the Vietnam experience, it is that the organizational process of problem identification, information sharing, and problem solving, if mishandled, can undo the work of the finest, most logical, and experienced individual decision maker.

Second, the experience suggests that decision making is an individual process and that therefore the skills of logical analysis and problem solving (described in Chapter 9) are sufficient to produce high-quality decisions. However, decision making in organizations is also a social process. Organizational functioning requires an unending stream of decisions great and small. These decisions are identified, made, and communicated by individuals throughout the organization. As a manager you depend on the decisions of others and the information they bring you. You also delegate decisions and share information about them with others. Part of a manager's role is determining who in the organization has the information, experience, and wisdom needed to make a particular decision. Another part is understanding who are the stakeholders in each issue who need to be involved because their acceptance of the outcome is crucial. Seeing decision making as a social process means that the manager is responsible for determining *how* the problem is to be solved, but not necessarily the solution. The sense that any decision is made alone in an organization is an illusion. There are those who feel that Richard Nixon's greatest failure was falling prey to this illusion. Those who knew him say that he was a brilliant analyst and individual problem solver. Yet his Achilles' heel was his inability to develop an effective social process of decision making that involved others in appropriate ways.

The focus of this unit is on managing the process of decision making, as opposed to the problem-solving skills of making a specific decision. It further focuses on the social aspects of that process and the alternative ways of making decisions

---

[1]For an interesting discussion of decision making, see Morgan McCall and Robert Kaplan's book, *Whatever It Takes: Decision Makers at Work* (Englewood Cliffs, NJ: Prentice Hall, 1985).

with other people: the costs and benefits and the appropriate application of these decision-making methods in different situations.

The decision-making alternatives you used in the prework section reflect a contingency theory of leadership. The continuum ranges from *autocratic* decision-making behavior, in which the leader decides alone, to *participative* styles, which involve consultation to *delegation.* The choice of style depends upon the problem at hand. Once again, managerial effectiveness depends upon having the skills required to analyze the problem in question and the ability to vary one's leadership behavior accordingly.

To understand the decision-making *process,* we must first examine the nature of effective organizational decisions and the components of decision effectiveness. The effectiveness of a decision can be judged in terms of three outcomes:

1. The *quality or rationality* of the decision, which is defined as the extent to which decisions influence employee performance.

2. The *acceptance* of the decision, defined as the degree of employee commitment to executing the decision effectively.

3. The amount of *time* available to make the decision.

The extent to which these three criteria of quality, acceptance, and efficiency are critical varies from one decision to another. For some decisions, particularly those you will implement yourself, acceptance is not critical, but high quality may be absolutely essential, as, for example, in decisions about how to program the computer for inventory control. Other decisions have very little quality requirement but involve great acceptance. The decision about how the secretarial pool will cover the phones at lunch time is an example of this type of decision. The solution devised has little in the way of a logical requirement, but it must be acceptable to the people involved. Efficiency is usually an important consideration in everything we do in organizations, but other objectives, such as developing subordinates or learning, sometimes take priority.

It is therefore important to be able to diagnose decision situations to determine the quality, acceptance, and efficiency requirements and the method of decision making that will maximize these requirements. No single decision-making method or management style is appropriate for all jobs or even all decisions in a single job. For some situations, the authoritative decision is best, for others the consultation style, and still others require a participative approach.

Victor Vroom and his associates[2] have developed a formal model that helps us to analyze specific decision situations and to determine the decision-making approach that is likely to be most effective. The model is constructed in the form of a decision tree based on ten rules (shown in Table 13–2) that were derived from research on problem solving and decision making. It poses eight questions for managers to ask about a decision:

A. Is there a quality requirement such that one solution is likely to be more rational than another? Does the technical quality of the decision matter?

B. Do I have sufficient information to make a high-quality decision?

C. Is the problem structured (i.e., is it a repetitive and routine problem for which a definite procedure has been developed)?[3]

D. Is acceptance of the decision by subordinates critical to effective implementation?

[2]Victor H. Vroom and P. Yetton, *Leadership and Decision Making* (Pittsburgh, PA: University of Pittsburgh Press, 1973).

[3]Unstructured problems are novel, and no procedures have been developed to handle them because they occur infrequently and/or are very complex.

TABLE 13-2   Rules Underlying the Vroom-Yetton Model

RULES TO PROTECT THE QUALITY OF THE DECISION

1. **The leader information rule.** If the quality of the decision is important and the leader does not possess enough information or expertise to solve the problem by himself or herself, then AI is eliminated from the feasible set.

2. **The goal congruence rule.** If the quality of the decision is important and subordinates are not likely to pursue the organization goals in their efforts to solve the problem, the GII is eliminated from the feasible set.

3. **The unstructured problem rule.** In decisions in which the quality of the decision is important, if the leader lacks the necessary information or expertise to solve the problem by himself or herself and if the problem is unstructured, the method of solving the problem should provide for interaction among subordinates likely to possess relevant information. Accordingly, AI, AII, and CI are eliminated from the feasible set.

RULES TO PROTECT THE ACCEPTANCE OF THE DECISION

4. **The acceptance rule.** If the acceptance of the decision by subordinates is critical to effective implementation and if it is not certain that an autocratic decision will be accepted, AI and AII are eliminated from the feasible set.

5. **The conflict rule.** If the acceptance of the decision is critical, an autocratic decision is not certain to be accepted, and disagreement among subordinates in methods of attaining the organizational goal is likely, the methods used in solving the problem should enable those in disagreement to resolve their differences with full knowledge of the problem. Accordingly, under these conditions, AI, AII, and CI, which permit no interaction among subordinates and therefore provide no opportunity for those in conflict to resolve their differences, are eliminated from the feasible set. Their use runs the risk of leaving some of the subordinates with less than the needed commitment to the final decision.

6. **The fairness rule.** If the quality of the decision is unimportant but acceptance of the decision is critical and not certain to result from an autocratic decision, it is important that the decision process used generate the needed acceptance. The decision process used should permit the subordinates to interact with one another and negotiate over the fair method of resolving any differences, with full responsibility on them for determining what is fair and equitable. Accordingly, under these circumstances, AI, AII, CI, and CII are eliminated from the feasible set.

7. **The acceptance priority rule.** If acceptance is critical and not certain to result from an autocratic decision, and if subordinates are motivated to pursue the organizational goals represented in the problem, then methods that provide equal partnership in the decision making process can provide greater acceptance without risking decision quality. Accordingly, AI, AII, CI, and CII are eliminated from the feasible set.

Source: V. A. Vroom, "A New Look at Managerial Decision Making," *Organizational Dynamics,* Vol. 2 (Spring 1973), p. 67.

    E. If I were to make the decision by myself, is it reasonably certain that it would be accepted by my subordinates?

    F. Do subordinates share the organizational goals to be attained in solving this problem?

    G. Is conflict among subordinates likely in preferred solutions? (This is irrelevant to individual problems.)

    H. Do subordinates have sufficient information to make a high-quality decision? (This applies only to individual problems.)

By answering these questions sequentially and tracing the answers through the model's decision tree (see Figure 13–1), the manager is led to a set of effective decision alternatives for the problem. There are eighteen effective decision sets, one at the end of each branch of the decision tree. The decision-making methods listed in the effective decision sets are those described at the beginning of the chapter. The

A. Is there a quality requirement such that one solution is likely to be more rational than another?
B. Do I have sufficient info to make a high-quality decision?
C. Is the problem structured?
D. Is acceptance of decision by subordinates critical to effective implementation?
E. If I were to make the decision by myself, is it reasonably certain that it would be accepted by my subordinates?
F. Do subordinates share the organizational goals to be attained in solving this problem?
G. Is conflict among subordinates likely in preferred solutions? (This is irrelevant to individual problems.)
H. Do subordinates have sufficient info to make a high-quality decision? (This applies only to individual problems.)

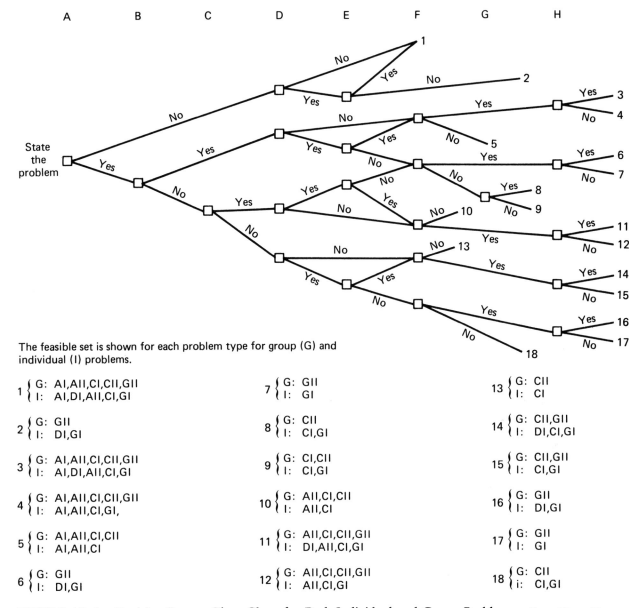

The feasible set is shown for each problem type for group (G) and individual (I) problems.

1 { G: AI,AII,CI,CII,GII
    I: AI,DI,AII,CI,GI

2 { G: GII
    I: DI,GI

3 { G: AI,AII,CI,CII,GII
    I: AI,DI,AII,CI,GI

4 { G: AI,AII,CI,CII,GII
    I: AI,AII,CI,GI,

5 { G: AI,AII,CI,CII
    I: AI,AII,CI

6 { G: GII
    I: DI,GI

7 { G: GII
    I: GI

8 { G: CII
    I: CI,GI

9 { G: CI,CII
    I: CI,GI

10 { G: AII,CI,CII
     I: AII,CI

11 { G: AII,CI,CII,GII
     I: DI,AII,CI,GI

12 { G: AII,CI,CII,GII
     I: AII,CI,GI

13 { G: CII
     I: CI

14 { G: CII,GII
     I: DI,CI,GI

15 { G: CII,GII
     I: CI,GI

16 { G: GII
     I: DI,GI

17 { G: GII
     I: GI

18 { G: CII
     i: CI,GI

FIGURE 13–1   **Decision-Process Flow Chart for Both Individual and Group Problems**   *From Victor H. Vroom and Arthur G. Jago, "Decision Making as a Social Process: Normative and Descriptive Models of Leader Behavior," Decision Sciences, Vol. 5 (1974); by permission of the American Institute for Decision Sciences.*

method listed first in a set indicates the approach that minimizes person-hours (i.e., is most efficient given quality and acceptance constraints). The method listed last is the approach that maximizes participation, given quality and acceptance constraints. Thus, the decision tree eliminates those decision-making methods that would jeopardize quality and acceptance requirements of a given problem. The manager can then choose from the methods remaining in the effective decision set depending on whether he or she aims to maximize efficiency or participation.

To summarize and understand how the model works, let us analyze an actual case problem using Vroom's model.

You are on the division manager's staff and work on a wide variety of problems of both an administrative and a technical nature. You have been given the assignment of developing a universal method to be used in each of the five plants in the division for manually reading equipment registers, recording the readings, and transmitting the scorings to a centralized information system. All plants are located in a relatively small geographical region.

Until now there has been a high error rate in the reading and/or transmittal of the data. Some locations have considerably higher error rates than others, and the methods used to record and transmit the data vary between plants. It is probable, therefore, that part of the error variance is a function of specific local conditions rather than anything else, and this will complicate the establishment of any system common to all plants. You have the information on error rates but no information on the local practices that generate these errors or on the local conditions that necessitate the different practices.

Everyone would benefit from an improvement in the quality of data as it is used in a number of important decisions. Your contacts with the plants are through the quality control supervisors, who are responsible for collecting the data. They are a conscientious group committed to doing their jobs well but are highly sensitive to interference on the part of higher management in their own operations. Any solution that does not receive the active support of the various plant supervisors is unlikely to reduce the error rate significantly.

First, we can see that this is a group problem, since it potentially affects all the plants. Then by answering the eight diagnostic questions and tracing them through the decision tree, we get

A—quality?	Yes, since a system that accurately records and transmits data is necessary.
B—leader information?	No, since error variance seems to depend on local conditions that you don't know about.
C—structured problem?	No, you don't know what is causing the errors.
D—acceptance necessary?	Yes, a solution that does not receive active support of the various plant supervisors is unlikely to reduce error.
E—unilateral decision accepted?	No, QC supervisors are highly sensitive to interference on the part of higher management.
F—goal congruence?	Yes, they are a conscientious group committed to doing their jobs well.
H—subordinate information?	Irrelevant to this *group* problem.

This leads then to feasible set 16 or 17, which has only one feasible decision method for this group problem—GII. Thus, the model recommends a group consensus decision in deciding how to develop a universal data system for all the plants.

Procedure for Group Meeting

The purpose of the group exercise is to compare your individual approaches to the case problems in the premeeting preparation to the recommendations proposed by Vroom's model for these cases and to identify and discuss reasons for differences between what the model recommends and what you would do.

STEP 1.   Each learning group should record its answers to the five cases on the chalkboard or flipchart so that all members can view one another's approach to the cases. The following Case Analysis Record Form provides a format for recording the data.

STEP 2.   The learning groups should discuss the cases and arrive at a group recommendation (30 minutes).

STEP 3.   The instructor takes the class through the cases using Vroom's model, answering the eight questions for each case (30 minutes).

STEP 4.   The class discussion should focus upon the comparison between the class and Vroom's recommendations which are listed on page 360. Answer the following questions:
a.   Did your recommendations differ from Vroom's? If so, how and why do they differ?
b.   What assumptions does the model make?
c.   What assumptions did you make with the cases?
d.   What factors are missing from this model?

Case Analysis Record Form

PARTICIPANT NAMES	CASE 1	CASE 2	CASE 3	CASE 4	CASE 5
Group recommendation					
Vroom model recommendation					

IV
Follow-up

A normative model, like the Vroom model, raises three questions: (1) When managers utilize the Vroom model, how likely are their decisions to be effective? (2) Do managers really make decisions like this? and (3) If not, why not?

First, research has shown that when managers choose one of the alternatives within the feasible set, a greater percentage of their decisions were found to be effective. In one study, when the managers used the leadership style indicated by the model, 68 percent of their decisions were effective; when they did not, only 22 percent of their decisions were successful.[4] Another study of 45 retail cleaning franchises discovered that managers whose leadership behaviors conformed to the Vroom model had more satisfied employees and more productive operations than other managers.[5]

Second, research comparing the Vroom model with the actual behavior of managers has shown that there is a general correspondence between the model recommendations for a specific situation and a manager's behavior in that situation. Vroom and Jago report, "In approximately two-thirds of the problems, nevertheless, the behavior which the manager reported was within the feasible set of methods prescribed for that problem, and in about 40 percent of the cases it corresponded exactly to the minimum man-hours solution."[6] Thus, managers seem to be using an intuitive notion something like the Vroom model to manage the decision-making process in their organizations. In some ways, however, the *differences* between model recommendations and managerial behavior are more interesting, in that they shed light on the assumptions on which the model is based and on the particularly difficult issues in managing the decision-making process.

For example, when we have asked managers how they would solve the engineering work assignment case described in the prework to this unit, many of them chose an AI or AII decision. Most resisted strongly the idea of bringing the group together for decision making either in the CII or GII modes. The Vroom model GII solution brought cries of "No way!" or "It will never work!" Further discussion of differences between individual styles and the Vroom GII decision recommendations raised some interesting comments:

- "The group wouldn't be able to deal with a difficult problem like this."
- "I wouldn't know how to control the conflict this situation creates if it were made a group decision."
- "In most groups the members would expect the manager to make this decision, and they would have to live with it."

These comments bring out some of the assumptions underlying Vroom's model and hence define some of the problems in its application. These assumptions are

1. Managers are equally skilled in using the different decision-making alternatives.

---

[4]Victor H. Vroom and Arthur G. Jago, "On the Validity of the Vroom-Yetton Model," *Journal of Applied Psychology* (April 1978), pp. 151–162.

[5]C. Margerison and R. Glube, "Leadership Decision Making: An Empirical Test of the Vroom and Yetton Model," manuscript, 1978.

[6]Vroom and Jago, "Decision Making as a Social Process," p. 754.

2. Groups are equally skilled in their adaptation to these decision-making alternatives.

3. Organizational history and the resulting organizational climate have no impact on a single decision analyzed by the model.

What the model does is analyze a specific decision dispassionately in terms of its quality, acceptance, and efficiency requirements without regard to the preceding assumptions about managerial and group skill or organization climate. Yet in any specific situation, these issues must be considered to ensure that decisions are effective.

In conclusion, we suggest the following considerations in applying the Vroom model to actual managerial situations:

1. Intuitive managerial decision-making models are more simplified than is the Vroom model. They do not account for some of the interactions among decision rules portrayed in Figure 13–1. This is supported by Vroom and Jago's research.

2. Managers tend to underemphasize the importance of acceptance and commitment components of decision effectiveness. This is also supported by Vroom and Jago's research.

3. Managers tend to use decision-making procedures they are skilled at and avoid procedures they feel uncomfortable with. For many, this means avoiding the more difficult group decision-making procedures.

4. Organization history and climate will affect the decision-making method chosen, independent of the logical dictates of the situation. Organization climate affects decision making in several ways:

   a. Group members will adjust to norms about "the way things are decided around here" and may have little experience or skill in other methods, such as group consensus.

   b. Managers may use a particular decision-making method because their boss uses it and be constrained in their flexibility of decision making by the style dictated from above. If your boss is AI with you, you have nothing to be GII with your subordinates about.

   c. Answers to the eight diagnostic questions may be influenced inaccurately by organizational norms. For example, in the military, where obeying orders is a pivotal norm, managers may tend to believe wrongly that their authoritative decision will be accepted (question E).

These considerations suggest that the Vroom model is useful in determining how the decision-making process *should* be conducted, but the application of this ideal requires management development for skills in all of the decision-making methods, team development in the various forms of group decision making, and organizational development to create norms that value quality, acceptance, and efficiency as the primary criteria for effective decision making.

Vroom and his colleagues[7] have recently developed a more complex model of the decision-making process. It consists of four decision trees, two for group decisions and two for individual decisions. At the individual and group level there are separate trees for use when decisions must be made quickly and when time is not such an important consideration. Their new model allows for greater situational complexity and comes equipped with computer software. However, it is so new that there is little research available on its effectiveness.

---

[7]V. Vroom and A. G. Jago, *The New Leadership* (Englewood Cliffs, NJ: Prentice Hall), 1988.

V
Learning Points

1. Individual decisions are not independent, solitary events. Instead they are closely connected to previous decisions and are influenced by the process that brought the decision point to a head.

2. Although decision making at very high levels is frequently characterized as a lonely individual struggle, decision making is also a social process. Decision making involves information sharing and interdependence among organization members. The manager's job is to determine the best way to solve a given problem by assessing what information and what players need to be involved.

3. Vroom's model is a contingency theory of leadership. Leadership styles range from autocratic to participative to delegative.

4. The effectiveness of a decision can be judged in terms of three outcomes:
   a. The quality or rationality of the decision.
   b. The acceptance or commitment on the part of subordinates to execute the decision effectively.
   c. The amount of time required to make the decision.

5. Utilizing groups to make decisions involves more time but results in greater acceptance of the decision and more likelihood of successful implementation.

6. The Vroom model helps managers analyze specific decision situations and determine which approach will be most effective.

7. The Vroom model utilizes the following factors in determining the appropriate approach: quality requirements, source of necessary information, goal congruence, type of problem (structured or unstructured), and potential acceptance and conflict by subordinates.

8. Managers whose leadership behavior approximates the model are more likely to make effective decisions than managers whose behavior does not conform to the model.

9. The Vroom model is a normative model (i.e., a "one best way" to figure out which decision making alternative to use). In reality,
   a. Managers' intuitive models for making decisions are simpler than Vroom's.
   b. Managers tend to underemphasize the importance of employee acceptance and commitment.
   c. Managers tend to use the decision-making procedure with which they feel most skilled and comfortable instead of the one that would be most effective.
   d. The organizational history and climate strongly affects the choice of decision-making method.

VI

Tips for Managers

- One of the most important factors for a manager to bear in mind when decisions are being made is the concept of setting precedents. With individual problems, solutions for one person or group often serve as a precedent for others. If you want to establish a reputation for fairness, it's worthwhile to consider whether you would want a given decision to be a guide for future ones. With both group and individual problems, the criteria used for making the decision should reflect the cultural values you are trying to promote within the organization.

- Some decisions eventually become obvious with time. The trick lies in knowing which decisions (or which parts of them) can be postponed and which need to be made immediately. This is learned by experience.

- Decision making is learned by experience, which is why it's desirable to start employees out making decisions at the lowest possible level. Too often the first decisions employees get to make are when they are promoted to supervisor and find themselves overwhelmed. Teaching employees good decision-making techniques, explaining why you made the decision you did, asking what decision they would make in your shoes, and delegating as many decisions as possible are all ways to develop good decision makers *before* they find themselves in the hot seat.

- Decisions are only as good as the information upon which they are based. Therefore it's important to have reliable and accurate information sources. In some organizations the higher one goes, the more difficult it is to have accurate information because people are busy telling you what they think you want to hear or information that reflects well upon them. Kotter found that the aggressiveness with which managers sought out information distinguished effective managers from less effective ones.[8]

- Test the water about possible solutions with well-chosen people (i.e., informal opinion leaders, graybeards, powerful people who are interested in the issue). Yes-men and -women or people with a narrow perspective or self-serving approach are obviously not good choices.

- It is not uncommon to have second thoughts about decisions. Indeed, it's a natural cognitive phenomenon. Knowing this can help you be more patient when employees (or even you) have second thoughts, even when a decision seemed to be final and everyone was in agreement.

- People can only process so much information because our brains are limited. Furthermore, it is sometimes impossible to have all the information that is needed to make a good decision. Thus there is often an element of ambiguity involved with decision making. People have different tolerance levels for ambiguity, which affects their decision-making process.

- Part of the psychological contract regarding employee input on decisions concerns the manager's response. When managers request input from employees, they "owe" them the courtesy of explaining what the final decisions were and why or why not the employee suggestion was used. When managers do not do this, employees are likely to say, "I don't know why I bothered; they just

---

[8]John Kotter, *The General Managers* (New York: Free Press, 1982).

went ahead and did what they wanted to anyway." In the future, such employees may be less forthcoming with their suggestions. However, when managers do explain how decisions were made and why an employee suggestion could not be used, they are both recognizing the employee's contribution and training him or her to make decisions in the future. Employees are not always aware of the broader contingencies their managers face. Sharing the rationale behind decisions is a way to develop employees. Managers do not have to use employee suggestions but they do have to explain why they didn't use them.

■ Chester Barnard, one of the first writers about management, introduced the "zone of indifference." Within that zone, employees will accept directives without questioning their boss's power, but ask them to do a task that lies outside that zone and they will resist.[9] We can adapt this concept to employee participation in decision making. Answering "yes" to Vroom and Yetton's question, "If I were to make the decision by myself, is it reasonably certain that it would be accepted?" implies that this problem falls within the employees' zone of indifference. Asking for participation on such issues wastes time and can even frustrate employees. The wise manager understands when employee involvement in decisions is important and when it is not.

■ Table 13–3 presents a realistic approach to decision making.

TABLE 13–3   Some Apparent Realities of Decision Making in Complex Organizations

SOME THINGS A MANAGER CANNOT EXPECT TO DO MUCH ABOUT	SOME THINGS INDIVIDUAL MANAGERS CAN DO	SOME THINGS THE ORGANIZATION CAN DO
The fact that decision making in organizations is not a totally rational, orderly process	Exercise choices in the problems to work on, which battles to fight and where, and when to cut losses	Set values and tone to support problem solving and risk
The nature of managerial work: the juggling of problems and conflicting demands	Develop intimate knowledge of the business and good working relationships with the people in it	Design organizational structure, reward, and control systems to support action rather than bureaucracy
People are flawed: they are limited information processors, have biases and emotions, and develop vested interests	Know yourself: know your strengths, weaknesses, and hot-buttons, and when to ask for help	Provide assignments where decision-making skills can be developed
Fundamental forces in the business environment	Develop the diverse set of skills necessary to act in different situations	Keep business strategy focused on things about which management is knowledgeable
Basic organizational components determined largely by the business one is in		

Morgan W. McCall, Jr., and Robert E. Kaplan, *Whatever It Takes: Decision Makers at Work* (Englewood Cliffs, NJ: Prentice-Hall, 1985), p. 115.

[9]Chester Barnard, *The Functions of the Executive* (Cambridge, MA: Harvard University Press, 1938).

VII
Personal Application Assignment

This decision is to choose a decision-making experience to write about. If you have trouble deciding, you can always use the Vroom model to analyze a decision with which you were involved.

A. *Concrete Experience*

1. *Objectively* describe the experience ("who," "what," "when," "where," "how" type information—up to 2 points).

2. *Subjectively* describe your feelings, perceptions, and thoughts that occurred *during* (not after) the experience (up to 2 points). Does this section have too much detail? (If so, delete 1 point).

B. *Reflective Observation*

1. Look at the experience from different points of view. How many points of view did you include that are *relevant* (up to 2 points)?

2. Use these perspectives to add more meaning to the incident (up to 2 points).

C. *Abstract Conceptualization*
   1. Relate concepts from the assigned readings and the lecture to the experience (i.e., what theories have you heard in the lecture or read in the *Reader* that relate to your understanding of this incident?). Make reference to at least two sources. Use standard referencing format and include the page number to which you are referring. How many sources did you use and how clearly did you explain their theories (up to 4 points)?
   2. You can also create an original model or theory, but it should not replace course concepts.

D. *Active Experimentation*
   1. Write about what you will do in the future that will improve your effectiveness. Use rules of thumb or action resolutions.
   2. Are they described specifically, thoroughly, and in detail (up to 4 points).

E. *Integration, Synthesis, and Writing*
1. Did you write about something personally important to you (up to 1 point)?
2. Was it well written (up to 2 points)?
3. Did you integrate and synthesize the different sections (up to 1 point)?

Leadership and Decision-Making Case Answers

(Do Not Read Until You Have Completed Chapter 12)
ANALYSIS

Case	A Quality?	B Leader's Information?	C Structured?	D Acceptance?	E Prior Probability of Acceptance?	F Goal Congruence?	G Subordinate Conflict?	H Subordinate Information?	PROBLEM TYPE	FEASIBLE SET
1	Yes	No	No	No	—	Yes	—	Yes*	14, Group	C11, G11
2	Yes	No	No	Yes	No	No	—	—	18, Individual	C1, G1
3	No	—	—	Yes	No	—	—	—	2, Group	G11
4	Yes	No	Yes	Yes	No	No	Not applicable	—	8 or 9, Individual	C1, G1
5	Yes	Yes	—	No	—	Yes	—	No*	4, Group	A1, A11, C1, C11, G11

*The question pertaining to this attribute is asked in the decision tree, but it is irrelevant to the decision outcome in these group cases because it applies to the individual DI alternative only.

14

LEADERSHIP: THE EFFECTIVE EXERCISE OF POWER AND INFLUENCE

OBJECTIVES By the end of this chapter, you should be able to:

A. Explain the four styles of personal power and influence.

B. Understand when each style is most appropriate.

How to Manage the Boss

Peter F. Drucker

Most managers, including of course most chief executives, have a boss. Few people are as important to the performance and success of a manager as the boss. Yet while management books and courses abound in advice on how to manage subordinates, few if any even mention managing the boss.

Few managers seem to realize how important it is to manage the boss or, worse, believe that it can be done at all. They bellyache about the boss but do not even try to manage him (or her). Yet managing the boss is fairly simple—indeed generally quite a bit simpler than managing subordinates. There are only a few Dos, and even fewer Don'ts.

The first Do is to realize that it is both the subordinate's duty and in the subordinate's self-interest to make the boss as effective and as achieving as possible. The best prescription for one's own success is, after all, still to work for a boss who is going places. Thus the first Do is to go to the boss—at least once a year—and ask: "What do I do and what do my people do that helps *you* do your job? And what do we do that hampers *you* and makes life more difficult for *you?*"

THE CORRECT DEFINITION

This sounds obvious—but it is rarely done. For even effective executives tend to misdefine a "manager" as someone who is responsible for the work of subordinates—the definition of 50 years ago—and thus tend not to perceive that they have any responsibility for the boss's performance and effectiveness. But the correct definition of a manager—as we have known it for at least 40 years—is someone who is responsible for the performance of all the people on whom his own performance depends.

The first person on whom a manager's performance depends is the boss, and the boss is thus the first person for whose performance a manager has to take responsibility. But only by asking, "what do I do to help you or to hamper you?"—the best way to ask is without beating about the bush—can you find out what the boss needs and what gets in the boss's way.

Closely related is the need for awareness that your boss is a human being and an individual; no two persons work alike, perform alike or behave alike. The subordinate's job is not to reform the boss, not to re-educate the boss, not to make the boss conform to what the business schools and the management books say bosses should be like. It is to enable a particular boss to perform as a unique individual. And being an individual, every boss has idiosyncrasies, has "good words" and "bad words," and, like the rest of us, needs his own security blanket.

To manage the boss requires thinking through such questions as: Does this individual who is my boss want me to come in once every month—but no more often—and spend 30 minutes presenting the performance, the plans and the problems of my department? Or does this individual want me to come in every time there is anything to report or to discuss, every time there is the slightest change, every time we make a move? Does this individual want me to send the stuff in as a written report, in a nice folder, complete with tabs and a table of contents? Or does this individual want an oral presentation? Is this individual, in other words, a reader or a listener? And does this boss require (as do for instance most financial executives) 30 pages of figures with everything as his security blanket—and should it be tables or graphs?

Does this individual need the information to be there when he gets to the office in the morning, or does this boss (as do a good many operating people) want it at the end of the day, say around 3:30 on Friday afternoon? And if there is disagreement among the management group, how does this boss want to have it handled? To have us iron it out and report our consensus (as did Gen. Eisenhower and as President Reagan clearly does)? Or for us to report our disagreements in full detail and with complete documentation (as did both Gens. George Marshall and MacArthur)?

What are the things the boss does well? What are his strengths? And what are the boss's limitations and weaknesses—the areas in which the subordinate needs to support, to buttress and to supplement the boss? A manager's task is to make the strengths of people effective and their weaknesses irrelevant—and that applies fully as much to the manager's boss as it applies to the manager's subordinates. If for instance the boss is good at marketing but uncomfortable with financial figures and analysis, managing the boss means to bring him into the marketing decision but to prepare the financial analysis beforehand and in depth.

Managing the boss means, above all, creating a relationship of trust. This requires confidence on the part of the superior that the subordinate manager will play to the boss's strengths and safeguard the boss against his or her limitations and weaknesses.

KEEP THE BOSS AWARE

The final Do: Make sure the boss understands what can be expected of you, what the objectives and goals are on which your own energies and those of your people will be concentrated, what your priorities are, and, equally important, what they are not. It is by no means always necessary that the boss approve—it is sometimes not even desirable. But the boss must understand what you are up to, must know what to expect and what not to expect. Bosses, after all, are held responsible by their own bosses for the performance of their subordinates. They must be able to say: "I know what Anne (or Joe) is trying to do." Only if they can say this will they be able to delegate to their subordinate managers.

And now two Don'ts:

Never expose the boss to surprises. It is the job of the subordinate to protect the boss against surprises—even pleasant ones (if any such exist). To be exposed to a surprise in the organization one is responsible for is humiliation, and usually public humiliation. Different bosses want very different warnings of possible surprises. Some—again Ike is a good example—want no more than a warning that things may turn out differently. Other bosses—President Kennedy for example—demand a full, detailed report even if there is only a slight chance of a surprise. But all bosses need to be protected against surprises. Otherwise they will not trust a subordinate—and with good reason.

Never underrate the boss! The boss may look illiterate; he may look stupid—and looks are not always deceptive. But there is no risk at all in overrating a boss. The worst that can happen is for the boss to feel flattered. But if you underrate the boss he will either see through your little game and will bitterly resent it. Or the boss will impute to you the deficiency in brains or knowledge you imputed to the boss and will consider you ignorant, dumb or lacking in imagination.

But the most important thing is not what to do or what not to do. It is to accept that managing the boss is the responsibility of the subordinate manager and a key—maybe the most important one—to his or her own effectiveness as an executive.

I

Premeeting Preparation

    A. Answer the following questions:

        1. Think about someone who handles power very well. How does he or she do it?

        2. What's the difference between someone who handles power well and someone who does not?

        3. What do you want to learn about power?

        4. What are the significant learning points from the *Readings?*

    B. Complete the Influence Style Self-diagnosis.

    C. Read the Topic Introduction.

Personal Influence Style Diagnosis

The focus of this chapter is the effective exercise of power and influence. Before reading the topic introduction, do a simple self-assessment of your style of influencing others. Generally speaking, how descriptive is each of the following styles of your typical influence behavior? Using the key provided, record your rating (from 1 = not descriptive to 5 = very descriptive) in the space to the left of each paragraph. Then read the topic introduction.

1	2	3	4	5
Not at All Descriptive of Me		Somewhat Descriptive		Very Descriptive of Me

Influence Self-Style Diagnosis

_____ I am direct and positive in asserting my own wishes and requirements. I let others know what I want from them, and I am quick to tell others when I am pleased or dissatisfied with their performance. I am willing to use my influence and authority to get others to do what I want. I skillfully use a combination of pressures and incentives to get others to agree with my plans and proposals, and I follow up to make sure they carry out agreements and commitments. I readily engage in bargaining and negotiation to achieve my objectives, using both tough and conciliatory styles according to the realities of power and position in each situation.

_____ I am open and nondefensive, being quick to admit when I do not have the answer, or when I have made a mistake. I listen attentively to the ideas and feelings of others, actively communicating my interest in their contributions, and my understanding of their points of view. I am willing to be influenced by others. I give credit for others' ideas and accomplishments. I make sure that everyone has a chance to be heard before decisions are taken, even when I do not agree with their position. I show trust in others, and I help them to bring out and develop their strengths and abilities.

_____ I appeal to the emotions and ideals of others through the use of forceful and colorful words and images. My enthusiasm is contagious and carries others along with me. I bring others to believe in their ability to accomplish and succeed by working together. I see and can communicate my vision of the exciting possibilities in an idea or situation. I get others to see the values, hopes, and aspirations that they have in common, and I build these common values into a shared sense of group loyalty and commitment.

_____ I produce detailed and comprehensive proposals for dealings with problems. I am persistent and energetic in finding and presenting the logic behind my ideas and in marshalling facts, arguments, and opinion in support of my position. I am quick to grasp the strengths and weaknesses in an argument and to see and articulate the logical connections between various aspects of a complex situation. I am a vigorous and determined seller of ideas.

II

Topic Introduction

Power and influence have negative connotations for many people. They conjure up unpleasant images such as the misuse of power by politicians, the high-pressure tactics of some salespeople, and the destructive behavior exhibited by military dictators. These negative connotations have, until recently, made it very difficult to examine the role of power and look objectively at its potential positive as well as negative consequences.

We learned in Chapter 4 that McClelland identified a need for power as a basic motivator, even though it is difficult in our society to acknowledge this need because we are suspicious of power. McClelland[1] resolved this dilemma by referring to the two faces of power. While a need for power always refers to a desire to have a strong impact upon others, one face of power is an unsocialized concern for personal dominance. It is characterized by an I win–you lose perspective and a need to dominate others. The second face of power is socialized. People who are high in this motive need show a concern for group goals, empowering others and a win-win approach. This second face of power, the socialized version, is required for long-term success in organizations. Indeed, McClelland and Burnham discovered that the most effective managers had high needs for power, used this power to achieve organizational goals, employed a participative management style, and did not focus on developing close relationships with others.[2] In our society we often say that "power corrupts," and we believe that even people who started out with needs for socialized power degenerate into a selfish concern for personal dominance. While this may not always be the case, it is essential to examine one's personal needs for power. This is another instance where it is important to know oneself. What is your need for power? What has been your experience with power and influence, and how does this affect the way you use power and influence with other people?

The power and status differences that exist between supervisors and subordinates are *real* and *natural*. They cannot be ignored or wished away. Indeed, in its simplest, most basic form, your role as a manager is to *make a difference* in the behavior of your subordinates. Your responsibility as a manager is to behave in ways that add to your subordinates' ability to do their jobs effectively and efficiently. The issue is not, therefore, whether or not managers have power, but how they choose to exercise the power demanded by the role and with what consequences. One does not "make a difference" without exercising power and influence somewhere, somehow, sometime.

Traditionally, managers have relied almost exclusively upon the power inherent in their position. "I'm the boss. I have the right and responsibility to tell you what to do, and if you don't perform, I retain the ultimate power of reward and punishment" would be the extreme form of this condition. Increasingly, however, managers are finding their positional power being eroded: union contracts, governmental equal employment opportunity regulations, and a shifting value structure among younger employees are all forces contributing to this erosion. Finally, those in staff positions and consultant roles recognize that they have little, if any, positional power in the first place. Instead, they rely upon the power that comes from their expertise and relationships.

---

[1]David McClelland, "The Two Faces of Power," *Reader* (1984), pp. 59–72.

[2]David McClelland and David Burnham, "Good Guys Make Bum Bosses," *Organizational Behavior Reader,* 1990.

Given the weakening of formal or positional power, what is the manager to do to continue to make a difference? Recent work by Berlew and Harrison[3] has shed considerable light on this dilemma. Effective managers, in their view, will need to develop an expanded range of *personal* power and influence behavior and skills and be able to match these skills to situational requirements. There will be times, in other words, when the exercise of "raw" positional power will (1) not be feasible, (2) will be inappropriate to the task at hand, or (3) will create negative consequences (i.e., resistance and/or rebellion). Under these conditions, one or some combination of personal power and influence behaviors will be essential. Berlew and Harrison have identified four typical patterns of behavior reflecting the exercise of power and influence. These will be described as four pure types for the purposes of conceptual clarity, recognizing that few people, if any, ever use (or should use) only one style exclusively.

REWARD AND PUNISHMENT

If the first style listed in the Influence Style Diagnosis was descriptive of your behavior, then you see yourself using reward and punishment as a style of influencing others. *Reward and punishment* is the use of pressures and incentives to control others' behavior. Rewards may be offered for compliance, and punishment or deprivation may be threatened for noncompliance. Naked power may be used, or more indirect and veiled pressures may be exerted through the use of status, prestige, and formal authority.

This influence style is characterized by "contingency management": letting others know clearly what they must do to get what they want and avoid negative consequences through your use of bargaining, negotiating, making offers, and threats. The use of the word "if" often signals the use of this style: "If you do X, I'll do Y."

Both reward and punishment and assertive persuasion (discussed shortly) involve agreeing and disagreeing with others. The difference is that in assertive persuasion, one agrees or disagrees with another's proposal because it is more or less effective, correct, accurate, or true. In using reward and punishment, on the other hand, the judgment of right or wrong is an evaluation based on a moral or social standard, a regulation, or an arbitrary performance standard. The person making the evaluation sets himself or herself up as the judge instead of appealing to a common and shared standard of rationality.

People using reward and punishment are very comfortable, generally, in situations of conflict. They are comfortable giving clear feedback—both positive and negative—and are very direct about prescribing their goals and expectations. Very often, however, the consequence—the "then" part of the "if" statement—is left implicit or vaguely defined.

As you reflect on the description just given, it will be clear that any individual, regardless of formal position, can effectively utilize many reward and punishment behaviors. Anyone, theoretically, can make evaluative statements involving praise and criticism. Similarly, if a meeting were dragging, anyone could prescribe a goal and expectation ("We've got to finish our work by six o'clock"). The crunch is most clear around "incentives and pressures." The ability to follow through on (1) an evaluation and/or (2) a prescribed goal or expectation is dependent on one's access to and control of meaningful rewards and punishments (incentives and pressures). Many managers recognize that subordinates can and do exercise significant incentives and pressures. By withholding support, dragging their heels, carrying out or-

[3]The ideas and materials here (with permission of Situation Management Systems, Inc.) are part of a series of training programs originally developed by David Berlew and Roger Harrison on positive power and influence. For more detail on the actual program, contact Situation Management Systems, Inc., Box 476, Center Station, Plymouth, MA 02361.

ders they know to be inappropriate ("I'm safe because I'm doing exactly what my boss told me to do!"), and other forms of subtle "sabotage," subordinates are demonstrating that bosses are not the only ones who have reward and punishment power.

PARTICIPATION AND TRUST

The second style in the Influence Style Diagnosis is, in some ways, opposite to the first. Unlike reward and punishment, where influence is exerted by *pushing* others to behave in ways you define as desirable, the use of the *participation and trust* influence style *pulls* others toward what is desired or required by *involving them*. By actively listening to and involving others, an influencer using participation and trust increases the commitment of others to the target objective or task. Follow-up and close supervision, therefore, become less critical. This is in sharp contrast to the reward and punishment style in which compliance (not commitment) must be monitored frequently.

People who use participation and trust are generally rather patient and have developed the capacity to be very effective listeners. They are very good at reflecting back to people (paraphrasing) both the content and feelings of what the person has said. They build on others' ideas and are quick to credit others for their contributions.

In addition to the foregoing, people who use participation and trust as an influence style are readily able to admit their own areas of uncertainty and mistakes. By openly acknowledging their own limitations and taking a nondefensive attitude toward feedback, they help others to feel more accepted for what they are.

On the surface, participation and trust may appear to some to be a weak and wishy-washy style of influence in contrast, for example, to the toughness of assertive persuasion or reward and punishment. It is not. It can be very powerful by building the trust and commitment needed to implement actions and with it a willingness to be influenced. As with the other influence styles, participation and trust can be misused to manipulate others. The manager who tries to involve subordinates in a consensus decision-making process when the manager already has the solution is treading on thin ice. If there is one best way to go or only one way you can accept, the assertive persuasion or reward and punishment mode of influence is probably more appropriate.

COMMON VISION

This third style of influence aims to identify a *common vision* of the future for a group and to strengthen the group members' belief that through their collective efforts, the vision can become a reality. The appeals are to the emotions and values of others, activating their personal commitment to private hopes and ideals and channeling that energy into work toward a common purpose. Common vision also has an intellectual component achieved by clear articulation of goals and the means to achieve them. The well-known speeches of Martin Luther King, Jr., and John F. Kennedy are classic examples of the effective use of common vision, although it is by no means a style that is useful in only large-group or political settings.

Within the everyday world of organizations, there are numerous opportunities for the effective use of common vision. Many an organizational meeting becomes an exercise in competing assertions. In such situations, the ability to help the group to pull together around a common goal can provide a much needed spirit of collaboration and inspiration: "What we can accomplish *if* we work together."

People who use common vision are generally very emotionally expressive. They are aware of what they feel (it is hard to create enthusiasm if you yourself feel bored) and are willing and able to project and communicate their feelings articulately. They talk in emotionally vivid imagery and metaphors. They are often called charismatic.

ASSERTIVE PERSUASION

The fourth style is considered the bread and butter of the business world—*assertive persuasion*. The essential quality of assertive persuasion as an influence style is the use of facts, logic, rational argument, and persuasive reasoning. While the influencer may argue forcefully with great élan and spirit, the power of assertive persuasion does not come from an emotional source. Facts and logic are, by definition, emotionally neutral. A person may react to a fact emotionally and thereby be persuaded to behave in a certain way. The feelings of the person using assertive persuasion are meant to be kept out of their argument. The facts are supposed to speak for themselves.

People using assertive persuasion to persuade others are usually highly verbal and articulate. They are forward with their ideas, proposals, and suggestions and can support their proposals with rational reasons. They tend to listen selectively to others' attempts at assertive persuasion, hoping to find a weak spot so that they can effectively reason against others' proposals.

THE VALUE ISSUES—POSITIVE VERSUS NEGATIVE POWER

None of the styles described here is inherently right or wrong, good or bad. All are important and relevant and can be used in a variety of ways. Think about a time when you felt really powerful. While the exact words will differ, most probably you felt strong, perhaps even on top of the world. What were the stimuli of those feelings? Were you uplifted by a moving speech? Did someone else recognize, comment upon, and reward you by acknowledging your competence? Maybe you were asked to become involved in solving a sticky organizational problem or even given resources and latitude to go it alone.

"It is not always that way. . . . There are times when we feel powerless . . . weak, turned off, at the bottom of a pile of garbage. Perhaps you felt put down by someone else's exercise of power: an autocratic boss, pushy friend, power hungry political leader or whatever. There are, indeed, two faces of power."[4]

The important distinction, therefore, has to do with how the exercise of power and influence is experienced: What is its impact? Assertive persuasion, reward and punishment, participation and trust, and common vision can be used in a way that results in other people feeling stronger. They can also be used to make people feel weaker—to feel like pawns in the hands of someone else. Common vision, for example, will result in people feeling weaker if it is used only to raise people's hopes and expectations without anything ever being realized or gained. People will thus feel "had" and become cynical to further influence attempts. On the other hand, we recognize that there are some situations in which it is extremely difficult to exercise needed influence and leave people feeling stronger. Firing someone is never a pleasant experience, and the dismissed person is bound to feel bad.

The need to exercise power and influence is an inherent part of the managerial role. Effective managers develop the skills needed to have a positive versus a negative effect whenever the situation allows that potential. During the upcoming class session, you will have an opportunity to explore each of these styles in more depth and practice ways of using power positively. For the living person, power is not a theory, but an ever-present reality that must be confronted, used, enjoyed, and struggled with many times a day.

[4]D. C. McClelland, "The Two Faces of Power," D. A. Kolb, I. M. Rubin, and J. McIntyre, *Organizational Psychology: Readings on Human Behavior in Organizations,* 4th ed. (Englewood Cliffs, NJ: Prentice Hall, 1984), pp. 59–72.

THE WIZARD OF ID reprinted by permission of Johnny Hart and Field Enterprises, Inc.

III

Procedure for Group Meeting: Influence Styles Role Plays

The core of this unit involves practicing each of the influence styles in four-person groups. The group leader can leave this group formation process to the students. Alternatively, groups could be formed to ensure that at least one person in the group felt that each of the four styles was very descriptive of how they typically behave.

STEP 1. Discussion of influence style self-diagnosis prework in four-person groups. (20–30 minutes)

Since the core of this unit involves practicing and getting feedback on the use of the influence styles, it is important to take time to be clear as to how people see themselves initially.

Each person should therefore take a few moments (about 5 minutes) to reflect upon and share with the others reactions to the following:

a. Self-assessments (i.e., how descriptive were each of the four styles of how you see yourself?).

b. Personal examples of having experienced positive and negative power from someone else (i.e., times when you felt stronger and weaker as a result of someone else's use of power).

c. Taking each of the four styles in turn,

(1) What about the style you find yourself *liking* and/or *disliking* (e.g., I like the clarity that reward and punishment provides, but I dislike the carrot and stick image)?

(2) What aspects of the influence style would be relatively easy for *you to use* from a behavioral point of view? What aspects would be relatively *difficult* for you to carry out?

(3) What aspects of the style would be relatively easy for you to *respond* to as a receiver (i.e., if someone were trying to influence you) and relatively difficult for you to respond to (i.e., if someone used that style on you, you'd be inclined to resist or not be influenced)?

It will be useful for the group to have a summary of this discussion on newsprint so it can be referred to later in the unit. An example format might look like that in the accompanying table.

Styles

	REWARD AND PUNISHMENT	PARTICIPATION AND TRUST	COMMON VISION	ASSERTIVE PERSUASION
Individual self-assessment				
Elements of style liked by individuals				
Elements of style disliked by individuals				

STEP 2.   Preparing for role plays: individual work. (10 minutes)
           On the pages that follow you will find six potentially stressful influence situations. Individuals should read these situations carefully and select one (to start) that best meets the following criteria:

   a. It seems real to you (i.e., you have been in that situation and/or could easily imagine yourself being in that situation).

   b. You would expect yourself to experience at least a moderate level of stress in dealing with that situation.

   c. You feel you could learn something of value about your influence style from getting involved in the situation on a practice basis.

   Jot down your response to questions (a) through (d) in each situation in the space provided following the situation you have chosen to work on.

STEP 3.   Conducting and critiquing the role plays. (minimum 1 hour) The basic structure will be as follows:

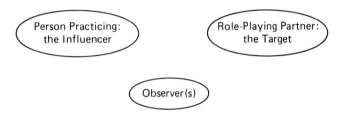

The sequence will be as follows:

   a. One person volunteers to go first. That person (the influencer) selects a partner (the target). The others are to be silent observers. (See Observer Form on page 405).

   Very briefly (2–4 minutes), the influencer tells his or her partner what the other person (boss, child, friend, etc.)—the target—is like, how they are likely to act. Partners should, within reason, behave in a way to produce the moderate stress level desired.

   b. Enact the situation. (5–6 minutes) It is *critical* that as the influencer you remember that you should *not* be acting. You are being yourself in the situation chosen. Only your partner is acting. It is very important, therefore, for you to be as "real" as you can. Only in this way will you have a chance to learn more about your own influence styles.

   c. Feedback discussion. (8–10 minutes)

      (1) Influencer *begins* by sharing responses to (a) through (d) for the situation chosen.

      (2) Observers then share their observations, following the Observer Form.

      (3) The target partner then shares his or her reactions using the following guidelines:

      ■ What influence styles did you experience the influencer using a lot? less often?

      ■ What influencer behaviors used made you feel stronger? weaker?

      ■ What two or three specific suggestions would you offer the influencer to enhance their impact in the situation chosen? in general?

      The influencer should focus on listening to and understanding this feedback (i.e., use of participation and trust style) and *not* try to convince the others why their observations are wrong or misinformed (i.e., use of reward and punishment and/or assertive persuasion.)

Then repeat the procedure so that each person has at least one practice opportunity. (If time permits, the entire small group can select a second stressful influence situation and repeat the entire practice process, steps 2 and 3.)

STEP 4. Review of initial discussion. (20 minutes)

If time permits, there is value in systematically reviewing the discussion held during step 1, in light of the practice experience offered by steps 2 and 3.

a. To what extent did people's preferences and intentions before the fact (i.e., styles people said they liked/disliked; felt it would be easy/difficult to deliver, etc.) fit their actual behavior in the situation chosen?

b. To what do you attribute any differences observed between intention and actual behavior? actual degree of style flexibility on the influencer's part? style used by the target person? the nature of the situation itself (what aspects seemed most critical)?

c. What connections can you make between this exercise and the readings?

Situation 1

It's 2:00 A.M., Sunday morning. The police have just delivered your son (daughter) to your home. There was a car accident; the driver, a friend of your child's, was drunk, and the police found several bottles of liquor in the car and some drugs. The police have just left the house. Since no one was seriously injured and it was a first offense, they have agreed to take no legal action this time. It's now time for you and your son (daughter) to "have a talk."

    a. How real does this situation seem to you? Has it happened to you or can you imagine it happening?

1	2	3	4	5

Very unreal   Very real

    b. How much stress would you expect to experience in this situation?

1	2	3	4	5

No stress at all   Very high stress

    c. Based on your responses to the Influence Style Diagnosis, the reading in the Introduction, and the discussion you just had, rank order (1 = most likely to 4 = least likely) the likelihood of your using each of the four styles in this situation.

             _____ Reward and punishment   _____ Common vision
             _____ Participation and trust   _____ Assertive persuasion

    d. *Independent* of your ranking of likelihood of use (ignoring your ability from a skill viewpoint or comfort from an attitude viewpoint), take a moment to reflect on and record the way in which each style might be useful in this situation (i.e., around what needs or issues might the style help you to "make a difference"?).

    (1) Ways in which reward and punishment might be useful:

    (2) Ways in which participation and trust might be useful:

(3) Ways in which common vision might be useful:

(4) Ways in which assertive persuasion might be useful:

Situation 2

You and your boss had what you thought was a really great performance appraisal session last month. You were clearly led to expect a 15 percent salary increase and have begun to plan on it. Wham! Your increase notice comes through with only a 9 percent cost-of-living increase. You are about to enter your boss's office to "have a talk."

a. How real does this situation seem to you? Has it happened to you or can you imagine it happening?

1	2	3	4	5
Very unreal				Very real

b. How much stress would you expect to experience in this situation?

1	2	3	4	5
No stress at all				Very high stress

c. Based on your responses to the Influence Style Diagnosis, the reading in the Introduction, and the discussion you just had, rank order (1 = most likely to 4 = least likely) the likelihood of your using each of the four styles in this situation.

_____ Reward and punishment _____ Common vision
_____ Participation and trust   _____ Assertive persuasion

d. *Independent* of your ranking of likelihood of use (ignoring your ability from a skill viewpoint or comfort from an attitude viewpoint), take a moment to reflect on and record the way in which each style might be useful in this situation (i.e., around what needs or issues might the style help you to "make a difference"?).

(1) Ways in which reward and punishment might be useful:

(2) Ways in which participation and trust might be useful:

(3) Ways in which common vision might be useful:

(4) Ways in which assertive persuasion might be useful:

Situation 3

You've been spot-checking your subordinates' expense reports on a periodic basis. One in particular caught your eye because it was higher than the rest, so you've been carefully reviewing his/hers for the past several weeks. While you cannot be 100 percent certain, you have strong reason to expect something "funny" is going on (e.g., excessive mileage charges, very high entertainment expenses). This subordinate is about to enter your office for a meeting you have called.

a. How real does this situation seem to you? Has it happened to you or can you imagine it happening?

1	2	3	4	5
Very unreal				Very real

b. How much stress would you expect to experience in this situation?

1	2	3	4	5
No stress at all				Very high stress

c. Based on your responses to the Influence Style Diagnosis, the reading in the Introduction, and the discussion you just had, rank order (1 = most likely to 4 = least likely) the likelihood of your using each of the four styles in this situation.

_____ Reward and punishment   _____ Common vision
_____ Participation and trust   _____ Assertive persuasion

d. *Independent* of your ranking of likelihood of use (ignoring your ability from a skill viewpoint or comfort from an attitude viewpoint), take a moment to reflect on and record the way in which each style might be useful in this situation (i.e., around what needs or issues might the style help you to "make a difference"?).

(1) Ways in which reward and punishment might be useful:

(2) Ways in which participation and trust might be useful:

(3) Ways in which common vision might be useful:

(4) Ways in which assertive persuasion might be useful:

Situation 4

You've recently hired a new secretary. You somehow were not aware of it at the time, but she has turned out to be a staunch feminist. She let you know this in no uncertain terms recently, and while it bugged you, you made an effort to alter your own behavior. Now you find out that she has been carrying on a campaign of sorts with other secretaries (e.g., telling them how wrong it is to get their boss's coffee), and your colleagues are really putting the pressure on you. You are really burned at having to deal with this issue and have buzzed her into your office.

a. How real does this situation seem to you? Has it happened to you or can you imagine it happening?

1	2	3	4	5
Very unreal				Very real

b. How much stress would you expect to experience in this situation?

1	2	3	4	5
No stress at all				Very high stress

c. Based on your responses to the Influence Style Diagnosis, the reading in the Introduction, and the discussion you just had, rank order (1 = most likely to 4 = least likely) the likelihood of your using each of the four styles in this situation.

     _____ Reward and punishment   _____ Common vision
     _____ Participation and trust   _____ Assertive persuasion

d. *Independent* of your ranking of likelihood of use (ignoring your ability from a skill viewpoint or comfort from an attitude viewpoint), take a moment to reflect on and record the way in which each style might be useful in this situation (i.e., around what needs or issues might the style help you to "make a difference"?).

(1) Ways in which reward and punishment might be useful:

(2) Ways in which participation and trust might be useful:

(3) Ways in which common vision might be useful:

(4) Ways in which assertive persuasion might be useful:

Situation 5

One of your subordinates has been promising to finish a report now for three weeks. Every time you inquire as to how it's going, what you get back is, "Oh, it's coming along. It's more complicated than either one of us imagined." The grapevine has informed you that your subordinate's marriage is going through some rocky spots. While you want to be fair, your boss is putting the screws on you to get the report in. The pressure on you is really mounting and something has to give. The "last straw" meeting you called is about to begin.

a. How real does this situation seem to you? Has it happened to you or can you imagine it happening?

1	2	3	4	5
Very unreal				Very real

b. How much stress would you expect to experience in this situation?

1	2	3	4	5
No stress at all				Very high stress

c. Based on your responses to the Influence Style Diagnosis, the reading in the Introduction, and the discussion you just had, rank order (1 = most likely to 4 = least likely) the likelihood of your using each of the four styles in this situation.

_____ Reward and punishment   _____ Common vision
_____ Participation and trust   _____ Assertive persuasion

d. *Independent* of your ranking of likelihood of use (ignoring your ability from a skill viewpoint or comfort from an attitude viewpoint), take a moment to reflect on and record the way in which each style might be useful in this situation (i.e., around what needs or issues might the style help you to "make a difference"?).

(1) Ways in which reward and punishment might be useful:

(2) Ways in which participation and trust might be useful:

(3) Ways in which common vision might be useful:

(4) Ways in which assertive persuasion might be useful:

Situation 6

Several months ago, unbeknown to anyone else, you lent a good friend $1,000 to help him out of a real bind. You were supposed to be repaid in two weeks—that was three months ago. You've asked about it half-heartedly a few times, but there always seemed to be a "good reason" for the delay. Now your spouse is wanting to take a winter vacation and proposed using your special joint savings account to do so—the one from which you took the $1,000 to loan your friend! You and your friend get together every week for lunch, and this friend has just waved hello and is approaching the table.

a. How real does this situation seem to you? Has it happened to you or can you imagine it happening?

1	2	3	4	5
Very unreal				Very real

b. How much stress would you expect to experience in this situation?

1	2	3	4	5
No stress at all				Very high stress

c. Based on your responses to the Influence Style Diagnosis, the reading in the Introduction, and the discussion you just had, rank order (1 = most likely to 4 = least likely) the likelihood of your using each of the four styles in this situation.

_____ Reward and punishment   _____ Common vision
_____ Participation and trust   _____ Assertive persuasion

d. *Independent* of your ranking of likelihood of use (ignoring your ability from a skill viewpoint or comfort from an attitude viewpoint), take a moment to reflect on and record the way in which each style might be useful in this situation (i.e., around what needs or issues might the style help you to "make a difference"?).

(1) Ways in which reward and punishment might be useful:

(2) Ways in which participation and trust might be useful:

(3) Ways in which common vision might be useful:

(4) Ways in which assertive persuasion might be useful:

Observer Form

INFLUENCE STYLES

OBSERVATIONS CATEGORY	ASSERTIVE PERSUASION Logic, Facts, Rationality, Ideas, Proposals, Reasons For and Against	REWARD AND PUNISHMENT Evaluations, Use of Incentives and Pressures, Bargains, Stating Own Personal Goals and Expectations	PARTICIPATION AND TRUST Active Listening, Recognizing Others' Contributions, Involving Others and Getting Their Contributions, Disclosing Own Areas of Uncertainty	COMMON VISION Building a Sense of Group Spirit, a *We* Feeling, Creating a Superordinate Group Goal, Shared Identity
Examples of where style was used to strengthen the other person (positive power)				
Examples of where style was used to weaken other person (negative power)				
Missed opportunities (i.e., example of where the style might have had a positive impact but was not used).				
Nonverbal behaviors that signaled a particular style				

On balance, rank the person you observed from two perspectives.

I. *Frequency of use* (1 = most frequent to 4 = least frequent)

       ___ Assertive persuasion   ___ Participation and trust
       ___ Reward and punishment   ___ Common vision

II. *Effectiveness of Use* (1 = used most effectively to 4 = used least effectively)

       ___ Assertive persuasion   ___ Participation and trust
       ___ Reward and punishment   ___ Common vision

IV

Follow-up

In their day-to-day work, managers are continually faced with a host of questions about the process of leadership. How can I get the job done most effectively? What is the "best" leadership style? How can I build commitment and loyalty among the members of my work team to me and to the company and its objectives? When should I listen and when should I give orders? If I become too friendly with my subordinates, will I lose their respect?

These are all contingency questions—there is no one right or wrong answer. One approach that attempts to deal with this complexity was developed by Robert Tannenbaum and Warren H. Schmidt.[5] As shown in Figure 14–1, it conceives of a continuum of leader behavior, ranging from leader-centered strategies to group-centered strategies.

Toward the middle of the continuum, the process becomes more consultative. The effective use of common vision at these points can serve to rally the group around the problem as defined by the leader. Participation and trust skills will be important as well, to ensure that everyone's ideas are freely shared, understood, and considered.

As the situation dictates the extreme of a group-centered approach, the effective use of all the power and influence styles becomes critical. A group consensus meeting moves through a series of predictable phases or stages. In the early stages, the essential process is one of amplification. The objective is to generate as many ideas as possible—to brainstorm.

At some point, however, a filter process will need to take place. The many ideas will need to be sorted and evaluated against agreed-upon criteria, and the reasons for and against will need to be carefully explored.

In terms of power and influence behaviors, the appropriate style is one that matches the needs of the situation. During the amplification state, common vision and participation and trust can be expected to predominate. Evaluations that characterize reward and punishment could dampen people's willingness to think creatively. Asserting one idea over another (assertive persuasion) is not appropriate at this stage.

The situation changes significantly during the filter phase. While brainstorming is fun and important, there is a problem to be solved. All alternatives cannot be implemented. Alternatives are not likely to be equally good—some will be better than others. Assertive persuasion will now rise in predominance. Participation and trust will still be important to ensure that everyone's assertive persuasions are clearly understood. Reward and punishment during the phase is probably most effective when used to influence the process of the discussion, not the content (i.e., to continue to remind the group that there is a time constraint, that there are consequences of their not solving the problem, and so on).

Some managers mistakenly believe that the more power they give to their employees, the less power they have for themselves. This is true only if you impose a win-lose framework on the situation and see power as a limited commodity. In fact, power is often paradoxical—the more one gives to others, the more one has for oneself. Managers who work hard to develop and empower their employees are

[5]R. Tannenbaum and W. H. Schmidt, "How to Choose a Leadership Pattern," *Harvard Business Review* (March–April 1958), pp. 95–101, and updated version, *Harvard Business Review* (May–June 1973), pp. 162–175.

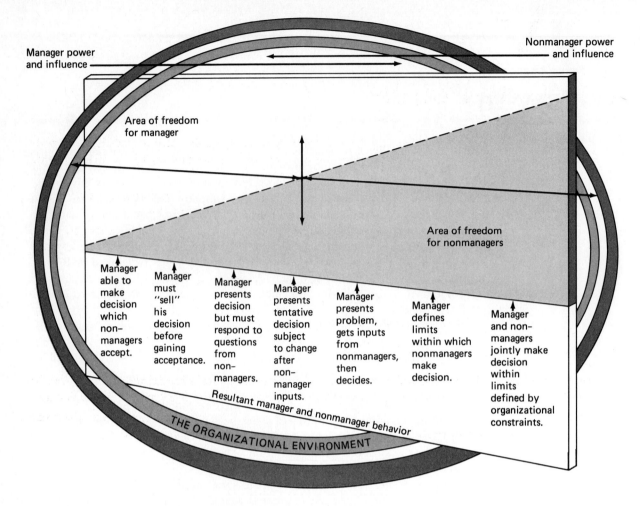

FIGURE 14–1   Continuum of Manager-Nonmanager Behavior

examples of people who accrue power by giving it to others. McClelland stated it well when he wrote, "This expresses the ultimate paradox of social leadership and social power: to be an effective leader, you have to turn all your so-called followers into leaders."[6]

In summary, inherent in the leadership roles is the exercise of personal power and influence. Learning to utilize power effectively is one of the most crucial tasks managers face. Effective leaders understand their natural stance and needs regarding power and have the diagnostic ability to assess the demands of the situation and the behavioral flexibility to act appropriately.

[6]McClelland, "The Two Faces of Power," D. A. Kolb, I. M. Rubin, and J. M. McIntyre, *Organizational Psychology: Readings on Human Behavior in Organizations,* 4th ed. (Englewood Cliffs, NJ: Prentice Hall, 1984), p. 67.

V
Learning Points

1. Power often has negative connotations for people, but it is a crucial part of leading and managing. A manager cannot "make a difference" without exerting power and influence over employees.

2. Power has two faces: a negative, unsocialized need to dominate others and a socialized concern for group goals and empowering others.

3. Managers traditionally relied upon the power inherent in their position. Changes in both society and the workplace demand that managers be proficient in several influence styles.

4. Berlew and Harrison identified four influence styles:

   a. Reward and punishment.

   b. Participation and trust.

   c. Common vision.

   d. Assertive persuasion.

5. Effective managers diagnose the situation and determine which style would be most effective. This reflects a contingency approach to power and influence.

6. Power is paradoxical in that the more a leader empowers others, the more power he or she receives.

VI

Tips for Managers

- Naked ambition seems to generate distrust as peers and others sense that a person would not let human considerations stand in the way of their quest for success.

- Political power refers to attempts to seek personal gain outside the normal channels. Political behavior can never be totally eliminated within organizations, but it is possible for top-level management to curb such behavior by not rewarding it and by establishing norms against it. Condoning political behavior sets a bad precedent within organizations and encourages cynicism about how decisions are really made.

- There are several ways to acquire power that are unrelated to one's position in the hierarchy within a system. Possessing a scarce expertise, serving as a liaison between two groups who have difficulty getting along, having access to information or people with hierarchical power, having a personal network that facilitates both tasks and information gathering, as well as being seen as an objective source of sound judgment are all ways to accrue power.

- Then again, there is the perennial favorite of getting power by ingratiating oneself with the boss. While this tactic may do wonders for your vertical power quotient, it accomplishes less with peers and, from their point of view, throws into question both your competence and trustworthiness.

VII

Personal Application Assignment

This week's assignment is to write about a situation involving leadership and influence (or lack thereof). Choose an experience about which you want to learn more. You could try out a different influence style than you normally use and write about that experience.

    A. *Concrete Experience*
      1. *Objectively* describe the experience ("who," "what," "when," "where," "how" type information—up to 2 points).
      2. *Subjectively* describe your feelings, perceptions, and thoughts that occurred *during* (not after) the experience (up to 2 points). Does this section have too much detail? (If so, delete 1 point.)

B. *Reflective Observation*
   1. Look at the experience from different points of view. How many points of view did you include that are *relevant* (up to 2 points)?
   2. Use these perspectives to add more meaning to the incident (up to 2 points).

C. *Abstract Conceptualization*
   1. Relate concepts from the assigned readings and the lecture to the experience (i.e., what theories that you heard in the lecture or read in the *Reader* relate to your understanding of this incident?). Make reference to at least two sources. Use standard referencing format and include the page number to which you are referring. How many sources did you use and how clearly did you explain their theories (up to 4 points)?
   2. You can also create an original model or theory, but it should not replace course concepts.

D. *Active Experimentation*
   1. Write about what you will do in the future that will improve your effectiveness. Use rules of thumb or action resolutions.
   2. Are they described specifically, thoroughly, and in detail (up to 4 points).

E. *Integration, Synthesis, and Writing*
   1. Did you write about something personally important to you (up to 1 point)?
   2. Was it well written (up to 2 points)?
   3. Did you integrate and synthesize the different sections (up to 1 point)?

15

SUPERVISION AND EMPLOYEE DEVELOPMENT

OBJECTIVES By the end of this chapter you should be able to:

A. Understand the interdependence between leaders and followers.

B. Describe the stages newly assigned managers undergo.

C. Explain how leadership can be perceived as a helping relationship.

Leader as Developer
David Bradford and Allen R. Cohen

During the conference when we were discussing difficult subordinates, I realized that I had completely written Mike off and had stopped any effective communication with him. Mike was a 53-year-old sales representative who had been with the company for over 12 years. He was well liked by the central office staff but had not met his sales plan for five of the last six years. Furthermore, I was starting to hear complaints about him from some of our clients.

I first tried to put myself in Mike's shoes. What must it be like to be near the end of one's career and starting to go downhill? If I were Mike, how receptive would I be to criticism? I might then be able to understand one of his habitual behaviors that had been particularly annoying to me: his tendency to look only to external factors for his failures, to blame "bad luck," the market, competitors who used unfair tactics, and the like.

Still, before meeting with Mike, I did two things. I considered what would be a reasonable goal for him in six months—what exactly did I expect of him in terms of sales level, generating new business, and the like. Then I thought, "What is it in Mike's behavior that would cause him trouble in making sales? Is it something in his style or is some knowledge lacking?"

I then sat down with Mike and began by acknowledging that our relationship had deteriorated, that I had been dissatisfied with him but hadn't confronted him before, and also that I probably hadn't helped him as much as I could have. Mike immediately blamed me for everything that had gone wrong. It was fortunate that I had thought this out before, because my first response was defensive, to attack back. What helped was that I had already thought about why Mike must be hurting—clearly his pain was greater than anything I was now feeling about his comments.

After Mike had vented his feelings, I repeated that I wanted to change our relationship so that I could be more helpful. In return, we needed to get agreement on some specific goals for Mike. Although I would help him, it would be his responsibility to meet certain objectives. He was to be accountable for them, and if he failed to meet or substantially reach them in six months, he would be placed on probation. We mutually negotiated these goals. When I felt he was setting them too low, I pointed out what other sales personnel would do. We ended up with my original list modified, but in a way both of us could live with.

I then asked Mike what he thought might cause him difficulty in going about reaching his goals. In what areas did he need more training, and were

Excerpted from *Managing for Excellence* by David Bradford and Allen R. Cohen (N.Y.: John Wiley, 1984), pp. 157–158.

there ways he behaved that caused problems? (I also asked him to discuss what he thought was easy for him—what his especially strong areas were.) As he shared his self-perception, I also shared my perception. I tried to point to specific behaviors at specific times that illustrated the problem areas I saw. At one point, he got very defensive and offered external reasons why the problems I identified were not his fault. I used his response as an illustration of what I was pointing out in his behavior.

In this discussion, we agreed to specific areas in which he could benefit from training. I sent him to a training program to work on his time-management problem. Also, we set up regular meetings (every two weeks) when we would review progress. I said that I was always available if he had a question, but that the initiative was up to him.

Mike did not meet the goals at the end of six months. I placed him on probation, with notice of termination in three months. I again met with him on a regular basis to offer assistance and coaching. Seven days before the end of his probation, Mike came in and said that the fit between him and the job was not right and quit.

As a result of this process, there was minimal reaction by the office staff (who had very much liked Mike). There was neither a decrease in morale nor a rise in paranoia among others. Mike found another job in an area both of us had discussed as being more in line with his skills. Perhaps most gratifying to me, he expressly thanked me for my concern. He is doing well in his new position and is much happier.

I

Premeeting Preparation

A. Answer the following questions:

1. Think about when you were in a supervisory position and had to help another employee. What was it like? What made it effective or ineffective?

2. What would you like to learn about supervising and helping employees?

3. What were the significant learning points from the *readings?*

B. Read the Topic Introduction.

C. Gather material. Each four person group in the Tower Building Game will require the following materials:

1. Two blindfolds.

2. Approximately 30 to 40 toy building blocks (if toy blocks are unavailable, sugar cubes may be used).

II

Topic Introduction

There is an inherent mutuality in the leadership transaction that is highlighted in the following anecdote about a production manager:

> A new production manager decided it was important to establish himself as "boss" immediately. Upon arriving on the job, he walked out onto the shop floor and called over to the union steward. In "no uncertain terms," he communicated to the union steward (who was also his assistant) that he, the manager, was in charge of this department. He expected to have things done his way.
>
> The union steward listened carefully, turned to the men on the shop floor, and gave a nonverbal signal with his hands. Work immediately stopped and the room became silent. He then turned to the manager, with a slight smile on his face, and said, "Okay, boss, it's *all* yours. Let's see you run this department!"

This naive production manager clearly did not realize that superiors and employees are dependent upon one another. While he assumed that his employees needed him—after all, he was their boss—he found out dramatically that he needed them as well. Without their acceptance of his power, he, in fact, had little power at all. Without followership there is no leadership. Employees *always* have the choice of accepting or not accepting someone's attempt to provide leadership. This situation of mutual dependence adds one further element to the complex demands of the leadership transaction.

For many people, becoming a manager or supervisor for the first time presents quite a challenge since it may require skills which were not necessary in previous positions.[1] Managing people well is different from performing an individual job well. Often promoting the outstanding performer to a management job can result in failure, unless the person has a propensity or a willingness to learn how to manage. Hanging onto old tasks that would be better delegated to others and discomfort with giving orders (and perhaps going overboard or underboard with authority) are common with new supervisors. Mary Parker Follett,[2] an early writer about management, contributed many helpful concepts regarding authority. She acknowledged the dependence of leaders upon followers and proposed the idea of depersonalizing the giving of orders and taking "the situation as the boss." This means that by examining the situation, it becomes evident to everyone, regardless of their hierarchical position, what needs to be done. Giving orders is replaced by mutual definition of the work. Handling authority well, like so many other areas of management, requires understanding one's own attitudes and tendencies and those of the individual employee or group involved, plus understanding what the situation requires.

There are many learning demands made upon new managers or supervisors. However, experienced managers also face heavy learning demands when they assume new positions. John Gabarro,[3] who studied 17 newly assigned managers, dis-

---

[1] For a practical guide for new managers, see Loren B. Belker's *The First Time Manager* (New York: AMACOM, 1986).

[2] Elliot M. Fox and L. Urwick (eds.). *Dynamic Administration: The Collected Papers of Mary Parker Follett* (New York: Hippocrene Books, 1982).

[3] John Gabarro, *The Dynamics of Taking Charge* (Boston: Harvard Business School Press, 1987).

covered that "taking charge" consisted of five predictable and alternate stages of learning and action (making organizational changes). These stages are similar to those in Kolb's learning cycle: concrete experience, reflection, abstract conceptualization, and active experimentation. During the first stage, *taking hold* (3 to 6 months), managers try to learn as much as possible and act upon obvious problems they know how to fix. They form a cognitive map of the situation and expend a good deal of effort in evaluating and assessing both subordinates and the situation.

The second stage, *immersion* (4 to 11 months), is characterized by fewer organizational changes but deeper learning about the organization. This is also a time when managers may question basic issues like structure or staffing. Stage three, *reshaping* (6 months), marks a return to action. Roughly 30 percent of both personnel and structural changes occurred during this period as managers act upon their learning during the immersion stage.

Stage four, *consolidation* (4 to 8 months), is another action period aimed at completing and consolidating the implementation plans of the previous stage. It includes assessing the results of those changes and adjusting to any unanticipated consequences that arose from them. By the final stage, *refinement,* the manager has "taken charge." The degree of learning is less during this stage and relates to the daily problems of the job rather than the manager's newness or need to make major changes. No major organizational changes occur during this stage.

By the end of the taking charge period, and Gabarro says it can last as long as two to two and a half years at middle and upper levels, the manager should have established the relationships and the power base necessary to be effective. The importance of establishing good working relationships with peers, superiors, and employees cannot be overlooked. Indeed, the failure to do so is one of the reasons some on the fast track falter when they become managers.[4] The definition of management, "working through others," involves a variety of roles and adaptation to individual employees and situations. In addition to the need to be personally flexible and adaptive, the effective leader must also be skilled as a helper and consultant. It is only with a recognition that the roles of leader and helper are substantially overlapping that managers will be able to help their subordinates help them (the manager) be more effective.

The leadership role of helper and consultant, while an element of managerial behavior on a day-to-day basis, is perhaps most clear in two specific situations: performance appraisal and goal setting. The discussion of performance appraisal in Chapter 16 highlights the dilemma managers face as they are asked to be helper-coaches in the feedback process and judges regarding salary and promotion decisions.

With respect to goal setting, some organizations utilize a process called *management by objectives* (MBO).[5] Again while the specifics may vary, the fundamental steps of MBO are as follows:

1. Superior and subordinate set mutually acceptable performance goals for the subordinate for some time period.
2. Periodic review sessions are held to measure progress against objectives with the supervisor providing feedback and counseling.
3. The extent of goal attainment is used as a major input into promotion and salary decisions.

Here, again, the supervisor is put into the difficult position of being both helper and evaluator. While certain structural changes can help to alleviate this dilemma,

[4]B. E. Kovach, "The Derailment of Fast-Track Managers," *Organizational Dynamics* (Autumn 1986), pp. 41–48.

[5]Henry L. Tosi, Carroll Tosi, Jr., and J. Stephen, "Some Factors Affecting the Success of Management by Objectives," *Journal of Management Studies,* Vol. 7 (May 1970), and Steven Kerr, "Overcoming the Dysfunctions of MBO," *Management by Objectives,* Vol. 5, no. 1 (1976); *Readings.*

the conflict is built into the very fiber of the leadership situation. The formal power to reward and punish cannot be wished away. Nor can the manager's responsibility to help subordinates grow and develop.

The inevitability of this dilemma means that effective managers need to understand the dynamics of the helping relationship. In the following section, a model of the helping relationship will be described. While most of the research on this issue has come from psychotherapy and counseling, the points have clear relevance and application to the dilemmas of supervision and employee development.

THE HELPING RELATIONSHIP: A GENERIC MODEL

The way to an effective helping relationship is fraught with many psychological difficulties that can either sidetrack or destroy the relationship. The process of sharing wealth, knowledge, or skill with one who happens to have less of these valuable commodities is far from being a simple exchange, easily accomplished.[6] Carl Rogers, in his classic article, "The Characteristics of a Helping Relationship," defines a helping relationship as one "in which at least one of the parties has the intent of promoting the growth, development, maturity, improved functioning, improved coping with life of the other."[7] This definition would include parent and child, teacher and students, manager and subordinates, therapist and patient, consultant and client, and many other less formally defined relationships.

Figure 15–1 depicts a model of the helping relationship that will serve as a focus for this class session. The model emphasizes five key elements in the helping relationship: (1) the task or problem around which the helping relationship develops, (2) the helpers with their motives (achievement motivation, power motivation, and affiliation motivation and self-image), (3) the receivers of help with their motives and self-image, (4) the environment and psychological climate in which the helping activities occur, and (5) the information feedback that occurs during the helping process.

The Task

The tasks around which helping relationships develop are widely varied—they range from tying a shoe to changing attitudes about birth control to conducting a performance appraisal review session to improving the effectiveness of an organization. It is possible to classify all tasks on a single dimension, namely, the extent to which it is required that the receiver of help be capable of accomplishing the task independently when the helper is no longer present. At one end of this dimension are tasks defined as assistance, situations in which there is no emphasis on the receiver's independent task performance. Giving a vagrant money for a cup of coffee is a good example of this end of the continuum. Many welfare and foreign relief programs are close to this end of the dimension. The emphasis is on the solution of an immediate problem, with no provision for handling recurrences of that problem or similar problems. This type of assistance, aimed only at symptom relief, is likely to induce a dependency on the helper,[8] making termination of the helping interaction difficult. When the interaction has been concluded, the receiver may blame the helper for inadequate help if he or she cannot replicate a successful result.

At the other end of the continuum is education. Here the emphasis is on increasing the receivers' ecological wisdom (i.e., their ability to solve problems that are similar to the present one by developing their ability to make use of the resources of their natural environment). The helper avoids using the special knowledge, skills, or other resources he or she may command to relieve the receiver's immediate need,

[6]See G. C. Homans, *Social Behavior: Its Elementary Forms* (New York: Harcourt Brace Jovanovich, 1961), for a discussion of two very relevant concepts, exchange and reciprocity.

[7]Carl C. Rogers, *On Becoming a Person* (Boston: Houghton Mifflin, 1961), pp. 34–40.

[8]Much of the reactions of ghetto residents and the poor to welfare programs can be understood in these terms—a sense of dependency often leads to hostile responses.

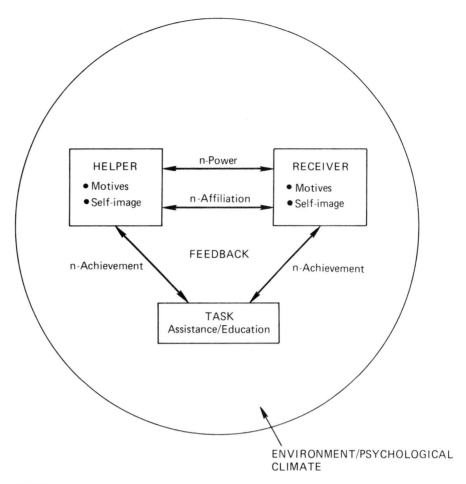

FIGURE 15–1   A Model for Analysis of the Helping Relationship

but instead works with persons in their frame of reference to increase their problem-solving ability.

While the educational approach often holds the greatest potential for the receiver's long-term benefit, it can cause great frustration to a person with strong needs for symptom relief. In addition, the educational approach will frequently be seen by receivers as an intrusion on their privacy and an escalation of their problem. At the international level, for example, India was quite willing to receive assistance in the form of surplus food in the 1970s, but grew resentful at U.S. insistence that such assistance be coupled with an educational program to solve their basic problems of food production.

The Helper and Receiver of Help

The personal characteristics of the helper and receiver of help are major factors influencing the process and outcome of the helping relationship. Two types of characteristics are particularly important: the motives and self-image of helper and receiver. At least three motives seem necessary in understanding the dynamics of the helping relationship[9]: power motivation (n-Power), affiliation motivation (n-Affiliation), and achievement motivation (n-Achievement). These motives are important because they determine how the helper and receiver will orient themselves to one another and to their task.

The helper's and the receiver's power motivation determines how much they

[9]These motives have been treated in detail in Chapter 4, dealing with motivation. Motives other than these, for example, security, can also influence the helping relationship.

will be concerned with influencing and controlling one another. By asking for and/or receiving help offered, the receivers place themselves in a dependent position, where they often feel weaker and more vulnerable to the source of help. The helper, at the same time, must deal with tendencies to feel superior, thereby letting the satisfactions of power and control overshadow the sometimes elusive goal of acting in the receiver's best interest. If the helper and receiver are unable to resolve power struggles and bring about a situation of power equalization, the relationship can degenerate into rebellion and passivity by the receiver or rejection by the helper ("She doesn't appreciate what I am trying to do for her"). One empirical example of the detrimental effects of a helper's overconcern with power can be seen in Prakash's[10] study of effective and ineffective organization change agents. He found that ineffective change agents were more concerned with their personal goals and with their political position within the organization than were the effective change agents who were more concerned about task accomplishment.

The helper's and receiver's affiliation motivation determines how much they will be concerned with the factors of intimacy and understanding. To be helpful, the helper must know his or her receivers and understand how they perceive their problem. The intimacy required for effective understanding is difficult to achieve in situations where the helpers have impossible demands on their time, even though a lack of intimacy can leave the helper and receiver in two different worlds, speaking two different languages. Too great a concern with affiliation by the helper and the receiver, on the other hand, can produce pressure toward conformity and mutual sympathy, which may cause the helper to lose perspective of the receiver's problem and the receiver to lose respect for the helper's expertise.

The achievement motivation of the helper and receiver of help influences how concerned they will be about accomplishing their task or solving their problem. A major question here is, "How is the goal of the helping relationship defined? Does the helper decide what is good for the receiver or does the receiver retain the power to decide what help he wants?" In the first case, the receiver is likely to have little motivation to accomplish the helper's task; and in the second, the helper's motivation is likely to be reduced. Only when the interpersonal issues of influence and intimacy have been resolved does it appear possible that the helper and receiver can agree on a goal to which they are mutually committed. Even if this is accomplished, a problem still remains of what are often strong desires to achieve the goal of the helping relationship. Help is often so late in coming that both helper and receiver feel a compulsion to accomplish *something*. The result is usually assistance programs designed to eliminate the receiver's immediate desperation rather than programs of education designed to help the receivers diagnose the causes of the problem and learn to solve the problem themselves.

There is an interaction among motives in any helping relationship. It is possible for the helper and receiver to be so highly power motivated that they become preoccupied with controlling one another at the expense of understanding one another and/or accomplishing their task. Similarly, as we have suggested, high achievement motivation can cause the helper and receiver to orient themselves to accomplishing the task without attending to the interpersonal processes of influence and understanding necessary if the receivers of help are to learn to solve the problem on their own. In a case such as this, the offer of "Here, let me help you" by the helper is often his or her cue to push the receiver aside and do the task him or herself, leaving the receiver in an unresolved state of ignorance about how to solve the problem. And finally, high affiliation motivation can lead to concerns about intimacy and understanding that preclude attempts to influence others and accomplish tasks.

The implication of this analysis for helping relationships is that moderate levels of achievement, affiliation, and power motivation in the helper and receiver are

[10]S. Prakash, "Some Characteristics of an Effective Organization Development Agent," unpublished Master's thesis, Sloan School of Management, Massachusetts Institute of Technology, 1968.

optimal for effective help to take place.[11] The dynamics of the helping relationship are such that influence, intimacy and understanding, and a concern for task accomplishment are all necessary for effective help to take place; yet excess concern in any one area can lead to the deterioration of an effective helping relationship.

The self-image and attitudes of the helper and receiver are also important defining variables in a helping relationship. Receivers must see themselves as capable of improvement and willing to receive help. If this is not so, a major portion of helping activity must center on building self-confidence and optimism before learning can take place. Helpers, on the other hand, must see themselves as capable of helping and yet, at the same time, must not feel that they are the "know-it-all" expert. This latter point is related to the issues of influence and intimacy discussed earlier. The helper must be willing to influence and at the same time have empathy with the feelings of the person being helped.

THE ENVIRONMENT AND PSYCHOLOGICAL CLIMATE

It is a truism in contemporary social psychology that behavior is a function of both the person and the environment. While one could imagine many environmental variables that could influence the process of helping—such as comfort of surroundings, freedom from distraction, and so on—we have limited ourselves for the present time to a consideration of those environmental factors that are related to influence, intimacy and understanding, and task accomplishment. As noted in Chapter 4, on motivation Atkinson and Feather have argued that the tendency (T) to act in these three ways can be predicted by the strength of the individual's motivation (M) for power, affiliation, and achievement; times the individual's perceived expectation (E) that action in terms of one or more of these motives will be rewarded; times the reward value (R) of the power, affiliation, and achievement rewards that he or she expects to get. Thus, the individual acts to maximize satisfaction following the formula $T = M \times E \times R$ for three motives: power, affiliation, and achievement. While M refers to the individual's motivation, E and R refer to the individual's perception of the environment.[12]

This analysis has important implications for predictions about effective helping; for if the environment tends to reward one motive disproportionately, it can alter the behavior of an otherwise moderately motivated helper and receiver. One example of this occurs in the Peace Corps where volunteers who might otherwise establish very effective relationships with host country nationals become bogged down in issues of power and control because the host country people (and sometimes the volunteers themselves) perceive the Peace Corps to be a political agent of U.S. foreign policy. Growth-promoting climates in which it is easier to both ask and receive help are characterized by mutual trust, active listening, acceptance, respect, and encouragement.

Feedback

The last element of the model is the information feedback that occurs during the helping process. Skillful giving and receiving of feedback is an essential element in the process of enhancing and developing personal effectiveness. As in a guided missile system, feedback helps individuals to keep behavior "on target" and thus better achieve their goals. Achievement-oriented people, in particular, want and need frequent and specific feedback to continue performing at optimal levels.

The purpose of feedback is to provide people with information that they may

---

[11]See David A. Kolb and Richard Boyatzis, "On the Dynamics of the Helping Relationship," Working Paper 372-69, Sloan School of Management, Massachusetts Institute of Technology, 1969, for empirical validation of this hypothesis.

[12]J. Atkinson, *An Introduction to Motivation* (Princeton, NJ: D. Van Nostrand, 1964), and J. Atkinson and N. T. Feather, *A Theory of Achievement Motivation* (New York: John Wiley, 1966). See also Chapter 18 on organization climate.

or may not choose to utilize. In a work setting there may well be consequences for not utilizing the information, but feedback offered in the spirit of helpful data is less likely to arouse defensiveness or lack of attending. Effective feedback has the following characteristics:

1. Effective feedback is descriptive as opposed to evaluative. For example, to tell a person "When you interrupt and don't let me finish my statements (description), it makes me feel as if you don't value my ideas (personal reactions)" has a very different impact from the evaluative statement, "Boy, you sure are a power-hungry s.o.b." The latter is bound to cause a defensive reaction. While the former may not be totally pleasant, it is nonetheless easier to hear or listen to because it is more descriptive than evaluative.

   In this sense, a household thermostat is a nonevaluative feedback device. It only measures and reacts to the temperature in the room—it does not decide what is too hot or too cold. The person setting the thermostat maintains control over that assessment.

2. Effective feedback is specific rather than general. To be told that one is "not performing well" will not be as useful as being told "your last three shipments were sent without the proper paperwork." Vague feedback is generally very hard to translate into the specific development goals that are so important to improvement.

3. Effective feedback is directed toward behavior that the receiver can control. To be told that "short people don't get ahead very fast in this company" is frustrating (as well as of questionable legality!).

4. To the extent possible, it is better for feedback to be solicited rather than imposed. If people can formulate the questions they feel a need to explore, their motivation to listen carefully is significantly enhanced. While this is an "ideal" to be reached, there are, nonetheless, times when you, as a manager, will see a need to give an employee some unsolicited feedback. Even under these circumstances, you can share the control and provide the employee with an opportunity to participate by saying, for example, "I've noticed a few things I think it would be good for us to talk about. Is now a good time to talk? If not, when would be a good time for you?"

5. As is pointed out in the preceding example, effective feedback is well timed. It does the receiver little good to find out that six months ago he or she did something "wrong." Feedback, generally, is most effective at the earliest opportunity after the behavior in question has occurred.

In summary, the five rules of thumb for giving effective feedback in a way that increases productive discussion and decreases defensiveness are

- Descriptive rather than evaluative.
- Specific rather than general.
- Directed toward controllable behaviors rather than personality traits or characteristics.
- Solicited rather than imposed.
- Close to the event under discussion rather than delayed for several months.

The five rules of thumb just outlined will contribute significantly to managing the inherent anxiety that characterizes behavior-oriented discussions between people. Another major question raised about the characteristics of helpful feedback is whether this feedback should be positive (pleasant for the receiver to hear) or negative (unpleasant). While there are those who feel that negative feedback is sometimes helpful in that it serves to unfreeze the receiver's self-satisfied concept and increase motivation to change,[13] most learning theorists have concluded that in the long run, reward is more effective than punishment. Rogers, too, places heavy emphasis on the importance of positive feedback to the receiver in his or her concept of unconditioned positive regard.[14] "I find that the more acceptance and liking I feel toward this individual, the more I will be creating a relationship which he can use. By acceptance I mean a warm regard for him as a person of unconditional self-worth—of value no matter what his condition, or his feelings. . . . This acceptance of each fluctuating aspect of this other person makes it for him a relationship of warmth and safety, and the safety of being liked and prized as a person seems a highly important element in a helping relationship." To support his conclusion, Rogers cites psychotherapy research by Halkides,[15] which showed that therapists who demonstrated a high degree of unconditional positive regard for their clients were more successful than were those who did not. Positive regard is also one of the competencies of high-performing managers that Boyatzis identified.[16]

[13]Warren G. Bennis, Edgar H. Schein, David E. Berlew, and Fred Steele, *Interpersonal Dynamics* (Homewood, IL: Dorsey Press, 1964).

[14]Rogers, *On Becoming a Person,* p. 34.

[15]G. Halkides, "An Experimental Study of Four Conditions Necessary for Therapeutic Change," unpublished Ph.D. dissertation, University of Chicago, 1958.

[16]Richard E. Boyatzis, *The Competent Manager: A Model for Effective Performance* (New York: John Wiley, 1982).

Procedures for Group Meeting: The Tower Building Game

(Time Allotted: 1 Hour, 30 Minutes)

For this exercise, the class should divide into four-person teams. The simulation is called the Tower Building Game. To maximize your opportunity to learn about leadership and the helping relationship, the Tower Building Game is designed to simplify the task to be managed and to focus on the essential human elements of the supervisory relationship. In the simulation, the worker's task is to stack blocks with his or her nondominant hand while blindfolded, symbolizing the restricted access to resources and information that usually exists in hierarchical supervisor-employee organizational relationships. Managers in the game as in real life have the responsibility to facilitate work and maximize productivity.

The basic game will be played four times. In this way, each member of a four-person team will have the opportunity to be a manager, an observer, an employee (twice). The basic structure is as follows:

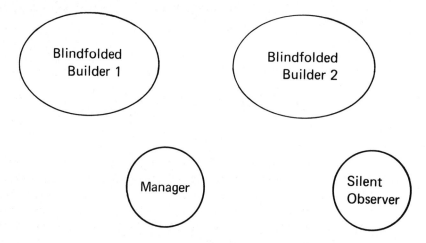

As soon as the order of rotation has been decided, the first two builders should don their blindfolds and leave them on until their production periods have been completed. Managers can talk to their builders, but they should not personally touch them or any of the building materials.

STEP 1. There are two production rounds during each phase of the game. Round 1 has no time limit; it is untimed. Round 2 is timed—there is a limit of 2 minutes for building the two towers after the goals have been set. Each builder's task is to construct as high a tower as he or she can using the *nondominant hand only* (left hand only for right-handers, and vice versa) while totally blindfolded.

STEP 2. Observer role. Observers should begin immediately to record their observations using the Tower Building Record Form on page 426 as a guide. These data will be an important part of the discussion after the entire game is completed. Successful supervision often hinges on aspects of management style that are subtle but powerful, such as tone of voice and nonverbal behavior. Careful observation can identify these factors for later examination and discussion by the quartet.

STEP 3.   Goal setting and scoring procedure. At the start of each of the two rounds, the manager should indicate to the observer the goal that has been set for each builder individually. The observer will record these on the Tower Building Record Form.

The *score* for each person will be determined by the achievement of this goal in the actual size of the tower. In other words, if the goal is 8 blocks and the person stacks 10 blocks, the final score is only 8. If, on the other hand, the goal is 8 blocks and the person stacks only 7 blocks, the score is 0. If at any time any part of the tower should collapse, the round is over and the score is 0. *Blocks must be stacked singly,* one on top of the other, with no double block foundations.

STEP 4.   Total group meeting after first cycle of tower building. (30 minutes) The meeting is important because everyone can gain ideas about how to improve the helping process during subsequent cycles of the Tower Building Game.

After each group has completed the first two production periods (one untimed and one timed), the entire class should reconvene for 30 minutes to analyze the process of helping that occurred during the first cycle of the Tower Building Game. One way to proceed in the meeting is to place the following chart on the chalkboard and have the members of each four-person team share their reactions. The observers should give their observations first, then the employees (receivers), and finally the manager (helper).

Analysis of the Supervisory Helping Relationship

EMPLOYEE'S ACTIONS THAT		SUPERVISOR'S ACTIONS THAT	
Helped	Hindered	Helped	Hindered
1	1	1	1
2	2	2	2
3	3	3	3
4	4	4	4
5	5	5	5

This total group meeting is often viewed as an unnecessary disruption. Many people, however, gain significant insight during this discussion, which helps them directly during subsequent rounds of the game. Although the specifics are impossible to predict beforehand, the major learnings often come from the insight that the receiver (the person who needs the help) can behave in ways that facilitate or hinder his or her ability to get help.

This half-hour total group meeting is still another example of the helping relationship process in that the group will be trying to help each individual benefit more from the remainder of the exercise. When the listing of forces that helped or hindered and subsequent discussion has been completed, members should return to their quartets for the three remaining cycles of the Tower Building Game.

STEP 5.   Completing the Tower Building Game. Each four-person team should now complete the remaining three cycles of the Tower Building Game.

DISCUSSION OF TOWER BUILDING GAME
(Time Allotted: 30 Minutes)

The discussion of the game is probably best conducted, at least initially, within the same four-person teams to make most productive use of the data generated and recorded by the observers. Observers should begin the discussion by sharing their observations of the manager's behavior (helper), the employees' behavior (receiver) toward the manager, and the nature of the helping relationship that developed. Others should *listen* and strive to hear and understand what is being said without reacting defensively. In sharing your observations, you are in effect involved in another helping relationship—you as observer are the helper and the manager and the employees are the receivers.

After the observer inputs have been made, the manager and employees should add their reactions and observations.

If there is time for a class discussion, answer the following questions:

1. What did you learn about helping from this exercise?
2. What did you learn about yourself?
3. What connections can you make between this exercise and the readings?

Tower Building Record Form

	Name of Manager				
	BUILDER 1		BUILDER 2		
	Untimed Round	Timed Round	Untimed Round	Timed Round	
Goal					Timed rounds for 2 minutes
Score					
	Total builder 1 =		Total builder 2 =		

OBSERVER QUESTIONS

1. *Definition of the task.* Where along the assistance-education task continuum did the manager and the employees fall? Were they primarily concerned about immediate production or development?

2. *Relationship between helper and receivers.* In what behavioral ways did the helper's/receiver's motivation for affiliation, power, and achievement manifest themselves? With what consequences?

3. *Information control and feedback.* How much information and feedback did managers provide employees? At what points in time? With what consequences? Did managers *solicit feedback* from employees during the building process? Did employees *initiate* (offer) *feedback?* What prevents managers and employees from asking for or giving direct feedback in the work setting?

4. *Goal setting.* How were goals set? Who most controlled the process of setting them? What happened after an initial success or failure (during the untimed round)? Did helpers become more controlling? Receivers more dependent?

5. *Differential management.* How were the two builders managed (helped)? The same or differently? If differently, how? With what consequences?

6. *Management turnover.* You each had the chance to be a builder under two different managers. Did you meet any problems in the transition? Did the manager take into account your "experience"? How could manager and employees have helped each other over this transitional period?

IV
Follow-up

To be effective, a manager must be capable of occupying many roles—leader, teacher, team member, politician, problem solver, and many others. This chapter has focused on the key managerial tasks of supervision and employee development. The changing demands of organizational life are making it increasingly imperative that the manager be both a skilled helper and skilled receiver of help. Two of the more important of these changes are worth noting here. First, the knowledge explosion is making human obsolescence a critical problem in nearly all modern organizations. The result is that managers must dedicate time and energy to the continuing development of their staff by helping them acquire the new skills required to stay on top of their changing jobs. At the same time, they must stay on top of their basic job by effectively using help that is available from others. Second, the nature of organizations is itself changing. Bureaucratic organization structures with highly programmed static activities are giving way to organizations that emphasize dynamic systems that are formed to accomplish a new task or solve an emerging problem that the organization faces, and are disbanded when the problem or task is no longer important. The manager of these temporary groups must be a highly effective consultant in defining the group's role in accomplishing tasks and in bringing the appropriate resources to bear on a problem. Then the group itself becomes a consultant to various parts of the organization and a receiver of help from those agencies whose resources it needs to accomplish its mission.

In the Topic Introduction, the formula $T = M \times E \times R$ was discussed, where M referred to an individual's motivation, while R and E referred to perceptions of the environment, or the psychological climate. The concept of climate has relevance for managers and the helping process at two levels. First, it has relevance to the extent that the reward system within an organization reinforces a manager's efforts at employee development. Many organizations pay lip service to this aspect of a manager's role but, in fact, communicate a different message by a reward system that emphasizes short-term productivity over employee development goals. The long-run success and adaptability of an organization depends on the establishment of an organization climate that is conducive to the maintenance of mutual managerial helping relationships throughout the organization. Second, as discussed earlier, managers sometimes feel they must be clairvoyant (or at least omniscient!) to be an effective helper who is capable of understanding another's needs, motives, or problems. True, certain skills are needed to be an effective helper—developing trust, listening accurately, and so on. These same skills, however, will help managers to develop a climate within their work group which will facilitate the helping process: people will feel safer seeking help and be more willing to accept help when it is offered. Effective management and effective helping are closely intertwined.

V
Learning Points

1. Without followership, there is no leadership.

2. First-time managers face the challenge of acquiring managerial skills that may not have been required in previous jobs. Thus it takes time to grow into the role and learn to handle authority.

3. Employees who are conditioned to taking orders from superiors may come to see the boss-subordinate relationship as an antagonistic one and find it difficult to take responsibility. Managers can avoid this problem by emphasizing joint study of problems or situations and taking orders from the situation.

4. Experienced managers go through a transition period when they assume a new position. The "taking charge" process involves five predictable stages that alternate between learning and action (making organizational changes). The stages are: (1) taking hold, (2) immersion, (3) reshaping, (4) consolidation, and (5) refinement.

5. An important managerial role is that of the helper-consultant.

6. The helping relationship model consists of

   a. The task or problem.

   b. The helpers with their motives and self-image.

   c. The receivers of help with their motives and self-image.

   d. The environment and psychological climate.

   e. The information feedback.

7. Moderate levels of achievement, affiliation, and power motivation in the helper and receiver are optimal for effective help to take place.

8. Self-image is important in the helping process because receivers must see themselves as capable of improvement and willing to receive help. Helpers must see themselves as capable of helping but not as "know-it-alls."

9. The rewards and psychological safety found in the environment influence the helping process.

10. Effective feedback is objective rather than judgmental, descriptive rather than vague, directed toward controllable behavior, solicited rather than imposed, and well timed.

VI

Tips for Managers

- One technique that some managers use to enter a new organization or position is to ask each employee to describe, either in verbal or written form, their job and also what they think their job should be. This helps the new manager to gather data about the situation and provides an opportunity for each employee to communicate with the boss without competing for attention.

- Developing employees sometimes means giving up tasks that one enjoys and does very well (at least in your own eyes) and turning it over to someone who will perhaps do a worse job with it until they have mastered it. Or the employee may do it differently, which can also be hard to accept. Letting go of tasks and delegating is an investment that should pay off in the future with competent employees who free up your time to look at the broader picture.

- Many new managers are shocked by the amount of time they must spend counseling or helping employees. Like any other role it can be overworked, but it is important to have good helping skills.

- Active listening is a key part of helping because often people determine what is bothering them or what decision they want to take by talking things out with another person. In presenting their story to a listener, many people imagine how the listener is reacting. Even though the listener may never give an opinion, this provides the speaker with another perspective.

- Professional helpers (social workers, psychologists, and therapists) are taught the concept of client self-determination. This means that the receivers have to decide for themselves what they want to do and take responsibility for their own actions; in general, helpers should not tell others what to do because this further increases feelings of dependency.

- New managers sometimes feel the need to make sweeping changes in the beginning of their tenure to "show people who's boss" or compete with a successful predecessor. In one organization, four successive first-time directors came in and unilaterally changed the same procedure. The record-keeping method went from A to B and back again twice. Each director was scornful of the previous director's method and bragged about his new "innovation." None took the time to investigate the history of the procedure; they just assumed that their predecessors hadn't been as smart as they were. Some changes obviously need to be made quickly, but it's always good to ask yourself, "Am I making this change for the good of the organization, or is it motivated by personal reasons?"

VII

Personal Application Assignment

The topic of this assignment is to write about an experience that involved supervision and/or employee development. Choose an experience that was significant to you and about which you are motivated to learn more. Alternatively you may want to experiment with the skills taught in this unit and write about the outcome.

A. *Concrete Experience*

    1. *Objectively* describe the experience ("who," "what," "when," "where," "how" type information—up to 2 points).

    2. *Subjectively* describe your feelings, perceptions, and thoughts that occurred *during* (not after) the experience (up to 2 points). Does this section have too much detail? (If so, delete 1 point.)

B. *Reflective Observation*

    1. Look at the experience from different points of view. How many points of view did you include that are *relevant* (up to 2 points)?

    2. Use these perspectives to add more meaning to the incident (up to 2 points).

C. *Abstract Conceptualization*

   1. Relate concepts from the assigned readings and the lecture to the experience (i.e., what theories that you heard in the lecture or read in the *Reader* relate to your understanding of this incident?). Make reference to at least two sources. Use standard referencing format and include the page number to which you are referring. How many sources did you use and how clearly did you explain their theories (up to 4 points)?

   2. You can also create an original model or theory, but it should not replace course concepts.

D. *Active Experimentation*

   1. Write about what you will do in the future that will improve your effectiveness. Use rules of thumb or action resolutions.

   2. Are they described specifically, thoroughly, and in detail (up to 4 points).

E. *Integration, Synthesis, and Writing*
   1. Did you write about something personally important to you (up to 1 point)?
   2. Was it well written (up to 2 points)?
   3. Did you integrate and synthesize the different sections (up to 1 point)?

16

PERFORMANCE APPRAISAL

OBJECTIVES   By the end of this chapter, you should be able to:

A. Explain the importance of performance feedback.
B. Describe the process of performance appraisal.
C. Identify the components of effective appraisals.
D. Demonstrate some of the skills required for a good appraisal.

A Description of Rejection

Ellen Goodman

She was brilliant. Everyone involved in the case agreed about that.

She was unattractive. Everyone agreed about that, too.

She was overweight, whiny, argumentative, unkempt—the list goes on—sloppy, hypercritical, unpopular.

The life of Charlotte Horowitz—whose dismissal from a Missouri medical school became a Supreme Court case this week—has become painfully public. A description of rejection.

From all reports, she interacted with the world like a fingernail on a blackboard. She was punished for the crime of being socially unacceptable.

Charlotte Horowitz was older than most of the other students when she was admitted to the University of Missouri, Kansas City, Medical School in 1972. She was also brighter, a misfit from New York who won her place despite the admissions officer's report that read, "The candidate's personal appearance is against her . . . ".

By the school's "merit system," she was tops in her medical school class. As her advisor wrote: "Her past record is the best in the school. Her examination scores are at the very top of the school. She has functioned at a high level and has had no problems with a patient at any time." Yet she was dismissed by the dean on the verge of graduation. The grounds were tardiness, bad grooming, and an abrasive personal style.

Of course, the case in front of the Supreme Court won't judge those grounds. It will deal with the issue of due process: whether she was given proper notice and a fair hearing; whether universities and professional schools have to extend certain legal rights to their students.

But the theme of this difficult, emotional story is prejudice. The most deep-rooted way in which we pre-judge each other. The sort of discrimination which is universal, almost unrootable. Prejudice toward appearance. Discrimination against what we "see."

The most unattractive children in the classrooms of our youth had their lives and personalities warped by that fact. Their painful experiences of rejection nurtured in them an expectation of rejection. That expectation, like some paranoia, was almost always fulfilled.

It is a mystery why some "unattractive people" wear it in their souls and others don't. Why one becomes Barbra Streisand and another a reject. But often, along the way, some people give up trying to be accepted and become defensively

Boston Globe, November 1977. © The Boston Globe Newspaper Co./Washington Post Writers Group. Reprinted with permission.

nonconforming. They stop letting themselves care. They become "unkempt, argumentative, abrasive." And the list goes on.

Everyone's self-image is formed in some measure by the way they are seen, the way they see themselves being seen. As their image deteriorates, their personality often shatters along with it. At that point, the rest of us smugly avoid them, stamping them "unacceptable," not because of their "looks" but because of their behavior.

It happens all the time.

There is no law that can protect children from this sort of discrimination. We are all, in that sense, the products as well as the survivors of our childhood. But the cumulative, spiraling effect of appearance on personality is worse for women than for men. If Charlotte Horowitz had been a man, surely her brains would have alleviated her physical unattractiveness. As a woman, her unattractiveness was further handicapped by brains.

As Dr. Estelle Ramey, a professor at Georgetown Medical School and former head of the Association for Women in Science, said: "If the bad fairy ends up the last one at your crib, you'll be cursed as a brilliant unattractive woman."

But this case isn't a question of the curse, the birth penalty, the "life isn't fair" sort of discrimination. It's a story of a university so "blinded" that its officials felt they had the right to throw away a life and a mind because it was housed in a body that was "overweight, sloppy, and hypercritical."

"What's been lost in all this," says Dr. Ramey, "is the contribution a brilliant human being might have made in a field which needs all the fine minds we have."

You see, Charlotte Horowitz was brilliant. Everyone involved in the case could, at least, see that.

I

Premeeting Preparation

A. Think back on the best performance appraisal you ever received whether it occurred in a work setting, school, or extracurricular activity. Write down what was good about it.

B. Think about the worst performance appraisal you ever received or gave. What made it so ineffective?

C. Write a list of the conditions you think are necessary for an effective performance appraisal.

D. What were the significant learning points from the readings?

E. Consider your performance in this course:
1. What have you done so far that has contributed to your own learning and that of your learning group?

2. What have you contributed to the general atmosphere of the class?

3. Are there extenuating circumstances that have affected your performance in the course?

4. What have been your weaknesses and strengths so far?

5. What would you like to do to improve in your performance?

6. How do you plan to do it?

II

Topic Introduction

Performance appraisals are often one of the least favorite activities of managers. Yet they can be a valuable managerial tool for maintaining and improving performance. An analogy is sometimes made between performance appraisal systems and seat belts—people believe in them but do not want to use them personally. Without such systems, however, personnel decisions about promotions, raises, and terminations might have little objective basis. Appraisal systems can never be totally objective because humans operate them, but they do represent the organization's attempt to evaluate employees fairly using a standardized method.

Given what we know about the correlation between feedback and high performance, it is surprising how many organizations do not evaluate employees in a systematic fashion. Even when organizations have systems in place, many managers fail to comply. In such instances employees often interpret skipped or late reviews as an indication that their manager is not concerned about them and does not appreciate their work. It is not uncommon to find organizations in which reviews hold great significance for employees but are perceived as little more than a waste of time by their managers.

Why the difference in opinion about performance reviews? At the organizational level, some appraisal systems are outdated and cumbersome and seem to measure only that which can be quantified. It's difficult for managers to take such systems seriously and see how they have any positive results. On the personal level, some managers resent the time consumed by appraisals and feel uncomfortable sitting in judgment upon another person. McGregor argued that the conventional approach to performance appraisal:

> unless handled with consummate skill and delicacy, constitutes something dangerously close to a violation of the integrity of the personality. Managers are uncomfortable when they are put in the position of "playing God." The respect we hold for the inherent value of the individual leaves us distressed when we must take responsibility for judging the personal worth of a fellow man. Yet the conventional approach to performance appraisal forces us, not only to make such judgments and to see them acted upon, but also to communicate them to those we have judged. Small wonder we resist![1]

Those systems that force managers to compare and rank all their employees goes against the values some hold about the importance of valuing people in their own right and not creating "losers" merely to comply with a bureaucratic requirement. Many people are uncomfortable giving negative feedback to people and fear that doing so may make a bad situation even worse.

In contrast to these reasons why managers tend to avoid appraisals, we know that managers who see appraisals as a useful tool can utilize their human resources more effectively. Research has shown that monitoring and providing feedback on

---

[1]Douglas McGregor, "An Uneasy Look at Performance Appraisal," *Harvard Business Review,* Vol. 35, no. 3 (May–June 1957), pp. 89–94.

performance is one of the most effective ways to improve performance.[2] Appraisals allow managers the opportunity to give feedback on performance as well as to set goals for future performance that, as we learned earlier, is an effective way to motivate employees.

Furthermore, performance feedback serves a variety of functions for the employee:[3]

1. Contributing to the development of one's self-concept.
2. Reducing uncertainty about the appropriateness of one's goal behavior and how it is perceived by others.
3. Signaling which organizational goals are most important in relation to the others.
4. Helping individuals to master their environment and feel competent.

An awareness of these functions may help managers to realize that a performance appraisal session means more to employees than just finding out what their salary will be for the next year.

Let's return to McGregor's statement that managers feel uncomfortable when they are put in the position of "playing God." To an extent, this is determined by the attitude the manager has toward appraisal. If the manager's underlying approach is to help the employee develop, his or her feedback is more likely to be effective and well received. The theory-in-use that underlies this approach is one that acknowledges the role of enlightened self-interest. In other words, if employees understand what is required of them and what they need to do or stop doing to be promoted or receive good performance ratings, they will do it. Managers utilizing this approach see their function as presenting employees with objective feedback about their performance and career plans. A less successful managerial approach to appraisal is the judgmental "gotcha," which is more likely to result in defensiveness than in the behavioral changes the manager desires.

The performance appraisal activity requires that leaders or managers switch into the helper and consultant role. As we found in the previous chapter, it is only with a recognition that the roles of leader and helper are substantially overlapping that managers will be able to help their subordinates help them (the managers) to be more effective.

The leadership role of helper and consultant, while an element of managerial behavior on a day-to-day basis, is especially clear in the performance appraisal situation. While the specific mechanics of implementation will vary across organizations, the "ideal" performance appraisal system is designed to achieve four basic objectives:

1. Provide feedback to subordinates to facilitate their ability to achieve organizational (and personal) goals).
2. Provide management with data to make salary and promotional decisions.
3. Motivate employees to be more effective workers.

Depending on how this process gets implemented, managers often find themselves in a role conflict. On the one hand, they are asked to be helper-coaches in

[2]D. A. Nadler, C. Cammon, and P. Mirvis, "Developing a Feedback System for Work Units: A Field Experiment in Structural Change," *Journal of Applied Behavioral Science,* Vol. 16 (1980), pp. 41–62, and D. R. Ilgen, C. D. Fischer, and M. S. Taylor, "Consequences of Individual Feedback on Behavior in Organizations," *Journal of Applied Psychology,* Vol. 64 (1979), pp. 359–371.

[3]S. J. Ashford and L. L. Cummings, "Feedback as an Individual Resource: Personal Strategies of Creating Information," *Organizational Behavior and Human Performance,* Vol. 32 (1983), pp. 370–398.

the feedback process; on the other hand, they serve as judges—linking performance assessment to salary and promotion decisions. Some research on the performance appraisal process points strongly to the need to separate these roles.[4]

The inevitability of the dilemma between being both helper and evaluator means that effective managers need to understand the dynamics of the helping relationship that were presented in the preceding chapter. In addition to these skills, it's important to understand the unique aspects of the performance appraisal process, which are presented in the next section.

PERFORMANCE APPRAISAL

Too often managers see appraisals as a once-a-year event. In reality, appraisal is a process that begins long before the appraisal interview and consists of the following steps:

1. Translating organizational goals into individual job objectives or requirements.
2. Setting clear expectations for job performance and communicating both expectations and instructions clearly.
3. Providing employees with the job training or coaching that they require to meet the expectations.
4. Supplying adequate supervision and feedback throughout the year.
5. Diagnosing employees' relative weaknesses and strengths and presenting them objectively during the appraisal interview.
6. Using the appraisal interview to establish a development plan with the employee, which includes an action plan for improved performance or further education and the efficient future use of the employee's abilities.

Framing performance appraisal as a process rather than an annual interview, means that appraisal is better integrated with the rest of the organization's functions. For example, if promotions are closely tied to appraisals, managers are more likely to be held responsible for the quality of their appraisals and more likely to give them the attention they require to have an impact upon performance or morale. We know that people generally focus their energies on that which is evaluated. If leaders measure only tangibles (such as financial and output figures), the intangibles (like service orientation, ability to get along with coworkers, etc.) are given less importance. The same phenomena can be observed with performance appraisal systems. Organizations that evaluate managers on how well they develop their subordinates are more likely to give the appraisal process the attention it requires to be effective.

There are four common responses to appraisals that wise managers seek to avoid:

1. "I never knew that's what the boss expected me to do!"
2. "Why didn't they tell me before they weren't happy with my work?"
3. "I wish I had known all along that they liked my work. I wouldn't have wasted so much time worrying about it!"
4. "I got a poor review because my boss doesn't like me."

By clarifying expectations carefully, giving immediate feedback throughout the year, and demonstrating a concern for fairness, managers can avoid some of these

[4]H. H. Meyer, E. Kay, and T. R. P. French, Jr., "Split Roles in Performance Appraisal," *Harvard Business Review,* Vol. 43, no. 1 (1965), pp. 123–129.

reactions. The importance of expectations has been discussed in Chapters 1 and 4 on psychological contracts and motivation.

Providing immediate feedback has several advantages. First, it offers an opportunity to improve performance. Second, it gives employees an idea about how their supervisor sees them so that the appraisal does not come as a shock. Third, it can keep the channel of communication open between managers and employees. Often new supervisors see an employee doing something incorrectly but are not sure how to give feedback. Instead, they become more and more angry with the employee and either "dump" the feedback when they can no longer contain themselves or save it for the appraisal interview. This is sometimes referred to as "gunny-sacking." In the meantime, their relationship with the employee can suffer, and they may have rounded out the employee's character with negative attributions that are inaccurate. The feedback given during the appraisal interview, be it positive or negative, should never come as a surprise to employees.

The fairness issue with appraisals relates to the necessity for managers to know themselves and their personal tendencies. The research on similarity and attraction indicates that people prefer those who are similar to themselves.[5] To describe corporations, Moore employed the metaphor of a "bureaucratic kinship system" based upon "homosexual reproduction," in which men with the power to hire and promote, reproduce themselves.[6] It is not uncommon to look around a table of senior managers and discover that they resemble one another, either physically or socially. Thus, it is easy for managers to perceive an employee they like more positively than the person really deserves. The opposite can occur with employees that managers either dislike or perceive as different from themselves. This is what occurred in this chapter's vignette, "A Description of Rejection," in which a medical student was not judged upon her outstanding test scores and patient care, but upon her "differentness," which was apparently unacceptable.

Attribution theory maintains that we make attributions about the causes of the behavior of both others and ourselves to understand what we see occurring.[7] We guess or infer the causes of people's behavior and base our reactions to their behaviors on these inferences rather than on the way they really are or behave. A practical example of attribution theory might be the "golden boys or girls" who surface, to the puzzlement of their peers, in some organizations. While such people usually possess a certain degree of talent, they are seldom as outstanding as their superiors apparently need to believe. Attributions, like perceptions, sometimes have more to do with the observer than with the person being observed. Appraisals are yet another instance when managers have to step back and ensure that their decisions and evaluations are not overly biased, either positively or negatively, by their personal values and likes.

[5]For a fascinating description of a corporation, see Rosabeth Moss Kanter's *Men and Women of the Corporation* (New York: Basic Books, 1977).

[6]Wilbert Moore, *The Conduct of the Corporation* (New York: Random House, 1962), p. 109.

[7]J. Jaspars, F. D. Finchman, and M. Hewstone, *Attribution Theory and Research: Conceptual Developmental and Social Dimensions* (London: Academic Press, 1983).

III

Procedure for Group Meeting: Performance Appraisal Role Plays

CLASS PERFORMANCE APPRAISALS
(Time Allotted: 1 to $1\frac{1}{2}$ Hours)

This exercise provides you with an opportunity to practice the "consummate skill and delicacy" McGregor mentioned. The class should divide into four-person teams. The exercise simulates a performance appraisal interview between two team members who will take on the roles of supervisor and employee, while the other two members act as observers. Roles will be rotated so each person has a chance to perform every role. The performance to be evaluated is performance in class. Class participants prepared for the Employee role by doing the Premeeting Preparation.

STEP 1. Decide whom each person will evaluate so that everyone has an opportunity to both evaluate and be evaluated once in the four rounds of the exercise.

STEP 2. Take 10 minutes for everyone to plan the appraisal interview for the person you will evaluate. Use the following questions to help you prepare for the supervisor role.

a. What has the employee done so far that has contributed to his or her own learning and that of your learning group?

b. What has the employee contributed to the general atmosphere of the class?

c. Are there any extenuating circumstances that have affected the employee's performance in the course?

d. Is there anything you are doing that has hindered the employee's performance in the class? What could you do to help the employee improve or maintain his or her performance? Is there anything that you could suggest that might utilize the employee's talents better in the classroom or the learning group?

e. What are the employee's weaknesses and strengths so far?

f. Choose at least one strength and one weakness that you have observed in the employee's performance in class to discuss during a 5-minute interview. Base your choice on which behaviors could make a significant difference if they were to be changed. Write down how you could phrase the employee's weak point to him or her in case it's not brought out in his or her self-evaluation.

STEP 3. Read the Performance Appraisal Interview Guidelines below.[8]

STEP 4. The supervisors should conduct a 5-minute performance appraisal interview with the employee while the two observers watch and fill out the Observers' Worksheet on page 445.

STEP 5. After the interview the observers and the supervisor and employee should talk about how it went and what, if anything, could have been done differently.

STEP 6. Perform the interviews with the other three dyads, and critique them.

STEP 7. Class debriefing session:

    a. What did you learn about performance appraisal interviews from this exercise?

    b. What did you learn about yourself in this process?

    c. What did you learn about other people from this exercise?

    d. What connections can you make between this exercise and the readings?

Performance Appraisal Interview Guidelines

Prior to the interview,

1. Fix a time and date for the interview that allows the employee enough time to prepare the self-appraisal.

2. Ask the employee to prepare the self-appraisal and provide an outline for doing so.

3. Don't postpone the interview or come late to it. Employees interpret these actions as lack of interest in them and the appraisal process. To do any good, appraisals have to be taken seriously by managers.

4. Choose a private location where you will not be interrupted.

5. Set aside enough time (1 to 2 hours) so that you will have time to complete your discussion.

6. Gather all the materials and relevant information about the employee's performance. Some managers also give copies of this information to the employees.

7. Choose which parts of the employee's performance should be included in the interview. Decide how to phrase these points.

[8]This list is adapted from Patricia King's extremely helpful book, *Performance Planning and Appraisal* (New York: McGraw-Hill, 1984), pp. 73–74, 88.

During the interview,

8. Explain the format and purpose of the performance appraisal interview:
   a. To discover the employee's opinions regarding their performance, problems, motivations, and career goals.
   b. To provide your appraisal of the employee's performance.
   c. To problem solve together about performance.
   d. To plan for the next period.
9. Ask the employee to present their self-appraisal.
10. Respond to the employee's self-appraisal and convey feedback. First, tell the employee the parts of the self-appraisal with which you agree and then identify parts with which you disagree. Next, provide other feedback that would impact performance. In doing this,
   a. Support the person even when you are criticizing his or her behavior.
   b. Avoid defensiveness (on both your parts).
   c. Encourage participation.
11. Ask if there are any conditions or problems that have been hindering the employee's work.
12. Problem solve with the employee regarding what both of you could do to improve the employee's performance.
13. Together set objectives and design a plan for the next period.
14. Discuss the employee's long-term career goals and the training and experience needed to reach them.
15. Fill out the performance appraisal form *after* the interview so the employee sees that his or her input was included.

Observers'
Worksheet

1. Did the supervisor explain the purpose of the appraisal interview?

2. Did the supervisor give the employee sufficient time to present their self-appraisal?

3. Did the supervisor do a good job of presenting his or her feedback?

4. Did the supervisor use active listening, or did he or she do most of the talking?

5. Did the supervisor create a nondefensive climate and refrain from becoming defensive himself or herself?

6. Did the supervisor take a problem-solving approach, or did he or she spend too much time giving advice or orders to the employee?

7. Did the supervisor jointly set specific goals for the future with the employee?

8. Other comments:

IV

Follow-up

Doing appraisal interviews may be uncomfortable in the beginning, but it is a skill that can be mastered with practice. The opening vignette in Chapter 15 is an example of a successful performance appraisal process with a problem employee. Managers who use performance appraisals well can utilize their human resources more fully. It is a mechanism for increasing the communication and dialogue so essential to effectiveness.

V

Learning Points

1. Performance appraisals are used to improve performance and motivate employees.

2. Feedback serves the following functions for employees:
   a. Helps to form their self-concept.
   b. Reduces uncertainty about whether their behavior is on track.
   c. Signals which organizational goals are most important.
   d. Helps them to master their environment and feel competent.

3. The attitude managers bring to performance appraisal determines the effectiveness of that appraisal. Managers who are sincerely trying to develop their employees and provide them with objective feedback are more successful than are those who take a judgmental approach.

4. Performance appraisal requires that the managers take on the role of helper-consultant.

5. The "ideal" performance appraisal system is designed to achieve four basic objectives:
   a. Provide feedback to employees to facilitate their ability to achieve organizational and personal goals.
   b. Provide management with data to make salary and promotional decisions.
   c. Identify areas for improvement to facilitate employee career development.
   d. Motivate employees to be more effective workers.

6. Performance appraisal is a process that begins with translating organizational goals into clear expectations for each individual, training people to do their jobs, providing effective supervision, determining strengths and weaknesses, and developing plans for the employee. It is not a once-a-year event but an ongoing activity.

7. Providing immediate feedback gives the employee an opportunity to improve, ensures that the appraisal is not a surprise, and keeps the employee-manager channel of communication open. Saving up negative feedback and "dumping" can cause a defensive reaction.

8. Fairness is always a matter of concern with appraisals. People tend to rate those who are similar to themselves more highly than those who are different.

9. Attributions or inferences about why people behave the way they do can also bias the appraisal process.

VI

Tips for Managers

- A major purpose of an appraisal interview is to provide the interviewees with data that will allow them the opportunity to change their behavior if they so desire. You cannot make them change their behavior, but you can outline the likely consequences of their behavior in an objective fashion.

- The appraisal interview can be an occasion for great anxiety for some individuals. This means that their ability to take in information may be impaired, so verbal or written summaries of what has been said are useful. People with low self-concepts may hear only the negative feedback, while others will hear only positives and completely miss the changes you would like to see made.

- Being evaluated evokes authority issues for many individuals and results in defensive communication. Taking care to posture yourself more as a counselor than a judge and creating a nondefensive climate by the way you communicate are two ways to decrease defensiveness.[9]

- When people succeed, they are likely to attribute their success to the internal qualities they possess (e.g., tenacity, intelligence). When they fail, some are likely to blame external conditions (e.g., their boss, the company's policies). Assigning blame is not as important as is trying to figure out ways to improve in the future.

- Managers are sometimes guilty of keeping their employees from performing well. For that reason, this issue should be addressed by managers. Employees are less likely to bring this subject up, though it may well be on the tip of their tongue. Sessions involving mutual feedback are usually more effective than one-way feedback. If you give feedback, you should expect to receive it.

- No matter how objective managers try to be, there is always a possibility of bias or misperception. Incorrect evaluations are very demotivating. There are two ways to avoid making incorrect evaluations. One is to collect good data and even check out your perceptions with other colleagues. The second way is to allow the employee the opportunity to present their self-evaluation first and carefully consider the employee's viewpoint. This does not mean that managers should back down from their statements if an employee disagrees. There are times when people cannot agree because of perceptual processes or ego defenses. The message here is to beware of possible biases or lack of information and collect enough data so you are well prepared.

- When employees have an opportunity to present their self-evaluations and explain contingencies that have affected their performance, they are more likely to see the appraisal as valid. For this reason effective managers ask the employee to prepare a self-evaluation before coming to the interview and either wait until after the interview to prepare their own review or prepare only a draft that can be modified on the basis of information received during the interview.

- Some managers focus more on what employees do wrong than on what they do right. If you think you have this tendency, force yourself to sit down and

[9]See Chapter 6, on Interpersonal Communication, and Jack R. Gibb's article, "Defensive Communication," *Readings.*

compile a list of the positive contributions made by employees and/or seek a different perspective from someone else in the organization who picks up on positives.

■ When employees set specific, rather than general, goals for the future, their performance is more likely to improve.

VII

Personal Application Assignment

This assignment is to write about a performance appraisal experience that you want to explore further. (You may wish to write about the classroom experience of giving or receiving a performance appraisal.)

A. *Concrete Experience*
   1. *Objectively* describe the experience ("who," "what," "when," "where," "how" type information—up to 2 points).
   2. *Subjectively* describe your feelings, perceptions, and thoughts that occurred *during* (not after) the experience (up to 2 points). Does this section have too much detail? (If so, delete 1 point.)

B. *Reflective Observation*
   1. Look at the experience from different points of view. How many points of view did you include that are *relevant* (up to 2 points)?
   2. Use these perspectives to add more meaning to the incident (up to 2 points).

C. *Abstract Conceptualization*

1. Relate concepts from the assigned readings and the lecture to the experience (i.e., what theories that you heard in the lecture or read in the *Reader* relate to your understanding of this incident?). Make reference to at least two sources. Use standard referencing format and include the page number to which you are referring. How many sources did you use and how clearly did you explain their theories (up to 4 points)?

2. You can also create an original model or theory, but it should not replace course concepts.

D. *Active Experimentation*

1. Write about what you will do in the future that will improve your effectiveness. Use rules of thumb or action resolutions.

2. Are they described specifically, thoroughly, and in detail (up to 4 points).

E. *Integration, Synthesis, and Writing*

1. Did you write about something personally important to you (up to 1 point)?
2. Was it well written (up to 2 points)?
3. Did you integrate and synthesize the different sections (up to 1 point)?

17

ORGANIZATIONAL ANALYSIS: THE ORGANIZATION AS AN OPEN SYSTEM

OBJECTIVES By the end of this chapter, you should be able to:

A. Explore the implications of the open systems view of organizations.

B. Identify and analyze your own personal theory of organizational functioning.

C. Explore relationships between theories of organization and managerial action.

Organizational Analysis: Matsushita and the 7-S's[1]

R. T. Pascale and A. G. Athos

Matsushita is one of the 50 largest corporations in the world and one of the major players in the electrical appliance industries. Back in 1918, its founder, Konosuke Matsushita, was an apprentice in a bicycle shop when he was inspired by Thomas Edison's discoveries to gamble on the electrical industry.

When forming his business, Matsushita devised the following unique *strategy*. First, in contrast to prevailing Japanese norms, he created his own distribution system and dealt directly with retailers. Later he introduced the use of point-of-purchase displays and installment sales. Next Matsushita's management focused upon building market share, passing on the cost savings generated from high production volume to consumers in the form of lower prices. To this day, Matsushita does not introduce new products; rather, it concentrates on improving the quality and price of imitations. Four percent of its sales revenues are invested in twenty-three R&D labs that analyze and improve upon competing products. The assumption behind Matsushita's strategy is that profits are tied to growth. In fact, the success of the company has affirmed Konosuke Matsushita's belief that investments that promote growth eventually pay off in long-term profits.

In addition to Matsushita's winning strategies, the innovative *structure* of the organization has also contributed to its success. In Japan, Matsushita introduced decentralization as a way to keep his company entrepreneurial. He wanted each product to be independent so (1) progress could be clearly measured, (2) managers would be self-sufficient and close to consumers, (3) small divisions could maintain their flexibility, and (4) employees would gain the seasoning and training for the general manager positions the company would later need. This type of structure helps the company's various operations to implement their own independent strategies.

However, Matsushita also foresaw the dangers of decentralization—(1) decreased control, (2) less interdivisional cooperation, and (3) reduced perspective and strength to cope with major threats to a whole product group—and, hence, centralized four key functions: accounting, a company "bank" for divisional

---

[1]The 7S's, a framework for analyzing organizations, are strategy, structure, systems, staff, style, skills, and shared values. In their ground-breaking book, *The Art of Japanese Management*, Athos and Pascale accused U.S. companies of devoting less time than the Japanese to the four "soft" S's—style, skill, staff, and shared values. They maintain that, to succeed, companies must focus on all seven areas and that these areas must complement each other. Athos and Pascale used Matsushita of Japan as an example of a company that did just that.

Adapted from *The Art of Japanese Management: Applications for American Executives* (New York: Simon & Schuster, 1981), pp. 28–57.

profits, personnel, and training. His concern with personnel and training stemmed from his belief that people are the key resource of the company.

One of the *systems* Matsushita put into place to accomplish his goals is the planning system. The planning system is composed of three steps: a five-year plan, a two-year plan, and the highly important six-month operating plans. The six-month plans are highly detailed and comprehensive; they are reviewed on a monthly basis, and each variance from the plan must be explained. While an entrepreneurial atmosphere is carefully cherished in the company, it is balanced by the rigor of the planning process. Performance is measured by the success of the six-month operating plans and rewards are distributed accordingly. "Putting their money where their mouth is" by tying the performance and reward systems with the planning process reinforces the importance of planning and reaching objectives.

Matsushita's *style* has also played a major role in his success. Matsushita believes in "developing extraordinary qualities in ordinary men." He and his second-in-command, Takahashi, have a strong "hands-on" approach. Matsushita talks with division managers daily and stresses that they need to spend time on the factory floor and with customers. Managers are expected to take initiative and isolate problems at the level where they occur and fix them. The company's management style is characterized as tough-minded, pragmatic, and energetic. Matsushita and Takahashi are both very direct and encourage healthy competition and conflict. However, conflict is seldom interpersonal. Instead, facts are presented and "reason" is allowed to speak for itself. Disagreements and decisions have "acceptance time" built in—so people have time to accustom themselves to thinking about a situation in a different way.

The following quotations from Matsushita reveals part of his managerial style: "When I meet with my managers, it is seldom formal. We communicate knee to knee. A crucial element is their independence, so, however pointed my question and direct the implication, I refrain from giving orders. We must respect the pride of different individuals and honor the traditions of their companies." We can see how this type of style would complement the entrepreneurial strategy and structure of the company.

The *shared values* of Matsushita are extremely important. Each employee receives training in these values, which are clearly articulated:

BASIC BUSINESS PRINCIPLES

- To recognize our responsibilities as industrialists.
- To foster progress.
- To promote the general welfare of society.
- To devote ourselves to the further development of world culture.

EMPLOYEE'S CREED

Progress and development can be realized only through the combined efforts and cooperation of each member of our Company. Each of us, therefore, shall keep this idea constantly in mind as we devote ourselves to the continuous improvement of our Company.

THE SEVEN SPIRITUAL VALUES

1. National service through industry
2. Fairness
3. Harmony and cooperation
4. Struggle for betterment
5. Courtesy and humility

6. Adjustment and assimilation
7. Gratitude

The company has a very strong shared belief system, which is another way of managing over 200,000 people successfully.

Matsushita has always believed that an enterprise is no better than the people in it. This has resulted in some extraordinary *staffing* policies. Like many Japanese companies, Matsushita devotes great time and attention to training. All professionals start out by spending six months selling or working in a retail outlet. They also spend time working on an assembly line. The seven spiritual values are part of the training program. The message is conveyed that what counts at Matsushita is "knowing the customer and getting marketable products to the point of sale at minimum cost." All promotions are accompanied by new training in the Matsushita philosophy and "refresher course" experiences in retail outlets and production.

In addition to their training efforts, Matsushita has other staffing policies that reinforce what management is trying to accomplish in other areas. For example, 5 percent of the employees are rotated to different divisions to promote the integration made necessary by a decentralized structure. Lifelong employment is another way to maintain the continuity of shared values. The company actively solicits employee suggestions and rewards them with money. However, employee suggestions are also quantified and used as a measure of division morale. This approach to suggestions also encourages the initiative and problem solving that is a hallmark of the Matsushita style.

The final component of the 7S framework to be discussed is *skills*. Matsushita himself is a highly skilled manager. In fact, many observers see him as one of the greatest managers of the century. His ability in the areas of innovation, efficiency, and managing people are exceptional. Over the years, he has played a variety of roles dictated by circumstances—sometimes heavily involved, other times standing back to allow others to develop. As a result, others in the company have developed some of the same skills Matsushita possesses. Furthermore, Matsushita has had the wisdom and skill to design an organization in which all aspects are constantly reinforcing the others. The result of this is a strong and dynamic company capable of both growth and environmental adaptation.

I
Premeeting Preparation

(Time Allotted: 1–1$\frac{1}{2}$ Hours)

A. Form subgroups. Since this exercise involves building and comparing personal theories about how organizations function, it is useful if group members build their theories in reference to the same organization or type of organization. Prior to the group meeting for this unit we therefore recommend that the total group divides into subgroups of about four to six persons who share a common interest in building their theory about a particular organization (e.g., Acme Products, the City Hospital, the fraternity) or a particular type of group, but a common reference point will make it easier within each subgroup to examine different individual ways of seeing the organization as a system during the class session. In addition, comparison among the subgroups will allow examination of how different types of organizations operate.

B. Read the Topic Introduction.

C. Complete the Premeeting Preparation Assignment described on pages 461–63.

D. What are the significant learning points from the readings?

Note: An alternate approach that in some cases is more productive is for the whole group to focus on a single organization that they have in common (e.g., the university they are attending or the company for which they work). In this case, the four- to six-person groups can be formed on any basis the group desires.

II

Topic Introduction

Today's business managers are confronted with ever-increasing complexity. They participate in a global economy characterized by high degrees of uncertainty and tough competition. They operate in a physical environment in which pollution has become an international issue. They are confronted with technological change that occurs at a rapid, if not furious, pace, which necessitates major retooling of equipment, reeducation of employees, and dramatic changes in ways of doing business.

Mergers and acquisitions have caused great upheaval in the lives of both companies and employees. In the past, businesses did not have to devote as much time and money fending off takeover attempts. While some of the merger mania may be responsible for more efficient companies, employees have paid a high price. Buffeted by change and uncertainty, they find themselves threatened by either termination or wary membership in companies quite different from the one they joined. One of the hidden costs of downscaling and merger mania has been decreased organizational loyalty.

Within organizations managers are confronted with a bifurcated work force—on the one hand, highly sophisticated and well-educated individualists who demand participation and opportunity, but don't necessarily expect to pay for it with loyalty, and, on the other hand, an unskilled segment so poorly prepared and educated that remedial education must be provided before the workers can perform their tasks. Traditional career paths have been disrupted with the phasing out of middle management positions in an effort to achieve lean and mean organizational charts and with the influx of baby boomers competing for fewer senior management positions.

All these factors add up to greater complexity for managers. The juggling act that managers have always performed is complicated further by the addition of complications from outside the firm. No longer can the manager, or even the salesperson, focus primarily on what occurs within their organization. Many of our theories about organizations were developed in simpler times when people had a greater internal focus. The classical theories of management, as we saw in Chapter 2, addressed the problem of how to organize clearly and efficiently without consideration of environmental problems. Compared with today's world, the environment in the early part of the century was relatively benign and free of problems. Nowadays an outward focus is essential to survival. Indeed, some say that organizations should not even be conceived as discrete entities with finite boundaries. The theory that first acknowledged the influence of outside factors upon the primary mission of the organization is *open systems theory,* which is described in the next section.

ORGANIZATIONS AS OPEN SYSTEMS

This dramatic increase in the interdependency of organizations with their environment has increased the need for organization and management theories that describe how organizations adapt and survive in their environment. Perhaps the most promising theoretical approach to date comes from general systems theory. This approach, which began in biology, has identified common organizational characteristics in all living systems—from the single cell to society. From this perspective, the central characteristic of living systems at all levels is that they are open to their environment—they take in matter/energy and information from the environment, transform it in some systematic way, and return it to the environment by means of information or matter/energy output. In a factory the raw materials and human labor are the input, the patterned activities of production are the transformation of matter/energy, and the finished product is the output. Maintaining the system requires continued inputs, which in social systems depend in turn on the product or output. Thus, in a successful system the outputs furnish new matter/energy for the initiation of a new cycle. The auto manufacturer sells the firm's products and by so doing obtains the means of securing new raw materials, compensating the labor force, and refining production technology, thereby assuring the continuation and growth of the organization. In addition, systems require an information return in the form of negative feedback, which allows the system to correct deviations from its goals. For the manufacturer this information takes the form of sales figures, return of poor-quality products, return on investment, and so on.

With this overview of open systems theory, let us now examine the basic components of an open system (see Figure 17–1).

1. *Definition of system.* First, we must understand what is meant by the concept "system." Basically, a system is a set of units or elements actively interrelated and operating in a regular fashion as a total entity. The importance of this definition is that it focuses on processes of relationship and interdependence among structural components rather than on their constant attributes.

2. *Closed versus open systems.* Theoretically, a closed system has totally impermeable boundaries and receives no matter/energy or information from the environment and exports no matter/energy or information to the environment. No such systems exist in nature. Thus, systems are only relatively open or closed, depending on the extent of a continuing flow of matter/energy and information between the system and the environment.

3. *Inputs.* Inputs in organizational systems are matter/energy in the form of raw materials, human labor, power, and so on and information in the form of data about the environment, knowledge of production techniques, and so on. Organizational systems have input subsystems to cope with the input process (e.g., personnel departments to hire and train workers, supply departments for production materials, and market research groups for analyzing market data).

4. *Creative transformation.* Through work processes of various kinds, inputs are transformed into outputs by means of transformation subsystems—energy is transformed, products are created and produced, information is analyzed,

FIGURE 17–1   Components of an Open System

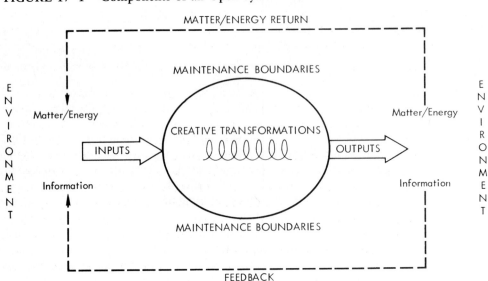

people are trained, services are organized. The basic tendency in systems is for these transformation subsystems (as well as input and output subsystems) to become more differentiated and specialized, requiring successively higher levels of integration and coordination to hold the system together.

5. *Outputs.* System outputs include products, knowledge, or services useful to the system's survival and waste. In organizations, these outputs are managed by output subsystems, such as sales or pollution control.

6. *Maintenance boundaries.* Systems develop maintenance boundaries to control input and output processes and define the system's identity. In some cases, these boundaries are physical, such as a fence around a plant to keep out unauthorized personnel or to prevent pilferage. Boundaries are also symbolic, as in the case of bookkeeping systems for transferring money into and out of the organization. More intangible are cultural and psychological boundaries, such as norms for membership and inclusion in the system. Systems vary in how permeable their boundaries are—on how open or closed they are. Prisons, for example, are relatively closed organizational systems physically, symbolically, and culturally, whereas a community organization such as the YMCA is more open.

7. *Matter/energy returns.* According to the second law of thermodynamics, all systems have a tendency toward entropy or maximum disorganization and disorder. Thus, to survive, systems must achieve a steady state by taking in inputs of higher complexity than their outputs. In this way, the system acquires energy for the transformation process, for internal repair, and for reserves to ensure a comfortable survival margin. For example, an organization buys coal, transforms it to ashes, and uses the energy released to produce products that are sold, thus providing resources for the acquisition of other resources the system needs and profits for the organization.

8. *Feedback.* To control its activities and maintain a steady state, a system needs feedback from its environment to alert it to deviations from its course (called *negative feedback*). A thermostat controlling room temperature is a simple example of this negative feedback process. In complex organizations and environments, identifying and analyzing the information needed to control systems processes is much more multifaceted and complex. Without adequate negative feedback controls, no system will survive.

9. *The environment.* In general systems theory the environment of a system includes the suprasystem or systems of which it is a part. The body is the suprasystem of the heart, defining relationships among the heart and other organs. Organizational suprasystems include the community and the wider society of which it is a part. These suprasystems define the organization's physical, economic, political, and social relationships with other subsystems of the society.

| The Relationship Between Theories of Organization and Managerial Action | The open systems view of organizations is not so much a theory as it is a perspective or a vantage point from which one can build a theory of how particular organizations function. Since general systems theory is of necessity formulated at a high level of abstraction to encompass living systems at all levels from single cells to society, it needs to be translated to a more concrete level to be useful for a particular manager in a particular organization. The value of the open systems approach is that its perspective rises above that of a particular job or function to encompass a systematic framework for interrelating specific components of an organization. That is, it can help managers to rise above priorities and prejudices of their jobs and departments and to see how their work fits into the total picture of the organization's adaptation to the environment. |

All managers have a personal theory of organizations that they use to make sense of their organizational lives. For some it is very explicit and systematic; for others it is more implicit or "intuitive." No theory is absolutely more correct or better than any other theory. The value of a theory depends on the user's style and what the theory is used for. Theories are guides to perception and action. It is important, therefore, that we understand our personal theories and how they influence our behavior. Many people, for example, do not realize how situation-specific their theories are. When they enter a new situation, they apply their old theory and are chagrined to find out that something is wrong. The more firmly entrenched their theory is, the more likely they are to blame others for their failure ("They just don't accept my leadership") rather than to modify their theory.

Just as our perceptions of other individuals are subject to a series of potential biases or limiting filters, our theory of organization is subject to a similar set of potential distortions. The basic dilemma is that we all must have a theory to organize our experience and action. In the absence of some theory, however narrow or implicit, the world becomes a jumble of chaotic possibilities. Kuhn points out with respect to the scientific theories:

> In the absence of a paradigm (theory) or some candidate for a paradigm, all the facts that could possibly pertain to the development of a given science are likely to seem equally relevant. As a result, early fact gathering is a far more nearly random activity than the one that subsequent scientific development makes familiar.[2]

As soon as a theory becomes formalized and accepted, however, the other horn of the dilemma begins to operate. Facts that are outside the boundary of the theory are either not examined at all or are examined with a biased eye. The basic theory, in other words, becomes very resistant to change.

Argyris and Schön describe this phenomenon as the "self-sealing" nature of most theories.[3] In part to reduce uncertainty and anxiety, our personal theories are often designed to create a self-fulfilling prophecy. They are untestable. We need, therefore, to build into our theories what Argyris and Schön call a "double-loop learning" capacity. We need to act and at the same time test the appropriateness of our actions to revise our personal theories when experience dictates a need for such revision.

This is by no means an easy task. In the upcoming class session you will have an opportunity to sharpen your understanding of your own personal theory of organizational functioning. By sharing and discussing your view with others, you can gain a better grasp of the assumptions and values on which it is based.

The exercise that follows is designed to help you build your own personal theory of organizational functioning by translating the abstract concepts of systems thinking into the particular case of your own experience in organizations. It is designed to help you systematically review your thinking about your organizational experience and to explore the action implications of your theory.

[2]T. S. Kuhn, *The Structure of Scientific Revolutions* (Chicago: University of Chicago Press, 1970), p. 15.

[3]C. Argyris and D. Schön, *Theory in Practice: Increasing Professional Effectiveness* (San Francisco: Jossey-Bass, 1974), and C. Argyris, "Double Loop Learning in Organizations," *Harvard Business Review* (September–October 1977), *Readings.*

Premeeting Preparation Assignment

Your task before the class meeting is to analyze the organization or type of organization that your subgroup decided to focus on in step A of the premeeting preparation. The forms provided in this assignment will help you to construct your own personal theory or model of how the organization you chose functions. A personal organizational theory or model is simply a representation or picture of the components of an organization and how they function together. This "picture" can be crude and simple or very detailed and complex. It can be accurate or inaccurate. The purpose of the exercise in this unit is to help you refine and increase the accuracy of your organizational model by systematically analyzing the organization using the general framework provided by open systems theory and by sharing your analysis with others to broaden your view and correct misperceptions you may have about the organization or type of organization in question.[4]

The preparation assignment has three main parts: (1) defining the boundaries of the organization you are examining, (2) analyzing the organization's environment, and (3) analyzing the organization's internal functioning.

PART I: DEFINING THE BOUNDARIES OF THE ORGANIZATION

The first step in creating your organizational theory is to focus sharply on the organizational entity you want your theory to describe. For many individuals, this represents the single organization in which they are currently working and living. For some, their focus is on the immediate locale or departmental environment. For others, the focus includes a broad network of organizations. The important task here is to define just what portion of your organizational experience you want your theory to explain. It may be useful to pick an organization of moderate size to avoid making the analysis too complex and time consuming. (You may want to create this description with other members of the subgroup you formed in step A of the premeeting preparation.)

Complete the following:

The organization my theory seeks to explain includes:

_____

_____

_____

_____

What is the organization's mission (its primary function or long-term goal)?

_____

_____

_____

_____

---

[4]*Organizational Behavior: Practical Readings for Managers*, D. A. Kolb, I. M. Rubin, and J. S. Osland, contains two articles that discuss the use of open systems theory for describing organizations. You may want to read these articles before building your model. The articles are Clark and Krone, "Toward an Overall View of Organization Development in the Seventies," and D. Nadler and M. Tushman, "A Congruence Model for Diagnosing Organizational Behavior."

Is the organization a part of a larger system? (For example, a company may be owned by a larger corporation, or a state university will be a part of state government and the looser system of higher education in the United States.) List the larger system or systems of which your organization is a part:

_____

_____

_____

_____

PART II: ANALYZING THE ORGANIZATION'S ENVIRONMENT

This step involves identifying the environmental entities that interact with the organization and are critical to its survival. These entities can be organized groups or organizations (e.g., unions), clusters of people (e.g., customers or the labor market), individuals; bodies of knowledge (e.g., the body of research on chemistry), governments, or even more abstract entities (e.g., changing values of young people). These entities can be loosely grouped into three types: those that provide *inputs* to the organization (e.g., suppliers), those that consume *outputs* from the organization (e.g., customers), and those that *maintain* the boundaries of the organization by defining what it can and cannot do (e.g., regulatory agencies). These are somewhat arbitrary categories, however, since the organization will engage in transactions with each of the entities critical to its survival that involve both *giving* something and *getting* something in return. For example, a manufacturer will give money to get coal from a supplier (input) and get money from customers for giving them its products (output). The form on page 464 provides space for you to list the significant entities that you see transacting with your organization. After listing each significant entity, specify in the space provided the nature of the transaction the organization makes with that entity—what the organization gives and what it gets in return.

PART III: ANALYZING THE ORGANIZATION'S INTERNAL FUNCTIONING

In this portion of the analysis of your organization you will be building a model of how the organization functions internally to transform inputs into outputs and maintain its boundaries. The forms provided will assist you in examining three aspects of internal organizational functioning.

1. The way in which the organization is *differentiated*—that is, how the organization divides itself into specialized subgroups to accomplish its major tasks.
2. The way in which the organization is *integrated*—that is, how the organization draws together and coordinates the work of various specialized subgroups.
3. The important *creative transformations* that the organization must perform to survive and be effective—that is, the tasks and processes that the organization must manage and control to cope with its environment and achieve its mission.

Organizational Differentiation

The form on page 465 provides space to list the major formal and informal groups in the organization. Formal groups are often easy to identify because they appear on organizational charts and are often clearly defined by physical location, task, and so on. As anyone who has looked at an organization knows, formal groups can often be identified at several levels of detail (e.g., division, department, section, work group, etc.). For this analysis, it is best to use major groupings without going into subsections of those groups.

Informal groups are more difficult to identify and require a more intimate knowledge of the organization you are analyzing. Nonetheless, in many organizations informal groups such as a black caucus, a regular luncheon meeting of key executives, or a group of friends often perform significant functions for the organization.

When you have completed your list of major groups, list each group's major task or tasks and the major environmental entities that the group transacts with (if any).

Organizational Integration

The next step is to analyze how the work of these different groups gets coordinated to make the organization function smoothly as a unit. The form on page 466 is designed to assist you in this analysis. In the circles provided, put the name of the major formal and informal groups you identified in the differentiation analysis. Then draw lines connecting groups that coordinate their activities with one another. Write on the line *how* that coordination takes place. For example, if marketing and sales coordinate their work via the formal hierarchy with a common supervisor, you might write on the line connecting marketing and sales "common boss." On the other hand, marketing might coordinate with research via task forces, committees, or informal liaison; some groups may not coordinate with others at all.

Key Creative Transformations

The last task in building your model is to identify the key processes that the organization must manage to survive and be effective. To do this you will need to examine the model you have created thus far and examine your own experience with the organization to identify those aspects of the organization's operation that are central to its operation—either because they are necessary for its survival or because they are problematical for the organization at this time. To assist in this examination, we have listed on pages 467–68 a variety of factors that can be important to an organization's functioning. On these pages circle those issues that are critical management issues for your organization, and briefly note in each circled box why it is critical. For example, in a rapidly growing organization *size* may be a critical issue to manage. You would circle that box and write "to manage rapid growth." If you identify key management issues not listed on these pages, relabel an unused box, circle it, and note why it is critical.

Components of the Organization's Environment

SIGNIFICANT GROUPS OR ENTITIES	Nature of Transactions	
	WHAT THE ORGANIZATION *GIVES*	WHAT THE ORGANIZATION *GETS*
Input Entities		
Output Entities		
Maintenance Entities		

Analysis of Organizational Differentiation

MAJOR ORGANIZATIONAL GROUPS	PRIMARY TASK(S)	ENVIRONMENTAL RELATIONSHIP(S)
Formal 1		
2		
3		
4		
5		
6		
7		
8		
9		
10		
Informal 11		
12		
13		
14		
15		
16		

Analysis of Organizational Integration

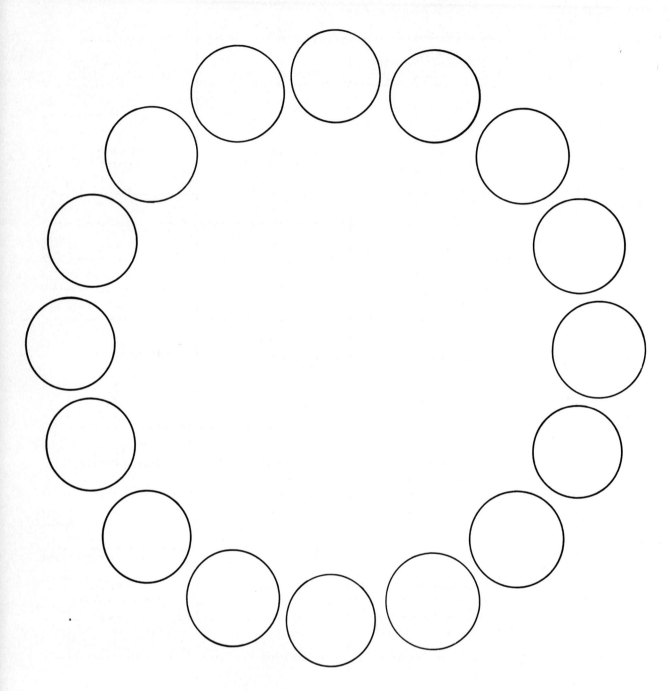

1 Architectural/ Physical Facilities	2 Capital	3 Career development
4 Cliques and Interest Groups	5 Community Relationships	6 Compensation/ Benefits
7 Conflict	8 Control Process	9 Costs
10 Culture/Shared Values/Beliefs	11 Decision-Making Methods	12 Efficiency, Waste
13 Formal Authority Structure	14 Formal Information System	15 Formal Reward System
16 Government Relationships	17 Influence Styles	18 Informal Communication
19 Informal Rewards	20 Strategy	21 Interpersonal Relationships
22 Job/Role Definitions	23 Job Satisfaction of Employees	24 Management Style

25 Market Relationships	26 Morale/Employee Attitudes	27 Motivation
28 Systems	29 Organization Climate/Norms	30 Performance Appraisal
31 Employee Skills	32 Planning Process	33 Policy and Procedures
34 Problem/ Opportunity Identification Process	35 Problem Solution Process	36 Profits
37 Return on Investment	38 Scheduling	39 Selection Procedures
40 System Goals	41 Team Functioning	42 Technology
43 Time Demands	44 Training/ Education	45 Turnover/ Absenteeism
46 Unions/Worker Organizations	47 Work Flow	48 Size

III

Procedure for Group Meeting: Building Theories of Organization

STEP 1.   Subgroups meet to compare and refine individual models. (30 minutes) The groups formed in step A of the premeeting preparation should meet together to share the models they created in the prework assignments. Each person in turn should share his or her model with the others and solicit their reactions. The group may want to pool the individual models to form a consensus model of how their common organization or type of organization functions. This will facilitate discussion and evaluation of the organization's health and effectiveness in step 2.

STEP 2.   Each subgroup joins with another subgroup to compare models and evaluate the organization's health and effectiveness. (1 hour, 15 minutes) Before beginning, everyone should read the Follow-up with special emphasis on the ten criteria for organizational health and effectiveness described at the end of the Follow-up. There are two tasks for the combined subgroups. First, they should briefly describe to one another the models they have built for their respective organizations. And, in this sharing process, they should explore how their organizations are different and what seems to account for these differences (different mission, environments, technologies, for example).

STEP 3.   Use your analysis to evaluate the health and effectiveness of the organizations using the ten criteria outlined in the Follow-up. Your first clue about an organization's health and effectiveness may well come from how difficult *you* found it to build the organizational models. Some organizations have clear missions and clear structures with key management issues well defined. Others seem disorganized and confusing; that is, the organization itself lacks a clear model of how it functions or should function to be maximally effective. The group should examine each criterion in turn rating their organizations on how well it meets these criteria. For example in criterion 1, does the organization recognize and deal effectively with the important entities in its environment or does it have a more closed view focusing only on customers or financial returns?

DEBRIEFING QUESTIONS

1. What personal values seem to underlie your own personal theory of organizations, for example, "Organizations should/should not . . . ".

2. What implicit assumptions, if any, are you making about human nature? About human motivation? About the purpose of your organization?

3. In the field of human behavior in organizations there are a series of what we might call continuing dilemmas, such as

   a. The relationship between "a people orientation" versus "a productivity/task orientation."

   b. Organization profit versus social responsibility.

   c. Individual goals/needs versus organizational goals/needs. What dilemmas seem inherent in your own personal theory? What is your own personal position around these dilemmas?

4. How generalizable is your theory? Does it apply only to your organization? Or is it useful in understanding other organizations as well?

5. Does your managerial action flow directly from your theory as described here? Or is your "theory in action" different than this expressed theory?

6. Is your theory "self-sealing"? Do you have feedback that would allow "double-loop learning"?

7. Given your theory, what would you be likely to overlook? Where might you be biased?

8. What connections can you make between this exercise and the readings?

IV

Follow-up

ORGANIZATIONAL HEALTH AND OPEN SYSTEMS APPROACH TO ORGANIZATIONS

It is increasingly clear that there is no longer "one best way" to organize and manage. The appropriate organization structure and management depends on the demands of the organization's environment, the tasks it must accomplish, and the people who are its members. Modern organizations must, in other words, be viewed as open systems. In this view, organization effectiveness is governed by three major factors: the individuals who make up the organization, the organization itself, and the environment in which the organization exists. Effective management of the interfaces between these factors—between the individual and the organization and between the organization and its environment—is central to organizational success. Figure 17–2 illustrates this model of organizations.

A. The major input resources to an organization are its human resources. People bring to their jobs a diversity of skills, needs, goals, and expectations. They are socialized into the organization through its personnel recruitment, hiring procedures, and job experiences.

B. The interface between the individual and the organization is critical to the full utilization of human resources. The individual and the organization establish a "psychological contract." The individual member expects to make certain

FIGURE 17–2 The Open System View of Organizations

INDIVIDUALS	I/O INTERFACE	ORGANIZATION	O/E INTERFACE	ENVIRONMENT
Skills Goals Motives Expectations Perceptions	Psychological contract Socialization Culture Motivation Job design Appraisal/reward Leadership Supervision Employee development	Division of work among individuals and groups Coordination and integration of work done by individuals and groups	Problem-solving process Goals Strategic plans Feedback	Demands from relevant parts of environment such as: Government Customers Suppliers Special interest groups Labor market
	GROUP MEMBERSHIP	**G/O INTERFACE**		
	Group dynamics	Decision making Communication Power and influence Conflict management Management of diversity Problem solving		

contributions to the organization and to receive certain rewards in return. The organization expects to provide certain rewards to the individual in return for certain contributions. It is at this interface between the individual and the organization that issues such as leadership, organizational climate, job motivation, job design, and the appraisal-reward process become important.

C. The organization itself provides the major transformation or throughput function. Individual and group tasks are identified and assigned according to the demands of the organization's technology; this leads to division of labor or specialization. However, specialization creates an equally important requirement to integrate the work of individuals and the various groups in which they work. It is here that such variables as job clarity, delegation of work and responsibility, decision making, communications, and conflict management become important.

D. An organization exists to act upon the environment, to have certain transactions with the environment. The desired nature or effect of these transactions defines the mission and goals of the organization. Feedback from the environment is required to determine the quality of these transactions, or how effectively the organization is performing its mission. This critical interface between the organization and its environment is defined by the problem-solving process that determines the organization's goals and strategic plans and the feedback procedures that the organization uses to measure its impact on the environment.

E. The environment impacts on the organization in many ways. For example, within many organizations today, governmental agencies are demanding changes in employment practices. This demand clearly has an influence on the individuals who are brought into the organization (A), on the way in which individuals respond to leadership and climate (B), and on the appropriate form of organization (C). Special interest groups (e.g., environmental protectionists) can and do have an impact on organizational goals (E) and the human resources available to the organization (A).

ORGANIZATIONAL HEALTH AND EFFECTIVENESS

The open systems model helps to describe an *effective* organization. An effective organization is one that is able to accomplish the following. It attracts skilled and motivated individuals (A) and manages them in such a way as to increase their skills and motivation (B). It separates tasks and allocates them to appropriate individuals and groups (C) without producing gaps and overlaps (i.e., the authority structure produces clear assignment of authority and responsibility). It develops effective formal and informal work units (C). It effectively coordinates the work of different individuals and groups (C). It has an effective problem-solving procedure for setting and reviewing goals and plans (D). It has clearly defined and well-communicated goals and plans that reflect the organization's basic mission and that are based on a careful analysis of the demands of relevant parts of the environment (E), and it obtains and uses feedback from the environment to evaluate effectiveness (D). More specifically, the following characteristics of organizational health or effectiveness can be identified.[5] These dimensions are much like the "vital signs" (e.g., temperature, pulse rate, blood pressure) that a physician would diagnose. Their main value is that they can signal a potential problem somewhere in the system, although they do not, in and of themselves, represent a complete diagnosis of specific organization problems.

1. The organization and its parts see themselves as interacting with each other *and* with a *larger* environment. The organization is an "open system."

[5]Adapted from Richard Beckhard, *Organization Development: Strategies and Models* (Reading, MA: Addison-Wesley, 1969), pp. 10–11.

2. The total organization, the significant subparts, and individuals manage their work against *goals* and *plans* for achievement of these goals.

3. Form follows function (the problem, or task, or project determines how the human resources are organized).

4. Decisions are made by and near the sources of information regardless of where these sources are located on the organization chart.

5. There are minimum inappropriate win-lose activities between individuals and groups. Constant effort exists at all levels to treat conflict and conflict situations as *problems* subject to problem-solving methods.

6. There is a shared value, and management strategy to support it, of trying to help each person (or unit) in the organization maintain his or her integrity and uniqueness in an interdependent environment.

7. Communication laterally and vertically is *relatively* undistorted. People are generally open and confronting. They share all the relevant facts, including feelings.

8. There is high "conflict" (clash of ideas) about tasks and projects, and relatively little energy is spent in clashing over *interpersonal* difficulties, because they have been generally worked through.

9. The reward system is such that managers and supervisors are rewarded (and punished) comparably for all of the following:

   a. Short-term profit or production performance

   b. Growth and development of their subordinates

   c. Creating a viable working group

10. The organization and its members operate in an "action-research" way. General practice is to build in *feedback mechanisms* so that individuals and groups can learn from their own experience.

THE 7S FRAMEWORK

The 7S framework described in the chapter opening vignette is another popular model for analyzing organizations. It emphasizes the importance of "fit" among the internal components of an organization. However, the strategy component must still be in line with the external environment. Table 17–1 portrays the seven S's and

TABLE 17–1   The Seven S's

COMPONENT	DEFINITION
Strategy	Plan or course of action leading to the allocation of a firm's scarce resources, over time, to reach identified goals.
Structure	Characterization of the organization chart (functional, decentralized, etc.)
Systems	Proceduralized reports and routinized processes such as meeting formats.
Staff	"Demographic" description of important personnel categories within the firm (engineers, entrepreneurs, MBAs, etc.). "Staff" is *not* meant in line-staff terms.
Style	Characterization of how key managers behave in achieving the organization's goals; also the cultural style of the organization.
Skills	Distinctive capabilities of key personnel or the firm as a whole.
Superordinate goals/ shared values	The significant meanings or guiding concepts that an organization imbues in its members.

their definitions. The "hard" S's are strategy, structure, and systems. The "soft" S's are style, skill, staff, and superordinate goals. This last category is also referred to as "shared values." The 7-S framework is a summary checklist that highlights the complexity of organizations, but in a manageable way. Within each of the S's, the analysis can be expanded into great detail. The crucial learning from this model is that all seven areas are important and must complement one another.

V

Learning Points

1. Today's managers are confronted with increasing complexity both within and without their organizations.

2. Open systems theory highlights the necessity of maintaining the basic elements of the input–creative transformation–output process and for adapting to the larger environment surrounding the organization.

3. All managers have their personal theory of organizations.

4. These theories are guides to perception and action, bringing order to what would otherwise be chaotic stimuli; however, they also determine what we see and can, according to Argyris and Schön, be "self-sealing."

5. Successful managers recognize that theories may not always be transferred from one situation to other situations. Therefore, managers should build "double-loop learning" into their theories.

6. Healthy, effective organizations are characterized by
   a. Acknowledgment of interdependence among subparts and the larger environment.
   b. A unified approach to common goals.
   c. Form following function.
   d. Decisions being made closest to the source of information.
   e. Conflicts viewed as problems to be solved, not as win-lose situations.
   f. A high level of personal integrity.
   g. Relatively undistorted communication.
   h. High conflict over tasks, not over interpersonal difficulties.
   i. Managers rewarded for profit or performance, growth and development of subordinates, and creating a variable work group.
   j. Feedback mechanisms that enable learning from experience.

7. The 7S framework consists of three "hard" Ss—strategy, structure, and systems—and four "soft" Ss—staff, style, skills, and shared values. Organizations must pay attention to each of these areas.

VI

Tips for Managers

- List all departments and organizations that operate in your system. Identify what each entity wants and needs from you and your unit.
- Changes in one part of the system will reverberate throughout the system.
- Always build feedback loops into work processes and units.
- Managers sometimes pay attention to and analyze only those organizational aspects that interest them. The open systems model and the 7S framework encourage managers to broaden the scope of their attention and take their analyses to greater depth.

VII

Personal Application Assignment

This assignment is to analyze your own organization using the 7S model, which is described in the article by Waterman, Peters, and Phillips entitled, "Structure is not Organization." This article is found in Kolb et al.'s *Organizational Behavior* reader (1990) or in *Business Horizons,* June 1984 (pp. 14–26).

Write about each of the seven aspects of your organization. If you are not currently employed, try the model with another organization you know well (your church, academic department or school, athletic team, orchestra, etc.).

Strategy—

Structure—

Systems—

Staff—

Style—

Skills—

Superordinate Goals/Shared Values—

Is there a "fit" among these seven components? Why or why not?

18

ORGANIZATION DESIGN

OBJECTIVES   By the end of this chapter you should be able to:

A. Explain the difference between formal and informal organizational structures and communication networks.

B. Describe the differentiation-integration dilemma found in organizations.

C. Identify both formal and informal integrative mechanisms.

D. Understand the advantages and disadvantages of one-way and two-way communication networks.

R&D Challenge: Getting It Out of the Lab

Michael A. Verespej

The biggest U.S. companies excel in basic research. But, with a few exceptions—like IBM, General Electric, Hewlett-Packard, and 3M Co.—they have had remarkably little success in turning that advantage into a competitive edge in the world marketplace.

American firms repeatedly have allowed companies in other countries—most notably, Japan— to beat them at applying technology to create new products.

U.S. executives don't deny that the Japanese are superior at applying technology. Yet, too often, they cling to the mistaken belief that being first on the table with new technology will enable them to stave off the competition.

Never mind that no nation discovers more technology than the U.S. And never mind that no one spends more—about $80 billion annually—on nondefense research than the U.S. The harsh reality is that the R&D race no longer goes to the man who invents something first.

"U.S. companies," says one corporate research director, "have not yet learned that speed to market is absolutely critical."

Falling behind. Although U.S. industry remains the leader in such key markets as computers and computer software, aircraft engines and components, biotechnology, artificial intelligence, and pharmaceuticals, it has fallen behind—technologically and in market share—in electronics, semiconductors, ceramics, machine tools, steel, low-cost manufacturing and process technology, advanced materials, and consumer electronics.

"There is no evidence that we don't do at least as well [in research] as the Japanese in areas we target," says management consultant Richard N. Foster at McKinsey & Co., author of *Innovation: The Attacker's Advantage,* an authoritative book on using R&D to gain a competitive edge. "But the problem is this: We target too much research at the end of product life cycles. We are not getting into new areas—and that's where the other guys have got ahead of us. American business has to learn that when winter turns to summer, you stop knitting sweaters."

Adds Dr. Lee W. Rivers, director of corporate planning at Allied-Signal Inc. and consultant to the President's Science Advisor: "The U.S. does more basic research than anyone else. But other people have found more effective ways to turn [U.S.-born] scientific knowledge into products, goods, and services." And, quite simply, that's the measure of R&D success today.

"The leading edge of research today is right up against the cutting edge of application," asserts Dr. Roland Schmitt, senior vice president and chief scientist

Industry Week, May 4, 1987, pp. 33–36.

at General Electric, president of the Industrial Research Institute, and chairman of the National Science Board, the policymaking arm of the National Science Foundation. "And that is where the Japanese excel."

Differences in approach. Take ceramics, for example, which many see as a key material for the future. While U.S. firms have set a research target of reducing the grain size of the ceramic powder, the Japanese approach has been to start at the applications stage, says advanced-materials expert Michael Eckstut at Booz, Allen & Hamilton Inc. Japanese ceramic companies work with automakers to develop useful products, he notes. "The Japanese know that what is important to the end customer is not grain size or [process] characteristics, but a product that can withstand so many degrees for 50 hours, or something you can bang on 50 times. That is the technology leverage, not the grain size."

So while the U.S. outspends Japan in ceramic research, the Japanese are spending where they're more likely to get results.

That's one reason Japan is faster at getting ideas to the market. Another is that manufacturing engineers have greater status in Japan.

In the U.S. the order of preference is: research, design, and then manufacturing, observes Dr. Robert Stratton, director of the Central Research Laboratories for Dallas-based Texas Instruments Inc. (TI). "To make the technology transfer from the lab to manufacturing, you need talented people. And there are not enough top-quality people in manufacturing. We have to make manufacturing engineering more important in universities and provide attractive opportunities for people with that background to move up the corporate ladder."

Not listening. Another problem is inadequate linkage between R&D and the marketplace, say corporate research directors. U.S. firms have a tendency to shoot for the best technology or massive markets while ignoring other, less glamorous products for which there is a market demand.

"The Japanese move into markets with adequate, but not forefront, technology—while we take the time to perfect the technology instead of just getting a technology that will work," asserts GE's Dr. Schmitt. "Many failures arise from that conflict. *Pushing back the frontiers of knowledge has always been much more appealing [to U.S. firms] than writing product specifications or doing process engineering.*"

Most major U.S. companies simply aren't interested in small markets—even though those small markets can provide the learning curve needed for success in the big markets they're drooling over. "You can't get the CEO of a $5 billion company excited about a $100,000 market like ceramic scissor blades or razor blades," says Allied-Signal's Dr. Rivers. "We shoot right from the start for the ceramic [automobile] engine. We don't want to go through the learning process in smaller markets."

There are exceptions. One U.S. industry that focuses on the long term—and on applications—particularly well is the pharmaceutical industry. But part of that is due to the nature of the industry. Because it takes eight to ten years to develop a drug, companies have become conditioned to long-term thinking.

WHERE WE MISS THE MARK

Why do Japanese firms do a better job of applying technology? Granted, they are less stifled by government-built roadblocks. But there are other reasons that, quite simply, stem from U.S. management failures. For instance:

■ Paying lip service to the importance of technology, but not backing it up with commitment.

■ Failure to integrate research and development with corporate planning, business units, and manufacturing.

- Refusal to abandon "the not-invented-here" syndrome.
- The desire for "big-bang" projects.
- The emphasis on short-term profits.
- Failure to effectively allocate R&D dollars.

Cultural edge. Clearly, the Japanese culture provides an R&D edge. Japanese companies don't face the antitrust barriers or high cost of capital that U.S. firms do. And Japanese firms are willing to invest heavily in technology and accept lower profit margins, since they face less pressure for strong quarterly earnings. Thus, corporate R&D expenditures in Japan are often as high as—if not higher than—net income. Some examples from fiscal 1985: Sharp Corp. had $380.4 million in profits and spent $355 million on R&D. Matsushita Electric Industrial reported $1.64 billion in profits, $1.6 billion invested in R&D. NEC Corp.'s $1.45 billion R&D outlay dwarfed its $662 million in profits.

"They have a belief that technology is the root that supports the company," says Dr. Thomas J. Savereide, executive director of 3M Co.'s Central Research Labs. Dr. Savereide headed an Industrial Research Institute team that visited Japan to study the Japanese approach to R&D. "They worry about the seeds that are coming up and how to connect them to the needs of the customer," he reports. "They see it as survival issue."

And the Japanese don't worry about whether the technology was invented in-house. In fact, many of the technologies they've applied or advanced originated in U.S. corporate, university, or government laboratories.

Unlike U.S. companies where financial, legal, and marketing backgrounds dominate the CEO ranks, Japanese CEOs usually have strong technology backgrounds. "In every company in Japan the technology is tied to the top," says Norm Johnson, vice president for R&D at Weyerhaeuser Co., Tacoma, Wash. "The chief R&D officer sits on the board and can influence technology direction."

"That's where we suffer a deficiency in this country," says Allied-Signal's Dr. Rivers. "We have less appreciation at the CEO level of the technological contribution to business success. We don't elevate the importance of the chief technical officer's input or weave R&D into the fabric of manufacturing."

Chuck wagon technology. That irks research directors. While they see the need to integrate R&D into the total operation, they have a difficult time selling that message within their companies.

"You have got to have the business units in the kitchen with you when you're cooking up technology," says GE's Dr. Schmitt. "Too much of what is done in the U.S. is chuck wagon technology—the technology guys dish it out and say to manufacturing, 'Here, do something with it.'"

If American efforts are disjointed, it is largely due to the rapid growth and prosperity of the early 1960s that led U.S. companies to regard manufacturing and lab work as "separate functions, each with its own empire," says Lester C. Krogh, 3M's vice president for R&D. "But that's deadly because the product of a lab is not new products, but information that has to be transferred to someone else to use."

How Japan integrates R&D. U.S. research directors believe that their companies—and the rest of U.S. industry—could benefit greatly by studying and mimicking the ways the Japanese integrate R&D into the entire manufacturing process.

The Japanese get a consensus on objectives beforehand—not after research work has begun, says Don Roberts, vice president for scientific affairs at Kendall Co., Boston. "They do a deep, up front investigation of what the customer's requirements are, and then take a comprehensive, complex series of steps to relate that to product characteristics."

The consensus is reached through a relentless examination by marketing, manufacturing, and research to identify the research goal, points out Weyerhaeuser's Mr. Johnson. "They do a good job of defining what they are going to do before they do it." Too often, he says, the U.S. approach is: "Let's not waste time, let's get to work."

But without linkages between manufacturing and marketing, "you are likely to end up with a lot of technically interesting little projects that are well-linked to the business, but that exert little or no leverage in the market," warns GE's Dr. Schmitt. "You have got to have that partnership on the front end. You have to bang heads with operations until you identify the critical paths of the critical businesses."

Strategic workshops. One U.S. company that works to get a consensus early is TI.

One useful TI approach: strategic workshops. These pull together people—usually more than 100—from R&D, marketing, and the product divisions to discuss "where the technology and markets are going," says Dr. Stratton. "It gives you a good base to start your technology planning and to learn how technology can be exploited in markets."

Just as important as reaching interdepartmental consensus is getting different scientific disciplines in sync. Increasingly, the "real breakthroughs are coming at the crossover points between the sciences," says Allied-Signal's Dr. Rivers.

"To design a new material, you need more knowledge than can be found in any one field of specialization," says Edward L. Hennessy Jr., Allied-Signal's chairman and CEO. "You need chemists who know what molecular changes are needed, physicists who can measure and understand bulk properties, and engineers who can figure out how to make new materials in a cost-effective way."

POOR ALLOCATION

One common criticism of U.S. companies is that they don't do a good job of allocating research dollars. Too many dollars, critics contend, are directed to technologies on the wane, instead of to next-generation research.

"If I had one wish to help American industry, it would be to take 20% of what companies spend on R&D and reallocate it, "says McKinsey's Mr. Foster. "You could double the output of scientific advances."

Mr. Foster, who made pioneering use of "S-curves" in R&D—to depict the relationship between technology investment and results—explains: "I would take [investment] from the top of the S-curve and put it in the middle where the productivity from research is five times greater.

"Too much is being invested in old technologies and too little in new ones," he contends. "Too many companies are at the high point of the S-curve." He suspects that 70% to 80% of all research dollars are "concentrated on improvements in existing products for which there may be no market in five years."

One example: While the Japanese were advancing transistor-based technology, U.S. companies were still working to improve the fast-fading vacuum-tube technology.

Three pitfalls. Research investments tend to be inadequate, excessive, or improper. "Companies often make inadequate investments to maintain technological leadership once they have established it," says management consultant Bill Sommers at Booz, Allen. "They stop just short of developing a proprietary technology—or fail to invest heavily enough when they have a time window."

Conversely, he says, many companies spend excessive amounts of money to develop new products that have little potential for high yields in a mature business. Another pitfall is investing in technologies where it's impossible to gain a competitive position.

One of the reasons that many U.S. companies fail in that regard is that they don't know when to pull the plug on old research projects. "Too many projects take on a life of their own," asserts Warren Stumpe, vice president and chief technology officer at Rexnord Inc., Milwaukee. "Companies need to recognize failure when it occurs so they don't commit any more dollars to the project."

Too much hedging? Many companies fail to narrow their choices. But consultants point out that that can spread R&D dollars too thin. Or it can allocate research dollars to areas that aren't company strengths.

"You need to pick and choose the programs critical to the company, and learn how technologies relate to competitiveness," declares Booz, Allen's Mr. Eckstut. "Otherwise, you lose sight of what's really important, get a very disjointed approach, and spend too many dollars on projects disproportionate to the attractiveness of the business or the chances of success."

Most companies rationalize the shotgun R&D approach by arguing that you can't predict where innovation will occur, says McKinsey's Mr. Foster. "They don't believe research can be managed. They think innovation and scientific advance are a matter of luck." But you can "focus research toward an end result," he says—or down the path toward greater probability of success.

How the S-curve helps. That where Mr. Foster's S-curve is particularly useful, say research directors. "It helps you understand whether the rate of return from your R&D investment is leveling off, and whether it's time to go on to a new S-curve," explains S. Allen Heininger, vice president-corporate plans at Monsanto Co., St. Louis.

Adds Keith McHenry, vice president for research and development at Amoco Oil Co.: "It helps up determine whether we are beating our heads against some kind of fundamental limit."

Mr. Krogh at 3M recommends a simple test: "Ask how much a project would be worth if it succeeded, or how much annual revenue a project would bring in in relation to its cost."

By looking at the economic value, suggests Booz, Allen's Mr. Eckstut, R&D can be placed within the framework of corporate priorities. "You can manage R&D, allocate resources, set priorities, design technology programs, and link R&D to the business' direction."

Oftentimes, he says, the only way that this message gets across is when a new CEO comes in and tells R&D people to start justifying what they do.

R&D profit centers. While it may sound like a drastic measure, many research scientists think the U.S. would be better off if companies viewed research centers as "profit centers," rather than as sinkholes which drain off millions of dollars in the hope of making some discovery.

"There is no need to have a corporate lab that doesn't produce several times more business value than its cost," argues GE's Dr. Schmitt. Adds Rexnord's Mr. Stumpe: "If companies look at R&D centers just as cost centers, that's all they are going to get. They are not going to get technical excellence."

Another problem research managers face: persuading CEOs in their companies to make R&D a higher priority. "While CEOs and senior managers publicly embrace the importance of technology, they're frequently uncomfortable with it, few approach it as a strategic issue, and they can't recognize its value," says Mr. Stumpe. "They are too attuned to short-term results."

Leaps of faith. Mr. Stumpe says too few research directors realize that it's part of their job to constantly communicate the R&D story. The most successful research chiefs, he believes, are those who are not only good scientists, but also great communicators. "You have to preach the value of research and retell that story at every single opportunity. You have to tell CEOs what they are getting for their money and show them how companies have failed by neglecting R&D.

"You have to convince CEOs to accept R&D as a leap of faith," he says, "because those companies who don't make a leap of faith eventually pay the price."

A change in attitude toward R&D must occur at the top, says Allied-Signal's Dr. Rivers. "Otherwise, no sooner will you get the green light to start, than you'll get the red light to stop."

"We have got to break down the attitudinal and institutional barriers to research in this country," asserts Dr. Rivers. "We could tolerate them in the past because we created basic technology and controlled the pace at which it was converted into goods. But we no longer control the latter, and we're losing the battle."

I

Premeeting Preparation

A. Read the Topic Introduction.

B. Read "The Family Hotel," pages 495–500. How would you redesign this organization?

C. What are the significant learning points from the readings?

II

Topic Introduction

The personal, interpersonal, and group dynamics issues discussed thus far in this book are essential elements in understanding human behavior in organizations. The focus in this chapter will be on the next higher level of analysis: the structure of an organization. The organizational structure forms the context within which personal, interpersonal, and group issues take place and are managed.

The formal structure of an organization consists of what is typically depicted in an organization chart. The boxes and the lines that connect them are important elements of the organization's role, authority, and communications structures. The boxes themselves reflect the functions that have been identified to accomplish organizational tasks. The "line functions" are those directly involved in task accomplishment (i.e., marketing, finance, production). Equally important are those "staff functions" designed to provide administrative or support services to the line functions. The lines connecting the boxes reflect two phenomena. One involves authority: who has control over whom. This hierarchy often corresponds very directly to one person being able to hire and/or fire others in lower positions: a key element of positional power. In addition, these lines reflect a communication network: the chain of command to be followed for certain forms of communication.

SOME TYPICAL PICTURES: THREE PURE MODELS OF ORGANIZATION STRUCTURE

While no organization chart will look exactly like any of the three examples offered here, the basic ideas behind these three pure forms can be presented by using a hospital organization as our example.

FIGURE 18–1   Functional Form of Organization

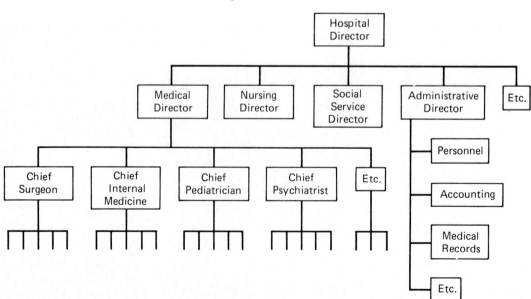

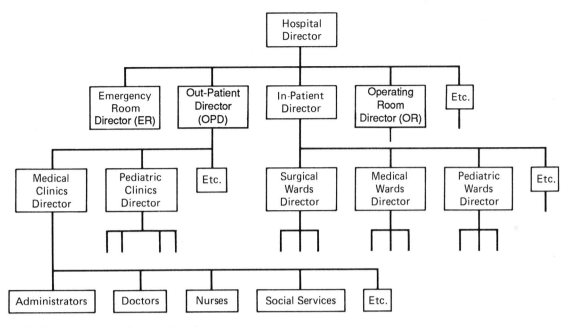

FIGURE 18–2   Product or Service Form of Organization

Functional Form

In this model the organization is differentiated primarily by the functional specialties (e.g., nurses, physicians) required to accomplish the organization's mission. Each organization member, throughout the chain of command, reports to his or her functional superior (e.g., a nurse reports to a head nurse who reports to a nursing director). A health care delivery system may be functionally organized as shown in Figure 18–1.

Product or Service Form

In this model the organization is differentiated primarily by the products it manufactures or the services it dispenses (see Figure 18–2). Each organization member in this system reports directly or indirectly to a manager in charge of a particular

FIGURE 18–3   Matrix Form of Organization

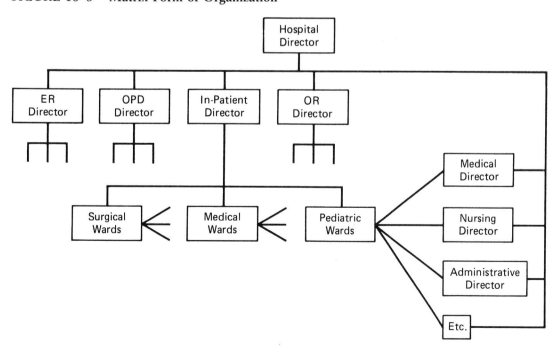

product or service (e.g., a pediatric nurse reports to the director of the pediatric clinics).

| Matrix Form | In this model the organization is differentiated both by function and product, and most members have two or more reporting relationships, or bosses (see Figure 18–3). For example, a nurse working in the pediatric ward would report both to the pediatric clinic director and to a nursing director for the hospital in general. |

ADVANTAGES AND PROBLEMS

One way of thinking about the differences in these three models is to consider who has the authority to hire and fire and prescribe the duties of organization members. In the functional model, it is the functional supervisor; in the product service model, it is the product service director; and in the matrix model, it is a joint decision of some kind. Each form has some pros and cons.

Functional models of organization enable the system to develop and maintain higher levels of expertise in the various functional areas or specialties. Organization members' loyalties are to the function, or specialty, and its standards of performance. In addition, each functional department can maintain subspecialists in various areas and allocate their time across the various services (e.g., inpatients, outpatients) being performed by the organization. If the system is organized by product or service, it becomes very expensive to maintain all the same subspecialists in each service area. In other words, in functional structures—one cardiologist, for example—could serve inpatients, outpatients, and the operating room; under a product management structure, however, maintaining the equivalent expertise in each area would require hiring several cardiologists who may not even be fully utilized. Often this same duplication of resources in product-oriented structures extends to support services and equipment as when each product-service area requires its own clerical system, data processing systems, records systems, and so on.

On the other hand, under a functional structure, it is often very difficult to perform the integration and coordination of services and inputs required by the organization. Problems in the various service areas become difficult to manage since the various functional representatives in that department often do not have a strong direct reporting relationship to the service director. For example, pediatricians in the outpatient department under a functional structure may see themselves more responsible to the chief of pediatrics than to the outpatient director. If coordination of doctors, nurses, and social workers is important in the outpatient department, and each health professional is responding to a different functional director, then coordination becomes difficult and problems may develop. These problems can be in the form of inability to agree on schedules to ensure proper coverage, difficulty in developing work responsibilities for each function in a given service, problems in developing procedures for coordinating activities in the service, or even trouble agreeing on the goals and objectives of the service. The product or service form of structure reduces these coordination problems by placing everyone in a given service area under one coordinating authority, although as indicated, it sometimes does so at the expense of duplication of resources in the total organization.

Also, in dealing with professionals in organizations, it is often important to maintain high levels of collegial interaction for purposes of maintaining professional standards, creativity, and morale. The product or service structure sometimes reduces opportunities for this type of interaction.

The matrix form of organization evolved out of the need to provide both the advantages of functional specialization and the coordination of product service management. By maintaining the functional organization, the subspecialists can be retained and allocated where needed in the organization, and the functional director can provide for in-service education and screening to maintain professional standards. At the same time, the product or service managers having authority over the functional representatives when they are in their service areas enable the managers to carry out their coordinative functions. Unfortunately, the existence of two or more bosses for the various organization members involved can often lead to situations of role conflict. The matrix structure, then, requires functional and product service directors to develop skills in managing these conflict areas.

This requires skills in allocating decision-making responsibility (who has authority over organization members under various situations), managing role conflicts, and so on. Thus, matrix management can provide the advantages of both other systems of organization, but it does so at the cost of increasing complexity and management skill requirements. Therefore, matrix organization structures should be used only where the nature of the organization's tasks requires high degrees of both functional expertise and coordination of services.

ORGANIZATION DESIGN: THE ISSUES AND PRINCIPLES

These three pure forms and the numerous variations possible can be viewed as choices available to those responsible for designing the fiber and structure of an organization. The issue then becomes, "How does one choose among the options available?" There are several crucial principles involved in this choice.

First, it is important to recognize that there is no "one best way to structure an organization." The overriding design principle is that *form follows function.* The contingency approach, therefore, dictates a focus on the appropriateness of the structure (the *form*) to the job or task at hand (the *function*). It is immediately clear, using just this principle, that the appropriate structure for an R&D department may well look very different from the appropriate structure for the production department. Both the entire organization and various subparts need to be designed with this principle in mind.

Second, and flowing directly from the foregoing, is the basic differentiation-integration dilemma of organization design. All complex organizations must somehow subdivide their total task (differentiation). Indeed, the driving force behind the need for an organization in the first place had to do with the job being more than one person could handle alone.

Once the differentiation decision is made, the organization's designers must then confront the second horn of the dilemma—integration. Differentiated elements must be coordinated. The pieces must be put back together and kept moving in a particular direction to achieve the organization's basic purpose. Herein lies the basic dilemma of organization structure and design. The more complex the overall task, the more complex is the required level of differentiation. The greater the required differentiation, the more complex and essential are the choices around integration.

Let us examine several of the more typical of these integrative mechanisms or choices.

Formal Integration Mechanisms

1. *Formal rules.* All organizations have formal rules and procedures, operating manuals, or policy books. The purpose of these, from an organizational structure and design point of view, is to eliminate the need for ad hoc information processing and decision making. When a situation or problem comes up, the individual employee refers to the policy book and finds the right answer. Carried to an inappropriate extreme, use of formal rules and procedures as a way of coping with needed integration results in our stereotyped image of the ossified bureaucracy. Rules proliferate, policy manuals abound and are continuously updated, and "nothing happens unless it is written in the rules."

2. *Formal hierarchy.* A major reason, from an organization structure and design point of view, for the existence of the formal hierarchy is to deal with exceptions. Since it is not possible to develop rules for every task situation, people (bosses) are needed to process certain information and make certain decisions

about exceptions to the rules. If the same exception occurs frequently enough, it may result in a new rule or policy.

As task complexity increases, the hierarchy also tends to become overloaded. "I'm overloaded with day-to-day fires and have no time for longer-range issues such as employee development and planning," is a common lament of the "overexceptioned" manager. When this condition develops, the organization must look to a third integrative mechanism.

3. *Formal targets or goals.* Through the use of specific subunit goals, budget limits, completion dates, and so on, subunits are able to work on their differentiated tasks with less continuous information processing and decision making. The pieces come together—assuming that everyone meets his or her agreed-upon targets as expected. Some tasks, however, do not lend themselves easily to such mechanisms. It is harder for the R&D department, for example, to agree to "be creative" by X date than it is for the production department to agree to Y units by X date. This is *not* because the employees in these departments are dramatically different personalities, although this is a typical assumption. Rather, the nature of their tasks is different.

Organization design is buttressed by appropriate reward systems. No matter how well designed an organization appears on paper, if the desired behaviors that will reinforce or implement the design are not rewarded, the design will fail. There is a very close relationship between rewards and punishment and organization design issues. For example, in an organization that severely punishes mistakes and deviation from the rules, one can expect many exceptions to rules that will be bumped upstairs. The hierarchy is likely to become overloaded with exceptions, and as a result, rules and procedures grow like Topsy. In contrast, if mistakes are tolerated and managers are encouraged to exercise discretion in interpreting the rules, there is no need to create a rule for every conceivable situation. These examples show that the behaviors that are rewarded and punished, that is, the reward system, affect the integration mechanisms and the organizational design.

In many organizations you can hear "Always ask for twice what you need because they will cut your budget in half anyway" or "If we set a realistic goal and met it, they'd expect us to do it faster next time" or "I know it can't be done that fast, but if that's what they want to hear, that's what I'll tell them, and then I'll try to blame the other shift for the delay." Such comments are a sign that the use of formal targets as an integration mechanism is being subverted by the reward system. When people are penalized for setting accurate goals and targets, they resort to deception.

The Informal Organizational Structure

The points just discussed focus upon the formal organizational structures. An organization chart, as we have noted, specifies the nature of the formal organizational structure and the path that should be taken for the transmission of information through the organization. The actual path taken often departs markedly from this formal structure. In fact, informal networks often develop because the formal network is not satisfying key individual needs. Brown discusses this distinction between formal versus informal organizations in terms of secondary and primary groups and points out,

There is, therefore, no abrupt point of distinction between primary and secondary groups. But the contrast remains a valid one; the secondary group tends to be organized for a formal purpose (in the case of a factory, for the production of goods), its structure is more or less rationally designed towards that end, and its members are not all intimately known to each other. The primary group may have a specific practical goal, and when in pursuit of that goal will organize itself logically to that end, but essentially it is based on social satisfaction and personal choice, and, quite apart from any practical goal, it seeks to maintain itself as a unity.[1]

Brown's "primary" group reflects the informal organization and his "secondary" group refers to the formal organization. Further on, in a discussion of "things people should observe if they are trying to understand the behavior of people in organizations," Brown suggests that

> It is useful, therefore, to distinguish between those actions which are fundamentally technical, those which are sociotechnical[2] and those which are purely social. . . . Clearly technical and sociotechnical behavior is an aspect of formal organizations, whereas social behavior belongs to the informal structure of the factory.[3]

The importance of understanding the distinctions between formal versus informal organizations and the problems that can arise if the two are not understood is at no time clearer than when one attempts to introduce a technical change into an organization and encounters great resistance. Such was the case in Trist's study of an attempt to change the process by which coal was mined.[4] The anticipated production increases from the new method were not being realized, and upon investigation it was observed that the new technology substantially altered the social system that had developed within this mine. The men were used to working in close-knit teams characterized by loyalty and mutual help. The new technology involved factorylike, individualized work stations that disrupted the group behavior that made their jobs satisfying. The point here is that, whereas a formal organization chart can be redrawn to account for the effects of a technological change, the informal social system, which does not appear on an organization chart, is also influenced by the technological change. Both must be taken into account.

Informal Integrative Mechanisms

We have already discussed several integrative mechanisms that are a part of the formal organizational structure. At this point, we need to explore the integrative mechanisms that are a part of the informal organizational structure.

1. *Informal rules—norms.* The informal counterpart to the formal use of rules in an organization is the concept of norms. A norm is an unwritten, informal "rule" that governs individual behavior in an organization. All social systems develop norms; they are an inherent consequence of social interaction. Consequently, the existence of norms is neither inherently good nor bad. The diagnostic question is whether or not the norms that arise function to support or reinforce or to inhibit the organization's primary formal function. Let us examine how norms influence the organization's primary formal mission or function. Imagine an A&D group whose primary function is the generation of new, creative ideas. This group has a formal leader, a boss.

   One might observe in such a group that ideas are freely exchanged and critically examined, with one exception. The boss's ideas tend to go unchallenged. When the boss states an opinion, the group behaves as if it were a decision, a fact. Now, if the boss possesses a unique technical expertise, one

[1]J. A. C. Brown, *The Social Psychology of Industry: Human Relations in the Factory* (Baltimore, MD: Penguin Books, 1954), pp. 128–129.

[2]"Sociotechnical" refers to social groupings that are determined by the technology used for the task. Offshore-platform oil well personnel, for instance, have a different social system than on shore oil well people, as the technology requires them to be together for long periods of time, sharing in eating, sleeping, and recreation.

[3]Brown, *The Social Psychology of Industry,* p. 131.

[4]E. Trist as reported in Warren G. Bennis et al., *The Planning of Change,* 2nd ed. (New York: Holt, Rinehart and Winston, 1969), pp. 269–281.

"And so you just threw everything together? ...
Mathews, a posse is something
you have to *organize*."

could argue that this is a functional norm. However, it is possible that, for a variety of reasons, people have come to believe that some form of punishment will befall anyone who does not agree with the boss—the "yesman" syndrome. This norm would be potentially dysfunctional to the group's efforts to fulfill its primary formal function.

Let us carry the example one step farther. A new person joins the group. As the "new kid on the block," he or she does not yet know all the rules of the game—the norms. The person, at some point, may vigorously try to persuade the boss that his or her idea has some serious flaws. A norm has been violated. There is some anxious laughter in the group, some uneasy shuffling around in chairs. After the meeting, an old-timer pulls the newcomer aside for a "Dutch uncle" talk. "Look, friend, let me tell you something for your own benefit. In this group, you never take on the boss the way you did today. It's a no-no, a taboo." Unless an organization is willing to consciously examine its norms—a norm in itself—it runs the risk of having this element of the informal structure act counter to the organization's primary formal function. Norms will develop in all social systems. The issue is one of diagnosing their appropriateness to the task of the organization and instituting new norms where necessary.

2. *The informal hierarchy—status differentials.* An important source of status in any organization is one's position in the formal hierarchy. Bosses are differentiated from subordinates in terms of the formal power associated with their position—power to control certain rewards, to make certain decisions, to resolve certain exceptions to formal rules, and so on. In many organizations, one finds other less formal dimensions along which people differentiate one another. Any element of difference can be a source of status and power. For example, in some organizations, a comment made by a male would be treated much more seriously than if the same comment were made by a female—a sex

differentiation. An age-seniority differentiation is also common: "These young turks are really something. They think a college education gives them all the answers!" The perceived status of one's educational background can also act as a source of differentiation. Many organizations find themselves to be heavily dependent on a particular task function: "We're a marketing-oriented company" or "We're an R&D-oriented company." The perceived consequence may be "When push comes to shove, the top positions always go to people from Marketing." The impact of these status differences can be positive or negative in terms of the organization's primary formal function. Again, the critical issue is one of appropriateness to the organization's primary formal function. Differentiated subunit tasks must be integrated—coordination is essential. Age-seniority, sex, educational background may have little to do with the issue at hand. Integrative decisions influenced by the informal hierarchy may, therefore, ultimately be dysfunctional to the accomplishment of the organization's primary formal functions.

3. *Informal goals—individual needs and goals.* The degree to which individual goals and organizational goals can be integrated has and will continue to be a major source of concern to organizational theorists and practicing managers. Many approaches exist and are being implemented to maximize the degree of overlap, such as goal-setting procedures, management by objectives, participative performance appraisal systems, and flexible and adaptive formal reward systems. The less the agreement between formal targets and goals (a formal integrative mechanism) and individual needs and goals, the more difficult it will be to achieve the needed integration of formally differentiated subtasks to ensure fulfillment of the organization's primary formal function.

Examples of these informal goals are not easy to see because they tend to be defined as "antiorganizational" and therefore operate under the table. Such comments as "She always has a hidden agenda" or "He's always trying to build his own little empire" are indicative of the tension between formal organizational goals and informal individual goals. In the specific context of group decision making, this tension has been discussed more fully as an example of self-oriented behaviors.[5]

A typical example of this dilemma can be seen operating on many assembly lines. A formal goal or target has been set—X units per hour per employee. This becomes the group norm or standard. Along comes a capable individual who wants to get ahead (perhaps someone with a high achievement need). Efforts on this person's part to better the formal standard are met with group pressures to get back in line—the group punishes rate busters. Here individual needs to belong to the group (an affiliative need) may take precedence over the formal goal of increasing productivity.

MAPPING ORGANIZATIONAL STRUCTURES

The usefulness of mapping the formal and informal aspects of an organizational structure is demonstrated in several research studies. Allen,[6] for example, finds that, in addition to the formal organization structure, the informal structure, as represented by patterns of friendship and extraorganizational social encounters, has an important effect on the flow of technical ideas. Scientists were found to discuss technical ideas with many of the same people with whom they interacted on a social basis.

Allen's research also uncovered the existence within research and development

---

[5]For more details on this concept, see Chapter 8.
[6]T. Allen, "Communications in the Research and Development Laboratory," *Technology Review,* Vol. 70 (1967), pp. 31–37.

laboratories of people he called "technological gatekeepers." These few people, much like the opinion leaders identified in early research on voting behavior, were mentioned very frequently as sources of critical information. These gatekeepers act as a link between the organization and the outside environment, as evidenced by their attendance at professional meetings and reading of professional and technical periodicals. Knowledge of who these gatekeepers are and of the nature of the existing sociotechnical and social networks within an organization can serve as important inputs into many organizational decisions. One would not, for example, want to make an architectural decision that would act to break up an effective informal communication group by moving its members apart from one another.[7]

A second important set of insights comes from research in the impact of different communication networks.[8] Suppose that you are the manager of a group of six subordinates. You are given the task of communicating to your group the following diagram:

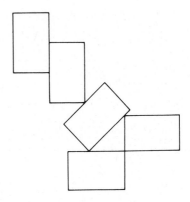

One approach would be for you to face *away* from the group (so that all they can see is your back) and verbally (use no pictures) try to convey your message. The group must remain silent—no questions allowed of you or each other. This approach would approximate many organizational structures of the following form:

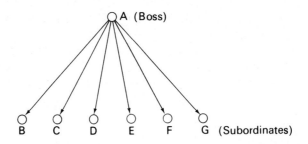

This has been called the closed, one-way communication network. A can communicate with B, C, D, and the rest, but they "cannot" communicate with each other and seldom do they communicate with A (short of saying "yes").

A second approach would be for you to face your group, verbally try to convey your message, and allow (and encourage) them to ask questions of you and each other. This approach would approximate a substantially different organizational structure, which could be represented as follows:

[7]The architecture of an organization is an important element of its formal structure. For more detail on this element see Fred I. Steele, *Physical Settings and Organization Development* (Reading, MA: Addison-Wesley, 1973).

[8]See, for example, P. Lawrence and J. Lorsch, *Developing Organizations: Diagnosis and Action* (Reading, MA: Addison-Wesley, 1969).

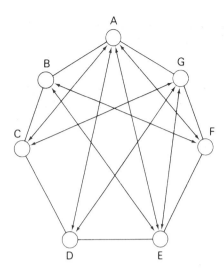

This has been called the open, two-way communications network. Full and open communication is encouraged between each and every group member.

In experimental investigations with these two (pure and extreme) networks, the following effects have been observed. For a given task, the closed network is considerably faster than the open network—the boss finishes sending the message sooner in the closed network. The closed network is considerably less efficient, however, in terms of accuracy—more of the members get the wrong message. In a series of related experiments, the open group has been found to be more adaptable to changes in task requirements.

With respect to morale, the members of the open network are more satisfied and feel more involved in the task. In the closed network, only A (the boss) feels satisfied and involved. In the open network, every member has the opportunity to assume a position of leadership. The open network, therefore, provides a training ground for the development of future managerial talent. These very simple experiments demonstrate clear relationships between the structure of a group (or organization) and the content of the communication, and demonstrate the process by which information is communicated in a way that influences people's feelings of satisfaction, involvement, commitment, and future capability to assume leadership positions.

The interdependence of formal and informal structures is often complex and difficult to map. However, in the process one may gain surprising insights into the real communications process of a group or organization.

THE FAMILY HOTEL

The Schmidt family started out with one hotel. Through judicious investment, they gradually grew to a corporation which owned six upscale hotel properties and a food distribution business. The father and three sons were extremely active in running the hotels. The father was the president of the company. Each son was in charge of a different functional area at the corporate level—vice presidents of finance, food and beverage, and sales and marketing. The other two vice presidents, in personnel and accounting, were new hires who were not family members. Although each of the properties had a general manager (GM), most employees considered the family members to be the real bosses in the organization. The family occasionally countermanded the order of the GM's and older employees contacted the owners directly when there were problems. The corporate vice presidents sometimes came to the properties and visited the staff in their functional areas without notifying the GM of their presence. Sometimes the GM's were first informed of new corporate policies and changes by their own subordinates. In their defense, the turnover rate at the properties was so high that the family felt they had to intervene, and the family members were all fairly competent and knew the business. But the GM's dissatisfaction with their intervention resulted in even more turnover.

In 1985, the business reached a turning point. Because of their success, the family decided to expand their business and hotel ventures to different parts of the country. But this decision caused dissension within the family. One of the sons disagreed with this strategy and opted to leave the family business for awhile to see if he could succeed on his own. Another son, who was tired of his father's authoritarian style chose to return to school and complete his graduate education. The third son wanted to focus solely on the expansion and his father wanted to do what he enjoyed most—making deals and pursuing new ventures. Since the family was no longer capable of overseeing the operations themselves, they hired an operations manager to run the business.

The formal organizational chart for the company is shown in Figure 18–4. But the new operations manager, Glen Chase, suspected that this chart did not reflect reality. He found himself in a delicate situation. From working with other family businesses, he knew that it was difficult for founders to relinquish authority and control to others. However, after talking with the staff comprising the executive committee at one of the properties, Chase also knew the organizational structure had to be modified and it had to be done quickly before the positions at corporate were filled.

Jack Wilson had been a general manager (GM) for ten years, although many of those years were spent working for other hotel chains. Jack said that he didn't feel he could really do his job because so many directives came from corporate headquarters that he spent all his time responding to them. Furthermore, policies and procedures that were appropriate for another hotel in a different geographic area were inappropriate for him. He felt his hotel's problems were somewhat unique and resented being told how to run his property. He also said that in the past the family and the different staff people who came from headquarters had given him conflicting advice. He handled that by always doing what the family said, since they had the power to fire him. However, his relations with other staff members had

FIGURE 18–4   The Family Hotel Formal Organizational Chart

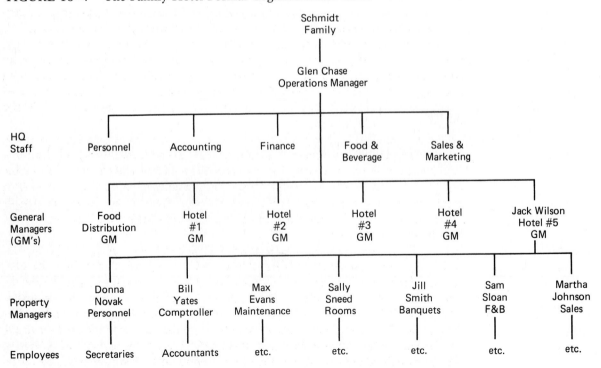

suffered as a result and he worried about his reputation at headquarters. He also felt he had to walk a narrow line with the employees. If they didn't like something, they called headquarters, and a family member would come swooping down to investigate. Sometimes he would not be informed of the complaint until that time. Because of the cronies who were friends of the family, Jack wasn't sure how far he could go in making changes in the hotel or even talking about problems openly with anyone in the organization.

Donna Novak was the personnel director. She had previously worked in manufacturing firms that had formalized HR programs. She was still a bit shocked by the comparatively unsophisticated personnel practices that are common in much of the hotel industry. She complained that she felt she had to hire whomever the family referred, whether or not they were qualified for the job. However, her main problem was keeping the hotel staffed. Turnover was high, and unskilled workers were at a premium in this community. She was convinced that some of the hotel's policies, like the lack of retirement benefits, were causing turnover. She also feared that the autocratic and arbitrary management practices of some of the department heads were responsible for high turnover. The hotel chain has a reward system that gives bonuses to department heads based upon their productivity. However, the salaried and hourly employees receive no bonuses, and some of them feel they are being taken advantage of by the department heads just so their bonuses will be earned. For example, some of the department heads are slow to put in requests for people to fill positions; the employees assume these managers are saving money on salaries, while the employees have to do the work of two people.

Sam Sloan was the food and beverage director, a position that is usually second in prestige only to the general manager on the property. Sam complained that he spent all his time preparing profit and loss statements for headquarters by hand since the hotel operations were not computerized. He said he understood the importance of keeping records and was very interested in the food and beverage figures but had no time left to check out trends in the industry. He was afraid he was falling behind in his field. The only opportunity he had to keep up came with the visits of the F&B vice president who did a good job of passing on the new ideas he had collected in his travels.

Jill Smith, the banquets manager, stated flat out that she had the most stressful job in the hotel. She said the salespeople promised the moon to prospective customers but often failed to tell her specifically what the clients had requested. Her waiters and waitresses had to fight over tableware with the restaurant servers. Furthermore, the chef gave her a hard time because she could not give him the exact count of meals needed until everyone showed up for their banquet. All day long and most nights she raced from meeting room to meeting room, handling irate customers and upset employees, until she did not have time for anything else in her life.

Bill Yates, the comptroller, was fairly satisfied with his job and the company with the exception of the financial control system. He said that the figures from the departments were sent directly to headquarters and they weren't sent back to the hotel until it was too late to use them for either controlling or forecasting. As a result, budgeting was a nightmare, and when the GM or the department heads looked bad as a result, they tended to blame him. Bill was hoping that automation would help the situation.

Martha Johnson, the sales director, had worked her way up in the organization from the banquet department. She talked at length about the difficulties between sales and the other departments in the hotel. Since the salespeople are the only ones who go home at five o'clock, they are not taken seriously by the others. They have their reputation and credibility to worry about with customers, but they depend heavily upon other departments to satisfy the customers. Martha says she has to check many things herself to make sure banquets or the kitchen are following the customer's request form, but the other departments resent her checking up on them. However, if she doesn't, mistakes happen. Martha said she has a running feud with the F&B director because he tries to bury some of his costs in her budget. Martha also wishes she had more sales expertise. She was grateful to move up within the company but suspects there is more she should be doing to modernize the sales office.

Sally Sneed is one of the few college graduates on the property. She studied education but found she disliked classroom teaching. She is the rooms manager and is responsible for the reservations and rooms functions. She gets along well with the other departments and, other than occasional communication problems with sales, has no major problems. She was, however, very concerned about the competition that the hotel faces. Room occupancy had dropped since two new hotels were constructed in the vicinity. Sally felt that the hotel had to offer something unique so it could keep its clientele. She thought one of the biggest problems was lack of renovation. The property was getting a little shabby, but all the capital expenditures were determined at headquarters and renovation requests took a long time to approve.

Sally's concerns about capital expenditures were shared by Max Evans, the maintenance department head. He'd worked at the property for two years and had recently been promoted. His crew was tired of patching carpets and trying to make old kitchen equipment hold together a while longer. He wished the kitchen people were trained to take better care of the equipment, because he thought they might cut down on some of the repair jobs. His major problem though was keeping all the department heads happy. Some of them expected him to stop whatever work was in progress and do their jobs first. He felt as if he were being pulled in several directions at once. Sometimes he just gave up and had his men go to whatever department was yelling the loudest.

After talking with the managers on the property, Glen also learned that the department heads met with Jack once a week in their executive committee meeting. At this time Jack just read them the latest directives from headquarters. There were few attempts at problem solving, presumably because all answers came from corporate and everyone knew Jack had limited power. Glen was worried about the problems he had uncovered and also felt the hotels needed to be more innovative. Since many of the managers had worked their way up through the system, some of them had never seen alternative ways of doing business. Glen thought a few of them had fallen behind the times. He himself wanted to try out some innovations. He was very aware that certain properties were losing out to the competition and wanted to turn that situation around quickly. As the organization was currently structured, he was afraid that wasn't possible. So he dug out his OB textbook, last seen in graduate school, and reread the chapter on organizational structure and tried to come up with a new design.

Answer these questions before coming to class:

1. What type of formal structure does the company currently have?

2. What type of informal structure does the company have?

3. What are the strengths and weaknesses of the informal structure?

4. What can you figure out about the communication networks that exist? Draw dashed lines on the chart in Figure 18–4 to show the communication patterns.

5. What are the issues for each of the participants?

PERSON	ISSUES
Jack, general manager	
Donna, personnel	
Sam, food and beverage	
Jill, banquets	

PERSON	ISSUES
Bill, comptroller	
Martha, sales	
Sally, rooms	
Max, maintenance	
Glen, operations manager	

6. What kind of a structure could better address these issues?

7. How would you try to resolve the integration problems between the property and the headquarters and at the property level?

We left Glen Chase, the operations manager, rereading his OB textbook. He'd figured out some ideas about a better organizational design and had flipped to the chapter on implementing change. There he read that changes are more likely to be implemented when the people involved have a chance to participate in the decision. He decided to test this out and called a meeting of all the department heads at the property he'd visited.

Prepare to run the following role-play session as Glen Chase. You may wish to refer back to the problem solving chapter to refresh your memory about what to consider in such a meeting.

III

Procedure for Group Meeting: The Family Hotel Role Play

(Time Allotted: 30 Minutes)

STEP 1. Choose volunteers to play each of the managers. The volunteers should be seated around a table. Leave an empty chair for people from the rest of the class who may want to join in for a few minutes.

STEP 2. Glen Chase starts the meeting off in his or her best problem-solving style and asks the other managers for their input on creating a new organization design. The group should draw a new organizational chart that includes their suggested changes.

STEP 3. Debriefing (20 minutes)

a. What kind of organizational design did the role players devise?

b. What was the rationale behind their choices?

c. What are the strengths and weaknesses of this design?

d. How did they resolve the differentiation-integration issue? How else could it be resolved?

e. What connections can you make between this exercise and the readings?

IV

Follow-up

Glen Chase convinced the Schmidt family to decentralize and allow the properties to have more autonomy. He decided that the informal structure they'd been operating with was really a functional structure or a matrix that refused to acknowledge itself. He tried to strengthen the GM's position by developing a GM's council and encouraging them to make decisions with him rather than merely trying to figure out what the family wanted. A bonus system was set up for each property which rewarded the GMs for innovations in their hotels. The executive committees on the properties were encouraged to solve problems and work as teams. However, so many of the managers were young and lacking in managerial skills that integration problems still occurred.

Chase's tactic with the vice presidents at headquarters was to have them do project work on system problems and/or innovations. This kept them too busy to do the daily monitoring that occurred in the past and caused them to be seen as special resources by the staff on the properties. The system evolved into a matrix form in which the GMs became the primary authority on the properties and the corporate staff were technical resources and back-up support for the hotel employees.

The design of an organization should depend upon the environment, the technology, the people, and the strategy. Far from being a negligible factor, the design of the organization has a direct influence upon effectiveness. As the opening vignette showed, design issues can be crucial to an organization's ability to compete.

V
Learning Points

1. Organization structure refers to the pattern of roles, authority, and communication that determine the coordination of the technology and people within an organization.

2. The functional form of organizational structure is organized around the functional specialties required to accomplish the organization's mission. It allows for greater development of functional expertise but may make organizational coordination more difficult.

3. The product or service form is organized around the products or services offered by the organization. Coordination problems are reduced in this structure, but it runs the risk of having duplicated resources and decreased opportunity for collegial interaction among people of the same function.

4. The matrix form is organized around both functions and products. It is an attempt to profit from the advantages of both functional and product structures. However, having both a product and a functional boss can cause confusion and conflict.

5. A guiding rule is "form follows function." Therefore, different parts of the organization may well be designed very differently.

6. The basic problem faced by any organization structure is that of differentiation-integration. Complex organizations have to divide the work (differentiation), but how then do they coordinate (integrate) the different parts to achieve the organization's goals?

7. Formal integration mechanisms are:
   a. Formal rules.
   b. Formal hierarchy.
   c. Formal targets or goals.

8. Informal integration mechanisms are:
   a. Informal norms.
   b. Informal hierarchy.
   c. Informal individual needs and goals.

9. Organization design is reinforced or weakened by the reward system. Whether or not individuals are rewarded for cooperating will help determine the success of integration efforts.

10. Both formal and informal aspects of organization design are important. The informal aspects refer to social behavior and relationships.

11. Closed, one-way communication networks are quicker but less accurate and more dissatisfying for members other than the boss.

12. Open, two-way communication networks, while slower, have the advantage of greater accuracy, higher morale and satisfaction, and increased adaptability to changes in task requirements. These networks are better for developing future managers because they provide shared opportunities for leadership.

13. Organization design should be determined by strategy, environment, technology, and people.

VI

Tips for Managers

- Looking at a problem, it's important to ask, "What is the problem, not who?" Unless managers are sophisticated about design issues, they are likely to see individuals, rather than structure, as the problem.

- When a succession of people fail in a position, it is often a signal that the position or the organization design is at fault. Some jobs and even departments are simply doomed to failure by poor designs, and it's a manager's job to determine that and rectify it.

- There is a saying, "When in doubt, reorganize." Don't reorganize unless you have undertaken a thorough analysis and are positive that design issues are really the culprit.

- Make sure the informal structure is well understood before any changes are made. Some organizations succeed in spite of their structure because the informal structure is stronger than the formal structure.

- It's difficult to see what the unanticipated consequences will be from new structures. Doubtless there will be some. Therefore, it is worthwhile to try to brainstorm possible consequences and leave some room for later modifications.

- A change in organizational design will often result in resistance. It is upsetting to most people to participate in reorganization. Getting employee participation in the process of developing a new design is one way to reduce resistance. See the contents of Chapter 20 regarding change.

VII

Personal Application Assignment

In this assignment you are to write about the design of an organization you know well by answering the following questions:

1. How would you diagram the structure of your organization?

2. How would you describe its communication networks?

3. How does your organization deal with the differentiation-integration issue?

4. What are the strengths and weaknesses of your organization's design?

5. What improvements could you suggest?

19

JOB DESIGN AND JOB INVOLVEMENT

OBJECTIVES   By the end of this chapter, you should be able to:

    A. Define and describe the historical roots of work alienation.

    B. Identify characteristics of job situations that motivate people.

    C. List and describe six methods for increasing job involvement.

Improving Quality: Lessons From Hewlett-Packard

John A. Young

I'm sure most business managers believe that their companies already produce high-quality products. We have always stressed product quality at Hewlett-Packard Co., and we have always believed—until recently—that the "find it and fix it" method of ensuring good quality was adequate and cost-effective.

But customers in recent years have come to expect much higher quality than ever before. Recognizing this, we decided several years ago to analyze in detail our methods and the costs of achieving good product quality. To our surprise, we calculated that as much as 25% of our manufacturing assets were actually tied up in *reacting to quality problems*. Using assets in this way, of course, drives up production costs and product prices, making us less competitive, in a relative sense, than we could be.

Were we, then, doing a good job of producing quality products at a fair price? And if we weren't, were other American businessmen doing any better? Was it any wonder that U.S. industry was having its problems?

As we thought about this problem, it became apparent that we were facing an intriguing management challenge. With above-average quality standards already well established at Hewlett-Packard, it would be difficult to ask for better results. Yet it was apparent that major improvement was needed for us to retain a leadership position in the long run. Clearly, a bold approach was needed to convince people that a problem existed and to fully engage the entire organization in solving it.

The proper place to start, we concluded, was with a startling goal—one that would get attention. The goal we chose was a tenfold reduction in the failure rates of our products during the 1980s. We knew this represented a difficult challenge. But we also suspected that anything less dramatic wouldn't convey the importance we attached to this issue. By establishing a far-reaching goal and getting people to feel in their guts that the goal was reasonable, we felt some serious movement would begin to occur. We also knew the close linkage between higher quality, lower cost and increased productivity would lead to other beneficial results for the company.

With the goal firmly established, the second step was to identify a nucleus of leading-edge people in our organization to champion the quality cause. But to do that, we had to find ways of showing them what was possible in the quest for improved quality.

We decided to send a dozen first-line and second-line managers from manufacturing, product assurance and related fields on a fact-finding tour of

Japan to see what kinds of approaches worked well there—an interesting reversal from a few short years earlier.

Not surprisingly, our study team returned with tales of impressive quality achievements and low-cost manufacturing—always in combination. What's more, they described the Japanese quality-assurance technique in remarkably simple terms: "Doing it right the first time." More than any other experience, this visit confirmed our feelings that quality improvements weren't only possible but perhaps essential to driving down prices, increasing productivity and maintaining our long-term competitiveness. And it triggered an almost crusade-like motivation among members of our study team to project this message companywide.

The next challenge was to find ways to spread the genuine enthusiasm and insight of these people throughout the organization. Several methods were available for this, and we used them all: training classes, newsletters, informal discussions and so on. But the one that seemed to have the greatest impact was peer competition—one of the strongest motivational forces available to any organization.

It was interesting to watch this type of competition take effect. People who long had thought they were doing a good job began to question long-accepted practices. Quality and productivity became the leading topics of many a coffee-break conversation, and in time more than 1,000 quality teams sprang up around the company.

When W. Edwards Deming and J. M. Juran, noted authorities on quality who helped rebuild Japanese industry following World War II, came to lecture at Hewlett-Packard, they drew packed audiences. Reports of even minor quality or productivity gains spread quickly throughout the company, inspiring others to emulate and perhaps exceed the original achievement. In time, the original nucleus of people had convinced just about everybody that much higher quality wasn't only attainable but would actually drive down costs because of productivity gains associated with doing things right the first time.

As we monitored the progress of this program, it became obvious to us that timely access to information is indispensable. Managers and supervisors who could easily call up on a computer terminal the latest parts-failure data, process schedules, rework information and so on could study cause-and-effect relationships much more clearly and make consistently better business decisions.

The logical fourth step, then, was to accelerate the spread of information-management tools throughout the company. Our intention, simply stated, was to ensure that a broad range of people were given an opportunity to access needed information, experiment with it and get instant feedback on their decisions. Perhaps more than any other factor, this process has greatly increased our knowledge of our business and made a major contribution to our overall approach to the quality/productivity issue.

What kinds of tangible results have we seen in the past few years? At one Hewlett-Packard product division, the cost of service and repair of desk-top computers was reduced 35% through improved design and manufacturing techniques. At another division, production time for two of our most popular oscilloscopes dropped 30% and product defects declined substantially, allowing us to cut prices 16%.

Vendors have been asked to become part of the total quality solution. As a result of workshops, performance evaluations and clearly stated quality specifications, there have been major improvements in the quality of parts we purchase from outside suppliers. In one case, a supplier of logic chips for our HP 3000 business computer achieved a tenfold reduction in chip-failure rates in just 15 months—to the point that we are no longer required to inspect every part that comes in.

In addition, the quality drive has helped us cut inventory companywide from 20.2% of sales at the end of fiscal 1979 to 15.5% at the end of 1982.

Based on 1982 sales of $4.2 billion, that 4.7% decrease represents nearly $200 million we don't have tied up in inventory.

By our best estimates, we are perhaps a third of the way to our 10-year goal of a tenfold reduction in product-failure rates. We haven't seen any flagging in the eagerness with which our people are addressing this issue, and they continue to find new areas ripe for improvement. It may take a few more years before we know that the goal is fully within grasp, but the results to date already have made the effort well worthwhile.

I

Premeeting Preparation

A. Read the Topic Introduction.

B. Using the instructions provided at the end of this chapter, learn to fold the moon tent and the shallow water cargo carrier (see instructions, pages 521–24 and 529–32).

C. What are the significant learning points from the readings?

II

Topic Introduction

Without work, all life goes rotten, but when work is soulless, life stifles and dies.

CAMUS

Ever since people ceased working for themselves as farmers and craftsmen and cast their fate with organizations, worker motivation and involvement has been a matter of both interest and concern. The Industrial Revolution and its effect upon the nature of manual work and the social structure focused greater attention on the concept of alienation.[1] Karl Marx[2] put an inflammatory finger on part of this concept when he stated that the separation of labor from ownership and the means of production resulted in *powerlessness* among the laboring class. Durkheim stated that the reduction of work into small, repetitive segments led people to see their jobs as *meaningless*.[3] He also applied the term "anomie" to describe a social system in which normative standards are weak. Anomie conveys a sense of disorientation, anxiety, and isolation in individuals; Durkheim maintained that the switch from an agrarian to an industrial society created anomie because there were fewer norms or rules to regulate the urban industrial society which evolved in the 1800s in Europe. Mayo,[4] who researched the Hawthorne experiment (described in Chapter 2), claimed

[1]For an interesting history and summary of the research done on both work alienation and job involvement, see Rabindra Kanungo's *Work Alienation: An Integrative Approach* (New York: Praeger, 1982).

[2]Karl Marx, *Economic and Philosophical Manuscripts* (Moscow: Foreign Languages Publishing House, 1844/1961).

[3]Emile Durkheim, *The Division of Labor in Society,* trans. G. Simpson (New York: Free Press, 1956), and *Suicide* (New York: The Free Press, 1951).

[4]Elton Mayo, *The Human Problems of an Industrial Civilization* (New York: Macmillan, 1933), or see *The Social Problems of an Industrial Civilization* (Cambridge, MA: Harvard University Press, 1945) for a better summary of Mayo's theory.

that factories that prevented social interaction resulted in worker *isolation* and affected productivity. Mayo disagreed with the prevailing assumptions of economic theory and industrial practice that he called the "rabble hypothesis." There were three tenets to that hypotheses, said Mayo, and he took exception to all three: society consisted of unorganized individuals—discrete atoms rather than natural social groups; each individual acts according to calculations of his or her own self-interest rather than being swayed by group norms; and each individual thinks logically, rather than being swayed by emotions and sentiments.[5]

As a result of the Industrial Revolution, workers found themselves performing small, simple, boring, repetitive jobs that had limited meaning and challenge for them. Precisely because jobs were so simple, workers were easily replaced, giving further justification for the belief that workers were merely cogs in the industrial machine. The cost of this efficiency was alienation, defined as self-estrangement, on the part of workers.

Alienation has been studied in connection with various aspects of modern life—politics and religion—and certain members of society—women, ethnic groups, youth, drug-users, and so on. In 1968 a Louis Harris survey proclaimed that 33 million Americans felt alienated.[6] While alienation was once seen as the consequence of an unjust economic system, it is now also seen as a basic reaction to society.[7] This reaction is characterized by estrangement, noninvolvement, aggressive anxiety, and lack of commitment.

Seeman[8] developed a definition of alienation that is composed of six aspects:

1. *Powerlessness:* the sense of low control versus mastery over events.

2. *Meaninglessness:* the sense of incomprehensibility versus understanding of personal and social affairs.

3. *Normlessness:* high expectancies for (or commitment to) socially approved means versus conventional means for the achievement of given goals.

4. *Cultural estrangement:* the individual's rejection of commonly held values in the society (or subsector) versus commitment to the prevalent group standards.

5. *Self-estrangement:* the individual's engagement in activities that are not intrinsically rewarding versus involvement in a task or activity for its own sake.

6. *Social isolation:* the sense of exclusion or rejection versus social acceptance.

Work alienation is an area of particular interest to the field of organizational behavior. Many causes have been identified, but most of them are related to one of the following broad historical trends[9]:

1. The Industrial Revolution

2. The urbanization of workers

3. The division of labor and resultant narrowed job scope

4. The bureaucratic reorganization with its emphasis upon formalized and centralized authority

5. The changing technology that produced mechanization and automation

[5]Charles Perrow, *Complex Organizations: A Critical Essay* (New York: Random House, 1986), p. 59.

[6]Louis Harris, "Harris Survey: 33 Million Americans Feel Alienated," *The Washington Post,* December 16, 1968, Section A, p. 21.

[7]Kenneth Kenniston, "Alienation and the Decline of Utopia," *The American Scholar,* Vol. 39 (1960), pp. 161–200.

[8]Melvin Seeman, "On the Meaning of Alienation," *American Sociological Review,* Vol. 24 (1959), pp. 783–791, and "Alienation Studies," *Annual Review of Sociology,* Vol. 1 (1975), pp. 91–123.

[9]Robert Blauner, *Alienation and Freedom: The Factory Worker and His Industry* (Chicago: University of Chicago Press, 1964).

Characteristics of a typical alienated worker are "lack of communication, poorly defined self-concept, apathy, lack of goals, resistance to change, and limited exercise of alternatives, choices, and decisions."[10] The "blue-collar blues" are perhaps the most common manifestation of worker alienation and are described as "general dissatisfaction with life, blunted aspiration, aggressive feelings toward other kinds of people, low political efficacy, mild but debilitating health reactions."[11] Labor distrust and strife, union grievances, reduced productivity, tardiness, absenteeism, and subversion signal the presence of alienated workers in the workplace.

Individuals react differently to their alienation. Some resort to fatalism, withdrawal, revolutionary impulses to reorder either work or society, involvement in orderly change, subversion, or sabotage. A common response to work alienation is to compartmentalize one's life and focus upon leisure and/or consumption.

In 1964 Robert Blauner wrote a book entitled *Alienation and Freedom: The Factory Worker and His Industry,*[12] which is considered a classic in the field of worker alienation. Blauner looked at four industries characterized by varying degrees of technology: craft, machine tending, assembly line, and continuous process automation. He studied the printing, textile, auto, and chemical industries to determine which types of alienation were present using four of Seeman's categories (powerlessness, meaninglessness, isolation, and self-estrangement). Blauner discovered that workers in the printing industry were the least alienated, due primarily to the control they had over their work and the pride they showed in both their work and profession. The most alienated group were the autoworkers who evidenced each of the four types of alienation. They had no control over their work on the assembly line, worked on only a small percentage of the finished product, lacked informal social structure and status structures, and viewed their jobs only as a means to further other ends.

The textile workers were the next most alienated group because they, too, had limited control and were even more powerless than autoworkers due to the lack of strong union representation. However, the fact that most textile workers lived in milltowns with a strong social structure where kinship ties and religion played a major role, isolation alienation was not found in this group. While some of the male textile workers experienced self-estrangement, the women, immigrants, and rural southerners who worked in the mills were not seen as manifesting the same needs for self-expression as workers in other industries or as northern textile workers.

Blauner found the chemical workers were more alienated than the printers but less alienated than the auto and textile workers. This was attributed to the fact that they were responsible for monitoring machines rather than being at the beck and call of machines as was the case for the textile and autoworkers. Like printers, chemical workers had freedom to control various aspects of their work and could easily see the meaningfulness of their work. The technology allowed them to have social contacts and work in teams. Chemical workers were seen as being loyal to their employer and enjoyed the opportunity to master the work and troubleshoot when a machine broke down.

Blauner's conclusion was that the type of technology determined the degree of worker alienation. He also predicted that automation was a positive improvement over mechanized technology and heralded a less alienated future for factory workers.

---

[10]Robert Cooper, "Alienation from Work," *New Society,* January 30, 1969, pp. 161–163.

[11]Stanley E. Seashore and J. T. Barnowe, "Behind the Averages: A Closer Look at America's Lower-Middle Income Workers," *Proceedings of the 24th Annual Winter Meeting, Industrial Relations Research Association* (December 1971), pp. 358–370.

[12]Ibid.

Although the assembly line is the most efficient design when one considers only the task, few companies have succeeded in ameliorating the mind-numbing quality of working on one. As Garson wrote after observing life in an auto factory: "The underlying assumption in an auto plant is that no worker wants to work. The plant is arranged so that employees can be controlled, checked, and supervised at every point. The efficiency of an assembly line is not only in its speed but in the fact that the workers are easily replaced. This allows the employer to cope with high turnover. But it's a vicious cycle. The job is so unpleasantly subdivided that men are constantly quitting and absenteeism is common. Even an accident is a welcome diversion. Because of the high turnover, management further simplifies the job, and more men quit. But the company has learned to cope with high turnover. So they don't have to worry if men quit or go crazy before they're forty."[13]

While automation has not eliminated alienation, Blauner was certainly correct in his assumption that technology has an impact on the way that work is designed and the way it affects the social system, that is, the people who use it. Technology helps or hinders the development of relationships and determines many of the areas of latitude for employee decision making. Technology also dictates how meaningful a job appears to an employee. Therefore, the crucial factors in work motivation are often limited by the "sociotechnical" system operant in the organization. Successful changes in work design must address both the technology and the social system.

The exercise that follows is designed to allow you to experiment with different sociotechnical systems. You will be asked to consider your learning group as manufacturing companies. During the first round you will work in assembly-line fashion; in the second round you may organize as you wish. By using a questionnaire to keep both productivity records as well as satisfaction indices, you will be able to examine the factors that influence work motivation and productivity.

[13]Barbara Garson, "Luddites in Lordstown," in *Life in Organizations*, by Rosabeth Moss Kantor and Barry A. Stein, eds. (New York: Basic Books, 1979), pp. 216–217.

III

Procedure for Group Meeting: Moon Tents and Shallow Water Cargo Carriers Simulation

STEP 1. *Company formation and organization.* Each learning group will form a company that will make moon tents and shallow water carriers.

STEP 2. *Choice of manager.* The instructor will choose a person to play the role of general manager (GM) from each learning group. The GM will be in charge of making purchases and production decisions. The GM will then choose an assistant general manager (AGM) who will be in charge of organizing the assembly line, quality control, and sales. The rest of the group will be assembly-line workers. The GM's instructions are found on page 515. The AGM's instructions are found on page 517. The workers' instructions are located on page 519. WORKERS SHOULD SIT QUIETLY—NO TALKING ALLOWED—WHILE THE GM AND THE AGM READ THEIR INSTRUCTIONS.

STEP 3. *Preparation for production of the moon tent.* (allow 10 minutes) After reading the GM's instructions, the GM should make decisions about production goals and materials purchasing, following the steps in moon tent production forms beginning on page 525.

Meanwhile the AGM should be setting up the assembly line and assigning tasks to workers. Workers should sit in a row and perform one or more steps in the construction and then pass the moon tent on to the next person. WORKERS ARE NOT ALLOWED TO TALK TO EACH OTHER; THEY MAY ONLY ADDRESS THE GM OR THE AGM. Workers should practice their step of the production under the direction of the AGM, who should also establish quality control procedures.

STEP 4. *Production of the moon tent.* (allow 15 minutes) The GM should conduct the 6-minute production run as specified on the moon tent form. Following production, the instructor should buy those products of acceptable quality from each company's AGM. The GM or the AGM should compute the company's profit and loss and each person should complete the Moon Tent Questionnaire on page 527.

STEP 5. *Production of shallow water cargo carriers.* (40 minutes) There are two major modifications in your instructions for the production of the shallow water cargo carriers:

   a. In this round the production steps have been expanded. Your company will be allowed to make an initial bid, do a time trial, and rebid before making the final production run.

   b. Also, *your company may organize in any way and establish whatever work procedures it wishes.* Workers may talk whenever they like. Managers are freed from the authoritarian role they were asked to play during the last round. You may find the data from the Moon Test Questionnaire useful in planning your production of the shallow water cargo carrier.

Instructions for the General Manager (GM)

Your task is to be an authoritative manager of an assembly line. There's no need to exaggerate your role, but you and your AGM are the only ones who understand what needs to be done. Just tell the workers what to do; they're probably not interested in the details. You've had trouble with them in the past because they sometimes loaf on the job. Your success, however, depends upon their producing lots of moon tents. Don't waste time establishing a relationship with these workers because turnover is high at this plant.

1. Don't let the workers do much talking. Remember time is money and your bonus is at stake here. The more moon tents they make, the more money you make.

2. Make sure your AGM is carrying out his or her task of lining the workers up correctly and assigning them to their "Steps in the Assembly Production Line" found on page 521.

3. Read the "Steps in Moon Tent Production" so you understand your responsibility for setting production and profit levels for your unit. Make these decisions by yourself so everyone knows you have real managerial potential.

4. Make your production level decisions, tell the workers what their quota levels are, and carry out the production run.

5. Figure out your profit statistics or ask your AGM to do so.

Instructions for the Assistant General Manager

Your job is to supervise the work of the assembly-line workers. *Don't let them talk on the line or valuable seconds will be lost.* Don't let them give you any advice or you'll look weak. Try to make all the decisions so your boss will be impressed by your authoritative manner.

1. Arrange the workers in a straight line.

2. Divide the number of steps (14) in the assembly-line production (see page 521) by the number of workers you have to find out how many steps each one must perform. For example, if you have five workers and 14 job steps, four workers should do 3 steps each and one should do 2 steps.

3. Assign each worker the steps for which he or she is responsible. Don't have any duplication of effort.

4. Inspect each moon tent when it is done. Use the Quality Control Points on page 524 to guide you.

5. Do whatever else your GM tells you to do.

Instructions for Workers

Guess what? Two more college-educated people have been brought in to run your production unit. You wonder how much they know about making moon tents, but you're smart enough to know it doesn't pay to talk on the assembly line. Just keep your mouth shut and do what you're told. Last time you made a suggestion, they called you a troublemaker.

Steps in Moon Tent Assembly Production Line

The following are directions for making a moon tent. For each step there is a picture showing you what to do and another picture showing how it should then look. Check this before going on to the next step. There are 14 steps.

1. You should have a piece of paper that is blank on one side and looks like this on the other side:

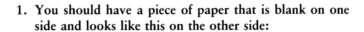

2. Turn the paper over so that the *blank side* is facing up and the pattern is nearest you.

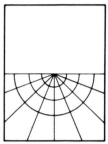

printed pattern at this end   YOU

3. Fold AB to CD.

It should look like this:

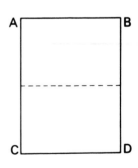

4. Fold G to F.

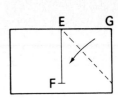

It should look like this:

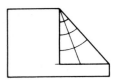

5. Bend down H to F.

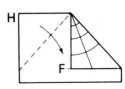

It should now look like this:

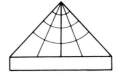

6. Fold one layer of paper (up direction) along JK.

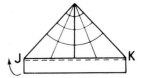

It should now look like this:

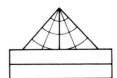

7. Turn the moon tent over to the other side. It should now look like this:

8. Fold (up direction) along LM.

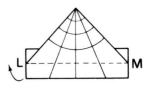

It should now look like this:

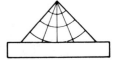

9. Tuck section N (just the top layer of paper) back around the edge of the tent, so it is between the back of the tent and the back layer of paper.

Fold section O (back piece) toward you over the edge of the tent and press flat.

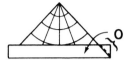

It should now look like this:

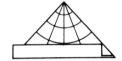

10. Do the same thing to the *left end* (don't turn it over). It should look like this:

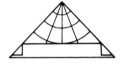

11. Pick up the tent and hold it in your hands with open side (P) down.
Open up P with your fingers and keep pulling it apart until points Q and R meet.

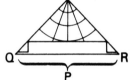

Turn the paper so that Q is facing up and R is underneath. It should look like this:

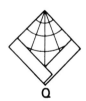

12. Fold up Q along ST.

It should now look like this:

13. Turn over so that R is facing up. Fold up on UV.

It should now look like this:

14. Open up W and stand up your Moon Tent!
   For "quality control" make sure Q and R stay up along
   the tent.

Passes Quality Control →

Not Good ⟶

QUALITY CONTROL POINTS FOR THE MOON TENT

1. The top of the tent must come to a point.
2. The printing must be on the outside of the tent.
3. The turned-up points at the base of the tent must lie flat against the tent sides.

Steps in Moon Tent Production

The instructor or a nonparticipant should record original bids, final bids, product accepted, and profit and loss on a chalkboard or newsprint so that all may see the bids of all companies. The instructor should also act as the buyer and final approver of product quality. Cost and profit information for the moon tent, as well as typical assembly times for one unit are as follows.

1. Cost and Profit Information for the Moon Tent

NUMBER OF SETS PURCHASED	TOTAL COST	TOTAL SELLING PRICE	TOTAL PROFIT
3	$147,900	$150,000	$ 2,100
4	195,000	200,000	5,000
5	240,000	250,000	10,000
6	279,000	300,000	20,100
7	319,900	350,000	30,100
8	360,000	400,000	40,000
9	400,000	450,000	50,000
10	440,000	500,000	60,000
11	474,000	550,000	76,000
12	519,600	600,000	80,400
13	559,650	650,000	90,350
14	599,900	700,000	100,100
$14 + n$	$599,900 + 40,250n$	$700,000 + 50,000n$	$100,100 + 9,750n$

2. Assembly Times for One Moon Tent
This table gives assembly times for one moon tent based on the actual *individual* performance of people who have assembled them.

- Fast assembly time (top 10%)   35–45 seconds
- Average assembly time   45–55 seconds
- Slow assembly time (low 10%)   over 55 seconds

3. Production Decision
Record here the number of moon tent sets you decided to produce: _____

4. Maximum Potential Profit
Your maximum potential profit can be computed in the following manner: From the information provided in the cost and profit table (step 1), you can determine the profit associated with reaching your *final* production decision (step 3). Enter the total profit here: _____
Production of the Moon Tent: You now have 6 minutes to produce the number of Moon Tents for which you purchased materials. Only units that meet quality control specifications will be accepted for sale.

5. Postproduction Inspection
Carefully inspect the units you have produced for quality and record the acceptable number of completed products here: _____(Wait for the leader or inspector to inspect your products.)

6. Actual Profit Earned

To determine the actual amount of your net profit (or loss, if negative),

a. Enter here the total selling price (see cost and profit table) for the number of products of satisfactory quality you have completed:

$a = $ _____

Note: You cannot sell more products than your final production decision (item 3).

b. Enter here the total costs (item 1) for the final number of products you decided to produce (item 3):

$b = $ _____

c. Your actual net profit or loss can then be computed in the following manner:

Net profit or loss $= a - (b + c) = $ _____

7. Possible Profit Ratio

Your percentage of possible profit earned is the ratio between net profit (6c) and maximum potential profit (4a). Enter that ratio here _____

8. Each person should fill out the Moon Tent Questionnaire.

Company (Team) Name _____

Moon Tent Questionnaire

1. How satisfied were you with your group?

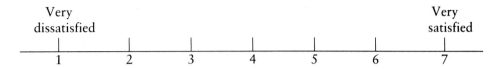

2. How productive was your group?

3. What did you like about your work?

4. What did you dislike?

Directions for Making the Shallow Water Carrier

These are directions for making a shallow water cargo carrier. The first 9 steps are the same as for the moon tent. For each step there is a picture showing what to do, and another picture showing what it should then look like. There are 14 steps.

1. Hold the sheet of paper so the printing on it is facing up, the letters SWCC nearest you are upside down (ƆƆWS).

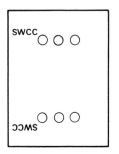

   It should look like this:

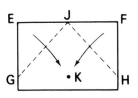

2. Fold AB to CD.

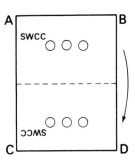

   It should now look like this:

3. Fold in along JG and JH so that E and F meet at point K.

   It should now look like this:

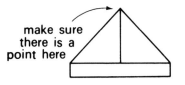

make sure there is a point here

4. Fold *one layer* of paper (up direction) along LM.

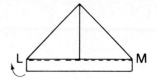

It should now look like this:

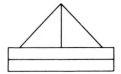

5. Turn your shallow water cargo carrier over to the other side. It should look like this:

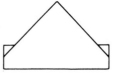

6. Fold (up direction) along NP.

It should look like this:

7. Tuck section Q (just the top layer of paper) back around the edge of the carrier, so it is between the back of the carrier and the back layer of paper.

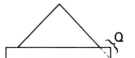

Fold section Q (back piece) toward you over the edge of the carrier and press flat.

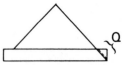

It should now look like this:

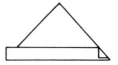

8. Do the same thing to the *left end (don't turn it over)*. It should now look like this:

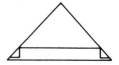

9. Pick up the shallow water cargo carrier and hold it in your hands with the open side (R) down. Open up R with your fingers and keep pulling it apart until points S and T meet.

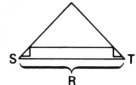

Turn the paper and fold so that S is facing up and T is underneath. It should now look like this:

10. Fold up S to U.

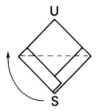

It should now look like this:

11. Turn over so that T is facing up (side without printing on it). Fold up T to U.

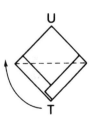

It should now look like this:

12. Pick up the carrier and hold it in your hands, with the open side, V, down. Open V with your fingers and keep pulling it apart until points W and X meet. Turn the paper so that W is facing up and X is underneath. It should look like the diagram shown here:

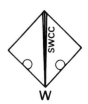

13. Fold W to A and then *bring W back down* again to its original position. There should now be a crease at BC.

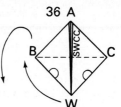

Turn over so that X is facing up. Fold X to A and then *bring X down* again to its original position. There should now be a crease at DE.

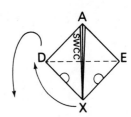

Grab Y (front and back at the top left point) with left hand, and Z (front and back at the top right point) with right hand and pull apart as far as it will go.

It should now look like this:

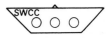

14. Stand it up. You have finished making your shallow water cargo carrier!

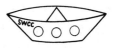

QUALITY CONTROL POINTS
FOR THE SHALLOW WATER CARGO CARRIER

1. The lettering SWCC must appear on the outside of the boat.
2. The middle point must be a point, not a curve.
3. The middle point must come even with or above the sides of the boat.

Steps in Shallow Water Cargo Carrier Production

Cost and profit information for the shallow water cargo carrier, as well as typical assembly times for one unit, are given as follows.

1. Cost and Profit Information for the Shallow Water Cargo Carrier

NUMBER OF SETS PURCHASED	TOTAL COST	TOTAL SELLING PRICE	TOTAL PROFIT
3	$267,000	$270,000	$ 3,000
4	352,000	360,000	8,000
5	420,000	450,000	30,000
6	450,000	540,000	90,000
7	483,000	630,000	147,000
8	512,000	720,000	208,000
9	540,000	810,000	270,000
10	570,000	900,000	330,000
11	605,000	990,000	385,000
12	636,000	1,080,000	444,000
13	663,000	1,170,000	507,000
14	700,000	1,260,000	560,000
$14 + n$	$700,000 + 37,000n$	$1,260,000 + 90,000n$	$560,000 + 53,000n$

2. Assembly Times for One Shallow Water Cargo Carrier
   This table gives assembly times for one SWCC based on the actual performance of people who have produced them.

   ■ Fast assembly time (top 10%)   40–50 seconds
   ■ Average assembly time   50–60 seconds
   ■ Slow assembly time (low 10%)   over 60 seconds

3. Tentative Decision
   After building your model and inspecting the information given, make a tentative decision about the number of units you wish to buy for production in a 6-minute period. Record that number here _____.

4. Timed Trial Run
   Now that you have made your tentative production decision, prepare for a timed practice trial. When you are ready, take a timed practice assembly. Record the construction time it took to complete one unit here _____.

5. Profit Reduction Resulting from Change of Decision
   Having taken the time trial, you may wish to change your decision about the number of SWCCs you can produce in 6 minutes. Production decision changes invariably cost money. The following table tells how much this change will cost.

CHANGE	PROFIT REDUCTION
1 more or 1 less	$12,000
2 more or 2 less	19,000
3 more or 3 less	27,000
4 more or 4 less	36,000
5 more or 5 less	46,000
6 more or 6 less	57,000

6. Production Decision
   After making your final decision, record here the number of sets you decided to produce _____.

7. Maximum Potential Profit
   Your maximum potential profit can be computed in the following manner.
   a. From the information provided in the cost and profit table (item 1), you can determine the profit associated with reaching your final production decision (item 6). Enter that total profit here:
   $a =$ _____
   b. If your final production decision (item 6) is different from your tentative production decision (item 3), you must subtract from the profit entered in a the correct profit reduction indicated in the table provided in item 5. Enter that amount here:
   $b =$ _____
   c. Enter your maximum potential profit here; subtract b from a:
   $c =$ _____

   Production of the shallow water cargo carrier: You now have 6 minutes to produce the number of SWCCs for which you purchased materials. Only units that meet quality control specifications will be accepted for sale.

8. Postproduction Inspection
   Carefully inspect the units you have produced for quality and record the acceptable number of completed products here _____. (If you are working in a group, wait for the leader to inspect your products.)

9. Actual Profit Earned
   To determine the actual amount of your net profit (or loss, if negative):
   a. Enter here the total selling price (see table, item 1) for the number of products of satisfactory quality you have completed:
   $a =$ _____
   Note: You cannot sell more products than your final production decision (step 6).
   b. Enter here the total costs (item 1) for the final number of products you decided to produce (item 6):
   $b =$ _____
   c. If your final production decision (item 6) was different from your tentative production decision (item 3), enter here the correct profit reduction as indicated in the table provided in item 5:
   $c =$ _____
   d. Your actual net profit or loss can then be computed in the following manner:
   Net profit or loss $= a - (b + c) =$ _____

10. Possible Profit Ratio
    Your percentage of possible profit earned is the ratio between net profit (9d) and maximum potential profit (7c). Enter that ratio here _____.

11. Each person should fill out the Shallow Water Cargo Carrier Questionnaire.

    Company (Team) Name _____

Shallow Water Cargo Carrier Questionnaire

1. How satisfied were you with your group?

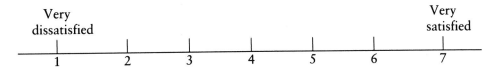

2. How productive was your group?

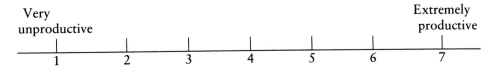

3. What did you like about your work?

4. What did you dislike?

STEP 6. *Work and motivation discussion.* (30 minutes, entire group) Tabulate the data from the two questionnaires by teams and display them on chalkboard or newsprint. The discussion should explore the following questions:

a. What were the most dramatic data differences between the first and second rounds? In which teams did they occur?

b. Have the teams with the greatest differences discussed the reasons for them? Did similar things happen in other teams? List them.

c. In general, what were the factors that led to satisfaction and productivity in the first round? In the second round?

d. If you had to continue working in this kind of production, which arrangement of work would you prefer? Why?

e. What conclusions can you now come to about improving the quality of work life in organizations? What kinds of things are helpful in sustaining interest and motivation?

f. Had there been a different technology and task, what would the effect have been on the way you went about the work?

g. How might you redesign the jobs you had to increase productivity? Satisfaction?

h. What connections can you make between this exercise and the readings?

IV

Follow-up

You have just finished a simulation designed to allow you to create your own work situation and try it out. You have probably drawn some conclusions about how work of this type can be best organized to maximize productivity and employee satisfaction, and quite probably your conclusions differ from those of some others in the class. In that regard you are not much different from other managers and the behavioral scientists who have worked in the area of motivation. Just about everything conceivable has been tried to improve employee motivation and productivity, from incentive plans to piped-in music, all with some success, but also some failures.[14]

The term "alienation" is not as popular as it once was; we are more likely to hear about the other side of the coin, "job involvement." However, we still hear managers complain that their workers are not motivated.

In recent years the satisfaction and productivity of the American worker has become a focal point for national attention and concern. In manufacturing organizations across the country, workers are singing the "blue-collar blues," and American worker productivity, once the leader of the world, is now widely blamed as one of the factors responsible for our faltering position in international competition. There are those who blame workers for this state of affairs, citing "lack of worker motivation" and the general decline of the "work ethic" as reasons for apathy and poor quality in the workplace. This reasoning, however, is limited and superficial; for, as was pointed out in Chapter 4, on individual motivation, there are no "unmotivated" human beings. When managers say their workers are unmotivated, they really mean that they are not motivated to do the tasks assigned them. These same workers are likely to show great motivation in other areas of their life, at home, in hobbies, in community affairs, and so on. The practical implication of this distinction for worker satisfaction and productivity is that time and effort spent lamenting lazy workers might be better spent in examination of the nature of the work itself and in the redesign of these tasks and jobs to add the personal autonomy, need satisfaction, and challenge that stimulate the motivation to work. The intrinsic motivation of the employee is very important, but job motivation is also affected by the situations in which workers find themselves.

Before we look at situations that are motivating, let's briefly touch upon some of the theories about personal motivation that were described in Chapter 4. McClelland identified three needs that motivate people: power, achievement, and affiliation. Notice how closely these parallel three of the aspects of alienation: Marx's powerlessness, Durkheim's meaninglessness, and Mayo's isolation. Attempts to create situations that are most motivating to people with high needs for achievement have also been productive for other people. Litwin and Stringer,[15] for instance, created three mock companies in the same business which they varied only by the style of the manager and the organizational climate he created. At the end of the two-week experiment, the company based upon achievement principles had outperformed the other two companies that were organized on "authoritarian" and "friendly" principles. In general, high achievers want:

[14]See W. A. Pasmore, "Turning People on to Work," in *Organizational Psychology: Readings on Human Behavior in Organizations,* ed. by Kolb, Rubin, and McIntyre (Englewood Cliffs, NJ: Prentice Hall, 1984).

[15]G. H. Litwin and R. A. Stringer, Jr., *Motivation and Organizational Climate* (Boston: Harvard University, Graduate School of Business Administration, Division of Research, 1968).

1. *Immediate, concrete feedback.* They want to know as soon as possible how well they are doing. If they are not doing well, they also want to know that so that they may adjust their performance to meet their personal and/or organizational goals.

2. *Moderate risk-taking situations.* They like the kind of situation that is a personal challenge, not one that is going to be left to fate. They operate best in the area where the probability of success at a task and its incentive value are about equal. A task that is too simple will not offer enough of a challenge and will not capture their interest for very long, unless it is a component of a more challenging goal. In short, they like situations in which they can be successful most of the time, as long as they give it their best shot.

3. *Personal responsibility for their own success or failure.* This is an outgrowth of both (1) and (2). When high-achievement-motivated people fail at a task, they want to know why, not alibi. They learn from facing the data squarely so as not to repeat their mistakes.[16]

Maslow developed a hierarchy of needs that ranged from physical needs, security needs, social belonging, prestige, to self-actualization. According to his theory, once lower-level needs are satisfied, they are no longer motivating. Maslow's self-actualization need relates to the desire to learn and develop oneself. Dead-end jobs with no possibility of greater learning or advancement provide little opportunity for self-actualization and decrease the likelihood of job involvement for people with strong self-actualization needs.

The work of Frederick Herzberg has been helpful in learning what it is about a work situation that increases satisfaction and productivity. Herzberg has differentiated between factors in a work situation that are motivating to the employee and those that we often assume are motivators but are really "hygiene factors."[17] Examples of hygiene factors are supervision, work conditions, relationships, pay and security, and company policies. A hygiene factor is never a motivator but will decrease motivation if it is not present or if it is present in inadequate ways. A motivator is a condition of the way the work is done that keeps satisfaction and productivity high. Motivating factors are achievement, recognition, the work itself, responsibility and advancement and growth.

Based upon what we know about alienation and motivation, job situations that motivate people have the following characteristics:

1. *Skill variety*—the degree to which a job requires a range of personal competencies and abilities in carrying out the work.

2. *Task identity*—the degree to which a job requires completion of a "whole" and identifiable piece of work, that is, doing a job from beginning to end with a visible outcome.

3. *Task significance*—the degree to which the job is perceived by the employee as having a substantial impact on the lives of other people, whether those people are within or outside of the organization.

4. *Autonomy*—the degree to which the job provides freedom, independence, and discretion to the employee in scheduling the tasks and in determining the procedure to be used in carrying out the tasks.

5. *Job feedback*—the degree to which carrying out the job-related tasks provides the individual with direct and clear information about the effectiveness of his or her performance.

[16]David C. McClelland, *The Achieving Society* (Princeton, NJ: D. Van Nostrand, 1961).

[17]Frederic Herzberg, *Work and the Nature of Man* (Cleveland, OH: World Publishing Company, 1966), and "One More Time: How Do You Motivate Employees?" *Harvard Business Review* (January–February, 1968), pp. 53–62.

6. *Dealing with others*—the degree to which a job requires employees to deal with other people to complete their work.

7. *Friendship opportunities*—the degree to which a job allows employees to talk with one another on the job and to establish informal relationships with other employees at work.[18]

Skill variety, task identity, and task significance are geared toward replacing the sense of meaningfulness that was lessened by dividing jobs into small, repetitive segments. Granting employees autonomy over their jobs encourages them to feel responsible (powerful and in control) for the outcome of their work and reduces legalistic approaches to work, for example, "That's not my job" or "If they're gonna give me a robot's job to do, I'm gonna do it like a robot! Anyway, it just lowers my production record to get up and point out someone else's error."[19] Job feedback allows employees to receive immediate feedback from the work itself, not from a supervisor. This relates to one of the conditions McClelland found to be most favorable for people with high needs for achievement—immediate concrete feedback that allows them to adjust their performance to meet their personal and/or organizational goals. Jobs that involve dealing with others and have friendship opportunities are ways of encouraging social belonging and combating the social isolation that Mayo reported.

It is possible to design jobs that are more congruent with human needs and motivation. The major ways of doing so are briefly described as follows:

1. *Job rotation* programs that move people from one job to another to decrease their boredom and allow them to learn different skills.

2. *Job enlargement* policies increase the number of tasks performed by an individual. In an assembly-line example, a worker would perhaps install an entire door panel rather than securing only one part of the door. Herzberg called the addition of interrelated tasks "horizontal job loading."[20]

Job enlargement can meet employees' motivational needs because it allows more ownership over a product or process and decreases monotony. It also provides an opportunity for workers to feel more competent, since they may get to use more of their skills. Being responsible for a larger task may increase the meaningfulness of the job in the worker's eyes. However, remember the comment of one critic, "You combine seven boring jobs and what do you get?"

3. *Job enrichment* methods attempt to change the nature of the job by broadening responsibilities, giving more autonomy for decision making, creating client systems and direct feedback systems, and generally enlarging the scope of jobs. Herzberg called this type of job design "vertical job loading" because it also includes tasks formerly performed by someone at a higher level—planning and control functions.[21] For example, a sales support clerk who formerly handled only one piece of the paperwork for the entire sales staff is now given responsibility for all the paperwork in one district. He is encouraged to deal directly with the sales staff and quickly becomes an important resource for them. He also has discretionary control over the scheduling of his work and the responsibility for making sure he has made no errors. A feedback system is established so he can gauge both the quality and

---

[18]This list is composed of factors identified by J. Richard Hackman and Greg Oldham, *Work Redesign* (Reading, MA: Addison-Wesley, 1980), pp. 77–80; J. R. Hackman, G. R. Oldham, R. Janson, and K. Purdy, "A New Strategy for Job Enrichment," *Readings;* and Henry P. Sims, Jr., Andrew D. Szilagyi, and Robert T. Keller, "The Measurement of Job Characteristics," *Academy of Management Journal,* (June 1976), p. 197.

[19]Garson, *Luddites in Lordtown,* p. 235.

[20]Frederic Herzberg, "One More Time: How Do You Motivate Employees?" *Harvard Business Review* (January–February 1968).

[21]Ibid.

quantity of his output. Both contact with the sales staff and the monitoring of his work were formerly performed by his supervisor.

What is motivating about job enrichment? It resolves the problems of meaninglessness, powerlessness, and isolation. Job enrichment not only has the same motivational advantages as job enlargement, but the effects with job enrichment are stronger and enrichment has the added benefit of granting workers autonomy. With all the publicity about entrepreneurs who want to run their own show, we can see how important autonomy is to many employees. Autonomy allows people to utilize even more skills and to exercise their creativity and capacity to learn and develop.

4. *Sociotechnical system* interventions attempt to match the necessary technology of the job with the social needs of the employees. Their goal is to produce a fit or integration of these two components. It's noteworthy that the basic unit of work design here is usually the group rather than the individual. Job rotation, enlargement, and enrichment focus upon individual rather than group needs.[22]

The most common example of sociotechnical systems are *autonomous work teams*. Such teams are totally responsible for assigning the work, determining the work schedule, work process, quality control procedures, reward structure, and so on. Perhaps the most famous example of autonomous work teams is Volvo's Kalmar plant. Instead of using an assembly line, the cars remain stationary while teams of approximately 20 workers install an entire system, such as instrumentation, electrical systems, interiors, and so on. Each group contracts with Volvo for a certain level of productivity. However, how the group organizes itself, who performs what tasks, and when breaks are taken are decided by the groups themselves. The groups inspect their own work and are given feedback by a computerized quality control system feedback. Absenteeism at Kalmar is half that reported in Volvo's traditional plant, and productivity is 20 percent higher than what the company expected.[23]

Sociotechnical systems have the advantages of all the previous design systems plus the added benefit of group membership. Interdependent work teams anchor people firmly within a social system, thus avoiding isolation and normlessness. Furthermore, groups are more creative and productive than are individuals when it comes to complex technology.

5. *Vision-led* organizations are predicated on the importance of meaning and significance to workers. Workers are pulled forward by a vision of accomplishing a certain goal.[24] Shared values rather than close supervision and controls are the glue that keeps employees motivated and producing well. Companies like the ones Peters and Waterman describe in *In Search of Excellence* are examples of vision-led organizations.[25]

6. *The quality movement* was started by Edward Deming,[26] an American management consultant who taught his famous 14 principles to the Japanese in the

[22]An entire issue of the *Journal of Applied Behavioral Science,* Vol. 22, no. 3 (1986), edited by W. Pasmore and W. Barko, is devoted to sociotechnical systems and includes information about autonomous work teams. See also the article by Schoonhoven on "The Sociotechnical Considerations for the Development of the Space Station: Autonomy and the Human Element in Space" in D. A. Kolb, I. M. Rubin, and J. S. Osland, *Organizational Behavior: Practical Readings for Managers* (Englewood Cliffs, NJ: Prentice Hall, 1990).

[23]For descriptions of the Kalmar plant, see P. G. Gyllenhammer's *People at Work* (Reading, MA: Addison-Wesley, 1977), and B. Jönsson, "The Quality of Work Life: The Volvo Experience," *Journal of Business,* Vol. 1 (1982), pp. 119–126.

[24]See Richard Walton's article, "From Control to Commitment in the Workplace" in the *Harvard Business Review,* Vol. 63 (March–April 1985), or "A Vision-Led Approach to Management Restructuring," *Organization Dynamics,* Vol. 14 (Spring 1986).

[25]Thomas Peters and Robert Waterman, Jr., *In Search of Excellence: Lessons from America's Best Run Companies* (New York: Harper & Row, 1982), and David Bradford and Allan Cohen's book, *Managing for Excellence: The Guide to Developing High Performance in Contemporary Organizations* (New York: John Wiley, 1984).

[26]See Myron Tribus's article, "Deming's Redefinition of Management" in D. A. Kolb, I. M. Rubin, and J. S. Osland, *Organizational Behavior: Practical Readings for Managers* (Englewood Cliffs, NJ: Prentice Hall, 1990).

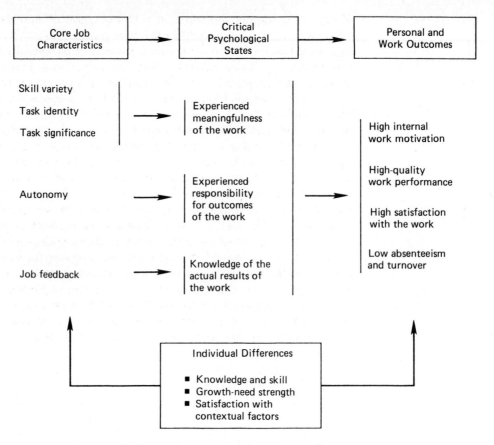

FIGURE 19–1 **Job Characteristics Enrichment Model** *J. R. Hackman and G. R. Old-ham,* Work Redesign © *1980, Addison Wesley Publishing Co., Inc., Reading, Mass. Adapted from p. 90. Reprinted with permission of the publisher.*

1950s, at the time the "Made in Japan" label was synonymous with poor quality. Japan's current reputation for producing goods of extremely high quality is credited in large part to Deming. Quality programs focus on managing the process of the work rather than people and give workers the challenge of constantly trying to improve the quality of the work processes and placing primary emphasis upon the customer. This provides workers with a sense of meaning. Such programs teach statistics as a common language that is used to measure variances from the perfect quality standard. Each employee is taught to inspect his or her own work so that defects and reworks are reduced or even eliminated. This emphasis on immediate feedback on quality stimulates needs for achievement. Since improving quality often needs more than one mind and the cooperation of more than one department, quality programs generally involve group problem-solving efforts, which meet people's need for affiliation. Quality programs focus on the requirements of the task, but their manner of doing so also meets the motivational needs of employees.[27]

Job redesign attempts such as those mentioned earlier have been made in many organizations. Some have succeeded while others have not.[28] The reasons for failure may have more to do with the way they were implemented than the particular merit of the new design. In some cases successful interventions have resulted not only in greater job involvement and satisfaction, but also in greater productivity.

In their Job Characteristics Enrichment Model, which appears in Figure

[27]David A. Garvin's book, *Managing Quality: The Strategic and Competitive Edge* (New York: Free Press, 1988), provides a good starting place for reading about the quality movement.

[28]V. Macaluso, W. McCreedy, D. Bond, S. King, and P. Forkel, *Work in America* (Cambridge, MA: MIT Press, 1972). This study was commissioned by HEW to examine the results of work redesign projects.

19–1, Hackman and Oldham[29] show that the positive outcomes of job enrichment characteristics are high internal work motivation, high-quality work performance, high satisfaction with the work, and low absenteeism and turnover. However, these outcomes occur at a maximum level only when all three of the critical psychological states are experienced: (1) experienced meaningfulness of the work, (2) experienced responsibility for work outcomes, and (3) knowledge of the actual results of the work. Hackman and Oldham also note that there are three types of individual differences that must be taken into consideration when planning job redesign projects. The first is the *knowledge and skill of the employee*—is the employee capable of performing an enriched job? The second is *growth-needs strength,* which refers to the individual's personal need for learning, self-development, and challenge. This is similar to Maslow's self-actualization need and Alderfer's growth-needs concept (see Chapter 4). People with low growth needs may well prefer repetitive jobs to enriched ones. The final individual difference is *satisfaction with contextual factors.* This refers to Herzberg's hygiene factors (salary, work conditions, policies, etc.), which were also discussed in Chapter 4. Job redesign efforts are unlikely to be successful if employees are dissatisfied with contextual factors.

Ensuring that the work situation is one that employees find motivating and one that encourages job involvement is a major, ongoing task of managers. Because of the close relationship between well-designed jobs and productivity, it is an area that managers and organizations cannot afford to overlook.

V

Learning Points

1. The changes in the nature of work and the social system brought about by the Industrial Revolution resulted in feelings of
   a. Powerlessness (Marx).
   b. Meaninglessness (Durkheim).
   c. Social isolation (Mayo).
2. These feelings came to be known as "alienation," which is simply defined as self-estrangement.
3. The cause of work alienation is usually traced to the Industrial Revolution, urbanization of workers, the division of labor that led to narrowed job scope, bureaucracy, and the switch to mechanized and automated technology.
4. Characteristics of work alienation are lack of communication, poorly defined self-concept, apathy, lack of goals, resistance to change, and limited exercise of alternatives, choices, and decisions.
5. Blauner found that the type of technology affected the degree of alienation found within four different industries. Workers in craft technologies and automated technologies had less alienation than did workers in mechanized technologies such as assembly lines.

[29]J. Richard Hackman and Greg R. Oldham, "Development of the Job Diagnostic Survey," *Journal of Applied Psychology,* Vol. 60 (1975), pp. 159–170.

6. Motivation is an internal state. However, it is also affected by work situations that encourage or discourage its expression.

7. Three theories of internal needs that motivate people are those of
   a. McClelland: power, achievement, and affiliation.
   b. Maslow: physical survival, security, social belonging, prestige, and self-actualization (self-development).
   c. Herzberg: challenging work, responsibility, achievement, recognition, advancement and growth.

8. These needs are met to a degree in jobs that have the following characteristics:
   a. Skill variety
   b. Task identity
   c. Task significance
   d. Autonomy
   e. Job feedback
   f. Dealing with others
   g. Friendship opportunities

9. Methods of job redesign and motivating employees are
   a. Job rotation—switching different jobs.
   b. Job enlargement—horizontal job loading, which combines related tasks.
   c. Job enrichment—vertical job loading, which increases job scope by including planning and control functions formerly held by supervisors. It also includes client contact and direct output feedback.
   d. Sociotechnical systems—integration of the needs of both people and technology. The basic work unit is usually the group rather than the individual. Autonomous work teams are an example.
   e. Vision-led organizations—employees are motivated by a common vision and shared values.
   f. Quality movement—employees are motivated by the constant challenge to improve quality.

10. Job redesign efforts have been found to improve both satisfaction and productivity in some cases. However, job enrichment programs are also contingent upon the individual worker's (1) knowledge and skill; (2) need for growth, self-development and challenge; and (3) satisfaction with contextual factors.

VI

Tips for Managers

- The key to success in redesigning work often lies in the way changes are implemented. Therefore, it's important to pay attention to implementation and the "fit" between the new design and other aspects of the organization.

- Whenever a new system of work design is implemented, it's realistic to expect that production may drop until employees master the new system and work their way up the learning curve.

- Job enrichment cannot take the place of decent pay and job security. Bear in mind Maslow's hierarchy, which states that pay and security are lower-level needs that must be satisfied before the higher-level needs met by job enrichment come into play.

- One way of checking up on job design is to do a flowchart on each work process. Find out how many different people need to "touch" a piece of paperwork before it is completed. Any time a paper is passed to other people for handling, it must then compete for their attention with all the other papers in their in-basket. If speed is important, it makes more sense to have as few people as possible touching a document.

- Some people are very happy to perform jobs that are perceived by others as boring. These people may not welcome job enrichment. Sometimes the best solution is to leave them where they are and design around them. Job enrichment should be made available for as many employees as possible, but not everyone will want to take advantage of it.

- Focus on providing motivating situations for those who desire it, *within* the organization's capabilities. There may well be people whose ambition or need to grow outstrips the opportunities an organization can provide. Rather than go overboard (remember Quinn's positive and negative circles in Chapter 2 and the danger of emphasizing employee needs at the cost of productivity?), counsel such employees to look for work elsewhere. Once again, managers have to exhibit good judgment and a knack for balance. If a manager ignores the motivational needs of employees, low productivity, alienation, and high turnover and absenteeism may result. On the other hand, too much attention to employee needs without equal emphasis upon the needs of the organization encourages people to fixate on themselves. The "Me-Generation" cannot be allowed to lose sight of the greater good so redesign programs have to be closely tied to the success of the organization.

- Statistics show that a greater number of Americans are now living alone and that the majority of households is no longer the traditional nuclear family. This may mean that more employees are seeking to meet their social needs at work than was true when family and community ties were stronger.

- Conditions that affect the success of work design interventions are organizational culture, technology, union support or lack therof, and the nature of the work force itself.

VII
Personal Application Assignment

The assignment for this chapter is to focus upon an experience you've had with job involvement and design in an organization. Choose a significant incident or situation related to the concepts discussed in the chapter that occurred at work or elsewhere. (This course or your academic program may be eye opening.)

A. *Concrete Experience*

1. *Objectively* describe the experience ("who," "what," "when," "where," "how," type information—up to 2 points).

2. *Subjectively* describe your feelings, perceptions, and thoughts that occurred *during* (not after) the experience (up to 2 points). Does this section have too much detail? (If so, delete 1 point.)

B. *Reflective Observation*

1. Look at the experience from different points of view. How many points of view did you include that are *relevant* (up to 2 points)?

2. Use these perspectives to add more meaning to the incident (up to 2 points).

C. *Abstract Conceptualization*

1. Relate concepts from the assigned readings and the lecture to the experience (i.e., what theories that you heard in the lecture or read in the *Reader* relate to your understanding of this incident?). Make reference to at least two sources. Use standard referencing format and include the page number to which you are referring. How many sources did you use and how clearly did you explain their theories (up to 4 points)?

2. You can also create an original model or theory, but it should not replace course concepts.

D. *Active Experimentation*

1. Write about what you will do in the future that will improve your effectiveness. Use rules of thumb or action resolutions.

2. Are they described specifically, thoroughly, and in detail (up to 4 points).

E. *Integration, Synthesis and Writing*

1. Did you write about something personally important to you (up to 1 point)?

2. Was it well written (up to 2 points)?

3. Did you integrate and synthesize the different sections (up to 1 point)?

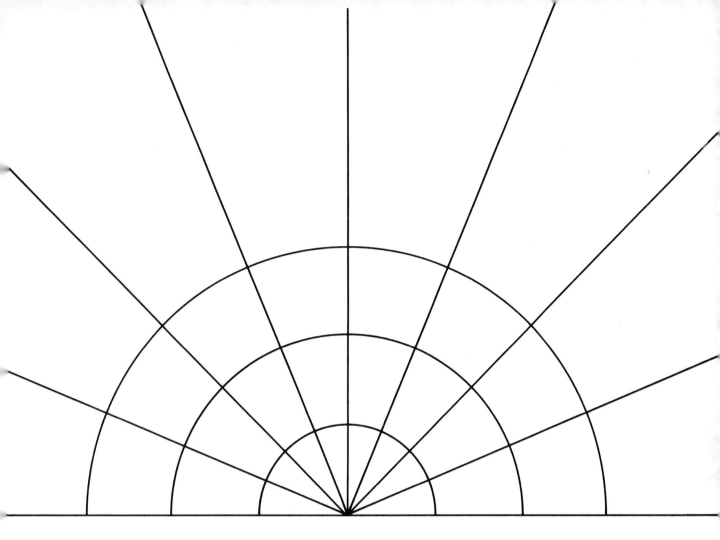

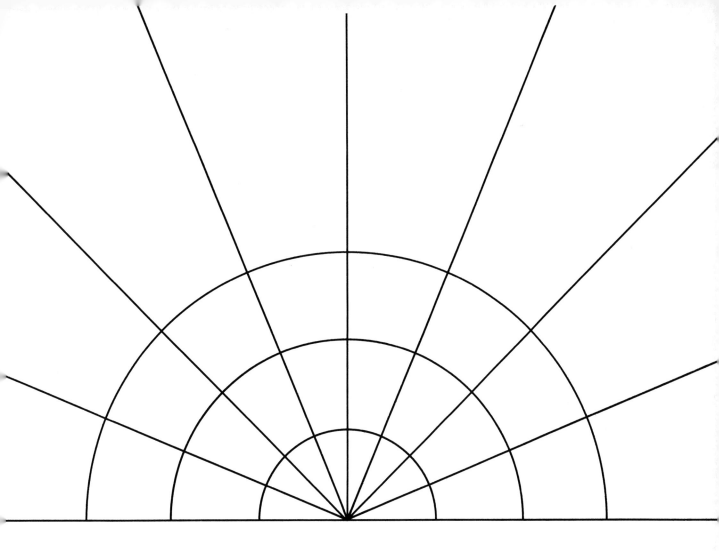

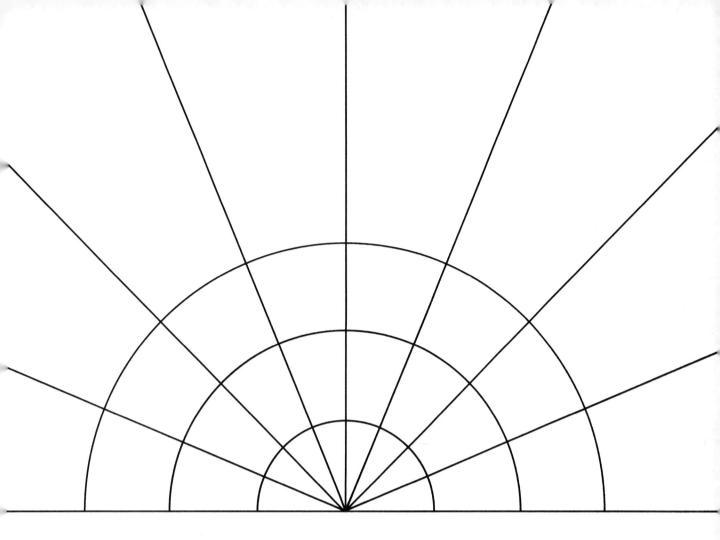

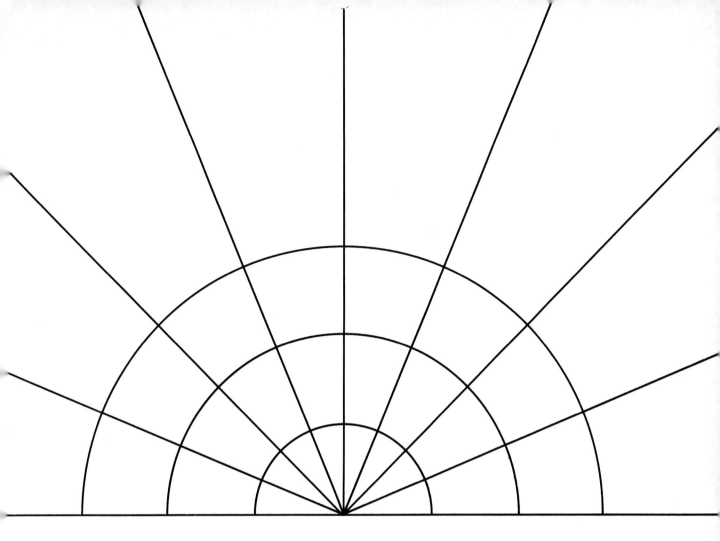

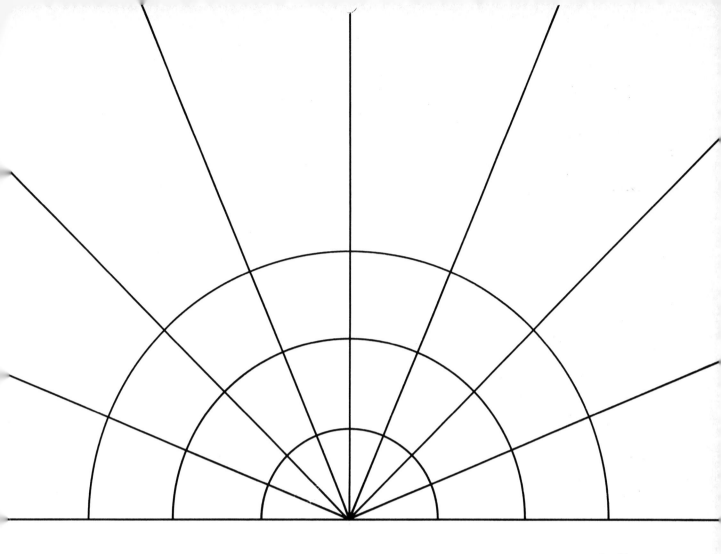

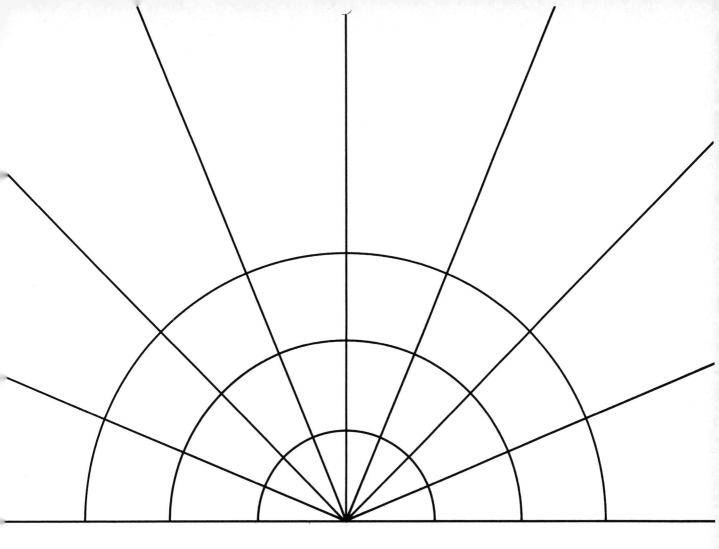

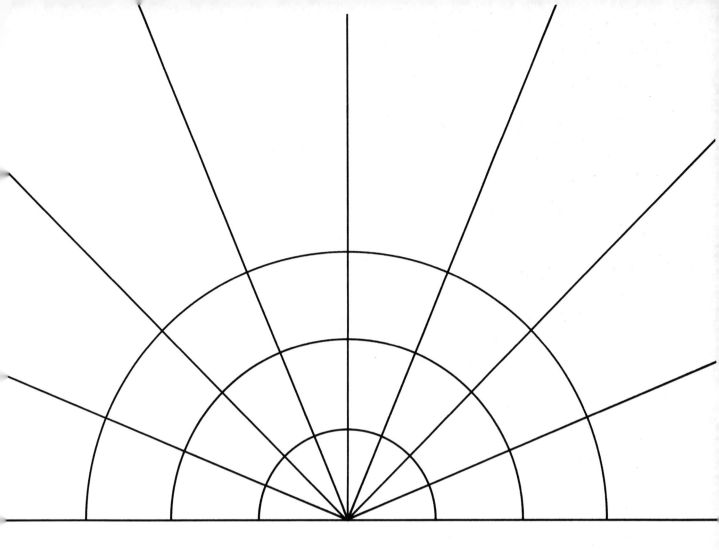

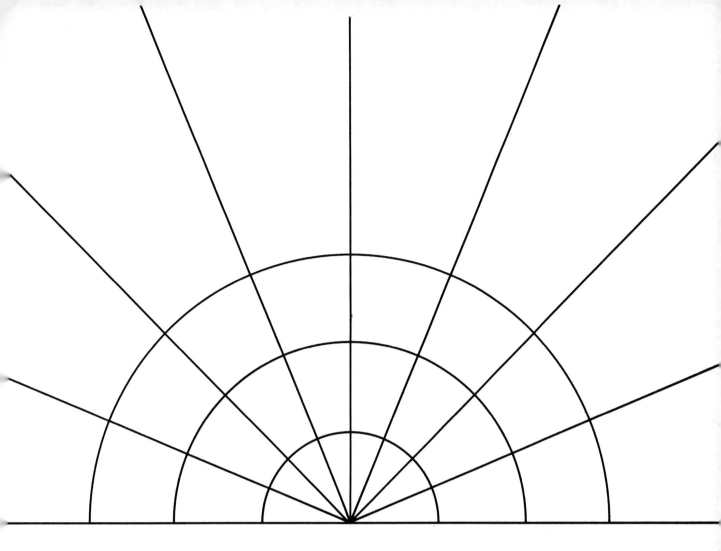

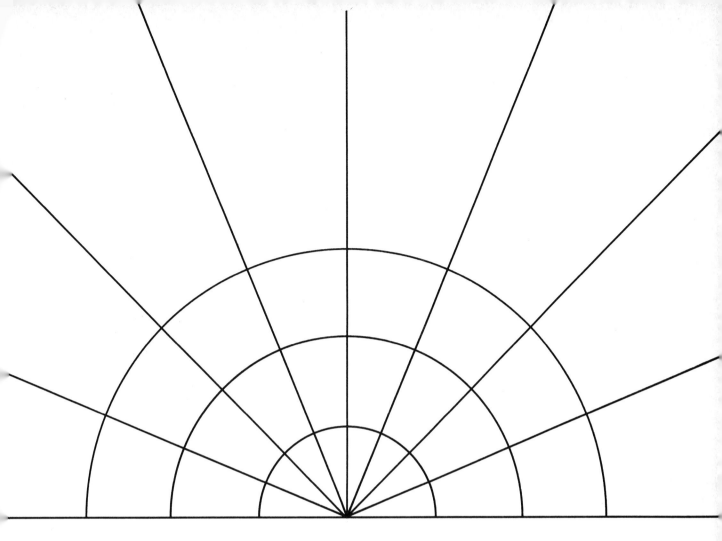

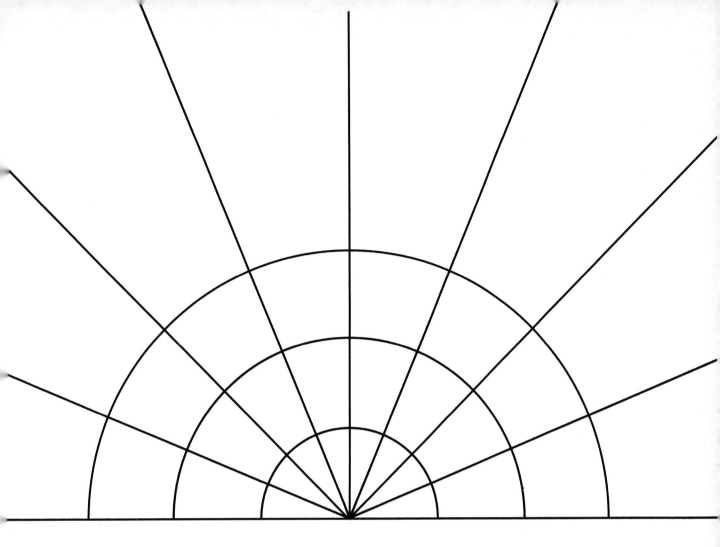

SWCC

 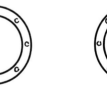

SWCC

SWCC

SWCC

SWCC

SWCC

SWCC

20

MANAGING CHANGE

How to Live in a Fad Culture

Stanley Bing

Every so often a guy like Kip Breen descends from corporate Mecca, all teeth and gray twill, to spread ultrasenior management's latest instant credo with beamish zeal and a steel fist. That year it was something called Negative Task Evaluation, and it made us dance like Saint Vitus before it disappeared into the mists of corporate time, as fads do.

"It's pretty simple," Kip said benignly, easing a glossy, user-friendly packet across my blotter. "We want each manager to break down his ongoing activities, then derive the amount of time each chore requires as a percentage of the total workweek. Then you just work out a couple of simple graphs to see who is spending an inappropriate amount of time on matters of minor importance."

And fire them, I thought.

In the coming months, I filled out more graphs than an infertile couple. People were evaluating one another all over the place, and relationships grew formal. We needn't have worried, though, because while middle management was diddling with its new Tinkertoy, the big guys were seized by a more terrible trend than careening around the horn: decentralization. Out of the window went the assiduously kept charts. With them flew 400 nice folks, willy-nilly. Nothing has been heard of Kip since, except over booze, when we survivors haul out his memory just for a hoot. Then we get back to work.

You'll have to excuse us guys on the inside if we get a little giggly each time the next new dogma comes along. We've been converted before, after all. We've managed in a minute and Theory Z'd, spotted megatrends, spun matrices, woven grids; we've hammered ourselves into hard-networking intrapreneurs, and sat in stupefaction before lanky preachers nagging us to Be Excellent! Some of us, thank God, have even found Wellness. We're willing to give each new creed a chance, until its hasty priests begin torturing the innocent into false confessions. The damned thing is, when the right idea is given the chance to mellow, spread, and ooze deep into the culture, it can actually do some good. But don't hold your breath.

Even when the idea is right—which it rarely is—most corporations still get it wrong. "You can go back to Management-by-Objective, Son of Management-by-Objective, Management-by-Objective meets Appraisal-and-Counseling," says E. Kirby Warren, professor at Columbia University's Graduate School of Business. "Most of these fads would have some real value if senior management took the time to ask themselves: (1) How do I adapt the idea to our culture and business? (2) What has to be changed to reinforce that thing we're talking about? and (3) Are we committed to staying with it long enough to make it work?"

Reprinted from *Esquire,* Aug., 1986. With permission of publisher and author.

But in today's overheated environment, most firms are too desperate to wait for results. "When we're facing intense competition from Asia, and money is relatively expensive, and technology is available and moves rapidly, it's not surprising that people reach out for a way of getting a handle, and what they tend to reach for are what you call fads," says Joseph Bower, professor at Harvard Business School. "If you take almost any one of them and discuss it with the author, it's a perfectly qualified view of how a set of ideas can run a company. But if it's treated as a kind of cookbook, as a single tool carried to an extreme, you get nonsense."

Still, when the guys with liver spots get that nutsy gleam in their eyes, you may have to snap to. Here are some pointers on how to survive.

It must be an autocracy, because democracy doesn't squeeze like that. The guys put in charge of forging the new culture aren't usually the Mother Teresa type. They take things personally, and they're not long on patience. Don't be fooled by warm and fuzzy verbiage designed to win your heart. This is a full-blown drill. Get out on deck and run around.

Keep your mouth shut. Yes, the anal graphs and rah-rah lingo may seem absurd, but develop some instant naiveté—I've seen more than one astute critic mailed overnight to the Elmira office for being a party pooper. "It's a religion," says a friend currently being strangled in the noose of a Quality circle. "To openly question or be cynical about it—you're more than grumpy, you're an apostate."

Charts are not enough. The need to play with neat fad gewgaws doesn't call off your actual job. "I had this subordinate who insisted on spending six months doing a PERT chart, while completely ignoring his other duties," recalls Wes, strategic-planning director at a multinational. "I love the memory of Frank pouring over a chart as big as a barn door that was supposed to govern our actions for the next year. He finally finished it, and we never looked at it again." Frank is out on the Coast now, by the way, teaching people how to do PERT charts.

General Pinochet! I had no idea you were dropping by. There's a healthy whiff of authoritarian zealotry in many fads, and some big boosters may think they've been named Ayatollah. Push them gently off your back. Unostentatious resistance to excess—even excess orthodoxy—is rarely questioned. "One of the darker moments last year was when the Productivity Czar asked everyone to sign a 'Petition of Commitment,'" recalls my friend Andy, a marketing manager at a retail firm. "It was invasive and ridiculous. I tried to kid him out of it. It turns out a lot of other people did, too. He was even advised against it by some of his peers, who felt it was sort of like reading the Bible in the office." The loathed petition now resides on the czar's wall, half full. Not one of the missing was punished.

Dare to be sold. A little credulity can be a beautiful thing. Several years ago I worked for a manufacturing company that decided to dedicate itself to Excellence. The propaganda campaign we inflicted on our workers was fierce. Management spent actual money to improve service. Worker initiative was rewarded. And, unbelievably, the elephantine organism began to lumber forth, to feel pride and a determination to succeed. It was corny and inspirational. We were a team, suddenly, and felt it. I wouldn't have missed it for the world.

A year into the program, the corporation was abruptly sold to a group of midwestern investors who broke it down and resold its body parts for cash. So long Excellence. Hello Leverage. What the hell: One good fad deserves another.

I

Premeeting Preparation

A. Please answer the following questions:

1. Think back on a time when a major change effort took place within your organization or group. What was the change? What preceded it? What happened when the change occurred? How did people react to it? Was it successful?

2. What theories do you have about organizational change? What factors might determine success or failure?

3. What skills are necessary for instituting change?

4. What do you want to learn about organizational change and development?

5. What were the significant learning points from the readings?

B. Read the entire unit.

C. Practice building the spaceship *Enterprise* following the blueprints on pages 609–12.

II

Topic Introduction

Change is becoming a way of life, and managers' jobs today are more and more preoccupied with coping with change thrust upon them, initiating change and improvement, and managing the process of implementing change. In planning for these changes, administrators and managers too often tend to move immediately from a superficial diagnosis of a problem to the action steps. Yet more effective results and fewer tensions in the system will occur if a more thorough diagnosis is made of the situation to be changed and the change process is managed systematically. Kolb and Frohman have developed a sequence for initiating and managing change that is a simple, seven-stage process (see Figure 20–1).[1]

The model emphasizes two important facets in the management of change:

1. It is a sequential process, with each step equally important.
2. Much of the success of the change effort will depend on the manager's relationship to those who will be affected most by the change and the appropriate participation of those people in the change process.

As with most models of behavior, the steps may blur into one another, but the articulation and recognition of them can help steer a clearer course through a change effort. The central issues for the change manager are summarized next for each stage of the change process.

[1]This model of the planned change process was generated through the collaborative efforts of Frohman and Kolb. For a more detailed description, see David A. Kolb and Alan L. Frohman, "An Organization Development Approach to Consulting," *Sloan Management Review,* Vol. 12 (1970), pp. 51–65.

FIGURE 20–1   The Process
of Planned Change

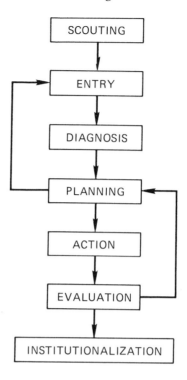

SCOUTING

Although many managers feel they have an adequate knowledge of their own systems, it is beneficial in the beginning to test that assumption. At this stage, the manager is determining readiness for change, identifying obvious obstacles, and observing what is going on. This stage involves a passive diagnosis of the situation to size up costs and benefits of intervention (Is it worth "rocking the boat"?). The key task is to find the entry points for initiating a change, those individuals whose permission is needed, and key informal leaders in the system. The scouting phase of change is important because the choice of an incorrect entry point may doom an improvement to failure before it is begun. For example, individuals who are most receptive to new ideas are sometimes "deviants" in their own group, while the group's leaders will be more cautious and conservative. To align oneself with the less respected "deviants" may cause difficulties in gaining the wider acceptance and legitimacy necessary to carry out the change.

ENTRY

Once the entry point(s) has (have) been chosen, the manager and the system to be changed begin to negotiate a "contract" through the entry point representative(s) that will define if and how the succeeding stages of the planned change process will be carried out. The term "contract" is set in quotation marks because this process implies more than a legal document agreed upon at the outset of a project. The emphasis here is on a continuing process of sharing the expectations of the change manager and the system and agreeing on the contributions to be made by both parties. It is important to emphasize the continuing process of contract renegotiation, because as the planned change process enters succeeding stages, the nature of the problem may change and the resources needed for its solution may increase or decrease. Another aspect of the continuing negotiation process is represented by the feedback loop that reenters the entry stage from the planning stage (see Figure 20–1). As the diagnosis and planning stages proceed, the entry point into the system may have to shift or expand to include those parts of the system that are affected by and/or are responsible for the problem. For example, the personnel department of a company might begin work on the problem of high turnover among first-level management. Diagnosis of the problem may well reveal that the reasons for this turnover lie in poor morale in the line operations. Since responsibility for the ultimate solution of this problem lies with the line managers, the entry contract must be expanded to include these managers in the change process.

The main issue around which the contract negotiation process centers is power—gaining the influence necessary to implement the new program or method of operating. There are four primary sources of this power:

1. The legitimately constituted authority of the system (e.g., the president says one should do this)

2. Expert power (e.g., the prestige of a consultant, or the compelling logic of a solution)

3. Coercive power

4. Trust-based power (the informal influence that flows from collaborative problem definition and solutions)

5. Common vision power, which taps into a common vision which many people share for the future

While in most change projects power from all four of these sources is brought to bear in implementation of the change, the power derived from collaborative problem definition is often especially critical to the success of those planned change efforts where the system's formal power structure and experts are seen as part of the problem to be solved.

DIAGNOSIS

Diagnosis, as much as possible, should be a collaborative effort involving as many of the affected parts of the system as possible. It focuses on three elements: the perceived problem, the goals of the group or organization, and the resources available.

1. *Problem definition:* The first step in defining the specific problem is to identify the subpart(s) of the system where the problem is located and identify the relationship between that subpart and other parts of the system. This is necessary to anticipate the effect of change in one part of the system on other aspects of the system's functioning. If more and/or different problems surface as the diagnosis progresses, the group can assign priorities and focus attention on the most important problem or the problem that must be solved before other problems can be attacked.

2. *Identification of forces that promote and resist change:* Lewin[2] saw change as a dynamic balance of forces working in opposite directions. He devised the "force field analysis," which assigns pressures for change and resistance to change to opposite sides of an equilibrium state. For example, several years back Ford found itself pressured by foreign competition, declining market share, and stakeholder complaints to change the company. These were some of the forces that promoted change at that time. However, within Ford there were also forces that inhibited change such as an entrenched adversarial union-management relationship, and both managers and workers who were accustomed to a way of working that was less efficient and innovative than their

---

[2]Kurt Lewin, *Field Theory in Social Science* (New York: Harper & Row, 1951).

competition. In Ford's case the pressures for change were stronger than the resistance, allowing the company to make some innovations. Identifying the forces for and against change is a useful aid in diagnosing the situation. Managers have three choices: to increase the strength of a pressure(s) to change, to decrease or neutralize the strength of a resistance(s) to change, or to try to convert a resistance into a pressure for change. The key point here is the conception of change as a dynamic process in which a state of equilibrium is reached.

3. *Goal definition:* At this point goals do not need to be as precise and measurable as they should be later. It is usually sufficient to articulate in broad outline the state you would like the organization or group to reach as a result of the change effort. Broadly stated, goals can give direction to the planning effort without overly constraining it.

4. *Resource identification:* Since people in the system will be involved in implementing the change (indeed, they are the major resources in many cases), their abilities, motivation, and commitment must be used if the change effort is to proceed properly. As these are identified, the manager will also want to ask, "What resources from outside our system do we need to use to reach our goal?"

PLANNING

The results of the diagnostic phase form the starting point for the planning phase. Depending on the findings, these results may require a renegotiation of the entry contract. During the planning phase, the entry contract should be expanded to include those members of the system who will be responsible for implementing the change and/or will be immediately affected by it.

The first planning step is to define the objectives to be achieved by the change. Once clear-cut objectives have been established, alternative solutions or change strategies should be generated. Following this, some attempt should be made to simulate the consequences of each of the alternatives. Often this is done simply by thinking through the implications of each change strategy, but more sophisticated simulation methods, such as computer simulation, can be used. The final change strategy is then chosen from the alternatives available.

Intervention plans can be classified on two dimensions: the source of power used to implement the intervention (formal power, expert power, coercive power, and trust-based power) and the organizational subsystem to which the intervention is addressed. The six organizational subsystems are as follows:

1. The *people subsystem.* Two general types of interventions can be used in this subsystem: personnel flow interventions and education. The personnel flow interventions affect the selection, placement, rotation, and retention of organization members. Educational programs have been designed to change motives, skills, and values. Some common educational interventions include seminars, university programs, data collection and feedback, role playing, and on-the-job training.

2. The *authority subsystem.* The authority subsystem has a formal and an informal aspect. Changes can be made in formal authority relationships—in job titles and responsibilities, in the span of control, in the number of organizational levels, and in the location of decision points. In addition, informal leadership patterns can be the object of change interventions. For example, a team-building program may be designed to base leadership more on team members' expertise than on organization titles.

3. The *information subsystem.* This subsystem also has a formal and an informal aspect. The formal information system of the organization can be redesigned to give priority and visibility to the most important information and to provide

mechanisms for getting information to the right place at the right time. Much of the organization's information, however, is carried by the informal system, which is often faster than the formal system. Many work team development programs focus in part on this process, using interventions designed to improve the quality of communications among organization members.

4. The *task subsystem*. The two identifiable parts of this subsystem are the human satisfactions offered by the job and the technology on which the job is based. Job enlargement, an increasingly important area of organizational development, has done much to redesign jobs to obtain a better match between the job holder's motives and the satisfactions provided by his job. Several schemes have been developed for classifying technology and exploring the implications of each classification for the organization of the firm and for the individual holding the job.[3] Likewise, the impact of technological change on the organization has been studied in detail, although little has been done to plan systematic technological changes with a consideration for their impact on other organizational subsystems or on the total development of the organization.

5. The *policy/culture subsystem*. As the name implies, this subsystem has a formal, explicit aspect and an informal, implicit aspect. The policy subsystem is made up of rules concerning working hours, promotion, the formal reward system, and work procedures. The culture subsystem consists of the norms and values of the organization—what type of behavior is rewarded, how conflict is handled, what is expected among peers. Perhaps the most common focus of organization change is on the formal policy system. Less common and more difficult are attempts to change the culture or climate of an organization.

TABLE 20–1   Planning Checklist

SUBSYSTEM	PROBLEM DEFINITION	PROPOSED SOLUTIONS	POSSIBLE EFFECTS ON OTHER SUBSYSTEMS
1. People		1. 2. 3.	1. 2. 3.
2. Authority		1. 2. 3.	1. 2. 3.
3. Information		1. 2. 3.	1. 2. 3.
4. Task		1. 2. 3.	1. 2. 3.
5. Policy/culture		1. 2. 3.	1. 2. 3.
6. Environmental		1. 2. 3.	1. 2. 3.

[3]See Jay R. Galbraith, "Organization Design: An Information Processing View," *Readings;* also J. Thompson, *Organizations in Action* (New York: McGraw-Hill, 1967), and J. Woodward, *Industrial Organization: Theory and Practice* (New York: Oxford University Press, 1965).

The Grid OD program is one example of a systematic and comprehensive approach to cultural change.[4]

6. The *environmental subsystem*. The environment can be divided, somewhat arbitrarily, into the internal physical environment and the external environment. One important component of the internal environment is architecture. The spatial relationships of organization members, for example, can have a great impact on the information subsystem.[5] The external environment has many characteristics that affect the organization: rapidity of change, uncertainty, quality and quantity of labor supply, financial and material resources, political and legal structures, market, and so on. An organization chooses its environment when it begins operation. It can subsequently redefine certain elements of its environment. For example, an organization initially conceived to serve a specific market can redefine its objective and self-image to that of a growth company in a wider market, thereby relating more to uncertain rather than stable aspects of its environment. This redefinition will have implications for all the other organizational subsystems.

The six organizational subsystems can form a checklist to be used by the manager when planning or executing any action intervention. An example of such a checklist is shown here as Table 20–1. The primary purpose of the checklist is to remind the manager that a change in one subsystem will affect other organizational subsystems. The list can be useful for selecting the best leverage point and for identifying the other subsystems most likely to be affected by the intervention. It may be easier, for example, to redefine jobs than to change motives, an indication that the manager should at least start with the task subsystem rather than the people subsystem. In addition, the manager must plan the intervention in such a way that both aspects of the subsystems are kept in harmony: educational programs and personnel flow interventions must be compatible, the formal and informal authority systems must be mutually supportive, the design of a formal information system must take into account the existing informal flow of information, a program that will redesign jobs must consider the human satisfaction factor as well as the existing technology, policy changes are doomed to subversion if they are not supported by cultural changes, and a close relationship must be maintained between the internal and the external environment.

The checklist can also be useful in identifying the sources of power available for bringing about change and for determining which source, or combination of sources, is the most appropriate for the type of intervention planned. Certain combinations may not be enough to implement even the best plan. The lack of trust-based power, for example, could doom the intervention to failure, as in the case of one consultant who was hired by the head office to do work in the field offices. Perceived as a representative of the head office, with which most of the field offices had great difficulty working, the consultant was unable to develop trust-based power. The intervention in the people subsystem of the field offices therefore met with little success. The consultant's own "postmortem" noted that it was the inability to establish trust with each field office that prevented acceptance of the change program.

[4]Robert R. Blake and J. Mouton, *Building a Dynamic Corporation Through Grid Organization Development* (Reading, MA: Addison-Wesley, 1969).

[5]For a systematic treatment of the impact of architectural and physical settings, see Fred I. Steele, *Physical Settings and Organization Development* (Reading, MA: Addison-Wesley, 1973).

ACTION

The action phase of a planned change effort can encompass a wide range of activities from management training, to creation of new information systems, to changes in organization structure, to changes in architectural and spatial relationships. No matter what the changes are, there is likely to be some *resistance to change*.[6] This resistance, when it occurs, is often treated as an irrational negative force to be overcome by whatever means; yet, in some cases, resistance to change can be functional for the survival of a system.[7] If an organization tried every new scheme, product, or process that came along, it would soon wander aimlessly, flounder, and die. The positive function of resistance to change is to ensure that plans for change and their ultimate consequences are thought through carefully. The failure of most plans for change lies in the change's *unanticipated consequences*. In industry, these failures often take the form of technical changes (e.g., a new information system, a new production process) that fail to anticipate and plan for the social changes that the technical changes cause (e.g., increases and decreases in power at different levels of the organization in the information system example or new working relationships and/or more or less meaningful work in the new production process example). The result is that managers and administrators are annoyed at the stupidity of those subordinates who resent this very logical improvement. Yet the subordinates often are not resisting the logic of the improvement (and hence logical arguments for the change do not help) but, rather, the social changes that management has not recognized and planned for.

Another cause of resistance to change can be the sudden imposition of changes in someone's environment without that person's prior knowledge of, or participation in, the change. To have an important part of one's environment suddenly changed by forces outside one's knowledge and control can cause great anxiety, even panic. The human response to this experience is hostility toward the source of change and resistance to the new method. The process of growth and maturation is one of gaining mastery over one's environment. Management, by imposing change, serves to arrest this process by denying subordinates the opportunity to live in an environment they can understand and control. People who spend their lives in organizations managed by imposed change can become helpless, passive victims of the system, cursed by management for their stupidity and lack of initiative.

These dysfunctional aspects of resistance to change can be alleviated by careful preparation for the action phase. If system members can be involved at the appropriate stages of the scouting, entry, diagnosis, and planning phases, the plan for change can be made more intelligent and more appropriate to the system's needs, both technological and social.

EVALUATION

The tradition in the scientific evaluation of change projects has been to separate the evaluation phase from the action phase. To ensure unbiased results, an independent researcher is often hired to evaluate the change efforts. While this approach has some benefit from the standpoint of scientific objectivity, it has some cost in terms of the effective implementation of change. It should be clear in this model that the evaluation phase is an integrated part of the change process.

The evaluation of the action strategy is conducted in terms of the specific objectives defined during the planning phase as well as interim task goals designed to determine if the change is progressing as desired. Members of the system therefore

---

[6]Paul Lawrence, "How to Deal with Resistance to Change," *Harvard Business Review* (May–June 1954), pp. 49–57, and Rosabeth Moss Kanter, "Managing the Human Side of Change," *Reader,* 1989.

[7]As stated in Chapter 10, Managing Multigroup Work, too little conflict or resistance can be as serious a problem as too much.

know on what dimensions they are being evaluated. The potential bias created by this knowledge can be overcome by careful choice of objective evaluation indices that cannot be manipulated. For example, the goal of an action intervention may be to increase the quantity of patentable products produced by a research group. The validity of the results obtained from using the number of patents as the evaluation index will not be affected by the group's knowledge of the intervention goal, whereas the use of self-evaluation ratings of creativity might.

To develop within the system the ability to use the information generated for self-analysis, the group or organization should monitor the progress of the action phase and evaluate the data itself. The results of the evaluation stage determine whether the change project moves to the institutionalization stage or returns to the planning stage for further action planning and perhaps to the entry stage for further contract negotiation among the participants.

INSTITUTIONALIZATION

If the steps so far outlined have been followed, a great deal of effort will have gone into the change, excitement about reaching change goals will have been high, and the natural tendency will be to experience a letdown once the change has been implemented. Institutionalization should not mean a rehardening of the organization's arteries, but a new way of working that combines stability and flexibility. If the change is seen as "complete," those arteries will harden. If it is seen as "continuous," there will be mechanisms in place for continuing to flex and change as situations demand. Some of these conditions necessary for the maintenance of change are as follows[8]:

1. Management must pay conscious attention to the "continuous transition."
2. Explicit processes or procedures for setting priorities for improvement should be instituted.
3. There should be systematic and continual processes of feedback.
4. The reward system should reward people for time and energy spent on these processes.

[8]Richard Beckhard and Reuben Harris, *Organizational Transitions: Managing Complex Change* (Reading, MA: Addison-Wesley, 1977).

III

Procedure for Group Meeting:
The Enterprise Acquisition Game

THE ACQUISITION GAME

This exercise is designed to simulate some of the organizational processes that occur when two companies merge. During the exercise, the group will divide into two corporations—the Enterprise Corporation, which manufactures spacecraft, and the Merger Corporation, a conglomerate that has just acquired the Enterprise Corporation. The exercise focuses on a visit by a management consulting team from the Merger Corporation to the production facility of the Enterprise Corporation. The two corporations have agreed that Merger Corporation would visit Enterprise, observe their production process, and help Enterprise improve its operations by implementing new managerial and production systems.

STEP 1.   Choose a game coordinator. The group should first choose someone to act as game coordinator. This person will act as leader and time keeper for the exercise, the government inspector and buyer of Enterprise's product, and the postgame discussion leader. (The instructor often plays this role.)

STEP 2.   Form the Enterprise and Merger Corporations. The group should divide itself approximately in half to form the two corporations. (If there are more than 20 people in the total group, it will be easier if the group subdivides so that the game is run in two parallel sections with two game coordinators, two Merger Corporations, and so on.) The game coordinator should flip a coin to determine which group is the Merger Corporation and which is the Enterprise Corporation. (See the instructions for Merger Corporation and for Enterprise Corporation in the following sections.)

STEP 3.   Timetable and overview of game procedure. The procedural steps in the exercise are summarized in Table 20–2. The game coordinator may want to copy this summary on a blackboard so that the procedure is visible to everyone.

STEP 4.   Instructions for the game coordinator. While the two corporations are preparing for the first production period, you should read the instructions for the total unit. Your most important tasks are to

    a. Keep the time schedule described in Table 20–2.

    b. Sell materials to Enterprise Corporation during production periods 1 and 2.

    c. Inspect and buy acceptable spacecraft materials from Enterprise Corporation during production periods 1 and 2 (see Quality Control Points on blueprints).

    d. Record and average numerical responses for each team on the change analysis scale, and lead the discussion which follows.

INSTRUCTIONS FOR THE ENTERPRISE CORPORATION

Your previous successful experience in the aerospace industry has just won you a government contract to produce as many *Enterprise* spacecraft as your production facilities will allow during the next two months (represented in this exercise by the

TABLE 20–2 Timetable for the Acquisition Game

STEP	ACTIVITY		TIME
A	Read Procedure Overview; Elect Game Coordinator; Form Corporations		10 min
B	*Merger Corporation* Develop plan for helping Enterprise improve Observe Enterprise's man- agement and production process	*Enterprise Corporation* Organize management and production process Build spacecraft mockups Buy materials Prepare to produce	20 min
C	Continue observation	Produce spacecraft	5 min
D	Coordinator evaluates, buys, and computes profit		2½ min
E	Merger Corporation implements new management/ production system		30 min
F	Merger observes	Enterprise production period 2	5 min
G	Coordinator evaluates, buys, and computes profit		2½ min
H	Game Coordinator leads analysis of the change process— discussion		45 min
		Total time	120 min

two 5-minute production periods). The government has given you a set of blueprints for the spacecraft as well as a number of quality control points (see page 613). You must buy raw materials from the game coordinator as determined by the price schedule in Table 20–3.* Your profit is determined by the number of spacecraft you sell to the government at a price of $5,000,000 each minus the cost of materials

TABLE 20–3 Materials' Costs of Enterprise Spacecraft

NUMBER OF SETS PURCHASED	COST PER SET
0–4	$4,500,000
5–9	4,400,000
10–14	4,300,000
15–19	4,200,000
20–24	4,100,000
25–29	4,000,000
30–34	3,900,000
35–39	3,800,000
40–44	3,750,000
45–49	3,700,000
50–100	3,650,000
Over 100	3,600,000

Caution: The materials you buy may be slightly faulty. Apparently it is difficult to print the spacecraft perfectly. If you receive raw materials with nose cone lines that don't start at the exact corner of the paper, ignore the lines and make your fold from the true corner of the paper. We're sorry for the inconvenience but we hear that real life government contractors sometimes have the same problem.

(other factors, such as overhead, materials, and waste, have been eliminated for simplicity). Only completed vehicles of acceptable quality can be sold. No materials can be returned.

In the 20-minute preparation time, you can organize your members in any way you wish to make purchasing and production decisions. During this time, the corporation is allowed two free sets of materials *for each member* to use in any way the corporation wishes to establish production techniques and time estimates. Any additional materials used during this time must be purchased at full cost. These materials cannot be used during the production periods.

Your agreement with Merger Corporation is that they may observe your activities during this time, but that they are not to interfere in any way.

When you have decided how many units you want to produce, tell the game coordinator how many sets of materials you want to buy and record that information on the Enterprise Corporation Accounting Form (page 603).

INSTRUCTIONS FOR THE MERGER CORPORATION

Your task during the first 20 minutes is to decide how best to work with Enterprise Corporation after the first production period to help them increase their profit during production period 2. You can organize yourself in any way you want to do this (e.g., you can choose one or two members to act as consultants and feed information and ideas to them, work one-to-one with members of the Enterprise Corporation, or use any other model you may choose).

During the 30 minutes before production period 2 begins, help the Enterprise Corporation in any way you see fit. *Once the second production period begins, however,* Merger Corporation is only allowed to observe. During round 2, Enterprise Corporation can have no more members than the number they had during round 1. Personnel transfers are, however, legitimate. In other words, the total number of people in Enterprise during round 2 must be the same, but specific people can be shifted from Merger Corporation to *replace* someone in Enterprise.

Enterprise Corporation Accounting Form

	MATERIAL SETS PUR-CHASED	COST PER SET	TOTAL COST	NUMBER OF UNITS SOLD AT $5,000,000 PER UNIT	TOTAL RECEIPTS	PROFIT OR LOSS
Production period 1						
Production period 2						

Analysis of the Change Process

Merger Corporation has just attempted to effect an improvement in the way in which Enterprise Corporation produces spaceships. On the whole, how successful do you think Merger was? Draw a circle around the number that most closely represents your opinion:

| 1 | 2 | 3 | 4 | 5 | 6 | 7 |

Completely
unsuccessful

Completely
successful

(The game coordinator will record and average scores for both corporations before proceeding with the discussion.)

Before beginning the discussion of the exercise, take a few minutes to respond to the following questions with short, written phrases. When you have done this, the game coordinator will lead the discussion in which you may share the written responses.

1. Scouting:
   a. How did Merger go about scouting Enterprise?

   b. How effective was it? Be specific.

2. Entry:
   a. Was the psychological contract clarified?

   b. Was a feeling of collaboration established? How?

   c. Was the entry conversation well timed?

3. Diagnosis:
   a. What data were considered in defining the problem?

   b. How was the problem defined (e.g., a production problem, a quality control problem, a finance problem, a government relations problem)?

   c. Were resources identified and used?

   d. How involved was Enterprise in the diagnosis?

4. Planning:
   a. Were the proper subsystems identified and changed?

   b. Which subsystem(s) was (were) worked on, and with what effect?

   c. Was the approach taken by Merger primarily technical (e.g., how to fold better) or social (e.g., emphasizing cooperation and teamwork between Merger and Enterprise)?

5. Action:
   a. Where did resistance appear? What seemed to cause it?

   b. How was it dealt with?

6. Evaluation:
   a. Were Merger's objectives met?

   b. Were evaluation questions asked (e.g., "Is this being helpful to you?")

7. Institutionalization (and flexibility):
   a. Would Enterprise improve if a third round were held?

   b. What was done to ensure continued improvement?

8. What connections can be made between this exercise and the readings?

Directions for Making the Spaceship *Enterprise*

The following are directions for making the spaceship. After each step, there is a picture showing what to do and another picture showing what it should look like. Make sure you check this before going on to the next step. There are 11 steps.

1. You should have a piece of paper that has one blank side, and one side that looks like this:

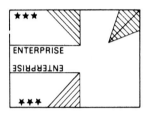

2. Turn the paper over so that the *blank side* is facing up and the word "ENTERPRISE" is on the left-hand underneath side.
   It should now look like this:

   "ENTERPRISE" lettering on this end

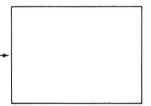

3. Fold corner A to B at the bottom of the paper.

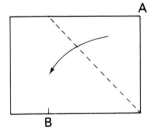

   It should now look like this:

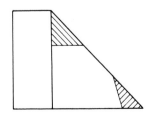

4. Fold corner C to D.

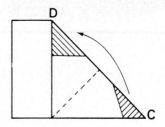

It should now look like this:

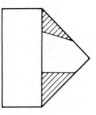

5. Fold E to F.

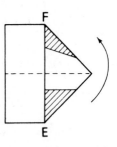

It should now look like this:

6. Fold on GH by starting with the part with the stars (* * *) on it and folding down so that the fold comes along the printed solid line. *There are three thicknesses of paper—make sure you only fold the first layer.*

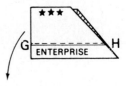

It should now look like this:

7. Make a fold (up direction) about 1 inch from the bottom along JK.

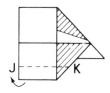

It should now look like this:

8. Turn the spaceship over and round so that L is on the left side.

It should now look like this:

9. Fold on MN by starting with the part with the stars (* * *) on it and folding down so that the fold comes along the printed solid line. *There are two thicknesses of paper—make sure you only fold the top one.*

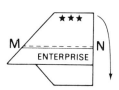

It should now look like this. *Make sure this sticks up in the center.*

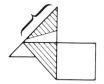

10. Make a fold (up direction) about 1 inch from the bottom along OP.

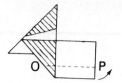

It should now look like this:

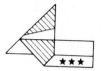

Read all of step 11 and then go back and do it part by part.

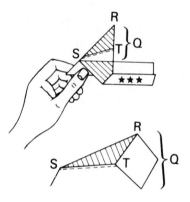

   a. Hold spaceship in hand.

   b. Open up Q with finger and flatten the lined area (/ / / / /) by bringing central point R toward the main body of the plane.

   c. Fold along ST to keep it flat.

   d. Make wings level so that plane can fly.

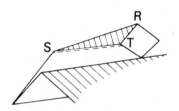

Finished plane should look like this:

    side view   top view   front view

1. Printed lines should be in the position shown on the diagram.
2. The wingtips must be turned up enough to let the stars show completely.
3. The "pilot's cabin" (step 11) must be puffed out noticeably. Skinny cabins crowd the astronauts. Cabin folds must be creased on printed lines.
4. The two wings must be level and even with each other (i.e., the entire wing deck should be at the same level).
5. The nose of the spaceship should be pointed.

The game coordinator will buy only those spacecraft that meet these quality control points.

IV

Follow-up

The preceding exercise often highlights one of the most common reactions to change: human resistance. Kanter states that resistance to change comes from (1) feeling out of control, (2) excess uncertainty from not knowing where the change will lead, (3) lack of time to mentally adjust to changes, (4) stress caused by too many changes and forced attention to issues that were formerly routine, (5) feeling compelled to defend the status quo because doing otherwise would involve a loss of face, (6) concerns about future competence when the ground rules seem to be changing, (7) ripple effects to personal plans which will be affected by the change, (8) greater work and energy demands necessitated by the change, (9) past resentments, and (10) the real threat posed by a change in which some people will be winners and others will be losers.[9] She concludes that all resistance to change is certainly not irrational and managers who understand the reasons for resistance are better able to deal with it constructively.

The dynamic changing environment to which most of today's organizations must adapt has added a new dimension to the classic managerial functions of planning, organizing, motivating, directing, and controlling. Today's managers must also manage the process of change—they must be able to diagnose problems and to plan and implement changes in such a way that they are accepted and carried out by the system itself. Part of the skill required for making successful changes depends upon the ability to determine readiness for change. David Gleicher of Arthur D. Little developed the following formula for determining readiness for change:

$$C = (abd) > x$$

In this formula, C = change, a = level of dissatisfaction with the status quo, b = clear or understood desired state, d = practical, first steps toward a desired state, and x = cost of changing. As Beckhard states: "For change to be possible and for commitment to occur, there has to be enough dissatisfaction with the current state of affairs to mobilize energy toward change. There also has to be some fairly clear conception of what the state of affairs would be if and when the change were successful. Of course, a desired state needs to be consistent with the values and priorities of the client system. There also needs to be some client awareness of practical first steps or starting points toward the desired state."[10]

Once readiness has been determined, to be successful, a change must have two characteristics. It must be a *high-quality solution* to the system's problem in terms of its technical and logical soundness, and it must be *acceptable* to the members of the system. Unfortunately the quality of a solution and the acceptability of a solution do not always go together. The acceptability of a change is often determined less by the quality of the problem solution and more by the *process* through which the change is introduced.[11] For example, changes that are imposed by administrative decree are often actively or passively resisted because the members of the system are

---

[9]For an interesting account of managing organizational change in today's environment, read Rosabeth Moss Kanter's *The Change Masters* (New York: Simon & Schuster, 1983), or an excerpt, "Managing the Human Side of Change," in *Readings*.

[10]Richard Beckhard, "Strategies for Large System Change," in D. A. Kolb, I. M. Rubin, and J. S. Osland, *Organizational Behavior: Practical Readings for Managers* (Englewood Cliffs, NJ: Prentice Hall, 1990).

[11]Alfred J. Marrow, David G. Bowers, and Stanley E. Seashore, *Management by Participation* (New York: Harper & Row, 1967).

FIGURE 20-2 A Model for Induced Change

AWAY FROM:	AND	TOWARD:
Generalized goals ────────────────▶		Specific objectives
Former social ties built around previous behavior patterns ──────▶		New relationships which support the intended changes in behavior and attitudes
Self-doubt and a lowered sense of self-esteem ──────▶		A heightened sense of self-esteem
An external motive for change ──────────────▶		An internalized motive for change

not aware of the problem that the change is intended to solve. On the other hand, involvement of system members in the total process of diagnosing the problem, planning alternative solutions, and implementing a chosen alternative are more likely to produce solutions that will be acceptable to the system.

The study of human behavior reveals that people do not easily change long-term behaviors. Anyone who has tried to give up a cherished "bad habit" understands that behavioral change can be tricky, if not downright difficult or impossible. Lewin[12] described the process of change as unfreezing, moving, and refreezing. *Unfreezing* is accompanied by stress, tension, and a strong felt need for change. The *moving* stage refers to relinquishing old ways of behavior and testing out new behaviors, values, and attitudes that have usually been proposed by a respected source. *Refreezing* occurs when the new behavior is either reinforced, internalized, and institutionalized or rejected and abandoned. Dalton found that in addition to this process of unfreezing, moving, and refreezing, there are also subprocesses in which movement occurs in successful change efforts.[13] These subprocesses—interaction patterns, feelings about oneself, type of objectives and motivation regarding the change—are shown in Figure 20-2. The four processes are characterized by movement.

In initiating a change in the status quo of a relationship, a program, a procedure, a communications pattern, an organization, or a way of work, the person wishing to initiate the change can improve the change effort by[14]

1. Diagnosing the present condition, including the need for change, and pressures and resistance to change.

2. Setting goals and defining the new state or condition after the change.

3. Defining the transition state between the present and future.

4. Developing strategies and action plans for managing this transition.

5. Evaluating the change effort.

6. Stabilizing the new condition and establishing a balance between stability and flexibility.

[12]Kurt Lewin, "Frontiers in Group Dynamics," *Human Relations,* Vol. 1 (1947), pp. 5–41.

[13]Gene W. Dalton, "Influence and Organizational Change," in *Organizational Psychology,* ed. by David Kolb, Irwin Rubin, and James McIntyre (Englewood Cliffs, NJ: Prentice Hall, 1984).

[14]Beckhard and R. T. Harris, *Organizational Transitions* (Reading, MA: Addison-Wesley, 1987).

V

Learning Points

1. Managing change is becoming a crucial part of the manager's role.

2. Much of the success of the change effort depends on the manager's relationship to those who will be affected most by the change and by the appropriate participation of these people in the change process.

3. Change is a sequential process and each step is equally important.

4. Kolb and Frohman's process of planned change consists of seven steps:

   a. Scouting.

   b. Entry.

   c. Diagnosis.

   d. Planning.

   e. Action.

   f. Evaluation.

   g. Institutionalization.

5. Scouting involves a discrete diagnosis of the situation to determine whether change is feasible and worthwhile and to identify the appropriate entry point, that is, the people who have the necessary power and interest in the change.

6. The entry phase involves negotiating a contract about the expectations of the manager and the system regarding the change.

7. The diagnosis stage consists of problem definition, identification of pressures for and against change, goal definition, and resource identification.

8. The planning phase establishes the objective of the change and the alternative change strategies. It is also necessary to identify the possible consequences of each strategy upon the other subsystems that will also be affected by any change.

9. The six organizational subsystems are:

   a. People.

   b. Authority.

   c. Information.

   d. Task.

   e. Policy/culture.

   f. Environment.

10. The five possible sources of power which can be used to implement a change are:

    a. Formal power.

    b. Expert power.

    c. Coercive power.

    d. Trust based power.

    e. Common vision.

11. The action phase can consist of a number of change interventions. Resistance to change should be viewed, not as an obstacle, but as a natural reaction that can improve the final result.

12. In the evaluation phase the group or organization monitors the progress of the action phase and determines whether the change should be institutionalized or returned to the planning stage.

13. Institutionalization refers to the maintenance of the change effort that implies continuous attention to feedback on its progress and ensuring that policies and reward systems reinforce the change.

14. Human resistance to change comes from a variety of sources: loss of control, excess uncertainty, surprises, too much change, loss of face, concerns about future competence, ripple effects, more work, past resentments, and the real threat of the change.

15. Readiness for change is determined by the following formula: $C = (abd) > x$, where C = change, a = level of dissatisfaction with the status quo, b = clear or understood desired state, d = practical first steps toward a desired state, and x = cost of changing.

16. Successful changes have two characteristics: high-quality solutions and acceptability to members of the system. Acceptability of a change is determined less by the quality of the solution and more by the *process* through which the change is introduced.

17. Lewin described the change process as unfreezing, moving, and refreezing.

VI
Tips for Managers

- Don't make changes just for the sake of making change. Too much change in a system is just as frustrating to employees as the feeling that any change is impossible. Think through the pros and cons of any change very carefully before taking action. For some people making changes has more to do with their own need to impact the system than the needs of the system.

- As a manager leading a major change effort, the best analogy is that of a surfer riding the crest of a wave. If few others see the need for change, it probably won't happen.

- Almost all organizations should focus a good bit of energy on innovation and change on a regular basis. But not everyone in the organization needs to be involved in this. Some organizations utilize parallel or collateral organization structures. Parallel organizations have the freedom and flexibility to do the innovating and problem solving, while the "maintenance organization" carries on with business as usual. People who dislike uncertainty and who cherish a fondness for the status quo are more satisfied in maintenance organizations, while the creative, entrepreneurial types prefer the parallel organization. Managers who point out that both of these structures and types of employees are equally valuable to the organization can avoid potential conflict between these groups.[15]

- Trust is an important aspect of any change project. Often clients do not make significant movement until they begin to trust the consultant(s) involved. Employees do not believe management's new visions for the future unless their trust has been won. Trust allows people to unfreeze and move. Therefore, it's very important that managers do not make promises they cannot keep.

- Successful change efforts seem to be characterized more by a desire to capitalize on some identified potential or strengths than by a focus solely to the negative aspects of the organization. Moving toward a desired state seems to produce more of the energy needed for change than merely moving away from a negative state.

- The more people have been allowed to participate in the change effort, the more commitment there will be to its success.

- Change efforts require extensive support from the top of the organization.

- New programs require careful attention and nurturing. Having the head of a new program report directly to the CEO until the program is well established is one way of ensuring its survival.

- Change is not always a rational, linear process. Where major organizational transformation is required, change involves a leap of faith to move the organization to another plane which cannot always be seen from the point of departure. For this reason, such changes emphasize shared values and symbolic gestures by managers.

---

[15]For more information on parallel organizations, see C. E. Miller, "The Parallel Organization Structure at General Motors: An Interview with Howard C. Carlson," *Personnel* (September–October 1978), p. 65, and B. A. Stein and R. M. Kanter, "Building the Parallel Organization: Creating Mechanisms for Permanent Quality of Work Life," *Journal of Applied Behavioral Science*, Vol. 16 (1980), pp. 371–388.

■ People sometimes go through a period of "mourning" in large-scale change projects. Letting go of old ways of behaving, old psychological contracts, old conceptions of their organization, and old relationships is not easy. Accepting this difficulty, acknowledging it with employees, and even planning ritual celebrations like farewell parties help people to get through this period more easily.

VII

Personal Application Assignment

This assignment is to write about a change effort or a consulting project you were part of or observed. Choose one about which you are motivated to learn more.

- **A.** *Concrete Experience*
    1. *Objectively* describe the experience ("who," "what," "when," "where," "how" type information—up to 2 points).
    2. *Subjectively* describe your feelings, perceptions, and thoughts that occurred *during* (not after) the experience (up to 2 points). Does this section have too much detail? (If so, delete 1 point.)

- **B.** *Reflective Observation*
    1. Look at the experience from different points of view. How many points of view did you include that are *relevant* (up to 2 points)?
    2. Use these perspectives to add more meaning to the incident (up to 2 points).

C. *Abstract Conceptualization*

1. Relate concepts from the assigned readings and the lecture to the experience (i.e., what theories that you heard in the lecture or read in the *Reader* relate to your understanding of this incident?). Make reference to at least two sources. Use standard referencing format and include the page number to which you are referring. How many sources did you use and how clearly did you explain their theories (up to 4 points)?

2. You can also create an original model or theory, but it should not replace course concepts.

D. *Active Experimentation*

1. Write about what you will do in the future that will improve your effectiveness. Use rules of thumb or action resolutions.

2. Are they described specifically, thoroughly, and in detail (up to 4 points)?

E. *Integration, Synthesis, and Writing*

1. Did you write about something personally important to you (up to 1 point)?

2. Was it well written (up to 2 points)?

3. Did you integrate and synthesize the different sections (up to 1 point)?

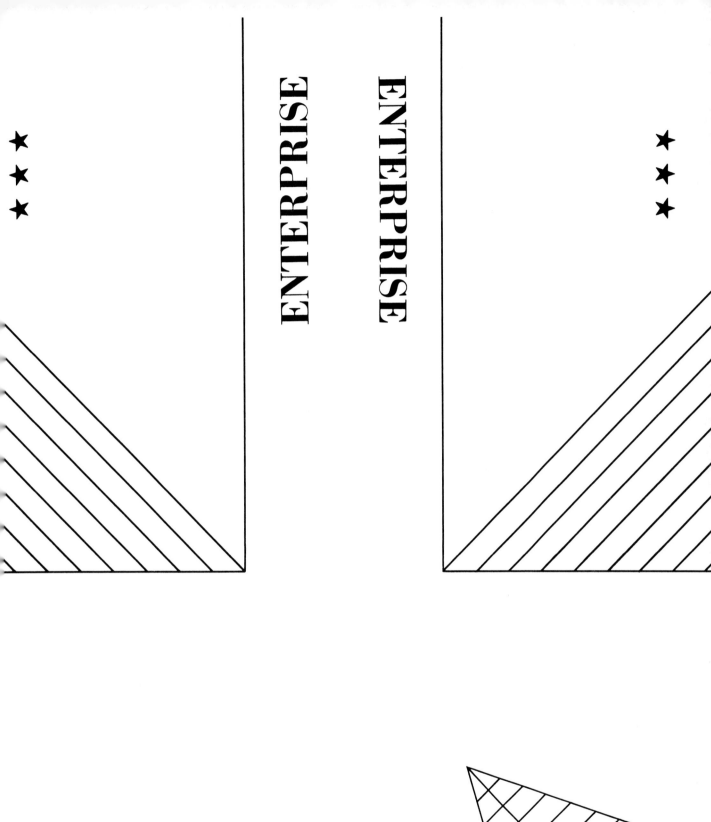

ENTERPRISE

ENTERPRISE

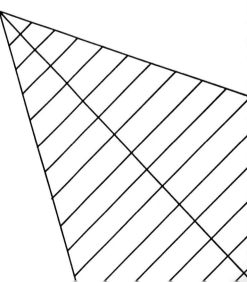

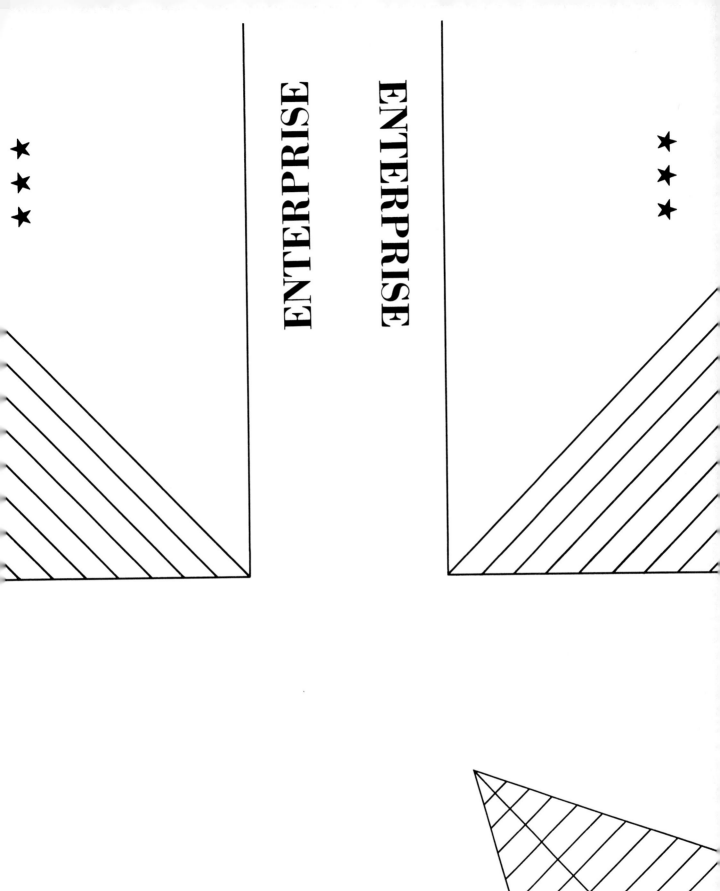

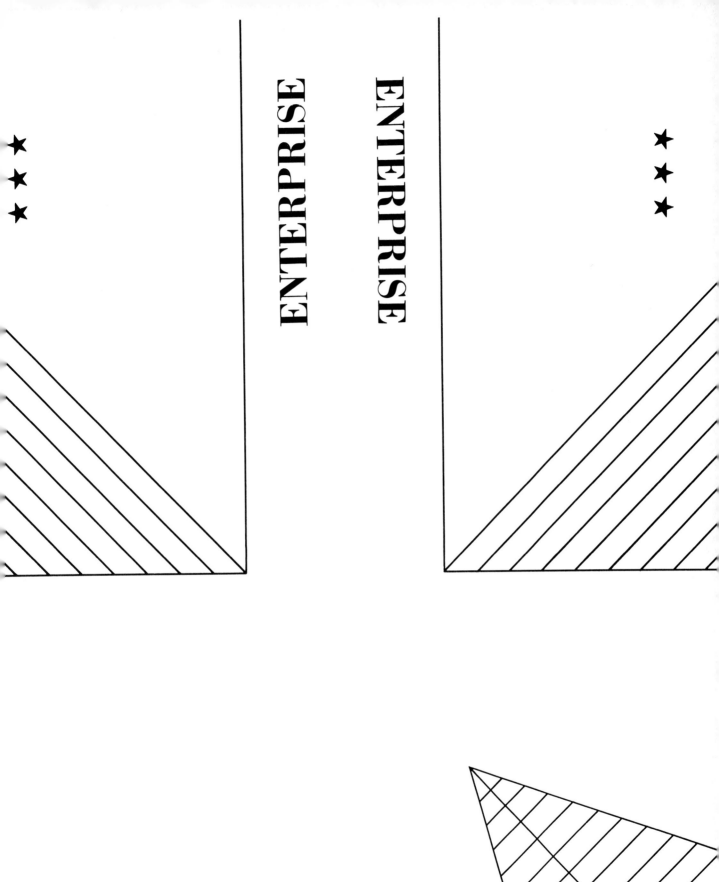

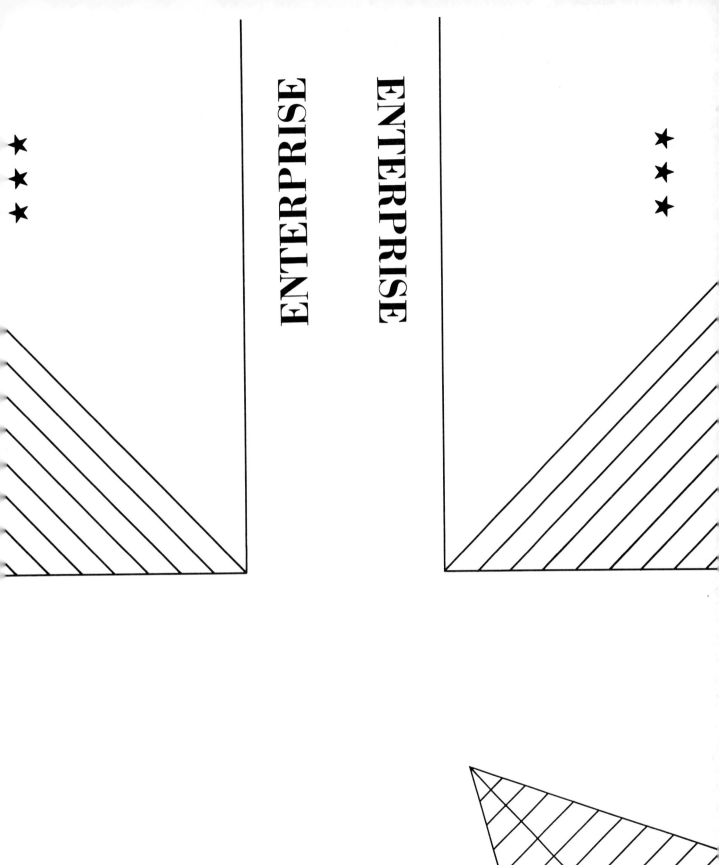

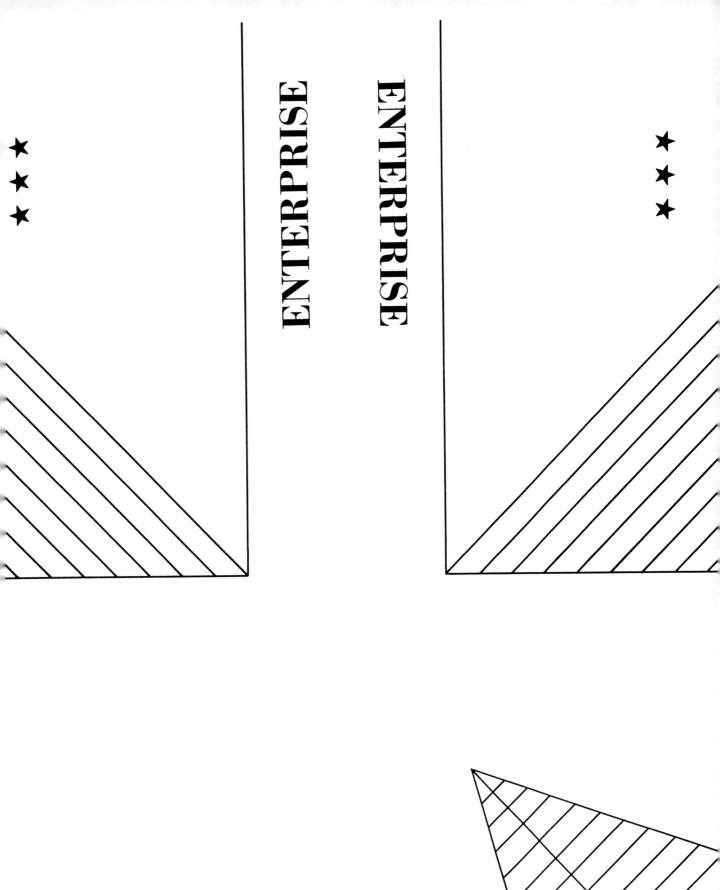

ENTERPRISE

ENTERPRISE

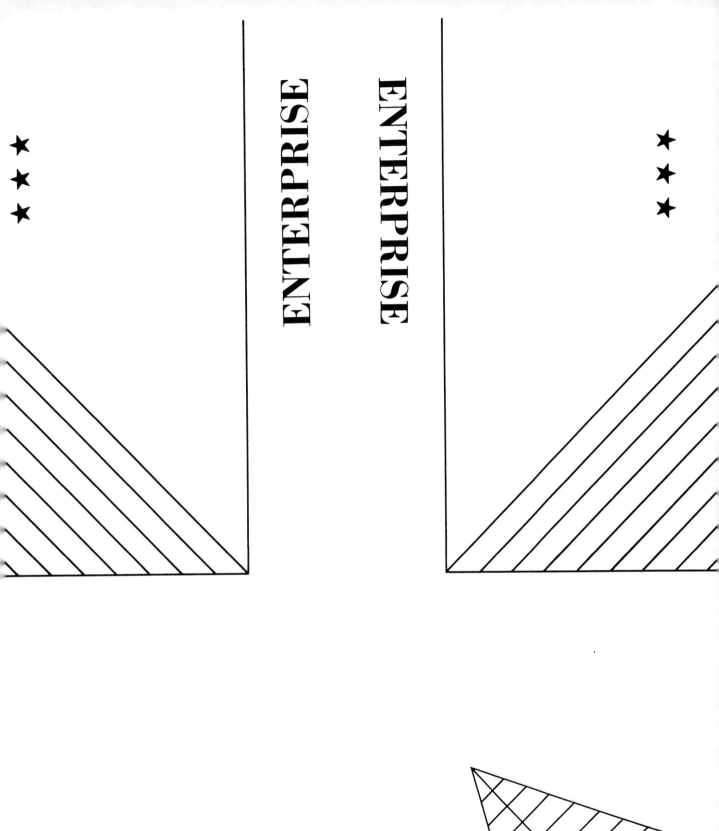

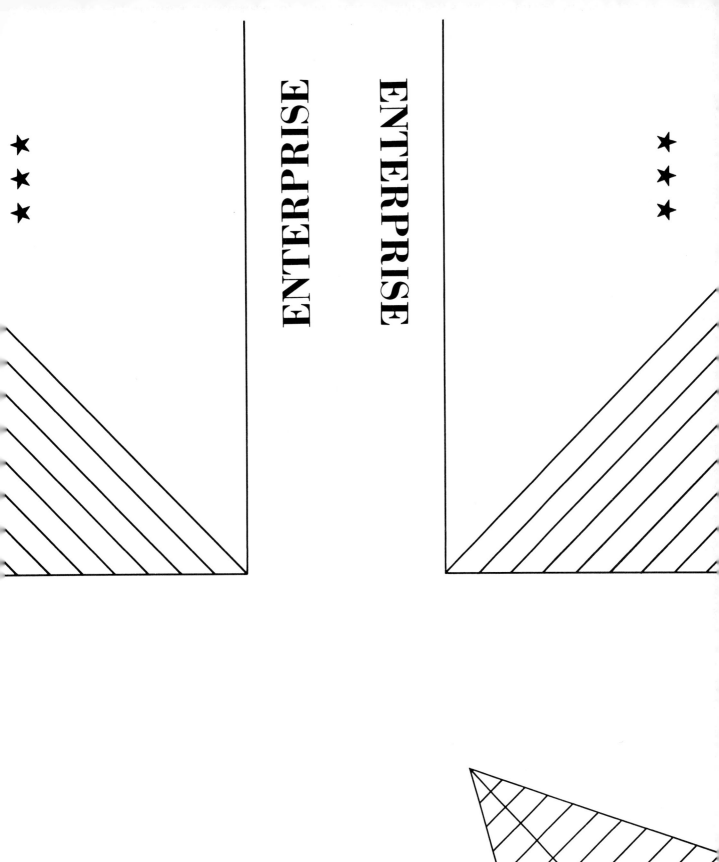

ENTERPRISE

ENTERPRISE

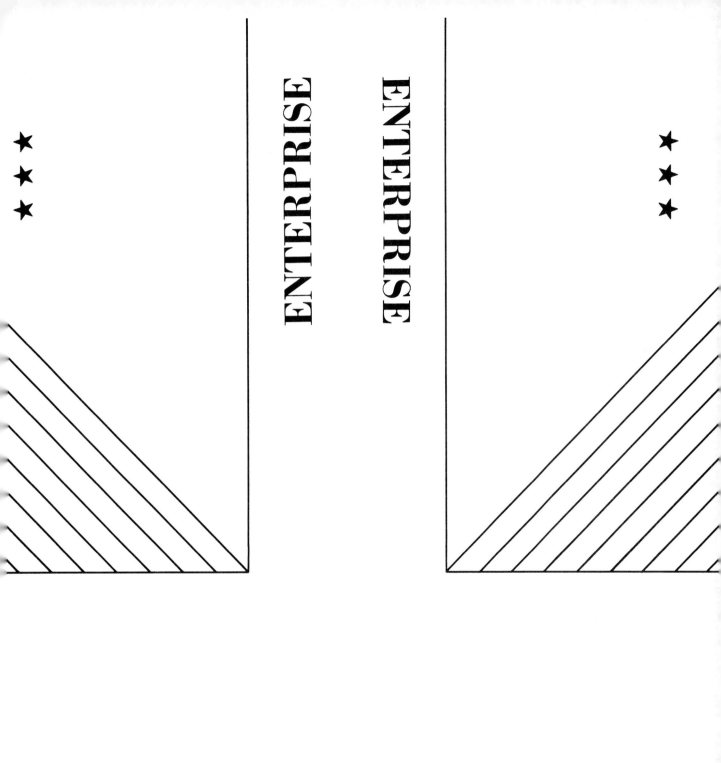

ENTERPRISE

ENTERPRISE

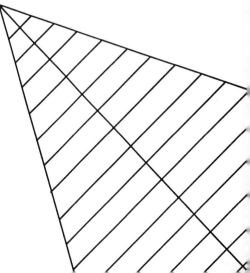

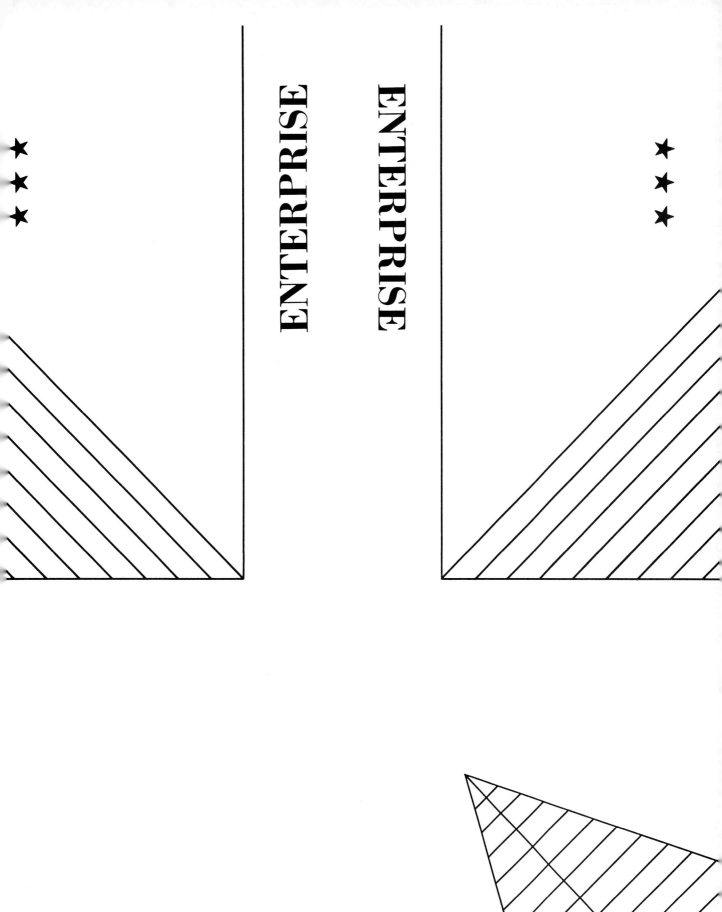

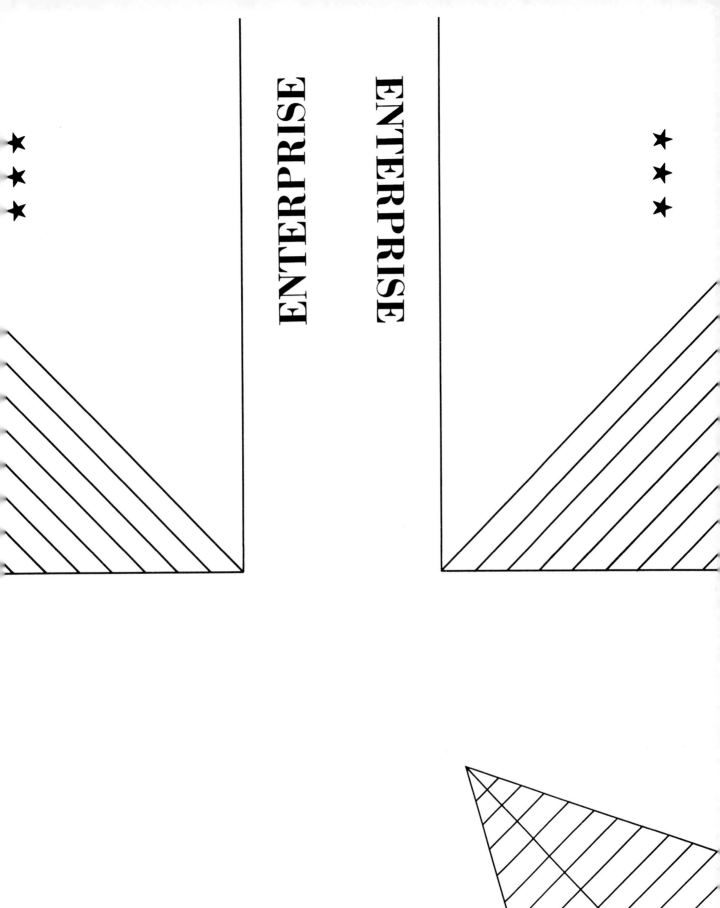

ENTERPRISE

ENTERPRISE

THE YELLOW PAGES
OF LEARNING
EXPERIENCES

I. PURPOSE

This section of the book[1] is intended as an aid to those students who would like to continue their learning beyond the classroom and the readings. It is a way of completing the learning loop (see the chapter, Learning and Problem Solving) by moving into the active experimentation stage, experimenting with approaches to new questions that have been raised by the experiences of each chapter.

The directory is divided into two major parts:

1. An index of key words and concepts related to organizational psychology
2. The listings of suggested experiments, readings, films, and experiences, under the following four headings:
   (I) Individuals, I-1 through I-50
   (G) Groups, G-51 through G-65
   (O) Organizations, O-66 through O-82
   (C) Culture and Environment, C-83 through C-90

These categories are meant to help you identify the relevant focus of your questions. A question raised by the motivation chapters, for example, may have implications for your own motivation, its effect on groups, its relationship to organization climate, or the effect of achievement motivation on the economic growth of a culture. It is up to you to choose your own level of learning and to look up appropriate entries in the directory.

---

[1]This section in the second edition was developed in collaboration with Margaret Fox.

II. USE

At the end of each chapter in the book there are two questions related to key concepts in the chapter *from your perspective*. After writing down those key concepts, take the key words in your statement and look for them in the index. If the exact words are not there, think of similar words, other ways of expressing the concepts. There should be some representation of your questions somewhere in the index.

If your concerns are about *conflict resolution* or *interpersonal competition,* for example, pertinent resources may be found somewhere in the four categories of learning resources: individual suggestions, 1 through 50; group suggestions, 51 through 65; organization suggestions, 66 through 82; and culture and environment suggestions, 83 through 90. Not all the index words have listings in each of the four categories, so it will be up to you to match the key concept with a learning resource in the appropriate category for your learning goal. Learning in a group situation may have precedence over the exact key word, for example, so you might find a group exercise to approximate the particular concept you have in mind.

In effect, the directory of learning resources is conveniently arranged to meet many kinds of learning needs, and your use of it will no doubt vary from unit to unit. Wherever possible, books have been listed by their paperback editions to minimize cost, and information as to how to obtain films is included.

III. ATTITUDE

The way in which you approach the use of this directory will determine how much learning you can gain from it. The books and films are not unusual listings for students who are used to reading bibliographies, but the exercises are not the usual fare. It will take a commitment on your part to the process of experimentation to learn from these experiences, but you should find your ability to learn from everyday situations considerably enhanced as you make use of the directory.

The ultimate goal of these suggestions is *to increase your ability to learn from everything you do or observe*. It is hoped that the process can be started here, knowing that in the study and understanding of human behavior there is no such thing as "time out."

PART I
INDEX TO THE YELLOW PAGES
OF LEARNING EXPERIENCES

The following index of key concepts highlight some of the major areas of learning about individuals in organizations and about organizational processes and structures. These key words will refer you to the entries in each of the four categories—Individuals (I-1 to I-50), Groups (G-51 to G-65), organizations (O-66 to O-82), and culture and environment (C-83 to C-90)—that are appropriate to the concept.

Perception (cont.)
Grp. 52, 56, 58
Org. 76, 77
Cult. & Env. 84, 85

Planning
Ind. 6, 14, 15, 20, 23
Grp. 64
Org. 67–69, 79–82
Cult. & Env. 83

Play
Ind. 4, 16, 21
Grp. 55, 63, 65
Cult. & Env. 89, 90

Power
Ind. 11, 14, 21, 22, 27, 41
Grp. 55, 57, 61
Org. 68, 72, 74–76, 78
Cult. & Env. 83, 88, 90

Prejudice
Ind. 22, 29, 48
Grp. 52, 58, 62
Org. 68, 72, 78
Cult. & Env. 85

Problem Solving
Ind. 17, 39
Grp. 61, 64
Org. 69, 70, 72, 78, 80, 81
Cult. & Env. 87

Responsibility
Ind. 3, 50
Grp. 55, 57, 59
Org. 66, 67, 78, 79, 81
Cult. & Env. 87, 89, 90

Risk Taking
Ind. 3, 43, 50
Grp. 65
Org. 70, 72, 78
Cult. & Env. 90

Roles
Ind. 7, 13, 19, 24, 31, 41, 47
Grp. 51, 53, 61
Org. 67, 71, 78
Cult. & Env. 87, 89, 90

Self-image
Ind. 7, 11–13, 18, 19, 23, 24, 45, 46
Grp. 51, 54, 56
Org. 66
Cult. & Env. 88–90

Self-oriented Behavior
Ind. 23, 31
Grp. 60, 63
Org. 69, 72

Socialization
Ind. 8, 19, 36, 38
Grp. 51, 56
Org. 66, 75, 77, 78
Cult. & Env. 84, 86, 89

Space
Ind. 9, 10, 32, 42, 46
Grp. 53, 54
Org. 74, 77
Cult. & Env. 87, 89

Stereotypes
Ind. 19, 22, 29, 48
Grp. 52, 56, 58

Stereotypes (cont.)
Org. 68, 76
Cult. & Env. 85

Stress
Ind. 3, 6, 13, 23, 36
Grp. 52
Org. 69, 75

Structure
Ind. 9, 32, 34, 42, 46
Grp. 54, 57, 61
Org. 72, 74, 78, 80, 82
Cult. & Env. 84, 87

Systems
Ind. 37
Grp. 51
Org. 69, 72, 74, 78, 80–82
Cult. & Env. 83, 86, 87

Task-oriented Behavior
Ind. 21
Grp. 55, 60, 63
Org. 67, 69, 72
Cult. & Env. 87, 89

Trust
Ind. 27, 31, 36, 40, 41, 47–49
Grp. 54, 57, 60
Org. 77
Cult. & Env. 85, 89, 90

Values
Ind. 7, 8, 12, 14, 22, 26, 27
Grp. 54, 63
Org. 66, 76, 78
Cult. & Env. 86, 87, 89, 90

PART II
LEARNING EXPERIENCES

I. LEARNING ABOUT INDIVIDUALS

The exercises and references in this section are mainly concerned with learning about behavior, your own as well as others', at the individual level. Some require interaction with other people, but the majority of these learning resources may be used individually.

The relevance to organization behavior of some of the suggested activities may seem remote at first, but the individual must be seen as the basic unit of any organization. What helps us understand ourselves and other individuals also helps us in understanding collections of people in groups and organizations.

The following resources (I-1 through I-39) can be used by you individually, although you may want to share your learning experiences with another person or several persons.

I-1. How many F's do you see in the following paragraph?

FINISHED FILES ARE THE RESULT OF YEARS OF SCIENTIFIC STUDY COMBINED WITH THE EXPERIENCE OF MANY YEARS:

Answer: There are six F's. How many did you find? Which ones did you miss? Why?

I-2. Construct something with modeling clay. Spend about two minutes building it and then destroying it. Experience what it feels like to destroy something you create.

a. Build another object, creating it until you reach a point where you decide you can't destroy what you build. Then destroy it. How much time did you put into creating it?

b. How valuable are your products? By what standards? What does the quality of what you build or the amount of effort put into building it have to do with how you feel about destroying it?

c. There is considerable attention these days on the process of job enlargement in organizations. What are the pros/cons of having people "feel" personal ownership in a whole product vs. being responsible for only one small piece (as on the typical assembly line)?

I-3. Test yourself for stress on this Social Readjustment Rating Scale, designed by Dr. Thomas H. Holmes and Dr. Richard H. Rahl.*

It includes one year's life events that would involve significant stress.

If you score 200 points or above, you may experience high levels of stress that can be associated with emotional or physical illness.

The description of the life event is followed by the number value of the stress caused by the event.

Events	Score
1. Death of spouse	100
2. Divorce	73
3. Marital separation	65
4. Jail term	63
5. Death of close family member	63
6. Personal injury or illness	53
7. Marriage	50
8. Fired at work	47
9. Marital reconciliation	45
10. Retirement	45
11. Change in health of family member	44
12. Pregnancy	40
13. Sexual difficulties	39
14. Gain of new family member	39
15. Business readjustment	39
16. Change in financial state	38
17. Death of close friend	37
18. Change to different line of work	36
19. Change in number of arguments with spouse	35
20. Mortgage over $10,000	31
21. Foreclosure of mortgage or loan	30
22. Change in responsibilities at work	29
23. Son or daughter leaving home	29
24. Trouble with in-laws	29
25. Outstanding personal achievement	28
26. Spouse begins or stops work	26
27. Beginning or ending school	26
28. Change in living conditions	25
29. Revision of personal habits	24
30. Trouble with boss	23

*Reprinted with permission from *Journal of Research,* Thomas H. Holmes and Richard H. Rahl, "The Social Readjustment Rating Scale." Copyright 1967, Pergamon Press, Ltd.

31. Change in work
hours or conditions   20
32. Change in schools   20
33. Change in recreation   19
34. Change in church
activities   19
35. Change in social activities   18
36. Mortgage or loan
less than $10,000   17
37. Change in sleeping habits   16
38. Change in number
of family get-togethers   15
39. Change in eating habits   15
40. Vacation   13
41. Christmas holidays   12
42. Minor violations of law   11

I-4. Create the most beautiful thing you can.

I-5. Sensory awareness may often be enhanced through sensory deprivation. Using blindfolds, earplugs, nose clamps, and heavy gloves, deprive yourself of your senses one at a time.
a. In what ways did your remaining senses change?
b. Did other senses compensate for the loss? How?
c. Vary the experiences; for example, while blindfolded, peel an orange, listen as you separate the sections, smell the newly released aroma, taste the sweetness of the pulp. Describe it to someone.

I-6. *Adult Development*
Current research suggests that contrary to Freudian assumptions, growth and development continue beyond childhood. For portraits of the dramatic changes in adult life, see
a. Gail Sheehy, *Passages* (New York: E. P. Dutton, 1974).
b. Daniel Levinson, "The Mid-Life Transition: A Period in Adult Psycho-Social Development, *Psychiatry,* Vol. 40 (1977). pp. 99–112.

I-7. *Congruency Exercise*
Write 10 to 15 spontaneous completions to the statement "I believe. _____." Categorize these responses into one of the following:
Something I believe/value that
● I've never shared with anyone publicly

● I've shared publicly with a few people
● I've shared publicly with many people
a. For each of the responses, if possible, list several behaviors in which you have engaged that you feel are congruent with one of these values. List behaviors that are incongruent with one or some of these values.
b. This activity can help you become more aware of blind or hidden aspects of your self-image, can provide insights into conflicts within yourself, and can provide clues as to how these conflicts become manifest in your interpersonal relationships.

I-8. Within a language, certain words have a dramatic impact upon the nature of human interactions. Consider the following:
A child tells his mother that he has spilled milk on the floor.
a. In what way would the subsequent interaction be different if the mother responded with "How?" with "Why?" What implications do these words have—what implicit meanings?
b. Make a list of words that have value implications (e.g., "should," "ought").
According to some of the general semanticists, one way we hide

our specific feelings from ourselves is through the use of general verbs. Try to speak for extended periods of time without using any of the forms of the verb "to be" (is, are, was, etc.).
a. How much difficulty did you have in doing this?
b. Did the experience force greater concreteness? How?
Think of how you address the people you know (e.g., formally, by first name, nickname) and how they address you.
a. What do these communications tell you about your relationships with these people?
b. See Roger Brown, *Social Psychology* (New York: The Free Press, 1965), Chapter 2, for conceptual help.

I-9. Rearrange the furniture in your room or, the next time you clean it, pay attention to the organization of your things, where you place certain objects, and so on.
a. Where in relation to windows and doors, do you feel most comfortable? Where do you place furniture such as a desk, sofa, bed, or a chair in your room? Try a new arrangement that helps you organize your personal life more efficiently.
b. What objects did you find behind furniture, under rugs, and

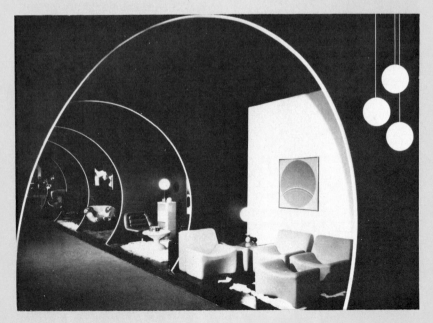

so on? How did you feel about finding them again?

c. Managing one's own life or space is, in some ways, similar to managing a group. How flexible versus structured are you? What differences, if any, are there in your "managerial" approaches?

I-10. Notice your own and others' behavior when entering a relatively empty restaurant.

a. Do you head for a corner? Center of the room?

b. Is it important for you to have a wall at your back? To choose a booth rather than a table?

c. Describe your feelings when such a choice has to be made whether you are alone or with a friend.

I-11. Experiment with a tape recorder and get feedback on your voice and style of communication.

a. Analyze your speech for affect level, logical ideas, precision of meaning, and so on.

b. Analyze the word content for n-Ach, n-Pow, n-Aff.

You can talk into a recorder while alone or try to record several live interactions. When real situations are used, you can check after the fact to see if you said what you thought you were saying. In addition, you can check your listening—what do you hear now that you didn't hear the first time?

I-12. Line up your books and magazines in order of preference.

a. What kinds of books do you like best/least? How do these books and magazines differ from each other in size, appearance, and content?

b. How do you arrange your books and magazines? Which ones do you want other people to know you have/don't have? What "image" do you project to others by your books and magazines? Analyze the books and magazines of another person in this way.

c. What aspects of these books do you most remember? What do you "know" as a result of reading them? Is it content knowl-

edge? What feelings did you have while reading them?

I-13. Analysis of your own dreams is a good way to improve your understanding of your hidden feelings, motives, and desires, but since dreams are constructed so as to "hide" feelings and motives by symbols and distortions, it is more useful to record several dreams and to pull together recurring themes for analysis.

a. Before you go to sleep at night, tell yourself to "dream" several times and then "will" yourself to remember your dreams when you wake up. A conscious effort such as this often proves useful for remembering.

b. When you awake, try to write down the feeling tone of the dream even if you can't remember the sequence of events or the details. In writing, allude to parts that are unclear or "blank." Concentrate for the next 10 minutes on reconstructing the dream until you are satisfied with it as a "whole" dream. Throughout the day, think about the dream several times to pick up any parts you may have left out or failed to remember earlier. (With practice, this will become easier.)

c. Look for recurring themes, significant persons, the affect level (what emotions are being expressed in the dream?), and pay attention to your reactions to the dreams and their meaning to you as you remember them.

d. One way to increase recall and to understand meaning in dreams is to use the "role-play" method of Gestalt therapy. Attempt to get back into the dream by acting out your own actions, perceptions, and movements. Then continue by role playing all the other things, animate or not, in your dreams (since even inanimate things are results of your own fantasies, they all have personal meanings). You should find your recall becoming clearer and your understanding of feelings deeper.

I-14. Career choice reflects personal values and personality traits.

One way that motives and needs often become manifest is by a person's choice of career. What career are you in now/considering at this time?

a. What careers seem appealing/disagreeable to you? Write a list of those you would consider and those you would reject.

(1) What factors in those careers that appeal to you reveal your need for affiliation with other people, your need for achievement and independence, your need for power and control over situations and other people?

(2) What factors in the careers that you would reject reveal your needs and motives?

b. What factors in the careers that appeal to you reflect your style of goal setting; short- or long-term, individual or joint decision making?

c. Almost all career choices involve some kinds of conflicting feelings (job vs. family; commitment vs. comfort, etc.). List, in the order of their importance, the conflicts you feel.

d. Can you think of career paths that might help you manage these conflicts? What changes in you and your relationships will be necessary to manage them?

e. The following short story may be helpful in understanding how a career choice affects an individual's life:

"The Trap of Solid Gold," in *The End of the Tiger*, John D. MacDonald (Greenwich, Conn.: Fawcett Books, 1965). To all outward appearances, his career is going well. His income is high. The problem is that the company's demands force him into a life-style he can't afford.

I-15. Think of changes going on in the world at this moment. What trends do you see in motion that will affect your present career choices?

a. Write a scenario about the immediate environment you will be living in 10 years from now.

How is it different/similar to the present?

b. What does this forecast tell you about career choices?

c. How do you feel about the possibility of changing careers several times during your lifetime (many people will!)? What do these feelings tell you about your own resistance to/comfort with the process of change?

d. See the Open Systems Planning Model (O-81) for a personal career development tool.

I-16. Play a musical instrument you have never played before, but with which you can make sounds. Express your feelings with the sounds.

a. How does the strangeness of the instrument affect your expressions? Are you able to express a full range of emotions (e.g., anger to tranquility)?

b. Does trying the instrument as a means of expression make you want to learn to play it? In what way is this different from taking lessons?

c. Does the absence of a teacher affect your feelings? Your ability to learn? Can you learn to play a song on your own?

I-17. For a fascinating theory of how the mind works, see Edward de Bono, *The Mechanism of Mind* (New York: Pelican Books, 1971). De Bono describes different styles of thinking and why "lateral" creative thinking is difficult. Also see William Gordon, *Synectics* (New York: Collier Books, 1962).

I-18. *Self-Perception*
Make a list of the ways you would predict how others see you. Check it out with them.

a. How accurate do you think they were in describing you? To what

do you attribute the differences, if any, in people's perceptions of you?

b. A film on perception, *Eye of the Beholder,* may be helpful to you. A crime seems to have been committed, but eyewitnesses disagree due to previous stereotypes. (Available from Harvard Business School, Audio-Visual Dept. Boston, Mass. 02163.)

I-19. *Personal Change and Growth*
Develop a list of behavioral habits/patterns/attitudes you think you exhibit that you believe have become expectations that others hold of you. These can cover a variety of factors—supporting a particular sports team, playing a particular role in groups (friendly helper), lending people your car, and so on.

a. As an experiment, try to alter one of these patterns in some significant way. Monitor your own reactions/feelings and the reactions/feelings of those whose expectations you have "violated."

b. Consider these data in light of their relationship to concepts like roles, expectations, norms, resistance to change, personal growth.

I-20. Write a scenario about a day in your life 10 years from now.

a. What do you want to be able to say about yourself?

b. What trends are in motion in your life now that will facilitate/hinder your reaching these statements/goals?

c. What trends are in motion in society that will affect your future goals? How?

d. What do you need to do now to achieve your future goals?

I-21. Play in a stream of running water. Create dams, divert the stream's path, make bridges and waterfalls.

a. What do you enjoy most about this kind of activity? Is it the freedom of playing as a child? The power of changing or building part of the environ-

ment? The sound and feel of running water?

b. Does it feel like a "waste of time"? Why or why not?

c. Hard-driving, aggressive, achievement-oriented people often have considerable difficulty with leisure time/play activities. Are these inborn characteristics or socially induced?

d. In what ways do organizations contribute to/help one cope with the work versus leisure conflict many people experience?

I-22. Listen carefully to the words of some songs you consider your favorites. What can you infer about your own motives, values, needs, and present concerns? What emotions do these songs elicit in you?

Analyze the themes contained in the "top 40." Does this give you any insight into the values and concerns of the youth subculture?

a. How are these songs in accord or discord with the values of society?

b. Find out why people of other subcultures dislike the music typically liked by youth, what kinds of emotions, stereotypes, attitudes it evokes, and so on.

I-23. *Time Management Exercise*
Keep a log for several days of how you spend your time. The more frequent the entries (e.g., every 1 to 2 hours) the better will be your data base for subsequent analysis and reflection.

a. Examine these data in terms of initiation by self versus others, wanted versus had to do, present-oriented demands versus potentially growth-producing activities, useful versus wasteful with time (after-the-fact).

b. How congruent is your daily living or life-style with your self-image? Which do you intend to modify?

c. In what way is your personal time management style related to/different from your style of managing other people?

I-24. *Who Am I Exercise*
On 10 separate sheets of paper answer the question "Who Am I?" as quickly as possible. Then go back

and rank order each of these statements: give a number 10 to the statement you would be *most* willing to discard and so on until you reach number 1, the statement you would be *least* willing to discard.

a. Reflection and analysis of these rank-order statements can provide clues to the cognitive map you use in thinking about yourself (e.g., did you use role descriptions, adjectives, verbs (action-oriented)?).

b. With a partner (friend, spouse), this exercise can yield insights into the hidden and blind parts of your self-images (Johari window), by asking them to make a similar set of rank-ordered cards about you and sharing them with you.

c. After doing this exercise, try writing a scenario about yourself ten years in the future (see I-15, I-20). Does the "Who Am I?" data change your perception of your future? In what ways?

I-25. *Tough and Tender Learning,* David Nyberg (Palo Alto, Calif.: National Press Books, 1971). Written by a creative teacher, this book emphasizes the differences between teaching and learning, with particular emphasis on developing individual learning styles.

I-26. *The Silent Language,* E.T. Hall (Greenwich, Conn.: Fawcett Premier Books, 1959). A general treatment of the ways in which nonverbal behavior communicates cultural norms and values.

I-27. *Leadership Style Questionnaire Source:* Adapted from M. Scott Myers, *Every Employee a Manager* (New York: McGraw-Hill Book Company, 1970).

This instrument is designed to help you better understand the assumptions you make about people and human nature. There are 10 pairs of statements. Assign a weight from 0 to 10 to *each statement* to show the relative strength of your belief in the statements *in each pair.* The points assigned for each pair must in each case total

10. Be as honest with yourself as you can and resist the natural tendency to respond as you would "like to think things are." This instrument is not a "test." There are no right or wrong answers. It is designed to be a stimulus for personal reflection and discussion.

1. It's only human nature for people to do as little work as they can get away with. ___(a)
   When people avoid work, it's usually because their work has been deprived of its meaning. ___(b)
   10

2. If employees have access to any information they want, they tend to have better attitudes and behave more responsibly. ___(c)
   If employees have access to more information than they need to do their immediate tasks, they will usually misuse it. ___(d)
   10

3. One problem in asking for the ideas of employees is that their perspective is too limited for their suggestions to be of much practical value. ___(e)
   Asking employees for their ideas broadens their perspective and results in the development of useful suggestions. ___(f)
   10

4. If people don't use much imagination and ingenuity on the job, it's probably because relatively few people have much of either. ___(g)
   Most people are imaginative and creative but may not show it because of limitations imposed by supervision and the job. ___(h)
   10

5. People tend to raise their standards if they are accountable for their own behavior and for correcting their own mistakes. ___(i)
   People tend to lower their standards if they are not punished for their misbehavior and mistakes. ___(j)
   10

6. It's better to give people both good and bad news because most employees want the whole story, no matter how painful. ___(k)
   It's better to withhold unfavorable news about business because most employees really want to hear only the good news. ___(l)
   10

7. Because a supervisor is entitled to more respect than those below him in the organization, it weakens his prestige to admit that a subordinate was right and he was wrong. ___(m)
   Because people at all levels are entitled to equal respect, a supervisor's prestige is increased when he supports this principle by admitting that a subordinate was right and he was wrong. ___(n)
   10

8. If you give people enough money, they are less likely to be concerned with such intangibles as responsibility and recognition. ___(o)
   If you give people interesting and challenging work, they are less likely to complain about such things as pay and supplemental benefits. ___(p)
   10

9. If people are allowed to set their own goals and standards of performance, they tend to set them higher than the boss would. ___(q)
   If people are allowed to set their own goals and standards of performance, they tend to set them lower than the boss would. ___(r)
   10

10. The more knowledge and freedom a person has regarding his job, the more controls are needed to keep him in line. ___(s)

The more knowledge and freedom a person has regarding his job, the fewer controls are needed to ensure satisfactory job performance. ___(t)

10

The theory behind this instrument is discussed in detail below. To get your scores, add up the points you assigned to the following:

Theory X score = sum of (a), (d), (e), (g), (j), (l), (m), (o), (r), and (s).
Theory Y score = sum of (b), (c), (f), (h), (i), (k), (n), (p), (q), and (t).

Assumptions About People and Human Nature—Personal Values

One of the forces that operates to shape leadership style is the basic assumption we hold about people and human nature. McGregor described two ends of a continuum of such assumptions, labeling them Theory X (traditional assumptions) and Theory Y (emerging assumptions). These two sets of assumptions are summarized as follows.

The Personal Analysis of Leadership Style Questionnaire is designed to help you assess the extent of your own Theory X versus Theory Y assumptions about people. Understanding these assumptions is of crucial importance because of the potential that exists for self-fulfilling prophecies. In other words, if you believe people are lazy, irresponsible, and so on (Theory X assumptions), you will manage them in a way that is consistent with these assumptions (e.g., watch over their shoulders all the time). This behavior can cause your subordinates to feel that they really have no responsibility in their job, which could lead them to work hard only when you are watching them closely. A self-fulfilling prophecy has thus begun and will be continually reinforced.

McGregor's conceptualization also highlights the inherent complexity of human behavior. People are not motivated by a single driving force. Instead, people seek many satisfactions and these needs are dynamic, changing as people grow and develop. This fact reinforces the need for flexible, adaptive behavior on a manager's part for differential leadership styles.

I-28. Domestic pets interact with your personality traits. Describe the relationship you have with a pet

THEORY X ASSUMPTIONS (Traditional)	THEORY Y ASSUMPTIONS (Emerging)
SOURCE: Douglas McGregor, *The Human Side of Enterprise* (New York: McGraw-Hill Book Company, 1960).	
1. People are naturally lazy; they prefer to do nothing.	1. People are naturally active; they set goals and enjoy striving.
2. People work mostly for money and status rewards.	2. People seek many satisfactions in work: pride in achievement; enjoyment of process; sense of contribution; pleasure in association; stimulation of new challenges, etc.
3. The main force keeping people productive in their work is fear of being demoted or fired.	3. The main force keeping people productive in their work is desire to achieve their personal and social goals.
4. People remain children grown larger; they are naturally dependent on leaders.	4. People normally mature beyond childhood; they aspire to independence, self-fulfillment, responsibility.
5. People expect and depend on direction from above; they do not want to think for themselves.	5. People close to the situation see and feel what is needed and are capable of self-direction.
6. People need to be told, shown, and trained in proper methods of work.	6. People who understand and care about what they are doing can devise and inprove their own methods of doing work.
7. People need supervisors who will watch them closely enough to be able to praise good work and reprimand errors.	7. People need a sense that they are respected as capable of assuming responsibility and self-correction.
8. People have little concern beyond their immediate, material interests.	8. People seek to give meaning to their lives by identifying with nations, communities, churches, unions, companies, causes.
9. People need specific instruction on what to do and how to do it; larger policy issues are none of their business.	9. People need ever-increasing understanding; they need to grasp the meaning of the activities in which they are engaged; they have cognitive hunger as extensive as the universe.
10. People appreciate being treated with courtesy.	10. People crave genuine respect from their fellow men.
11. People are naturally compartmentalized; work demands are entirely different from leisure activities.	11. People are naturally integrated; when work and play are too sharply separated both deteriorate; "The only reason a wise man can give for preferring leisure to work is the better quality of the work he can do during leisure."
12. People naturally resist change; they prefer to stay in the old ruts.	12. People naturally tire of monotonous routine and enjoy new experiences; in some degree everyone is creative.
13. Jobs are primary and must be done; people are selected, trained, and fitted to predefined jobs.	13. People are primary and seek self-realization; jobs must be designed, modified, and fitted to people.
14. People are formed by heredity, childhood and youth; as adults they remain static; old dogs don't learn new tricks.	14. People constantly grow; it is never too late to learn; they enjoy learning and increasing their understanding and capability.
15. People need to be "inspired" (pep talk) or pushed or driven.	15. People need to be released and encouraged and assisted.

and how it differs from your relationships with other members of the group you live with.

a. How does your pet respond when you are friendly/angry/involved with another person or task?

b. For a week, keep a diary recording the behaviors of your pet. Assess what you think are your pet's needs and what your own needs are in relation to the animal. Whose needs are met the most and how?

c. Do you relate to/manage your pets in ways similar to your style with other people? What characteristics of you/them affect these relationships?

I-29. Observe a stranger on a bus or subway. Watch his or her movements, expressions, mannerisms, dress, and so on.

a. What can you infer about this person—social status, race, religion, occupation, marital status, nationality?

b. What stereotypes come to mind about this person's personal habits, work habits, family life, attitude about sex, crime, responsibility?

c. If possible, interview the person. Specifically, check the validity of your stereotypes.

I-30. Watch a favorite talk show on television.

a. Observe the reactions of guests to the questions they are asked. What things do they say or do to "avoid" the issues? Why do you think they are avoiding them?

b. How does a public audience affect an individual on television? What kinds of things do you think the M.C. wants to ask but doesn't?

c. Compare your analysis to your own reactions to "being on stage." How does an audience influence your behavior? How do you prepare yourself psychologically to "walk on stage"?

I-31. *Games People Play,* Eric Berne (New York: Grove Press, 1961, also in paperback). This book can help to enhance your under-

Courtesy: The New York Zoological Society (The Bronx Zoo).

standing of the behavioral effects of different motives, the dynamic way in which motives interact, and the impact of self-fulfilling prophecies.

I-32. *Spatial Language*
Visit the office of an executive in an organization. Examine the way in which his or her office is laid out.

a. How does the arrangement of the furniture affect you? Does the desk act as a "barrier" to communication? How accessible is this person to you in this room?

b. Is the office conducive to thinking and reflecting or doing things?

c. How formal or informal can you be in this room?

d. If you can, interview the person to see if he or she had any goals in mind in arranging the office. Find out how the person feels about working in the office,

talking with others, just relaxing and reflecting.

e. For conceptual help see *Physical Settings and Organization Development,* Fred I. Steele (Reading, Mass.: Addison-Wesley Publishing Co., Inc., 1973).

I-33. "Learning how to learn" has been postulated as the cornerstone to self-renewal and adaptation for individuals and organizations. To learn something is to "know" it. A crucial step, therefore, in learning how to learn is to understand our own definitions of knowledge.

a. What does it mean to you to "know something"?

b. Do you feel your knowledge base has increased if you "know," for example, that being dependent on someone else makes you angry? What difference, if any, would it make if no one else/many other people "know" the same things as you or feel the same way you do?

c. What can you do to expand your definition of knowledge? Would you have to change your learning style? How?

d. Predict the patterns your friends or family will score on the Learning-Style Inventory. Show them your predictions and explain to them the basis for your predictions. What "traits" give you clues as to their learning styles? How accurate were you in your predictions?

I-34. *Contrary Imaginations,* Liam Hudson (New York: Schocken Books, 1966). The learning styles of groups of boys are divided into two broad categories: *convergers,* who do well in structured situations, and *divergers,* who prefer situations that are more open ended and who show higher creativity.

I-35. *The Teachings of Don Juan: A Yaqui Way of Knowledge* and *A Separate Reality: Further Conversations with Don Juan,* Carlos Castaneda (New York: Pocket Books, 1972). Personal and fascinating accounts of a young anthropologist's apprenticeship to a Yaqui Indian's world of "nonordinary reality." Castaneda struggles to grasp a system of knowledge totally different from his familiar concepts of Western civilization.

I-36. The following books describing the inner experiences of people who became mentally ill or "schizophrenic" give insight into the disruptive effects of socialization on individuals and how inner conflicts can lead to total ineffectual behavior and distrust of human relationships.

I Never Promised You a Rose Garden, Hannah Green (New York: Signet, 1964). A very moving account of a young girl's struggle to find her way out of the world of mental illness. Many insights can be gained as to how personalities develop, how various motives manifest themselves in fantasies, dreams, and behavior. The help-

ing relationship with her doctor is enlightening and encouraging.

The Bell Jar, Sylvia Plath (New York: Signet, 1971). Six months in a young creative woman's life in which she descends into sickness. A good account of how the inner world and the outer world of a person collide.

I-37. *I'm OK—You're OK,* Thomas A. Harris (New York: Harper & Row, Publishers, 1969, also in paperback). Harris outlines his theory of transactional analysis, a system of "script" writing between parents and children. Offers insight into how we develop (internalize) the parent, child, and adult in ourselves.

I-38. Think of the ways in which a person's childhood influences his or her behavior today—values, goals, achievements, motives. Some biographies and novels that illustrate the impact of early years on later life are

Cheaper by the Dozen, Gilbreath and Cary (New York: Bantam Books, 1959).

To Kill a Mockingbird, Harper Lee (New York: Popular Library, 1963).

Hitler: A Study in Tyranny, H.R. Trevor-Roper, (New York: Harper & Row, 1962).

A Puritan in Babylon, W.A. White (New York: Capricorn Books, 1965).

The Education of Henry Adams, H. Adams (Boston: Houghton-Mifflin Co., 1973).

I-39. Look at the squares below and count how many squares you see.

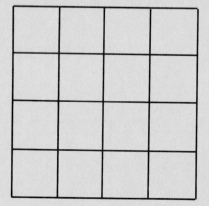

a. Ask somebody else to count the squares. Do you perceive the same number of squares? Share how you arrived at your answers.

b. What feelings do you have when you can't perceive the same number as somebody else? How are your problem-solving methods the same or different?

c. How does your problem-solving method correspond to your learning style?

Learning resources I-40 to I-50 call for interaction with a partner to benefit from the exercises.

I-40. With a friend, mirror each other's movements and behavior. One person is the mirror, the other the viewer. The mirror follows the viewer's actions. Do this for 5 to 10 minutes.

a. Switch roles for another 5 to 10 minutes.

b. For the next 5 minutes mirror each other at the same time.

c. In discussing your experiences, pay particular attention to issues of shifts in control, the nature and quality of the sharing process, the ways in which you competed vs. collaborated.

d. Leadership and followership go hand in hand. How did it feel when your partner would not/could not easily follow your lead? As "leader," did you exercise power in a way which made your follower feel like an origin or a pawn? With what consequences?

I-41. *Role Reversal Game*
Arrange with another person (friend, spouse, child) to switch roles for about one hour. You behave like the other person and he or she behaves like you.

a. Pay attention to the feelings you have about losing the status of your normal role, your feelings about playing the role of the other person, about experiencing your normal role from another point of view.

b. Discuss with your partner such interpersonal processes as styles of influence, decision making and conflict resolution, perception, control, dependency, and the psychological contract.

I-42. Boundary Game

With another person, discover where both of your "psychological boundaries" are—where proximity to the other person "violates" the space around you that you feel is your space. Do this nonverbally once.

a. What feelings and reactions do you have when the other person "enters" your territory? What expectations do you have of him or her when this happens? What kind of "contract" do you establish?

b. How does your partner react when you enter his or her space?

c. In conversing with another person, what is your "effective communication distance" (the distance at which you usually stand to converse with another person)?

d. What are the different reactions you get from violating another person's space?
   (1.) in encounter with the same sex
   (2.) in encounter with the opposite sex
   (3.) in encounters where there are clear status differences

e. In what ways do boundary issues manifest themselves in organizations? office locations, lunch facilities? With what consequences?

I-43. Interview a "successful" entrepreneur and somebody who failed in business.

a. How does each spend his or her time? What things do they enjoy?

b. What frustrations or obstacles did each encounter in their business and how were they met? What kinds of risks did they take?

c. What part did interaction with other people play in the success or failure of the business?

What part did self-directed achievement play?

d. In what ways do their experiences influence your desires to become/not become an entrepreneur? Your feelings about entrepreneurs? How do you regard "failure" in business after the interview?

e. For conceptual help, see *The Achieving Society,* David C. McClelland (New York: The Free Press, 1961). McClelland explores the relationship between the entrepreneurial spirit (achievement motivation) in a culture—as found in its literature—and the probability of a subsequent economic growth.

f. Achievement Motive Exercises can be obtained from Education Ventures, Inc., 209 Court St., Middletown, Conn. 06457.

I-44. Communicate nonverbally with another person for about 10 minutes.

a. What facial expressions, body expressions, gestures did you use?

b. What was the "language" of your partner?

c. What feelings, motives, thoughts could you communicate nonverbally? What was difficult for you to communicate in this way?

I-45. Draw or paint a picture of yourself or create a self-descriptive collage.

a. Show your picture or collage to a partner and describe yourself.

b. How do colors and designs reveal your personality? What words do you use in expressing yourself? What kinds of expressions?

c. How difficult is it to communicate thoughts and feelings about yourself?

d. The U.S. Navy, for example, is struggling with the pros and cons of allowing sailors to "express themselves" (e.g., hair style, pictures by their beds). What could you tell the Navy—as an "expert" in organizational psychology—that would

help them make the best decision about this issue?

I-46. Let someone be a consultant to you for this exercise. Ask him or her to describe your room in terms of an organization.

a. What things in your room tell about your feelings, your personality, your activities, your ideas? How does your room reflect your personality?

b. How does color and design reveal personal information about you?

c. How does the organization of the room reflect your personality? What kind of "image" does this organization (or lack of) give to your consultant? What kind of advice do you get?

d. Analyze the room of a partner or a friend in the same way.

I-47. Empathy Triads

(Empathy: "The projection of one's own personality into the personality of another in order to understand him better." *Webster's New World Dictionary.*)

With a partner spend about 10 minutes playing the role of an empathic friend or consultant, and then for another 10 minutes play the role of a person receiving empathy from a friend or consultant. A third person may observe and help process the interaction.

a. What did you say or didn't you say that was most helpful? Least helpful? What did your helper say to you or didn't he or she say that was helpful? What facial and behavioral cues did you use in giving empathy?

b. Did you find "Why" questions or "How" questions to be most helpful in giving empathy?

c. Can you define the kinds of techniques that seem to be most effective in giving empathy to another person?

d. How empathic do you feel you are capable of being, for what kind of people, in what kind of situations?

e. What functional role, if any, does empathy play in organizational life? Why should/should not a manager try to increase his empathic skills?

f. Why should/should not an organization try to be empathic with the needs of others (e.g., the privileged, the handicapped)?

I-48. *Operation Empathy*

Think of someone who is very different from yourself (for example, a corporation president might feel that a hippie is his or her "opposite"). Jot down the ways in which you think this person is different from/similar to yourself. Then seek out such a person and try to find out how this person sees the world—try to "get into his or her shoes." (If you do this in a triad, the third person may observe the interaction and provide useful feedback.)

a. How empathic did you feel toward this person? What were your first impressions, perceptions, projections, stereotypes of this person that changed during or after the interaction?

b. Which impressions, stereotypes, and so on remained the same?

c. How different/similar do you feel this person is to you now?

d. What barriers did you find that made it difficult for you to be empathic to this person? Did you discuss these with him or her? Why or why not?

I-49.
There are many books available with suggested activities for enhancing your awareness of how you communicate to another individual, for increasing your sensitivity to another's feelings, how to build trust, and so on. Some of these (available in paperback) are

What to Do Till the Messiah Comes and *Below the Mind,* Bernard Gunther (New York: Collier Books, 1971).

Gestalt Therapy, F. Perls, R. Hefferline, P. Goodman (New York: Delta, 1951).

Joy: Experiencing Human Awareness, W. Schutz (New York: Grove Press, 1967).

Supervisory and Executive Development: A Manual for Role Playing, Norman Maier et al.

(New York: John Wiley & Sons, Inc., 1964).

I-50.
Find a dart game and a partner. Play a few rounds.

a. Did you set any goals for the number of points you wanted to score each round? How did you react to reaching or not reaching your goals?

b. What can you learn from your risk-taking posture according to how near or far you stand from the dart board?

c. What difference does another person make in your behavior, the goals you set, your reactions to success or failure?

d. While playing, announce your goal before each dart throw. Give yourself your announced goal points if you make it or better it. If you miss your goal, score zero. Does this affect your risk taking? Concentration? Use of feedback on performance?

e. Of what use are the insights of this game to organization (e.g., goal setting, feedback, interpersonal competition)?

G. LEARNING ABOUT GROUPS

Although groups are made up of individuals, they tend to develop in ways that are more than just the sum of the parts. Individuals take different roles in groups, and the group itself will establish consistent patterns of interaction over periods of time.

In organizations, the problem of intergroup competition and conflict often leads to decisions that are less than optimal and, to a high degree, resistant to change. Change is often feared for possibly upsetting the equilibrium between groups and giving one group more power.

The following learning resources will add to your knowledge of group dynamics as well as to your own relationship to groups.

G-51. *Intergroup Relations*

All of us belong to multiple groups because we are members of many systems. One way to better understand the nature of intergroup relationships is to draw a map of our own multiple group connections. This can be called a role set analysis. (For a related approach at the organizational level, see O-66.)

a. Make a list of all the groups of which you feel you are a member (e.g., fathers, wives, students, members of a political party, fans of a particular sports team).

b. To what extent is your membership in each of these groups central (very important) or peripheral (relatively minor) to you?

c. Which of your group memberships create a conflict for you? What is the nature of the conflict? Do the people in your most central group tend to share other roles and groupings with you?

d. How do these conflicts affect your relationships with others within your most central group? In your more peripheral group?

G-52. *Intergroup Conflicts*
Intergroup conflict is one of the most pervasive of all organizational phenomena. Think of a group membership which is important to you. It could be a fraternity, a particular department in a company, or residence in a particular location.

a. Identify another group with which you and your group feel some conflict or competition.

b. How do you think that other group sees your group and the people in it in terms of strengths and weaknesses, likes and dislikes?

c. Interview several members of the other group to find out how they do, in fact, see your group.

d. Which of your predictions was verified? Which were not? To what do you attribute any misperceptions? How sure are you that the people you inter-

viewed were being absolutely honest about their perceptions of your group?

G-53. Observe a dinner discussion (at home or in a restaurant).

a. What kinds of things are discussed, not discussed here? By whom?

b. What does the arrangement of people at the table tell you? What roles do people play?

c. How does conflict at the dinner table get expressed? Resolved?

G-54. *Sociometric Game*
Creating human sculptures and arranging people in seats are some concrete ways of making affiliation with others explicit. Such an activity helps to highlight group issues such as inclusion, exclusion, trust, distrust, and closeness versus distance. When a group is having difficulty determining which people distrust others and which people feel close to others, the following exercise can help to illustrate the reality of affiliation or lack of affiliation in a group.

a. Ask members in the group to place themselves in relation to

the center of the room depending on how close or distant they feel to the rest of the group members. They should also try to place themselves near those individuals to whom they feel closest. Concentric circles or "rings" of people may be defined in this way.

b. Discuss how it feels to be in the position you have chosen. Find out how others feel about your being in that position.

c. Another exercise is to have each member of the group place each of the other members around him or her according to how he feels about them. The other members of the group become his or her "sculpture." Each person should have a chance to do this if time permits.

G-55. *Tinkertoy Game* (for either a small or large group)
As the leader or teacher of a group of people, experiment with two distinct styles of leadership: nondirective and democratic versus directive and authoritarian. Pass out several pieces of a Tinkertoy set to each person seated around

a table and put the remaining pieces in the center of the table.

a. In the first round, tell people they may choose six pieces to construct an object. When everybody has the pieces they want, tell them to begin building until each person completes something.

b. In the second round, tell them to find a stick and a square piece, then to take a yellow round piece and attach it to the other end of the stick, and so on, giving *specific* directions for completing a six- to eight-piece model (they all will look alike if built as directed).

c. Process the two rounds and compare motivation and feelings toward the leader, creativity and so on; compliance and defiance to directions given, task performance, and so on.

G-56. Go to the zoo.

a. Which animals remind you of yourself, of other people you know? Why?

b. What animals do you feel afraid of, puzzled by, amused by, and so on?

c. What behaviors of animals resemble human beings? How do groups of animals express cooperation, conflict? Can you distinguish the leader, the outcast, or the scapegoat? How do animals enforce group norms?

d. Engage a monkey's attention nonverbally. Try to get it to imitate you. What cues did it pick up from you? Imitate it imitating you. How does it react? How does this relate to interpersonal behavior?

e. Experiences such as visiting a zoo/farm or reading Desmond Morris' book, *The Human Zoo* (New York: Dell Publishing Co., 1969) can highlight such concepts as leadership, group norms, status/power, motivation, and interpersonal behavior, particularly as they relate to our biological heritage and development from lower animals.

G-57. *Master-Slave Game* (for a group of about 10 to 12 people)

Perception of power is a vital factor in any group or organization's leadership. The execution of power by leaders depends to a great extent on the perception of power by the subordinates in a group, their need to give others power, and their inability to designate power to themselves. The following game illustrates how groups vary in leadership dynamics depending on these variables.

Divide into two teams. Each group of Slaves has the task of selecting two Masters for their group who will exercise "absolute power" over the group during the game.

a. Masters should meet for about 5 minutes alone (in pairs) and each group of Slaves should meet for about 5 minutes together before the game begins.

b. Each team meets in a separate room for 20 minutes with their Masters. Neither group should be aware of what is going on in the other group.

c. Both groups then reconvene to discuss what happened, what issues came up, and how power was exercised. The Masters should explain to everybody what their "plans" were (strategies, for example) and the Slaves should reveal what went on in the pregame meeting.

d. How were the two teams different/similar in the 20-minute period? What differences in perception and execution of power were there?

e. Most groups in formal organizations have *designated* leaders. How could these leaders (Masters) behave to mitigate the suspicions, resentment, hostilities that often develop? How could subordinates (Slaves) behave to improve the relationships between the "have" and the "have nots"?

G-58. *Lemon Exercise*
The following game highlights the concepts of stereotyping, first impressions, individual versus group traits, and differentiation in a group.

a. Gather a group of 10 to 12 people and show them a lemon. Ask people to describe the lemon by writing characteristics down on a piece of paper.

b. Next, give all members a lemon and ask them to "get to know" their lemon. In a few minutes, ask all players to put their lemons in the middle of the floor, scramble them, and then identify their own lemon.

c. Next, ask the players to get even more familiar with their own lemon. The final task will be to

identify their lemon with their eyes closed (have people label their lemon with a marker first).

d. Discuss how people found their lemons (a majority of people will be able to do this) and what cues or traits they used to identify their lemons. Compare final methods of identification with the initial descriptions or impressions of the lemon held up to the whole group.

G-59. *Blindfold Game* (for three people)

In managing people, there are obviously many styles of helping. The following exercise will help you better understand your own personal helping style, how you feel about being a helper or a helpee, and the effect your style has on another individual.

a. One person dons a blindfold (A), one is a helper (B), and a third person acts as a silent observer (C). A should wear the blindfold for about 20 to 30 minutes and try to be as active as possible (e.g., eating a meal, taking a walk). Just sitting still will be of no value.

b. B is A's helper while C is the silent observer. As the helper in this exercise, pay attention to how comfortable you feel "helping" A, how dependent or independent you want him or her to be with you, the ways you go about helping A to do what he or she wants to do (or whoever decides what he will do).

c. Switch roles until everybody has a chance to be blindfolded. Discuss the issues of responsibility for another person, what "help" really means in a concrete situation, how it feels to be dependent and to give and receive support and empathy. What other feelings are elicited by the exercise? Did anybody feel resentment or hostility at helping or being helped?

d. In what areas and in what ways is a manager a helper? What are the personal (in both parties) and organizational barriers (e.g., reward systems) to the development of effective helping relationships?

G-60. *The Benefactor Game* (for 6 to 10 people)

Gather together a group of people. The following exercise will highlight various aspects of a group decision-making process: competition versus collaboration, task-oriented versus maintenance-oriented versus self-oriented behavior and motives, styles of group decision making, conflict resolution, and interpersonal influence. This exercise is *for real and is not just a game.*

Place in an envelope a sum of money large enough to be meaningful to any one of the members of the group. Someone in the group must *in fact* receive this money—so do not expect it

back. Place the envelope on a table in front of the group. The instructions to the group are as follows:

A sympathetic benefactor has decided to leave a sum of money to one of your members. For a variety of reasons, however, he decided not to choose the recipient himself. You, therefore, have the following task: decide by *group consensus* which member of your group is to be the recipient of the money. The following conditions must be adhered to:

(1) One, and only one, person can receive the money.

(2) The recipient must use the money for his or her *own personal satisfaction,* he *cannot,* for example, offer to buy everyone drinks or offer to split it up in some other way later.

(3) The group must be able to state the criteria and rationale for its final choice.

(4) It will be the recipient's to keep and cannot be given back to the benefactor or his or her representative after the decision.

Failure to adhere to these conditions within the allotted time of 30 minutes will result in forfeiture of the money. This is a real exercise—not a game.

G-61. Meetings are a good way to observe groups in the decision-making process. Even though you may not know all the facts about the issues on the agenda, you will be able to observe some basic dynamics in any decision-making group. Often at a meeting where there are set limits (a time schedule, an agenda, etc.) power strategies and interpersonal dynamics make themselves apparent even to an outside observer. Sit in on a group that has to make a decision, a committee meeting, or a voting membership meeting of some small organization.

a. What is the style of leadership in this meeting? How are

"agenda items" presented for discussion and decision making?

b. Who has the most influence in this group? How is it exerted? Who has the least influence on the decision-making process?

c. What kinds of roles do people play in this meeting? What needs make themselves apparent? What are the main concerns of the group members?

d. If the group makes a decision, what effects does it have on the group members and their relationship to each other? If no decision is made, what are the consequences?

G-62. Often group norms are implicit rather than explicit and may even be difficult to define explicitly. Individuals, of course, are influenced by group norms even when they are not aware of what norms are. When you are aware of group norms, it is easier to understand your own behavior in terms of a group context. Describe the three most salient norms that operate in the group that is most important to you.

a. What are the feelings and assumptions behind them? How do these norms get communicated to others?

b. What happens to people who violate these norms? How does the group "police" itself? How does it feel to "go against" the group norms?

c. Has the group ever systematically examined its norms and tested its present relevance?

d. How do new norms develop and old norms get discarded? Understanding this process can help you consciously manage the process of change—both individually and in a group.

G-63. Paint a mural with some friends. This joint project will highlight several facets of group dynamics: decision making, teamwork, influencing, task-oriented versus self-oriented behavior.

a. Whose ideas get executed? How is this done?

b. How does talent or inspiration translate into work? What definition of work is generated by this project?

c. How does the finished mural compare to the original conception of it? What changes were made along the way to alter the original plan? How were these decisions made? How would you improve the teamwork of the group if you were to paint another mural?

d. With others in a group or organization to which you belong, create a mural or collage that is representative of that group or organization. Discuss together the following questions:
   (1) What new insights do you have about the group?
   (2) What did the group learn about its norms, climate, values?

G-64. *Modified Delphi Technique*
The Delphi technique is usable as a means of reaching group consensus when prioritizing a list of items or any other task that requires the group to come to a mutually agreeable rank ordering.

It was originally used as a method for future forecasting aiming for agreement among experts on the likelihood of certain events. In the modified form shown here, it is still usable for forecasting and planning, but is also adaptable to more immediate tasks.

a. Display the lists of items to be ranked so that all may see them.

To the right of the items, construct a matrix with the names of participants across the top.

b. Ask participants to rank order the items on a separate sheet of paper. It is important that they be written so that participants do not adjust their ratings due to group pressure.

c. Collect the rankings and enter them in the appropriate places in the matrix, determining the mean and range:

d. *Discussion:* The purpose of the discussion is to
   (1) Bring out the reasons for the extremes in those items with the largest range
   (2) Attempt to reduce that range by discussing criteria used by individuals and attempting to get new agreement on the best criteria for rating the items

e. If consensus is apparent, the group may want to move toward it at this point without going through another round. If there is still some disagreement, repeat the ranking process.

f. If two cycles of ranking do not reduce the range enough to reach consensus, stop and discuss the process issues that may be interfering with decision making.

G-65. *Serious Games,* Clark C. Abt (New York: Viking Press, 1970). The author, whose company specializes in simulations for learning and problem solving, has provided both theory and examples of the usefulness of experiential learning for groups.

	JIM	PEG	IRV	DEB	DAVE	CHERYL	BILL	MEAN	RANGE
Item 1	4	4	3	4	3	4	4	3.7	3–4
Item 2	2	1	1	2	1	1	2	1.4	1–2
Item 3	1	2	2	1	4	3	3	2.3	1–4
Item 4	3	3	4	3	2	2	1	2.5	1–4

SOURCE: We are indebted to Charles Case, Cleveland State University, for this modification of the Delphi technique.

O. LEARNING ABOUT ORGANIZATIONS

This section is concerned with organizations—collections of individuals who come together to carry out transactions with the environment that would be impossible to do separately. They are also composed of groups of people who are often in conflict with other groups within the organization, usually as a result of competition for resources, influence, and recognition.

The study of individuals and groups yields an awareness of a high level of complexity. The study of organizations is even more complex. The exercises and references in this section are intended to help with thinking and learning about organizations, and ways of acting on them to precipitate planned change.

O-66. *Socialization*

Socialization experiences take place continually and in a variety of contexts. Each of us has had numerous experiences with socialization already: as a child in the family, every new grade or class we enter in school, new jobs we take, new group experiences, etc. Seldom, however, do we think explicitly about this recurring process.

a. Think of a recent new group, organization, or class you have joined.

b. Using the framework at the right, try to articulate the "contract" as it existed at the point of entry.

c. Review your entries and consider the following:

   (1) In what ways did you and the organization communicate these expectations to each other?

   (2) In what areas can you identify the greatest matching? The greatest mismatches?

   (3) How were mismatches handled at entry? During your life with the organization? With what conse-

quences or satisfactions (in terms of productivity, satisfaction, etc.)?

d. Think about the many organizations of which you have been, are, or will be a member.

   (1) Is there a pattern to what you expect to get/give?

   (2) Is there a pattern to what you think the organization will expect to get from/give to you?

   (3) To what extent are any patterns related to your individual needs? Your theory of organizations?

O-67. *Responsibility Charting*

A recent technique that has proven useful in clarifying roles and responsibilities in project management is *responsibility charting*. The first step is to construct a grid with the tasks that must be done on the left side, and the people most likely to be involved listed across the top (see the example on p. 530).

The chart is used to indicate each person's responsibilities for each decision or task that must be done. There are four levels of involvement possible for each person in each task or decision:

1. *Responsibility ("R")*. The person with this designation under his or her name would be responsible for action to make sure decisions are carried out.

2. *Approval required, or the right to veto ("A–V")*. This item must be reviewed by the person(s) designated, who will *either approve or reject it.*

3. *Support ("S")*. Provides logistical support and resources for this task or decision.

4. *Inform ("I")*. Must be informed of decisions, but cannot influence them.

Each item is considered and responsibility (R) is assigned. It is essential that there be only one R for any one horizontal line. A consensus must be reached or an authoritarian decision made on who has responsibility. If there is lack of agreement, it is often because the task is defined too broadly. At that point the group should attempt to draw another horizontal line or two and break down the task into components, assigning R for each.

O-68. *Pecking Orders*

Pecking orders in an organization can tell you a lot about the nature of the organization: its hierarchy of power and affiliation between members, the kinds of status that are important to individuals, and so on. Visit several different types of organizations (e.g., a supermarket, a hospital, a police station). In each case, try to develop a picture of the "pecking order" or status hierarchy that exists.

INDIVIDUAL (YOU)		ORGANIZATION OR GROUP	
Expect to Get	Expect to Contribute	Expect to Get	Expect to Contribute

a. Pay attention to the multiple ways in which this pecking order is communicated (e.g., forms of dress, locations of work space, forms of address). What can you infer about the degree of openness versus closedness, flexibility versus rigidity, assumptions about people, and so on of these various types of organizations?

b. Interview several people in these organizations and try to check the accuracy of your own diagnosis.

c. In what ways do aspects of the "pecking order" in an organization vary as a function of the task (e.g., military organization versus a volunteer welfare organization)?

O-69. *Force Field Analysis*

There are several diagnostic tools available in diagnosing and planning for change. Application of these tools should increase the skills of the administrator in bringing about effective improvement in organizations, groups, and individual relationships. One such diagnostic tool is called force field analysis. In physics, there is a concept that a body is at rest when the sum of all the forces operating upon it is zero. The body will move in a direction determined by the unbalancing forces. This concept can be applied to situations involving human factors, for example, the production level of work teams in a factory, which often is constant (within small limits) around a certain level. The level stays reasonably constant be-

cause the forces tending to *raise* the level are just counteracted by forces tending to *lower* the level.

This kind of analysis can be applied to a wide range of situations involving human behavior. For example, suppose you are a member of a group and another member remains silent and uncommunicative. In an effort to understand his behavior better, you might make up a force field diagram. Some *increasing* forces might be

Pressure from other group members (A)

Rewards given for amount of participation (B)

Relevant topics he or she knows about (C)

Some *restraining* forces might be

Desire to avoid hurting other members (D)

Fear of retaliation if he or she does talk (E)

Anxiety about exposing himself or herself (F)

There could be any number of forces, of course, and of varying intensities.

As long as the total strength of the *restraining forces* exceeds that of the *straining forces* exceeds that of the *increasing forces,* the group member will reduce the amount of talking he or she does. He or she will maintain the same rate of talking if the forces match exactly, and increase the rate if the *increasing forces* outweigh the *restraining.*

There are two different strategies one could employ in an attempt to help the person in the illustration talk more. One is to increase the strength of the in-

creasing forces (e.g., apply more pressure). This may temporarily raise the present rate of talking. The problem with this strategy is that it tends to increase the tension in the system, causing new restraining forces to appear. As a result, this approach may result in changes that are temporary in nature.

A second approach is to eliminate or reduce the strength of the restraining forces. In this way, the rate of talking rises to a new, higher level without any resulting increase in tension. To understand why this second approach is less frequently used, we must understand certain characteristics of the forces people generally see operating.

Most forces fall into one of three categories:

Self—having to do with oneself as a person

Others—people other than oneself

The environment—nature of facilities, time available

In diagnosing a problem, most people, if they see themselves at all related to the problem, see themselves as increasing forces while others and environment are the restraining forces. One reason for this is that they may implicitly be aware of the effects of the two change strategies outlined above. In other words, if I recognize the part I might be playing (my attitudes or my behavior) in *holding back* problems, I may be the one who has to change! In the example presented, my tendency to dominate may be the most powerful force keeping others (restraining) from talking—and to help them talk more, I will have to be less dominant

Force field analysis can be a powerful diagnostic tool in helping to uncover possible problem areas in planning a change effort. From the change agents' point of view, it can help them to diagnose a system's readiness, capability, and potential for change. It can help them to understand their own motives and goals for being involved.

SUE	BOB	JOHN	BETH	DICK	RALPH	JIM	
I	A-V	R	A-V	S		I	Task₁
A-V			R	A-V	A-V	I	Task₂
	S	S	I	R		A-V	Task₃
S	A-V		I	R		S	Task₄
R		S		A-V		I	Task₅

SOURCE: Richard Beckhard and Reuben Harris, *Organizational Transitions* (Reading, Mass.: Addison-Wesley Publishing Co., Inc., 1977).

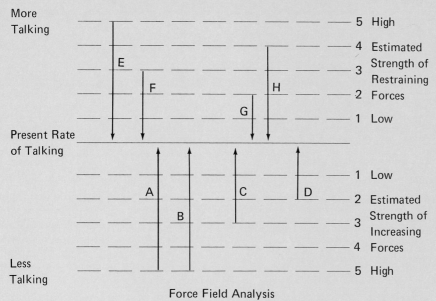

More
Talking

E	F	H
		G

5 High
4 Estimated
3 Strength of
Restraining
2 Forces
1 Low

Present Rate
of Talking

A	C	D
B		

1 Low
2 Estimated
3 Strength of
Increasing
4 Forces
5 High

Less
Talking

Force Field Analysis

O-70. *Organizational Decision Making*

Many organizations claim they operate to "maximize" performance or growth. Simon (1947), on the other hand, argues that people are not maximizers but satisficers (they will settle for results that satisfy without being optimal).

a. Think of several organizational decisions you have been part of.
b. Were they optimizing or satisficing decisions?
c. What are the forces (individual, group, organizational) that operate to create satisficing decisions? Maximizing decisions?
d. Can an organization ever make an optimizing decision? Under what conditions?

O-71. Management literature that may add further understanding of organization theory:

Managing with People, J. Fordyce, R. Weil (Reading, Mass.: Addison-Wesley Publishing Co., Inc., 1971). A practical handbook for managers of all types with suggestions for long-range development as well as immediate results.

Parkinson's Law, C. Northcote Parkinson (New York: Ballantine Books, 1957). A classic antidote to the deadly seriousness of management literature.

Supervisory and Executive Development: A Manual for Role Playing, N.R.F. Maier et al. (New York: John Wiley & Sons, Inc., 1964). A good source for understanding the dynamics behind group effectiveness.

Up the Organization, R. Townsend (Greenwich, Conn.: Fawcett Books, 1970). A successful manager describes his use of Theory Y assumptions and leadership to revitalize an ailing company.

O-72. A good understanding of how "top management" operates in an organization can be gained by sitting in on a political meeting (town, city, state, or federal) and observing intergroup dynamics of a political organization structure such as group loyalty, intergroup conflict and resolution of conflict, power strategies, influencing, decision making, and policy-making tactics. Observe the communication channels that are both overt and covert (implicit).

a. Which groups in the meeting are in conflict with which other groups? What issues are most salient to each group? What determines group loyalty and group factions—around what political issues?
b. What behaviors communicate power-motivated individuals, affiliation motivation, achievement motivation? What individuals appear to be self oriented, task oriented, maintenance oriented?
c. What is the organizational climate of this meeting? Which people are ready to fight, eager to cooperate, most likely to conform or be influenced by others? Who holds the most persuasive power?

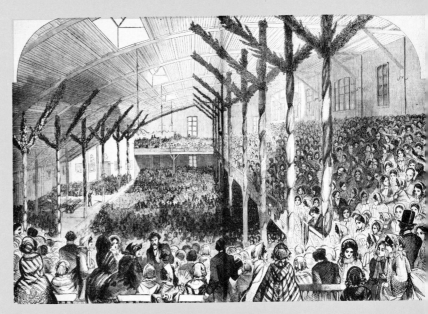

The Republicans in Nominating Convention in Their Wigwam in Chicago, May 1860.

d. If possible, interview one of the members after the meeting and find out what his or her motivations were, whether this person's needs were met by the decision made, how he or she viewed the process of the meeting.
e. How would you, as an organizational psychologist, go about trying to improve the functioning of such a complex organization? Consider changes you would make at the level of the individual, small subgroup, organization, and environment (e.g., constituency, relationship to other political structures, and so on).

0-73. The fiction of management and business can be a good source of learning. Although most novelists have dealt with themes of interpersonal relations, some writers have made management a major theme. Some popular fiction recommended for your enjoyment are

The Boss Is Crazy Too, Mel Lazarus (New York: Dell, 1963). Imagine a publishing company in which the president can become wealthy by driving the company into bankruptcy.

Banking on Death by Emma Lathen (New York: Pocket Books, 1975). Thatcher, vice president of a Wall Street investment banking house, continually encounters murder while about his business. Fine inside insights into the irrational workings of a supposedly rational organization.

John D. MacDonald has written 65 or so novels (Fawcett Books), many about business. Recommended are

The Crossroads (about family business)

Slam the Big Door (land development)

Pale Gray for Guilt (a swindler is swindled in an amazingly clever financial transaction)

Rich Man, Poor Man, Irwin Shaw (New York: Dell Publishing, 1969). A bright young man goes through a number of successful careers as an entrepreneur, manager, and politician.

0-74. Understanding how architecture and spatial arrangements within an organization affect personal interaction can give you insights into the organization's assumptions about people, the group norms that exist, the hierarchy of status, and the kind of work climate that exists. Visit a state or private mental hospital and try to "analyze" the organizational climate by observing a patient ward, talking to workers, and, if possible, talking to inmates.

a. How comfortable do you feel being around people who are diagnosed as mentally ill? How comfortable are you talking to nurses, attendants, doctors about the institutions?
b. What rules do you observe? What are the behavioral norms for patients, for the attendants, nurses, and doctors? What kinds of structures exist that seem to encourage mental health or mental illness? What kinds of "authority" issues do you think are necessary or unnecessary? In what ways do you feel patients may be dehumanized?
c. Find out how doctors set goals in helping patients terminate their illness. How do they determine prognosis of patients? What are the motivations of those persons in a helping role? Try to predict what their learning styles might be. How open/closed do you feel they are to their own personal growth and change.

0-75. The climate of an organization has a dramatic impact on the individuals who are part of it. In some cases, our family and educational organizations contribute to a person's inability to cope with their environment, a situation we have labeled "mental illness." Some popular books that offer insight into how culture, environment, and organizations may initiate and sustain such effects are

The Politics of Experience, R. D. Laing (New York: Ballantine Books, 1967). A maverick British psychiatrist looks at the damage we do to each other through our institutions and attitudes, particularly the way his profession perceives mental illness.

Myth of Mental Illness and *The Manufacture of Madness,* Thomas S. Szasz, M.D. (New York: Dell Publishing Co., 1970). Szasz challenges the underlying assumptions of mental illness and presents the concept of mental illness as a misused part of a strategic struggle for power.

One Flew Over the Cuckoo's Nest, Ken Kesey (New York: Signet Books, 1963). A novel about a ward in a mental hospital in which the authority ("Big Nurse") is so dedicated to running a smooth ward that she punishes anyone who shows signs of recovery.

0-76. *Organizational Diagnosis*
Just as we have cognitive maps that influence our perceptions of other people, we also have our own theory of organizations that may "filter" our perceptions of an organization's climate and structure. These implicit theories consist of a set of key variables, concepts, and a map of the relationships among them.
a. Walk into an organization and write down your immediate conclusions about its climate. Take time afterward to check those conclusions with people at several levels in the organization. Are your conclusions supported or disconfirmed? Now go back and write down the data you used to come to the initial conclusions. What do they tell you about your filters?
b. Think of an organization you are presently working with, have worked with recently, or one you'd like to work with (either full-time or in some consulting, training, or other part-time capacity). If someone who is unfamiliar with this organization asks you to describe it briefly, how would you respond?
c. Suppose you have been asked by an appropriate person in this organization to do an organizational diagnosis in order to understand it as a preliminary step to helping it change. What data would you collect (categories or variables, *not* method) to use in the diagnosis? Why?
d. Now go over your responses to (b) and (c) and try to consider the following:
   (1) What is your cognitive map of organizations? What key variables or categories of variables do you use in describing an organization?
   (2) How would the variables you examined in your diagnosis relate to each other? Which variables are causally related? What does this map tell you about how *you* would go about making organizations more effective?
   (3) How do your own motives (n-Ach, n-Aff, etc.) influence your own theory of organizations?
(See the chapter The Organization as an Open System.)

0-77. A simple comparative study of organization climates can help you to understand the implications that architecture, furniture arrangements, personnel systems, and group norms have for the joining-up process in an organization. You may want to "pretend" you are seeking employment in order to establish what the criteria for joining up in an organization are.
a. What does it feel like to approach the building or office when you enter the organization? Compare this process of walking into a bank, hospital, courthouse, or police station with some informal operation such as a small restaurant, store, or volunteer organization.
b. What aspects of the physical structures induce feelings of acceptance or informality? Feelings of distrust or defensiveness? How are you greeted? What effects do the spatial arrangements have on you? How do they relate to the behavioral norms of the employees?
c. What can you infer about what it is like to work in these organizations from the style and manner of communication of the personnel? from the employees? What are the prevalent attitudes of the employees about the management of the organization?
d. What mixed messages do you get about what it is like to work in each of the organizations you visit?

0-78. *Political and Military Organizations*
Although they tend to have different goals (control, defense) from those of profit-making or helping organizations, governmental and military organizations share the same problems. The following books provide insights into organization behavior by chronicling patterns of organizations under stress.
Inside the Third Reich, Albert Speer (New York: MacMillan, 1970). From his position as an insider, Speer provides detailed accounts of how this "organization" was built, functioned, and was eventually defeated. In addition to an excellent analysis of Hitler's style of leadership, important insights can be gained into such concepts as organization structure (project versus functional versus matrix organization), centralization versus decentralization and organizational decision making, patterns of organizational communication, planned organizational change, resistance to change, individual versus organizational goals.
The Caine Mutiny, Herman Wouk (Garden City, N.Y.: Anchor Books, 1961). A good description of what happens when an organizational task under the leadership of a strict authoritarian figure becomes a focus for rebellion—leading to organizational breakdown. See also *The Arnheiter Affair,* Neil Sheehan (New York: Dell, 1973).
Patton, Ladislas Farago (New York: Dell Books, 1970). An excellent portrayal of a general's impact on the military organization—his leadership style, military goals, and personal values and needs in conflict with the military organization.
Power, Adolf A. Berle (New York: Harcourt, Brace and World, 1969). A lengthy treatise on the realities of political power from

one who has both participated in government and observed as an academician.

Rules for Radicals, Saul D. Alinsky (Vintage Books, 1971). The master organizer of mass political action has set down his laws for forcing change. Although they would seldom be part of an organizational planned change effort, they do provide stimulation for thinking about the effective use of power.

0-79. *Planned Change*
Argyris (1971) has argued that, in all that he does, the effective change agent should strive to accomplish three objectives:

To increase the availability of valid information.

To increase the possibility of free choice by the client.

Through these two objectives, to help the client generate internal commitment among employees and members to those choices.
a. Think of several change agents you have known.
b. To what extent did they seem to operate within the Argyris ideal?
c. What consequences can you see or predict that would occur from not adhering to these criteria (e.g., forcing a solution rather than maximizing free choice)?
d. What would a brainwasher in a P.O.W. camp say about these criteria?

0-80. *Planned Change*
The Kolb-Frohman model of planned change (see Planned Change and Organizational Development chapter) is essentially a collaborative model of the change process. Significant change can also occur in a more spontaneous, power oriented, or forced manner. In these cases, it is usually "planned change" as well, but the planning takes place in a unilateral way.

Think of a specific change at the level of the individual (e.g., deciding to get married), group (e.g., change of leadership), organization (e.g., change of work procedure), and environment (e.g., civil rights acts, abortion decisions).

Consider the ways in which the Kolb-Frohman model might have been used—implicitly or explicitly.

Consider the impact on the individual or organizational or social changes that are spontaneous, power oriented, and forced rather than collaboratively planned. Which is more permanent? Which has more unanticipated consequences?

0-81. *Open Systems Planning*
Complex organizations are open systems. As such, an effective, proactive organization does not wait to react to the environment, but tries to anticipate, plan for, and influence the nature of the environmental demands placed upon it. One procedure for such activity is open systems planning.

This procedure may be used productively with any organization of which you are a member, as long as it has an anticipated life of at least a few years. Fraternities, campus organizations, families, and companies are all good places to use the system. The seven phases are:

Phase One—Identify the Planning Unit
The first step is to identify who the planning unit is and to determine for what level of the system planning is being undertaken. This can range from individual plans for each member of a group to a plan for a group that represents only part of an organizational subunit, to a plan for an organizational subunit or a total system. Generally, it becomes more difficult to draw meaningful action steps from the OSP process when plans are made that members have no authority or responsibility to carry out or when critical members of a unit are not present for unit planning.

Phase Two—Defining the Mission
The second step in this process is to come to a common definition of the core mission/goal of the system. In forming this mission statement, you should explore all initial differences as fully as possible (i.e., resist the premature conclusion that "It's probably a matter of semantics").

Phase Three—Present Demands
Once having defined your mission in your own view, the next step is to identify all of the other relevant systems making demands on the present system.

Phase Four—Present Responses
For each of the demands identified in Phase Three, what is the present pattern or mode of response?

Phase Five—Projected Future
Looking two to four years ahead, predict the likely demands of these other systems on your group, given normal inertia and trends. In other words, if you took no proactive steps, what would the future look like?

Phase Six—Ideal Future
What would we like each demand system to be asking of us two to four years from now?

Phase Seven—Action Steps
What short-range (e.g., three to six months) and long-range steps must we take to have them demand of us what we would like in Phase Six?

0-82. In planning change, Jay W. Forrester contends that we tend to try to provide simple, immediate solutions to only the most obvious parts of the problem, and fail to take into consideration the total system and how it will respond. His following books provide a philosophical framework for large system change, and computer models for anticipated long-range consequences:

Industrial Dynamics, Jay W. Forrester (Cambridge, Mass.: Massachusetts Institute of Technology Press, 1961).
Urban Dynamics, Jay W. Forrester (Cambridge, Mass.: Massachusetts Institute of Technology Press, 1969).
World Dynamics, Jay W. Forrester (Cambridge, Mass.: Wright-Allen Press, 1971).

C. LEARNING ABOUT CULTURE AND ENVIRONMENT

The fourth critical area for organizations is the larger societal system in which they exist. To ignore cultural and environmental factors in making organization decisions is to miss extremely important data. Political, economic, and social change affect every organization.

This section of learning resources can provide a beginning for the manager or student who wishes to expand his or her knowledge of the wider context in which an organization functions and changes.

C-83. Change agents who work on larger political systems (Gandhi, Martin Luther King, Jr., Jesse Jackson, etc.) and on organizations from the outside (Ralph Nader, Saul Alinsky) usually have a different approach to initiating change than the manager or organization development consultant.
a. What assumptions do these "cultural" change agents make about the nature of social systems?
b. What are their models of the change process? How do they deal with resistance to change?
c. To what would you attribute the success or failure of such change agents in their major projects (Indian independence, the Montgomery bus boycott, Operation Breadbasket, auto safety, minority employment)?
d. There are numerous examples of national experiments in

change, such as civil rights laws, the Equal Rights Amendment, abortion laws and decisions, pollution control, etc. Use the Force Field Analysis (page 531) to analyze the forces that led to one of these changes.
e. Do another Force Field Analysis of the forces that are pushing for success and forces pushing for failure of these changes.
f. A good film on the process of planned change is *A Time for Burning* (William Jersey Organization, New York). The minister of a large urban church attempts to bring about change in the racial attitudes of his parishioners. His heart is in the right place, but his methods are doomed to failure from the beginning.

C-84. *Society and the Individual* There are many current books written by social analysts that offer insight into the cultural trends and changes that affect the individual's life, his values, goals, and attitudes about change itself. Some popular books dealing with these issues are:
New Rules: Searching for Self-fulfillment in a World Turned Upside Down, Daniel Yankelovich, (New York: Bantam, 1981). Describes the new emerging American philosophy embodying personal freedom and responsibility—"a genuine, cultural revolution whose ultimate goal may be to humanize our industrial society."
Megatrends, John Naisbitt (New York: Warner Books, 1982). Describes changes in the 80s, as

Future Shock did for the 70s; details ten new directions of change that will transform our lives.
Pursuit of Loneliness: American Culture at its Breaking Point, Phillip Slater (Boston: Beacon Press, 1970). An analysis of the relationships between our self-imposed subservience to technology and the quality of life in the United States, why it is destructive, and proposed changes that will alter the values and motives underlying most organizations and institutions existing today.
The Temporary Society, Warren Bennis and Phillip Slater (New York: Harper & Row, Publishers, 1968). An insightful analysis of the growing temporality of relationships in Western culture. The short-term "task force" and the matrix organization are organizational correlaries.
Future Shock, Alvin Toffler (New York: Bantam Books, 1970). The rapidity of technological innovation in the West is leading to a new kind of psychological disorientation, induced by change. It affects individuals and their relationships to work and to others, and the pace is picking up.
Twelve Angry Men (United Artists) is a film highlighting group decision making and influence. A jury of 12 men is charged with the responsibility of deciding the guilt or innocence of a young boy charged with the murder of his father. On the first ballot, the vote is 11 guilty and 1 not guilty. The ensuing 70 minutes dramatizes the process by which each

of the other 11 jurors "becomes convinced" of the boy's innocence. When used as a training input, viewers are asked to predict the order in which the jurors will change their minds.

C-85. Foreign customs are often strange to us when we don't understand what they mean or how they are similar or different from our own. We have a tendency to defend our own customs when in the company of foreigners until open communication allows us to discover those areas in which we are alike. Go to dinner with a foreign friend.
a. How are your eating customs different, the same? How do your cultural differences affect your ability to communicate?
b. How do you overcome language barriers? What words do you have the most trouble defining?
c. Find out what life is like in an organization in your friend's country. In what ways do cultural differences influence appropriate leadership styles? Styles of decision making? Modes of conflict resolution? The meaning and value of work vs. leisure?

C-86. Children are often the best mirrors for viewing cultures, particularly cultures in which there is conflict. These three novels of childhood and adolescence provide some startling insights.
Lord of the Flies, William Golding (New York: Capricorn Books, 1955). A group of boys shipwrecked on an island go about organizing their own adultless society with results that reflect contemporary organizations and society.
A High Wind in Jamaica, Richard Hughes (New York: Signet Books, 1956). Some children are taken aboard a pirate ship in a routine raid. They adapt quickly to what they think are pirate values, so much so that it is difficult to tell which group is more dangerous.

The Heart is a Lonely Hunter, Carson McCullers (New York: Bantam Books, 1940). A young girl growing up in a southern town is faced with conflicting demands, values, and loyalties.

C-87. If there are any countercultural organizations (communes, self-help groups, free universities, etc.) in your vicinity, you may find a visit to one of these types of organizations valuable in understanding how different values, roles, and attitudes affect the climate and structure of an organization. In many cases, there may appear to be *no* organization in the traditional sense.
a. How does such an organization manage its internal problems—decision-making processes, task division, maintenance and so on?
b. What are the motives or incentives for working or living in such an organization? For leaving one? Try to talk to somebody who has lived or worked in the organization about how it compares with other more traditional structures. How do people relate to each other, work together, resolve conflicts?
c. What are the underlying values and norms in a countercultural organization and how do they contradict the values of similar but more traditional structures? What are the assumptions about people?
d. See *The Greening of America,* Charles A. Reich (New York: Bantam Books, 1971). Reich postulates three levels of consciousness among Americans and forecasts new conflicts that will differ from traditional ones due to the newer sets of values held by the emerging "counterculture."

C-88. *Dreams and Deeds,* R. A. Levine (Chicago: University of Chicago Press, 1966). Cross-cultural differences are clearly illustrated in this analysis of the dreams of adolescent boys from two cul-

tures in one country. The group with dreams full of achievement imagery is much more successful than the group with high power imagery.

C-89. *The Children of the Dream,* Bruno Bettelheim (New York: Avon Books, 1970). In reflecting on the ways organizations socialize new members, it is helpful to look at the ways that societies socialize their children. This study of Israeli kibbutzim focuses on the transfer of values and norms from adults to children, particularly around sharing and interdependence. It also offers insights into the kibbutz as a social system that is intentionally different.

C-90. The question of effective helping style is of critical concern to the manager. One source for learning about various ways of helping and their effects on people is found outside management in the area of psychotherapy and humanistic psychology, a rather recent cultural phenomenon. Various schools of psychology have developed helping techniques that transcend the social biases individuals encounter in their process of growing into adulthood. Another current trend in therapy centers is the encounter group, sensitivity group, or self-awareness group method of discovering who oneself really is and how one feels about being that self. Some psychological films which illustrate these therapy techniques are:
Three Approaches to Psychotherapy (Carl Rogers, Albert Ellis, and Fritz Perls). A good presentation of three contrasting helping styles: non-directive (client-centered), rational therapy, and Gestalt therapy.
Humanistic Revolution. Interviews with some of the leaders—Maslow, Perls, May, Watts, Tillich, Rogers, and others.
Journey into Self. Classic film of the encounter phenomena, Dr. Carl Rogers and Dr. Farson co-lead an intensive basic workshop. Academy Award-winning documentary.

Target Five. Virginia Satir, eminent family therapist, demonstrates the actualizing relationship to be reached when people and families discard the manipulative relationships that hamper growth and development.

In the Now. Dr. James Simkin gives an excellent demonstration of Gestalt therapy principles and techniques with three different subjects.

All these films may be obtained on a rental basis for about $30 a day from Psychological Films, Orange, California.

Dr. Gordon Allport. An interview with Dr. Allport in which he discusses self-development, personality development, and socialization and existentialism.

Games People Play. Eric Berne and transactional analysis—theory and practice.

Nude Marathon. Paul Bindrim conducts a workshop filmed by the Canadian Broadcasting Corp. for Canadian T.V.

Rollo May: Human Encounter. Dr. Rollo May discusses his philosophy and therapy principles.

All these films may be obtained on a rental basis from the University of Pennsylvania Film Center.

Primal Scream. A documentary film showing progress of patients of primal therapy under the care of Dr. Janov (Primal Institute, Los Angeles, California).

WORKBOOK EVALUATION

In an effort to model the importance of asking for feedback and because we're very interested in your comments, we would appreciate it if you would fill out this form and return it to us. We'll use the feedback to guide the revision of the next edition.

1. Please rate the workbook overall on the following points:

Relevance of the content:

Poor   1   2   3   4   5   Excellent

Clarity of the writing:

Poor   1   2   3   4   5   Excellent

Usefulness of the exercises:

Poor   1   2   3   4   5   Excellent

2. What did you like about the workbook?

3. Was there anything you disliked about the workbook? If so, what?

4. What suggestions do you have for improving the workbook?

5. What else, in the way of topics, exercises and the like would you like to see included in the next edition?

Please return this form to:

> Dr. Irwin Rubin
> 37 Kawananakoa Place
> Honolulu, Hawaii   96817

Thank you for your assistance with the above.